Gettysbu
The First Day

CIVIL WAR AMERICA

Gary W. Gallagher, editor

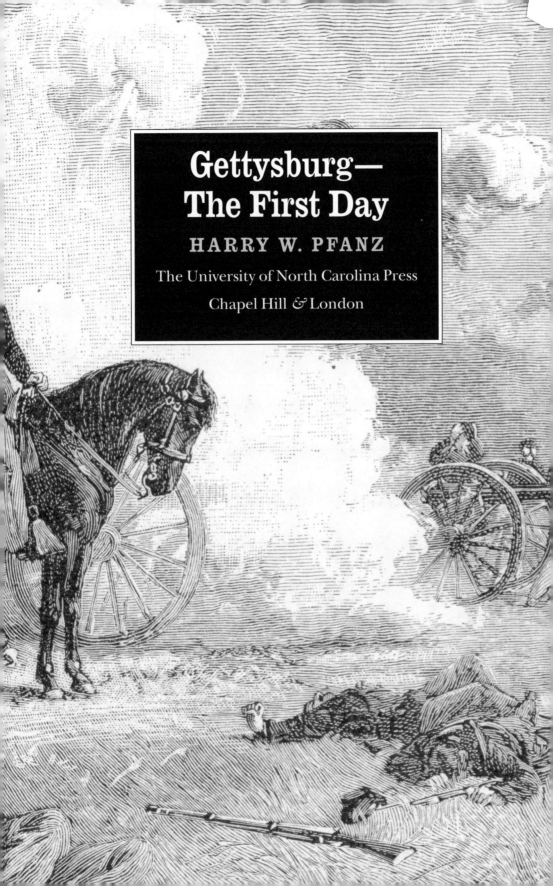

Gettysburg— The First Day

HARRY W. PFANZ

The University of North Carolina Press

Chapel Hill & London

© 2001 The University of North Carolina Press
All rights reserved
Manufactured in the United States of America
Set in New Baskerville and Clarendon types
by Keystone Typesetting, Inc.
The paper in this book meets the guidelines for permanence
and durability of the Committee on Production Guidelines for
Book Longevity of the Council on Library Resources.

Library of Congress Cataloging-in-Publication Data
Pfanz, Harry W. (Harry Willcox), 1921–
Gettysburg, the first day / by Harry W. Pfanz.
p. cm. — (Civil War America)
Includes bibliographical references (p.) and index.
ISBN 978-0-8078-2624-9 (cloth: alk. paper)
ISBN 978-0-8078-7131-7 (pbk.: alk. paper)
1. Gettysburg (Pa.), Battle of, 1863. I. Title. II. Series.
E475.53 .P479 2001
973.7'349—dc21   00-048927

cloth   07   06   05   04   03   7   6   5   4   3
paper   13   12   11   10   09   5   4   3   2   1

For

Sarah, John, and Matthew Pfanz

and

Elizabeth and Katherine Ake

CONTENTS

MAPS

ILLUSTRATIONS

PREFACE

This is an account of the battle of 1 July 1863 at Gettysburg and of certain relevant events and decisions immediately preceding it. The battle was a "meeting engagement"; neither Gen. Robert E. Lee, commander of the Confederate Army of Northern Virginia, nor Maj. Gen. George G. Meade, commander of the Federal Army of the Potomac, planned to give battle at Gettysburg. Events and subordinate commanders took measures that made Gettysburg the battle site. They included Lt. Gen. Ambrose Powell Hill, commander of Lee's Third Army Corps; Maj. Gen. Henry Heth, one of Hill's division commanders; Brig. Gen. John Buford, commander of the First Division of the Army of the Potomac's Cavalry Corps; and Maj. Gen. John F. Reynolds, the commander of that army's temporary left wing.

The battle commenced about 8:00 A.M. approximately three miles west of the town when Union cavalry videttes opened fire on a Confederate column advancing on Gettysburg. There was skirmishing as the horsemen fell back toward Gettysburg and their support. Close to 10:00 A.M., as cavalry units formed on the low ridges west of the town, infantry of the Union First Corps reached the field. There was a sharp but brief fight between two Confederate and two Union infantry brigades, and the Confederates fell back.

There followed a lull of some three hours punctuated by the crack of skirmishers' rifles and occasional cannon shots, as strong reinforcements reached the area. The Union First and Eleventh Corps took defensive positions west and north of Gettysburg, and arriving Confederates from Hill's and Lt. Gen. Richard S. Ewell's corps formed opposite them. Full-scale fighting resumed about midafternoon as the Confederates attacked first from the north and then from the west. There was a short but violent fight, and soon after 4:00 P.M. the two Union corps retreated through the town south to Cemetery Hill. There they rallied, and the Confederates did not continue their attack. The remainder of both armies reached the

Gettysburg area that night and on the following day, setting the stage for the battles of 2 and 3 July.

The battle has spawned a number of suppositions. One is that a battle at Gettysburg was inevitable because of the concentration of roads there. Another proposition holds that Union cavalrymen, by hard fighting, delayed the Confederates' arrival at Gettysburg until Union infantry was at hand. Many people believe that a Confederate sharpshooter shot General Reynolds. One of the greatest clichés is that Union forces were defeated on 1 July because of the poor performance of the Eleventh Corps. In addition, it has been accepted by many that only Lt. Gen. Richard S. Ewell's vacillation and his failure to press an attack against the Union forces rallying on Cemetery Hill prevented the Confederates from achieving a complete victory. I address these and other matters in the following text.

Information on battles is usually spotty and less than we would like. This is true of the battle of 1 July. Although the outlines of the day are plain enough, some details escape us. For instance, we do not know where on Oak Hill O'Neal's and Ramseur's brigades formed for their attacks and the exact locations there of the positions of the batteries that supported Rodes's division. On the Union side our knowledge of locations of the regiments of Schurz's division and the positions of Dilger's and Wheeler's batteries are equally vague. We may well wonder, too, how so many of the regiments of Baxter's brigade fitted into the limited front on Oak Ridge at the time of Iverson's assault, and just where Cutler's and Baxter's brigades were on Oak Ridge before they retreated into the town. The lack of such information makes for difficult plotting of the battle on maps.

Here it may be well for me to note that we cannot be certain about some terrain features on the field. For instance, was the orchard on Oak Hill by the Mummasburg Road there during the battle and, if so, were its trees large enough to affect the posting of batteries on the hill? If so, how much? None of the men who fought there mentioned it. Some of the prominent terrain features such as Sheads's Woods or the Springs Hotel Woods did not have names known to the combatants or to us today. In such cases I have identified these features by using names that were obviously applied after the battle or might not have been in common use at all. The name Herbst Woods, applied now because a John Herbst owned it at the time of the battle, was commonly called McPherson Woods by soldiers and veterans. Because of this, I have opted not to use the present-day "Herbst" designation.

Portions of the First Day's battlefield have been lost to development, sad to say, though most of the core of the field is in park ownership. Most visitors will not be bothered so much by these undesirable modern intrusions as by the heavy traffic that infests the roads and park avenues that pass through the area. This portion of the battlefield is well worth a visit, but such a visit must be made with care. This problem seems destined to worsen in the immediate future, for there is no easy solution — certainly none that the National Park Service alone can effect.

ACKNOWLEDGMENTS

Many people have been of help to me in the long course of this study. I cannot name the numerous librarians and archivists who helped me, but I deeply appreciate their assistance, particularly that of John E. White at the Southern Historical Collection of the University of North Carolina's Wilson Library.

My son Donald, author of *Richard S. Ewell* and a historian at Fredericksburg and Spotsylvania National Military Park, was of special help to me. He provided information on source materials, shared his opinions, and read and made numerous comments on drafts of my manuscript that improved it greatly. As always, Robert K. Krick at that park was generous with his special knowledge of sources, particularly those relating to the Army of Northern Virginia.

Special help came from two friends: Edwin C. Bearss of Arlington, Virginia, and Fred Mende of Charlotte, North Carolina. Both men read and commented on my manuscript. Ed carried chapters of it on his almost constant tours and speaking engagements. In addition to reading the manuscript, Fred shared his views with me by mail and during several visits to the field.

I received much cooperation, help, and hospitality, as always, from D. Scott Hartwig and his colleagues at Gettysburg National Military Park. Without doubt, these good people are the final authorities on matters relating to the Gettysburg Campaign. In addition to Scott, I take pleasure in thanking others on the Gettysburg staff, including John Heiser, Eric A. Campbell, Paul Shevchuk, Kathleen Georg Harrison, Winona Peterson, and Bert Barnett.

There were other Gettysburgians who helped me. They included my old friend Col. Jacob M. Sheads, Dr. Charles H. Gladfelter of the Adams County Historical Society, and battlefield guides Wayne E. Motts and Timothy H. Smith. I am pleased also to include a Maine man now residing in the Gettysburg area, Dr. Thomas A. Desjardin, whose interests extend far beyond the 20th Maine Regiment.

I spent many days at the U.S. Army's Military Institute at Carlisle Barracks, Pennsylvania. There, as before, I received generous help from Dr. Richard J. Sommers, David H. Keough, Pamela Cheney, Michael Winey, Randy Hackenburg, and Louise Arnold Friend.

Dr. Gary W. Gallagher of the University of Virginia has been of immense and essential help with this effort as he has with my two previous Gettysburg books. He has been a friend in need.

Two men were of special help in reconstructing the brickyard fight. These were Mark H. Dunkleman, who has done much research on the 154th New York Regiment and Amos Humiston, and George W. Conklin of Edison, New Jersey, who has written a history of the 134th New York Regiment.

There are others who have provided me with information and helpful opinions. They include Charles T. Jacobs of Gaithersburg, Maryland; Earl B. McElfresh of Olean, New York; Arnold Blumberg of Baltimore; Ralph Kirshner of Chapel Hill, North Carolina; David Vermillion of Newark, Ohio; Bryce A. Suderow of Washington, D.C.; Alfred Young of Burtonsville, Maryland; Jeffrey Keene of Trumbull, Connecticut; and Michael Dreese of Middleburg, Pennsylvania.

I must also acknowledge the aid and patience of the staff of the University of North Carolina Press. I thank especially Ron Maner and Stephanie Wenzel.

It takes a number of years for me to complete such a project as this; it requires numerous trips to libraries and endless hours to write it up. Of course, it could not have been done without the encouragement and cooperation of my family, particularly my wife, Letitia Earll Pfanz, who not only served as a clerical assistant on our road trips but accommodated my day trips to the battlefield and the work at home. I must also acknowledge the support of our daughter Marion Ake and Jim Ake; Donald's wife, Betty; and our son Lt. Col. Frederick W. Pfanz and his wife, Carol. Their support was invaluable to me.

Gettysburg—
The First Day

INTRODUCTION
Fredericksburg
to the Potomac

Its drums were beating, its colors flying, as the 900 officers and enlisted men of the 26th North Carolina Regiment, "beaming in their splendid uniforms," filed from their camp at Fredericksburg, Virginia. It was a beautiful morning on 15 June 1863, and the 26th, with its three sister regiments of Brig. Gen. James Johnston Pettigrew's brigade, was heading off on its first campaign with the vaunted Army of Northern Virginia. "Everything seemed propitious of success," recalled a veteran in later years. It was heady stuff for the virtually unbloodied Tarheels who had been guarding the coastal areas of their native state from Federal invasion. But in a month their uniforms would be worn, and the North Carolinians would learn that war can be horror and hardship as well as beating drums and flaunted colors.[1]

Pettigrew's brigade belonged to the new Third Corps of the Army of Northern Virginia. The corps had sprouted from the wreckage of the battle of Chancellorsville, fought a few miles west of Fredericksburg on 1–3 May 1863. It has been termed by some as Gen. Robert E. Lee's most brilliant victory. Lee and his army of about 60,000 soldiers had befuddled Maj. Gen. Joseph Hooker, commander of the U.S. Army of the Potomac. Lee stopped Hooker's campaign toward Richmond and intimidated him so that he ordered his army back north of the Rappahannock River. Lee's victory had been costly. Nearly 13,000 Confederates had been killed or wounded in the battle, including "Stonewall" Jackson, the commander of Lee's Second Corps. Not only could the South ill afford to lose so many men in an indecisive battle, but it seemed as though Jackson would be impossible to replace.[2]

Lee had no time to savor the plaudits of victory or to mourn for the dead and maimed. The campaigning season had opened, and he knew that the Federals would not delay to lick their wounds. He had to prepare for further operations.

His first priority was to reorganize his army and to find a successor for Jackson. The army's two corps of infantry and artillery, the First commanded by Lt. Gen. James Longstreet and the Second under the lamented Jackson, had been large and unwieldy. To remedy this, Lee divided the army into three corps having three divisions each. Newly promoted Lt. Gen. Richard S. Ewell inherited Jackson's old Second Corps, and Lt. Gen. Ambrose P. Hill received command of the new Third Corps. Ewell had commanded a division in the Second Corps until he lost a leg at Second Bull Run, and Hill had led the famed Light Division in that corps. Ewell would have three old divisions commanded by Maj. Gen. Jubal A. Early and two new major generals, Robert Rodes and Edward Johnson. Hill would have one old division, that of Maj. Gen. Richard H. Anderson, and two newly created divisions under recently promoted major generals, Henry Heth and W. Dorsey Pender. Both Heth and Pender had commanded brigades in the Light Division, and these brigades served as nuclei for their new divisions. Each of the army's three corps numbered more than 20,000 officers and enlisted men, and each of its nine divisions was upward of 6,000 strong. In addition to these three corps, the army had Maj. Gen. James E. B. Stuart's cavalry division. On 30 June the Army of Northern Virginia would number about 75,000 officers and enlisted men. Col. Armistead Long of Lee's staff believed that at that time it was "the best disciplined, the most high-spirited, and enthusiastic army on the continent."[3]

After conferring with President Jefferson Davis and Secretary of War James Seddon, General Lee started his army on a campaign that would take it north of the Potomac. In his two reports of the campaign Lee gave his reasons for this movement: It was not advantageous for him to attack the Army of the Potomac in its Fredericksburg position. Therefore he had to draw it away. By moving north of the Potomac, he would pull Hooker's army from Virginia, clear the Shenandoah Valley of Federal forces, and disrupt Federal campaign plans for the summer both in Virginia and elsewhere. Equally important, his army could find badly needed food, forage, horses, and supplies in the North. In addition, there were other valuable results that might be obtained by a military success. Surely they would have

Gen. Robert E. Lee (NA)

included the elusive recognition of foreign governments, the encouragement of the peace movement in the North, and, perhaps, independence.[4]

In the meantime Hooker was recovering from his traumatic defeat. As early as 7 May one of his staff officers wrote that Hooker would attack again in twenty-four hours. Although this was impractical thinking, it might have reflected expectations at Hooker's headquarters. In addition President Abraham Lincoln and Gen.-in-Chief Henry Halleck visited the army to talk with Hooker and with some of his ranking generals. Lincoln and Halleck believed that Hooker should not be entrusted with command of the army in another battle. Yet, though few candidates were available to succeed him, they delayed for nearly two months before appointing his replacement.[5]

Meanwhile Hooker was busy. He expressed a desire to open another campaign on Richmond, especially after he learned that all of Lee's army but Hill's corps had moved from his front. Lincoln responded to such proposals with often quoted homespun remarks and forbade such a movement. Although General Lee was able to move with his army essentially as he wished, the administration tethered the Army of the Potomac to Washington and insisted that it be a shield between Lee's army and the capital.[6]

{ INTRODUCTION }

3

Lt. Gen. Richard S. Ewell
(D. Pfanz)

Part of Hooker's resilience might have resulted from his ability to divert blame for his defeat. Instead of shouldering the responsibility for it, he laid the burden on the Sixth Corps for not advancing rapidly against Lee's rear and on the Eleventh Corps for its allegedly poor, if not disgraceful, performance on 2 May. The Eleventh Corps, which is a major subject of this study, was an easy target. It was relatively new to the Army of the Potomac and had a poor reputation. Its three divisions had come to the army from Maj. Gen. John Pope's Army of Virginia, the loser at Second Bull Run. The corps had been commanded by Maj. Gen. Franz Sigel, who was a leader in the German immigrant community but an undistinguished general. More to the point, it contained a number of regiments composed of German immigrants, and two of its division commanders, Adolph von Steinwehr and Carl Schurz, were natives of Germany. It is ironic that the division of the corps smashed at Chancellorsville was the one commanded by a non-German, though its First Brigade, led by Col. Leopold von Gilsa, was one of the first struck. The German officers of the corps were highly incensed by the blame heaped on them; they sought courts of inquiry and permission to publish their reports, but to no avail. Thus, when the Eleventh Corps embarked on the new campaign, many of its soldiers were subject to gibes and insults from men of other corps and had low morale.[7]

Although the Army of the Potomac had sustained 17,000 casualties at Chancellorsville and was losing about 23,000 officers and enlisted men whose terms of service had expired, Hooker did not attempt to reorganize it. Brig. Gen. Henry J. Hunt, its chief of artillery, wrote that its seven corps of infantry and artillery were too small and required too many commanders and staffs. Yet for a year nothing was done to remedy this problem. Perhaps it would have been politically impossible for Hooker to do so; he would have to rebuild the army's strength by acquiring new regiments by transfer.[8]

Lee opened his campaign on 3 June by sending Ewell's corps to Culpeper, and Longstreet's corps followed. Rebel cavalry, posted along the Rappahannock River, screened the move from prying Union horsemen and would continue to do so during the Confederate march through Virginia. The Union commanders were not aware of the infantry concentration at Culpeper, but they knew that the cavalry was there in force. They assumed that the Confederates were mounting a raid around the Union right. Hooker ordered Maj. Gen. Alfred Pleasonton, commander of the Army of the Potomac's cavalry corps, to "disperse and destroy" the Rebel force at Culpeper. Pleasonton's troopers struck Stuart's force at Brandy Station on 9 June. There was a slam-bang melee, the largest cavalry battle of the war. Although it was a draw, it revealed the presence of Confederate infantry in that area. It showed also that the Union cavalry was much improved and the peer of the Confederate mounted arm, and it boosted the morale of the Federal troopers. It also discomfited General Stuart, who was criticized for having been surprised. There were boasts of other accomplishments, including the gaining of valuable but nebulous intelligence and the breaking up of an imagined raid, but it did not impair General Lee's plans.[9]

Ewell resumed his march toward the Shenandoah Valley on the 10th, and his corps reached Cedarville north of Front Royal on the 12th. It met Brig. Gen. Albert Jenkins's cavalry brigade there; Jenkins had about 1,000 Virginia troopers divided into three regiments, two battalions, and a battery. Jenkins's brigade had been operating in the Valley area and beyond and was not accustomed to working with a large body of infantry. Ewell's corps followed Jenkins's troopers toward Winchester and Martinsburg while Longstreet's corps remained on the east side of the Blue Ridge to guard Snicker's and Ashby's Gaps.[10]

On the 14th and 15th Ewell's divisions captured Winchester and Martinsburg and much of their Union garrisons. Ewell's booty at Winchester included 23 cannon, 300 loaded wagons, 4,000 prisoners, and a lot of supplies. Rodes's divisions at Martinsburg captured another 5 guns, 6,000 bushels of grain, and 200 more prisoners. Ewell did not dally. He continued his march north down the Valley. On the 15th, three brigades of Rodes's division and Jenkins's brigade crossed the Potomac at Williamsport, where Rodes's footsore men took three days of rest. Johnson's division crossed the river on the 18th at Boteler's Ford downstream from Shepherdstown, and Early's crossed at Shepherdstown on the 22d.[11]

While Ewell moved north, Hill's corps remained at Fredericksburg to confront the Union Sixth Corps across the river from the town. The Sixth Corps made one feint across the river; otherwise it was a quiet time. After the Union forces left its front, Hill's corps, on 14 June, started for the Valley and Lee's army. By the 22d all of Ewell's corps was in Pennsylvania, and Lee ordered his two other corps to its support. Longstreet's corps left the gaps to the cavalry and crossed the Potomac on the 24th and 25th at Williamsport. Hill's corps waded the river on the 24th at Shepherdstown. Stuart and his cavalry remained in Virginia to guard the passes and the Confederate rear until the Union forces left their front. On the 25th at 1:00 A.M. Stuart led three of his brigades from Salem, Virginia, on their circuitous ride to Pennsylvania. That, too, is another story.[12]

The Army of the Potomac moved north also in an attempt to maintain contact with Lee's army and stay between it and Washington. This was a difficult task complicated by its having to remove or destroy its hospitals and the supply depot at Aquia Creek that had supported its operations in the Fredericksburg area. On 13 June Hooker announced that he was shifting his line of communications from the Potomac River to the Orange and Alexandria Railroad. Less that a week later, as Ewell's corps was crossing into Maryland, Hooker's army moved north to Leesburg and to confront the Confederates at Thoroughfare Gap and Aldie. On the 17th, 19th, and 21st, Union cavalry clashed with the Confederate horsemen at Aldie, Middleburg, and Upperville.[13]

Hooker was unable to discern Lee's intentions and the location of his army. The Confederate cavalry screen held the Union forces east of the Blue Ridge and away from the moving infantry. On the 21st, after the battles at Middleburg and Upperville, Hooker gave the Confederate cavalry a great compliment. He wrote President Lincoln that his own cavalry had "achieved wonders," but that the Confederate horsemen had "hitherto prevented me from obtaining satisfactory information as to the whereabouts of the enemy. They have masked all of their movements." That was the Confederate cavalry's primary mission, and it had performed it well.[14]

Although the Confederate march was hard, its generals knew their destinations and could plan their marches. The generals of the Army of the Potomac had to react to what they knew of the Confederates' progress, and their march was stop and go. The weather was hot, the roads were either dusty or muddy, and the warm uniforms were soiled and stinking. Many men dropped from the ranks because of heat exhaustion and fatigue. Brig. Gen. James S. Wadsworth's division rested a day at Centerville, where officers urged their men to take care of their feet. On the next day they countermarched before a halt at Herndon. By this time the troops were in a complaining mood and growled that officers conducting the march had been lost. In one way they were — Hooker could not accurately predict the movements of Lee's army and his own and assuage concerns felt by the president and others for the safety of Washington.[15]

During the march north the difficulties between Hooker and the administration approached a climax. All worked under pressure; Lee's campaign threatened the country's very existence, and they could not agree to a course of action to oppose it. On 15 June Hooker offered Lincoln some comments on the campaign. He concluded them petulantly by writing, "I do not know that my opinion as to the duty of this army in the case is wanted; if it should be, you know that I will be happy to give it." On the following day he observed that the president had long been aware that he, Hooker, had not enjoyed the confidence of Halleck. He continued, "I can assure you so long as this continues we may look in vain for success, especially as future operations will require our relations to be more dependent on each other than heretofore."[16]

President Lincoln gave a sharp response. He informed Hooker that he placed him in relation to Halleck as the commander of one army to the general-in-chief of all the armies. He summed it up by writing, "I shall direct him to give you orders and you to obey them." Later that day Halleck stated to Hooker, "You are in command of the Army of the Potomac, and will make the particular dispositions as you deem proper. I shall only indicate the objects to be aimed at."[17]

On 24 June Hooker concluded that Ewell's corps was across the river — he supposed for the purposes of plunder — and expressed the belief that the "yeomanry of that district should be able to check any extended advance of that column, and protect themselves from their extended aggression." This was wishful thinking, and it did not add to his credibility. He closed with a big "if." If the enemy did not throw additional forces across the river, he wanted to make Washington secure and then, with all of the force that he could muster, "strike for his line of retreat in the direction of Richmond."[18]

Maj. Gen. Henry Slocum, commander of the Twelfth Corps at Leesburg, recommended on 19 June that the Federals bridge the Potomac at Edwards Ferry. A crossing there, about five miles east of Leesburg at the mouth of Goose Creek, would enable his and other corps to be supplied over Maryland's roads and by the Chesapeake and Ohio Canal. Hooker so ordered, and by 9:00 A.M. on the 21st the engineers had placed a 1,340-foot pontoon bridge there. Hooker asked for another bridge on the 24th beside the first. The engineers assembled the bridging and on the 25th laid a second bridge that contained sixty-five boats. This efficient work of the army's engineers must rank as one of the highlights of the Gettysburg campaign.[19]

Hooker learned on the 24th that Lee's entire army was crossing into Maryland — Hill's corps was doing so at Shepherdstown. On that day, too, Hooker ordered his Eleventh Corps, which had been guarding the bridge site, to march to Sandy Hook, Maryland. Hooker also instructed Maj. Gen. John F. Reynolds to take the First and Eleventh Corps and a brigade of cavalry, cross the river, and seize Crampton's and Turner's Gaps as rapidly as possible. (Hooker believed correctly that the Confederates had not yet seized them.) Reynolds then was to direct his column toward Middletown. The Eleventh, First, and Third Corps crossed into Maryland on the 25th; army headquarters and the Second, Fifth, and Twelfth Corps, on the 26th; and the Sixth Corps on the 27th. General Reynolds complained at the time of the First Corps crossing that the Eleventh Corps had blocked the roads and bridges with "led horses and colts, evidently stolen." By the 28th the Army of the Potomac was concentrated around Frederick, Maryland.[20]

Hooker had rejuvenated the Army of the Potomac and had led it into Maryland in a highly credible manner. After the Confederates reached the Potomac, the town of Harpers Ferry and its garrison became a bone of contention. Halleck did not wish to abandon the town, but Hooker, who wanted to add its garrison to his army, believed it ripe for Confederate plucking. On the 27th Hooker visited the town and found it garrisoned by 10,000 men who were of "no earthly account" at Harpers Ferry and could be added to the Army of the Potomac. In a dispatch dated the 27th Hooker asked Halleck to present his views to the president and to the secretary of war. In a follow-up message he stated that he could not carry out his original instructions both to protect Washington and Harpers Ferry with the means at his disposal. He asked to be relieved from his command. Halleck referred Hooker's request to the president. In his report Halleck stated simply that Hooker was "at his own request relieved from the command, and Major-General Meade appointed in his place."[21]

CHAPTER 1
Ewell's Raid

At 2:00 A.M. on 15 June cavalry bugles blared. Jenkins's brigade, "fatigued but hopeful" and encouraged by its successes in the "glorious battle" at Martinsburg the day before, began its march to the Potomac and to Maryland and Pennsylvania. It forded the Potomac above Williamsport, turned right, and trotted into that little town, driving a few Union troops from it. Some of the local folks must have known of the brigade's coming, for they set up tables in a street and gave its men a breakfast of milk, bread, and meat. After a hasty meal, the Virginians hurried on toward Hagerstown. Ladies and children welcomed them there about noon with flowers and shouts of "Hurrah for Jeff Davis." Ladies begged them not to go on to Chambersburg where they might meet serious opposition, but the troopers pressed ahead for the Mason-Dixon Line and for Greencastle beyond. Before reaching Greencastle, Jenkins formed the brigade into two columns. Pistols in hand, the Virginians then charged into the village. Although they captured a lieutenant, his small command escaped. After burning Greencastle's railroad station and cutting telegraph wires, Jenkins's men rode ten miles north on the Valley Turnpike to Chambersburg.[1]

Albert Gallatin Jenkins, born in 1830, was from Cabell County along the Ohio River about as far west from Richmond as a person could get and still be in Virginia. Not only was Cabell County a place of strong Unionist sentiment, but Jenkins had been schooled among northerners at Washington and Jefferson College at Washington, Pennsylvania, and at Harvard. Jenkins was a lawyer by profession, and he had served in Congress. Although he had no military training until after the war began, he raised a Confederate unit called the Border Rangers. He subsequently became colonel of the 8th Virginia Cavalry and in August 1862 a brigadier general.[2]

After Jenkins's brigade joined Ewell, its primary task was to collect cattle, horses, and supplies for the Army of Northern Virginia. In addition, it was to perform the usual cavalry duty of screening and gathering intelligence. It is ironic that a brigade of strangers to the Army of Northern Virginia should lead that army on its most critical campaign while the army's integral cavalry units either guarded its rear or rode with Stuart to the east and out of touch with it.

Three brigades of Rodes's division crossed the Potomac at Williamsport on the fifteenth while the other two bivouacked south of the river. Rodes's men were sorely in need of rest, and their bruised and bleeding feet made a halt necessary. They rested at Williamsport until the nineteenth when Ewell ordered them on to Hagerstown. Johnson's division crossed the river at Boteler's Ford a mile downstream near Shepherdstown and bivouacked around Sharpsburg. Early's division, which was threatening Shepherdstown from Harpers Ferry, forded the Potomac at Shepherdstown on the twenty-second. During their short stay near the Dunkard Church at Sharpsburg, men of the 1st and 3d North Carolina regiments held memorial services at the graves of comrades who had been killed there nine months before.[3]

General Lee ordered Ewell's corps into Pennsylvania on 21 June. Because he did not know Hooker's intentions, he gave Ewell broad instructions about his advance. On 17 June he had told Ewell to send Rodes's division to Hagerstown. Ewell's troops were to take supplies that could be used by the army, repress marauding, and give out that Lee was going to Harpers Ferry. Two days later Lee cautioned Ewell to be governed by circumstances around him, to supply his corps with provisions, and to send surplus supplies back to the army. On the twenty-second Lee advised Ewell to move toward the Susquehanna River on routes encompassing Emmitsburg, McConnellsburg, and Chambersburg. However, his trains were to follow the Valley Turnpike, which arced northeast from Hagerstown through Chambersburg and to Carlisle and Harrisburg. Moving on a broad front, especially to the east, would relieve some of the congestion on the center route, and it would confuse the enemy and cause him to pursue Lee east of the mountains and away from Lee's line of communications. Lee instructed also, "If Harrisburg comes within your means, capture it."[4]

Lee was greatly concerned with the collection of supplies. He urged Ewell to use Jenkins's brigade for this and, if necessary, to send a staff officer with it to make sure that it operated in accordance with Lee's instructions. Lee reminded Ewell that whether or not the rest of the army could follow him depended on the amount of supplies that he obtained. If Stuart's three brigades joined him, they could help with the foraging.[5]

Lee was mindful that foraging had to be controlled tightly to discourage abuse, looting, and the erosion of discipline. In General Order 72 he stated that private property would not be injured or destroyed by any person connected with the army or taken by any persons except the commissary, ordnance, quartermaster, and medical chiefs or their agents. These officials would make requisitions on the locals, indicate where the seized supplies were to be delivered, and pay the market price for them with Confederate money. Should the citizens not comply with the requisitions, their goods could be taken, and if they refused money, they were to be given a receipt. In this way Lee hoped to subsist his army without destroying its discipline and reputation.[6]

Jenkins's brigade reached Chambersburg at 11:00 P.M. on the fifteenth and charged "like a tempest with a thousand thunderbolts" through its streets, waking its citizens. One Union account tells of how one charge culminated ingloriously in a collision with a mortar bed left in the street. The crash broke this brave charge, a gun fired accidentally, and the paladins fell into disarray. It could not have been a pretty sight; perhaps it was a reasonable outcome to a long and tiring day. Once the charging was over, the troopers bivouacked on the eastern outskirts of the town.[7]

Over the next two days Jenkins's men collected supplies from the town's stores, houses, and barns. They destroyed the railroad depot, cut telegraph wires, demolished a railroad bridge, and confiscated some weapons. They also drove off some Union troops who attacked their pickets. All went well until about 11:00 A.M. on the seventeenth, when a picket reported the approach of a "strong Yankee force." This could have been a squadron of the 1st New York Cavalry commanded by Capt. William Boyd or a small detachment of Maryland cavalry under Lt. Charles W. Palmer, both of which were in the area. Whichever it was, the picket's alarm prompted Jenkins to assemble his Virginians and retreat to Hagerstown, leaving Chambersburg to sixteen Federal troopers.[8]

Rodes became furious when he learned of Jenkins's retreat. He complained that Jenkins had been told to remain in Chambersburg until Rodes's division joined him there. Because of his retreat, Jenkins had lost much property useful to the Confederacy. From this time on, Jenkins operated directly under Ewell, who accompanied Rodes's division.[9]

Longstreet's corps crossed the Potomac at Williamsport on the twenty-fifth and twenty-sixth and reached Chambersburg on the twenty-seventh.

It rested there two days. Hill's corps forded the river at Boteler's Ford on the twenty-fifth. McGowan's brigade led Pender's division through the ford at Shepherdstown. Permission was given for the men of the 1st South Carolina to remove their pants and drawers if they wished, and most did. They then waded the river, which Capt. Thomas Littlejohn described as about 400 yards wide with a rapid current and water between knee and hip deep.[10]

Musician Julius A. Leinbach of the 26th North Carolina's band crossed the river naked below the waist. After he dressed, someone suggested that his band play "My Maryland." Leinbach refused. Soon a request came from General Pettigrew that Leinbach play the tune, and the band did so.[11]

Dr. LeGrand Wilson of Davis's brigade was with Heth's division when it crossed at Shepherdstown on the twenty-fourth. When he rounded a bend above the river, Wilson viewed a scene that "was enough to arouse enthusiasm in every southern heart." He could see a column of cheering soldiers, their bright arms glittering in the sunshine. Below him, he saw men fording the river holding their cartridge boxes high to keep them dry. Artillery was crossing a short distance downstream, and wagons and ambulances crossed above the column. Bands on the Virginia side played "Dixie," and those across the river played "My Maryland." Wilson thought the scene "grand and inspiring." G. W. Nichols of the 51st Georgia must not have been one of those cheering. He believed that the men did not want to cross the river. They had become tired of Maryland during the Antietam campaign in 1862, and they expected trouble north of the Potomac.[12]

Lt. John L. Marye of the Fredericksburg Artillery recalled that though the water was deep and the current swift, the artillery crossed without trouble, and the mounted men stayed dry. Meanwhile the infantry of Heth's division, with cartridge boxes and shoes slung around their necks, crossed in a column of fours with hands joined. Occasionally, to the amusement of others, an infantryman would step in a hole and get wet up to his neck. After they reached the Maryland bank, they sloshed north toward Hagerstown.[13]

Obeying Lee's orders, Ewell's corps advanced over three routes. Rodes's and Johnson's divisions and the corps' wagon trains followed the Valley Turnpike to Chambersburg, Shippensburg, and Carlisle. Early's division marched to the right over roads close to South Mountain via Waynesboro and Greenwood. It then turned east over the turnpike toward Cashtown Pass and Gettysburg. Before reaching the pass, it burned the iron furnace of Congressman Thaddeus Stevens and, in doing so, probably increased his already deep hatred of the South. After clearing the pass, Early's men marched toward York over two routes: White's cavalry (the 35th Virginia Cavalry Battalion) and Brig. Gen. John B. Gordon's brigade kept to the turnpike through Gettysburg to York and Wrightsville on the Susquehanna River. Early's three other brigades took lesser roads to the north through Mummasburg, Hunterstown, and East Berlin. In the meantime, George H. Steuart's brigade of Johnson's division and the 1st Maryland Cavalry Battalion feinted west from Greencastle to McConnellsburg and rejoined the main column at Chambersburg. It collected sixty cattle, forty horses, and some mules—hardly enough to have made such an arduous detour worthwhile.[14]

Jacob Hoke described the passing of one of Ewell's divisions through Chambersburg. First came some cavalry and then the brigades of infantry. Bands playing "Dixie" and "My Maryland" punctuated the column. Artillery followed the infantry brigades, and ammunition wagons followed the batteries. Teams of from four to six horses pulled the wagons, whose wheels made a grinding noise that suggested that they were heavily loaded. More artillery and more wagons followed, and a drove of 50 to 100 cattle brought up the rear. The soldiers wore various garb—some had portions of Union uniforms—but the color butternut predominated. Many men were ragged and dirty and had no shoes, but they were well armed and seemed to move as a vast fighting machine; they were not laughing as they might have been when marching at route order through the countryside. The division was an impressive sight.[15]

Apart from the brief alarm experienced by Jenkins's troopers in Chambersburg, only Gordon's brigade and White's battalion met any mentionable opposition. This was the 26th Pennsylvania Emergency Infantry Regiment, which had been sent to Gettysburg on a foolhardy and impossible mission: "to harass the enemy and to hold the mountains there." The 26th had existed for three or four days when, on 26 June, it passed through Gettysburg and out the Chambersburg Pike to somewhere near Marsh Creek. The regiment's 700 members were well uniformed in blue, but they were greener than grass and no more than sacrificial lambs, victims of Minuteman and militia myths that had created the illusion that such untrained Americans could successfully oppose well-trained troops. The 26th formed a line when White's battalion appeared. There were a few shots, and the tyros of the 26th fled the field toward Harrisburg with some of White's men in pursuit.[16]

Gordon's brigade reached Gettysburg on the twenty-sixth. Salome Myers

Stewart wrote with some exaggeration that several hundred cavalry arrived first, two of whom rode by her "brandishing their sabres and pointing pistols." "Several thousand" infantry followed, yelling like fiends and with "their old red flag flying." Some of them spent the night at the courthouse. They requisitioned supplies, and they left for York on the twenty-seventh after burning the railroad bridge over Rock Creek and some cars.[17]

The mayor of York surrendered his town when the Confederates approached, and Early occupied it. Gordon's brigade continued on to Wrightsville to seize its bridge over the Susquehanna. A few shots stampeded the militia guarding it, but they set fire to the great wooden structure and prevented the Confederates from capturing it. The fire spread into Wrightsville, and Gordon's men helped the civilians bring it under control. In the meantime others of Early's divisions burned railroad bridges in the area. They would have torched some factory and railroad buildings in York had Early not feared that the fires would spread.[18]

Ewell and Rodes's division reached Carlisle on the twenty-seventh after a halt of one day at Chambersburg to secure supplies. Ewell summoned Chambersburg's leading merchants to a meeting at a bank. They met with three members of his staff: Majors John A. Harmon, William Allen, and William J. Hawks — Ewell's quartermaster, ordnance, and commissary chiefs. Each had prepared requisitions. The merchants looked at their lists and claimed that the requisitions could not be filled. The officers replied that they had used county census records in making out their lists and told the merchants to collect what was wanted throughout the county. In reply the merchants submitted lists of what might be provided. Ewell did not like their offer and ordered them to go to their places of business, where details of soldiers visited them, took what they wanted, and paid for it in Confederate scrip.[19]

In his report Ewell summed up this part of the campaign in Pennsylvania by writing simply, "At Carlisle, Chambersburg, and Shippensburg, requisitions were made for supplies, and the shops were searched, many valuable stores being secured." A Shippensburg merchant claimed that the Rebels had plundered his town for four days and that five sergeants had visited his store at different times in search of drugs. He estimated that they had taken drugs worth $20,000 to $25,000 from Shippensburg alone. After Gettysburg's officials had declared their inability to furnish any supplies, the Confederates had searched stores and found only a small quantity. However, they did find about 2,000 rations in ten or so railroad cars parked on a siding there. These were given to Gordon's brigade, and they burned the cars. In York the authorities answered the Confederate requisitions by furnishing Early with 1,500 to 2,000 pairs of shoes, 1,000 hats, and 1,000 pairs of socks, but they produced only $28,000 instead of the $100,000 demanded. Early, who could be more lenient than his reputation suggests, believed that the York authorities had made an honest effort and asked for no more. Ewell sent a wagon train south from Chambersburg with medical and ordnance stores along with a drove of 3,000 cattle. In addition he notified the army's quartermaster of the location of 5,000 barrels of flour that had been collected. Getting so many barrels of flour back in Virginia would not have been easy to do.[20]

Gathering supplies from individual farmers was not always pleasant. Forage parties received little or no opposition, for the farmers were thoroughly frightened. A soldier in the 8th Louisiana wrote that it was sad to see women in Waynesboro crying and wringing their hands at the sight of the Confederates. People watched from a distance "with every appearance of fear, very much in the same manner as the wild beeves of Louisiana gather round a person creeping through the grass in hunting ducks." They were so afraid that they would give the Rebels anything that they wanted if only they would not destroy their property. Lieutenant Marye, who led details in search of horses, thought it a distasteful duty; it seemed that every other animal seized was a family pet, a favorite of the women and children who "with wailing and crying" begged that their pets might be spared. He believed that most of the draft horses taken were too large and clumsy for use by the artillery.[21]

Lt. John H. (Ham) Chamberlayne of Virginia's Crenshaw Battery hit the jackpot at a Dunkard church. Services were going on inside, and there were horses and buggies outside. While his men secured the horses, Chamberlayne passed out receipts to their owners. But his luck ran out. A Union patrol intercepted the artillerymen on their return to their battery, and Chamberlayne became a prisoner at Fort Delaware and at Johnson's Island.[22]

The Rebels took advantage of the Pennsylvanians' fear of them. Most seemed to rationalize that General Order 72 did not apply to food obtained without overt coercion. Therefore they were able enjoy the fat of the land — chickens, butter, buttermilk, cherries, and all else potable and edible — when they were not actively on the march. If their consciences bothered them, they were able to assuage them with the accepted truth that Union soldiers were doing worse things in the South. One soldier of the 7th Louisiana, described as not a "raw," went into a house near the regiment's bivouac and asked for some bread and milk. The housewife invited him to sit and then asked what regiment he belonged to. He replied, "7th Louisiana," and she fainted. She had good reason. Earlier the Confederate cavalry had told the Pennsylvanians that the Louisiana Tigers would "kill, burn & destroy everything & everybody in the country."[23]

Because the men of the Army of Northern Virginia have had the reputation of being well behaved while in the North, their lapses in good behavior and that of the "raws" stand out in bold relief. Hard liquor was plentiful. The commissary of the 9th Louisiana issued a half-pint of confiscated whiskey to the men of the regiment. Naturally the drinkers put the ration of the nondrinkers in their own canteens, and this "old Red Eye" was still having its effect in York three days later. Even officers were not immune. One soldier wrote that it was not unusual to see a mounted officer snoozing by the roadside. Col. John Fite of the 7th Tennessee illustrated why such dereliction was tolerated. When Fite went into Hagerstown to buy a hat, some convivial fellows from Hill's staff invited him to a saloon. After leaving them, he met Brig. Gen. James J. Archer in the company of a Dr. Gwynne, who invited the two Confederates to his home. There some ladies offered him more to drink, and being a gentleman, Fite could not refuse them. He rode back to his bivouac intoxicated in the rear of a wagon. Archer called Fite on the carpet later that day for another matter. During their discussion Archer told Fite that he was drunk and should be placed in arrest. Fite retorted that the only difference between them was that he had sobered up whereas Archer was still drunk. Archer closed their talk by asking Fite to have a drink. Fite obliged and returned to his regiment.[24]

J. D. Hufham Jr. recalled that "it wasn't often that our boys got a chance at liquor, and, when they did, they made good use of it." Pennsylvania was a land of opportunity. One expert forager kicked a haystack and found a whole barrel of whisky. They chopped open the barrelhead and dipped its contents out by the bucketful. Further, there was a lot of mint around and ice from icehouses. Therefore, "mint juleps in tin cans were plentiful." Whether or not they made juleps, on the twenty-ninth some men of the "Irish Company" of the 9th Louisiana drank too much and had a brawl in which a lieutenant got "badly used up." After others quieted them down, they fell asleep.[25]

Although some Confederates liked Pennsylvania whiskey, many had little good to say of the people themselves. LeGrand Wilson wrote that when Joseph Davis's brigade passed through Greencastle, 200–300 "bright girls" lined the road to watch them go by. The last of them, who wore a U.S. flag as an apron, "impudently asked the boys if they would not like to fight under it." Wilson regarded this as a sign that they were in enemy company. Others might have detected another message.[26]

After being in Pennsylvania for about three days, General Pender wrote Mrs. Pender that the country was magnificent but that the people were miserable, coarse, and dirty. He had yet to see a nice-looking young lady; those encountered were coarse and dirty and went barefoot. Capt. Thomas Hightower of Georgia echoed Pender's observations: the women in Green-castle were "pretty rough" and the homeliest he had seen. He thought that most of them were Irish and "red mouthed Dutch." He saw that even the women of sophisticated Carlisle were ugly and comical. A cynic might wonder if both men were trying to avoid giving their wives reason for jealousy. Lt. Henry R. Berkeley of the Amherst Artillery found Shippens-burg peopled by "Black Dutch," whatever that might have meant.[27]

But perceptions differ. Col. Cullen A. Battle of the 3d Alabama Regi-ment was provost marshal of Chambersburg. After spending two or three days there, he and some of his staff accepted a dinner invitation at a resident's home. When he left, a citizen's delegation thanked him for his courtesy and kindness. In Wrightsville a woman whose house had been saved from burning during the bridge fire by men of Gordon's brigade thanked them by having Gordon and some of his men to breakfast.[28]

Lts. J. Warren Jackson and William C. Gimsey of the 8th Louisiana "amused themselves extensively" in York, where they saw pretty girls and found the people friendly. Yet though some North Carolinians saw few women in the town, they met a lot of men. Many of the men mingled and drank with Confederate officers and said that they disapproved of the Lincoln administration. Capt. William Seymour of Brig. Gen. Harry T. Hays's staff said that some of the York people confessed to being Copper-heads. This should have pleased him, but he thought them a mean and sordid people who would claim anything to save their money and their property. Citizens told General Early that there were thousands of Knights of the Golden Circle in that part of the state. The Confederates had met people along the way who greeted them with mysterious gestures that were supposed to identify them as members of the Knights and Confederate sympathizers. But they had been gypped by two men who told them that the purchase of such memberships would afford them and their property protection from the invaders.[29]

Daniel's, Ramseur's, and Iverson's brigades occupied Carlisle Barracks, the army's cavalry post, while Doles's Georgians bivouacked on the campus of Dickinson College and provided the provost guard for the town. Ewell, who had been stationed at the barracks when he was a young man and had acquaintances in the town, observed that the residents "look as sour as vinegar, and, I have no doubt, would gladly send us all to Kingdom come if they could." However, he sent two officers of his staff on a kind visit to a family he had known to see if they were all right. Other Confederates had pleasant civilian contacts when they attended church services, and a few enjoyed talking with the college's professors at its library. In his report Ewell announced that "agreeably to the views of the commanding general, I did not burn Carlisle barracks." General Stuart and his cavalry would do that during their visit on 1 July.[30]

A memorable event took place at the barracks. During its stay there, the 32d North Carolina had the honor of receiving the first of the new Confederate flags, adopted on 1 May, that had reached the Army of Northern Virginia. They raised this flag, "The Stainless Banner," on the barracks flagstaff and held a ceremony to mark the occasion. It featured speeches by important officers, some of whom had had too much to drink. Years later a veteran recalled the affair with emotion: "Oh! it was a grand occasion — in striking contrast to the sad scenes witnessed by the same soldiers two days thereafter, on the blood-stained heights of Gettysburg."[31]

The march to the Susquehanna had been an exhilarating experience for the officers and men of the Army of Northern Virginia. Capturing Winchester, eating good food north of the Potomac, and being conquerors in a rich land raised their morale and made them feel invincible. General Lee was worried about the Army of the Potomac, but few men in the lower ranks were greatly concerned. Harrisburg lay just ahead and would be theirs for the taking.

As Rodes's division marked time in Carlisle, Ewell was planning to seize Harrisburg on the Susquehanna just eighteen miles away. The extent of his planning is unknown. The most overt action was a reconnaissance of Harrisburg's defenses west of the river by Capt. Henry B. Richardson, Ewell's chief engineer, and a detachment of Jenkins's cavalry. Jenkins's men had entered Carlisle on the morning of the twenty-seventh. When Rodes's infantry reached the town that afternoon, the cavalrymen accompanied Richardson to Mechanicsburg ten miles east on the road to Harrisburg. They halted that night about five miles from Mechanicsburg. During the night Union troops from Harrisburg's defenses harassed them and allowed them little sleep. The harassers were probably from the 1st New York

Cavalry Regiment or other experienced units that had escaped from Winchester, rather than emergency troops called up to defend the city. After reaching Mechanicsburg on the morning of the twenty-eighth, Jenkins demanded that the citizens deliver food for 1,550 men to the town hall. They brought ham, bread, and butter enough for the Virginians and more. One resident wrote that the Confederates seized horses and that the local mills were grinding and teams were hauling their produce away.[32]

Jenkins's men pushed to the outskirts of Harrisburg and drove off swarming Federals so that Richardson could see its defenses. Jenkins also ordered up Capt. Thomas E. Jackson's battery to exchange fire with Federal batteries in their front. At the same time Jenkins had to send a part of his force back toward Mechanicsburg to combat Federal horsemen who were stinging his rear. However, all of Jenkins's and Richardson's preparations to capture Harrisburg were to no avail. On 30 June Ewell ordered Jenkins back to Carlisle. The raid and the threat to Harrisburg were over. Ewell had to march his corps at once south to the Gettysburg-Cashtown area, where General Lee was concentrating his army.[33]

CHAPTER 2
Lee's Army Concentrates

On the night of 28 June at his headquarters east of Chambersburg, General Lee learned from Henry T. Harrison, a Confederate spy, that the Army of the Potomac had crossed that river and at least three of its corps were near Frederick, Maryland. Harrison told him also that General Meade had replaced Hooker as commander of the Army of the Potomac just that day. Lee should not have been greatly surprised that the Federal army was in Maryland; he had designed to draw it there, and he had learned on the twenty-third that it had bridged the Potomac at Edwards Ferry. Yet because General Stuart, his cavalry commander, had not told him that the Union army had crossed into Maryland, he believed that it was still in Virginia. Regardless of what Lee might have known or suspected of Federal movements prior to 28 June, it was Harrison's report that triggered immediate action. Lee sought to keep Meade's forces away from the Cumberland Valley and his line of communications by concentrating his army east of South Mountain. To this end, he directed that his three corps unite in the Gettysburg-Cashtown area without delay.[1]

Lee's messenger rode the thirty miles to Ewell and reached him on the twenty-ninth as the one-legged general was starting toward Harrisburg. Neither Ewell nor Rodes revealed the plans for taking the city, though Rodes reported that they had made a thorough reconnaissance of its defenses on the twenty-ninth. Rodes's division was rested and well supplied with rations, and every man in the division was said to have contemplated the movement with eagerness. In addition, Maj. Gen. Isaac Trimble, who at that time had no assignment in Lee's army, had arrived at Ewell's headquarters on the twenty-ninth and was brimming with advice. Trimble wrote in later years that immediately on his arrival he had informed Ewell of Lee's desire to take Harrisburg. He wrote also that Ewell had authorized him to take a brigade and a battery and seize it. Trimble explained that artillery could shell every part of the city from west of the river, but he did not say how the brigade would cross the wide river in the face of the unknown but sizable force protecting the city. Neither Ewell nor Rodes wrote of such a scheme and if Rodes would have been willing to turn over a portion of his division to another general for such a dubious operation.[2]

When he received Lee's orders to move his corps to the Gettysburg-Cashtown area, Ewell directed General Johnson to take his division and the corps trains back over the Valley Turnpike and approach the concentration area through Cashtown Pass. He also sent Capt. Elliott Johnson of his staff to Early with orders to rejoin the corps in the concentration area. On 30 June Ewell accompanied Rodes's division south over the Baltimore-Carlisle Turnpike through Papertown (Mount Holly Springs) to Petersburg (York Springs) and then south on the road linking Harrisburg with Gettysburg. The division bivouacked at the crossroads hamlet of Heidlersburg about ten miles northeast of Gettysburg. It rained much of that day, the roads were muddy and slippery, and the march was tiring. South of Petersburg Ewell ordered a band from Doles's brigade to pep up the troops with music. When the headquarters passed through Papertown, Ewell's cartographer, Jedidiah Hotchkiss, and others visited the paper factory to replenish their paper supply. On this march, as on others in Pennsylvania, the troops enjoyed the ripe cherries on trees near the road. Often they chopped or broke branches from the trees and ate the fruit from the severed limbs as they hiked along. General Order 72 apparently did not cover fruit.[3]

The 1st North Carolina Sharpshooter Battalion, commanded by Maj. Rufus W. Wharton, was the last unit to leave Carlisle. Wharton had been the military governor of the town. His orders were to wait there until all of the other Confederate units had left and then to bring up the rear. Just before daybreak on 1 July, as Wharton's battalion was preparing to march, Jenkins's cavalry turned several hundred prisoners — emergency militia — over to him. He discussed what should be done with them with a legal officer who was present, and the two decided that the docile fellows should be paroled and allowed to return home. In the light of a waning moon Wharton attempted to form the prisoners into a line so that they could be sworn not to serve again until properly exchanged. Wharton noticed that the prisoners moved gingerly. He looked at them more closely and saw that they were barefooted — the cavalrymen had taken their shoes.[4]

As Ewell prepared to seize Harrisburg, A. P. Hill's corps bivouacked near Fayetteville along the Gettysburg-Chambersburg Turnpike. Hill's orders were to move over this pike toward York, cross the Susquehanna, threaten communications between Harrisburg and Baltimore, and cooperate with Ewell. Though Ewell had already been ordered to return to the Cashtown area, Hill's report suggests that on the twenty-ninth he began his march to Cashtown before he received a change of orders from General Lee. Upon receiving the orders, Hill directed Heth's division to Cashtown, a cluster of houses and a tavern at the east portal of Cashtown Pass. Pender's division followed on the thirtieth. In spite of Harrison's report to General Lee about the nearness of the Union army, Hill seems not to have appreciated the likelihood that elements of it might be nearby.[5]

Heth's division, in the van of Hill's corps, marched to Cashtown on the twenty-ninth but went no farther. (Lee reported that "the weather being inclement, the march was conducted with a view to the comfort of the troops.") Hill likely learned that day that the army would be concentrated near Cashtown and that his corps should gather there. After his division reached that area, Heth took measures to secure it. The 52d North Carolina and the 2d Mississippi regiments went south on the road to Emmitsburg and placed pickets at Millerstown (Fairfield), where they had a brush with Buford's cavalrymen on the morning of 30 June. At the same time Col. John M. Brockenbrough, commander of the Virginia brigade in Heth's division, ordered Col. William S. Christian of the 55th Virginia to take his regiment east on the road to Gettysburg. Christian was to set up picket posts, and Brockenbrough warned him not to mistake friends for foes — some of Ewell's or Stuart's troops might be approaching from that direction. Christian asked other questions but learned that Brockenbrough and Heth did not have the answers; the orders had come from Hill. Since the sun was setting, Christian hurriedly marched his regiment a mile and a half east along the pike, placed it at a cemetery at a crossroads, and sent out patrols. The 55th remained there overnight without being disturbed.[6]

Dr. LeGrand Wilson related an incident that suggests that Hill's orders to pass east beyond Gettysburg had been changed. Davis's brigade had marched five or six miles from Cashtown and had bivouacked. Next day it served as an escort for engineers who were mapping the area. The engi-

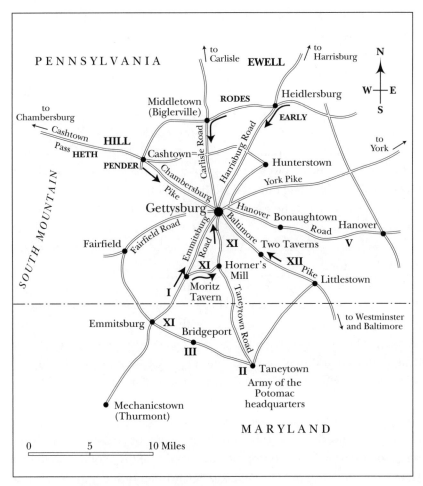

Map 2.1. Gettysburg Campaign, 30 June–1 July

neers worked rapidly, and the brigade was able to return to a bivouac above Cashtown on the evening of the thirtieth.[7]

Pender's division rested near Fayetteville on the twenty-ninth, a cloudy and rainy day. It had inspections in the morning. Pender had written a letter to his wife on the previous day. His letter brimmed with optimism: everything seemed to be "going along finely," and he hoped to be in Harrisburg in three days. His men had been marching well; they would go fifteen or twenty miles in a day "without leaving a straggler and hoop and yell on all occasions." He found it difficult to restrain the men from plundering; but the civilians were so scared that the soldiers had only to express a wish to them, and it was fulfilled. One woman was not intimidated. The

{ LEE'S ARMY CONCENTRATES }

band of the 13th North Carolina played "My Maryland" as it passed the house of an old woman who watched the passing Confederates from a rocking chair on her front porch. When the music stopped, she stood and shouted in broken English, "Oh, yes! Oh, yes! It's 'Maryland, my Maryland!' but when you come back it will be 'Fire in the mountains; run, boys, run!' " That said, she laughed loudly, sat down, and resumed her vigorous rocking.[8]

In keeping with the practice in both armies, the 26th North Carolina of Pettigrew's brigade held its muster at Cashtown on the morning of the thirtieth. After the muster, Heth sent Pettigrew's brigade toward Gettysburg in search of supplies, especially shoes, which were badly needed by the men of his division. Bandsmen of the 26th recalled that as they passed east through Cashtown Pass, their rations were short and they could buy nothing because the commissary and the quartermaster departments had "cleaned up things pretty well as they went." At the same time, Colonel Fite of the 7th Tennessee, with General Archer's approval, raided a large house in Cashtown. The party found goods of all sorts, including badly needed shoes, in the cellar. Their haul was so large that they had to carry it off in a wagon. That evening the Tennesseans bivouacked closer to Gettysburg at a farm with a barn that was "full of bacon" hidden beneath straw that the men were carrying off for bedding.[9]

Heth did not say why he believed that Gettysburg contained a lot of provisions. Perhaps he did not know that Gordon's brigade had passed through the town four days earlier and should have picked it clean. In response to Heth's order to go there for supplies, Pettigrew's brigade started for the town early on the morning of the thirtieth with three regiments — the 11th, the 26th, and the 47th North Carolina — plus three guns of Capt. Victor Maurin's Donaldsonville Artillery of Louisiana. Pettigrew also took several empty wagons to carry the goods that they hoped to garner. Heth told Pettigrew that the town might be defended by a "home guard," which he would have no trouble driving off. However, if he met troops capable of resistance or a portion of the Army of the Potomac, he should not attack. He was not to precipitate a fight.[10]

That morning, while breakfasting on "confiscated chicken" at the 55th Virginia's position near McKnightstown, five miles west of Gettysburg, Colonel Christian saw a large body of Confederates approaching from the direction of Cashtown. It was Pettigrew's brigade, and that general asked for the commander of the troops on picket. (This suggests that Christian did not stir himself to greet Pettigrew.) Pettigrew asked Christian to "attend" his column with the 55th. The wary colonel replied that the Virginians had spent a sleepless night on picket and, more importantly, he had heard nothing of this from Colonel Brockenbrough. This did not dissuade Pettigrew. He replied that while his own men were well drilled and equipped, they were rather inexperienced, and he wanted a seasoned regiment to go with them. Pettigrew's argument or rank proved persuasive, and the 55th joined him.[11]

Pettigrew's brigade trudged ahead, and according to Pettigrew's aide, Lt. Louis G. Young, General Longstreet's spy passed it. The spy soon returned from the town with the report that Buford's cavalry division, 3,000 strong, occupied it. A genuine Knight of the Golden Circle confirmed this. Pettigrew sent back to Heth for instructions. Heth repeated his orders and expressed belief that the Army of the Potomac had not reached Gettysburg.[12]

Pettigrew had a chance meeting with another man near Herr Tavern on Herr Ridge two miles west of Gettysburg's square. Dr. John W. C. O'Neal, a physician of the town and a native Virginian, was on his way to see a patient at Bream's Mill when he met Pettigrew's column. The general questioned him; O'Neal showed him his medical equipment and his list of calls and convinced the general of his identity. Pettigrew allowed him to go about his business, but O'Neal had not gone far when a rider overtook him and returned him to the general. As O'Neal expressed it, "Egad, those were the days when you were told to stop to stop." Pettigrew asked him if there were any Yankees in the town and if he had any newspapers. O'Neal, who had left the town early that morning, replied that there were no troops there when he left it. He added that he was a doctor and not an informant. Finally Pettigrew allowed him to go, but he did not permit him to enter the town.

O'Neal did not leave. He thought it safer to stay with Pettigrew than to go off and be arrested by a Confederate who might hold him prisoner. He saw some of Pettigrew's officers talking in front of the tavern and went with them east to Willoughby Run and to the tollhouse beyond it. When at the tollgate, they saw mounted men on the crest of McPherson Ridge 400 yards ahead. Pettigrew turned to the doctor and said, "I understood you to say that there were no Yankees in the town." He pointed toward the horsemen and continued, "Those are mounted men and are evidently from the town." O'Neal probably became embarrassed and afraid at this time. There had been no troops in the town when he left it, O'Neal replied, and he did not know who was there now. Pettigrew and his party returned to Herr Tavern. O'Neal believed that it was then about 10:00 A.M. Near Marsh Creek O'Neal met a doctor from Baltimore whom he knew and rode with him to Cashtown.[13]

Pettigrew's brigade returned then to Marsh Creek, followed by Union cavalrymen. Heth reported that Pettigrew had found a large force of cavalry supported by infantry in the town. In his *Memoirs*, Heth said that infantry drums had been heard beyond the town (there was no infantry nearby). Hill reported that Pettigrew had met mostly cavalry; Lee's report stated that being ignorant of the force in the town, and unwilling to hazard an attack with a single brigade, Pettigrew had returned to Cashtown. Lieutenant Young took issue with Lee's report. Since there was Union cavalry in the town, he argued, the Confederates could not have entered it without a fight. He believed that Pettigrew would have been willing to attack had his orders not forbidden him to do so. As the Confederates retired west over the pike, Young and Lt. Walter Robertson, also of Pettigrew's staff, followed behind, keeping an eye on the enemy cavalry. When Union troopers came to within 300 or 400 yards of them, the lieutenants would stop in the pike where the Union horsemen could see them. The Union riders would stop also and remain halted until Young and Robertson moved on. This happened a number of times as Pettigrew's men plodded west toward Cashtown.[14]

After he returned to Cashtown on the evening of the thirtieth, Pettigrew told Heth of his encounter with Union troops in Gettysburg. Heth thought that he must be mistaken. General Hill rode up while they were talking, and Heth asked Pettigrew to repeat what he had said. Hill, like Heth, did not believe that there was a Union force in Gettysburg "except possibly a small cavalry vidette." Pettigrew brought Lieutenant Young into the conversation, probably because Hill had known him when he had been on Pender's staff and his views might carry weight with the corps commander. Young told the generals that he had watched the Union cavalry column carefully and that its movements were those of well-trained troops and not "home guard." Yet Hill was not persuaded; he did not believe "that any portion of the Army of the Potomac was up." However, in emphatic words he "expressed the hope that it was, as this was the place he wanted it to be." Young reflected in later years that "blindness in part seems to have come over our commanders, who, slow to believe in the presence of an organized army of the enemy, thought there must be a mistake in the report taken back by General Pettigrew." Further, he doubted that any of the brigade commanders except Pettigrew believed that they were marching to battle, "a weakness . . . which rendered them unprepared for what was to happen." In 1877 Heth wrote that Hill had said that he had just come from General Lee, who told him that the information from his scouts corroborated that which Hill had received from his own scouts—that the enemy was still at "Middleburg" and had not "struck their tents." If said, this made no sense. Yet the ardent Heth, disregarding what one of his own brigade commanders had seen, replied, "If there is no objection, I will take my division to-morrow and go to Gettysburg to get those shoes." Hill replied, "None in the world."[15]

That night the 26th North Carolina Regiment bivouacked in a grove of trees by a creek. It put out pickets. Two ladies appeared, much distressed because the pickets separated them from their homes. Lt. Col. John R. Lane, as became a gentleman, assured them that the Army of Northern Virginia did not make war on women and children, and that he esteemed it his duty and privilege to protect them. In order that they not be inconvenienced, he advanced the picket line beyond their houses. That night some men of Heth's division bivouacked approximately three and a half miles from Gettysburg, and its men "quietly dreamed of home and loved ones in blissful ignorance of the momentous fact that Meade's great army was almost within their hearing."[16]

As Pettigrew's brigade made its foray toward Gettysburg, General Lee's headquarters moved east to the foot of the mountain near Caledonia. Johnson's division of Ewell's corps reached the Scotland area just northeast of Chambersburg. Anderson's division of Hill's corps remained at Fayetteville, while McLaws's and Hood's divisions advanced to nearby Greenwood. Pickett's division of Longstreet's corps stayed at Chambersburg. As these divisions collected west of South Mountain and Cashtown Pass, Pender's division marched from Fayetteville into the pass to support Heth's division. It rained during Pender's march; but the macadam pike had a hard surface, and the rain did not slow Pender's pace. During the morning the division passed by Thaddeus Stevens's still-smoldering ironworks, and it halted in the early afternoon at a basin high in the pass where there were farms and space to spread out. An order arrived for the men of the division to cook a ration for the next day and to be ready to march at 5:00 A.M.[17]

On 30 June Brig. Gen. Alfred M. Scales, who had just returned to the army, took command of the North Carolina brigade formerly led by Pender. Scales had commanded its 13th Regiment until he was wounded at Chancellorsville.

Since Scales had been unable to inspect the brigade in camp, he observed it critically as it marched. He was well pleased with the brigade's equipment and bearing; he saw no straggling and heard no complaints. The troops seemed cheerful and buoyant, and all manifested confidence in themselves and in General Lee. Scales expressed his pleasure to Pender; he said that the sooner they met the enemy, the better, for given an even chance, a glorious victory awaited them. Pender replied gravely that his old comrade would soon be gratified. Pettigrew had found Gettysburg occupied by cavalry and a large body of infantry, and indications were that they would have their hands full on the following day. Pender would prove a better seer than Heth and Hill.[18]

CHAPTER 3
Meade's Pursuit

"No one ever received a more important command." So wrote Gen.-in-Chief Halleck to Maj. Gen. George G. Meade when he ordered Meade to take command of the Army of the Potomac. Battle was imminent, and the fate of the republic fell suddenly and without warning upon Meade's shoulders.[1]

Halleck advised Meade that he would be hampered by no minute instructions and that he was free to act as he deemed proper. That said, Halleck reminded Meade that the Army of the Potomac was the "covering army" of Washington as well as the "Army of Operation" against the invading Rebels. Therefore, it must protect both the capital and Baltimore. Should Lee advance on either city, Meade would give him battle. Meade replied, "As a soldier, I obey it, and to the utmost of my ability will execute it." He met with Hooker at the Army of the Potomac's headquarters near Frederick, Maryland, and learned of the army's deployment and the orders that had been given it. Although Meade and the army's chief of staff, Maj. Gen. Daniel Butterfield, had small personal regard for each other, Butterfield consented to remain at his post and provide essential continuity at army headquarters at that critical time.[2]

After meeting with Hooker, Meade informed Halleck that it appeared to him that he should move the army toward the Susquehanna River and, at the same time, cover Washington and Baltimore. If the enemy gave up his attempt to cross the Susquehanna or turned toward Baltimore, Meade would give him battle.[3]

Meade's appointment gave general satisfaction to the officers and men of the army, though few outside the Fifth Corps knew much about him. Many would have preferred Reynolds or someone better known to them,

Maj. Gen. George G. Meade
(NA)

particularly George B. McClellan. Lt. Henry P. Claire, adjutant of the 83d New York, in a letter home lauded Hooker's removal but gave Meade only a month in command. Claire preferred McClellan and wrote that he sincerely prayed to God that if McClellan was not placed in command soon, that "Jeff Davis enters Washington hangs Lincoln and all his damnable associates proclaiming himself President." He would give a month's pay "to see Washington sacked & the present clique chased like bayed foxes with bloodhounds after them." Col. Samuel H. Leonard of the 13th Massachusetts expressed a more charitable but still cynical view of Meade's future when he announced the change of command to his regiment. He assured his men that this change was not the last one, "that we needn't be discouraged, as we might all yet receive the honor."[4]

Most of the army's ranking officers applauded the change. Of the commanders of the seven infantry corps, only Maj. Gen. Daniel Sickles regretted Hooker's departure. Reynolds, who, apart from Maj. Gen. Henry Slocum of the Twelfth Corps, was the ranking general of the lot and had declined the honor, was Meade's friend. Reynolds rode to headquarters to see his new commander. Meade told him that his appointment had been an unwelcome surprise and asked for Reynolds's support. Reynolds assured him that he was pleased with Meade's selection and that Meade could rely on him. The two discussed the military situation and were said to have "concerted" a plan that "resulted in the fighting of the battle of Gettysburg upon ground selected by Reynolds." Unfortunately, if there was such a plan, we know nothing about it.[5]

On 28 June, when Meade took command of the Army of the Potomac, Longstreet's and Hill's corps were near Chambersburg, and Ewell had two divisions at Carlisle and one in York. Meade spent the day taking hold of the army's command as it concentrated in the Frederick area. Meade was concerned especially with bringing his cavalry from south of the Potomac, where it had been been covering the army's rear during the Potomac crossing. He wanted the cavalry deployed so that it could screen the army's front and flanks on the march north. On the twenty-ninth, in keeping with Meade's statement to Halleck, the Army of the Potomac's seven corps were moving north from Frederick toward Pennsylvania on a twenty-five-mile front extending from Emmitsburg to Manchester, Maryland. The First and Eleventh Corps, on the left of the army, marched from Frederick to Emmitsburg.[6]

The soldiers of the First and Eleventh Corps found the march through Maryland memorable. These corps were the first to cross the Potomac, and both had marched to Jefferson and Middletown, where they could support the units that had seized and held the South Mountain gaps. It was hard marching. There was rain each day, and the wet roads were cut up by the wheels of wagons, caissons, limbers, and guns and churned by thousands of human feet and horses' hooves. In spite of their hardships, soldiers of the two corps recalled their first days in Maryland with pleasure.[7]

Maryland was an Eden when compared with war-ravaged Virginia. Capt. Stephen M. Weld, one of Reynolds's aides, described Barnesville as a "small old fashioned town with one or two cottages in it, with pretty gardens in front; quite the contrast to anything we have seen in Virginia." He wrote of the scenery between Barnesville and Jefferson as "very beautiful," having neat farmhouses, whitewashed fences, and grain ready to be harvested and seeming "like a perfect paradise." Jefferson, "a strong Union town with many pretty houses, and some three or four churches," was memorable to Weld because the First Corps headquarters was in one of its houses and Weld slept in a bed. Weld found the church bells in Middletown on the twenty-eighth "pleasant indeed." They reminded the soldiers of home.[8]

The 55th Ohio, an Eleventh Corps regiment, stopped at Jefferson, where some of its men pillaged. The people greeted them in a friendly way nonetheless, and they had some good things to eat. When the 14th Brooklyn passed through Jefferson, flags were flying from most of the houses. As it approached Middletown, its drum corps hustled to the front of the regiment, and the 14th paraded through the town with flags unfurled and with "vim and spirit." More importantly, "bright faced Maryland girls" watched from the windows and doors of houses as the New Yorkers passed. The 14th bivouacked nearby. When it marched on the next day, the girls came out to say goodbye and to volunteer to mail letters for the soldiers. The 143d Pennsylvania arrived in Middletown on a Sunday when a lot of women and girls were walking along the street on their way home from a Sunday school picnic. The regiment had guards posted, probably to discourage straggling. One sentry, Charley Wilson, halted some of the girls as they tried to pass his post and told them that they could not go by. When some began to cry, the magnanimous Charley allowed them to do so if they would kiss him. Some did. The girls also volunteered to post letters for the men of the 143d. This welcoming and sympathetic behavior boosted the morale of the Union soldiers and boded ill for the Confederacy.[9]

Both the First and the Eleventh Corps passed through the Frederick area. Troops paraded through the town on 28 June to the cheers of the populace. The First Corps passed through Emmitsburg on the twenty-ninth with drums beating and flags flying. At this time Reynolds knew that Ewell had pushed toward the Susquehanna and that the remainder of the Confederate army was near Chambersburg. Some of the information he received was accurate, but some was not, and it was difficult to discern true from false. On the twenty-ninth, after he had reached Emmitsburg, Reynolds forwarded outdated information received there to the effect that Hill's corps was moving on Chambersburg. That night, after a hard march in the rain, the First Corps bivouacked on the high ground north of Emmitsburg. Reynolds had selected the ground carefully with an eye toward confrontation with Rebels reported in Fairfield. After a rainy march from Frederick over heavy roads, the Eleventh Corps bivouacked south of Emmitsburg. Generals Oliver O. Howard and Schurz placed their headquarters at St. Joseph's College, a girls' school. Some of the Eleventh Corps occupied its grounds. Although they had had an arduous day, Schurz asked the band of the 45th New York to play a concert of songs, marches, and polkas for their hosts. Yet in spite of the parading and other festivities, a soldier of the First Corps detected a change in the faces of the officers. They were becoming grave, reticent, and more pensive.[10]

Although the approach of battle was sobering, it did not dim the soldiers' appreciation of pretty girls. Between Frederick and Emmitsburg, the Iron Brigade passed a young woman, about twenty years old, waving a flag at the gate of an imposing farmhouse. Lt. Col. Rufus R. Dawes of the 6th Wisconsin and his staff tipped their hats and bowed as they passed her. The men of Company B stared dumbfounded at her; the men of the German company gazed in silent admiration. Company C expressed its admiration in a more positive way. As it neared the girl, Lt. Lloyd Harris ordered, "Company C, Right shoulder, shift, arms!" The men dressed their lines and went to right shoulder shift. When they came opposite her, Harris commanded, "Carry, arms," and they gave her a marching salute "as if she were general of the army." The following companies of the Iron Brigade followed suit. It can be hoped that she appreciated the pleasure she had given, the honor accorded her, and the heroes who gave it.[11]

On 29 June Meade informed Halleck that he was moving the First and Eleventh Corps to Emmitsburg on the right of his line, which would extend east to New Windsor. At the same time he wrote of moving his army forward and inclining to the right. He stated that his main aim was to find and fight the enemy; to do this he would hold his army together and endeavor to fall upon some portion of Lee's army. Yet on the twenty-ninth he ordered the First Corps north from Emmitsburg to Marsh Creek, midway between Emmitsburg and Gettysburg. On 30 June Meade ordered Reynolds to take command of the three corps of the army's left wing — his own First Corps, the Third, and the Eleventh. Meade did not know the precise location of Hill's corps when he ordered Reynolds to Marsh Creek, but on the thirtieth he announced to his corps commanders that Longstreet and Hill were "at Chambersburg partly toward Gettysburg." At 10:45 A.M. he informed them that Hill was in Cashtown Pass. By that time he had no definite location for Longstreet's corps.[12]

On the morning of 30 June the First Corps began to stir. Orderlies galloped around more than usual, and officers seemed to be waiting for something to happen. In a while an order came for the troops to fall in. After a delay, Col. Roy Stone's brigade of the Third Division moved off, not in a hurry but "more slowly as tho we were afraid of running against something. All was seeming uncertainty." One of the boys of the 143d Pennsylvania said that "he could smell a fight." When the Pennsylvania regiments crossed the Mason-Dixon Line, they gave the "wildest demonstrations of joy" and sang "Home Sweet Home." The First Corps advanced to Marsh Creek and formed a defensive line there. Wadsworth's division covered the road to Gettysburg and deployed the 19th Indiana Regiment of the Iron Brigade on a picket line astride the road about two and a half miles north of the creek. Maj. Gen. Abner Doubleday's division watched the road to Fairfield, and Brig. Gen. John C. Robinson's division took a reserve position to the rear but north of the Maryland line. The Eleventh Corps remained at Emmitsburg but shifted its position to encompass the ground north of the village.[13]

While waiting by Marsh Creek, the First Corps had its bimonthly muster but was not disturbed. It was a day of mizzly rain; but it was warm, trees gave shelter, and the troops did not suffer much. The 14th Brooklyn Regiment was in a field near a large farmhouse. The farmer asked Col. Edward Fowler to move his regiment, and Fowler replied that this was impossible. The farmer threatened to hold Fowler responsible for anything taken from his farm. As befitted the colonel's surname, almost every man had chicken to eat while there, and the colonel took no notice of it. It was probably during this halt that the men of the 56th Pennsylvania bathed in a mill pond, and some of Robinson's soldiers found a still, got drunk, and had a brawl.[14]

While the First Corps was at Marsh Creek and the Eleventh rested near Emmitsburg, the cavalry screening the army's left wing moved toward it from beyond South Mountain. Maj. Gen. Julius Stahel's division, on loan from the Department of Washington, had been operating with Reynolds in place of the army's integral units that were still south of the Potomac. Stahel's troopers had guarded the South Mountain gaps and patrolled toward Hagerstown, where they found no Confederates but saw that the Confederates were sending supplies back across the Potomac at Williamsport. On 28 June Brig. Gen. Joseph T. Copeland and two regiments of his Michigan brigade had ridden into Gettysburg. The citizens, who feared the return of Early, were glad to see the Michigan men and welcomed them with buckets of drinking water. Copeland reported Gordon's passing through Gettysburg two days earlier and sent back a dispatch taken from a Rebel courier. He bivouacked his regiments east of the town and picketed the roads to York, Hanover, Chambersburg, and Hagerstown.[15]

Stahel's operations came to a sudden end. On 26 June Reynolds complained to Butterfield that Stahel's cavalry did nothing; they bivouacked behind the infantry and sent small squads on patrols. On the same day Hooker wired Secretary of War Edwin M. Stanton a request that Stahel be ordered to report to Maj. Gen. Darius Couch at Harrisburg to organize the cavalry raised there — a pointless assignment. Hooker stated that Stahel, who outranked Pleasonton, his chief of cavalry, would embarrass Pleasonton and "retard his movements." In short, Pleasonton could not order Stahel's cavalry about so long as Stahel commanded it. Halleck ordered Stahel to report to Couch on the twenty-eighth. Most of the regiments in his division were assigned then to the Army of the Potomac and became its Third Cavalry Division. Hugh Judson Kilpatrick, a newly promoted and controversial brigadier, received command of the new division. This unheralded reorganization must have prompted Copeland's sudden recall from Gettysburg. Kilpatrick's and Brig. Gen. David McM. Gregg's divisions would operate toward the right of the advancing army, leaving its left to the First Cavalry Division, commanded by Brig. Gen. John Buford.[16]

Buford had been born in Versailles, Kentucky, to a family of Virginia origins, but after age ten he lived in Rock Island, Illinois. Following schooling at Cincinnati College and Knox Manual Labor College, he entered West Point's class of 1848. While at the academy, he no doubt became well acquainted with A. P. Hill and Henry Heth, who were in the class of 1847. Buford was an excellent horseman and after graduation joined the 1st Dragoon Regiment. He later transferred to the 2d Dragoons, with which he served in the West until the war began. As a dragoon officer he would have been well versed in outpost duties and in mounted and dismounted skirmishing. Although born in Kentucky, Buford made his Union sympathies clear when he declined a request by Kentucky's governor to serve with the Confederacy. Buford spent the first year of the war unhappily as a major in the inspector general's office in Washington. Maj. Gen. John Pope rescued Buford from this assignment by making him a member of his staff and then giving him command of a brigade of cavalry. Buford, as a brigadier general, participated with distinction in various Virginia cavalry operations, beginning with Second Bull Run, and eventually became commander of the First Division of the Cavalry Corps.[17]

Gen. John Gibbon described Buford as slow of speech but "quick enough in thought and apt in repartee." Col. Theodore Lyman of Meade's staff considered him one of the best Union cavalry officers, "a compactly built man of middle height with a tawny moustache and a little triangular gray eye, whose expression is determined, not to say sinister. His ancient corduroys are tucked into a pair of ordinary cowhide boots, and his blue blouse is ornamented with holes; from one pocket thereof peeps a huge pipe, while the other is fat with a tobacco pouch. Notwithstanding this get

Brig. Gen. John Buford and staff (LC)

up, he is a very soldierly looking man. He is of good disposition but not to be trifled with."[18]

Buford's three brigades, those of Col. William Gamble, Col. Thomas Devin, and the Reserve Brigade under Maj. Samuel H. Starr of the Sixth Cavalry, had moved from Aldie, Virginia, via Leesburg and Edwards Ferry to Poolesville, Maryland, on 26 June. On the twenty-seventh they had marched over poor roads and had crossed the Monocacy River at a "wretched ford." They had bivouacked about three miles from Jefferson because they could not pass the wagons of Stahel's division, which filled the road over Catoctin Mountain. From the top of the mountain above Jefferson, the soldiers delighted in the "magnificent prospect," and they received cheers from the citizens as they rode through the village a day behind the First Corps. The division went into camp at Middletown on the twenty-seventh so that it could shoe horses and refit. On the twenty-eighth, as a part of the new cavalry reorganization, recently promoted Wesley Merritt replaced Major Starr as commander of the Reserve Brigade.[19]

Buford's division spent only a day at Middletown. On 29 June Merritt led the Reserve Brigade to Mechanicstown (Thurmont) via Frederick. It remained there until 2 July. On the twenty-ninth Buford led Gamble's and Devin's brigades on a wide swing west across South Mountain to Boonsboro and Cavetown and then back across the mountain at Monterey Gap. The brigades bivouacked east of the mountain near Fountaindale, south of Fairfield, "within a short distance of a considerable force of the enemy's infantry." It had been a pleasant ride; Maj. John L. Beveridge of the 8th Illinois Cavalry Regiment remembered it as the most delightful of his army life. The day was perfect, the roads were good, and they enjoyed scenic views as they crossed the mountain. Further, people cheered them and gave them food. A mounted trooper of the 17th Pennsylvania Regiment, holding a guidon, marked the Pennsylvania border for them. The soldiers from Company G of the 17th, whose homes were in the nearby Waynesboro area, received permission to visit their families that night with the understanding that they would return to the regiment by sunrise the next morning. All of them did. At Monterey officers who, as usual, had to provide their own food were able to have a supper of bread, butter, apple butter, ham, and coffee.[20]

Buford became disgruntled during his stay at Fountaindale. Although the inhabitants knew of his arrival there, and might have known the location of the enemy's camp, none of them would give him information on the enemy's presence or even mention it. (It seems unlikely that they would have known very much about the Confederates.) The entire community seemed afraid to speak, giving the excuse that if they did, the enemy would destroy their houses.[21]

The two brigades started for Fairfield at first light. When they reached the outskirts of the village, which was concealed by fog, they ran unexpectedly into a Confederate picket post. It was manned by men of either the 2d Mississippi or the 52d North Carolina, both of which had spent the night in that area. The 6th New York and the 8th Illinois advanced as skirmishers, and there was a small fight. A ball knocked Thomas Withrow of the 8th Illinois from his horse. Withrow took cover in a barn and fired from it. The Union force pushed ahead and then fell back. Withrow's horse, which had been drilled to act with the other horses, moved off with them, leaving Withrow on foot and hiding in the barn until a farmer helped him escape. Capt. Benjamin Little of the 52d North Carolina wrote simply that his regiment skirmished with a force of the enemy and swept it away. Buford, who believed that two Confederate regiments and a battery were in the area, reported that he would have had to use artillery to drive the Confederates from the place. However, he had decided not to do so for fear that a fight there, far from the route he was expected to follow, might "disarrange the plans of the general commanding." Therefore he turned the column southeast toward Emmitsburg and traveled from there to Gettysburg without further enemy contact.[22]

The last day of June was somber — calm, cloudy, and drizzling. Colonel Gamble's brigade led Buford's column with the 8th Illinois Regiment in front. Buford supposed that Copeland and his two Michigan regiments were still at Gettysburg when in reality they had returned to Frederick. Buford's brigades passed the First Corps bivouacs, and as they did so, Buford visited Reynolds, probably at Moritz Tavern. We know nothing of their conversation, but we can assume that when it was over, Buford had an understanding of Reynolds's intentions. An officer of Reynolds's staff accompanied Buford when he left, and the officer returned to Reynolds that night with a report of Buford's discoveries at Gettysburg.[23]

Buford's column entered Gettysburg over the Emmitsburg Road about midday and probably filed through the town over Washington Street. Theirs was a triumphal procession of little pomp; tired and dirty men rode horses over streets lined with cheering civilians who regarded them as deliverers. Lt. John H. Calef, commander of the horse battery supporting Buford's brigades, wrote of schoolchildren dressed in white standing at street corners singing patriotic songs. Pvt. Frederick A. Harter of the 8th Illinois was touched by "The Battle Cry of Freedom" and the enthusiasm it aroused in the troopers. Sarah Rogers remembered the cavalrymen as being enthusiastic: "We sang for them," she wrote, "and they cheered." The townsfolk distributed cold water, bread, and butter. When Calef passed through the town at the head of his battery, a little girl presented him with a large bouquet. Since he had no way of keeping the flowers, they might have become dessert for his horse.[24]

Gamble's brigade turned out the Chambersburg Pike. It bivouacked beyond the seminary and sent one or two squadrons forward in search of the enemy. Two squadrons of the 8th Illinois found Confederates; perhaps

Col. William Gamble and staff (LC)

they were the troops who shadowed Pettigrew's brigade on its return to-ward Cashtown. They and others of Gamble's brigade remained on picket near Marsh Creek until the following morning.[25]

The picket line probably ran from the Hagerstown Road north along the high ground east of Marsh Creek to Oak Ridge and to Keckler's Hill and then east across the Gettysburg Plain, and beyond Rock Creek to the York Pike. Devin's brigade had the responsibility for the longer but less threatened segment of the line that extended between the York Pike and the Mummasburg Road. The 17th Pennsylvania's reserve was at the junction of the Newville and Carlisle roads, and its pickets were a mile or so to the front. Col. William Sackett of the 9th New York Cavalry Regiment, who commanded the pickets of Devin's brigade, had his headquarters back at the seminary.[26]

Buford sent dispatches during the day to report what he knew of the enemy. At 5:30 A.M. when at Fountaindale, he stated that the enemy was in strength behind Cashtown and that a patrol "toward Mummasburg" had met a superior force strongly posted. (Perhaps this was a portion of Heth's division near the Chambersburg Pike.) A third party sent north skirmished with Confederates and captured a soldier, perhaps a straggler or courier, from Rodes's division. Buford's dispatch also spoke of a patrol toward

{ MEADE'S PURSUIT }

Memorial, "17th
Pennsylvania Cavalry"
(H. Pfanz)

Littlestown that learned of the cavalry battle in Hanover, though it did not take place until late on the morning of that day.[27]

Buford's dispatches to Reynolds and to Pleasonton at 10:30 and 10:40 P.M. told of the extensive operations of the horsemen after they had reached the Gettysburg area that day. He wrote of Pettigrew's brigade's being a half-mile from the town when his troops entered it. However, he erred when he wrote that Pettigrew's force probably "was terribly exaggerated by reasonable and truthful but inexperienced men," and that his troops had pushed it back toward Cashtown. He determined that Hill's corps was at Cashtown and that Pender's division had come up that day. He learned, too, that Ewell was crossing the mountain from Carlisle and that Rodes had reached Petersburg. He found out that there were no major units on the roads running east from Cashtown north from Gettysburg but that the area was infested with Confederate cavalry detachments. He also heard rumors of the enemy's advancing on him from York. Buford commented that he had to check out some of these reports, which caused him to overwork his horses and men. He complained that he could get no forage and rations and that Early's troops had seized every horseshoe and nail that they could find. He grumbled that there was no grain "in the country" and that people were talking instead of working to provide it. He did not say what he expected them to do. Although the civilians furnished his men with food, he could not "stand that way of subsisting" because it caused "dreadful straggling."[28]

Buford's brigades set up camps on the west side of Seminary Ridge — Gamble's brigade south of the pike, and Devin's north of it. Buford placed his own headquarters at the Eagle Hotel in the northeast corner of the intersection of Chambersburg and Washington streets. At 10:40 P.M., in a dispatch to Pleasonton, he stated as fact that Hill's corps was massed back of Cashtown and that its pickets were in sight of his own. In short, by 10:40 P.M. Buford had learned and reported information that was essentially correct. Meade, Pleasonton, and Reynolds had heard a lot about the Confederates that they needed to know. Whether or not they could determine the accuracy of the information is another thing.[29]

That evening Buford talked with Devin and others in Devin's camp. It was a scene to command an artist's talent. On leaving Devin's tent, after discussing the situation that they faced, Buford remarked to Devin that the enemy's concentration was a certain thing, that a battle would be fought the next day, and that he was afraid that it would begin before the infantry arrived. Devin disagreed. He said that his troops could handle any attack made against his front in the next twenty-four hours. To this Buford is said to have made the often quoted reply, "No, you won't. They will attack you in the morning and will come 'booming,' skirmishers three deep. You will have to fight like the devil to hold your own until supports arrive. The enemy must know the importance of this position, and will strain every nerve to secure it, and if we are able to hold it, we shall do well." Buford was right.[30]

CHAPTER 4
Meade and Reynolds

"I am moving at once against Lee," wrote General Meade to Mrs. Meade on 29 June when he told her of his appointment to the command of the Army of the Potomac. He asked for her prayers. Later that day he wrote to her again, saying, "I am going straight at them, and will settle this thing one way or the other." These were personal and private comments devoid of posturing. In a dispatch to Halleck on the twenty-ninth he announced his plans to advance the army that day to a Westminster-Emmitsburg line, inclining right to cover the Baltimore-Harrisburg Road. He hoped to guard Baltimore and to fall upon Lee's rear if the Confederates were attempting to cross the Susquehanna. He intended to hold his army "well together, with the hope of falling on some portion of Lee's army in detail." In writing of Stuart's move around his right at that time, he stated that "my main point being to find and fight the enemy, I shall have to submit to the cavalry raids around me in some measure." Meade's attitude should have pleased the powers in Washington. Some expression of determination to fight was to be expected of a newly appointed army commander, but people acquainted with Meade knew that he was no humbug and that he meant what he wrote.[1]

Meade, a Philadelphian born in Spain in December 1815, had graduated from West Point in 1835, served two years in the artillery in Florida, and then resigned to work as a civil engineer. He returned to the army as a lieutenant of engineers in 1842 and served in Mexico, principally with Taylor's army, where he won a brevet for gallantry in Monterrey. After the Mexican War, he returned to army construction work. At the outbreak of the Civil War, he held the grade of captain and was erecting a lighthouse near Detroit. He sought active field service and in August 1861 received a brigadier's star and command of the Second Brigade of the Pennsylvania Reserves. John Reynolds, who was five years his junior in age but had eleven days' seniority in rank and far more service with troops of the line, commanded the First Brigade. The two generals became friends and confidants.

Meade led his brigade on the Peninsula until he was wounded at Glendale on 30 June 1862. He was back on duty in time to command his brigade at Second Bull Run. At Antietam he led a division and, after Hooker was wounded, temporarily commanded the First Corps. He became a major general on 29 November 1862 and commanded the Reserves division at Fredericksburg. He fought with particular distinction there, nearly breaking the Confederate line. At Chancellorsville Meade commanded the Fifth Corps and urged aggressive action instead of a retreat across the Rappahannock. Meade had proven to be a capable combat commander at brigade, division, and corps levels. He had avoided politicking and cabals and had gained the respect of most of his peers, save generals Sickles and Butterfield perhaps. It should be no surprise, then, that President Lincoln and Halleck considered him for the command of the Army of the Potomac and that he received the appointment after Reynolds turned it down.[2]

When Meade took command of the Army of the Potomac on 28 June, he had no plan of operations of his own, of course; he would not necessarily have known the locations of its major units other than those of his own corps. He learned that Hooker had no plan except to move his army north in three columns toward Gettysburg and the North Central Railroad between Harrisburg and Baltimore. According to Meade, Hooker was "waiting for the exigencies of the occasion to govern him," much as Meade had to do later. Maj. Gen. Daniel Butterfield, Meade's chief of staff, testified that Meade had adopted his suggestion that Hooker's orders for the twenty-eighth be implemented. Meade, in turn, testified that his intent was to move along the main axis from Frederick to Harrisburg, extending his wings on both flanks, and to do so until he either met the enemy or had reason to believe that the enemy was about to attack him. It was his firm intention to secure advantages for himself while denying them to the enemy and to give battle as soon as he could find his foe.[3]

Meade moved the army's left wing north from Frederick to Emmitsburg on 28 June, his first day in command. The First Corps continued its march north to Marsh Creek on the thirtieth as the two cavalry brigades of Buford's division went on to Gettysburg. In the meantime, army headquarters moved to Middleburg on the twenty-ninth and to Taneytown on the thirtieth.[4]

By then Meade knew that Ewell had reached Carlisle and York and that Longstreet and Hill were "at Chambersburg partially toward Gettysburg." At 11:30 A.M., in a dispatch from Taneytown to Reynolds, he indicated his lack of specific knowledge about the enemy's location and plans by stating that the enemy occupied the Cumberland Valley "from Chambersburg, in force," but whether or not the Rebels held Cashtown Pass for offensive or defensive purposes remained to be seen. However, he suggested to Reynolds that Buford ought to be able to advise him of any enemy advance. In case the enemy did move against Reynolds or against Howard at Emmitsburg, Reynolds was to draw his corps back to Emmitsburg, where Meade would reinforce him with the Third or Twelfth Corps. Meade believed that he had concentrated his army as his knowledge of the enemy dictated. He had his cavalry out and would move again after he had made plans based on concrete intelligence. In the meantime, if the enemy advanced toward his army, Meade would concentrate where he showed the most force.[5]

On 30 June the First Corps bivouacked along Marsh Creek, the Eleventh was at Emmitsburg, and the Third moved to Bridgeport on the Monocacy about five miles east of Emmitsburg. Meade gave Reynolds command of the left wing constituting these three corps. The Second Corps was at Uniontown; the Fifth, at Union Mills; the Twelfth, at Littlestown; and the Sixth, far to the east at Manchester, Maryland. His cavalry was at Gettysburg and at Mechanicsville (Thurmont) and Littlestown, Pennsylvania, and New Windsor, Maryland. Meade had deployed his army so that each corps had supporting corps close by. This was particularly so on the left; the Sixth was rather isolated from the others but was positioned to block an increasingly unlikely turning movement around the Union right toward Baltimore. Meade explained to Reynolds that he had ordered the move to Marsh Creek more with the intention of an advance toward Gettysburg, in support of Buford, no doubt, than as a move to a defensive position. At 4:30 P.M. he wired Halleck of the locations of his troops. Meade intended to push toward Hanover, but he feared that if his army moved too fast, its men would break down and require a day of rest.[6]

In truth Meade knew that battle was imminent, and he sought to cover his bases while leaving his options open. On 30 June he issued a circular reminding the troops of their duty, a statement that offended some who believed that they needed no reminder. But there was practical advice as well: Meade was afraid of wearing out the men and animals with too much marching. Believing that the Confederates were turning from the Susquehanna, he urged that positions be occupied that would permit men and horses to rest. He ordered that impedimentia be reduced, columns be "put in light marching order," trains be parked, rations for three days be issued, and every soldier have sixty rounds of ammunition. Corps commanders were to familiarize themselves with roads leading to other corps. The situation was becoming tense. If Lee had halted his advance toward the Susquehanna, then, Meade reasoned, Lee would have to find and fight him if the Army of Northern Virginia was to stay in Pennsylvania. The day of reckoning was at hand. Meade confided to his wife that he was "much oppressed with a sense of responsibility and the great interests entrusted to me," but he thought that in time he would become accustomed to this.[7]

Since the battle of Gettysburg, learned people have looked at maps of that region with the advantage of hindsight and have observed sagely that the road network made the town an obvious concentration point and prize for the army that could seize and hold it. Perhaps Buford saw these advantages after he arrived in the area, but the benefits of seizing the town were not compelling to either Lee or Meade. Lee was planning to concentrate his army closer to Cashtown and the Cashtown Pass, and Meade had other locations in mind. Meade's engineers and other staff officers were busy on the morning of 1 July looking for such positions. On 30 June Meade had authorized Reynolds to fall back from Marsh Creek to Emmitsburg if, in his opinion, the left wing would have a better position there. Brig. Gen. Andrew A. Humphreys, an engineer and commander of the Second Division, Third Corps, looked for potential positions in that area. Brig. Gen. Gouverneur K. Warren, Meade's chief engineer, selected contingency positions between Manchester and Ridgeville, Maryland, and had a more familiar site under consideration behind Big Pipe Creek just below the Mason-Dixon Line. General Meade selected the "Pipe Creek Line" as the position of choice and on 1 July issued the "Pipe Creek Circular." This circular designated the portions of the Pipe Creek Line to be occupied by the various corps should the enemy assume the offensive and attack. Although the upcoming battle was fought at Gettysburg, Brig. Gen. Henry Hunt, Meade's chief of artillery, wrote in later years that it probably would have been better if it had been fought at Pipe Creek.[8]

On the evening of 30 June General Howard, commander of the Eleventh Corps, was anticipating a night's rest at St. Joseph's College when he received an invitation to have a talk with Reynolds at his headquarters. Reynolds was at Moritz Tavern, a large brick house on the Emmitsburg

Maj. Gen. John F. Reynolds
(CWLM)

Road a mile south of Marsh Creek. Howard arrived there about dusk and joined Reynolds and his staff for supper. After the meal the two generals studied maps and reviewed the day's messages.[9]

Howard had served with Reynolds at West Point and had a high opinion of him. Reynolds was widely admired. He belonged to a leading Lancaster family, and his father had been a friend of President James Buchanan from whom John had received help in obtaining some desired assignments. John Reynolds attended private schools before receiving an appointment to West Point's class of 1841, where he had the opportunity to become acquainted with Doubleday, Seth Williams, and Confederates Longstreet, Lafayette McLaws, and Richard Anderson, who were in bracketing classes. Reynolds graduated in the middle of his class and went into the artillery.

Reynolds was an outdoorsman and a fine horseman, and he took well to field service. In Mexico he fought as a subaltern in Braxton Bragg's famous battery and gained two brevets and considerable fame. Between wars he served in both coastal and field batteries and participated in the Utah Expedition. By 1860 he was commandant of cadets at West Point, and in May 1861 he became a lieutenant colonel in the 14th Infantry. When the Civil War opened, Reynolds was forty-two years old, had twenty years of solid service, and ranked two grades above many of his contemporaries.

After the war began, Reynolds became a brigadier general and commander of a brigade of Pennsylvania Reserves. He was military governor of Fredericksburg, Virginia, for two months in the spring of 1862, and he distinguished himself in the battle of Gaines's Mill, where he was captured. He was released from captivity and held only six weeks, partly because the citizens of Fredericksburg petitioned for his release. During the Antietam campaign he had the fruitless and frustrating task of trying to organize Pennsylvania's militia to resist the Confederate invasion. He led a division at Second Bull Run and the First Corps at Fredericksburg and at Chancellorsville. It is generally believed that he was offered command of the Army of the Potomac after Chancellorsville and refused it. Reynolds was Meade's strong right arm as Meade prepared to meet Lee in Pennsylvania.[10]

There were "abundant and conflicting" messages for Reynolds and Howard to ponder and discuss on the evening of 30 June, messages from army headquarters, Buford, scouts, and alarmed citizens. From them Reynolds and Howard concluded that Lee's army was close by and in force. Howard received the impression that Reynolds was depressed. At 11:00 P.M., when orders for the following day had not come, Howard made the hour's ride back to his bed at Emmitsburg. About midnight, presumably after receiving Buford's 10:30 P.M. dispatch telling of Hill's massing at Cashtown and reports of Ewell's presence at Petersburg (York Springs), Reynolds forwarded this information to Meade. Then he rolled himself into a blanket and fell asleep on the tavern floor.[11]

Not long after Howard had fallen asleep in Emmitsburg, an orderly's knocking awakened him. A courier had arrived from Meade's headquarters on his way to Reynolds. He carried a sheaf of orders and stopped to show them to Howard. After looking at them, Howard relayed them to Reynolds. The orders for 1 July sent the First Corps to Gettysburg, the Eleventh to Gettysburg or in supporting distance of the First, and the Third to Emmitsburg. They announced also that Longstreet's and Hill's corps were at Chambersburg — partway toward Gettysburg — and that Ewell's corps was still at Carlisle and York. Clearly these orders had been written before Buford's latest intelligence had been received. But how were Reynolds and

Howard to reconcile the order to advance with that of 30 June instructing them to fall back in the event that the enemy advanced against them?[12]

Meade was doing two things: he was preparing contingency plans in case the Confederate army attacked, and he was looking for an opportunity to bring the enemy to battle if he could do so to an advantage. The situation was changing rapidly. On the morning of 30 June, insofar as he knew, the enemy was still marching toward the Susquehanna. By that night it became apparent that Lee's incursion was ebbing and that he had to fight if he was to stay north of the Potomac. It was necessary that Meade select defensive positions in advance if his army was to occupy the best ground available. Yet Meade could not permit the enemy to move at will. In his talk with Reynolds, after taking command of the army, Meade had said that he wanted to bring the enemy to battle "whenever and wherever found." Knowing Meade, Reynolds would have believed that. He knew that the Confederates were in force around Cashtown and that Buford's division had been sent forward to flush them out. In marching to Gettysburg on 1 July, Reynolds would be in a position to support Buford in case of trouble and would, with the strong left wing, be leading the army to where the enemy was showing the strongest force.[13]

The product of the reconnaissances of 30 June for defensive positions was the controversial Pipe Creek Circular, dated 1 July. It announced that Meade no longer intended to assume the offensive unless he could be certain of success, and it gave directions for occupying a defensive position along Big Pipe Creek in northern Maryland. It did not reach Reynolds and Howard, and we cannot know what effect it would have had on their movements on 1 July. If Reynolds had a firm understanding of Meade's intentions and concerns, it might well have had none.[14]

Meade relied on Reynolds's judgment and probably would have endorsed any decision he made. This is apparent from a dispatch that he wrote to Reynolds on 1 July that was probably drafted about the same time as the Pipe Creek Circular and that also failed to reach him. In it Meade observed that if the enemy was concentrating to the right or east of Gettysburg, it would not seem "a proper strategic point of concentration for the army." If instead Lee was concentrating to the front or left of Gettysburg, Meade had insufficient knowledge of the country to judge it as an offensive or defensive position. He wanted Reynolds's views on this. He was interested also in Reynolds's opinion of the army's morale and proportionate strength as compared with its last returns — presumably those of 10 or 20 June. Meade, like most other ranking officers, greatly overestimated the strength of Lee's army. He told Reynolds that he believed the Confederates to have 92,000 infantry and 270 cannon. Yet he believed that the Army of the Potomac's strength equaled it and, with the expected arrival of the Harpers Ferry garrison, ought to exceed it.[15]

Meade had prepared his army for both attack and defense, and battle was imminent. The first of July would be an eventful day in the country's history.

CHAPTER 5

Reconnaissance in Force

"None in the world" was General Hill's answer to Maj. Gen. Henry Heth. On the evening of 30 June Heth had asked Hill if Hill had any objection to his marching his division from Cashtown to Gettysburg to get a large quantity of shoes that Heth believed were stored there. Why should Hill object? The Confederates were in Pennsylvania to gather supplies for the Confederacy, and Heth's division needed shoes. Apparently neither Hill nor Heth had known or given thought to the scouring Early's division had given that very area for supplies less than a week before. Besides, both Heth's and Pender's divisions were in the Cashtown area, and Hill probably considered Gettysburg to be within his zone of operations. The town was only a short distance away; Pettigrew's brigade had been on its outskirts that very day and had seen some Union troops there. But these troops were not the sort to pose a great threat; even General Lee believed that the Army of the Potomac was still far to the south.[1]

Not everyone thought that Gettysburg was free of capable defenders. Lt. Louis B. Young, Pettigrew's aide, wrote in later years that Pettigrew and he could not convince Hill and Heth that the Union troops that they had seen near Gettysburg had been veterans and not just men called up for the emergency. Young wrote in retrospect, "This spirit of unbelief had taken such hold, that I doubt if any of the commanders of brigades, except General Pettigrew, believed that we were marching to battle, a weakness on their part which rendered them unprepared for what was about to happen."[2]

And what did Hill do? In his report Hill stated that he had accompanied

Pender's division to Cashtown on 30 June and, on arriving there, learned that Pettigrew had found Union troops in Gettysburg. Hill then sent orders back to Maj. Gen. Richard H. Anderson at Fayetteville to bring his division forward on 1 July and dispatched a message to General Lee telling him that Pettigrew had seen some Union troops in Gettysburg. Hill also sent a courier to General Ewell to tell him that he intended to advance to Gettysburg early on the morning of 1 July to determine what troops were in his front. Presumably he told General Lee this as well, unless he believed that Lee expected him to continue his advance to the east. Pender's division and Lt. Col. David McIntosh's battalion of artillery followed Heth, but Hill did not say why he believed that Pender's support was needed. Hill was sending two of his three divisions on a reconnaissance. Such a large force, if opposed, might well commit Lee's army to battle on a field that Lee had not seen and before his army was assembled — under such circumstances that Lee was prompted to report that "it had not been intended to fight a general battle at such distance from our base, unless attacked by the enemy." Lee's headquarters were on the west side of South Mountain, and he did not ride through Cashtown Pass until midmorning of 1 July. Did Lee approve of Hill's advance? He did not say; in his report he stated only that Hill had gone to Gettysburg.[3]

Heth's division, accompanied by Maj. William J. Pegram's battalion of artillery, began its march at 5:00 A.M. Unfortunately Heth did not give the starting points of the four brigades of his division when the march began. Pettigrew's brigade might have spent the night no more than a mile west of Marsh Creek, and Archer's brigade was at Cashtown itself. Archer's brigade led the column, and Davis's brigade followed on its heels. Pettigrew's and Brockenbrough's brigades brought up the rear. Capt. Edward A. Marye's battery, the Fredericksburg artillery, was near the front of the column. The 5th Alabama Battalion and fifty men of the 13th Alabama Regiment of Archer's brigade led the division, probably marching on the turnpike until the enemy came into view. The approach march was uneventful until the head of the column reached the brow of the Marsh Creek floodplain.[4]

As Heth's and Pender's divisions hiked toward Gettysburg on the morning of 1 July, the bivouacking troopers of Buford's division groomed, fed, and watered their horses, cleaned their carbines, and ate. Many officers went into the town to get breakfast and groceries for their messes, for they had to secure their own food. Two miles west of Gamble's brigade's bivouac, Capt. Daniel Buck's squadron of the 8th Illinois Cavalry Regiment picketed the turnpike from the high ground to the east of Marsh Creek.

Buck's headquarters were in an inn, probably Herr Tavern, a mile and a half west of the brigade's bivouac. Buck had sent Lt. Marcellus Jones forward with Company E to set up picket or vidette posts overlooking Marsh Creek. Jones placed three posts south of the pike and two north of it in unidentified locations, and one on the pike itself. Sgt. Levi S. Shafer headed the detachments on the picket line, and Pvts. Thomas B. Kelley, George Sager, James Hale, and H. O. Dodge manned the post at the pike. Lieutenant Jones was with the picket reserve about 250 yards to the rear at the top of the ridge. Behind the picket squadron on Herr Ridge a squadron of the 8th New York Cavalry guarded the approach to Gettysburg from Fairfield, while posts manned by the 3d Indiana and the 12th Illinois regiments were off to the north.

Although the videttes could see Confederate campfires on the high ground to the west and surmised that there would be a battle the next day, they spent a monotonous night at their posts. On the morning of 1 July a dozen men of the 8th New York patrolled the Hagerstown Road without seeing Confederates, but Privates Kelley and Hale at the pike saw Heth's column marching toward them. Sergeant Shafer was absent at that moment, so Kelley rode back to the reserve to warn Lieutenant Jones of the Confederate approach. Jones told the reserve to follow him and galloped forward to Shafer's post.[5]

The Confederates had been advancing without skirmishers until they reached Marsh Creek. After all, General Archer had been told that there were no worrisome enemy forces in the Gettysburg area, and the column was behind its own picket line much of the way. As the head of the column neared the Marsh Creek bridge, an officer on a gray horse pulled up at the bridge to allow some of the infantry to cross ahead of him.[6]

At this time Jones reached the picket post overlooking the bridge and saw the approaching Confederates about 700 yards away. Private Sager raised his carbine to fire, but Jones stopped him, saying, "Hold on, George, give me the honor of opening this ball." Jones vaulted from his saddle and asked Sergeant Shafer, who had returned, for the loan of his carbine. Resting it on a fence rail, Jones shot at the officer on the gray horse. It was 7:30 A.M., and the battle had begun.[7]

Jones's shot, and the others that probably followed, warned Archer and his men of the opposition ahead. The Illinois cavalrymen saw the Rebel column halt and a line of skirmishers deploy in their direction. Jones's picket reserve reached the picket post in a few minutes, and horse holders led the cavalrymen's mounts to the rear. In the meantime a courier from

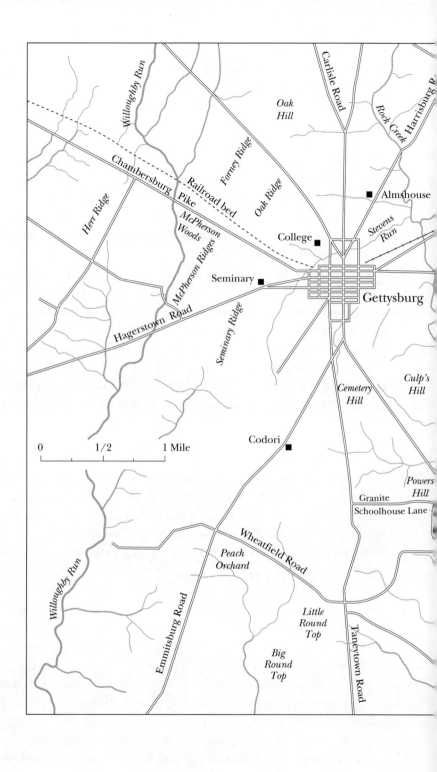

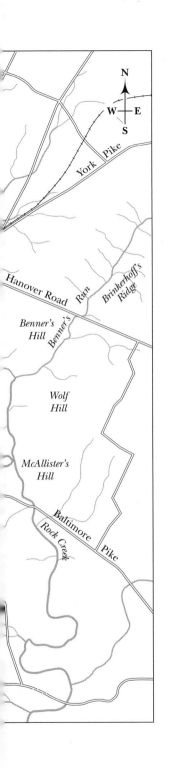

Captain Buck galloped to the brigade's bivouac to tell Maj. John L. Beveridge, commander of the 8th Illinois and the ranking officer then in the camp, that Confederates, "infantry and artillery in column," were approaching over the pike. Beveridge hurried a squadron of the 8th Illinois forward to support Buck's men and sent gallopers into the town to tell Buford and Gamble of the Confederate approach and to recall whatever troops were there. Buglers sounded "Boots and Saddles" and "To Horse," and Beveridge readied the brigade for action. Buford and Gamble soon arrived at Gamble's brigade's bivouac.[8]

Lt. Col. John A. Kress of General Wadsworth's staff rode up as Buford was leaving the Eagle Hotel and saw the hubbub there. Buford asked, "What are you doing here, sir?" Kress replied that he was looking for shoes for Wadsworth's division. Buford told him to return to his division. Kress asked, "Why, what is the matter, General?" As Buford swung into his saddle, a cannon barked off to the west. "That's the matter," Buford replied as he galloped off.[9]

Persons interested in "firsts" might credit Lieutenant Jones with firing the first shot of the battle; a small monument near where Jones fired Shafer's carbine is called the "First Shot Monument," and its inscription claims that Jones fired the shot at 7:30 A.M. Of course this is impossible to prove beyond doubt, and there were about five others who claimed the distinction. Further, there were men in Fairfield or on patrol to the north on 30 June who might have claimed the "first shot" honor. The most tenacious opponents of the Illinois claim were the veterans of the 9th New York Cavalry Regiment. They maintained that Cpl. Alpheus Hodges fired the first shot from a vidette post at the Chambersburg Pike bridge over Willoughby Run at 5:00 A.M. on 1 July. They held that Hodges saw a mounted party advancing over the pike. After notifying the picket reserve, Hodges rode forward for a closer look at the approaching riders. Deciding that they were Confederates, he started to leave, and they fired at him. He shot back, and the Confederates rode away. The 9th's veterans were so eager for Hodges to be recognized for firing the first Union shot that they took their case to the board of the Gettysburg Battlefield Memorial Association and established their claim to the board's "entire satisfaction." Yet there are obvious questions concerning the 9th's claim that ought to be answered: Who were the mounted Confederates seen by Hodges? How did they get by the picket posts manned by the 8th Illinois videttes? Capts. Wilbur G. Bentley and Newel Cheney of the 9th New York did not identify the Confederates but left the assumption that they had come from the west over the pike. They explained that the Confederates were able to reach Hodges's post because the 8th Illinois did not have a picket post out by Marsh Run until after Hodges's contact. Only then did Gamble place the picket post above Marsh Creek. Yet none of the few Confederate chroniclers of Heth's activities mention an early morning reconnaissance by mounted men, and the 8th Illinois Cavalry veterans insisted that they were on picket throughout the night. Further, as stated by James McLean in his analysis of first shot claims, Buford would not have permitted his outposts to be so close to the main body as Hodges's was said to have been, and in a creek bottom dominated by higher ground at that.

The New Yorkers were honorable men, and Hodges must have shot at someone. Although he denied it, Hodges might have been at another bridge and fired much later than he thought. Perhaps a detachment spawned by the cavalry units working with Ewell who infested the area north of Gettysburg had wandered down from there. We cannot know.[10]

Archer's brigade and the column behind it halted while the 5th Alabama Battalion; Companies B, C, and G of the 13th Alabama Regiment; and probably sharpshooters from the 1st Tennessee deployed as skirmishers. Although the few veterans who wrote of this deployment placed the skirmish line south of the pike, there must have been skirmishers north of it as well. Col. Birkett D. Fry ordered the 13th's color-bearer to uncase his flag, thereby announcing to the Tennesseans that they were about to fight.[11]

It was at this time, perhaps, that Marye's battery dropped trail and opened fire. Local tradition holds that it did so near the Samuel Lohr farm about a quarter-mile west of Marsh Creek. The Confederates saw men on a hill somewhat to their right. Maj. William Pegram, the artillery battalion commander, thought that they might be some of Longstreet's troops who were said to have been on a road to their right. When a sergeant who had seen Longstreet's corps far to their rear dispelled this idea, Pegram ordered Marye to open fire with one gun. As they readied one of the battery's three-inch rifles to fire, a man rushed from the house and yelled, "My God, you are not going to fire here are you?" On seeing that they were, he threw up his hands and disappeared into the house. After the gun fired several shots, there was no reply; the gun was limbered up and the infantry advanced.[12]

The Confederates pushed forward slowed by the marshy ground and the stubborn Union cavalrymen. When the skirmishing began, the cavalrymen on the forward line were mounted. After they fell back on their reserve, horse holders took the horses to the rear, and the carabineers fought on foot. It is probable that the riflemen on the Confederate skirmish line greatly outnumbered them. Buck's squadron and the one sent to support it would not have had more than 200 men, 50 of whom were horse holders, whereas the above three Confederate units alone would have had about 500 men on the skirmish line. Furthermore, Archer had help nearby if it was needed. Certainly the Confederates' firepower would have dominated the fight; although they might have had a slower rate of fire than the carbines, their rifles would have had greater range and accuracy. The Confederates pressed from front and flank, and the cavalry line slowly and reluctantly retired the mile and a half back to McPherson Ridge. Union cavalrymen formed on the ridge watched the battle come to them. First they saw the horse holders with the led horses cross Herr Ridge about three-quarters of a mile in their front. Then the retreating skirmishers fell back over the ridge. Finally, a Confederate skirmish line appeared, followed by a line of battle, and Confederate batteries rolled into position on the ridge.[13]

The Union cavalrymen had done their job; they had forced Heth's column to deploy skirmishers and had slowed the approach of his division. They had given Buford time to set up a cavalry line on McPherson Ridge to meet the Rebel onslaught and had provided Union infantry additional time to reach the field. Private Kelley, who had been with Jones when the battle opened, boasted almost thirty years later that "if anyone living thinks Johnny reb got this two and a-half miles or three miles from the 8th Ill. Cav., 'dismounted,' without winning every inch of the ground they got, he does not know the mettle we contained." Yet it had been skirmishing and not a knockdown fight—at least in the eyes of the Confederate infantrymen. The 5th Alabama Battalion's casualties numbered only seven men wounded. Colonel Fry called the cavalry's resistance "inconsiderable." Fry insisted that the cavalrymen had not retarded the Confederate advance or done them any damage. Only small parties appeared in their front, and though Fry saw individual instances of gallantry, the first intimation they had of a greater force was when they reached Herr Ridge and drew artillery fire. Perhaps then there was some reason for Lt. Col. Samuel G. Shepard, in his report for Archer's brigade, to write only that the enemy's pickets fell back gradually before them, and Heth offhandedly remarked that he supposed that the force opposing him was cavalry supported by a brigade or two of infantry. The rather small amount of Federal resistance west of Herr Ridge had been enough to slow the Confederate advance, but it had also contributed to Heth's and Archer's underestimation of the force that they would meet.[14]

Buford had come to Gettysburg to gain information and to fight. Any instructions that he received from Pleasonton, commander of the Cavalry Corps, and from Reynolds must have been given orally, for no written copies of orders to him seem to exist. Pleasonton testified that he had given orders to hold Gettysburg "to the last extremity until we could get there." But we can doubt him: Meade did not decide to order his army to Gettysburg until the battle was well under way, and Pleasonton, who testified with the benefit of hindsight, was in no position to force Meade's hand. Buford was the ranking Union officer on the field when the battle began, and Buford obviously believed that Reynolds would be pleased to march to his aid in case he became involved in a fight. With that assurance in mind, he made the decision to hold the Gettysburg position — for "entertaining" the enemy "until General Reynolds had reached the scene."[15]

Battery A, 2d Artillery, commanded by Lt. John H. Calef, was a key element in Buford's battle plan. Battery A was a "horse battery," the first of its kind in the army, and was called popularly "flying artillery." Because it supported cavalry, it had to keep up with it; therefore, unlike their comrades in standard field batteries who rode on limber and caisson chests or walked, cannoneers had their own mounts. Calef's battery had six three-inch Ordnance rifles whose wrought iron barrels weighed only about 816 pounds and were lighter and more mobile than the army's heavier Napoleons and ten-pounder Parrott rifles. The battery's six guns, as in all other Union and Confederate batteries, were organized further into three sections of two guns each. The battery should have had five officers, but it had only two, Calef and Lt. John Roder. John Calef, the battery's commander, had been in West Point's class of 1862 and had one of the best assignments the army could provide to an ambitious young officer.[16]

Calef's battery had parked on the east arm of McPherson Ridge south of the Chambersburg Pike on the evening of 30 June. Colonel Gamble told Calef to select his position on 1 July, and Calef decided to place his guns on the west arm of the ridge overlooking Willoughby Run facing west along the pike to Herr Ridge. Calef had fences opened that morning so that he could move his guns to their positions. No sooner had he done this than Buford sent for him. He found the general with Reynolds, who had reached the field ahead of the infantry. Calef's was Buford's only battery, and Buford wanted it spread out in order to give the impression of greater artillery strength. At Buford's direction, Calef placed Roder's section on the west ridge to the right of the pike. He placed the section commanded by 1st Sgt. Joseph Newman left of the pike between the pike and the McPherson barn, and the remaining section under Sgt. Charles Pergel on the east arm of the ridge near the southeast corner of McPherson Woods.[17]

As soon as it could be formed, Gamble sent the remainder of his brigade, about 900 officers and men, forward to the east arm of McPherson Ridge. The squadrons of the 8th Illinois not on the skirmish line occupied the ridge between the pike and the woods. The 8th New York was to their left and rear in and beyond the woods. The four companies of the 12th Illinois occupied the space between the pike and the railroad bed, and the six companies of the 3d Indiana extended Gamble's line north of the railroad bed. Col. George Chapman of the 3d commanded his six companies and the four of the 12th Illinois.[18]

Devin's brigade extended Gamble's line north to and beyond the Mummasburg Road. Colonel Devin sent the 6th New York to the Mummasburg Road and deployed one of its squadrons on foot to the front and left in extension of the 3d Indiana's line. Capt. William L. Heermance commanded this squadron. Portions of the 17th Pennsylvania Cavalry and the 9th New York patrolled to the north. About 8:00 A.M., when the Confederates were driving back the pickets of the 8th Illinois along the Chambersburg Pike, the squadrons of the 9th New York, in turn, were watering their mounts in Rock Creek. When summoned to the front, the buglers sounded "Boots and Saddles," and when they had finished watering, each squadron trotted to reinforce the line near the Mummasburg Road.[19]

In the meantime the Confederate column reached Herr Ridge. Archer's brigade filed off to the right of the pike; Brig. Gen. Joseph Davis's, to the left. After Archer deployed, Heth ordered Archer forward. Heth reported that Archer and Davis were "now directed to advance, the object being to feel the enemy; to make a forced reconnaissance, and determine in what force the enemy were — whether or not he was massing his forces on Gettysburg." Archer protested that his brigade was too "light to risk so far in advance of support." But after the order was repeated, the brigade advanced.[20]

Lieutenant Roder's left gun greeted the Confederates with a shot at Davis's brigade. This greeting prompted a reply from Pegram's guns, which had gone into position on Herr Ridge. Marye's four pieces, two three-inch Ordnance rifles and two ten-pounder Parrotts, were on the south side of the pike near Herr Tavern; Capt. Joseph McGraw's four Napoleons went in across the road, and three of Lt. William E. Zimmerman's four three-inch rifles (one gun was disabled when being brought

{ RECONNAISSANCE IN FORCE }

Lt. John H. Calef (MCLL)

into action) took position on the left of McGraw's. The Crenshaw Battery, Lt. Andrew B. Johnston commanding, galloped toward its position, its cannoneers clinging to their seats on its limbers and caissons. Just before turning from the pike, a wheel rolled off the limber of one of its guns, dropping the end of its axle to the road and pitching the cannoneers riding on the limber to the ground. No one was hurt, the cannoneers replaced the wheel, and the Napoleons of the battery went into position on Marye's right. Capt. Thomas A. Brander's battery, two Napoleons and two

Chambersburg Pike (postbattle), McPherson Ridge to Herr Ridge (MCLL)

three-inch rifles, joined the Crenshaw Napoleons on the right of Marye's guns. Marye's and Crenshaw's guns had opened on Calef's four pieces near the pike so that eight Rebel guns were firing at Calef's four. Calef ordered his guns to fire slowly and deliberately and discerned what guns were in his front. Calef wrote, "The battle was now developing, and the demoniac 'whir-r-r' of the rifled shot, the 'ping' of the bursting shell and the wicked 'zip' of the bullet, as it hurried by, filled the air."[21]

Archer's brigade, 1,200 officers and men strong, deployed on Herr Ridge; that is readily apparent, but exactly where its regiments and supporting regiments deployed and how they reached their positions is not known. Archer's principal objective was McPherson Woods and the cavalrymen it sheltered. Whoever held the woods controlled the terrain around it. After turning onto the road that ran by the tavern on the crest of the ridge, the 13th Alabama entered the timber, later called Springs Hotel Woods. The 13th was on the right of the line, and the 1st Tennessee on its left formed along the east edge of the woods. It seems likely that the remaining 600 officers and men of the brigade, with skirmishers 100 yards

{ RECONNAISSANCE IN FORCE }

to the front, would have ample space to form in the north portion of the woods opposite the west end of McPherson Woods just 600 yards to the east. After the 13th formed its line behind Lt. William Zimmerman's three three-inch rifles, Capt. Bailey A. Bowen of Company C took fifteen or so men off to screen the brigade's right. From the brigade line they could see their skirmishers following the Union skirmish line as it fell back to McPherson Ridge and a line of bluecoats that extended beyond their view.[22]

As Archer's brigade was deploying, a large dog bounded from a building on Herr Ridge. Its barking summoned a man in a leather apron with glasses on his forehead and a leather knife in his hand. The bewildered cobbler asked Lt. William F. Fulton's men what was going on. When told that Hill's corps was about to attack the Union cavalry and that there would be fighting, he became excited. According to men of the 5th Alabama he said, "Tell General Hill to hold up a little, as I turned my milch cow out this morning, and I wish to get her up before the fighting begins." On their way to their position the two leading companies of the 13th Alabama passed near a house inhabited by an old lady and her large yellow dog. (Perhaps it was the same animal as that described above.) When the dog attacked some of the soldiers, they shot him. The Alabamians also knocked over the woman's ash hopper and gave her good reason for berating the Rebels and calling them terrible fellows.[23]

Three regiments of Davis's brigade, the 2d and the 42d Mississippi and the 55th North Carolina, followed Archer's brigade along the pike. Dr. LeGrand Wilson saw a weeping woman and children and knew that the enemy was nearby. When the head of the brigade neared Herr Ridge, its skirmishers ran to the front. Soon after, Wilson saw a puff of smoke in the distance and heard the bark of a cannon, and a projectile whistled overhead. Calef's battery had welcomed them to the field. The brigade filed to the left of the pike on line with Archer's brigade, probably taking the road opposite Herr Tavern that led to the Mummasburg Road a mile to the north. The 42d formed on the brigade's right just north of the pike. The 2d Mississippi was in the center of the brigade line beyond the railroad bed and probably on the west side of Willoughby Run. It faced down the lane to the Bender farm buildings about 500 yards to the east. The 55th North Carolina was on the left. The brigade line numbered about 1,700 officers and men, and its skirmishers covered its front.[24]

Davis's line advanced just behind its skirmishers and abreast of Archer's line across the pike. Col. John M. Stone, commander of the 2d Mississippi and a future governor of that state, recalled that a lane bordered by a post-and-rail fence split his front so that most of his line was to its right. Although some of Davis's men recalled passing through a woods, maps show none in this area. East of the remembered woods was a rail fence and a field of grain, possibly oats. The men of the 2d climbed the fence, and as they formed in the grain field, a shell from Calef's battery hit the fence and sent rails flying. The Confederate line moved downslope at the double-quick toward the east branch of Willoughby Run in order to rout the Union skirmishers partially hidden by the brush along the stream. The Mississippians heard the "peculiar hiss of the minnie ball" but pressed ahead and drove the cavalrymen up the slope to their main line below the crest of Forney Ridge. When they approached this Union line, the 42d Mississippi and the two right companies of the 2d became hotly engaged. Colonel Stone tried to reach the right of his line, but he had to dismount to do so because a fence blocked his way. As he climbed the fence, a bullet hit him and removed him from the fight. One regimental commander was down. After a short firefight, Davis ordered his men to charge. His troops obeyed, and the cavalry line gave way. Davis's line pushed toward the ridge's crest and victory, but when it arrived there, the brigade received a big surprise.[25]

The 55th North Carolina on the brigade left faced the 6th New York Cavalry Regiment, whose weak skirmish line stretched beyond its flank. Maj. Alfred H. Belo deployed a company to counter this threat. Captain Heermance had dismounted his New Yorkers and had sent their horses back to Sheads's Woods on Oak Ridge. As Davis's line approached, a squadron from the 9th New York, which had come from Rock Creek, joined the 6th south of the Mummasburg Road near the Forney buildings. A detachment of twenty men from the 9th also rode out the Mummasburg Road about 400 yards beyond Forney Ridge to the vicinity of the Hoffman farm buildings. There it found Belo's men in force south of the road in Forney's Woods. The Rebels drove the cavalrymen back to the field east of the Forney buildings, where they formed a line across the road. Some North Carolinians soon reached the Forney buildings, but the New Yorkers drove them back in turn. When more North Carolinians appeared, the men of the 9th retreated to the stone wall at the crest of Oak Ridge. The cavalrymen waited there until they saw skirmishers creeping toward them through the tall wheat in the field to their front. The New Yorkers fired when the Rebel skirmishers came within carbine range and sent them running back beyond the Forney buildings. The cavalrymen remained on Oak Ridge until they were ordered away.[26]

Brig. Gen. Joseph R. Davis
(LC)

After his four guns near the pike opened fire on the Confederates in their front, Lieutenant Calef rode south beyond McPherson Woods to Sergeant Pergel's section. He met Buford and his bugler on the way. Buford was sitting on his horse, calmly smoking his pipe. He remarked to Calef, "Our men are in a pretty hot pocket, but, my boy, we must hold this position until the infantry comes up." He told Calef to withdraw his guns by section and by piece when the infantry arrived. In the meantime Calef was to fill his limber chests with ammunition from his caissons back at the seminary and await orders. Just as he finished speaking, a shell burst nearby, and their horses reared in fright. When Calef reached Pergel's section, he saw a Rebel line of battle coming from the woods beyond Willoughby Run. It was Archer's brigade, "and their battle-flags looked redder and bloodier" to Calef than ever before. Calef ordered Pergel's two guns to fire at the flags.[27]

As the Confederate line approached the low ground along Willoughby Run, its center and left passed beneath the trajectories of Pegram's guns. Shells from these supporting batteries whistled over their heads — the "sweetest music" that Pvt. William H. Moon of the 13th Alabama ever heard. Moon was a color guard to the left of Sgt. Thomas J. Grant, the color-bearer. Grant had imbibed freely that morning and was waving his flag and yelling loudly and in a manner sure to draw fire. Moon told him to be quiet or he would bayonet him. Just then a fusillade of minié balls zipped by them and calmed Grant down.[28]

The 13th advanced at a walk under small arms fire, its soldiers loading and firing as they went along. Near Willoughby Run the Federal fire became so hot that the skirmish line halted, and the main line went to the front. The 13th pushed ahead until it came to a strip of ground beside the stream. The steep bank on the east side gave the Alabamians some cover and provided a good place for them to reform, reload, catch their breaths, and cool down. One soldier noticed that the stream there was knee deep and had clear water and a pebbled bottom.[29]

As the 13th paused, Private Moon could see the 1st Tennessee on his left pushing into McPherson Woods. It was hotly engaged at close quarters, and the bluecoats were charging it in "column" rather than in a skirmish line, an indication that infantry had entered the fight. The Tennesseans were lying down, loading while on their backs and rolling to their bellies to aim and fire. Capt. Jacob B. Turney of the 1st Tennessee commented that the fire was severe for what seemed to him like thirty minutes and that powder smoke hovered near the ground, obscuring their view of the Union forces. From the 14th Tennessee toward the brigade left, Pvt. Robert T. Mockbee of the 14th Tennessee heard the brigade give a Rebel yell as it charged across the run after Calef's battery fired on it.[30]

The Union horsemen had given way grudgingly before the Confederate attack, but their time was running out. They knew that the First Corps should be marching to their aid, yet when the Confederates reached Willoughby Run, they feared that they must soon yield their position west of Gettysburg. The men of the 8th Illinois, posted between the pike and McPherson Woods, had a broad field of wheat in their front that extended 400 yards down to Willoughby Run. The grain stalks gave them some concealment, but the rounds fired by Pegram's guns at Calef's center section fell among them and gave them much concern. The Illinois soldiers had to fall back. As they did, an unusual thing happened. After lying concealed among the stalks of wheat until Archer's line was close upon him, a trooper jumped up and shouted in a loud voice, "Forward, forward — now we have them!" This so disconcerted the nearby Confederates that their line faltered. Buford remarked that he had never seen such a daring and successful thing.[31]

To the right of the 8th Illinois two squadrons from the 12th Illinois, three from the 3d Indiana, and one from the 17th Pennsylvania guarded the pike and supported Roder's section. Their troopers sweated through the morning's artillery duel and met the advance of the 7th Tennessee and the 42d and 2d Mississippi Regiments through the grainfields in their front. Although armed with breech-loading carbines that permitted them to fire slightly faster than men with muzzle-loading rifles, the troopers' thin cavalry lines were no match for the strong ranks of infantry bearing down on them. They had no choice but to fall back. Gamble's men on McPherson Ridge, unlike Devin's to their right, could retire 300 yards to the east arm of McPherson Ridge. Pergel's guns were already there. The red battle flags pushed toward these guns, and a squadron of the 8th Illinois received orders to charge the advancing Confederates in order to give Pergel's guns time to displace to the rear. When the Illinois squadron topped the ridge, "the rebels' fierceness and determination could plainly be seen by us in their faces; they were so near our boys."[32]

Calef told Pergel to move his section, one gun at a time, to his caisson park near the seminary. He then rode to the right to see to his other four pieces. As he spoke with Sergeant Newman about his section's withdrawal, a shell burst under one of the gun teams, killing or wounding four of its six horses. Newman was able to remove the gun with the remaining pair, but the Confederates were so close that he had to abandon the harness of the dead horses in the hope of recovering it at another time. Lieutenant Roder's section was moving off when Buford intercepted it. He ordered Roder to enfilade the railroad cut to its right, which was being used by the advancing Mississippians. As one of Roder's guns was dropping trail, probably in the low ground between the two arms of McPherson Ridge, one of the Rebels shouted, "There is a piece — let's take it." Cpl. Robert S. Watrous, the chief of piece, grabbed a double round of canister and ran forward to load it. The Confederates shot Watrous in the leg, but Pvt. Thomas Slattery snatched the canister from Watrous's hands and shoved it into the gun's muzzle. By the time the charge was rammed and fired, the Confederates were so close that the muzzle blast literally blew them away. Union infantry would soon deal with the remaining Confederates there.[33]

A Confederate victory seemed to be at hand, but as the 13th Alabama climbed from the Willoughby Run ravine into a field south of McPherson Woods, its men saw a Union line of battle a hundred yards to the front. Their officers, including Lt. Henry W. Pond, "one of those long, keen, good ones," urged them on. About this time, too, Lt. Col. Newton J. George of the 1st Tennessee asked Archer to have the 13th Alabama wheel to the left, facing the woods, to enfilade the cavalrymen still there. The regiment, or a portion of it, had wheeled and was shooting toward the men in blue when they were ordered to fall back to Willoughby Run. A heavy line of battle, Union infantry, had appeared through the smoke and was pouring fire into Archer's right. A new and ominous phase of the battle had begun.[34]

Writing of this overture to battle, Buford stated that Gamble's brigade had fought for nearly two hours and "had to be literally dragged back a few hundred yards to a position more secure and better sheltered." Calef's battery fought "as is seldom witnessed" and had held its own — gloriously at one time — as the target of a concentric fire of twelve guns. The cavalry had performed well and had slowed the enemy's approach. Its casualties were substantial but small when compared with those sustained by the infantry later that day. Gamble's brigade reported 99; Devin's, 28. Calef's battery had 12. Perhaps it is significant that the 8th Illinois, which did most of the skirmishing that slowed Heth's approach, had only 8 casualties, while the 3d Indiana had 32, the 12th Illinois had 20, and the 8th New York suffered 40. The three latter regiments participated in the critical afternoon's fight in Shultz's Woods, which will be discussed below, and it seems likely that most of their casualties occurred during that part of the day's battle. Though the cavalry's morning battle was essential to the Union success at Gettysburg, it seems not to have been the knock-down, drag-out fight that some of the cavalrymen claimed it to be.[35]

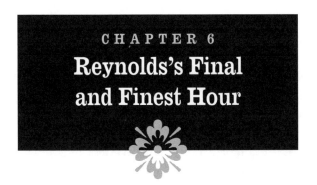

CHAPTER 6

Reynolds's Final
and Finest Hour

At 4:00 A.M. on 1 July, on a "muggy and disagreeable" morning, Maj. William Riddle, aide to General Reynolds, reached Moritz Tavern on the Emmitsburg Road, seven miles south of the square in Gettysburg, with dispatches from General Meade. He found Reynolds wrapped in a blanket and asleep on the floor. Riddle was reluctant to awaken the tired general, so he scanned the messages he carried to see if they required Reynolds's immediate attention. When he saw that there was an order to move, he awakened the general, who, resting his head in his hand, listened while Riddle read the movement order three times. The general then roused himself and went to a nearby room to awaken some sleeping members of his staff.[1]

Meade had ordered the First and Eleventh Corps to Gettysburg, and Reynolds took measures to start them on their way. He summoned Maj. Gen. Abner Doubleday, now acting commander of the First Corps, to his headquarters, and between 7:00 and 8:00 A.M. the two went over dispatches received from Meade and Buford. Reynolds also sent Howard a note saying that troops rather than supply trains would have priority on the roads. At 6:00 A.M. Howard notified Reynolds that Meade had ordered him to move the Eleventh Corps to supporting distance of the First at Gettysburg, and that he was marching it there. One division would follow the First Corps on the Emmitsburg Road. The others would turn east to Horner's Mill and approach Gettysburg over the Taneytown Road. In response Reynolds reminded Howard that the movements of the trains were subordinate to those of the troops and ordered that empty wagons be sent to the rear. Reynolds's orders reached Doubleday at 8:00 A.M., and he started immediately.[2]

But Reynolds did not seem to be in a particular hurry that morning. After all, he did not know of Heth's advance, he wanted to rest his troops, and he did not expect a battle that day. Col. Charles S. Wainwright, chief of artillery of the First Corps, breakfasted soon after sunrise and was busy with paperwork when he received an order from Doubleday to ready his batteries for an immediate move. It was standard practice to rotate the divisions in their order of march, and the Third Division, followed by the Second, was to lead the way. Brig. Gen. James S. Wadsworth's First Division, the closest to Gettysburg, was to bring up the rear. Wainwright ordered the two batteries not accompanying divisions to hook onto the Third Division's rear when it passed, and he rode ahead to find Reynolds and learn what the general thought about the prospects of a fight. Reynolds told him that he did not expect a battle; they were moving forward only to be within supporting distance of Buford's cavalrymen who were to push out from Gettysburg that day. Wainwright became so certain that the march would be short and uneventful, and that they would be in bivouac by noon, that he put his food and saddlebags in a wagon instead of carrying them. When his horse cast two shoes, he stopped at a farm to have them replaced and dallied there afterward for several minutes to avoid going out in a heavy shower.[3]

On his way to Gettysburg Reynolds stopped to see Wadsworth at his bivouac at Marsh Creek. He learned that Doubleday had ordered Wadsworth's division to follow the others and that Wadsworth was waiting for them to pass. Reynolds did not want it to delay so long and ordered Wadsworth to move it out immediately and take the lead. It was well that Wadsworth did so, for it took more than an hour and a half for the two rear divisions to call in their pickets and get under way. Capt. E. Clayton Rogers of Wadsworth's staff was delighted with the order to move; he had never seen a cavalry fight and was eager to reach a place where one might take place.[4]

Wadsworth's division had two brigades. The First, the Iron Brigade, commanded by Brig. Gen. Solomon Meredith, had the 2d, 6th, and 7th Wisconsin regiments, the 19th Indiana, and the 24th Michigan. The brigade had the reputation of being a hard fighting outfit and gloried in the nickname it had won at South Mountain. Its members could be identified by their broad-brimmed, black "Jeff Davis" hats instead of the more commonly worn kepi. The Second Brigade, commanded by Brig. Gen. Lysan-

Brig. Gen. Lysander Cutler
(CWLM)

der Cutler, had four New York regiments: the 76th, 95th, 147th, and 84th, commonly called the 14th Brooklyn, its militia designation. It also included the 56th Pennsylvania and the 7th Indiana, which had been left behind at Emmitsburg as a train guard. Cutler, a Massachusetts native born in 1806, was one of the oldest men in the army. He had entered the service as colonel of the Iron Brigade's 6th Wisconsin Regiment and was a no-nonsense commander.[5]

After the usual early "Reveille" the men of Wadsworth's division breakfasted on coffee, hardtack, and pork. With a battle in the offing, the nearly 500 officers and men of the 24th Michigan Regiment assembled for prayer. While the chaplain prayed, the commissary issued rations and the ordnance officer distributed ammunition. Two miles to the front, probably in the Greenmount area, the 19th Indiana assembled by the Emmitsburg Road. Its men had spent a rainy night on picket and had gathered to wait for the remainder of the brigade to come by. Col. Samuel J. Williams, its commander, had been told that the brigade would march at 8:00 A.M.[6]

Cutler's brigade led the march because it was ready to go when the order came to move out, and the Iron Brigade was not. Col. J. William Hofmann of the 56th Pennsylvania observed that Cutler was "one of those officers who always had his troops ready, and in the morning moved out at the designated time, breakfast or no breakfast." The leading brigade in the column was to be the advance guard and marched a mile and a half ahead of the troops that followed. The division moved in a column of fours at route step, although for reasons not given, some members of the 2d Wisconsin, which led the Iron Brigade, recalled that they had marched "cautiously."[7]

Pvt. James P. Sullivan, whose pen name was Mickey of Company K, wrote that the men of the 6th Wisconsin were in good spirits while on the march and that the soldiers of Company F, Germans from the Milwaukee Turnverein, struck up a "soul stirring" marching song "such as only Germans can sing." The regiment marched in step during the singing and gave Company F three cheers when it finished. Company K responded with a song whose lyrics began, "On the distant prairie where the heifer wild, stole into the cabbage in the midnight mild." It sang some others, too, including one called "Paddy's Wedding." They were in good spirits, buoyed by a rumor passed along the column by a staff officer that General McClellan was back in command of the army. The men cheered like mad at this news, and some shed tears of joy. The merriment ended when, as they approached Gettysburg, they heard the bark of artillery and saw smoke puffs from shell bursts.[8]

The jollity camouflaged a lot of somber thoughts. Cornelius Wheeler, orderly (first) sergeant of Company I, 2d Wisconsin, had conversations with two other sergeants during the march. Sgt. Joseph Williams of Company I told him that he did not feel quite right and that he would not make it through the day. Wheeler replied that he was foolish to feel so, for there seemed to be no trouble ahead that day, and if there was, he would come through all right. Soon after, Sgt. Maj. George R. Legate came up from the rear of the regiment and said, "Corny, we are going to have a fight today, and I will not come out alive." Wheeler replied that this was nonsense; they probably were not going to have a fight, and if they did, as sergeant major Legate could easily stay out of it. "No," replied Legate, "I will stay with the regiment whatever happens."[9]

A farmer standing beside the Emmitsburg Road about three miles south of Gettysburg at 8:30 A.M. would have seen some of the best units of the Army of the Potomac pass by. First came Reynolds and his staff and escort,

Company L, 1st Maine Cavalry. After a short interval Wadsworth and his staff passed, followed in turn by Cutler and his staff leading Cutler's 1,600-man brigade — the advance guard. The 2d Maine Battery, commanded by Capt. James A. Hall, came next, and after an interval of a mile and a half the Iron Brigade went by. A brigade guard, twenty men from each Iron Brigade regiment, brought up the rear of Wadsworth's division. The regiments trudged along at route step in a column of fours, colors cased, over a rutted and muddy dirt road.[10]

As they rode along, some of Reynolds's staff officers detected a change in their general. Although he had seemed depressed and taciturn since the battle of Chancellorsville, he now appeared to be in good spirits and chatted and laughed with them. As they passed through Gettysburg, Reynolds sent Capt. Joseph Rosengarten to warn the townspeople to stay in their houses. Rosengarten returned from this effort with his spectacles and face spattered with mud. He complained that the Gettysburgians were not heeding his warning. To this Reynolds joked, "Oh, they have been throwing dirt in your eyes."[11]

When Reynolds reached a point about about three miles south of Gettysburg, one of Buford's staff officers met him with the news that the Confederates were advancing over the Chambersburg Pike. This news galvanized Reynolds into action. He sent an aide back to Wadsworth to tell him to close up his division and to come on. Reynolds and his party then hurried toward the town and, when a half-mile from it, met a civilian on horseback who told Reynolds that the cavalry was fighting. Reynolds went on to the edge of town and stopped at the George house, a one-story stone cottage. He asked for directions before going into the town — probably over Washington Street. Reynolds did not tarry in the town; he hurried out Chambersburg Street in search of General Buford.[12]

Reynolds reached the fields west of Gettysburg just about the time that Archer's and Davis's brigades and Pegram's artillery battalion were deploying on Herr Ridge for their push against Buford's main line on McPherson Ridge. Buford was said to have learned of Reynolds's approach from Lt. Aaron B. Jerome, his signal officer, who had a perch in the cupola of the seminary building. He must have learned of it also from the staff officer who had met Reynolds south of the town. Jerome wrote that he had called Buford's attention to an "army corps" advancing over the Emmitsburg Road two miles away and identified it as the first corps by its flag — a questionable claim. Soon after, Reynolds galloped onto the field and hailed Buford.[13]

The generals examined the enemy deployment, and Buford no doubt briefed Reynolds about the situation as he knew it. After learning the "real state of the case," Reynolds must have decided at this time to fight at Gettysburg and to hold the high ground south of the town. Reynolds asked Buford to hold on to his position and promised to bring up the infantry as soon as possible. That done, he called his aides together and sent officers galloping to Meade, Howard, and perhaps Sickles.[14]

Reynolds selected Capt. Stephen Weld to go to Meade, telling him to ride as fast as he could even if it meant killing his horse. Weld departed at 10:00 A.M. and reached Meade in Taneytown at 11:20. He reported that the enemy was approaching Gettysburg in force and that Reynolds feared that the Confederates would seize the heights on the "other side" (south or east) of the town. Nevertheless, he would fight them all through the town and keep them back as long as possible. Meade is said to have replied, "Good God! If the enemy gets Gettysburg we are lost!" If made, this was an odd remark that might have been misunderstood; Meade's Pipe Creek Circular, issued just that morning, mentioned only withdrawing from Gettysburg, not holding it. It seems likely that at this time Meade would not have attached such significance to Gettysburg.[15]

Reynolds probably sent Major Riddle to Howard with orders "to come quite up to Gettysburg." Howard, in turn, sent Capt. Daniel Hall to Reynolds to facilitate communications with him. In a postwar paper Captain Rosengarten claimed that Reynolds ordered Howard to place two divisions on Cemetery Hill, but Howard denied that he had received such an order.[16]

After summoning reinforcements for Buford, Reynolds went back to the Emmitsburg Road to hurry Wadsworth's division along. When he came to the Codori farm buildings just south of the town, he asked his escort to open gaps in the fences in the fields to the west to provide a shortcut to the seminary area. As this was being done, Cutler's brigade reached and halted on the high ground at the Peach Orchard. Colonel Hofmann recalled seeing Reynolds from his place in Cutler's column; the general stood beside the road studying what appeared to be a large county map. Wadsworth rode ahead to speak with Reynolds. They briefly discussed setting up defenses in the town but quickly decided that doing so might result in the town's destruction. Besides, positions west of it would serve better. It seems likely that Reynolds would have already decided this. Certainly he would have equated Gettysburg with Fredericksburg and realized that Confederate batteries on Seminary Ridge would have dominated the town. Further, the town could be readily flanked and made untenable.[17]

The shortcut selected by Reynolds left the Emmitsburg Road near the Codori buildings and led to Seminary Ridge somewhere near the Hagerstown Road. It probably followed several paths. When Cutler's men reached the shortcut, they could hear cannon fire and musketry beyond the seminary and knew that there was a fight ahead. Regiments left their noncombatants, pack animals, and packs near the road and set off at a rapid pace. The 76th New York led the column, followed by the other regiments of Cutler's brigade and Hall's battery. After a large gap the Iron Brigade came in its turn. Although Reynolds's escort opened the fences, it would have been a hard job for cavalrymen without axes, and Cutler's pioneer detachment had to help with the work. Some regiments loaded their rifles as they crossed the fields; others did not. Two ladies at one of the houses ladled water from buckets for the soldiers until officers of one regiment kicked over the buckets because this kindness was disrupting the march. When Cutler's brigade reached the seminary area, the right of Buford's line was falling back to Seminary Ridge. The infantry was arriving in the nick of time.[18]

Reynolds had ridden ahead of Wadsworth's division and saw what had to be done. He selected a position for Hall's battery and sent Lt. Col. James M. Sanderson, the First Corps commissary officer, back for Captain Hall. Sanderson found Hall and his battery starting up the east slope of Seminary Ridge. He told Hall that Reynolds wanted to see him at once and that his battery was to come forward at a trot. Reynolds met Hall on the pike near the McPherson barn. Pointing to the ridge crest north of the pike where Calef's right section had been and then to some Rebel batteries on Herr Ridge, Reynolds said, "Put your battery on this ridge to engage those guns of the enemy." Hall's guns were to draw Pegram's fire from the infantry while it was taking position. Then, seeing his battery crossing Seminary Ridge south of the seminary building a half-mile to the southeast, Hall saluted Reynolds and galloped to meet it. He led the six three-inch rifles and their caissons north in the swale in front of Seminary Ridge and across the pike to the rear of his position area. Under shelling by Marye's guns, the battery swung "left into battery," its guns dropped trail on the broad crest of the ridge, and about 10:00 A.M. they opened with shot and shell.[19]

General Wadsworth rode up as Hall received his orders. Reynolds turned to Wadsworth and said, "Put a strong support on the right of this battery; I will look out for the left." Reynolds probably also designated Cemetery Hill as a fallback position at this time. Wadsworth directed Cutler to take his three leading regiments—the 76th New York, the 56th Pennsylvania, and the 147th New York—north in the swale in front of Seminary Ridge and across the pike and the unfinished railroad bed into the fields beyond. As the 147th neared the pike, Hall's battery came "tearing and galloping along" toward the ridge crest on the 147th's left. It broke through Cutler's column and forced the 147th to remain behind as the two lead regiments moved on.[20]

The 76th and 56th regiments marched north in the low ground far enough to allow space for the 147th between the bed and the 56th's left. Cutler ordered them into line facing west on the high ground (the south end of Forney Ridge) overlooking Willoughby Run. At that moment Davis's brigade appeared. The 56th completed its movement from column into line, and the 76th was doing so when Colonel Hofmann saw the Confederates approaching his front. He did not recognize them; he turned to Cutler and asked, "Is that the enemy?" Cutler, who had been watching the approaching line through binoculars, replied, "Yes!" Hofmann commanded, "Ready, Right Oblique! Aim! Fire!" The Union infantry was in the fight.[21]

As Cutler went beyond the railroad bed, General Wadsworth gave Col. Edward B. Fowler of the 14th Brooklyn charge of the 95th New York and ordered that the two regiments guard the left of Hall's battery. Reynolds spoke with Fowler as these two regiments took position near the McPherson farm buildings in time to meet cavalrymen being driven from McPherson Woods by Archer's line. The cavalrymen shouted, "They are coming, give it to them." Soon after, Archer's men fired on Fowler's line from the woods.[22]

After he saw that his own and Brig. Gen. John C. Robinson's divisions were on the march, General Doubleday, the acting commander of the First Corps, started for Gettysburg. About two miles south of the town, Doubleday and Colonel Wainwright saw powder smoke and heard cannon fire. They assumed that Buford was engaged in a cavalry action and were not alarmed. (Hill and Heth were not the only ones who were slow in grasping reality that morning.) A few minutes later as they approached the Peach Orchard area, one of Reynolds's staff officers galloped up with orders for Doubleday to bring up his and Robinson's divisions as rapidly as possible. Doubleday gave the necessary orders and hurried toward Gettysburg. He caught up with the Iron Brigade as it was crossing the fields toward Seminary Ridge. He pressed ahead and saw Reynolds on McPherson Ridge posting the left of Cutler's brigade. A staff officer sent by Doubleday to Reynolds returned with the request that Doubleday take watch of the Hagerstown Road, at the left of the Union line. Doubleday had no other contact with Reynolds on the field. Yet he was soon in command of the troops west of the town, and he developed a special concern for McPherson Woods, which he considered the key to the Union position.[23]

After Reynolds saw that Fowler's demibrigade was taking position north of the woods on the short west arm of McPherson Ridge, he rode back to the east arm of the ridge at the rear of McPherson Woods. The woods was an open grove with little underbrush, and Reynolds was able to see Archer's brigade advancing through it. It was a desperate situation; if not stopped, Archer's men could easily outflank the left of Cutler's line and meet the Iron Brigade from the height of McPherson Ridge. Knowing that the Iron Brigade was coming, Reynolds sent Lieutenant Colonel Kress back to bring it up. The 2d Wisconsin at the head of the brigade had just reached Seminary Ridge. It had marched north along the ridge to the Hagerstown Road and hurried into the swale between Seminary Ridge and McPherson Ridge without even pausing to load. Kress met the 2d there and told Col. Lucius Fairchild, its commander, to swing his regiment from column into line between the retiring cavalrymen and the enemy. It was to repel the Confederate assault on Pergel's section of Calef's battery, which was still at the corner of the woods to its front.[24]

The 2d went from column into line, Colonel Fairchild and his field officers dismounted, and at the command, "Forward, double-quick," the Badgers hurried up the slope to the ridge's crest. They jogged by Pergel's guns and enabled Pergel to haul them off. The Confederates blasted the men of the 2d with a volley, and many fell, including Lt. Col. George H. Stevens. In spite of the galling fire, Fairchild pushed the 2d ahead, obliquing it slightly to the right and into the woods. The Badgers loaded and fired as they went down the slope through the scattered trees.[25]

General Reynolds watched the arriving Iron Brigade from his "powerful black horse" in the company of his orderly, Pvt. Charles Veil. Veil wrote that Reynolds had led the 2d Wisconsin in its charge (except that he confused it with the 19th Indiana), but in this he was probably mistaken. None of the officers and men of the 2d mentioned this signal association, and they certainly would have had it occurred. Instead, Reynolds and Veil reached the 2d's rear as it made the charge. Knowing the gravity of the situation, Reynolds shouted, "Forward men, forward for God's sake, and drive those fellows out of the woods." Then he looked back toward the seminary,

Alfred R. Waud, "Death of Reynolds, Gettysburg" (LC)

probably to see if the rest of the brigade was coming up. As he did so, a minié ball struck the back of his neck at the base of his skull. Reynolds said no more; he reeled in his saddle and fell to the ground — dead.[26]

Veil vaulted from his horse and ran to Reynolds, who was lying on his left side and had a bruise above his left eye. Veil thought that he was stunned. He grasped the general under the arms; Capts. Robert W. Mitchell and Edward C. Baird joined him. Each took a leg, and they carried the general from the perils of the woods. The captains then hurried off to tell Double-day and probably Wadsworth of Reynolds's fall. They did not realize that their general was dead, but they surely knew that he was out of the fight. At one point Reynolds seemed to gasp, and Veil offered him water. What happened next is not clear. He must have been seen by a doctor. Lt. Henry H. Lyman, adjutant of the 147th New York, stated that Dr. John T. Stillman, surgeon of the 147th, examined the general and found him dead. They carried his body on a stretcher to the George house on the Emmitsburg Road. There Veil remembered seeing the general's wound for the first time; he recalled it as a small hole at the base of his skull that did not bleed.[27]

Captain Rosengarten joined the cortege at the George house, and he and Veil went into Gettysburg in search of a coffin. They could not find one and had to settle for a crate obtained from a stonemason. The crate was too short for the body, however, and could not be used until they knocked an end from it. They then secured an ambulance, and with Doubleday's approval, the party took the body to Taneytown, meeting General Winfield S. Hancock on the way. At Taneytown Rosengarten and the other officers spoke with Meade before they continued to the railhead at Westminster. At some point they were able to secure a more suitable container for the body and packed it in ice. Major Riddle and Captain Weld caught up with the party at Westminster. Riddle wept uncontrollably when he saw the general's body. The escorts placed the body on a train at 5:00 A.M. and reached Baltimore about noon. The general's sister and her husband met the escort there and presumably took charge of funeral arrangements. An undertaker embalmed the body, trimmed its moustache and beard, dressed it in Reynolds's major general's uniform, and placed it in a metal casket painted to resemble rosewood. They placed a plate on the casket engraved with the words, "John Fulton Reynolds, U.S. Army, July 1st 1863."

The funeral party left Baltimore by train at 8:30 P.M. and reached Philadelphia at midnight. The family took Reynolds's casket to the home of his sister, Catherine Landis, where it remained over 3 July. At Baltimore the military escort had been reduced to six men: Private Veil, Major Riddle, and Captains Mitchell, Rosengarten, and William H. Wilcox. During the pause in Philadelphia, the escort stayed in the Continental Hotel; Weld bought some trousers and visited some friends.

The funeral party left for Lancaster at 6:30 A.M. on the Fourth of July in a private car provided by the Pennsylvania Railroad. It reached its destination about noon. Lancaster's residents had decorated the city for the Fourth and adapted their decorations to Reynolds's death by lowering flags to half-staff and hanging crepe. The family and the six soldiers rode to the cemetery in carriages that Weld described as "old wagons," and former Pennsylvania Reserves served as pallbearers. The graveside service was a simple one of prayers and readings from the Bible by a local clergyman. Then, in the words of Weld, "Poor General Reynolds disappeared from us for some time to come."[28]

CHAPTER 7
Cutler's Cock Fight

The fire exchanged between Cutler's and Davis's brigades in the fields north of the railroad cuts signaled the debut of the Union infantry into the conflict at Gettysburg. What might have been little more than a skirmish between cavalry outposts and reconnoitering infantry was ballooning into a full-scale battle. Regardless of the intentions of the two commanders, the long marches of their armies were reaching a climax at Gettysburg.

Cutler's brigade and the Iron Brigade of Brig. Gen. James S. Wadsworth's division had opened the fight. It was well for the Union cause that they did so, for both brigades and the division commander had reputations as fighters. Wadsworth's reputation, though, was more complex. Like General Lee, he had been born in 1807 but in New York of old Connecticut stock. He had attended Harvard and had read law with Daniel Webster, but his greatest interest was in farming and the management of his large Geneseo, New York, estate. Once a Democrat, he became active in the antislavery movement and had turned Republican. He served as a volunteer aide on the staff of Brig. Gen. Irvin McDowell at Bull Run and, although he seems not to have had other significant military experience, he received a brigadier general's commission in August 1861. He commanded a brigade in McDowell's division for five months, and from March to September 1862 he was military governor of the District of Columbia. He then became the unsuccessful Republican candidate for governor of New York. In January 1863 he returned to the Army of the Potomac as commander of the First Division, First Corps.

Wadsworth lacked military training and experience, but he had other qualities that commended him to the men in his command. Captain Hall, the battery commander, wrote that he was a "glorious man. A braver man

Brig. Gen. James S.
Wadsworth (CWLM)

never lived." Lt. Col. Rufus Dawes of the 6th Wisconsin Regiment described him as a man of "venerable and commanding appearance, and was
absolutely fearless in exposing himself to danger." Colonel Wainwright
praised Wadsworth as being "active, always busy at something, and with a
good allowance of common sense." Wainwright observed also that Wadsworth "knew nothing of military matters." General Howard described him
as "of large frame . . . always generous and a natural soldier." Wadsworth
led his division without hesitation into the maelstrom at Gettysburg and
must have defined the character of its fighting there.[1]

When Wadsworth's right brigade, Cutler's, opened fire on Davis's Mississippians, the 147th New York Regiment was missing from its place on
the left of Cutler's line — the space between the ravine off the 56th Pennsylvania's left and the west railroad cut. When Hall's battery had trotted
forward to take its position on McPherson Ridge, it had severed the 147th

McPherson farm buildings from the east (postbattle) (GNMP)

from the column's head. This dramatic interruption, plus the movement of the 14th Brooklyn and the 95th New York to the ridge at the McPherson buildings, increased the normal confusion of the event and gave Lt. Col. Francis Miller an incomplete understanding of what the 147th was to do. As a result, he led the neophyte regiment to the swale between the arms of McPherson Ridge. Miller halted the 147th, called the Ploughboys, by the garden fence at the McPherson buildings while he tried to find out where the regiment was to go. While there, Pvt. Francis M. Pease was greatly impressed by the cannonballs that flew over their heads, "pretty thick, some of which struck just behind us and made the dirt fly fiercely."[2]

The McPherson buildings included a two-story house, a bank barn, and a wagon shed. The barn was at the north end of the grouping, about fifty yards south of the pike, and was set into the east slope of the west arm of the ridge. The shed stood between the barn and the house south of it. An orchard connected the buildings with McPherson Woods, and a fenced lane ran from the yard between the house and barn to the pike. Colonel Miller likely halted the 147th along the east side of the fenced lane.[3]

In the meantime the 76th New York at the right of Cutler's line had "a

{ CUTLER'S COCK FIGHT }

grand celebration of fireworks." Incoming artillery fire had harassed its march north across the fields, and Confederates hidden by wheat assailed it with rifle fire when it reached its position on the right of Cutler's line. Although the 56th Pennsylvania had replied at once to the Confederate attackers, the New Yorkers hesitated. Maj. Andrew J. Grover, their commander, did not know at first if the fire came from friend or foe, and he cautioned his men to hold theirs until the enemy could be seen. This happened soon, and the 76th blazed away. But there was new trouble. The 55th North Carolina Regiment appeared over the crest of the ridge well to the right of the 76th beyond Cutler's flank. Once Cutler's fire revealed his brigade's position, Davis's men "charged them in magnificent style" from front and flank. The 55th wheeled right against the Union right. As it advanced, Col. John K. Connally seized the 55th's flag, and he and the color guard rushed several paces ahead of the regiment's line. This rash act drew fire on the colonel and on the color guard that wounded Connally in the arm and hip. Maj. Alfred H. Belo asked Connally if he was wounded badly. "Yes," replied Connally, "but do not pay attention to me; take the colors and keep ahead of the Mississippians."[4]

When the North Carolinians struck the flank of the 76th New York, Major Grover ordered it to "change front to the rear." This faced the regiment's front away from the threat posed by the 2d Mississippi and toward that of the North Carolinians. Sgt. Edgar D. Haviland wrote that after they formed a line and opened fire, "men fell like sheep on all sides of me." A corporal hit by a cannonball fell into his arms, and "at such time a man don't have much time to take care of the men." As soon as he moved the corporal's body away, another soldier fell at his side. It was after the change of front that Major Grover, a Methodist minister and "an estimable man and gallant soldier," fell. Capt. John E. Cook took command.[5]

The 147th New York had a short stay at the McPherson farm buildings. A staff officer galloped to Colonel Miller and told him that Hall's battery would be flanked on the right in three minutes if he did not protect it. Miller ordered his 380-man regiment "by the flank and at a double-quick" past the rear of Hall's battery, which was off to his left. It crossed the railroad bed at the low area between the two McPherson Ridge cuts, and as soon as the rear of the regiment was across, Miller gave the order, "By the left flank; guide center!" The 147th, in line, moved west up the slope into the wheat fields on both sides of a rail fence that paralleled the railroad bed eighty yards to the north. As it advanced, its men heard the firing of its fellow regiments to its right. When it entered the active fight, it was about

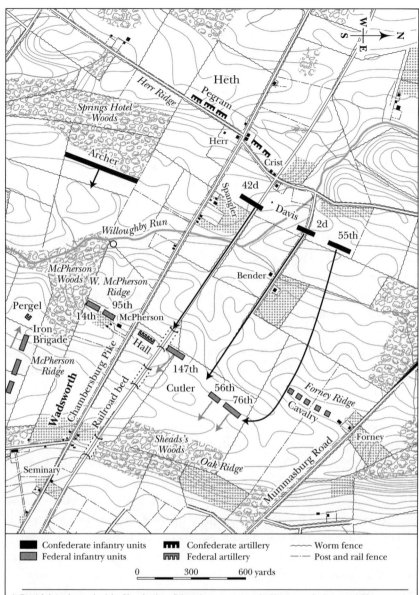

Confederate infantry units   Confederate artillery   ∿∿∿ Worm fence
Federal infantry units   Federal artillery   —·—· Post and rail fence

0   300   600 yards

1. Davis's brigade, north of the Chambersburg Pike, advances against the Union cavalry line on McPherson and Forney Ridges.
2. Cutler's brigade leads Wadsworth's division to McPherson Ridge and replaces the cavalry there. Two regiments form near the McPherson buildings on Hall's battery's left; the 56th Pennsylvania and the 76th and 147th New York regiments cross the railroad bed to confront Davis and to support Hall's battery on its right.
3. The 42d Mississippi drives off Hall's battery; the 2d Mississippi and the 55th North Carolina attack the three right regiments of Cutler's brigade and outflank their right.
4. Cutler's three right regiments retreat to Sheads's Woods, pursued by Davis's men.

Map 7.1. Davis Attacks Cutler

thirty-five yards behind the extension of the line of Hall's battery to the left and somewhat ahead of the 56th and 76th regiments to its right. As the 147th advanced, bullets struck the wheat around it causing the stalks and heads to shake. Dead men and wounded who could not go to the rear dropped among the yellow stalks. Finally the 147th's left reached the crest of the ridge and touched the railroad cut to the right of Hall's battery. When he saw an enemy flag about 150 yards to their front, Colonel Miller ordered, "Lie down! fire through the wheat close to the ground!"[6]

Cutler believed that the three regiments "fought as only brave men could fight, and held their ground until ordered to fall back." Wadsworth told Cutler to retreat the 300 yards back to Sheads's Woods on Oak Ridge. The 56th and 76th fell back in good order, but the Ploughboys stayed where they were. Had someone blundered? Not really. An aide had delivered the order to Colonel Miller, but Miller was shot in the head before he could relay it to his regiment. His frightened horse, having no restraining hand, bolted to the rear carrying the wounded Miller on his back.[7]

Maj. George Harney took command of the 147th. Since he did not know of the order to fall back, the Ploughboys fought on. The Rebel balls "whistled around their heads like hail." Capt. Nathaniel A. Wright, down on his hands and knees, pounded the ground and yelled, "give them h——." A bullet hit Capt. Delos Gary of Company A in the head. When Lt. Volney Pierce noticed that the fire in his front had slackened and the Confederates seemed to be shifting to his right, he advanced his company abreast of Company C. There he saw a Rebel skirmish line moving toward a rail fence and firing into Hall's battery. He saw also another body of Confederates in a fence corner on the other side of the railroad cut. He ordered, "Left oblique, fire!" and the two companies banged away at the skirmish lines until they retreated down the hill. The battery's two right sections had been shooting at the skirmishers while the left section fired toward the enemy artillery. Although Lieutenant Pierce saw the battery limber up and pull away when the enemy skirmishers fell back, Captain Hall reported that he ordered the battery to retire when he saw Cutler's brigade in retreat. Probably Hall referred to the 76th and 56th regiments rather than to the 147th.[8]

In the meantime the fighting increased in fury on the 147th's right. Zipping bullets cut the wheat, and wheat heads dropped on the prone New Yorkers who crawled to the ridge crest, fired, and wriggled back to cover to reload. The New Yorkers shot were hit in either the head or the upper body. To meet the threat from the right posed by the 55th North Carolina,

Major Harney swung the regiment's three right companies back from the ridgeline to the rail fence that ran through the regiment's line. But the pressure from the north increased, and the Ploughboys fell "like autumn leaves; the air was full of lead." Harney saw that the 147th's refused right would soon be outflanked by the 55th, and the regiment would be surrounded. He called a few nearby officers to him and presented his dilemma. The two regiments on their right had fallen back, and perhaps they should do so, too. Yet they had been placed there to support Hall's battery, and since they had not been ordered back, perhaps they should hold on. There seemed to be two alternatives: to surrender and save those still alive, or to fight and fall back with heavy loss. Among the officers consulted, there was no question of surrender.[9]

The 55th North Carolina pressed ahead; the troops on its left, which extended beyond the 147th's refused right, clambered over the rail fence in the New Yorkers' rear. As it was doing so, Lieutenant Pierce saw its colors droop to the front. He commented that "an officer in front of the centre corrected the alignment as if passing in review. It was the finest exhibition of discipline and drill I ever saw, before or since, on the battlefield." All this occupied only a few minutes. General Wadsworth, coming from left, saw the 147th's peril and asked one of his aides, Lt. Timothy E. Ellsworth, to ride into the boiling cauldron and order the 147th to withdraw if, in his judgment, there was no reason for it to remain where it was. Ellsworth did so; "his coal-black hair pressing his horse's mane, he came through the leaden hail like a whirlwind across the old railroad cut and up the hill to Major Harney." It did not take Harney long to decide that there was no reason for them to stay. After advising the Ploughboys to get rid of all of their equipment except rifles and cartridge boxes, he shouted the unorthodox command, "In retreat, double-quick, run!"[10] Some of them did indeed run.

There are two differing accounts of what happened next. Perhaps the refused companies on the right did one thing; those on the left closest to the railroad bed did another. Private Pease of Company F heard no orders to retreat until the Rebels got very close, and then he fled at a fast rate over the railroad bed. Adjutant Lyman wrote that "in getting off the field, no order or line was observed. Some kept to the north side of the old railroad over the second ridge . . . but the galling fire of the Second Mississippi and Fifty-fifth North Carolina, who were advancing from the north, drove most of them across the cut towards the Chambersburg Pike." As Lieutenant Pierce started for the rear, he saw wounded Pvt. Edwin G. Aylesworth lying wounded on the ground. Aylesworth begged not to be left behind. Pierce and Sgt. Peter Shuttz tried to help him away, but they had to lay him down if they were to save themselves. Aylesworth did not survive, and his plea, "Don't leave me, boys," haunted Pierce the rest of his life.[11]

Capt. James Coey of Company E had other recollections. On being ordered to retreat the men were to rise up, fire, and drop quickly so that the return fire of the Rebels would pass over their heads. Then, protected by the ridge, they were to march off at a quick-step carrying their rifles at the trail so that they could load as they went, turn, and fire. Coey wrote that when they turned and fired, the enemy shot back. "The scourge of lead that passed over us was terrible, and could almost be felt — not the zip of the bullets, but a rushing, forcing sound." The 147th's line seemed to melt away; 126 men fell by that fire, including the color bearer, a "Swede, six feet two, fair haired, blue eyed," who was shot several times and fell swathed in the flag that was thoroughly drenched with his blood. Sgt. William A. Wyburn unrolled the dead color-bearer from the flag, tore it from its staff, rolled it up, and raced to the rear. In the excitement of their pursuit, some Rebels neglected to draw their ramrods from their pieces and fired them. Coey remarked that the noise they made had a demoralizing effect. The enemy got so close to the fleeing New Yorkers that they hurled camp hatchets at them along with "vile and opprobrious taunts."[12]

Mississippians at the west end of the railroad cut raked it with rifle fire. It was crowded with men, particularly with wounded who had taken shelter in it on their way to the rear. Pierce and some others were able to climb from it and flee east through a meadow and into a peach orchard on the slope of Seminary Ridge near the Thompson house. Pease was not so lucky and was captured by Confederates who looked down on them from the ground above. During his flight Pierce met Sergeant Wyburn, who was carrying the flag. As they walked from the field, a minié ball hit Wyburn and knocked him down. Pierce thought that he was dead and tried to take the flag from him, but Wyburn revived and said, "Hold on, I will be up in a minute." He stood and carried the colors off.[13]

About seventy-five officers and men of the 147th rallied behind Oak Ridge. The survivors of the 56th Pennsylvania and the 76th New York were also there. In no more than a half-hour the three regiments had been reduced to about half of their original strength. Wadsworth ordered Cutler to take them farther back, and they walked over the railroad bed behind Seminary Ridge as far as Stevens Run at the edge of the town. There they found water and rested before returning to the fight.[14]

After the retreat, Cutler rode up to the 147th, which was then the size of two companies. Not seeing its colors, he said to Harney, or whomever was the ranking officer present, "You have lost your colors, sir." In reply the officer pointed back across the field and said, "General, the 147th never loses its colors." Coming toward them was a man, probably Wyburn, bringing in the flag. "Boys," Cutler replied, "I'll take it all back." He added, "It was just like cock-fighting today. We fight a little and run a little. There are no supports."[15]

The retreat of the 147th New York left Hall's battery without support on its vulnerable right. Hall had led his six three-inch rifles into position at a trot and had posted them hurriedly while under the fire of Pegram's guns. In the excitement of the occasion Hall did not notice the railroad cut only twenty yards beyond his right piece. Perhaps Hall was less concerned about his right than he ought to have been because he had heard Reynolds direct that Wadsworth place a strong infantry support there to protect it.[16]

Hall's guns opened on the enemy batteries on Herr Ridge 1,300 yards to his front and dueled with them for a half-hour. No one described the contest; Hall wrote that his pieces forced two enemy guns to move to the cover of the barn. It must be assumed that the exchange was no more than routine but occasionally terrifying artillery practice. After a half-hour, the battery's battle took a new turn. Lt. Frank Carr raised an alarm: a body of Confederates was within twenty yards of its right gun.[17]

General Buford had seen Confederates in the west cut from a vantage point to the rear. He sent one of the guns from Roder's section, Calef's battery, forward to drive them out. Roder placed one gun between the two arms of McPherson Ridge so that it could enfilade the west cut. The Confederates spotted Roder's gun and attacked it but were driven off. Likely it fired only a few times before Roder had to haul it off, for things were happening that rendered it useless there.[18]

When Hall heard the alarm raised by Lieutenant Carr, he rode to the right to ascertain its cause. When he saw a line of Confederates pointing rifles at him, Hall became convinced that his battery was in trouble. The Confederates, some of whom were wearing capes, had approached the battery unseen through the west railroad cut. They seemed to rise from the earth no more than sixty yards away and began to snipe at the horses and the cannoneers. Hall ordered his center and right sections to swing their muzzles to the right and to fire canister. Lt. William N. Ulmer, commander of the right section, had anticipated Hall's order, and his two pieces blazed away immediately with double canister. The blasts sent the Rebels tumbling back into the cut, from which they could continue their sniping. At this time Hall saw Cutler's troops, probably just the 56th and 76th regiments, pulling back in front of Davis's brigade's left. "Feeling that if the position was too advanced for infantry it was equally so for artillery," Hall ordered his battery to retire by sections.

Hall's intention was to move his vulnerable right section back to relative safety and, with the help of its fire from the rear, to save his four remaining guns. Ulmer's section "went back handsomely"; but by then the 147th New York had fallen back, and the Mississippians north of the railroad bed kept pace with the retreating guns. From the railroad bed they raked the gun crews and horses with minié balls. They killed all of the horses on one piece, and Ulmer's men had to try to draw it off by hand.

Seeing that Ulmer's section could not cover the center and left sections, Hall decided to pull them away. He instructed the section chiefs to reverse their limbers, which were below the crest and behind the guns. While they were doing this, the four guns fired rapidly in order to create smoke that would mask their withdrawal. The cannoneers rolled the guns down into the swale to the waiting limbers, hooked them up, and tried to draw them off. Hall described their retreat as "*hellish.*" The Rebel skirmishers pursued the guns. A high, stout fence along the pike and the enemy artillery fire that enfiladed the pike convinced Hall that his guns had to stay in the fields between the railroad bed and the pike until they crossed the east arm of McPherson Ridge. When they approached Seminary Ridge, the guns turned toward the pike and had to reach it by going through a gap in the fence and over its lower rails. Only one gun could pass through the gap at a time. The Confederate skirmishers fired briskly at them, and one bullet struck Hall's horse in the rump. The skirmishers crowded toward the last piece through the gap. They bayoneted the gun team's six horses, which fell dead at the fence. The gun's crew abandoned it.

Captain Hall met Wadsworth on the pike where it crossed Seminary Ridge. Not fully appreciating the infantry's plight, Hall complained that they had been cowardly to abandon his battery. Wadsworth told him to post his guns where they could cover a Union retreat. Hall replied that this should be done where they were standing, but Wadsworth said that they could not hold Seminary Ridge and that he wanted the battery to fall back "beyond the town." Hall said that he wanted to recover his lost gun before leaving, but Wadsworth "snappishly" ordered him on his way. Hall obeyed and took his battery, which now had only three guns, back through the town to Cemetery Hill and put them in position there. Hardly had he done this when an officer on Wadsworth's staff appeared and told him to return his battery to Seminary Ridge. Much had happened in the fields west of the town in the few minutes since Hall had left. The battle had taken a new turn, and there would be more fighting there.[19]

{ CUTLER'S COCK FIGHT }

CHAPTER 8
McPherson Woods

It was an "unadorned long-drawn-out line of ragged, dirty blue against the long-drawn-out line of dirty, ragged butternut, with no 'pomp of war' about it, and no show or style except our old black hats." So wrote Capt. Robert K. Beecham of the clash between Archer's brigade and the Iron Brigade in McPherson Woods on the morning of 1 July. Sergeant Pergel's two three-inch rifles had opened fire on battle flags of Archer's brigade as it left the cover of the Springs Hotel Woods, but the butternut line beneath the flags came on. As soon as the Iron Brigade's line passed Pergel's guns and entered McPherson Woods, General Buford ordered Pergel to the rear. A new phase of the battle had begun.[1]

Brig. Gen. James J. Archer commanded the attacking butternut brigade. Archer hailed from Maryland, had attended Princeton, and was once a lawyer. He had served as a captain in the war with Mexico and had been brevetted a major for gallantry at Chapultepec. In March 1855 he became a captain in the Regular Army's 9th Infantry and soldiered with it until May 1861. He entered the Confederate service as colonel of the 5th Texas. After becoming a brigadier general in June 1862, he received command of the Tennessee Brigade on the Peninsula and led it in subsequent battles to Gettysburg.

Archer was small in stature, rough and unattractive in appearance, irascible, and outspoken. Yet after serving under him, men found that he could be warm of heart and "the very God of War." They called Archer "The Little Game Cock." Mary Boykin Chesnut saw him in 1864 after he had been a prisoner of war and was probably in poor health. She described him then as hard faced and black bearded, with sad black eyes. He had become a tragic figure and would die that October.[2]

The infantrymen relieving Gamble's cavalrymen and Pergel's guns belonged to the 2d Wisconsin Regiment, 300 strong, which was leading the Iron Brigade to the field. The 2d, and the regiments following it, had crossed the fields from the Emmitsburg Road at the Codori buildings to Seminary Ridge and had moved north along that ridge to the Hagerstown Road and into the swale west of the seminary. Lieutenant Colonel Kress of Wadsworth's staff met the column and, not finding General Meredith, sent the various regiments as they arrived (the 6th Wisconsin excepted) forward into line to drive the Confederates from McPherson Woods. Col. Lucius Fairchild of the 2d Wisconsin had not expected a fight and had brought the 2d to the field with unloaded rifles. When the 2d neared Pergel's section, Fairchild commanded, "Forward into line," and its companies swung left from a column of fours into a two-ranked line of battle that measured about 100 yards from flank to flank. This was probably a ragged movement, for the Badgers had to cross a rail fence near the woods and load their pieces while jogging at the double-quick. As the regiment swung into line, its field officers vaulted from their horses, took their places behind the regiment, and went into the fight on foot.[3]

McPherson Woods, the focal point of the fighting south of the Chambersburg Pike, had the shape of a truncated triangle with its 400-yard base along Willoughby Run and its north side extending east from the run about 600 yards across the west arm of McPherson Ridge to the crest of the ridge's east arm. Although the floor of the south edge of the woods sloped west from the east ridge to the run, its north half included the nose of the west ridge and the swale between the two ridges. Thus troops moving through the north half of the woods from the east would have to go down the slope for about eighty yards into a broad marshy ravine, cross a rivulet, then proceed uphill to the crest of the nose of the west ridge before descending downhill 200 yards to the run. The woods contained oak and other deciduous trees spaced widely apart and had been used for grazing and picnicking. It had little undergrowth to impede vision and movement.[4]

Orderly Sergeant Wheeler wrote of his feelings as he went into the fight. In the past he had approached battle with some doubt and fear for his personal safety. This time, though, he felt "jubilant & free & fearless." He knew that ordinarily no thinking man could go into battle and not feel fear, but he never felt better than at this time at Gettysburg. The regiment approached McPherson Woods from the southeast and passed by the 8th New York Cavalry's line and to the right of Pergel's pieces. It double-quicked across the east arm of the ridge, never stopping until after it

Brig. Gen. James J. Archer
(LC)

entered the woods. There it received a volley from Confederates in the ravine that bisected the woods—likely from the 7th or 14th Tennessee. The deadly volley cut down an estimated 30 percent of the regiment. Apparently General Reynolds was shot at this time; Wheeler wrote that Reynolds was not more than a hundred feet from the 2d and that he saw the general fall from his horse.[5]

After pressing forward and firing for a few minutes, the 2d Wisconsin halted until the rest of the brigade came into line on its left. During this halt the 2d took stock of its casualties, which included Sergeant Williams, whose presentiment of death had been fulfilled. While the men of the 2d paused, enemy balls buzzed "phit phit phit" in the air around them, and bullets fired low made the leaves rustle at their feet. One struck the heel tap of Pvt. Emanuel Markle's shoe, smashed into his heel, and knocked him flat. Soon after Markle's fall, the 2d resumed its advance toward the run.[6]

Archer's brigade had crossed Willoughby Run. The 13th Alabama

McPherson Woods, site of
Reynolds's death (GNMP)

halted briefly beside the stream where its steep bank shielded the Alabamians from the cavalry's fire. The regiment reloaded its rifles, caught its breath, and tried to cool off. Yet Private Moon found that it was "hot, hotter, hottest" in the low and windless trough.[7]

In the meantime the 1st, 7th, and 14th Tennessee regiments to the 13th's left had crossed the stream and into the trees along its bank. They met the 2d Wisconsin, which was striving to drive them out. Lt. Furguson S. Harris of the 7th Tennessee climbed the slope east of the run and led his company 300 yards into the woods, probably as far as the ravine. There he saw a man in a large broad-brimmed hat carrying an immense U.S. flag. The Confederates wrote few details of the fight but believed that it lasted about a half-hour. They recalled well that the fighting was severe and that the powder smoke hovered near the ground, concealing the Union line from their view. Lt. Col. Samuel G. Shepard of the 7th Tennessee reported

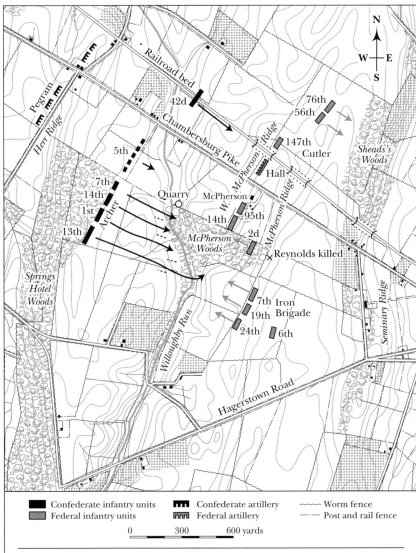

Confederate infantry units   Confederate artillery   ∼∼∼ Worm fence
Federal infantry units   Federal artillery   —·— Post and rail fence

0   300   600 yards

1. Archer's brigade forms on Herr Ridge in the Springs Hotel Woods. Batteries of Pegram's battalion occupy Herr
Ridge and duel with Calef's battery on McPherson Ridge.

2. Archer's brigade advances against Union cavalry in McPherson Woods and on McPherson Ridge.

3. Wadsworth's division of the Union First Corps arrives. Two regiments of Cutler's brigade take position at the
McPherson buildings, while three go north of the railroad bed. Hall's battery replaces Calef's north of the
Chambersburg Pike.

4. The 2d Wisconsin Regiment leads the Iron Brigade to McPherson Ridge. General Reynolds sends the brigade into
the woods to repulse Archer's advance. Reynolds is killed at the eastern edge of the woods.

5. The 7th Wisconsin, 19th Indiana, and 24th Michigan regiments form a line on the 2d Wisconsin's left,
advance, and strike Archer's brigade. They capture Archer and drive his brigade back to Herr Ridge.

Map 8.1. McPherson Woods, Morning

that they were not more than forty or fifty yards from the enemy when they opened fire and that the men shot with "great coolness and deliberation, and with terrible effect." Private Moon, looking toward the woods from the 13th's position, saw that the fighting was at close quarters. The Wisconsin men were charging, and the Tennesseans were lying on their backs before rolling to their stomachs to fire. Lieutenant Harris saw Lt. Billy Baber grab the hair of a fellow who was firing from behind the regiment's line. He pulled him to the front where, even if he did not shoot the enemy, he might not hit a friend. He also saw Capt. John Allen and Jack Moore, each on one side of a man called "Bully Ike," forcing him into the fight. When the firing ceased, Capt. Jacob B. Turney dropped to his knees, peered beneath the smoke, and saw Federal legs and feet moving toward their left. He reported this to General Archer, who did not become alarmed; he said that Davis's brigade was to occupy "that timber to our left." If so, Archer seems to have had no idea of the true location of Davis's brigade.[8]

To the right of the woods, men of the 13th Alabama viewed what they could see of the fight to their left with awe and wonder. Lt. Col. Newton J. George of the 1st Tennessee, who according to Private Moon was the only officer of the brigade to have gone into the fight on horseback, rode up to Lt. Col. James Aiken of the 13th Alabama or to Archer (Moon was not sure who it was). He asked the officer to have the 13th wheel left and take the 2d Wisconsin in the flank. After all, the 13th was not heavily engaged, and McPherson Ridge concealed the arriving Union infantry that would soon strike the Confederates south of the woods. The 13th complied; it wheeled left swinging its right uphill toward the crest area of McPherson Ridge just vacated by Pergel's guns and about seventy-five yards off the left of the 2d Wisconsin. There the Alabamians fired toward the 2d Wisconsin and the smoke that concealed them. The battle seemed to be going well for the 13th when suddenly it was ordered to fall back at once toward Willoughby Run. The men did not understand the order, but they obeyed. When they reached the run, they were told to lie down. The reason for their falling back was not readily apparent.[9]

Archer's brigade could not see it, but the rest of the Iron Brigade was entering the fight. The 7th Wisconsin, commanded by Col. William W. Robinson, was the first up. Kress ordered Robinson to deploy his regiment on the crest of the ridge in front of the cavalry as soon as possible. Robinson formed the 7th into line and led it to the top of the ridge at the double-quick. Like the 2d, the 7th had arrived with empty guns because, as Robinson wrote, "no one expected we were to be engaged so suddenly." He gave the command to load as the 7th ran forward so that it did not lose much time. Such haste proved unnecessary because it had to wait at the top of the ridge for the 19th Indiana and the 24th Michigan to join it. At this time the 2d Wisconsin was fighting in the woods about a hundred yards to the right and front of the 7th. Through the dense smoke that hung over the low ground in his front, Robinson could see troops whom he could not identify. They opened fire on the 7th.[10]

When this firing began, Capt. Craig Wadsworth, who was then serving as volunteer aide to General Doubleday, rode up to Colonel Robinson from the right. Robinson had become confused; the lay of the land in his front was not only unknown to him, but it was obscured by smoke. Robinson asked young Wadsworth if the troops firing at the 7th were friend or foe. Wadsworth pointed down to the left, and there Robinson saw a Rebel battle flag. Wadsworth told Robinson that Doubleday wanted the Confederates driven back. Robinson advanced the 7th far enough so that its men could see down the slope ahead of them. As soon as the regiments to be on their left came up, they delivered a volley and advanced.[11]

The 19th Indiana joined the 7th Wisconsin on its left. The Hoosiers had loaded their rifles the night before when they had manned the picket line in front of the corps. Although the weather had been moist and might have dampened their powder, they had not unloaded their pieces. They learned of Reynolds's being shot as they approached McPherson Ridge, and "the men set their faces resolutely to meet the foe and avenge his death." They paused briefly. A staff officer ordered the color bearer, Pvt. Burlington Cunningham of Company K, not to unfurl the flag, but when the line was formed, Cunningham turned to Pvt. Abraham Buckles of the color guard and said, "Abe, pull the shuck." Buckles pulled off the cover, and one of them tied it around his waist. Cunningham unrolled and shook out the flag and flaunted it above his head. The 19th was ready to enter the fight. As it crossed the fence at the ridge's crest, it received a volley from the wooded ravine to its right. More than a dozen balls pierced its flag, and Cunningham fell. Someone said to Buckles, "Abe, drop your gun and take the flag," and Buckles did so. The men of the 19th returned the Confederate volley, and at the command, "Charge," Buckles and his flag led the Hoosiers forward.[12]

Because General Doubleday had held the 6th Wisconsin in reserve near the seminary, the 24th Michigan was the last regiment to join the brigade line on McPherson Ridge. The 24th was relatively new to the brigade and reached Gettysburg with nearly 500 officers and men. Like the men of the other regiments, those of the 24th had not loaded their rifles. Col. Henry A. Morrow halted the regiment on the ridge's crest so that its men could do so, but before this was accomplished, a staff officer rode up and told Morrow to advance.[13]

As the other Iron Brigade regiments formed on its left, the 2d Wisconsin had resumed its push through the woods, its right flank along the fence that separated the woods from the open field to the north. As it advanced, Colonel Fairchild saw the 14th Brooklyn, distinguished by its chasseur uniform with red baggy pants, in the field off the 2d's right flank. The 2d pushed down the slope toward Archer's men in the ravine and onto the nose of the crest beyond. It moved slowly but inexorably, firing as it went as only a well-trained and disciplined unit could do. Colonel Fairchild wrote that his officers and men fell "with terrible rapidity." When Fairchild was about fifty yards into the woods, a minié ball shattered his left arm and forced him to relinquish command to Maj. John Mansfield. Mansfield continued to push the line close to the enemy.[14]

As the men of the 2d remembered it, some of Archer's men dodged from tree to tree. According to Lt. Dennis B. Dailey, who was with Company B on the right of the 2d's line, the Federals had pushed to within fifteen paces of the Rebel line before it gave way. Then the Badgers "pursued them vigorously." Mansfield reported that some of the retreating Confederates sought the cover of trees and attempted without success to reform their broken lines, while others took refuge in the large quarry hole just north of the woods by the bank of Willoughby Run. But their resistance was to no avail, for the 2d, with the help of the regiments on its left and right, forced the Rebels in the woods back to the stream.[15]

The charge of the left three regiments of the Iron Brigade was a straightforward movement. As the 24th Michigan, coming from the rear, neared the left of the 19th Indiana, General Meredith ordered it and the 7th Wisconsin to charge. Lt. Col. John B. Callis, whose horse had been killed and who was hit also by a Rebel volley, wrote that the 7th received a galling fire from Confederates in the woods. Callis thought that the regiment had no time to load, so he and not Robinson ordered its men to fix bayonets and advance. As the 7th's line moved off, a staff officer, whom Callis identified as Craig Wadsworth, rode up and ordered it to halt. But he was too late; "their rushing charge was irresistible." Pvt. William C. Barnes, a member of the 19th Indiana's color guard, recalled, "We went down at them pretty lively." It was heady stuff; yet in 1877 Lt. Col. William W. Dudley of the 19th wrote that a person not in such a charge could not imagine the mixed

{ MCPHERSON WOODS }

emotions of an officer at such a time: "His anxiety lest the fire of the enemy which his men cannot return, and the many obstacles which his line must encounter, may destroy the alignment and thus lose the momentum and break the face of his charge, and thus the precious lives entrusted to his care, which he sees strewn along the rear of the advancing line, be wasted; all these things are calculated to try his nerve and courage of the bravest officer."[16]

In its charge the 7th passed beyond the line of the 2d Wisconsin in the woods. Fortunately for the Iron Brigade its three left regiments sustained few casualties in their charge. Struck hard in front and in flank, the Confederates were unable to resist. Some fled; others threw down their arms and tremblingly asked where they should go, while others simply dropped their rifles and ducked through the Union formations to the Union rear. After the 13th Alabama had been ordered back to Willoughby Run, its men were told to lie down. Suddenly "the bluecoats soon covered the hillside in our front, ordering us to surrender." The Rebels, who had no rescuers close by, obeyed. Pvt. Elijah T. Boland did not know how many men surrendered, but all those "who had not grasped time by the forelock and left," when they realized that they were in a trap, did so. One officer rushed toward Lieutenant Colonel Callis, pointed his sword at him, and said, "I surrender." Callis replied, "Surrender, that is no way to surrender," as he struck the man's sword from his hand and just missed hitting his neck. Callis schooled the Confederate in what he deemed the etiquette of surrendering by saying, "If you surrender, order your men to cease firing, pick up your sabre and order your men to go to the rear as prisoners." The officer obeyed. Then, not far from the Union line, Callis saw a Rebel soldier pick up a regimental flag that had fallen to the ground. He was trying to wind it on its staff. Callis ordered Pvt. Dick Huftill to shoot the man. Huftill stepped to the front of the 7th's line, steadied his rifle on Pvt. Webb Cook's shoulder, and "brought the man and colors down together."[17]

The 7th went across the run and up the slope to a shelf on Herr Ridge and in the rear of the Confederates who were facing the 2d Wisconsin in the woods. From the shelf they could see a Confederate line on the ridge above them. The 19th Indiana advanced on the left of the 7th to Willoughby Run and captured soldiers of the 1st Tennessee Regiment. It went on up the ridge's slope and there spent an hour processing prisoners and destroying 400 captured rifles. As they did this, they saw Confederates on the ridge belatedly preparing to attack them.[18]

On the 19th's left the 24th Michigan had charged across the stream, swung around the right flank of Archer's brigade, and also went to the shelf on the hill. It halted there and sent skirmishers to its front and to the left, almost as far as the Harmon farm buildings. By crossing the run and climbing to the shelf about halfway to Springs Hotel Woods the Iron Brigade had made Archer's positions untenable and had doomed many men of his brigade to capture. The 2d Wisconsin and Cutler's two regiments to its right were one "door"; the left of the Iron Brigade, the other. A *New York Tribune* reporter wrote, "The great double doors of the Iron Brigade shut together, with the slam as of colliding mountains, folding between them 1,500 prisoners of war." Although Archer's brigade probably lost less than a third of the 1,500 reported, the amount was ample; this battering without interference from Heth's rear brigades suggests that Heth had not made adequate provision for Archer's close support.[19]

The capture of Archer himself underscored the completeness of this victory. He was the first general in the Army of Northern Virginia taken since Lee had become its commander. Although accounts by two soldiers of the 13th Alabama suggest that Archer was on the brigade right when captured, others more persuasive place him on the left, possibly with the 14th Tennessee. Capt. Thomas Herndon of the 14th, who was seized a few yards from Archer and at about the same time, wrote that Archer had ordered that every man was to take care of himself. Lieutenant Colonel Shepard of the 7th, who wrote the brigade's report, said that he saw Archer shortly before his capture and that "he appeared very much exhausted with fatigue."[20]

As the 2d Wisconsin drove the Tennesseans beyond Willoughby Run, Pvt. Patrick Maloney of Company G, "a brave patriotic and fervent young Irishman," spied General Archer among a small body of Confederates about thirty paces west of the stream. Archer wore a "splendid gray uniform" and must have stood out from the men around him. Maloney saw him, dashed into the midst of the Confederates, and grappled with the general, who, though weak and exhausted, resisted capture. The other Confederates seem not to have defended him, and Archer gave up the fight. Major Mansfield, in his report for the 2d Wisconsin, stated that Maloney brought Archer to him and that Archer gave him his sword. Mansfield wrote that he turned the sword over to Lt. Dennis Dailey, who, though an officer of the 2d, was then serving on the brigade staff. Dailey was to take prisoners to the rear and, presumably, turn Archer's sword over to General Meredith or someone else of rank.[21]

Dailey told another story. He wrote that the "sullen general," after being collared by Maloney, had asked him for protection from his captor. Dailey asked Archer to turn over his sword, its "beautiful steel scabbard," and sword belt. Archer protested, saying that courtesy permitted him to retain his sidearms. Nevertheless, he complied. Dailey sent Archer back to Meredith's headquarters and saw him no more. However, Dailey did take a fancy to the captured sword, which was lighter than his own. He kept it and sent his own sword to the rear. Dailey was wounded later that day and went to the home of Mary McAllister on Chambersburg Street. The Confederates captured him there, but not before he gave the sword to McAllister to hide for him. The Confederates took Dailey off, but he escaped on the night of 5 July and returned to Gettysburg for his sword. He learned that Colonel Morrow of the 24th Michigan, who had been wounded also and was at the McAllister house, had departed and had taken the sword with him. Morrow returned the sword to Dailey, however, and in the fall of the year Dailey gave it to General Meredith as a souvenir of the fight. After Meredith's death in 1881, the Merediths returned the sword to Dailey.[22]

Two postscripts need to be added. The Confederates killed Private Maloney later that day unfortunately, but capturing Archer gave him a small place in history. Archer, when taken to the rear, encountered General Doubleday, whom he had known in the Old Army. Doubleday greeted him, "Good morning, Archer! How are you? I am glad to see you!" To this Archer replied, "Well, I am *not* glad to see *you* by a —— sight."[23]

CHAPTER 9

The Railroad Cut

Lt. Col. Rufus R. Dawes was proud of his 6th Wisconsin Regiment. When the 6th, the last regiment in the Iron Brigade's column, reached the Peach Orchard area and he could see the spires of the town, Dawes prepared to show the Gettysburgians the 6th's "style of marching." After informing the adjutant and the 6th's company commanders of his intentions, he ordered its ranks closed, its colors unfurled, and its drum corps to the front, where it would play the regiment into the town. The drums rattled and thumped and the fifes shrilled "The Campbells Are Coming" as the regiment neared the town. But at the same time those men of the 6th away from the drumming might also have heard the thudding of distant cannon fire. Before reaching the town, the music stopped—there would be no parading; instead the 6th followed the brigade's path across the future field of Pickett's Charge to Seminary Ridge. As the 6th approached the ridge, Lt. Gilbert M. Woodward galloped up shouting, "Colonel, form your line, and prepare for action." Dawes turned in his saddle, stood in his stirrups, and shouted commands that swung the regiment from column into line and caused the men to load their guns as they moved forward. The 6th was hastening toward the left of the 24th Michigan and the left of the Iron Brigade when Lt. Benjamin T. Marten of General Doubleday's staff dashed up and told Dawes that Doubleday wanted him to halt his regiment. Dawes did so, and he ordered his men to lie down in the wheat that surrounded them. The brigade guard of 100 men, 20 from each of the brigade's five regiments, under the command of Lts. Lloyd G. Harris of the 6th and Levi Showalter of the 2d Wisconsin, joined the 6th there. Dawes divided them into two provisional companies, placing one on each flank of the 6th. They remained with it throughout the morning's fight.[1]

Lt. Col. Rufus R. Dawes
(MCLL)

The 6th did not rest long. A "very boyish staff officer," either Marten or Lt. Meredith L. Jones, came up with Doubleday's order for Dawes to move to the right at once. Dawes formed the 6th in a column and started it north in the swale west of the seminary. As he did so, Capt. James D. Wood, the brigade adjutant, rode to his side with orders to "go like hell," for the Rebels were driving Cutler's men. From high in his saddle Dawes could see Union troops in retreat beyond the pike, and Hall's guns displacing to the east. A strong but loose line of Confederates advanced over the ridge behind them in pursuit. Lieutenant Harris, who was with his half of the brigade guard in the rear of the column, saw "the 147th New York out-flanked, in full retreat with Gen. Joe Davis' Mississippi brigade in hot pursuit" (Harris could not have known these identities at that time). Sgt. James P. "Mickey" Sullivan remembered that a heavy line of battle was coming toward them. It must have been about this time that the 6th saw soldiers carrying a body to the rear in a blanket; it probably was General Reynolds, but they did not know it.[2]

Dawes saw that the 6th was on the enemy's flank and might be able to strike a hard blow, but it should do so in line and head-on. When west of the seminary building, he turned the 6th's column to the right and marched it parallel with the pike until the whole regiment was facing east. Then he commanded, "Battalion, by the left flank, march!" and the 6th faced the pike and the enemy in line of battle. Led by Dawes on horseback and carrying their rifles at right shoulder shift, the men of the 6th, their heads bowed "into the leaden storm," double-quicked toward the pike and the Confederate flank. They had gone but a few steps when Dawes's mare reared and plunged. Dawes tried to bring her under control, but she fell to the ground and sent Dawes sprawling. He got to his feet quickly and shouted, "I'm all right, boys," and the regiment opened its line enough to pass Dawes and the mare. The mare, which had been shot in the shoulder, hobbled to the rear on three legs. In the meantime the 6th had passed over a stubble field. It halted when it reached the rail fence on the south side of the pike. At Dawes's command to "fire by file," each man blazed away toward the Confederates in his front.[3]

The Confederates who fought at the railroad cut, primarily at the center cut, have left only sketchy accounts of their fighting there. It must have involved all three regiments of Davis's brigade. Like the Union troops opposing them, they were fatigued and sweating from their exertions and the heat of that sultry July morning. They had been driving Cutler's three regiments to the east when they saw Union troops making for their right. To meet this new threat, they attempted to change front to the south, and many took shelter in the center railroad cut and along its adjoining bed. The 2d Mississippi's color-bearer planted his flag about fifty yards east of the cut near the low point in the swale. The troops of the 42d were probably on the 2d's right in and beyond the deep portion of the cut, and those of the 55th North Carolina mingled with the 2d Mississippi and extended left "beyond the embankment." Maj. John A. Blair, commander of the 2d, wrote that "all the men were jumbled together without regiment or company." He was attempting to organize them for an advance when the Union attack came. Maj. Alfred H. Belo, then commanding the 55th North Carolina, believed that the side that charged first would "hold the field," and he suggested to Major Blair that they charge before Federal deployment was complete. Blair agreed, but before he could organize a charge, General Davis sent an order for the brigade to retreat and reform, probably back on Herr Ridge with the rest of Heth's division. The troops of the 2d and 42d were to slip away through the railroad cut while the 55th covered their

{ THE RAILROAD CUT }

Center railroad cut from the east in 2000 (H. Pfanz)

withdrawal. The plan might have worked had the order come sooner; but it was tardy, and the three regiments were too disorganized to carry it out in the face of Dawes's advance. The Confederates would have to fight it out where they were.[4]

The 6th Wisconsin and the Iron Brigade's guard were not quite alone. When Cutler's brigade reached the field, General Reynolds had placed the 14th Brooklyn and the 95th New York on the west arm of McPherson Ridge south of the pike to support Hall's battery and connect it with McPherson Woods. In effect they were a demibrigade commanded by Colonel Fowler. Col. George H. Biddle's 240 officers and men of the 95th wore a standard uniform; the 318 soldiers of the 14th wore a special chasseur uniform consisting of scarlet trousers stuffed into leggings, a short blue jacket, red vest, and kepi. (The 14th's memorial at the railroad cut has a statue of a man so garbed.) Both were veteran regiments, the service of the 14th extending back to First Bull Run.[5]

The main line of the two regiments was in the orchard and behind a rail fence north of the woods. The woods was to the 14th's immediate left, and both regiments faced west across a wheat field that sloped gradually to Willoughby Run's ravine about 300 yards away. No one mentioned it, but it is likely that both regiments had posted skirmishers to their front. It seems, too, that the 95th on the right would have deployed to support Hall's battery's left.

As the demibrigade took its position, enemy riflemen fired on it from the woods and hit several men. Two bullets struck Fowler's black horse in the head, and another bruised the colonel's thigh. Although the 14th fought back, it was the advance of the 2d Wisconsin through the woods that forced the Confederates from its flank.[6]

Since Archer's brigade did not have the men to cover the space between McPherson Woods and the pike with a solid line of battle, he must have covered it with only a skirmish line. Maj. Albert S. Van de Graaff, commander of the 5th Alabama Battalion, wrote of its being deployed only as skirmishers on 1 July and having a loss that day of only seven men wounded. These low casualties indicate that the battalion was not fighting the attacking regiments of the Iron Brigade and suggest that it was skirmishing on the quieter front opposite Fowler's demibrigade.[7]

After Archer's retreat, Fowler's men received fire from Davis's Mississippians in their rear. With surprise and consternation, Fowler saw that the enemy was off his right near the west railroad cut. Hall's battery was going to the rear, and the Confederates had shot all of the horses on one gun. Fowler first thought that his two regiments were lost. "Like lighting," he figured that if his two regiments attempted to retreat, all of their troops would be shot. Therefore his only alternative was to charge. At this time Fowler apparently did not know that Doubleday had already sent the 6th Wisconsin to Cutler's aid. Since the 6th was in the broad swale beyond the east arm of McPherson Ridge, it was probably out of Fowler's sight, and neither he nor Dawes saw each other.

Colonel Fowler faced his two regiments to the rear and, while under fire, marched them east, in line, until they were opposite that portion of the enemy in and west of the center cut. Fowler then faced his line toward the pike with the 95th on the right. Fowler's line advanced under enemy fire until it reached the fence along the pike. The fence offered some cover, and the New Yorkers paused on their bellies behind it. Fowler wrote that at this time "the 6th Wisconsin advanced bravely to our assistance and formed on our right." Fowler then ordered an advance by his whole line, including the 6th, shouting and cheering his men on as they advanced into the fire of the enemy posted at the railroad bed. The Confederate balls came so thick and fast that "the whirring noise they made sounded like the steady rhythm of machinery." Fowler's men wavered, Colonel Biddle left the field wounded, but they continued on. Fowler claimed to have re-covered one of Hall's guns in this charge.[8]

There is a more credible version of this tale, however. As Dawes related it, the two New York regiments tardily *joined the 6th* in this counterattack. When the 6th reached the fence beside the road, its men could see a line of yelling Rebels advancing east across their front and firing at Cutler's retreating men. Dawes ordered his men to fire, and they blazed away, some steadying their rifles on fence rails as they shot at the southerners' right flank. This flank fire checked the pursuit, "the rebel line swayed and bent, and the men suddenly stopped firing and ran into the railroad cut, which is parallel to the Cashtown turnpike." To Sergeant Sullivan, who did not know that there was a railroad bed, when the Confederates jumped into the cut, it looked as if the earth had opened up and swallowed them. Lieutenant Harris had a similar reaction; he had hoped that they would meet the Rebels in a "stand up knock down fight," but instead they had disappeared into the earth. Pvt. Augustus Klein called them "kowardly sons of bitches" for taking cover in the cut. Dawes ordered the 6th over the fence and into the pike. When writing his early accounts of this fight, Dawes forgot the two fences at the pike but was reminded of them later. He wrote that to climb the first fence "was a sure test of metal and discipline." But the 6th had "metal," iron perhaps, and climbed the fence. It reformed in the minimal shelter afforded by the pike and, perhaps, pulled down some of the fence in its front. It was probably in this brief interval that Lieutenant Harris, commander of the brigade's guard detachment on the 6th's left, ran to the right wing of the nearby 95th New York and shouted to the closest officer, "For God's sake why don't you move forward and join our left?" Harris wrote that the 95th failed to do so, but Dawes remembered differently.[9]

Dawes became aware of the nearness of the 14th and 95th after his troops climbed the first fence and were preparing to charge. After shouting to the 6th, "Forward, double-quick, Charge. Align on the color," he saw Maj. Edward Pye of the 95th approaching. He ran toward him shouting, "Let's go for them Major." Pye responded by waving his sword and shouting, "Forward guide right," and, wrote Dawes, the men of the 95th joined the 6th on the left. Dawes wrote also that the 95th was out in the field before the 14th Brooklyn started, and that the 14th advanced in echelon to the left and rear of the 95th.[10]

In his report Dawes commented that "the men of the whole line moved forward upon a double-quick, well closed, in face of a terribly destructive

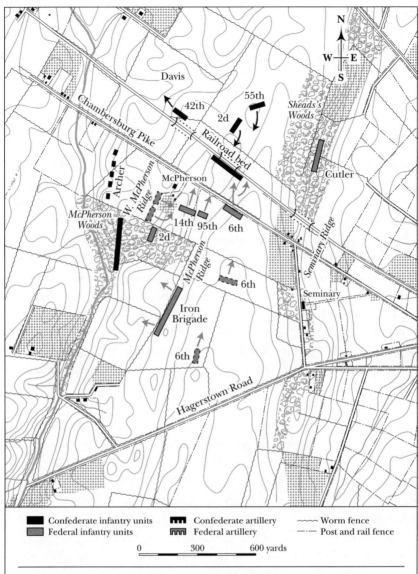

Map 9.1. Action at the Railroad Cut, Morning

1. Cutler's troops retreat toward Sheads's Woods; Davis's men pursue them north of the railroad bed.
2. General Doubleday orders Colonel Dawes to lead his 6th Wisconsin from behind McPherson Woods and strike Davis's men in the flank. The 6th marches north to the Chambersburg Pike. It pauses there and fires at Davis's men.
3. Although Davis orders his regiments back to Herr Ridge, many men take shelter from the 6th's fire in the center cut and along the adjacent railroad bed.
4. Colonel Fowler starts his 14th Brooklyn and 95th New York regiments from the McPherson buildings toward the pike on the 6th's left.
5. The 6th charges the Confederates in the railroad bed and in the center cut. Fowler's men join them on the left.
6. Two hundred Confederates are captured, but others escape to Herr Ridge.

fire from the enemy." The 420 men in Dawes's line had to cross a grassy field without cover to reach the enemy's position 175 paces away. The enemy fire chopped the 6th apart, and its flag fell several times. Every man in the color guard was killed or wounded. Even Dawes carried the flag briefly, but others were eager for the perilous honor of carrying it and leading the regiment forward. The regiment's dead and wounded marked its course across the field. Dawes believed that the regiment stuck together because its officers and men heeded his often shouted orders, "Align on the colors! Close up on that color! Close up on that color!" Cpl. Frank A. Waller remembered that the enemy had begun firing on them with a slow fire that became hotter as they neared the cut. When it left the pike, the regiment's line was straight and in good order, but soon it had a V shape with the colors at its apex. When the Wisconsin line was about fifty yards from the cut, the enemy fire suddenly slackened, and the veterans knew that the Confederates would soon fire a lethal volley. It crashed when the Wisconsin men were about fifteen feet from the cut, and it seemed to Sgt. George Fairfield of Company C that half of the 6th fell. Those men still on their feet made a mad dash for the railroad bed and the Confederates it sheltered.[11]

The charge of the 6th Wisconsin had been a heroic and tragic affair. Dawes estimated that 160 men of the 6th fell, not including the brigade guard, whose casualties he did not know. The charge lasted only minutes, but it engendered many memories, including Maj. John Hauser's shouting "Forwarts, Forwarts" in his thick Swiss German accent, and Capt. Joseph Marston, the "Tall Sycamore," herding Company C along with outstretched arms. Dawes mourned many deaths but mentioned Capt. John Ticknor's in his report. Like many other officers at Gettysburg, Ticknor had begun his service in the ranks, but his special talent for leadership had gained him a captaincy. He had a special reputation for a fine tenor voice that often led the 6th in song. Dawes thought that he had been shot when crossing a fence, where the bodies of several men dangled, but Sergeant Sullivan saw him fall soon after he had helped the sergeant remove a box of caps from the belt of wounded Cpl. Charles Crawford. Ticknor's body returned to Wisconsin in a metal coffin with its lid soldered shut. Pvt. A. Richard "Sleepy Dick" Marston was among the dead also. Marston had been a good soldier but one who required an unusual amount of sleep. He had fallen asleep while on picket duty on the night of 30 June and was placed under arrest. Lieutenant Harris, his company commander, knew that though it was very unlikely, Marston could be shot for this offense. On the morning of 1 July Harris pleaded Marston's special case to Dawes, General Meredith, and General Wadsworth ("glorious old man that he was") and got Marston a pardon. Thanks to Harris's intervention, Marston was at the railroad cut, where he "met sudden death like a true soldier and patriot." *Dulce et decorum est pro patria mori.*[12]

A minié ball struck Cpl. James A. Kelly of Company B in the chest during the advance. Kelly turned to Dawes, who must have been nearby, and in the turmoil opened his shirt to show him the hole made by a ball when it entered his chest. He asked Dawes to write to his parents and tell them that he had died a soldier. Dawes promised to do this, and Kelly turned away to die. At 2:00 P.M. that day Dawes penciled in his notebook, "If I am killed today let it be known that Corporal James Kelley [sic] of Company B shot through the breast, and mortally wounded, asked to tell his folks he died like a soldier."[13]

As the 6th neared the cut, the colors of the 2d Mississippi, flying from a staff stuck into the ground in front of the regiment, attracted much attention. Pvt. William B. Murphy, the color-bearer, wrote long after the war about his experience with the 2d's colors at the railroad cut. The Mississippians were intent on capturing Hall's battery when they reached the cut, which at that place was no more than two feet deep. The regiment halted in the railroad bed facing the pike, fired at the cannoneers, and drove them from one gun. They did not move to capture it though, and the color guard took position in front of the railroad bed about fifty paces east of the cut and ten south of it. Within five minutes after Dawes's attack, the Wisconsin men had killed or wounded all of the color guard, shot a dozen holes in the colors, and splintered its staff. A "squad" of Union soldiers rushed for the flag; all were shot but others took their place, and the Rebels shot down a dozen more "like sheep." Murphy thought it the most deadly struggle that he had witnessed during the war. He recalled a lieutenant's having been shot in the shoulder, and, of course, the man who took the flag from him — a large fellow who seized both him and the flag just as he tore it from its staff.[14]

There was a melee around the flag; no two men saw what happened just alike, so their accounts vary. Lt. William N. Remington was one of those who made a try for the flag and quite likely was the officer remembered by Murphy. He ran from his place with his company at the left of the line, behind the companies to his right, and through the 6th's center. He dashed to the front toward the red flag and received a slight wound in the neck almost immediately. This did not deter him. He was about fifteen feet from the flag when he saw a Confederate in the cut taking aim at him. He turned his side toward the man and kept running toward the flag until he was shot in the shoulder and knocked to the ground. That was enough; he got to his feet and walked backward to the 6th's line. He met Major Hauser and "got d — d" for going after the flag. (Majors are sometimes wiser than lieutenants.) Remington returned to his company. After being wounded twice, he admitted, "Flag taking was pretty well knocked out of me."[15]

Pvt. Jasper Donglis of the 2d Wisconsin, a member of the brigade guard, drummer Lewis Eggleston, and Pvt. Cornelius Okey tried to take the flag at the same time. Confederates wounded Okey and killed Eggleston. Pvt. John O. Johnson, Eggleston's messmate, whose rifle was fouled, tried to save Eggleston by stepping between him and the Confederates and striking them with his piece. Johnson himself fell wounded, perhaps by the same bullet that struck Eggleston. Flag taking, like flag bearing, was akin to suicide.[16]

Cpl. Frank Waller had not planned to try to take the flag, but he saw it near at hand and went for it. Waller jerked it from the color-bearer's hand, but he made no mention of its being on or off a staff. Waller thought that he was able to seize it because the man had been wounded, but perhaps he was wrong in this because Murphy said nothing of being shot. Waller thought first of carrying the flag to the rear, where it could not be retaken, but he thought better of this. Instead he threw the flag to the ground and stood on it as he loaded and fired his rifle twice before the fighting stopped. He was not aware of it, perhaps, but his brother Sam, who was nearby, saw a Rebel taking aim at him and parried the man's rifle with his own. Then he killed the man with his rifle butt. Frank Waller wrote also that a man from the 14th Brooklyn tried to take the flag from him as he was standing on it, but the man stopped when Waller threatened to shoot him. After the fighting ended, he turned the flag over to Lieutenant Colonel Dawes.[17]

While Waller was busy with the Mississippians' flag, his comrades were gainfully employed with the Mississippians themselves. Dawes wrote simply that when they approached the cut, the men of the 6th shouted for the Confederates to surrender and throw down their arms. He reached the cut where it was about four feet deep and looked down on "hundreds" of disorganized Rebels. As he did this, Lt. Edward P. Brooks, the regiment's adjutant, "with promptness and foresight," took twenty or so men and posted them across the railroad bed to the east where they could enfilade the cut. Yet in his report of the battle Colonel Fowler stated that he had "directed the Sixth Wisconsin to flank it by throwing out their right." Fowler might have sent such an order, but if so, it should have gone to Dawes, who made no mention of it and probably would have felt no obligation to obey it.[18]

Sgt. George Fairfield of Company C wrote that the Confederates near the east end of the cut lay in water, mud, and blood and may well have been in a state of fatigue and shock when they saw the grimy, blackened, and yelling devils who shouted down at them. Lt. Earl Rogers described the frame of mind of the men of the 6th at this time: "They seemed all unconscious to the terrible situation; they were mad and fought with a desperation seldom witnessed." There was killing enough. A Confederate fired up at Pvt. John Harland at close range and killed him. Harland's friend, Pvt. Levi Tongue, aimed at the Confederate, who now had an empty rifle. The Confederate dropped his gun and pleaded, "Don't shoot, don't kill me." Tongue shouted back, "All hell can't save you now," and shot the man. His body fell on Harland's. Four days later, after the Confederates had gone, a soldier of the 6th found Harland's body still lying beneath that of the man who had shot him.[19]

The melee did not last long, for the Confederates were unable to resist their attackers. Some of the Johnnies threw down their arms, but Sergeant Sullivan complained that before doing so, they would shoot at the Wisconsin men. Others, he said, simply ran to the rear. From the brow of the cut Dawes shouted down to the Confederates below him: "Where is the colonel of this regiment?" A Confederate field officer heard him and replied, "Who are you?" Dawes answered, "I command this regiment. Surrender or I will fire." Without further parley, the Confederate officer, Major Blair, handed Dawes his sword, and a half-dozen other officers followed suit. While he juggled the swords, Dawes told the major to fall his men in without arms, and the major did so. In the meantime Sergeant Sullivan had jumped into the cut, accepted a sword from a Confederate officer, and started through the cut "with the intention of stopping the Johnnies, who were limbering to the rear." When he began to climb from the cut, he saw a big Rebel fleeing. He called on him to stop and threw the sword at him when he did not do so. As Sullivan did this, a bullet hit him in the left shoulder and knocked him down. He thought at first that someone had clouted him in the shoulder with a gun butt, for the impact of a bullet can give that feeling. Sgt. John Tarbox came up and said to him, "They've got you down, Mickey, have they?" No sooner had Tarbox asked the question than he pitched forward dead. Sullivan complained that "some of the damned rebs who had surrendered" had shot him. A lot of this went on that day, he complained; he had never seen so many men killed in such a short time. If Sullivan was correct, the Confederates who did such shooting were courting a massacre.[20]

Major Belo of the 55th North Carolina was in the cut area when the Federals demanded their surrender. One Union soldier (could it have been Sullivan?) threw a sword at him and shouted, "Kill that officer, and we will capture that command." The sword missed Belo, and a North Carolinian shot the man who threw it. Belo and a number of his men then ran to safety.[21]

Like Sullivan, Sgt. George Fairfield went into the cut to roust out prisoners. He walked the cut from east to west sending the prisoners to the east until he ran into a gap in their crowd. There he saw what he deemed to be "the other two regiments" retreating to the west. He explained that they could not shoot at the escaping soldiers without hitting the prisoners and had to let them go. He thought that if the cut had not been so deep and the Confederates had been able to see the 6th and climb from it, they could have captured the Wisconsin men before the New Yorkers came up. After the New York troops arrived, it was too late.[22]

In his report of the battle, Colonel Fowler wrote that "all the enemy within our reach surrendered—officers, battle-flag, and men. Those in line on the left of my line escaped by following through the railroad cut." Major Pye, who commanded the 95th after Colonel Biddle's fall, stated that the two New York regiments had charged with the 6th Wisconsin, and they had taken many prisoners. Colonel Fowler grumbled that the Rebels went out of the cut to the right and surrendered themselves and their colors to the 6th Wisconsin, which "from its position made most of the captures." Sergeant Fairfield complained to Horace Greeley's newspaper for reporting that the 14th had taken the most prisoners, when in fact it had not come up on the left until after the surrender. In an 1865 letter Capt. John A. Kellogg of the 6th, who was on Cutler's staff, wrote that the 6th reached the cut three minutes before the New Yorkers. General Wadsworth credited all three regiments for the action, but Doubleday reported that Dawes had ordered the charge, "which was gallantly executed," and that the 14th and the 95th had joined in.[23]

There was no doubt in Dawes's mind about which regiment had carried the burden of the action. In a letter to the Reverend Charles B. Krauth of the Gettysburg Battlefield Memorial Association, Dawes stated plainly, "It is due the 6th Wisconsin Regiment for me to say that the regiment led the charge and by its dash forward substantially accomplished the results." To bolster his case he gave strengths for the regiments involved: 450 for the 6th, less than 100 for the 95th, and less than 250 for the 14th. These figures vary from those given on the memorials and elsewhere in favor of his argument. He lauded the 95th's help but disparaged that of the 14th and denied that Colonel Fowler had given him orders.[24]

After the charge, the 6th reported having 7 officers and 225 enlisted men as prisoners, and Major Hauser delivered them to the First Corps provost guard. As soon as Hauser marched the prisoners off, Dawes sent a line of volunteer skirmishers out to the west arm of McPherson Ridge to guard against a surprise return by the Rebels. Cpl. Frank Waller was one of the volunteers for this duty. As Waller moved to the west ridge, Lieutenant Colonel Dawes sent the flag that he had captured to the rear with Sgt. William Evans, who had been wounded in both thighs and was on his way to a hospital. Evans did not go by stretcher; he hobbled off using two rifles as crutches and had the flag tied around his waist.[25]

Evans reached the town, passed hospitals in it, and took refuge in the Jacob Hollinger house on the town's east side in the angle formed by the junction of the Hanover Road and York Pike. There the Hollinger girls, Liberty and Julia, "two very pretty and sensible young ladies," put him to bed. In a while Lieutenants Harris, Remington, and John Beeley, all with wounds but ambulatory, found their way to the house. While eating there, they regaled the family with their exploits. Late that afternoon, when the Rebels entered the town, Evans asked the girls to hide the flag. They stuffed it inside his bed tick and sewed the tick shut. The ambulatory officers left the house when the Rebels entered the town, but Evans remained until after the battle ended and the rebels had vacated the area. On the morning of 4 July Evans somehow made his way to the 6th's position on Culp's Hill, where he delivered the flag to Dawes and the regiment.[26]

CHAPTER 10

Noon Lull

Lt. Gen. A. P. Hill felt poorly on the morning of 1 July. Although two of his divisions were marching toward Gettysburg in a reconnaissance in force, Hill kept to his cot. He felt certain that Heth's division, which was in the lead, would find no serious opposition; after all, General Lee himself had said just the day before that the Army of the Potomac was far to the south. Therefore, in spite of Pettigrew's encounter the previous day, he had few qualms about letting Heth's and Pender's divisions go on without him. Both division commanders were experienced and competent officers who could take care of any situation that might reasonably arise. But as he rested on his cot, he heard the sound of distant gunfire, a dull rumbling that suggested that more than skirmishing was taking place. As Hill pondered this, General Lee appeared. He had been riding through Cashtown Pass when he heard the sounds of heavy firing. Leaving Longstreet to follow with his corps, Lee hastened forward to see what it was all about. He had tried to make it plain to all of his ranking generals that he did not want a general engagement until all of his army was at hand. The distant thundering suggested that a premature battle was building. Lee had reached Hill's headquarters in Cashtown as Hill was rising from his cot. He asked the general what he knew about the gunfire. "Nothing," Hill had to reply, but he would ride toward Gettysburg and look into it. He mounted his horse and hurried away. General Lee followed at a slower gait.[1]

Ambrose Powell Hill's performance at Gettysburg has been an enigma. The son of a prominent Culpeper, Virginia, family, he joined West Point's class of 1846 and at the end of his second year ranked twenty-third among the class's sixty-six cadets. Then disaster struck. On his way back to West Point from leave in Virginia in the summer of 1844, he stopped briefly in

Lt. Gen. Ambrose P. Hill
(NA)

New York City but was there long enough to sow a few wild oats. His harvest was gonorrhea, and his doctor placed him in the academy's hospital. When it became apparent that his recovery would be slow, the academy officials sent him home on sick leave. In 1845 when he returned after what must have been an embarrassing stay in Culpeper, he had fallen behind his class in his course work. Academy officials put him back a year to the class of 1847. Three members of his class would be generals at Gettysburg, and Hill and Heth became good friends.

After graduating in 1847, Hill served as an artillery subaltern in Mexico, the only member of his class to do so. He spent a year as an artillery officer in Florida, where in addition to having prostatitis he came down with yellow fever. In 1855, because Hill was physically unfit for field service, Secretary of War Jefferson Davis detailed him to the U.S. Coast Survey. He served with it in the grade of first lieutenant until Virginia's secession and his resignation from Federal service. Hill spent most of his Coast Survey years in Washington, where he was a sociable chap, fond of female companionship. He and his friend George B. McClellan both courted Ellen Marcy, the daughter of then-captain Randolph B. Marcy, but McClellan won the parents' blessing and her hand. Hill then directed his affections toward Kitty Morgan McClung, sister of John Hunt Morgan, the future Confederate general. The two became the happy parents of four girls.

Hill's Confederate career began with the colonelcy of the 13th Virginia Regiment, which he molded into a crack unit. He became a brigadier general in February 1862 and a major general in May, though his combat experience was limited to his having led a brigade in the battle of Williamsburg. His new command was a six-brigade division that, for reasons best known to him, he designated the Light Division. He made the division into what was considered by many to be the best in the Army of Northern Virginia.

Hill was deemed an excellent division commander, but he was a contentious fellow. The *Richmond Enquirer* gave Hill credit for successes in the Seven Days' battles that might well have been shared with his superior, Longstreet, and others. This resulted in squabbling, and Longstreet placed Hill under arrest. Hill requested a transfer. Finally, a threatened duel forced Lee to intervene, and he transferred Hill and his division to Stonewall Jackson's command. Hill got along poorly with Jackson, who placed Hill under arrest for failing to comply with Jackson's march procedures. Hill demanded that Jackson prefer charges; Jackson would not do so, and only Jackson's death brought this silly quarrel to an end. In spite of Hill's prickly and sometimes juvenile behavior, Lee regarded him on the whole as the best major general that he had, and when the army was reorganized in 1863, Hill became a lieutenant general and commander of the Army of Northern Virginia's Third Corps.[2]

While Lee and Hill rode forward, Heth took measures to bring order from the chaos of his morning's probe. He deployed his division for further action; "blood now having been drawn, there seemed to be no calling off the battle." No one bothered to record how Heth posted his brigades; presumably all but Davis's formed in the area whence Archer had launched his ill-fated morning attack. Pettigrew's large 2,000-man brigade occupied the center of Heth's line. It had been behind the gun line on Herr Ridge during Archer's attack, but afterward it advanced a half-mile to the east edge of the Springs Hotel Woods. It seems likely that the right of Pettigrew's brigade was at the present Old Mill Road, and its line ran north along the east side of the woods where Country Club Road is now. However, one account states that the regiments formed in echelon from the left, the 26th North Carolina being to the front, and that the regiments assumed a single line in the attack.[3]

Brig. Gen. James J. Pettigrew
(LC)

Heth placed Archer's battered brigade south of the Old Mill Road, to Pettigrew's right. It was in a woods whose east edge was in extension of that occupied by Pettigrew's regiments. Archer's brigade was probably about 1,000 strong at this time, and its right would have been near the Finne-frock buildings. Col. Birkett D. Fry of the 13th Alabama now commanded the brigade. Fry had attended the Virginia Military Institute and was in West Point's class of 1846, from which, after failing mathematics, he was dismissed. However, he gained practical military experience during the war with Mexico and on a filibustering expedition to Nicaragua. When the Civil War came, he left his job as a cotton mill manager to become colonel of the 13th Alabama. Prior to Gettysburg Fry had been wounded at Seven Pines; at Antietam, where his arm was shattered; and at Chancellorsville. He was of slight build and quiet manner, but he had a "gunpowder reputa-tion." Fry would be wounded a fourth time during Pickett's Charge.[4]

Brockenbrough's brigade, which had less than 1,000 men, formed be-tween Pettigrew's left and the pike. The brigade had been Heth's, but Col. John M. Brockenbrough of the 40th Virginia now commanded it. Brocken-brough, an 1850 graduate of the Virginia Military Institute and a farmer, entered the Confederate service as colonel of the 40th in May 1861, and though he commanded a brigade, he remained a colonel until he resigned

{ NOON LULL }

in January 1864 after a subordinate was promoted over him. Brocken-brough's brigade contained the 40th, 47th, and 55th regiments and the 22d Virginia Battalion. The brigade had arrived in a woods that morning, probably the Springs Hotel Woods. It advanced to Archer's aid but had fallen back to another woods when Archer's brigade retreated. Brocken-brough then formed his brigade on Pettigrew's left.[5]

Heth left Davis's brigade north of the pike. It had been so disorganized by the morning's battle that Heth thought it inadvisable to return it to action again that day. Further, by being north of the pike it would be better able to collect and reform its stragglers.[6]

Pender's division left its bivouac in Cashtown Pass at about 8:00 A.M., the hour that the Union First Corps began its march from Marsh Creek. It followed the Chambersburg Pike toward Gettysburg in support of Heth's division. When about three miles west of the town, probably at the present-day Knoxlyn Road, Pender deployed his division across the pike. He sent Perrin's (McGowan's) South Carolina brigade and Scales's North Carolina brigade to the right along the cross road and Lane's North Carolinians and Thomas's Georgians to the left. They formed with a strong body of skir-mishers on their right to screen that flank from cavalry. The division ad-vanced to Herr Ridge and, at Hill's orders, halted in Heth's rear. This was an indication that Hill had reached the field by this time.[7]

With one exception the batteries of Pegram's battalion remained in their morning positions. Capt. Thomas A. Brander's battery moved from near the railroad bed north to the far left, where it occupied high ground about 300 yards north-northwest of the Bender farm buildings. Later in the afternoon Capt. Victor Maurin's Louisiana battery of Lt. Col. John J. Garnett's battalion replaced an unnamed battery of Pegram's battalion that had exhausted its ammunition, an indication that it had done a lot of firing.[8]

Lt. Col. David McIntosh's artillery battalion came from Cashtown with Pender's division. It marched near its front. McIntosh sensed that the "smell of battle was already in the air," and the feeling that serious business was at hand had quieted the usual joking among the cannoneers. The battalion's batteries occupied their positions after Pender deployed his brigades in support of Heth's. Capt. R. Sidney Rice's four Napoleons and the two Whitworth guns of Capt. William B. Hurt's battery dropped trail near McGraw's battery just south of the pike. Rice's guns fired slowly at bodies of Union troops. Hurt's section shelled the woods to the right of the town — probably Shultz's Woods on seminary ridge, though we might wonder what targets it had there.

McIntosh placed Capt. Marmaduke Johnson's Virginia battery and Hurt's two three-inch Ordnance rifles to the far right near the Hagerstown Road. Although Union guns shelled them during the afternoon, they remained inactive. McIntosh's fourth battery, Lt. Samuel Wallace's 2d Rockbridge Artillery, unlimbered somewhere near the pike. Therefore, six guns guarded the Confederate right near the Hagerstown Road while seven batteries plus Hurt's Whitworths supported Hill's infantry.[9]

Hill's three remaining artillery battalions remained with Col. R. Lindsay Walker, Hill's artillery chief. Walker left Major John Lane's battalion with Anderson's division and brought Major William T. Poague's and Lt. Col. John J. Garnett's battalions toward Gettysburg. Poague's battalion did not take part in the fighting on 1 July; Garnett halted his batteries in a clover field along the pike. Since he did not expect to be ordered into the battle soon, Garnett allowed his drivers to unhitch their teams so that their horses could graze.[10]

During the lull that followed the repulse of Archer's and Davis's brigades, the remaining two divisions of the Union First Corps and the Eleventh Corps hurried toward the field. General Doubleday and Wadsworth's divisions had arrived at the same time, shortly before Reynolds's death. Doubleday did not speak with Reynolds; their contact was through Lt. Benjamin T. Marten, who carried Reynolds's orders for Doubleday to "attend to the Millerstown [Hagerstown] Road on the left of our line." Reynolds's death left Doubleday in full command of the First Corps and responsible for the contact of the battle west of the town. He had had little, if anything, to do with the repulse of Archer's brigade but had sent Dawes's against Davis and had thus contributed greatly to the Confederate repulse.

The deeds of corps and division commanders were seldom recorded unless they resulted in controversy, and we know little about the specific and routine actions of Hill, Doubleday, Wadsworth, Heth, and Pender on the afternoon of 1 July. Fortunately Doubleday's report and his other writings tell of his quandary at this time. He thought of McPherson Woods as a redoubt; its possession by the First Corps was essential to its holding McPherson Ridge. After Archer's repulse, Doubleday brought the Iron Brigade back from west of Willoughby Run and ordered its regiments to take defensive positions in the woods. About the same time he directed Cutler's brigade to resume its original position facing west. He decided to hold the First Corps where it was. It would have been disgraceful for it to

Maj. Gen. Abner Doubleday
(CWLM)

have abandoned the field without orders to do so. He assumed that Reynolds, who had Meade's confidence, had intended that it fight there. In his report he buttressed his decision with strategic reasons for holding the line west of Gettysburg, but it seems unlikely that they would have been in his thoughts at that critical and busy time.[11]

Doubleday is one of the intriguing figures at Gettysburg. During the Revolutionary War his grandfather had been at Bunker Hill and Stoney Point and had been a prisoner on a British hulk. Later he was an officer on a privateer. Doubleday's father, Ulysses, was a newspaper publisher in Auburn and in Cayuga, New York, and had served two terms in Congress. Perhaps Ulysses was responsible for his son's considerable ability as a writer, a skill that he would employ often in the postwar years.

General Doubleday was born in Ballston Spa, New York, in 1819. After working for two years in the field of civil engineering, he entered West Point and graduated in its class of 1842 with Longstreet, McLaws, Richard Anderson, and John Newton, all generals at Gettysburg. He served with the Third Artillery in Mexico and against the Apaches and Seminoles. When the 1860s opened, Doubleday was stationed in Charleston, South

Carolina, and ranked second to the commander there when the war began. Other officers there tended to get along well with the local people, but Doubleday did not. He was an outspoken abolitionist, and his views were not appreciated by them. Perhaps it is appropriate, therefore, that he is said to have fired the first shot from Fort Sumter. His rise in the wartime army was routine for an officer of his rank. He became a brigadier general in February 1862 and commanded a brigade at Second Bull Run and a division at South Mountain and in later battles. He became a major general in November 1862 and received command of the Third Division, First Corps, which he led at Gettysburg.

Although Doubleday must have performed reasonably well in his assignments and critiqued them in a scholarly way, he did not enjoy the confidence of some of his colleagues. Colonel Wainwright, who had close dealings with him, differed with him over artillery reorganization and probably was influenced by that experience. Wainwright wrote in March 1863 that Doubleday knew enough, but that he was entirely impractical and slow in getting an idea through his head. Later, when writing of the approach of the First Corps to Gettysburg, Wainwright declared that Doubleday complained because George Sykes, who was his junior, was a corps commander and he was not. Colonel Wainwright termed Doubleday a "weak reed to lean upon" in whom he had no confidence. Meade so lacked confidence in Doubleday that he replaced him on 2 July with Maj. Gen. John Newton.[12]

When Brig. Gen. Solomon Meredith's four Iron Brigade regiments returned from beyond Willoughby Run, they took up a line in McPherson Woods overlooking Willoughby Run. The 7th Wisconsin was on the brigade's right; it was about midway up the slope of the west arm of McPherson Ridge. The 19th, on the brigade's left, rested in the fringe of trees in the floodplain at the far southeast corner of the woods, and the 24th Michigan held the center of the line between the 7th and the 19th. The 2d Wisconsin, which had led the morning's charge, formed first in the field north of the woods where the 14th Brooklyn had been. It later turned this area over to Roy Stone's brigade and formed a support line in the woods. (The Iron Brigade's experiences in this position are presented at greater length in Chapter 22.)[13]

After the repulse of Davis's brigade, Cutler received orders to advance his three mauled regiments from behind Oak Ridge to the positions they had occupied at the beginning of the battle. The 95th New York joined them there, and the 14th Brooklyn and the 6th Wisconsin formed to the left in support of Calef's battery.[14]

After Davis's repulse Wadsworth sent Calef's battery back to the position between the pike and the west railroad cut that Hall's battery had vacated a few minutes before. Calef placed Pergel's and Newman's sections there. They began firing and immediately drew fire from three Confederate batteries on Herr Ridge. Soon after, Brander's battery nearly enfiladed Calef's four guns from its position north of the Bender buildings. After the guns began firing, the drivers of their teams found oats left by Hall's battery when it pulled out. The drivers fed them to their horses, "who ate them with as much relish and as little concern as though they were at the picket-rope, merely raising their heads if a shell burst near, some of them being killed while munching their grain." Soon Colonel Wainwright sent Gilbert Reynolds's battery to Calef's relief.[15]

Like the other regiments of Cutler's brigade the 14th was near some of the casualties of the morning's fight. Cpl. George W. Forrester of the 14th's Company C was lying wounded nearby. Although shells fired at Calef's battery were plastering the area, four men of the 14th tried to rescue him. They went to him and rolled him onto a shelter half; each man took a corner, and they started for the rear. A shell exploded among them and killed Forrester and three of his rescuers immediately. A fragment tore the leg off the fourth man and caused him to scream in pain. Comrades tried to carry the wounded man to a hospital, but he bled to death on the way.[16]

When General Reynolds set out for Gettysburg that morning, he asked Doubleday to bring up Robinson's and his own division commanded by Brig. Gen. Thomas Rowley. It took nearly two hours for the two divisions to pack their gear, call in their pickets, and take to the road. Col. Roy Stone's brigade of Doubleday's division led the way up the Emmitsburg Road, followed first by three batteries of the artillery brigade and then by Brig. Gen. Gabriel Paul's and Henry Baxter's brigades of Robinson's division. Rowley's brigade, temporarily commanded by Col. Chapman Biddle but accompanied by Rowley, marched with Cooper's battery over the Pumping Station Road, a country road that roughly parallels the Emmitsburg Road about two miles to the northwest.[17]

Biddle's brigade had been on the Fairfield side of the corps to cover its left flank and the approaches from Fairfield and Cashtown where the Confederates were known to be. After getting their bearings from a wall map hanging in the parlor of W. Ross White, who gave his name to the intersection of the Bull Frog and Pumping Station roads, the officers of the 121st Pennsylvania Regiment deployed it in a picket line. The line ran from the I. Bigham farm on Marsh Creek west to the C. Topper farm on Middle Creek. White's house and the nearby crossroads were near the center of this line. The 20th New York spent the night in a woods probably in support of the picket line, and the 151st Pennsylvania bivouacked on the George Spangler farm. It could not have been a pleasant camp; the troops not only had to be mustered for pay, but 30 June was rainy and the morning of 1 July was "lowery." On the night of the thirtieth the New Yorkers got orders to prepare three days of rations.[18]

About 8:00 A.M., after calling in its pickets, Biddle's brigade started for Gettysburg over the Pumping Station Road. A company of "sharpshooters" led the column, followed by the 121st Pennsylvania, which had skirmishers out on both flanks. Then came the 142d Pennsylvania, followed by the 20th New York Militia Regiment (also designated the 80th New York). Cooper's Pennsylvania battery brought up the rear. The road was unimproved and rough, but no one complained. No other troops had passed that way; it must have seemed far from the war, and the few hours spent on it must have been a pleasant respite.[19]

Capt. John D. S. Cook of the 20th New York contrasted the Pennsylvania countryside with that of Virginia. He fondly recalled its orchards, meadows, grainfields, comfortable houses, and "mighty barns." His reactions mirrored those of many Confederates who had been awed by the prosperous land of plenty. Unlike the Confederates, Cook did not disparage its inhabitants. He spoke of farm families who came to the road to watch them pass and gave them bread and butter. The loaves of bread were large, and the butter came in crocks. The women spread the butter with "one broad sweep of a huge knife." With "swift strokes" they sliced off the buttered ends as they were grabbed by soldiers who hurried off with the delicacy. Of course there was a fly in the ointment. Some soldiers of the 20th New York complained that they had been refused bread because they were not Pennsylvanians. In order to make sure that they got their share of bread and butter, thereafter they claimed that distinction.[20]

Rowley's brigade marched east three miles to Marsh Creek, went another half-mile to Willoughby Run, and then turned north. It followed the Black Horse Tavern and the Willoughby Run roads two miles to the Hagerstown Road and the Confederate right flank. Lt. David Slagle of Doubleday's staff met the brigade on the Pumping Station Road. Doubleday had sent him galloping across the countryside to tell Rowley to hurry

Col. Roy Stone (CWLM)

the division along. As the brigade approached the Hagerstown Road, its men could hear cannon fire and see the smoke of exploding shells. At about 11:00 A.M. it reached the Hagerstown Road, formed a line, advanced 200 or so yards north into a grove of trees with a "carpet of springy sod," and awaited orders.[21]

Col. Roy Stone's brigade of Doubleday's division marched somewhat abreast of Rowley's brigade on the Emmitsburg Road. The brigade's three Pennsylvania regiments — the 143d, 149th, and 150th — had bivouacked near the intersection of the Emmitsburg Road and Bullfrog Road. From there it could have gone to the aid of Rowley's brigade had its help been needed. But it passed an uneventful night in a woods that gave it some cover from intermittent showers. Capt. Francis Jones of the 149th spent the night under a rubber blanket on a pallet of rails propped against a fence. Pvt. Avery Harris of the 143d recalled that both officers and men were uneasy and in a state of expectancy; there was no joking, and "anxiety seemed to be settling down upon them." As he tried to sleep, Harris saw clouds scudding across the face of the moon as if to flee the Gettysburg area.[22]

Stone's men awakened on the morning of 1 July, not to bugles and drums but to the rousing of officers and sergeants who cautioned them against unnecessary noise. The morning was sultry and uncomfortable, and the commissary wagons were tardy in reaching them. The men of the 143d cooked rations they had drawn the day before, but officers, who had to provide their own food, went hungry because the wagons and pack animals had not come up. Some officers of the 150th asked permission to buy and butcher a sheep, but this was denied them. They had to make do finally with coffee and hardtack. In spite of awaking early, the brigade did not take to the road until after 9:00 A.M.[23]

Private Harris remembered that there was a lot of starting and stopping in the first half-mile of the march as though there was uncertainty over what they were to do. When they reached a crossroad, probably at Greenmount, a group of men, women, and children with horses, mules, and cattle entered on the Emmitsburg Road. A small boy and girl on a horse were crying as though their hearts would break. The party included a robust young man, eighteen or so years old, on a mule. Harris thought that he would rather have faced a battery of Napoleons than the taunts delivered by Stone's men at the young man, but he grinned and bore them. After all, no one would be shooting at him that day.[24]

After a time they heard the "plunk, plunk" of distant artillery. As they trudged slowly through a wooded area, probably where the road crossed Seminary Ridge, a staff officer galloped up in haste. He barely paused as he shouted to Colonel Stone or to Colonel Edmund Dana of the 143d before continuing his hard ride along the road. As the officer rode off, there were commands to close up and increase the pace to quick-time. The day was warm and sultry, and the sun burned down. Men began to fall out, and thirsty stragglers crowded at farm wells. When Capt. William P. Dougal of the 150th, the most corpulent man in the regiment, could not keep up, Col. Langhorne Wister allowed him to fall out but ordered him to bring up the regiment's other stragglers.[25]

The brigade double-quicked along the Emmitsburg Road to the Codori buildings, turned left into the fields in the path of Wadsworth's division, and hurried toward the seminary. The three regiments passed over Seminary Ridge south of the school and halted in the swale in its front. Confederate shells flew overhead; Doubleday and Rowley shouted some words of encouragement that were countered by the news of Reynolds's death. Stone's men unslung and piled their knapsacks and blankets in heaps pending their return. After loading their rifles and uncasing their colors, the regiments started forward amid a burst of merriment—Colonel Wister had forgot to order the 150th to load. After doing so, they resumed their advance.[26]

When they reached the west arm of McPherson Ridge, Colonel Stone relieved the 2d Wisconsin, which moved into the woods. He placed the 150th between the woods and the McPherson house, probably behind the fence on the orchard's west side. The 143d was on the 150th's right near the farm buildings, and the 149th went to the right of the line between the barn and the pike. Each regiment sent out a company of skirmishers, and the men were allowed to lie down. The troops near McPherson's well filled their stomachs and canteens with cold water drawn from the well with a sweep. The drinking ended abruptly when an officer cut the sweep's rope to prevent the dire effects that might occur when overheated men filled their empty stomachs with cold water. On the other hand Sgt. John Shafer of the 143d found a crock of "sour milk," perhaps buttermilk, in the cellar of the house. He carried it to the wagon shed, where he and others ladled the milk to their mouths with their unwashed hands. This drinking, too, ended abruptly when a shell crashed through the shed's roof.[27]

Recollections suggest that the 143d received its full share of cannon fire while in this position. If so, perhaps it was because the buildings nearby provided the Rebel gunners something obvious to aim at. After leaving the wagon shed, the milk drinkers saw a Rebel shell strike the barnyard floor and burrow like a mole through its muck. It was an awesome sight that caused one man to shout, "See the d——d thing go." "Bang, flup, thud," a shell hit behind the 143d. Another ricocheted along the 143d's line and ripped off a soldier's haversack. It was a near thing for him and deserving of comment. He obliged by remarking, "Well boys they have cut off my supplies." If the latter shell really did enfilade the 143d's line, it probably came from Oak Hill rather than from Herr Ridge, a serious eventuality that would prompt changes in the deployment of Stone's brigade.[28]

As Stone's brigade took position near the McPherson buildings, Doubleday sent Lieutenant Slagle again to bring up Rowley's brigade. He found it in the woods north of the Hagerstown Road where it had halted and started it toward the left of the First Corps line—the left of the Iron Brigade. Biddle faced the brigade right, and it trudged east through the open fields toward Willoughby Run. As it left the woods, a bullet felled a man, and the regimental surgeon leaped from his horse to help him in full view of his regiment as it passed. Captain Cook of the 20th New York remarked that the shooting "thrilled every one with a sense of danger as great perhaps as that felt during the battle itself." The brigade waded Willoughby Run between the road and the Finnefrock buildings, where some dismounted cavalry was skirmishing, and passed over McPherson Ridge into the swale behind it. It formed in the swale west of the seminary building with its right near the south edge of McPherson Woods and dropped knapsacks. In a few minutes it advanced over the ridge and down to the run to support the 19th Indiana, which was then off to its right. This was no place to be, under the guns of Rebel skirmishers concealed in the wheat field west of the run. Soon better sense prevailed, and the brigade was ordered back — the 20th New York to the crest of the ridge and the rest of the brigade behind it. Both brigades of the Third Division, First Corps, and Cooper's battery had reached the field and were ready for a renewal of the battle. The corps' remaining three batteries and its last division, Robinson's, were also nearby.[29]

The artillery brigade reached Marsh Creek on 30 June. Like the infantry, its officers and sergeants were busy with their monthly and bimonthly reports. They also received orders to send their wagons to the corps quartermaster. On the morning of 1 July, as he was finishing his returns, Colonel Wainwright received his orders for the day's march. He had three batteries at hand. Capt. Gilbert H. Reynolds's Battery L, 1st New York Light Artillery; Capt. Greenleaf Stevens's 5th Maine Battery; and Lt. James Stewart's Battery B, 4th U.S. Artillery, were to follow Stone's brigade and, in turn, would be followed by the Second Division.[30]

As he waited, Lieutenant Stewart had some breakfast and a brief visit from Capt. Craig Wadsworth. Wadsworth took a cup of coffee with him and invited him forward to watch the cavalry fight. Stewart liked the idea. He turned the battery over to Lt. James Davison with instructions to have "Boots and Saddles" sounded as soon as the men had finished their morning tasks and to have the battery ready to move. Then, with his bugler, he rode toward Gettysburg. According to Stewart's only account of the battle, he saw preparations being made for the fight ahead, and he promised General Wadsworth that he would post his battery at the east railroad cut. Then Stewart sent his bugler back for the battery. Unfortunately, as stated below, Stewart's account does not quite agree with Colonel Wainwright's report made only two weeks after the event. Wainwright claimed that Stewart had been posted initially 200 yards south of the seminary, and Wainwright is probably correct.[31]

When his batteries reached the Codori buildings, Wainwright turned them into the shortcut toward the seminary and rode ahead to see what was to be done. He found the situation fluid and decided to send the forges and battery wagons to the rear and to park the guns and caissons within easy reach. Reynolds's battery led the way. When it arrived, troops of cavalry relieved by infantry were falling back from the ridges to the west. The batteries halted behind Seminary Ridge where there was plenty of room. Reynolds's six guns and their caissons halted in a newly planted orchard. The drivers, whose clothes were matted with dust and mud, got down from their mounts to stretch their legs and walk about. The horses shook themselves beneath their harnesses and saddles and rubbed their heads against one another as they are wont to do. It was a short stop. Wainwright ordered the battery forward. Leaving the caissons behind, the six teams pulling the guns vaulted the remains of a fence in their front and pulled their jouncing guns over the downed rails. Wainwright placed Stewart's battery 200 yards south of the seminary building for a time before sending it to the east railroad cut. Stevens's Maine battery took Stewart's place.[32]

Robinson's two brigades were the last First Corps units to reach the field. They had bivouacked on the night of 30 June just north of the Mason-Dixon Line, and the 88th Pennsylvania spent the night on picket. Although some men recollected that they had begun their march to Gettysburg as early as 6:00 A.M., others thought that they had done so as late as 9:00 A.M., and they are probably right. Their march was uneventful and leisurely until a galloper from the First Corps headquarters told them to close their ranks and hasten forward.[33]

As the 90th Pennsylvania hurried past the Rogers house on the left of the road midway between the Peach Orchard and the Codori buildings, an elderly man stood in its yard along with his granddaughter, a "blooming lass of 14 or 15 years." Peter Rogers exhorted them in "beseeching, tremulous tones, 'Whip 'em, boys, this time. If you don't whip 'em now, you'll never whip 'em.'" The boys answered with "Bully for the old man" and "Hip hip for the girl."[34]

The division, as the First Corps reserve, went on to the seminary and halted on the west slope of the ridge. No sooner had it arrived than Adjutant Abner Small of the 16th Maine saw officers in the cupola of the seminary building pointing to the north. Doubleday soon ordered Robinson to send a brigade north to guard the right of Cutler's brigade from Confederates arriving from that direction. Col. Richard Coulter led his 11th Pennsylvania and the 97th New York beyond the railroad bed to Oak Ridge without delay, and the rest of Baxter's brigade soon followed. (This portion of the battle is discussed in Chapter 13.)[35]

In addition, Doubleday ordered Robinson to hold the seminary. Robinson had learned the value of breastworks at Glendale on the Peninsula and set Paul's brigade to work tearing down fences and piling up a crescent-shaped work in front of its position. Shot and shell fired from Confederate batteries on Herr Ridge and Oak Hill fell near Paul's men as they gathered and heaped the rails and piled up earth and other materials. They saw a ball fired from a Napoleon rolling slowly along the ground and witnessed a foolish act too often associated with inexperienced soldiers lacking good sense. A man "with great glee" put out his heel to stop a twelve-pounder ball that rolled so very slowly toward him. Ignoring shouts telling him to let it go by, he attempted to stop the ball with his foot. It mangled his leg so badly that it had to be amputated.[36]

While the men of Paul's brigade piled up breastworks, Capt. Stephen C. Whitehouse, commander of Company K, 16th Maine, spoke to Adjutant Small. Whitehouse stated that he wished that he felt as brave and as cool as Col. Charles Tilden seemed to be. Small replied that the colonel was probably as scared as any of them and that Whitehouse should cheer up, for " 'Twill soon be over." Whitehouse tried to be cheerful, but he did a poor job; "his face wore a look of foreboding, and his smile was a stiff mockery." They talked until they were interrupted by the command to fall in. Whitehouse said, "Goodbye, Adjutant, this is my last fight." He turned, shouted the command "Fall in!" to Company K, and Small never saw him again. The afternoon's hard fighting had begun, and for Whitehouse it was soon over.[37]

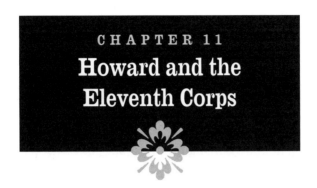

CHAPTER 11

Howard and the Eleventh Corps

Maj. Gen. Oliver Otis Howard, "Otis" to his family, had climbed high by July 1863. Howard had been born in Leeds, Maine, on 8 November 1830, the son of a farmer who had died when he was only nine. After his mother remarried, he made his home with an uncle, John Otis. He attended Bowdoin College, financing his tuition, in part, by teaching in the public schools. He graduated from Bowdoin in 1850, but though he had a fiancée, he had no career plans. Near the end of his stay at Bowdoin, his Uncle John, now a congressman, offered him an appointment to West Point. "To sacrifice ease to ambition," Howard accepted it and entered West Point's class of 1854.

Howard had no trouble with his studies at the academy and graduated fourth in his class of forty-six. Those of his class who fought at Gettysburg included Thomas Ruger, who graduated number three; Stephen Weed; and the Confederates William Dorsey Pender and J. E. B. Stuart. Custis Lee headed the class, and noted artillerist Henry L. Abbott of Boston was number two. Even then, Howard was controversial. He was ostracized for a time in 1851 by his fellow cadets, and Lee and Abbott were two of his principal antagonists. Why he was shunned is not known, though it was said that some cadets criticized him for visiting an enlisted man stationed there whom he had known in Maine. It must not have been a sectional antagonism, for Abbott was from Massachusetts and Stuart was one of his better friends.[1]

After graduation Howard became an ordnance subaltern serving at arsenals in the North and in Florida. In 1857 he and his family moved to

West Point, where he taught mathematics until June 1861. Howard resigned his first lieutenancy to become colonel of the 3d Maine Volunteer Infantry Regiment. By this time he had fathered three children, had been a superintendent of a Sunday school for enlisted men and their families, had founded a Bible school for cadets, and had studied theology under an Episcopal priest with the idea of trading his uniform for clerical garb.

At the time of his resignation from the Regular Army, he was thirty years old, slender, and about five feet, nine inches tall. He had thick brown hair, moustache and beard, and blue eyes. Frank Haskell, author of the classic letter about Pickett's Charge, described him as a "very pleasant, affable well dressed little gentleman." Maj. Thomas Osborn, his later chief of artillery, wrote in 1864 of Howard's kindness and bravery and also of a "nervous and unstudied gesture which to people unacquainted with him appears feminine."[2]

In June Howard took the 3d Maine to Washington, D.C. There it was brigaded with the 4th and 5th Maine and the 2d Vermont regiments, and Howard received the brigade's command. The brigade participated in the battle of Bull Run. Howard, like his future foe Stonewall Jackson, disliked fighting on Sundays and became unnerved briefly by the noise and carnage of the battle. He calmed his fears by praying to God that he might do his duty; he claimed later that the fear left him, never to return during the war.[3]

Howard became a brigadier general on 3 September 1861 and led a brigade in the Second Corps until he was shot twice at Fair Oaks on 1 June 1862 and lost his right arm. He recuperated in Maine but was soon back with the Second Corps in command of a brigade in John Sedgwick's division. Fortunately for Howard's career, Sedgwick fell wounded at Antietam, and Howard succeeded to the command of the division, which would not have happened had he dallied during his convalescence in Maine. He continued to command the division at Fredericksburg and became a major general as of 29 November 1862. After Fredericksburg, when General Hooker placed Daniel Sickles in command of the Third Corps, Howard, who outranked Sickles, protested. Hooker yielded to Howard's protests, and perhaps those of his Maine political supporters, by assigning him on 2 April to the command of the Eleventh Corps. Two years after resigning his lieutenancy and minus one arm, thirty-two-year-old Howard wore two stars and was in the upper echelon of the republic's principal army.[4]

Howard's appointment to the command of the Eleventh Corps was not popular with the members of that corps, however, particularly with its

132   { HOWARD AND THE ELEVENTH CORPS }

German regiments, who would have preferred Maj. Gen. Carl Schurz as Sigel's successor. The corps had been with John Pope's Army of Virginia until September 1862, when, under Sigel, it was transferred to the Army of the Potomac. It was not welcome; it had a reputation for having performed poorly under Sigel, who was a mediocre general but very popular with the numerous German immigrants in the corps. Approximately half of the corps' regiments were German, enough to give it a foreign cast and make it a target of criticism and a scapegoat for troops of other corps prone to be critical. Howard wrote that his reception was outwardly cordial, but that there was much dissatisfaction in the corps because of Sigel's departure. Then Howard and his brother, Maj. Charles H. Howard, got the idea that General Schurz, Howard's ranking subordinate and commander of his Third Division, was working against him. Further, Howard was not blessed with much of a sense of humor; he was a straitlaced teetotaler who believed that alcohol was a poison "injurious to the mental and moral life of a soldier." Thus it is likely that the nonpuritanical members of the corps, German or not, believed that he had little in common with them.[5]

Howard took some positive measures to gain acceptance. He kept much of the old corps staff, particularly Lt. Col. Charles W. Assmussen as chief of staff, despite the fact that Assmussen did some drinking when not in Howard's presence, and Lt. Col. Theodore Meysenburg as adjutant general, both of whom were German. Howard knew that Assmussen drank; in fact he seemed to notice everything. He could be tactful, too. While inspecting a bakery he heard a teamster swearing. Instead of berating the man in the presence of others, he took him aside to tell him that he wanted to hear no more such language. At another time he thanked an orderly who held his horse; it was a small gesture, but the orderly remarked to others that no one else had thanked him since he had entered the army.[6]

The reputation of the Eleventh Corps worsened, of course, after Stonewall Jackson's assault smashed and routed it at Chancellorsville. The onus fell on the German units; someone had to be blamed, though Gen. Henry Hunt in later years wrote that "under the circumstances no men could have withstood such a sudden attack as that made by 'Stonewall' Jackson on the flank and rear of the Eleventh Corps." John Bigelow Jr., in his exhaustive study *The Campaign of Chancellorsville*, wrote that "such a disaster would have happened to any body of troops situated as the XI Corps was when Jackson struck it." Schurz and others wanted the matter aired, the reports published, and a review by a court of inquiry, but this was not done. In addition, the corps had internal problems. Capt. Frederick C.

Maj. Gen.
Oliver Otis Howard
(CWLM)

Winkler, judge advocate general for the Eleventh Corps, had little confidence in it. He believed that jealousy and intrigue between officers, particularly those of the older regiments, had destroyed discipline. Beyond that the officers and men of the army, including those of the First Corps, had made up their minds. The "Flying Crescent," one of the names the corps was called derisively after Chancellorsville, had confirmed its disrepute in spades and carried the burden of its poor reputation to Gettysburg and its aftermath.[7]

The First and Eleventh Corps marched from Frederick on 29 June. While the First Corps went ahead to Marsh Creek on the thirtieth, the Eleventh halted in the Emmitsburg area. General Reynolds, the wing commander, thought that the Confederates might attempt to turn the Union left by cutting southeast from the Fairfield area to the Frederick road south of Emmitsburg. On the thirtieth, to be prepared for such a move, Howard shifted units of his corps from east to northwest of the village. He placed Francis Barlow's division north of it where the First Corps had been. Corps headquarters was at St. Joseph's College, and Schurz's division occupied the school's grounds and its environs. Howard sent patrols toward Monterey and Cashtown. Lt. Col. Edward Salomon led 100 men of the 82d Illinois to Fairfield, arriving there at 3:00 P.M., an hour after the Confederates had left the village; Capt. Emil Koenig took 100 men from the 58th New York south on the road to Creagerstown; and 3 officers and 100 enlisted men of the 75th Ohio scouted the countryside along the Greencastle Road. None of these parties met Confederates.[8]

Howard "yielded to the tempting offer of hospitality" by a Jesuit father and took up temporary residence at the college in a room with a comfortable bed. Schurz made his headquarters there also. Schurz did not await an invitation to do so; he called on the mother superior and asked for permission to use one of the "nunnery's" buildings, suggesting with "perfect sincerity" that the college would be protected by his presence. The mother superior took the hint and put a large frame building at his disposal. Schurz's staff received a tour of the college and a good dinner, and the nuns allowed an officer to play the chapel organ. In response Schurz had the band of the 45th New York play a concert of songs, marches, and polkas for their hosts.[9]

Sgt. Adam Muenzenberger of the 26th Wisconsin wrote that they had arrived in Emmitsburg worn out from hard marching "like dogs" in rainy weather and over bad roads. Although the rain was intermittent, it seemed to dominate the Emmitsburg bivouac. The pause there gave time for the bimonthly muster. Arriving mail gave those who received it great pleasure and prompted a lot of letter writing in return. Religious Catholics of Schurz's division had an opportunity to attend Mass in a church—no doubt a rare experience for them. There were also those who spent time on the picket lines. On the murky and misty night of 30 June, Lt. Clyde Miller of the 153d Pennsylvania commanded a picket line somewhere north of the town. In the darkness his pickets fired at a noise from a cornfield in their front that sounded like cavalry. When dawn came, they found dead sheep where the presumed cavalry had been.[10]

After the evening meeting with Reynolds at Moritz Tavern (described in Chapter 4), Howard returned to his comfortable bed at St. Joseph's College. An officer carrying dispatches from army headquarters to Reynolds awakened him there to show him the messages. One was a movement order for 1 July. Howard's sleep was over for the night. He issued orders that would enable his corps to comply with the instructions from Reynolds that he expected to receive. Barlow's division would follow the First Corps to Gettysburg via the Emmitsburg Road. About a mile north of Moritz Tavern, Schurz's and von Steinwehr's divisions and the five batteries of the corps would turn east from the Emmitsburg Road toward the Taneytown Road at Horner's Mill and march north from there to Gettysburg. This route was about three miles longer than Barlow's, but it had no other military traffic. At 6:00 A.M. Howard informed Reynolds of his plan; he stated that unless Reynolds desired otherwise, he would "encamp" two miles from Gettysburg at the crossroads at the "J. Wintz" place. After 2 July this area would be identified with the Peach Orchard and the battle there.[11]

Schurz reported that his division broke camp about 7:00 A.M.; on the other hand, Howard wrote that he received the order to move at 8:00 A.M., an hour that comports better with the movements of the First Corps. Once his divisions were on their way, Howard started with his staff and escort over the Emmitsburg Road to Gettysburg. To avoid the traffic on the road, they took to the fields beside it and pushed ahead as rapidly as they could. After two hours the party reached the Peach Orchard area where Howard had planned to halt. From the high ground there they could hear gunfire and see the town ahead and the troops of the First Corps taking a short cut across the fields from the Emmitsburg Road to Seminary Ridge. Here a messenger from Reynolds told him to "come quite up to Gettysburg." After being questioned by Howard, the staff officer told him to stop anywhere according to his judgment.[12]

Howard had sent Capt. Daniel Hall in search of Reynolds. Because he was two hours ahead of his divisions, Howard and Colonel Meysenburg made a reconnaissance of the area. After failing to find a place from which they "could get an extended view," they rode to Cemetery Hill. They saw that the hill commanded the town and the country to the west and north, that its gentle slope in those directions made for a good artillery positions, and that Culp's Hill could anchor the right of a defensive position there. Howard said to Meysenburg, "This seems to be a good position, colonel." Meysenburg promptly replied, "It is the only position, general." In writing of this, Howard stressed that both had meant "*position for Meade's army.*"[13]

Howard accepted credit for selecting Cemetery Hill as the bastion of the position south of Gettysburg. His was a correct but invidious claim for which Congress thanked him. Others insisted that Reynolds had recognized the hill's value, and they were probably correct also. The hill's significance ought to have been obvious to him and probably to Wadsworth as well. Wadsworth validated this claim for Reynolds when he sent Hall's battery to the hill later that morning when he thought that the First Corps might be driven from the fields west of the town. Yet Howard of his own volition saw the importance of the hill and took measures to ensure that Union troops occupied and held it.[14]

After observing the advantages of the hill, Howard rode into Gettysburg, where he tried to climb to the belfry of the courthouse. It was locked, but young Daniel Skelly, whose father operated a dry goods store in the Fahnestock building across Middle Street, offered to take him to the "observatory" on the roof of that building. There Skelly and a teenage friend, W. August Bentley, and some other townsfolk were watching the battle. Bentley remembered that a one-armed general, his staff, and an escort had come "dashing" down the street and had reined up in front of the building. Skelly led Howard and a German staff officer, who carried large field glasses, to the observatory. It provided a good view of the area, and Howard "swept the field long and anxiously." He saw firing beyond the seminary and masses of cavalry drawn up on the right. He also saw portions of the First Corps taking position near the railroad and another body of troops, a portion of Robinson's division perhaps, moving northeast along Seminary Ridge, and Confederate prisoners trudging through the town toward the Union rear. He and the staff officer, with some help from the townsfolk, were familiarizing themselves with the area's terrain when Sgt. George Guinn of Cole's Maryland Cavalry rode up and shouted from the street below, "General Reynolds is wounded, sir."[15]

Howard replied, "I am very sorry; I hope that he will be able to keep the field." Howard continued with his survey from the observatory for a few more minutes. At 10:30 A.M. his aide, Capt. Daniel Hall, appeared in the street and shouted up, "General Reynolds is dead, and you are the senior officer on the field." Maj. Charles Howard brought him the same message from Doubleday a short while afterward.[16]

A heavy burden had fallen on Howard. Since he was a religious man, he must have uttered a brief prayer. He said to those around him, "God helping us, we will stay here until the army comes." He immediately dictated orders by which he assumed command of the army's left wing. He sent Captain Hall to tell Schurz that he was appointed acting commander of the Eleventh Corps and to ask him to hurry to the field. Howard also sent Capt. Edward P. Pearson down the Emmitsburg Road to Barlow and to Sickles at Emmitsburg to tell them of Reynolds's death and to urge them to hurry to the field. Sickles was to pass the word on to Meade in Taneytown.[17]

Although the Twelfth Corps was not in the left wing, it marched to the hamlet of Two Taverns on the Baltimore Pike just five miles southeast of Gettysburg on the morning of 1 July. Maj. Gen. Henry W. Slocum, its commander, was senior to Howard. Howard informed Slocum, as he had Sickles, that the left wing was engaged with Hill's corps and that Ewell was advancing on Gettysburg from York. Slocum, a punctilious fellow, was agonizing over his compliance with the Pipe Creek Circular and did not answer this call for aide. Howard would attempt to seek help from him again later in the day.[18]

After sending these dispatches, if not before, Howard returned to Cemetery Hill and established his headquarters there. As he left the Fahnestock building, Mrs. Fahnestock asked, "Oh, sir, you are not going to let the rebels come into the town, are you?" Howard paused and replied, "Madam, no one can tell what may happen in war." To Daniel Skelly, Howard appeared "perfectly calm and self possessed." Howard's foremost objective was "to hold Gettysburg with one wing, which only amounted, with our small corps to 'an advanced guard,' to hold this strategic position till the army should come up."[19]

After returning to Cemetery Hill, Howard established his headquarters on its crest east of the Baltimore Pike. He was there to greet Schurz, who had hastened forward over the Taneytown Road in response to his summons. Schurz and the troops in his column had known nothing of the fighting at Gettysburg until Captain Hall delivered Howard's dispatch. Schurz turned his division over to Brig. Gen. Alexander Schimmelfennig, told him to bring it forward at the double-quick, and with his staff set out for Cemetery Hill four miles away. On his way he met terrified civilians fleeing the battle. One was a middle-age woman who carried a bundle in one hand and tugged a small child with the other. She recognized Schurz as a man of importance and tried to stop him, crying at the top of her voice, "Hard times at Gettysburg! They are shooting and killing! What will become of us!"[20]

The Eleventh Corps had a difficult march from Emmitsburg that began about 8:00 A.M. There was a drenching shower, perhaps a local one that the First Corps might have avoided. Barlow's division followed the First Corps up the Emmitsburg Road, which the First Corps had left even more rutted than usual. Schurz's and von Steinwehr's divisions found both the Taneytown Road and the road to Horner's Mill poor and stony at the outset and soon made much worse by the passing of troops and their heavy vehicles. They became so rutted that the infantry often found it easier to walk in the adjoining fields and leave the roads to batteries and trains. One bit of drama common to Pennsylvania units provided some diversion. When the men of the 153d Pennsylvania, marching on the Emmitsburg

Road, crossed the Mason-Dixon Line into their home state, they tossed their caps into the air and gave three cheers for Pennsylvania. That was a brief respite; the mud, the heat, and the humidity were constants. The march worsened, of course, after orders came to hurry, and the troops had to try to double-quick. This extra exertion prompted many of them to throw away clothing and equipment that weighed them down.[21]

The five Eleventh Corps batteries moved with Schurz's column. Capt. Hubert Dilger's Ohio battery marched with Schurz's division; Lt. William Wheeler's 13th New York Battery was with von Steinwehr. The remaining three, Capt. Michael Wiedrich's New York battery, Capt. Lewis Heckman's Ohio battery, and Lt. Bayard Wilkeson's Regular battery, bumped along at the rear of the column. Dilger, formerly of the army of Baden and hero of Chancellorsville, rode near the head of the column with Captain Winkler. While on the Taneytown Road, they heard cannon fire and tried to find a high point from which to see the batteries firing. Then the firing stopped, and they contented themselves with eating some of the cherries that were then so plentiful in the Gettysburg area. The sound of renewed and fierce fire caused them to hurry back to the column, and they learned that Schurz had gone on ahead.[22]

Howard had asked Major Osborn, his artillery chief, to hurry his guns to the front. Lieutenant Wheeler, who had been riding along "thinking of anything but an approaching fight," was aroused from his reverie by an aide who ordered his battery forward at a double-quick. In spite of his concern about the poor condition of the wheels on his vehicles and the stones in the road that might collapse them, Wheeler took his guns forward at a trot. The gun carriages jounced and rattled. The horse feed and equipment carried on the caissons broke loose and fell to the road. The cannoneers ran beside their sections both to spare their horses and because it was too dangerous for them to ride on the limber chests. Wheeler tried to keep this pace for four miles until the battery reached Cemetery Hill. After arriving, it halted to await further orders. As it did so, its breathless and sweating cannoneers caught up.[23]

After Schurz reached Cemetery Hill, he looked toward the seminary a mile to the northwest. He could see puffs of smoke and hear the crackle of musketry and the thudding of cannon fire, but the soldiers themselves were too distant to discern with the naked eye. The battle there seemed like a small affair when set against the rural landscape and the backdrop of South Mountain. It gained increasing significance when the ambulance bearing Reynolds's body passed on its way to Taneytown. At 12:30 P.M.

Wadsworth sent a note that reported wrongly that the enemy was retiring and urged an advance. A few minutes later Howard learned from Doubleday that he was not then concerned about his left but that he was worried about his right, which was hard pressed. He had every reason to be worried, for Rodes's division of Ewell's corps was moving toward it.[24]

On Cemetery Hill, Howard and Schurz were able to see Confederates on Oak Hill, but they could not estimate their strength. Schurz observed, "Either the enemy was before us in small force, and then we had to push him with all possible vigor, or he had the principal part of his army there, and then we had to establish ourselves in a position which would enable us to maintain ourselves until the arrival of re-inforcements. Either of these cases being possible, provision was to be made for both." To accomplish both ends, Howard asked Schurz, as acting corps commander, to post his and Barlow's divisions to the right of the First Corps on Oak Ridge while von Steinwehr's division and the extra batteries remained in reserve on Cemetery Hill.[25]

The leading elements of Schurz's division reached Cemetery Hill about 12:30. Its soldiers in dirty blue woolen uniforms soaked with sweat had come at a double-quick and were panting for breath. Schurz told Schimmelfennig, as acting commander of his division, to take it through the town and to deploy it in two lines to the right of the First Corps. This, he said, was done with "promptness and spirit." Yet because Rodes had occupied Oak Hill, Schimmelfennig had to post his troops in the plain facing northwest off the right and rear of the First Corps. Soon after, Barlow's division arrived and also hastened through the town. Initially Schurz intended that his (Schimmelfennig's) division form behind the First Corps right somewhere west of the Mummasburg Road, probably in the broad expanse south of the Hagy buildings. He ordered Barlow to place von Gilsa's brigade to the right of Schurz's division and on the west side of the Mummasburg Road; Brig. Gen. Adelbert Ames's brigade would form east of the road and to von Gilsa's right rear, where it could watch the Carlisle and Harrisburg roads. But Howard learned that Ewell's corps was approaching the Union right and that Schurz would have to deploy to protect that flank. He ordered Schurz to limit his support to the First Corps right to a heavy line of skirmishers and to prevent the Eleventh Corps right from being turned.[26]

The arrival of the Eleventh Corps excited and inspired Gettysburg's fearful citizens. Schimmelfennig's and Barlow's divisions flowed through the town over Washington Street like a river of blue. One soldier remembered that the townsfolk "were excited and scared to death, hurrying and scurrying in every direction," but another wrote that they would hardly venture from their doorways from which they handed out eatables and water. Most soldiers had no time for them. Schurz's men, in the lead, went at a double-quick. When Dilger's battery was ordered to the front of their column, it went at a gallop, its cannoneers now riding on its limbers and holding on for dear life. The infantry moved to the sidewalks to make way for the battery and cheered as it went by. From his house at the corner of Washington and Middle streets, Michael Jacobs saw that "they kept pace without breaking ranks; but they flowed through and out into the battle-field beyond, a human tide, at millrace speed." And then, when Barlow's division passed, he heard cheering that rolled toward him like some "high surge sweeping across the surface of a flowing sea." It followed a group of mounted men who rode at a brisk trot behind a colonel, probably Leopold von Gilsa, who seemed to be enjoying the acclaim. The colonel had just been released from arrest for failure to obey an order by Barlow, and the brigade was hailing his return. The 153d Pennsylvania of von Gilsa's brigade must not have been traveling at a double-quick, for it followed its band, which led it with drums beating "amid the rejoicing of the inhabitants, who greeted us as deliverers." Lt. Henry Hauschild of the 75th Pennsylvania, Wladimir Krzyzanowski's brigade, received special greetings. Hauschild had been a resident of Gettysburg and had friends there. He died a short while later in the fields north of the town.[27]

General Howard met Barlow's division as it passed from the Emmitsburg Road into Washington Street and rode with Barlow through the town. One of Howard's most vivid recollections of this ride in later years was that of a young lady who stood on her porch after all other civilians had been driven inside by cannon fire and waved her handkerchief at the soldiers as they passed. By this time, apparently, Rodes's division had occupied Oak Hill, and Carter's batteries were firing at the Eleventh Corps troops as they sallied from the town. Howard wrote that he accompanied Barlow to "Barlow Hill"; but he was confused, for Blackford's Sharpshooters would have been on Blocher's (Barlow) Knoll by this time, and he could not have gone there. By this time Howard knew of Ewell's approach and had sent Schurz instructions to look out for his right. He did not see Schurz while he was north of the town. Not long after reaching that part of the field, Howard sent his brother, Maj. Charles Howard, to see Buford in order to consult with the cavalry chief, reconnoiter, and send him information. At about 2:00 P.M. he sent Meysenburg, who had been with him, back to Cemetery Hill.[28]

After this brief stay on the Eleventh Corps front, Howard ascended Oak Ridge, passed behind Robinson's division, and stopped to talk with Wadsworth. Wadsworth testified later that Howard told him to hold on as long as possible and then retire. Howard quibbled over this statement; he believed that he had told Wadsworth that Doubleday would instruct him to hold his position. Howard might have been technically correct. Although Howard and Doubleday would have observed the chain of command and protocol, Wadsworth's reputation suggests that he would not have been concerned with such niceties at the time.[29]

Howard met with Doubleday about a quarter-mile beyond the seminary—where, he did not say—and examined the position of the First Corps. Oddly enough, Doubleday's writings do not mention Howard's visit. Howard asked Doubleday to look out for the First Corps left and said that he would protect its right. His concern for the First Corps left might have stemmed from a worry shared by Doubleday and Reynolds over cavalry reported in the Fairfield area and for troops in that direction that might interpose between the First and Third corps. But Doubleday saw no troops other than those of Heth's and Pender's divisions because there were none to see. Howard's promise to protect the First Corps right would soon prove rash.[30]

After his visit to the First Corps, Howard returned to Cemetery Hill, where he remained for the rest of that day's battle. Howard had requests for reinforcements from both Doubleday and Schurz. Howard sent Charles R. Coster's brigade and Heckman's battery to Schurz in a belated way, but he had no help for Doubleday. He instructed Schurz to send a regiment to Wadsworth if he could spare it, but Schurz had none to send. Similarly, he asked Buford to support the First Corps center, but that, too, was an empty gesture. Perhaps Howard would have responded more reasonably to such requests had he been closer to the fighting instead of at his headquarters on Cemetery Hill. Yet after Coster's brigade had been sent to Schurz, he had no help to give. Only Orland Smith's brigade and Wiedrich's New York battery were at hand, and Howard wisely kept them on Cemetery Hill to man that vital rallying point.[31]

Howard responded to the alarms of his corps commanders by urging them to hold on until the expected arrival of the Twelfth Corps. He had sent General Slocum a dispatch at 1:00 P.M. "informing him of the situation of affairs." This elicited no response. Slocum's seeming failure to

{ HOWARD AND THE ELEVENTH CORPS }

reply, though questionable in hindsight, had merit from Slocum's point of view. Slocum had received the Pipe Creek Circular, and he assumed that Howard had gotten it too. He had advanced to Two Taverns as ordered by the circular and had, therefore, complied with it. He had not been aware of the battle that morning and believed that going to Gettysburg would have been in violation of his orders. In Slocum's view Howard's dispatch seemed informational and not a summons for help.[32]

Slocum learned of the battle from a civilian. (This suggests that the Twelfth Corps had no communication with the nearby left wing and that it had no patrols to its front.) He sent Maj. Eugene W. Guindon forward to confirm what he had been told. Guindon did not have to travel far toward Gettysburg before hearing gunfire, and he returned with this news to Slocum. Slocum reported that he put his corps in motion without delay but possibly not until he received a second message from Howard.[33]

At 3:00 P.M., after his return to Cemetery Hill, Howard sent Slocum another dispatch by Capt. Daniel Hall. In it Howard announced that his right flank was under attack and that his force was in danger of being outflanked and driven back. He asked if Slocum and his corps were moving up. When he delivered the dispatch, Captain Hall briefed the general on the events of the day. Unfortunately Hall did not record Slocum's response, but Hall considered it to be anything but honorable, soldierly, or patriotic.[34]

About 4:00 P.M. Howard ordered Doubleday to fall back fighting to Cemetery Hill if he could no longer remain in his position west of Gettysburg. At the same time he sent Maj. Charles Howard to Slocum to "inform him of the state of affairs." He asked Slocum to send one of his divisions to the right of Gettysburg and one to the left. He also asked Slocum to come in person and take command. Charles Howard met Slocum on the Baltimore Pike near Powers Hill. Slocum had acted on General Howard's 3:00 P.M. dispatch in spite of Captain Hall's fears. Slocum told Charles Howard that a division had already been sent to the right (via Wolf Hill to Benner's Hill) and that he would send the other to the left. However, because he deemed it contrary to Meade's wishes, he did not want to come forward himself to take responsibility for the fight.[35]

A message from General Meade buttressed Howard's request. Capt. Addison Mason of Meade's staff reached Two Taverns with a dispatch that announced that Hancock had been appointed to command of the left wing. It urged corps commanders to push to Gettysburg with all possible haste. Slocum was no longer at Two Taverns; his corps were already marching to Gettysburg. After receiving the dispatch, Slocum wrote one addressed to "General Hancock, or General Howard." It announced that the Twelfth Corps was advancing and would come up about one mile to the right of Gettysburg. In his report Slocum wrote that "agreeably to suggestion from General Howard," probably in the dispatch carried by Hall, he put Williams's division in position on the right near Rock Creek facing Benner's Hill. In accordance with orders from Hancock, Geary's division was placed on the left of the line near the Round Tops.[36]

General Howard now faced the crises of the day. After taking command of the forces on the field, he had decided to fight at Gettysburg and had brought the Eleventh Corps to the battle. After it was posted, he remained on Cemetery Hill, which he regarded as essential to hold if the Army of the Potomac was to fight at Gettysburg. He did not intrude in the tactical direction of the troops west and north of the town. There would be hard fighting there, but it would be conducted by Generals Doubleday and Schurz.

CHAPTER 12

Ewell and Rodes
Reach the Field

Four Confederate generals met at the hamlet of Heidlersburg on the evening of 30 June to discuss orders received that day from General Lee. General Ewell, who had called the meeting, if it were so formal a gathering, was there with two of his three division commanders — Robert Rodes and Jubal Early. Maj. Gen. Isaac Trimble also sat in on the conversation. Generals Ewell, Rodes, and Trimble had come south from Carlisle that day with Rodes's division, and Early had brought his division west from York to its bivouac area about three miles to the east of the crossroads. Trimble had no assignment within the corps. Yet he is a principal, and biased, source for what happened both at this meeting and at Ewell's headquarters on the following day. Ewell, Early, and Rodes would have special responsibilities in the events of 1 July, while Trimble would affect their place in history.

Jubal Early ("Old Jube," "Old Jubilee," and probably some other nicknames, too — Lee referred to him as "my bad old man") was a Virginian, born on 3 November 1816. He was in West Point's class of 1837, along with Union generals Joseph Hooker and John Sedgwick, and after graduation he served as an artillery subaltern in Florida. He resigned his commission in 1838 to study law and practiced it in Rocky Mount, Virginia. Early participated in Whig politics and served a term in the state legislature. He was a major in the 1st Virginia Regiment in Mexico but saw no fighting there. He was a bachelor.

Early had opposed secession, but once Virginia seceded, he became an ardent Confederate. He entered the army as colonel of the 24th Virginia, became a brigadier general on 21 July 1861, and commanded a brigade at

Maj. Gen. Jubal A. Early
(CWLM)

First Bull Run. Although he was wounded at Williamsburg, he was back in the saddle in time for Malvern Hill, Cedar Mountain, and Second Bull Run. After capably commanding a division at Fredericksburg, he became a major general in April 1863 and fought at Chancellorsville. Yet his personality and appearance often overshadowed his accomplishments. He was six feet tall, thin, and bearded and had flashing black eyes. Unfortunately he suffered from rheumatism that caused him to be stooped and irritable. He could be a harsh disciplinarian, overbearing, and arrogant. Yet those persons close enough to see the inner man knew that he could be generous, magnanimous, and even genial. It took a strong man to stand up to Early, and perhaps Ewell deferred to him too much.[1]

Robert Rodes was a different sort of man. He had been born in Lynchburg, Virginia, in 1829 and was a graduate of the Virginia Military Institute. After being on the faculty of the institute, he went to Alabama, where he worked as a civil engineer and married an Alabama lady. He returned to the faculty of his alma mater just before the war began. Al-

Maj. Gen. Robert Rodes
(CWLM)

though he was in Virginia at the time of secession, he hurried back to Alabama and became colonel of the 5th Alabama Regiment. Rodes and his regiment went to the Virginia theater, and in October 1861 he became a brigadier general. He performed well in the Army of Northern Virginia's campaigns and was wounded at both Seven Pines and Antietam. He commanded a brigade at the outset of the Chancellorsville campaign, where he succeeded to the temporary command of D. H. Hill's division. He performed so well that he became a major general and received his own division.

Rodes was in his early prime, more than six feet tall, blonde, and had a moustache but no beard. His face had strong and sharp features. He seemed a dramatic contrast to his one-legged eccentric corps commander and to the stooped and irascible Early. One of his soldiers wrote that "decision of character was plainly written upon his countenance," not to mention a generous disposition, and that his "deportment in battle stamped him as a fearless brave soldier." Douglas S. Freeman wrote that he seemed to be a "Norse god." General Lee could well use that sort of division commander.[2]

General Lee had ordered Ewell to move his corps back from Carlisle and York, first to Heidlersburg and then to either Gettysburg or Cashtown "as circumstances might dictate." When at Heidlersburg, Ewell received a note from General Hill stating that Hill was at Cashtown. There might also have been an earlier dispatch telling of the Army of the Potomac's location in Frederick County and directing Ewell to move to "that point." At any rate the fog of war had become thick, and the course of the campaign had changed abruptly. There was a lot to talk about.[3]

Only Trimble wrote of the generals' meeting at Heidlersburg. Trimble had been born in Baltimore in 1802 and had graduated from West Point in 1822. After ten years of service, he left the army and embarked on a successful career in railroading. When war came, he became a colonel of Confederate engineers and later commanded a brigade in Ewell's division. Like Ewell, Trimble had been wounded at Second Bull Run, and he suffered long with osteomyelitis. His infirmity did not prevent his requesting promotion to the grade of major general, which he received in April 1863 under the assumption that he would be able to take command of Jackson's old division. He did not recover as soon as expected, however, and the division went to Edward Johnson. Trimble instead received command of the Valley District, which in the spring of 1863 was not active enough to sate his ambitions. As soon as he was able, Trimble rode north in the wake of the Army of Northern Virginia and caught up with Lee at Hagerstown. Lee talked with him about the area's topography and listened to his fanciful offer to capture Baltimore with a single brigade. According to Trimble, Lee also told him of a plan to strike the Union army in detail. Lee then suggested that Trimble ride on ahead to help Ewell take Harrisburg.[4]

Trimble reached Carlisle on 28 June. He told Ewell immediately that Lee wanted him to take Harrisburg. (Ewell knew that.) According to Trimble, Ewell asked what forces would be needed to take the town. Although he could have known little or nothing of the town's defenses and garrison, which must have been changing daily, Trimble asserted that it could be captured with a brigade and a battery of artillery. In reply, wrote Trimble, Ewell said that he could march on the city with a brigade the next day. This was the beginning of Trimble's service to the commander of the Confederate Second Corps.[5]

Jed Hotchkiss, Ewell's topographical engineer, noted in his diary that on the twenty-ninth Ewell was "quite testy and hard to please," disappointed because he could not go on to Harrisburg, and had everyone "flying around." That night Hotchkiss had to leave his cot to answer questions posed by Ewell and make a map for him — presumably of the country between Carlisle and the Gettysburg-Cashtown area. At an early hour the next morning, Rodes's division began its march over South Mountain to Heidlersburg about twenty miles to the south. Johnson's division and the corps train, which had followed Rodes's division up the Valley Turnpike to Chambersburg and Carlisle, did not follow. It went back the pike toward Chambersburg and would not rejoin the corps until 1 July. General Early, who had received the order to concentrate from Ewell on the evening of the twenty-ninth, put his division in motion on the morning of the thirtieth. He sent Lt. Col. Elijah V. White's 35th Virginia Cavalry Battalion (the Comanches) west on the pike to Gettysburg to screen his flank and marched his infantry west via Weigelstown and East Berlin. At East Berlin some of White's troopers ran into a scouting party of Federal cavalry, and Early received a request from Ewell to march toward Heidlersburg. That night his division bivouacked three miles east of that point.[6]

Trimble wrote that at the 30 June meeting Ewell read over Lee's order several times and commented on its " 'indefinite phraseology,' as he expressed it, in very severe terms." Ewell then asked each officer what the order meant by "according to circumstances." Such a phrase is not in Lee's dispatch to Ewell of 28 June; perhaps it was in a dispatch that we do not have. Both Early and Rodes gave "unsatisfactory opinions." Trimble then told them of his meeting with General Lee and of Lee's hope to defeat the Federal army in detail. He said that they had heard that the First Corps of the enemy was at Gettysburg. That, he claimed, was the "circumstance" that "directs you to march on that place." (This account by Trimble, cited here and below, was written more than twenty years after the event and contains obvious errors. At the time of this meeting the First Corps had not yet reached Gettysburg, and it seems unlikely that Ewell's people would have known of its location.) Trimble's explanation did not satisfy Ewell, who asked the rhetorical question posed countless times in history, "Why can't a commanding General have someone on his staff who can write an intelligible order?"[7]

On 1 July, soon after sunrise, Rodes's division, accompanied by Ewell and Trimble, marched west toward Cashtown via Middletown (now Biglerville). Early started his division about 8:00 A.M. with the intention of marching to Cashtown via Hunterstown and Mummasburg. By following these routes, each division could turn south toward Gettysburg if necessary. About 9:00 A.M., before reaching Middletown, Ewell learned from Hill that his corps was moving to Gettysburg. Ewell ordered his divisions to do the same. In addition, he sent Maj. G. Campbell Brown to Cashtown to tell General Lee that Rodes and Early were on their way to Gettysburg.[8]

Trimble was the only one to describe some of the details of this march. He recalled that after an hour or so of marching there was a halt, probably a routine stop to give the troops a brief rest. Ewell sat on a log, spread out a map, and "began again to comment in ill temper on the 'ambiguity of the order.'" But Trimble, according to his own recollection, was ready and willing to set the corps commander straight. He urged Ewell not to lose precious time. Pointing to Ewell's map, he suggested that they take the road to Cashtown and send to Lee for orders when they reached "Newtown" (possibly Middletown). This, of course, is essentially what happened, though how much Trimble actually had to do with it we cannot know.[9]

Major Brown had a unique position within Ewell's corps. He wore many hats: he was Ewell's adjutant, he was the son of Ewell's first cousin, he was Ewell's stepson, and to some extent he was his "Boswell" in the postwar years. Brown rode west from Middletown to the Chambersburg Turnpike near Cashtown and met General Lee there. At that time the battle had already begun, Hill's wagons jammed the pike, and troops, probably of Pender's division, were passing toward Gettysburg. Brown told Lee of Ewell's movements. Then Lee asked him "with a peculiar searching, almost querulous impatience, which I never saw in him before and but twice afterward, whether Gen. Ewell had heard anything from Gen. Stuart." Brown replied in the negative. Lee observed that Stuart had not complied with his instructions. He then impressed upon the major "'*very strongly*,' that a general engagement was to be avoided until the arrival of the rest of the army." After their meeting, which lasted about a half-hour, Lee rode on toward Gettysburg, and Brown returned to Ewell. On his ride east, Brown could see shells bursting in distant trees.[10]

While Brown searched for General Lee, Rodes's division turned south from Middletown on the road that led from Carlisle to Gettysburg. Ewell rode with it. No one recorded the division's order of march, but on the basis of its later deployment we can assume that Brig. Gen. Alfred Iverson's brigade was in the lead, followed by Col. Edward A. O'Neal's Alabama brigade. The four batteries of Lt. Col. Thomas H. Carter's artillery battalion, Junius Daniel's brigade, and George Doles's followed, but not necessarily in that order. The division's train would have followed the hindmost of these units, and Brig. Gen. Stephen D. Ramseur's brigade brought up the rear. When about four miles from Gettysburg, the Confederates

Brig. Gen. Alfred Iverson
(CWLM)

heard the distant grumbling of artillery fire and assumed that the enemy must be in Gettysburg in force.

South of the intersection of the road between Hunterstown and Mummasburg, where the Carlisle Road descends from the high ground of Oak Ridge to the Gettysburg Plain, Rodes's column, except for Doles's brigade, veered right from the main road. Rodes's main column followed a lesser road that paralleled Oak Ridge on the west and led to Herr Ridge at the Chambersburg Pike. Doles's brigade continued on the main road and descended into the plain to guard Rodes's left as the division approached the battlefield. At some unidentified point, the division encountered videttes of Devin's brigade. Iverson's brigade then deployed and advanced with increased caution.[11]

Brig. Gen. Alfred Iverson was a Georgian who had served in the Mexican War and afterward worked as a lawyer and railroad contractor. In 1855, with the help of his congressman father, no doubt, he secured a commission in the 1st U.S. Cavalry and served as a lieutenant in that regiment until Georgia's secession. He became a captain in the Confederate army and was posted in North Carolina, where in August 1861 he helped raise the 20th North Carolina Regiment. Though not a Tarheel, he became its colonel. Iverson was wounded in the Seven Days' battles, but he led his regiment in subsequent battles of the Army of Northern Virginia. When his brigade commander, Samuel Garland, was killed at South Mountain, Iverson replaced him. Promotion to brigadier general followed on 1 November 1862. Although Iverson must have performed reasonably well to this point, by the summer of 1863 he was not getting along with the officers of his brigade. Being a Georgian in a North Carolina unit might have contributed to his difficulties. Yet Rodes, who must have known him well, seems to have had confidence in him.[12]

Rodes's column moved intact until the tree cover at the crest of Oak Ridge widened beyond Iverson's front. Rodes deployed O'Neal's brigade to Iverson's left on the crest and east slope of the ridge. Cpl. Samuel B. Pickens of the 5th Alabama Regiment (not to be confused with the 5th Alabama Battalion in Archer's brigade) commented that his regiment was on the left of the brigade. When O'Neal's line went forward and wheeled left and right to come on line with Iverson's brigade, the men of the 5th had to double-quick over plowed fields, through wheat, and over fences, causing many fatigued soldiers to drop from the ranks. Pickens had never suffered so much in his life.[13]

In the meantime Doles's Georgians and a provisional sharpshooter battalion from O'Neal's brigade, commanded by Maj. Eugene Blackford, deployed on the Gettysburg Plain, the relatively flat area north of Gettysburg. There the brigade and the sharpshooters could cover the Carlisle Road and the ground to the east almost to the Harrisburg Road. They met more cavalry videttes in the plain as well as on the ridge — pickets whom Rodes described as "a few mounted men." No doubt Rodes consulted Ewell as his division proceeded south. General Trimble wrote that when the division was within a mile or so of Gettysburg, Ewell or Rodes asked him to lead it to a "good position."[14]

Devin's cavalrymen warned Union commanders of Ewell's approach. Unfortunately, accounts of the brigade's doings are fragmentary and scarce, and they contain statements that cannot be true. Devin's outpost line arced from Gamble's right, and the Mummasburg Road in particular, east across the Gettysburg Plain to the York Pike. The 17th Pennsylvania Cavalry manned a picket line that extended from the Mummasburg Road east to Rock Creek. Its reserve was at the junction of the Carlisle and Table Rock roads a half-mile north of the town. The three companies on picket had posts a mile or so farther to the front. The troopers did more than simply await the Rebels' arrival. Early's column found Union cavalrymen as far off as East Berlin on 30 June. That evening Capt. Theodore W. Bean of the 17th Pennsylvania led a reconnaissance three miles out the Carlisle Road and then east to Hunterstown before returning to the regiment. A patrol from the 9th New York Cavalry Regiment went northeast to Hunterstown and back over the Harrisburg Road on the same day. In the course of their ride the New Yorkers charged a Confederate patrol that was following them and captured one man. The man taken might have been Thomas Spates of the 35th Virginia Battalion, who was "picketing" in a cherry tree when captured. Another of the 9th's patrols found Confederates in Hunterstown on the morning of 1 July. That morning videttes picked up a civilian who brought word of the Confederate bivouacs at Heidlersburg. Therefore, Union commanders should have known that the Confederates were in great strength north of Gettysburg.

There were other claims. A member of the 17th Pennsylvania Cavalry wrote that its units were skirmishing with Confederates along the Carlisle Road at sunrise. Devin's report confirmed the exaggeration that the 17th Pennsylvania, supported by the 9th New York, held Early's division in check for two hours prior to the arrival of the Eleventh Corps north of Gettysburg in the early afternoon. Confederate accounts do not mention their being in these places in force at such early hours, nor do they mention a fight with cavalry there. However, it might be that Devin's men met cavalrymen other than those encountered on 30 June who were scouting ahead of Ewell's divisions and wrote nothing of what they did.[15]

When Rodes reached Oak Hill, he could see Hill's corps on Herr Ridge to his right front and much of the Union First Corps in the sector south of the railroad bed. He would not have been able to distinguish the sunken bed from the fields around it. After studying the situation in his front, Rodes decided that the positions occupied by O'Neal's and Iverson's brigades (we do not know just where they were except that they probably faced Gettysburg from somewhere along Oak Ridge to the north) would not allow him to "get at" the Federals properly. It was necessary to move the whole of his "command by the right flank, and to change direction to the right." This movement shifted the fronts of Iverson's and O'Neal's

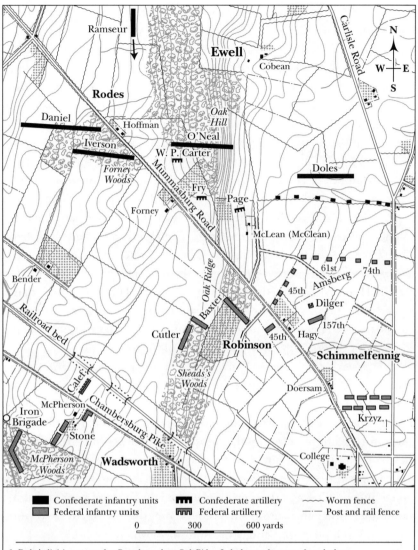

Confederate infantry units   **Confederate artillery**   〜〜 Worm fence
Federal infantry units   **Federal artillery**   ─·─ Post and rail fence

0   300   600 yards

1. *Rodes's division approaches Gettysburg along Oak Ridge. It deploys under cover of woods there.*
2. *Iverson's brigade forms in Forney Woods, with Daniel's brigade behind its right wing. Daniel's right likely extends beyond the woods but behind Forney Ridge.*
3. *O'Neal's brigade is on Oak Hill and on its east slope. Its 3d Alabama is on Daniel's left, with its 5th Alabama on its left in reserve.*
4. *Ramseur's brigade moves up from the rear.*
5. *Doles's brigade advances in the plain, its left near the Carlisle Road.*
6. *W. Carter's and Fry's batteries are on Oak Hill's south slope.*
7. *Cutler's brigade occupies Sheads's Woods. Baxter's brigade arrives and takes position north of Sheads's Woods facing west from behind a wall and north along the south edge of an oak grove.*
8. *Schimmelfennig's (Schurz's) division masses just north of town on the plain east of Seminary Ridge. The 45th New York, 61st Ohio, and 74th Pennsylvania advance as skirmishers.*

Map 12.1. Oak Hill and Oak Ridge, Early Afternoon

Brig. Gen. George Doles
(CWLM)

brigades to where they could face the right of the First Corps. It also permitted two batteries of Carter's battalion to take position on the hill.[16]

After this shift, Iverson's 1,300-man brigade occupied Forney's Woods south of the Mummasburg Road and fronted southeast toward the right of the First Corps. O'Neal's Alabamians formed off Iverson's left across the crest of Oak Hill and under cover of its trees. Their line extended down the ridge's east slope to the plain below. As his brigade formed, a soldier of the 6th Alabama on the brigade's right looked across Forney's fields of ripe wheat to the gray lines of Hill's corps "moving slowly but steadily on the long blue lines in his front" as it deployed for the afternoon's attack.[17]

While the other four brigades of Rodes's division made their way down the ridge, Doles's brigade — the 4th, 12th, 21st, and 44th Georgia regiments — plus Blackford's battalion of sharpshooters followed the Carlisle Road toward Gettysburg until it was about 2,200 yards north of the town. It deployed west from the road but was unable to close a gap between its right and O'Neal's left. The sharpshooters spread across Doles's front in a skirmish line that extended to the Harrisburg Road. Until Early's division arrived on the Harrisburg Road, it was the job of Doles's brigade to hold at bay any Federals who might come from the town to threaten Rodes's left. George Doles would prove equal to the task. He hailed from Milledgeville, Georgia, where he had been a businessman and captain of the Baldwin Blues. When war came, he became colonel of the 4th Georgia Regiment. When Roswell Ripley fell wounded at Antietam, Doles succeeded to the command of his brigade and became a brigadier general. He would be killed at Bethesda Church in June 1864.[18]

Daniel's brigade, Lt. Col. Thomas H. Carter's battalion of artillery, the division train, and Ramseur's brigade as train guard followed the leading brigades. When the sound of battle reached the division, the train left the column, and the rear brigades and artillery pushed close to Iverson and Doles. Daniel's brigade of about 2,500 officers and men was the largest in the division. After it double-quicked to Oak Hill, Rodes ordered Daniel to form his brigade about 200 yards in rear of Iverson's in such a way that its left wing was behind the right of Iverson's in Forney's Woods. Once in position, Daniel's North Carolinians lay down to avoid the artillery fire that might come their way.[19]

Brig. Gen. Stephen Ramseur's brigade was at the rear of the column. It did not hurry forward until the division train started for the rear. Ramseur rushed ahead of his brigade to see what was happening and found the other brigades already deployed. Rodes held Ramseur's men in reserve to support either Doles on the left, O'Neal in the left-center, or Iverson on the right as circumstances would demand.[20]

While the infantry brigades occupied the positions assigned them, trying to keep under cover of the woods, Ewell, Rodes, and Lt. Col. Thomas Carter posted William P. Carter's and Charles W. Fry's batteries on the south slope of the hill. Carter's two Napoleons and two ten-pounder Parrots were on the right, and Fry's two ten-pounder Parrotts and three-inch rifles were beside the woods on the left. Rodes could see Federals in his front but saw none facing in his direction. As soon as Carter's guns were ready to fire, they joined Hill's batteries in their duel with the Federal guns on McPherson Ridge. No doubt Ewell and Rodes intended to aid Pegram's guns on Herr Ridge, but Carter's help was really not essential at that time. In opening fire, Carter's two batteries advertised the presence of Rodes's division on Oak Hill and brought a hail of death in its direction. The Oak Ridge pot had begun to boil, and soon both armies would get a scalding.[21]

CHAPTER 13
Oak Ridge

Confederate projectiles "skipping in a playful manner" between the caissons and limbers of Calef's battery announced the arrival of Rodes's division on Oak Hill. To meet this new threat, to avoid enfilading fire from Oak Hill, and to take cover from the fire of the batteries on Herr Ridge, Calef's, Reynolds's, and Cooper's batteries moved back to the broad swale between the arms of McPherson Ridge and the rear of McPherson Woods. There they fronted north toward Carter's guns on Oak Hill. As Reynolds's New York battery took position east of the woods, Confederate shells fell near its guns, and Capt. Gilbert Reynolds was wounded in the face and blinded temporarily in his left eye. Captain Reynolds remained with his battery until Colonel Wainwright ordered him to the hospital, and Lt. George Breck took command of the battery. At the same time, a shrapnel ball grazed Wainwright's ankle. It stung, but the colonel's pride smarted more — Calef's battery had displayed greater skill in the displacement than had his First Corps batteries. Yet Wainwright reflected later that "it could not be expected that the crack Batt'y of the army should be outdone."

As soon as they were in their new positions, the First Corps guns opened fire on their Oak Hill antagonists. As they fired slowly at the Rebel cannon to the north, Colonel Wainwright sent Calef's battery to rejoin Buford. Reynolds's and Cooper's batteries continued to fire for nearly an hour at Rodes's guns and at the infantry around them.[1]

Rodes's arrival and the cannonading had an immediate effect on some of the First Corps infantry. The 143d and 149th Pennsylvania regiments of Stone's brigade, near McPherson's barn, changed front from west to north and took position in the swale and along the pike. They did this to shelter themselves from the fire of the batteries on Herr Ridge and reduced their vulnerability to Rodes's guns.[2]

Cutler's brigade was in the greatest peril. After repulsing Davis's brigade in the morning's fight, the 14th Brooklyn and the 6th Wisconsin went beyond the west railroad cut where they could support whatever battery occupied the exposed position between the cut and the pike. At General Wadsworth's order, Cutler placed his remaining four regiments north of the railroad bed where his brigade had opened the battle. This line turned out to be directly in front of Carter's batteries on Oak Hill. At a range of no more than a half-mile, Cutler's men were vulnerable to Carter's enfilading fire. Twelve years later Colonel Hofmann of the 56th Pennsylvania pondered the brigade's precarious position and wrote, "It must be admitted that a grave error was committed on our side in re-establishing our line of battle out in the open in front of Seminary [Oak] Ridge. It was ignoring all of our experience gained during two years of active warfare, and was never justified by the results upon any field down to the close of the war." Hofmann believed that the time spent there before the arrival of the Confederate batteries would have been better used in establishing a strong position on Oak Ridge in their rear.[3]

Rodes's threat from Oak Hill prompted Cutler to ask Wadsworth for orders; Wadsworth told him to take whatever position he thought proper. Cutler first "changed front to the right" and aligned his four regiments to face the enemy on Oak Hill. Although this shift eliminated the threat from enfilading fire, Cutler's regiments were still needlessly exposed. Soon Cutler moved them east to the shelter of Sheads's Woods on Oak Ridge and formed the brigade on the brow of the ridge's east slope.[4]

As Rodes's division arrived on Oak Hill, the lead elements of the Eleventh Corps filed from Washington Street onto the plain north of the town. Schurz had ordered Schimmelfennig to form the Third Division in two lines on the right of the First Corps, but Rodes reached there first. Therefore, Schimmelfennig deployed the division fronting north in the fields behind the First Corps right, where the north edge of the town is today. Although Schurz supported the First Corps right with a heavy line of skirmishers, there was still a gap on the slope of Oak Ridge between Cutler's brigade's right and the Eleventh Corps. By this time Howard learned from the cavalry that "the enemy was massing between the York and Harrisburg roads." He ordered Schurz to deploy Schimmelfennig's and Barlow's divisions so that the approaching enemy could not readily turn the Union right flank and to support the First Corps right with a "thick" line of skirmishers.[5]

The 45th New York and the 61st Ohio led Schimmelfennig's division to the field and set about to implement the new orders. The 45th was a regiment of German immigrants organized in New York City and commanded by Col. George von Amsberg, a Hannoverian from Hildesheim who had fought for Lajos Kossuth in the Hungarian revolution of 1848. Now, because of Schurz's and Schimmelfennig's temporary elevations, he commanded Schimmelfennig's brigade on the afternoon of 1 July. The rapid march to Gettysburg and through the town had caused straggling among the fatigued troops, but there was no time to wait for the stragglers and rear units to catch up. So while Schimmelfennig and von Amsberg strived to put the arriving troops into their proper formations, Capt. Francis Irsch of Company D led four companies of the 45th forward to the immediate support of the First Corps right. Irsch was to push toward McLean's (McClean's) red barn 700 yards to the north, holding his left to the Mummasburg Road and extending his line east as far as it would stretch. Lt. Col. Adolphus Dobke of the 45th would support him with the rest of the regiment as soon as it was assembled. The 61st Ohio and the 74th Pennsylvania extended the skirmish line to the right. From their vantage point on Oak Hill, Ewell and Rodes viewed with alarm the arrival of the Eleventh Corps north of the town.[6]

As Rodes formed on Oak Hill, the Second Division, Robinson's, of the First Corps was massing near the seminary. At Doubleday's orders, General Robinson sent the 11th Pennsylvania and the 97th New York regiments of Brig. Gen. Henry Baxter's brigade north beyond the railroad bed to Oak Ridge. They were to cover the gap between the First and the Eleventh Corps. Col. Richard Coulter, a veteran of the Mexican War and commander of the Eleventh, had charge of the two regiments. Not knowing what they would meet, Coulter's men advanced behind a skirmish line from the 97th. They filed north along the tree-covered slope of Oak Ridge a quarter-mile beyond the railroad bed. Capt. Isaac Hall of the 97th's Company A led the skirmishers almost to the Mummasburg Road, where they drew Confederate fire. In the meantime the main bodies of the two regiments formed behind the rail fence at the north edge of Sheads's Woods, and Coulter sent skirmishers from the Eleventh into the hay field in his front to roust Rebels hiding in the tall timothy. As the Eleventh deployed, Col. Charles Wheelock of the 97th pulled Captain Hall and his companies from the Mummasburg Road and sent them as skirmishers into the hay field to the right of the Eleventh. He ordered them to pass by the Eleventh's skirmish line and go to a high post-and-rail fence on the north edge of the hay field about 200 yards in their front. According to Captain Hall, "Every man moved forward with alacrity, though met with a galling fire." In spite of harassment by aggressive skirmishers in the wheat field between the hay field and the Mummasburg Road, Hall's men pushed to the fence between the two fields. They found no Confederates in the tall grass, but from the north side of the hay field they could see a portion of a Rebel brigade in a woods on Oak Hill.[7]

Soon after Coulter's force departed, General Baxter led his four remaining regiments north along Oak Ridge. Baxter had a fine war record. Although he was forty when the war began, he entered the army as a captain in the 7th Michigan Regiment and in August 1862 became its lieutenant colonel. He commanded the 7th at Fredericksburg and was wounded in a lung when he led it in an assault crossing of the Rappahannock River. He became a brigadier general in March 1863 in time to lead a brigade at Chancellorsville. At Gettysburg on the afternoon of 1 July, Baxter placed his four regiments to the right front of Coulter's men between Sheads's Woods and the Mummasburg Road. After he had formed his line on the ridge, the two regiments with Colonel Coulter joined them on the left, and Colonel Wheelock called the skirmishers from the hay field. Although the 97th's contingent was able to leave the hay field in less than five minutes, alert North Carolina skirmishers killed one of them and wounded others.[8]

When Coulter left Sheads's Woods for the ridgeline, Cutler's brigade moved from its position along the east edge of the woods, which it probably occupied after Baxter's brigade had passed that way. Its occupation of the woods meant that the First Corps right held Oak Ridge from the Mummasburg Road well into Sheads's Woods — a front of 500 yards. It was a strong position if attacked from the west, but it was very vulnerable to assaults from the north, where Rodes's division was preparing to strike it.[9]

While Carter's guns were firing and Rodes's brigades were deploying against the threatening Federals, Major Brown returned from his errand to General Lee. Brown found Ewell and Rodes busily posting one of Carter's batteries "to the right of the road leading from Middletown to Gettysburg" — the Carlisle Road, if Brown was correct. Brown did not identify the battery or its precise position. Probably it was either W. P. Carter's battery or Fry's battery on Oak Hill. Since much was happening about that time, and neither general was an artilleryman, it seems likely that the Confeder-

Brig. Gen. Henry Baxter
(CWLM)

acy would have been better served had the generals given their attention to other matters and left the battery to Colonel Carter. Brown gave Ewell General Lee's message: "A general engagement was to be avoided until the arrival of the rest of he army." Ewell acknowledged the message in his report by observing that by the time that he received it, Hill had already engaged the enemy and Carter's guns had opened "with fine effect." "It was too late to avoid an engagement without abandoning the position already taken up," Ewell explained, "and I determined to push the attack vigorously."[10]

Ewell and Rodes had watched the movements of the Federals in their front with interest and alarm. When the generals reached the hill, they saw no enemy troops facing them. But after W. P. Carter's and Fry's batteries opened on the Union guns near the Chambersburg Pike and before Rodes's brigades were deployed, Rodes saw Eleventh Corps troops advancing toward his division's positions from the town and others moving into Sheads's Woods. He must have been aware also that the 11th and 97th regiments had exchanged shots with his skirmishers, but he might have known nothing of the presence of the rest of Baxter's brigade. Ewell and Rodes misinterpreted these movements to mean that they were about to be attacked. There was only one thing to do; Rodes, with Ewell's approval no doubt, "determined to attack."[11]

Rodes's center would assault the First Corps right while Doles's Georgians confronted the Eleventh Corps units on his left. Doles's brigade numbered about 1,300 men and stretched across the plain north of the town between Oak Ridge and the Carlisle Road. Doles's skirmishers and Blackford's Alabama sharpshooters from O'Neal's brigade screened Doles's front and extended the Confederate skirmish line to the Harrisburg Road. Although they skirmished with Devin's cavalrymen and with skirmishers of the Eleventh Corps, the Confederate skirmishers were relatively passive, while Ewell and Rodes awaited Early's arrival on the Harrisburg Road.[12]

Col. Edward A. O'Neal's Alabama brigade consisted of the 3d, 5th, 6th, 12th, and 26th regiments. It still operated under Rodes's eye. Like many other Confederate brigade commanders, O'Neal had been a lawyer and a politician before the war. He entered the army as a major of the 9th Alabama. In the spring of 1862 O'Neal became lieutenant colonel of the 26th Alabama, and its colonel in April 1862. He had taken command of the brigade at Chancellorsville, where he received his third wound. Whatever his talent for command, by July 1863 O'Neal had considerable battle experience and the scars to prove it. Yet Rodes, who had cordial relations with him, had had reservations about his promotion and had urged the War Department to assign some other officer to command the Alabama brigade. His suggestion was not accepted, and O'Neal, the senior colonel in the brigade, became its commander. However, General Lee blocked O'Neal's promotion to brigadier general, and O'Neal was one of the few assigned brigade commanders with the army who were not generals. Obviously, if Lee distrusted O'Neal's ability as a brigade commander, Rodes would have to give special attention to his old brigade in the fight ahead.[13]

Rodes reported that all of his brigades except Doles's and a portion of O'Neal's formed "in the woods." O'Neal's position was not defined. He had three regiments in his main line; the 6th was probably on the left on the east slope of the ridge and abutted the 26th somewhere short of the crest. The 12th was on the right, probably in the trees that crowned the crest. The first position of the brigade made it vulnerable to fire from the Union First Corps batteries. Fire from an unidentified battery wounded a captain and several privates of the 6th Regiment. Rodes then moved the brigade back "abreast with Iverson's" to give it more shelter. This would have placed the right of O'Neal's line on the crest of the ridge where the woods widens and on a line directly east of the Hoffman farm buildings. Fry's battery would have been posted in its front.[14]

O'Neal's 3d and 5th regiments became subjects of misunderstanding and controversy. Rodes placed the 5th in reserve on the left of O'Neal's line. It was in reserve under Rodes's personal direction, and its task was to guard the gap between O'Neal's left and Doles's right. In addition, Rodes ordered Col. Cullen A. Battle to place his 3d Alabama regiment on the left of Daniel's brigade. Capt. William H. May of the 3d thought that his regiment had been detached from O'Neal's line because of a lack of space on O'Neal's right; whether it was space with tree cover, perhaps, or between the brigade line and Fry's battery he did not say. In his report O'Neal wrote that Rodes ordered his right regiment, the 3d, to connect with Daniel on its right and the 5th on the left. This suggests that, as the brigade formed, the 3d and 5th regiments might have constituted a second line. Whatever Rodes intended, O'Neal considered both regiments detached from his brigade and not under his command.[15]

In his report to Rodes, O'Neal complained of this. He understood that Rodes would command the two detached regiments himself. "Why my brigade was thus deprived of two regiments," he grumbled, "I have never been informed."[16]

O'Neal might not have understood the status of the 5th Alabama, but it seems apparent enough today. The 3d is another story. Unless Rodes wanted it under tree cover, it is not clear why he moved the 3d from O'Neal's right and placed it on Daniel's left. Colonel Battle, the 3d's commander, wrote that it was to "keep well up on Daniel's left." Rodes wrote also that O'Neal was to have formed the balance of the brigade on the 3d, but the gap between it and O'Neal's main line would have made this hard to do. If the 3d was on Daniel's left in Forney's Woods, and the main line was near the crest of Oak Hill, there must have been a gap of over 200 yards between the two. Further, we might wonder if Rodes's precise instructions to O'Neal included the movements of the 3d.[17]

Iverson's brigade was in Forney's Woods on the right of Rodes's forward line. Iverson reported only that it was in support of a battery, probably W. P. Carter's. Iverson's four regiments numbered about 1,300 men and, when deployed in the woods, must have stretched across its eastern half. Daniel's brigade, about 2,100 strong, formed 200 yards behind Iverson's right wing. So posted, it could have extended over 400 yards beyond Iverson's flank into the open fields west of the woods. This could have placed its right at the foot of the high ground surmounted by the road running south to Herr Ridge and to Hill's corps. Although Daniel's right would have been in the open, it was concealed from Union eyes by Forney Ridge, where Buford Avenue runs today. Rodes's fifth brigade, Ramseur's, continued to march from its place in the rear of the column to Oak Hill, where it constituted the division's reserve.[18]

Although only Blackford's "Battalion of Sharpshooters," Alabamians from O'Neal's brigade, has separate mention in the reports of Ewell's corps, each brigade, like Doles's, probably had its own provisional battalion that it used as skirmishers. It may be assumed, therefore, that if a brigade was in a forward line, its sharpshooters were posted as skirmishers in its front.[19]

Rodes did not leave a precise description of his attack plan. His report suggests that Iverson's brigade was to take the lead, supported by O'Neal on the left and Daniel on the right. Iverson could call on Daniel for support, and Carter's batteries would suspend their fire as his men "passed them." Neither Rodes nor Iverson gave Iverson's objective; Rodes reported only that he "caused Iverson's brigade to advance," presumably on Cutler's brigade in Sheads's Woods.[20]

Rodes reported that he personally ordered O'Neal to attack "at the same moment" that he sent Iverson forward, and that he had indicated to O'Neal the precise point toward which he was to direct the *four* regiments then under his orders. Daniel "was at the same moment instructed to advance to support Iverson, if necessary; if not to attack on his right as soon as possible." But the brigade commanders recalled their instructions somewhat differently. Iverson's report suggests that he believed that O'Neal would start off first. He sent a staff officer to see when O'Neal began to move and reported that his brigade did not advance until he learned that O'Neal's brigade had done so. Iverson notified Daniel also when his brigade began its advance. These varied views suggest a communication problem in the upper echelons of Rodes's division.[21]

Rodes has been criticized for placing brigades having seemingly less capable commanders in his first line. No one with the benefit of hindsight would disagree, but this must not have been apparent then. Rodes had long service with all of his brigade commanders but Daniel and must have known their strengths and weaknesses. Iverson, a Georgian, had not been getting along well with the North Carolinians of his brigade, but this was nothing new. Rodes knew how O'Neal had performed in battle as a regimental commander, and though he obviously had misgivings about O'Neal's being a brigade commander, he had to make do with him. Perhaps he intended to do this by assuming some of O'Neal's command responsibilities. Doles had an important semi-independent assignment, and Rodes, no doubt, considered Ramseur a capable commander. However, Ramseur's brigade was in the rear of the division column and could not have been moved to its forward line without considerable delay. Undoubtedly neither Ewell or Rodes, if they even considered it, could have deemed such a delay justified, especially when both believed that the enemy was about to attack them.[22]

Rodes saw "that the enemy was rash enough" to come out of Sheads's Woods to attack him and determined to "meet him" when he reached the foot of Oak Hill, probably at the Mummasburg Road. About 2:30 P.M. Rodes "caused Iverson's brigade to advance, and at the same moment gave in person to O'Neal the order to attack." The general engagement had begun.[23]

O'Neal wrote that his brigade stepped off after the artillery had been withdrawn. Perhaps he was referring to the shift of W. P. Carter's battery to assist the batteries of Channing R. Page and W. J. Reese in support of Doles's brigade in its growing confrontation with the Eleventh Corps. Rodes posted Captain Page's four Napoleons on the east slope of the hill near McLean's barn, where it supported O'Neal's attack against Baxter's brigade.[24]

Rodes thought that O'Neal's Alabamians advanced with alacrity but in some confusion. Unfortunately they were "making no impression on the enemy." Rodes went to the left to send the 5th Alabama forward to give O'Neal's attack added punch. He was surprised to find O'Neal with the 5th instead of with the brigade line. Oddly enough, O'Neal and his staff had no horses at hand, and Rodes had to lend him a staff officer to carry a message to the 3d Alabama. Because of O'Neal's lack of leadership, as Rodes saw it, the Federals quickly repulsed his attack. O'Neal's repulse left Iverson's left exposed.[25]

O'Neal's troops recorded little about their assault. Col. Samuel B. Pickens, a twenty-four-year-old graduate from the Citadel and commander of the 12th Alabama, was sparing with the written word. He reported that after an hour's artillery duel, O'Neal and the 12th attacked the enemy in his strong position. After a desperate fifteen-minute fight, the regiment on the left, either the 5th or 6th Alabama, was flanked by a larger force and gave way. Capt. David Ballenger wrote of "stern resistance," and Capt. Robert Emory Park of the 12th wrote of a fierce shelling that killed two men of his company. Throughout the whole fight Maj. Adolph Proskauer, the 12th's "gallant Jew Major smoked his cigars calmly and cooly in the thickest of the fight."[26]

The 5th Alabama advanced at Rodes's order, but it did not bring success to O'Neal's effort. Cpl. Samuel Pickens of Company D (not to be confused with the colonel of the 12th) wrote of the 5th's catching up with the brigade's left at a fence north of the McLean barn, and that Company D went ahead from there as "sharpshooters." The Company D men did a lot of brisk shooting from the barn. They did very little killing because the enemy was far off behind a fence in the oak grove. From there, he wrote, they shot back, "making bullets whistle over us." After the brigade line passed the barn, leaving Company D behind, the men of the company dashed forward from the barn, through an open field, and to a lane where the regiment had halted. Pickens wrote that the troops were scattered and that he had never seen such confusion. Both of Baxter's regiments in their front and the troops of the Eleventh Corps on their left were shooting at them. Soon they fell back to a fence where O'Neal and Rodes rallied them.[27]

The oak grove in O'Neal's front covered the east slope of Oak Ridge along the south side of the Mummasburg Road. It embraced two small fields that extended back about eighty yards from the road. No one described the grove, but it is likely that slope was not arable. Probably its trees were large and scattered like those in McPherson Woods, and there was little underbrush. A worm fence ran along its southwest side, and both a worm fence and a post-and-rail fence separated it from the Mummasburg Road.[28]

After forming his brigade along the crest of the ridge, General Baxter became aware of O'Neal's threat to his right. He deployed three regiments along the southwest side of the grove fronting north. Two companies of 12th Massachusetts faced the McLean barn and were on the left of the line. The 88th and 90th Pennsylvania and the 83d New York carried the line downhill to the foot of the ridge. The Eleventh Corps would extend their line to the right. Like the Alabamians, Baxter's men left little information about O'Neal's attack. Baxter's skirmishers crossed the Mummasburg Road into trees there and had discovered O'Neal's men moving south, "cocked and primed for the fight." There was a short but spirited action, Baxter's fire creating a "fleecy cloud of smoke" that rolled down the front of the brigade. "The minié balls zipped and buzzed with a merry chorus toward the Southern line, which halted, and after a brief contest, retired to the shelter of the woods." That was about all that Baxter's men had to say,

166   { OAK RIDGE }

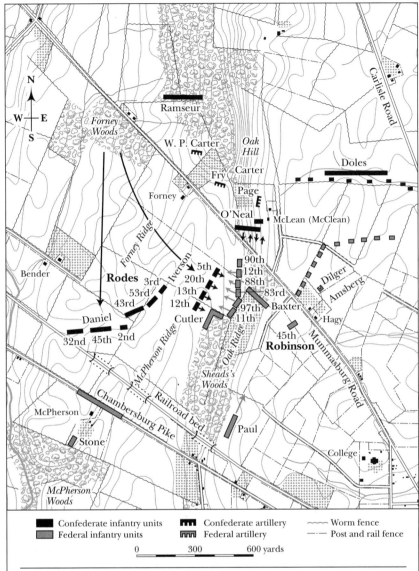

1. O'Neal's brigade attacks the First Corps right at the Mummasburg Road. It is repulsed by Baxter's brigade, the 45th New York Regiment, and Dilger's battery.

2. Iverson's brigade advances from Forney Woods and wheels left to attack Cutler's troops in Sheads's Woods and on Oak Ridge. Daniel's brigade follows in its support.

3. After repulsing O'Neal, Baxter's troops shift west to the crest of Oak Ridge to meet Iverson.

4. As Iverson's line advances from the bottom of the swale in front of Oak Ridge, Baxter's and Cutler's men fire on it, then rush forward and capture many of Iverson's men.

5. Regiments of Daniel's brigade and the 3d Alabama support Iverson on the right; skirmishers assail Baxter's men on the left; and Ramseur's brigade appears on Oak Ridge.

Map 13.1. Rodes's Division Attacks

possibly because later events loomed larger than this opening scrap along the Mummasburg Road.[29]

Although First Corps partisans were reluctant to admit it, Baxter's brigade had significant help from troops of the Eleventh Corps. Colonel von Amsberg had sent Captain Irsch of the 45th New York with four companies of skirmishers forward toward the McLean barn to ease the pressure on Baxter's right. Rodes's batteries greeted Irsch's men as they deployed in a wheat field on the Hagy farm but did them little harm. As Irsch's skirmish line advanced, it met the right of Blackford's line between the Mummasburg Road and Hagy's orchard and in the grainfields to the east. Blackford claimed that his men annoyed the Eleventh Corps skirmishers and held them off until the Confederate infantry regiments came forward, but the New Yorkers did not agree. They insisted that their four companies "pushed forward slowly, gaining ground under terrific artillery and sharpshooter fire," for 400 yards and sustained considerable loss. They then lay down behind some fences, perhaps those at the Hagy orchard, and continued to snipe with their Remington rifles at Page's battery and Blackford's sharpshooters. The remaining six companies of the 45th followed.[30]

Capt. Hubert Dilger's Ohio battery rolled into the field behind von Amsberg's infantrymen. Its six Napoleons unlimbered "on the highest point of the field," but it is unlikely that they were together. Lt. Clark Scripture's section was on the swell of ground just north of the Hagy buildings, and the other four guns were near the Carlisle Road. From their position near Hagy's, Scripture's two pieces exchanged shots with a four-gun battery, probably Page's, at 1,400 yards. Soon other Rebel batteries joined in, and Dilger's put all of his guns to work. Two Confederate cannon moved forward to a range of 800 to 1,000 yards, and Dilger's pieces fought "a heavy artillery duel" until, as he claimed, he silenced the enemy.[31]

Page's battery, by this time, had four men killed or mortally wounded and twenty-six who were "more or less badly wounded," plus seventeen horses that were killed or disabled. This crippling toll for a four-gun battery was "borne with unflinching courage." Colonel Carter had sent the battery to the east slope of the hill at Rodes's request but had not seen its position. After the battery had dropped trail, some of Dilger's guns arrived at a gallop from Gettysburg and "opened a flank fire on Page with their admirable percussion shells." Page's guns sat one above the other "like seats in an amphitheater." The battery "caught every shell & was almost torn to pieces." Page sent for Carter "in hot haste" to tell him of the battery's plight. In response Carter "dashed through a little skirt of woods

& down the slope to Rodes." He passed near enough to Page's position to see its predicament but did not stop to ask how it came to be that way. He confronted Rodes "as mad as a hornet" and asked, " 'General what fool put that battery yonder?' There was an awkward pause & a queer expression on the faces of all — Rodes included — & then he said quietly, 'you had better take it away Carter.' " As Carter started away, one of Rodes's staff told him in a low voice that Rodes had posted the battery. Later a contrite Carter observed in justice to Rodes that when Rodes placed the battery there, it was the proper thing to do. Carter had no time then to explain his outburst, and nothing ever came of it.[32]

Against the opposition of the Confederate batteries but with Dilger's support, Irsch's four companies renewed their advance until the captain saw troops of O'Neal's brigade stealthily advancing toward Baxter's right along the lane that led from the McLean buildings to the Mummasburg Road. The surreptitious Alabamians did not seem to be bothered much by Irsch's fire nor by that of Baxter's men, so Irsch asked Dilger to rake them with canister and case shot. Dilger's cannons fired over the heads of Irsch's men, who hugged the ground to avoid being hit. Although the enemy's formations wavered, the southerners pushed past the front of the 45th, whose skirmishers fired into their front, flank, and rear. In the meantime the six New York companies under Lieutenant Colonel Dobke veered left to plug the gap between the First and Eleventh Corps and shot at the Confederates. Baxter's men fired at the Confederates also, causing them to break and retreat toward McLean's barn. As they did so, Irsch's Germans peppered them once again and pursued them toward the barn. In the distance the New Yorkers could see Page's battery hauling off. O'Neal commented, "We were compelled to fall back as the regiment on the left, being flanked by the enemy, gave way." Irsch's four companies pursued the fleeing Alabamians, captured an alleged 300 of them, and took temporary possession of the barn.[33]

One of the Confederates captured at the barn asked after his brother, Cpl. Rudolph Schwarz of Company B, 45th New York. Companies A and B had taken most of the prisoners at the barn, and Corporal Schwarz was nearby. The brothers, who had not seen each other since the first left Germany, had a brief and joyful reunion. Tragically, as the Confederate Schwarz was taken to the rear, a Confederate ball killed his brother.[34]

While the Union forces were beating back O'Neal's attack, Iverson's brigade was advancing. The two brigades had jumped off at about the same time. A soldier of the 12th North Carolina remembered that Rodes himself had started them off with the words, "Boys, they are advancing upon us; go ahead and meet them!"[35]

Lt. Walter A. Montgomery of the 12th North Carolina wrote of the ambience along the brigade line just before the assault: batteries were firing, litter bearers were organizing, aides were galloping, and high-ranking officers sat "grave and silent on their mounts." That atmosphere, the thought of what lay before them, and the incoming artillery rounds produced terror, tension, nervousness, "and energy of bodily action, especially of the urinary function." However, according to Montgomery, these reactions passed when they fired their first shots. In their place came excitement, passion, energy, and the desire for victory. If such was the case — and the *complete* absence of fear seems highly unlikely for most men — the North Carolinians ran the gamut of these emotions.[36]

Iverson's brigade, which must have had a front of about 400 yards, advanced from the south edge of Forney's Woods and wheeled sharply left to close on O'Neal. It seems likely that the brigade would have turned after passing the tall east-west post-and-rail fence between Forney's wheat field and hay field, but one soldier mentioned climbing the fence. Forney Ridge screened the brigade from Union troops on Oak Ridge until Iverson's men crossed its crest. Once across, the brigade descended a gradual slope into the swale as it advanced toward the crest of Oak Ridge and Sheads's Woods about 600 yards to the east. As the Rebel line moved through the open fields, where there was "not a bush nor a tree," Federal batteries roared at it from beyond the Chambersburg Pike, and riflemen shot at it from Sheads's Woods and even from the Chambersburg Pike. After the line passed the bottom of the swale, its right regiment, the 12th, neared the northwest corner of Sheads's Woods while the brigade's left neared Oak Ridge south of the east-west fence. Some men claimed that Iverson was not present to correct the brigade's "false" alignment. We cannot know if Iverson would have done so, for at no time during the advance did the men of Iverson's brigade fully appreciate that Baxter's troops were waiting for them in strength all along Oak Ridge's crest. In effect, the North Carolinians were marching into an ambush.[37]

Only three of Baxter's regiments — the 12th Massachusetts, the 97th New York, and eight companies of the 11th Pennsylvania — faced west across Forney's fields when the attack began; the other regiments of Baxter's brigade were dealing with O'Neal. Baxter's personal attention also must have been directed toward the Alabamians. As Baxter's men were repelling O'Neal's attack, General Robinson rode into Baxter's sector in time to see Iverson's brigade approaching Baxter's thin left wing, whose weakness allowed "too great an interval between it and the line of the First Division." Robinson ordered Baxter to move his regiments from the oak grove to the ridge crest to strengthen the line in front of Iverson. He also ordered Paul's brigade to come from the seminary to occupy the grove where Baxter's right had been.[38]

Baxter's brigade formed a line on the ridge. The appearance of the ridge has changed significantly since the battle. Doubleday Avenue, constructed by the War Department for the convenience of battlefield visitors, now runs along the crest where there was no road in 1863, and there was no railroad at the east base of the ridge. There have been changes in the walls and fences too. A wall or fence ran diagonally downslope from the northeast corner of Sheads's Woods through the west end of the grove to the Mummasburg Road about 200 feet up from the McLean lane. There might have been a wall with a rider fence from the crest to the fence edging the grove and just a fence through the grove to the road. It was apparently removed soon after the battle. The fence along the crest east of the avenue, like the avenue, was not there during the battle. On the other hand, the wall that ran along the crest south from the road and overlooked the swale seems fifty yards shorter than it must have been on 1 July 1863.[39]

Baxter fitted his 1,400-man brigade into the 400-yard space between the road and Sheads's Woods. The 12th Massachusetts remained on the right with all of its companies fronting west, and the 11th Pennsylvania and 97th New York shifted left to reach Cutler's right and were down from the crest and behind the south end of the sloping wall. The 83d New York and 88th Pennsylvania occupied the gap between the 97th and the 12th. The 90th Pennsylvania swung left to the right of the 12th and extended Baxter's line across the road.[40]

The soldiers of Baxter's brigade watched the approach of Iverson's line with awe. The men of the 88th remembered the field as "swarming with Confederates, who came sweeping on in magnificent order, with perfect alignment, guns at right shoulder and colors to the front — to many a dead march." Capt. Vines Turner of the 23d North Carolina wrote that the North Carolinians marched through the grass field "in gallant style, as evenly as if on parade." Rodes, who reported that O'Neal's brigade had gone into action "in some confusion," described Iverson's as having "attacked handsomely." Yet he did not praise its commander.[41]

The men of Cutler's brigade probably were the first to see Iverson's line as it loomed into view above Forney Ridge and marched in their direction, but the nearby troops of the 11th Pennsylvania were the first to open fire on the North Carolinians. The Tarheels returned the greeting with a Rebel yell and came on. The yell and the musketry announced to the 97th New York that something was up, and its men hurried up the slope to their wall. Once there, despite the fact that they could not see over the ridge without craning their necks, they opened fire on the Rebel line. Soon it descended far enough into the swale to be out of their view. In the meantime, like their comrades to the right, the New Yorkers were targets of Confederate skirmishers in the wheat field to the north.[42]

The North Carolinians started upslope toward the crest of the ridge ignorant of what awaited them there. But there was more to it: the brigade's left advanced through the tall timothy in an oblique direction that exposed it to the 12th Massachusetts, the 90th Pennsylvania, and the other regiments on the right of Baxter's line. The 88th Pennsylvania hunkered behind the wall and "quietly awaited the enemy to come within short range." The order traveled along their line "to await command and aim low." To the left the 83d New York at the wall heard Baxter's admonishment: "Keep cool, men, and fire low."[43]

When the Confederates were about fifty yards from the wall and Baxter's line, Lt. Col. Joseph A. Moesch, the Swiss-born commander of the 83d, shouted, "Up men, and fire." Moesch rode behind his line cheering his men on, but they needed no urging. In the words of one, "The men are no longer human, they are demons; a curse from the living here, a moan from the dying there. 'Give them ——,' shouts one. 'See them run,' roars another."[44]

The surprise was complete; hit from both the front and the left, the North Carolina line reeled and staggered. The effect, wrote one, "was terrible, the one volley really striking down hundreds." Cpl. J. F. Coghill of the 23d described it as the hardest fighting he had ever seen. He wrote that they fought like tigers. Coghill's only company officer, Lt. Charles W. Champion, was among the killed. A veteran observed with pride that "the line did not recoil as O'Neal's had done."[45]

The Tarheels could not safely retreat over the open, bullet-swept field, and many who tried were shot down. Nor could they advance — "to rise from the ground meant certain death." Some attempted to continue their attack, but Northern bullets felled them in their tracks. Col. Daniel H. Christie of the 23d North Carolina tried to lead a charge from the swale and fell mortally wounded. "Unable to advance, unwilling to retreat," the brigade hugged the ground — some in muddy shallow depressions on the slope. For the men in blue on the ridge crest, it was like shooting fish in a barrel, except that some of the fish, along with the skirmishers near the Mummasburg Road, could shoot back. Sgt. Harry Evans and 1st Sgt. John Witmoyer, who were together behind the wall, shot at the North Carolinians "industriously." As they did so, they saw a brave color-bearer in front of the Confederate line defiantly waving his flag. Said Evans as he raised his rifle to his shoulder, "John, I will give those colors a whack." As soon as Evans said this, Witmoyer heard the dull thud of a bullet striking a body. He turned to Evans and asked if he was hit. "The sergeant did not reply, but slowly bringing his musket down, fell over dead, the ball having pierced his heart."[46]

Baxter's men steadied their rifles on the wall and shot away. Lt. Samuel Boone of the 88th saw that his men were behaving "splendidly" and that they needed little supervision from him. He took the rifle of a wounded man and some cartridges and caps and "done some wicked firing into the mass of Confederate soldiers lying down in the field within short musket range." (The Confederates captured Boone later that day. It may be wondered if they would have taken him alive had they known that he had sheathed his sword in order to have the pleasure of taking pot shots at them.)[47]

There was dismay along the Confederate line, for even those lying down were vulnerable to the vicious fire. One dead North Carolinian lay with his rifle clenched in his dead hands and five bullet holes in his head. There must have been a lot of head wounds that day. But on the right of the line, where the 12th had some cover, men were able to stand and shoot back. While firing his rifle, Sgt. Thomas H. White felt a stinging in his hand. He turned to his lieutenant, shaking it and saying, "That fellow stung me pretty sharp." Sharper than first thought: he turned pale and sank to the earth. The bullet had passed through his hand and a lung before leaving his body. Yet he survived, was taken prisoner, and lived to become a family man.[48]

Unlike Sergeant White, most of the men of the 12th North Carolina on the brigade's right did not share the bad luck of the regiments to their left. They were behind a "knoll" a hundred yards from the corner of Sheads's Woods. This swell of ground sheltered the 12th from the fire of Cutler's brigade in the nearby woods, the regiment being far enough from the gunfire to its left not to be overly damaged by it. So the men of the 12th bided their time, still under fire until the battle took a new turn.[49]

Under the circumstances it was not long before many of the Carolinians on the left waved "white flags"—handkerchiefs or whatever else they had to display their desire to surrender. This display puzzled some of Baxter's troops, and there was confusion in their response. In the 12th Massachusetts some shouted "charge bayonets," while others with hot rifles and hotter blood shouted "fire away." To those with cooler heads it seemed that the North Carolinians could be had for the plucking. Perhaps, as some North Carolinians later believed, Union commanders had seen Ramseur's brigade coming to the Carolinians' aid and determined to reap a harvest while they could. Some Union officers wondered about a Confederate trap, but Baxter resolved the dilemma by shouting, "Up boys, and give them steel."[50]

Near Baxter's left, Lt. Col. John P. Spofford of the 97th, who was on horseback and had a better view of the Confederate line than those around him, saw confusion in the Confederate ranks and shouted, "Boys of the 97th, let us go for them and capture them." At Spofford's command the New Yorkers and the men of the 11th Pennsylvania on their left followed their flags over the wall and rushed the Confederate line. Colonel Wheelock, the 97th's commander, was on foot at the time and did not see what Spofford had seen. He was taken by surprise by Spofford's action but approved it and followed his men.[51]

Col. James L. Bates of the 12th Massachusetts and his adjutant, Lt. Charles C. Wehrum, watched as O'Neal's men rallied near McLean's barn, and Bates observed some move toward his left. Seeing this, Wehrum rushed to the left wing of the 12th's line. He arrived in time to see many men in Iverson's prone line waving tokens of surrender. He heard confused shouting—a Babel of commands and advice. No one seemed to be in charge. Wehrum spoke to Sgt. George Kimball, who had been wounded but was resting his rifle on the wall in an effort to take a last shot. Wehrum asked, "What's the order?" Kimball replied, "Forward." Without hesitation, Wehrum, who was "always quick and impulsive," jumped the wall, shouting, "Forward 12th!" Fifty men followed him down the slope. As he vaulted the wall, Wehrum saw that a large number of troops from the regiments to his left were going forward also.[52]

After the war, Captain Hall of the 97th insisted that his regiment and the 11th Pennsylvania had gone out to bring in the surrendering North Carolinians, helped a little by a few men of the 12th Massachusetts. He denied the truth of Wehrum's accounts, which he had seen in the *National Tribune*. Hall contended that the 12th was formed north of the cross fence between the wheat field and the hay field and could not have gotten over it to take part in the movement. In turn, Wehrum denied Hall's argument, saying that Hall, as a company commander, should have been busy with his company and would not have known what the 12th was doing. Both men seemed to have forgotten that the 83d New York and the 88th Pennsylvania were on the line between them and took part in the action as well.[53]

There were those who thought that Baxter's advance was not a charge in the usual sense of the word. Sergeant Kimball wrote that "it was not a charge at all, only a run forward to drive in Iverson's men who were willing enough to surrender." Wehrum agreed. In truth, the North Carolinians probably did not know what to do; most of their leaders were dead or wounded, and many of the men were numbed and baffled. Some of them played dead; others waited helplessly to be shot. Suddenly Baxter's men were among them, brandishing bayonets and clubbed muskets in an attempt to herd them into captivity. Some North Carolinians dropped their pieces, stood, or ran to meet their captors and passed through their lines as prisoners. Lieutenant Boone, who had discarded his rifle and drawn his sword, met a Tarheel running toward him "still carrying his musket at trail arms." Boone assumed the man meant mischief and shouted, "Drop your arms, and get back quick." At the same time he swatted the man across the back with the flat of his sword's blade. Only then did he see that the man had been wounded and blood was running from beneath his cartridge belt. Boone figured later that the man had been too preoccupied to think of dropping his rifle. In the heat of the fight Boone had taken pleasure in potting the North Carolinians; now he felt sorry for hitting this wounded man and bore a feeling of guilt about it into the postwar years.[54]

General Robinson reported the capture of 1,000 men and 3 flags. The Tarheels surrendered in droves and went to the rear, where Capt. Benjamin F. Cook, the division provost marshal, collected them and turned them over to the Eleventh Corps. The 97th's writers claimed that Baxter's men captured 400 Confederates, and Colonel Wheelock reported that the 97th had taken 213 from the 23d North Carolina alone. The "Return of Casualties" for the Army of Northern Virginia listed 308 missing from Iverson's brigade, but that can hardly have been accurate. Iverson did not report the number captured; he mentioned only that he left 500 men lying "on a line as straight as a dress parade."[55]

Baxter's men captured the colors of the 20th and 23d regiments. Sgt. Sylvester Riley of the 97th brought in the colors of the 20th and turned the flag over to Lt. Ebenezer B. Harrington of Company C. In turn, Harrington gave it to Colonel Wheelock. Wheelock waved the flag defiantly and attracted fire. General Baxter witnessed this bravado and told Wheelock to send the flag to the rear for safekeeping. Wheelock supposedly replied, "My regiment captured those colors and will keep them." When Baxter ordered him in arrest, Wheelock responded by having an officer hold the staff while he cut the captured flag from it with his sword. Wheelock then waved the torn flag and the officer its staff "in a taunting manner." This foolishness ended when a bullet hit the officer in the forehead and killed him.[56]

The 88th Pennsylvania captured the flag of the 23d North Carolina in a two-man effort. Capt. Joseph H. Richard of Company E went for the flag, but the color-bearer refused to give it up. The two wrestled over it until 1st Sgt. Richard L. Gilligan came to Richard's aid. Gilligan knocked the color-bearer down with the butt of his rifle, and Richard took the flag. Gilligan later became a captain and in 1892 received the Medal of Honor for the job that he had done with his rifle butt. The gallant color-bearer, if he survived, had only a bashed head as his reward.[57]

The Union sweep forward must have been hurried, for danger loomed nearby. Confederate skirmishers had taken over the wheat field along the Mummasburg Road as soon as Dick Coulter's two regiments had gone to the left of Baxter's position. They had fretted Baxter's line with annoying and lethal shots, and they shot at Baxter's troops when they left the cover of their wall to round up Iverson's men. Unfortunately, their bullets were not discriminating; they struck the captives as well as their captors. The situation worsened when a line of battle appeared — perhaps it was from Ramseur's brigade, or it might have been the 3d Alabama in its search of a place to fight. It poured a "destructive enfilading fire" into the mass of men that Lieutenant Boone thought killed as many Confederates as their captors. Boone recalled that "the course of the bullets could be seen cutting the high grass as if done by electricity."[58]

In the meantime the survivors of Iverson's brigade not captured waited anxiously for help. It was not a long delay, for Ramseur was launching his brigade's attack. By this time smoke probably shrouded the swale and partially concealed the remainder of Iverson's line from the view of the Federals on the ridge. Corporal Coghill and other sharpshooters on the left were told to get away if they could. Coghill slowly retreated, looking back at the Federals and at Ramseur's brigade that was coming in as he went.[59]

The smoke, confusion, and distraction caused by the appearance of Ramseur's men permitted Capt. Don Halsey, Iverson's adjutant, to try to organize the brigade for further use. This must have been a nearly impossible task, for most of the field officers had been killed or wounded and the regimental organizations must have been a wreck. Only the 12th North Carolina had come out well. It had halted in a sheltered spot afforded by a slight rise in front of Sheads's Woods, and a gap separated it from the brigade line on its left. Lt. Col. William S. Davis, its commander, wrote that he and his 175 officers and men had felt very much alone. Fortunately Cutler's regiments had not been as aggressive as Baxter's and had not molested his small force.[60]

Baxter's brigade, now joined by Paul's, would soon be attacked again. Ramseur's brigade, with the help of Daniel's and some survivors of O'Neal's and Iverson's brigades, would soon give Robinson's division more than it could handle.

Rodes's opening attack had been bitter for both O'Neal and Iverson. Although criticized by Rodes, O'Neal retained the good will of his regimental commanders. Iverson did not. He had not gotten along with his officers before the battle, and afterward they pulled no punches in condemning him. They accused him of sending the brigade forward without a screen of skirmishers; they accused him of allowing it to have a "false" alignment that exposed its left to Baxter's line; but most of all they criticized him for not having gone forward with the brigade — in fact, one rumor held that he had remained in the rear behind a large chestnut log and that "more than once he reminded his staff that for more than one at a time to look over was an unnecessary exposure of person." Another rumor that was circulated by a member of Ramseur's brigade and probably retold throughout the division was that Iverson was "drunk . . . and a coward besides," and that he "was off hiding somewhere" and "his brigade, commanded by an unnamed lieutenant colonel, was beaten by the Yankees."[61]

Iverson's alleged conduct produced not only criticism but also threats. Col. Daniel H. Christie, commander of the 23d North Carolina, who had been mortally wounded while trying to launch a charge from the swale, had called the survivors of the 23d together in the yard of a house along the Mummasburg Road. From its front porch he had "with much feeling assured them that he might never live to again lead them [into] battle but he would see that 'The imbecile Iverson never should.' "[62]

Iverson's report suggests that he was less delinquent and more active than his critics were disposed to recognize. He did put out skirmishers — Corporal Coghill and probably the skirmishers in the hay field west of Oak Ridge were from his brigade. He prepared the brigade for its offensive, and he attempted to coordinate its attack with Daniel and O'Neal. During the assault he sought support from Daniel, and he tried to launch a charge at the end of the fight with the 12th North Carolina and the 3d Alabama, but the attempt failed. He had conferred with Ramseur on the enemy's position, and after Ramseur's attack began, he ordered his survivors into Sheads's Woods. Then, "going to the front," he stopped Ramseur's men from firing into his. Late in the day, "having few troops left," he attached them to Ramseur's brigade. But what he did not do outweighed his positive efforts. He did not lead his brigade in its advance, and because of its misfortune, that was unforgivable.[63]

Ewell's report mentioned Iverson in connection with "the unfortunate mistake" of telling Rodes that one of his regiments had surrendered. He also credited Captain Halsey, not Iverson, of rallying the brigade, assuming command, and restoring order to the line. Rodes's report said nothing personal of Iverson. Rodes reviewed what the brigade had done and even mentioned that Captain Halsey had tried to prepare its remnants for further action. At the close of his report, when Rodes praised and thanked selected individuals, including Captain Halsey for good performance, Iverson's name, like O'Neal's, was conspicuously absent. Iverson remained in command of the brigade until the end of the campaign, and then he went off to Georgia to organize its state troops. He did not return to the Army of Northern Virginia.[64]

After the war Capt. Vines E. Turner and Sgt. Henry C. Wall of the 23d regiment wrote an epitaph for the brigade at Gettysburg. It said, ". . . unwarned, unlead as a brigade, went forward Iverson's deserted band to its doom. Deep and long must the desolate homes and orphan children of North Carolina rue the rashness of that hour."[65]

CHAPTER 14

Daniel's and Ramseur's Brigades Attack

Brig. Gen. Junius Daniel's North Carolina brigade numbered about 2,100 officers and men. It was the largest in Ewell's corps and one of the strongest in the army. It was large, in part, because it had been posted in North Carolina and Virginia after the Peninsular Campaign and had not shared the Army of Northern Virginia's recent casualties. Daniel was born in the Old North State in 1828 and had graduated from West Point in 1851. He spent nine years in the army before resigning his lieutenancy in 1858 to manage a family plantation in Louisiana. When war came, he left his plantation to serve as colonel of the 14th North Carolina Regiment. He commanded a brigade on the Peninsula and became a brigadier general on 1 September 1862. Daniel's brigade joined Rodes's division in Virginia as a result of the army's reorganization after Chancellorsville and in time for it to take part in the invasion of Pennsylvania.[1]

After reaching Oak Hill, Daniel's Tarheels took position in the west half of Forney's Woods and the fields beyond. Their task was to support Iverson's brigade, to their left front, and to guard the division's right. To this end, Daniel posted the brigade's left wing 200 yards behind the right of Iverson's line. So placed, Daniel's brigade could have extended as much as 450 yards beyond Iverson's right 200 yards into the open fields not far from Davis's brigade—the left of Hill's corps. After his men filled this "skirt of woods," Daniel ordered them to lie down to avoid artillery fire that might come crashing their way.[2]

The shelling that bothered Iverson's and Daniel's brigades must have been directed at W. P. Carter's battery by the batteries of the Federal First

Brig. Gen. Junius Daniel
(CWLM)

Corps. If so, it seems unlikely that it would have been close enough to have threatened Daniel's brigade, but it did. Lt. Col. Wharton J. Green, a staff officer, and Daniel were standing with their horses in front of Daniel's line when a shell exploded nearby and killed or wounded thirteen men. During the hour and a half that the brigade waited there, Daniel told Capt. William M. Hammond that his only regrets were that some of his regiments were not "more thoroughly seasoned," and that many men, perhaps a great number of them, would not survive the fight.[3]

Unfortunately Daniel did not record the alignment of his regiments at the time of their advance. It seems likely that the 32d Regiment was on the right, connecting, in turn, with the 53d, 43d, and 45th regiments and with the 2d Battalion. The 3d Alabama of O'Neal's brigade was on Daniel's immediate left, and Daniel learned that the rest of O'Neal's brigade was on line with his own and that it would support Iverson's left. Daniel would shift the position of his units in his line as it approached the enemy.[4]

After an hour and a half, Daniel learned from Iverson that his brigade was advancing. Daniel's brigade set off behind it at an interval of at least

200 yards. Daniel rode ahead to reconnoiter. From the crest of Forney Ridge, perhaps, he saw that Iverson's brigade had changed direction to the left and was attacking the enemy in a "woods" on Oak Ridge in his front. In turn, the enemy was threatening Iverson's right — probably from Sheads's Woods. We can well wonder why Daniel had not known that Iverson's brigade was wheeling left, but we should not be surprised. A similar thing was to happen on the afternoon of 2 July when Benning's brigade lost contact with Law's in front of the Round Tops. Human frailty, informality, and inexperience, coupled with the noise, smoke, and confusion of battle, often made plans go sour.[5]

During Iverson's brigade's ordeal, Iverson sought out Daniel and asked for his support. Daniel offered him one regiment. Iverson thought one would be enough because the 3d Alabama was moving then toward his brigade's right, and Iverson assumed that it was coming to his aid. Iverson then pointed out a large enemy force, probably Stone's brigade, that threatened to outflank his right, and he asked Daniel to take care of it.[6]

Daniel's brigade would attack units of the Union First Corps in two locations: on Oak Ridge to Iverson's right and along the railroad bed at the west and center railroad cuts. Troops in either place could assault Iverson's right. As Daniel's line moved south, the 143d and 149th regiments of Stone's brigade shot at Daniel's line from their positions along the pike. These regiments were opposite Hill's front and arguably ought to have been the targets of that corps. However, since Hill's infantry was not yet attacking, Daniel had to deal with them without delay if his brigade was to assist Iverson's.[7]

The bronze statue of Rodes's primary adversary, Brig. Gen. John C. Robinson, surmounts a tall pedestal on the crest of Oak Ridge just south of the Mummasburg Road. This is an appropriate place for it; the portly, heavily bearded bronze figure stands firmly, feet apart, at the former site of the elbow in his division's line. It looks north toward Oak Hill and the advancing Confederate line in anticipation of what was to come and with determination to meet it head-on. Although the statue captures the spirit of the man and the moment, it has one major historical inaccuracy: the general fought that day on horseback and expected his regimental commanders to do the same. Robinson had two horses shot from under him that afternoon, but he emerged unscathed only to lose a leg at Spotsylvania ten months later. The Confederates found Robinson and his two brigades hard to move.[8]

When Baxter's men returned from the swale with their captives from

Iverson's brigade, they found Paul's brigade arriving to give them much-needed support. They welcomed these comrades, not only because they had sustained significant casualties and it was obvious that hard fighting lay ahead, but also because they had shot away most of their ammunition. Because Baxter's and Cutler's brigades were not resupplied with ammunition when it was needed, Paul's men had to hold the ridge almost alone.[9]

Little was written about the departure of some of Baxter's regiments and the joint occupation of the ridge by Paul's brigade and some of Baxter's units. There were two exceptions. First, when the 97th New York returned from its sortie against Iverson's hapless line, it found one of Paul's large regiments at its old position but facing north. With unusual tact, Captain Hall did not identify this unit. Although there was only firing on the skirmish line at that time, Hall wrote that the regiment became "unsteady" and that some of its men began to drift to the rear. Colonel Wheelock posted the 97th to "rally" it. After the regiment had become "tranquilized," Wheelock ordered the 97th back over the wall, and with the probable cooperation of others, it captured eighty more of Iverson's men.[10]

The second exception involved the 90th Pennsylvania, which was near the angle in Robinson's line. Confederates on Oak Hill assailed the right of the 90th with a withering fire. To meet it the Pennsylvanians had to change front from west to north. Maj. Alfred Sellers rushed to the front of the regiment, gesturing with his sword in an effort to direct the fire of the 90th north toward Oak Hill until Paul's troops relieved it. Sellers received the Medal of Honor for his act.[11]

Paul's brigade arrived at the salient with about 1,500 officers and men, a lesser number than Baxter and Cutler had there when the fight began. Paul's brigade consisted of the 16th Maine, the 13th Massachusetts, the 94th and 104th New York, and the 107th Pennsylvania regiments. Brig. Gen. Gabriel Rene Paul was a Missourian of French ancestry and a graduate of West Point in its class of 1834, and he had long service on the frontier. He became a brigadier general of volunteers in September 1862, and since October he had commanded brigades in the First Corps. Like Baxter, he would share his command functions with Robinson, who, after Baxter's departure, had only one brigade on this line.[12]

Paul's brigade marched north at Robinson's summons. At the command "Fall in! Forward Sixteenth!" this Maine regiment double-quicked to the right. After crossing the railroad bed, it slanted northwest into Sheads's Woods, where its 275 officers and men clambered over piles of rocks and

Brig. Gen. John C. Robinson
(CWLM)

brush and deployed into a thin line about 150 yards long. Its left fronted west, and its right curved around the north end of the woods behind a rail fence so that it faced the Mummasburg Road. The 94th New York formed on its left. Both regiments confronted Confederates advancing across the wheat fields to the north and opened on them. Captain Whitehouse of the 16th, who had predicted his death, and Cpl. William N. Yeaton of its color guard were among the first killed. Capt. William H. Waldron shouted for his Maine men to "keep cool and aim low" and was wounded in the neck. A Rebel ball struck the horse of Col. Charles W. Tilden, and both horse and rider went down. Tilden was soon on his feet again and in full command. At his order to "Charge bayonets," the men of the 16th leaped the fence with a cheer, and the Rebel line fell back from behind the fence beyond the hay field. Col. Adrian Root's 94th New York advanced with the 16th. Root considered going on through the wheat field beyond the hay field and silencing one of the Confederate batteries on Oak Hill; but this seemed inadvisable, and both regiments fell back to the woods.[13]

The 13th Massachusetts, followed by the 104th New York, double-quicked north along the east side of the ridge and formed a line at a fence at the south edge of the oak grove. A sunken section of the Mummasburg Road crossed their front. Their men could see Rebels around McLean's barn. Col. Gilbert G. Prey recalled that his 104th New York advanced with unloaded rifles. It fronted northwest across the acute angle made by the road and the ridge. The 104th had not been in this position long when General Robinson ordered Prey to form the 104th on the right of the 13th Massachusetts. Prey dutifully obeyed, but he soon heard Robinson bellow, "Colonel Prey, —— you, where are you going? Form on the left." Prey noticed that he could accomplish this simply by "flanking to the left" and did so "in as good style as General Robinson ever formed a regiment or that he ever maneuvered in a brigade drill." While administering this unspoken rebuke to his division commander, Prey ordered his men to load at will so that when they reached their position, they would be ready to fire.[14]

The 13th Massachusetts took position on the right of the First Corps line. Its men could see a line of Rebels near McLean's barn, and snipers, probably from the 5th Alabama Regiment, fired at them from the barn itself. Color Sgt. Roland G. Morris was one of the first Yankees shot. Morris was a bright young man, the life of his company. He had been a student at Heidelberg when the war began and had hurried home to enlist. During the march through Maryland he had thoughtlessly gone off without permission to visit some civilian friends, and for his transgression he had lost the post of color-bearer. On the morning of the battle he begged Col. Samuel Leonard to return the flag to his care, and after lecturing him, Leonard did so. Morris was again a happy man who joked and laughed his way to the Mummasburg Road. When a Rebel bullet struck him in the chest, he leaped into the air and fell to the ground where he struggled and cried in agony until two of his comrades carried him away to die.[15]

General Paul fell early in the fight. As he rode behind the 104th's line, a bullet struck him in the right temple and exited through the socket of his left eye. Although he lost his sight, Paul survived his wound and lived in darkness until 1883. His fall left the brigade without a commander. Prey went to Robinson and asked who was in command. Robinson asked where Colonels Root and Leonard were, and when Prey said that he did not know, Robinson told him that he was in command. If so, it was a momentary thing, for Leonard appeared and was soon wounded, and the command fell to Colonel Root. Now, as brigade commander, Root ordered his

94th to charge. It did so with a cheer. When it reached the Mummasburg Road, it opened fire on the enemy battery. However, Robinson ordered Root to return his line to its original position. As Root was seeing to this, a shell burst above his head. The burst stunned him, and Root rolled from his horse.[16]

The 13th Massachusetts's line extended along the south side of the oak grove upslope from the ridge's base. The 104th was on the 13th's left; its line ran diagonally up to the position of the 97th New York, which had remained on the crest. The 107th Pennsylvania continued the line to the south. After returning to the woods from their charge on the Rebel skirmish line, the 16th Maine and the 94th New York moved farther back in Sheads's Woods to carry Paul's line south along Oak Ridge.[17]

Cutler's and Baxter's brigades continued the First Corps line to the left along Oak Ridge. After being relieved by the 94th New York and the 16th Maine, Cutler's men fell back behind the ridge, where they waited for wagons to bring them ammunition. Exactly where they waited is unclear, but they were under enfilading fire from Confederate batteries to the north. While they paused, a staff officer rode up and requested that three regiments be sent to the seminary area to support First Corps batteries there. As he gestured in the direction they were to go, one man recalled, a shell took off his hand. The 14th Brooklyn and the 56th and 147th New York hurried to the new position, probably south of the railroad bed, where they received ammunition and awaited an attack.[18]

Baxter's regiments, with the possible exception of the 97th New York, ran out of ammunition and left the line. Like Cutler's troops, they moved south along the ridge to support Stewart's battery on the north side of the east railroad cut, but no one wrote specifically where they went or if they received more ammunition. After their earlier fight, those who wrote of the brigade's movements apparently regarded this episode as anticlimactic and not worthy of note. The men were "without water, lips parched and smeared with powder; in short, they were exhausted, and dropped out one by one as the weary hours wore on." They knew of no reinforcements at hand, but they could see Hill's corps on Herr Ridge to the west and Daniel's fresh brigade maneuvering a few hundred yards in their front as it prepared to strike them. Their situation seemed desperate.[19]

While Iverson's North Carolinians hemorrhaged in front of Baxter's position, Daniel's brigade tramped south on a divided mission. It had to support Iverson's brigade, of course, but at the same time Cooper's and Reynolds's batteries were pounding away at it from beyond the pike. Daniel saw that if he wheeled the brigade against the ridge in Iverson's support, it would be enfiladed not only by the enemy's batteries but by the infantry of Stone's brigade along the pike. Since Hill was not dealing with Stone's brigade, Daniel had to do it. Daniel would prove himself to be an able tactician in dealing with this problem. Probably there were other brigade commanders as competent as he, but few at Gettysburg would have such an opportunity to exhibit their skill. To solve his problem, Daniel sent the 32d and 45th regiments and the 2d Battalion straight ahead to strike the Federals along the pike. At the same time, he turned the 43d and 53d regiments against the Federals on Oak Ridge. After seeing that the 43d and 53d were posted properly, he turned his attention to the difficult problem of dealing with Stone's brigade.[20]

The 43d Regiment had moved with the brigade line for about a half-mile before it came under fire. Halting in a lane, probably the one between the Bender farm buildings and the fields east of them, the 43d waited there until Daniel ordered it to strike Oak Ridge just north of the railroad bed. The 53d went farther to the left to aid Iverson. It formed first off Daniel's left between the 3d Alabama and Iverson's right regiment, the 12th North Carolina; then it shifted to the 3d's right. It advanced to within fifty yards of the Union position in Sheads's Woods, where Union fire struck both of its flanks. By then the Union counterattack on Iverson was over, and the Federals were short of ammunition. Colonel Battle of the 3d Alabama called this fight "a desperate one." The Confederates compelled Cutler's men to abandon the woods to the care of Paul's brigade. After their attack was over, Daniel gave his two North Carolina regiments further orders, but Colonel Battle received none. Battle sent an orderly to Daniel for instructions, but Daniel had none for him — Battle was free to act on his own. Battle then moved the 3d to the right flank of Ramseur's brigade, which was preparing to attack Robinson's position at the Mummasburg Road.[21]

The departure of the 3d Alabama exposed the 53d North Carolina's left, and it, too, fell back about fifty yards to lessen the effect of Union fire against its flank. The 53d then fronted south, probably in reaction to the fire from First Corps troops along the pike. It would soon move back toward the 12th and Iverson's line and, fronting east, would advance with the 12th toward Sheads's Woods.[22]

As Daniel maneuvered his left and the 12th North Carolina against Cutler's and Baxter's regiments in Sheads's Woods, Paul's brigade contended with Rodes's sharpshooters and Ramseur's brigade. Ramseur's four

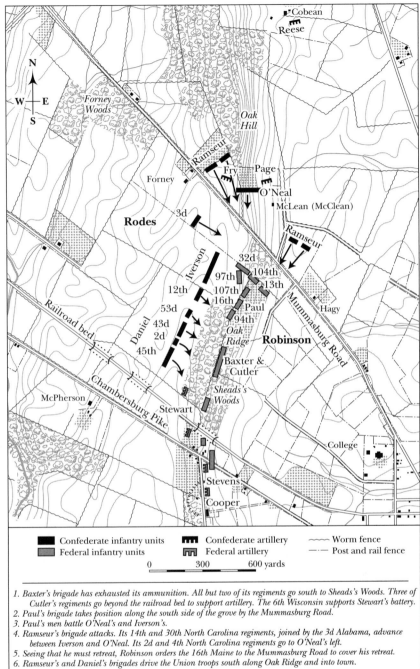

N
W E
S

Cobean
Reese

Forney
Woods

Oak
Hill

Ramseur

Fry — Page

O'Neal

Forney

McLean (McClean)

Rodes

3d

Ramseur

Iverson

32d

Railroad bed

12th

97th

104th

107th

13th

16th

Daniel

53d

Paul

43d

94th

Hagy

2d

Oak
Ridge

Robinson

Mummasburg Road

45th

McPherson

Chambersburg Pike

Stewart

Baxter &
Cutler

Sheads's
Woods

College

Stevens

Cooper

| ■ Confederate infantry units | ▥ Confederate artillery | ～ Worm fence |
| ▨ Federal infantry units | ▥ Federal artillery | ─·─ Post and rail fence |

0   300   600 yards

1. *Baxter's brigade has exhausted its ammunition. All but two of its regiments go south to Sheads's Woods. Three of Cutler's regiments go beyond the railroad bed to support artillery. The 6th Wisconsin supports Stewart's battery.*
2. *Paul's brigade takes position along the south side of the grove by the Mummasburg Road.*
3. *Paul's men battle O'Neal's and Iverson's.*
4. *Ramseur's brigade attacks. Its 14th and 30th North Carolina regiments, joined by the 3d Alabama, advance between Iverson and O'Neal. Its 2d and 4th North Carolina regiments go to O'Neal's left.*
5. *Seeing that he must retreat, Robinson orders the 16th Maine to the Mummasburg Road to cover his retreat.*
6. *Ramseur's and Daniel's brigades drive the Union troops south along Oak Ridge and into town.*

Map 14.1. Rodes Smashes Robinson's Salient

North Carolina regiments constituted Rodes's reserve. They were posted so that they could go to the support of either Doles, Iverson, or O'Neal. Minutes after O'Neal and Iverson advanced, Ramseur received orders to go to the support of both. But Ramseur would not have to attack alone; O'Neal's men were ready to try again, and the Alabama regiments, particularly the wandering 3d, would join the advance of Ramseur's brigade while Iverson's remnants kept Paul's men busy on Oak Ridge.[23]

There was heavy skirmishing before Ramseur's brigade made Rodes's final push. Some Confederates fired down into the left of the 104th New York from a stone wall where the road crossed the ridge's crest. It was effective shooting that could not be ignored. It downed seven men in the 104th's color guard, and Colonel Prey believed that if he allowed it to go on, the 104th would lose all of its men. Prey ordered his left wing to charge the snipers. When it hesitated, he stepped to the front shouting, "I'll lead you boys." They charged the sharpshooters and drove them from behind the wall. Then Prey went back to his right wing and with it captured sixty Confederates in the Mummasburg Road. Prey reported that when the detail of the 104th escorting these prisoners to the rear passed behind the 13th Massachusetts, Lt. Col. Walter N. Batchelder took charge of the prisoners and later counted them among the 13th's take.[24]

Meanwhile the 13th also captured Confederates in the sunken road. After reaching the oak grove, they saw a large body of Confederates in their front. The Yankees fired at them and advanced slowly. Sharpshooters on the ridge crest to their left enfiladed their line. One ball struck a sergeant in the left temple. Blood and brains oozed from it. The 13th left the sharpshooters to Prey and concentrated on the Rebels in its front. A Rebel "brigade" advanced toward the 13th and occupied the road. It was a mistake. As the Confederates scrambled up the road bank to charge the 13th, the Federals "let them have it in good shape." The Yankees shouted, "Give it to 'em for Fredericksburg," and so intimidated the Rebel attackers that many threw up their hats in token of surrender. The 13th captured 132 of them, all said to have been North Carolinians.[25]

Over on Paul's left, the 107th Pennsylvania, the 16th Maine, and the 94th and 97th New York battled Iverson's remnant and the 3d Alabama. The 107th fired from behind the stone wall, probably at Iverson's men and perhaps at the 3d Alabama. At one time some "excited fellows" on their right, possibly Prey's men, leaped over the wall in a charge, and the 107th joined them. The Confederates there punished them for their rashness by driving them back. The 107th remained behind the wall for the rest of the

Brig. Gen.
Stephen D. Ramseur
(CWLM)

fight. Eventually the 107th ran low on ammunition. General Robinson and his staff helped the regiment by gleaning cartridges from the boxes of the dead and wounded. On 1 July the First Corps ammunition supply did not keep up with its expenditure.[26]

After their charge from Sheads's Woods, the 16th Maine and the 94th New York formed on the left of Paul's line along with some of Baxter's men. They faced west from the crest of Oak Ridge toward the remnants of Iverson's brigade and probably the 3d Alabama Regiment. They beat off an attack and made what Abner Small, the 16th's adjutant, deemed a skillful defense of their position under the critical eye of General Robinson. During the fight Lt. George A. Deering picked up a loaded rifle and fired it without removing its ramrod. The ramrod flew off with a "crazy whizz" that set his company to laughing. The laughter sounded strange to Small in the presence of all the corpses lying around them, but it did not last long.[27]

Ramseur's brigade, supported by Fry's battery, made the final push against Robinson's salient. Brig. Gen. Stephen Dodson Ramseur was a rising brigadier known for being a fighter and for his skill in handling troops in battle. A member of his brigade wrote that he was "impetuous, impatient, aggressive" and regarded by some as foolhardy. Further, "if fighting was going on he was not satisfied if he was not permitted to take a hand." Ramseur, a North Carolinian, was in West Point's class of 1860 and, like many of the war's better officers, began his career in the artillery. He resigned his Federal commission on 6 April 1861, entered the Confederate service as a lieutenant of artillery, and in a year's time had become a major. He accepted the colonelcy of the 49th North Carolina Infantry and led it in the Peninsular battles until he was wounded at Malvern Hill. He received a wreath for his stars in November 1862 and command of the brigade that he led at Gettysburg. Ramseur's brigade, the smallest in the division, had four North Carolina regiments: the 2d, the 4th, the 14th, and the 30th, altogether numbering about 1,000 officers and men. He would need them all.[28]

After reaching its position behind the forward brigades, where the woods widened, Ramseur's regiments paused for about fifteen minutes. Robinson's men had just repulsed O'Neal's and Iverson's brigades, and in one officer's eyes, "things looked decidedly blue." Rodes ordered Ramseur to send two regiments to the right to help Iverson and two to the left to support O'Neal. When Ramseur led the 14th and 30th regiments to aid Iverson's brigade, he discovered that three of its regiments had been "almost annihilated." The 3d Alabama appeared at this time from Iverson's right. Colonel Battle asked Ramseur if he would allow the 3d to attack with his brigade. Ramseur replied enthusiastically, "Yes, N.C. will stay with you." To this Cpl. Henry Muldoon muttered sourly, "They haven't been a doing it."[29]

No one recorded just where Ramseur intended to strike with his right. Apparently he did not witness Iverson's tragic assault against the shank of Robinson's line and intended to attack over some of the same ground. Before he could do so, Lt. James Crowder of the 23d North Carolina, who was fighting with Iverson's sharpshooters, and another officer rushed to him and warned him of the dangers of attacking there. They persuaded Ramseur to focus his attack against the apex of the Union line instead. As Ramseur's left wing, the 2d and 4th regiments, was preparing to strike the right of Robinson's line, Rodes intervened. He sent them instead back to Oak Hill, where they prepared to meet an enemy advance — possibly the arrival of Paul's brigade. After a few minutes, when the Federals did not attack, the 2d and 4th regiments, under the command of Col. Bryan Grimes, moved back down the hill under scathing musketry from the 104th New York and the 13th Massachusetts and prepared to attack.[30]

General Robinson was aware of Ramseur's arrival and the threat that these North Carolinians posed. By the time that he received orders to withdraw, "all other troops" except Stewart's battery had begun moving to the rear. This would have included the right of the Eleventh Corps, whose retreat before Early's assault must have been apparent to him. Robinson's task was to get Paul's brigade off the ridge with as few losses as possible. He selected the 16th Maine to cover the brigade's retreat and sent a staff officer to order Colonel Tilden to post it at the intersection of the wall on the ridge's crest and the Mummasburg Road. Robinson rode up to Tilden immediately thereafter and repeated the order, stressing that the 16th was to hold the position "as long as there was a man left." Tilden protested — with only 200 officers and men the 16th could not possibly hold the position against the forces arrayed in opposition to it. Robinson was inflexible and replied, "Take the position and hold it at any cost." Tilden turned away and said to the Maine men standing nearby, "You know what that means." He then led the 16th north along the ridge to the road.[31]

Tilden posted the regiment's colors in the angle formed by the wall and the road. (A granite marker is there today.) He placed the 16th's right wing along the road facing north and the left behind the wall fronting west. As the Maine men took this position, they could see Hill's corps advancing far off to their left and Ewell's corps sweeping across the plain to their right. One of Ramseur's regiments appeared across the road; they saw its colors and heard its commander's shout to "fire." A volley crashed, and some of the Maine men fell. The 16th returned the fire and saw the North Carolinians' colors fall. Confederates shot at them from front and flanks. The Maine men looked for help, saw none, and began to fall back grudgingly along the ridge, firing as they went. They could not have delayed the Rebels long.[32]

Ramseur's 14th and 30th regiments plus Battle's 3d Alabama attacked the 16th's positions. They were not to be denied. The North Carolina regiments formed in the tree cover on Oak Hill, and the 3d Alabama rested in the fields to the west awaiting the signal to go forward. Col. R. Tyler Bennett of the 14th, which was on the left of this column, called out to Ramseur for permission to allow the 14th to swing to the left, envelop the enemy, and "lift him into the air." Ramseur replied, "No, let's go directly in upon them."[33]

At Ramseur's command the North Carolinians swept down the hill's slope at the double-quick, wheeling left against the 16th's position and what remained of the Union line on either side. Ramseur himself, the only Confederate commander said to have been mounted just then, led the charge on his gray mare. In later years Col. Francis Parker of the 30th, thinking of Gettysburg, wrote that "Ramseur could handle troops under fire with more ease than any officer I ever saw." A Union soldier shot Ramseur's mare as she neared the wall, but she did not fall just then. The troops of the right wing, in concentrating on the angle in the wall held by the 16th Maine, tended to converge and mass. Some mixing resulted that must have slowed their progress. Ramseur tried to move the attack along by shifting the 12th North Carolina to the right to threaten the rear of Paul's troops. At the same time, Capt. James I. Harris of the 30th extracted Company B from the mass and moved it sixty yards downhill along the wall. Colonel Parker strung the remaining companies of the 30th along the wall. As he did so, a bullet struck him below the right eye, passed through his face and nasal tubes and emerged below his left eye. He was a bloody mess, but in spite of his wound, Parker ordered the 30th forward. By this time the 16th Maine had fallen back to Sheads's Woods. The 30th pushed down into the plain, where it threatened the Union troops remaining in the woods and waited for the remainder of the brigade to come on line.[34]

As Ramseur led his right wing against the angle in the Union line, Colonel Grimes took the 2d and 4th regiments against Robinson's right. The regiments had moved under fire down the slope from Oak Hill to a jump-off position near the foot of the ridge. When the left wing advanced, Grimes's two regiments headed for the gap off the Union right. (Whatever gap there had been must have been widened by the erosion of Robinson's line and the need for the 45th New York to support Eleventh Corps troops on its right.) When Grimes's men advanced, they received a galling enfilading fire from the grove on their right, probably from Paul's regiments that had not yet fallen back. Grimes's two regiments wheeled right and then advanced around the enemy position. With the help of the brigade's left wing Ramseur drove Robinson's men from the field. The Union force left between 800 and 900 prisoners in their hands.[35]

The 16th Maine furnished its share of the prisoners captured by the Confederates that day. In spite of Robinson's order to hold its position in the nose of the salient to the last man, it fell back before the superior forces arrayed against it. When it reached the railroad cut, it halted. Not only was it being attacked from the north by troops of the 12th North Carolina and the 3d Alabama, but Daniel's 43d and 53d regiments pressed it and Robinson's other regiments from the west. For most of the Maine soldiers the options were surrender or death. An Alabama soldier pointed his rifle at Colonel Tilden at a distance of less than 100 feet and shouted, "Throw down that sword or I will blow your brains out." Tilden responded by sticking the sword into the ground and attempting to break it. His men were equally loath to surrender the colors. With Tilden's permission the color-bearers, Sgt. Wilbur Mower and Cpl. Sampson A. Thomas, tore the flags from their staffs and ripped them into pieces too small to become official trophies for the enemy but large enough to provide treasured mementos for the men who had fought beneath them. Adjutant Small and a few others ran the gauntlet into the town. They dashed south, crossed the pike, and made their way "in a fever of anxiety" to Cemetery Hill. Of 275 men who entered the battle with the 16th Maine, only 39 reached the hill. Capt. Daniel Marston took command there. In the regimental report Lt. Col. Augustus B. Farnham, who had not been in the battle, listed only 9 men killed, 52 wounded, and 162 missing. Its casualties in all categories numbered about 77 percent.[36]

Ramseur's, Iverson's, and O'Neal's brigades had butted heads with three Union brigades of the First Corps right on Oak Ridge. In the meantime Daniel's and Doles's brigades were fighting at the railroad cuts and the Chambersburg Pike and on the Gettysburg Plain.

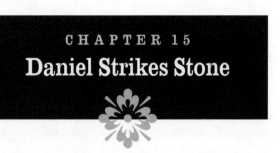

CHAPTER 15

Daniel Strikes Stone

Col. Roy Stone's brigade of Pennsylvania regiments was a keystone in the line of the Union First Corps. It had been intended that it form on the right of the Iron Brigade and McPherson Woods facing west. The arrival of Rodes's division changed that. After Rodes's troops appeared on Oak Hill, two of Stone's three regiments faced north to confront them. Thus, the brigade formed a bastion and a link between the First Corps troops in McPherson Woods and those in Sheads's Woods on Oak Ridge.

Stone's brigade numbered about 1,200 officers and men. All three regiments—the 143d, 149th, and 150th—were from Pennsylvania; two, the 149th and 150th, bore the title "Bucktails" and wore deer tails curled around their caps in imitation of Stone's former regiment, the 13th Pennsylvania Reserves, the original Bucktails. Stone, who had been a major in the 13th, had intended to form a brigade of marksmen modeled after the original Bucktails. However, if that project was not dead already, it must have bled to death at Gettysburg. In August 1862 Colonel Stone had recruited and received command of the 149th. He took command of the brigade in February 1863, and Lt. Col. Walton Dwight, nicknamed "Old Gobble 'em Up" since Chancellorsville, stepped into command of the 149th. The brigade's third regiment, the 143d, did not aspire to the Bucktail name, but in no way was it inferior to its comrades. All three regiments participated in a limited way at Chancellorsville, but Gettysburg would be their first major trial in battle.[1]

When his brigade arrived on the west arm of McPherson Ridge, on the Iron Brigade's right, Colonel Stone placed the 150th between the McPherson house and the woods. Its right connected with the 143d posted by the house and barn. The 149th was on the brigade right with "two-thirds" of its companies in McPherson's lane and the remainder in a "dry ditch" beside the Chambersburg Pike facing north. Two of the brigade's companies were absent: Company D of the 150th was guarding the White House in Washington, and Capt. James Glenn's Company D of the 149th was serving as provost guard for Rowley's division and was south of the seminary. Beyond that, each regiment had a company deployed as skirmishers along the fence near Willoughby Run. In addition, Capt. Zarah McCulloch's Company E of the 149th manned a skirmish line 100 paces north of the pike — probably along the railroad bed.[2]

The companies of the 149th along the pike were just north of the McPherson barn, which stands about seventy yards south of the road. Carter's batteries enfiladed the brigade and made its "position hazardous and difficult in the extreme." The crash of a shell among the branches of the cherry trees along McPherson's lane was the Pennsylvanians' first indication that Carter's guns were on Oak Hill. Stone ordered the remaining third of the 149th to the roadside. When all of it was there, Dwight ordered it to sidestep to the left so that as many men as possible could take shelter in the ditch. The 149th's position, as marked on the field, ran from the crest of the west arm of McPherson Ridge on the left to the center of the swale between the two branches of the ridge. The 143d Pennsylvania carried the line right to the crest of the ridge's east arm.[3]

Although its move to the south side of the pike reduced the 149th's vulnerability to artillery fire from the north, it increased the potential danger of enfilade from the west. The Confederates spotted the left of the regiment. Some of Hill's guns opened fire on it, bowling their rounds along the pike. This could not be tolerated. To avoid it, Colonel Stone decided to use the 149th's colors as a decoy to divert the enemy's fire. He ordered the two flags of the 149th placed behind a lunette of fence rails piled up by cavalry pickets on the brow of the ridge about fifty yards north of the pike and off the 149th's left. When propped against the rails, the flags would be visible to the Confederate gunners on Herr Ridge, while the wheat would hide the absence of the regiment, which the Confederates would assume to be with the flags. After Color Sgt. Henry Brehm of the 149th's color guard received his orders, he and five other men of the color guard planted the national and state flags at the rail lunette and flopped down behind it. Colonel Stone's ruse worked; the Confederates shifted their fire from the 149th toward the flags.[4]

Stone's men along the pike stretched prone to avoid the bounding balls from W. P. Carter's battery and the ricocheting shells from Fry's rifled guns. The tallest man in the 149th, who was lying beside Capt. Francis Jones, raised himself on his elbows for a look around. The instant that he lifted his head, a projectile knocked it off and flipped his body to the rear. The round, probably fired from one of Fry's rifled guns, burrowed into the ground behind Jones, and the headless man's blood spattered the captain's clothes. Jones's first thought was an odd one: he was thankful that he had not insisted that the man carry his extra clothes in his knapsack on the hot march to the field.[5]

Another shell struck the ranks of Company B. It killed two men and wounded five. One of the injured men crawled along the line on his hands and feet crying, "I am killed, I am killed." Lieutenant Colonel Dwight, who brooked no nonsense, shouted, "The hell you are killed, go back to your place." The man proved Dwight wrong by lying down on the bank of the ditch and dying. Soon after, a shell exploded under Capt. Albert J. Sofield of Company A and blew him apart. The same shell also killed Cpl. Nathan Wilcox and Pvt. Edwin Dimmick, both of Tioga County.[6]

As Rodes's division left its cover and deployed in the open fields by the Mummasburg Road, Stone could see enemy formations of Hill's and Ewell's corps extending for two miles, a line of "deployed battalions, with other battalions in mass or reserve." Rodes's formations faced a Federal position that did not parallel his own. His troops assaulting Oak Ridge would have to expose their right to Stone's line, while those attacking Stone would be vulnerable to fire from Oak Ridge. Therefore, an attack by Daniel on the lower part of Oak Ridge would require a simultaneous attack on Stone as well. When Iverson's brigade wheeled east against Robinson's position, Colonel Stone's two regiments fired at its right or at the right of the 3d Alabama or the 53d that supported it. The fire of the 143d and 149th Pennsylvania regiments was at a long range and could not have been very effective. Cpl. Simon Hubler of the 143d poured powder from two charges into the barrel of his rifle and rammed a ball on top of it. He set his sight at 900 yards and pulled the trigger. Shooting at such a range, even by Bucktails, must have wasted limited ammunition.[7]

THE FIRST ATTACK OF DANIEL'S BRIGADE

Stone's ineffectual fire attracted Junius Daniel's attention. Rodes's instructions to Daniel were "to protect the right of the division, and to support Iverson's right." While Daniel aided Iverson's right by sending his 43d and

53d regiments against Oak Ridge, he attacked Stone's line with his three right units. The 32d North Carolina Regiment on the right of his line, the 45th in its center, and the 2d North Carolina Battalion on the left advanced south against Stone's line. When they were about 500 yards from the Union position, probably at the ravine that crossed their front, Daniel ordered them to halt and lie down while Carter's guns fired over them. After some shooting, the North Carolinians heard the command "Up and charge!" and resumed their advance.[8]

When Stone saw that the 45th Regiment and the 2d North Carolina Battalion were headed toward him, he ordered the 149th north 160 yards to the railroad cut in the west arm of McPherson Ridge. The Pennsylvanians aligned themselves along its north side with their arms resting on the lip of the cut and their heads high enough to see across the field in their front. Pvt. E. A. Gearhart saw the Rebel officers stepping along in front of the gray lines and gesturing with their swords. Then they halted, a cloud of smoke belched from their line, and minié balls zipped above the heads of the Pennsylvanians in the cut. Dwight had ordered his men to "take deliberate aim at the knees of the enemy as he came up," and to hold their fire until the enemy was close enough for them to cut down "all three ranks" with a single volley. In response to the Confederate fire, the order rang along the line, "fire! fire!" The 149th fired a volley and then four or five rounds at will.[9]

As the Confederates approached Company E on the skirmish line, it fell back before them and formed on the 149th's right. Pvt. Avery Harris of the 143d and his comrades watched the maneuvers of Daniel's regiments and the 149th's advance to the cut with rapt interest. Harris, in retrospect, offered a running commentary: "But see yonder[,] boys: that line of Rebs coming from our right front. Don't they do that fine? But if they don't change direction, we will take them in flank. All eyes to the front now. They are swinging their right now, and that means us. Hark! Don't fire men until they get to the fence. But look now! There goes the 149th with their Tails just a bobbing. What does that mean? . . . I'll tell you what they mean — Old Roy Stone is after a big chunk of Glory for his Tails and don't intend the 143d shall have any of it."[10]

Obviously there was rivalry between the 143d and the 149th regiments. Thirty years later, when second thoughts were common, Stone claimed that he sent the 149th to the cut where it would fire a volley or two and then fall back under cover of the burning powder's smoke. He also re-

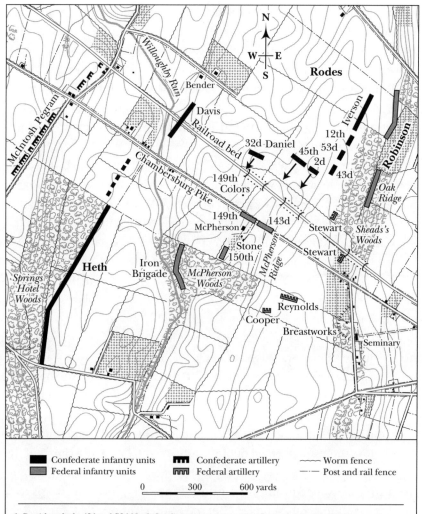

N
W—E
S

Willoughby Run

Rodes

Bender

Davis

Railroad bed

McIntosh Pegram

32d Daniel

Iverson

12th

45th 53d
2d

Robinson

43d

Chambersburg Pike

149th
Colors

Oak
Ridge

149th
McPherson

143d

Stewart

Sheads's
Woods

Stone
150th

Stewart

Heth

Springs
Hotel
Woods

Iron
Brigade

McPherson
Woods

McPherson Ridge

Reynolds

Cooper

Breastworks

Seminary

■ Confederate infantry units
■ Federal infantry units
▥ Confederate artillery
▥ Federal artillery
〰 Worm fence
–·– Post and rail fence

0   300   600 yards

1. Daniel sends the 43d and 53d North Carolina regiments to support Iverson's brigade's right.
2. With his 32d and 45th North Carolina regiments and 2d Battalion, Daniel advances south toward Stone's
   brigade at the Chambersburg Pike. The 45th and the 2d Battalion advance along the west arm of McPherson
   Ridge and in the swale east of it; the 32d is west of the ridge.
3. The 149th and 143d Pennsylvania regiments are along the road between the two crests of McPherson Ridge.
   The 149th's colors are fifty yards off its left front.
4. As Daniel attacks, the 149th advances to the west railroad cut. Firing from there, it repulses Daniel's attack.
5. Brander's Confederate battery enfilades the cut. The 149th falls back to the pike.
6. Davis's brigade does not support the 32d, which does not advance beyond the railroad bed.

Map 15.1. Daniel's First Attack

called sending the 149th's colors to the left front at this time, but in this he was confused.[11]

The 45th and 43d North Carolina regiments and the 2d Battalion met a "murderous fire" from Stone's riflemen and from Union batteries firing canister or case shot from Seminary Ridge. Daniel directed his 43d and 53d regiments toward the Union position on Oak Ridge in support of Iverson's brigade's right. He sent the 45th and the 2d Battalion to the important rail fence where "a slight eminence," a rise on the crest of McPherson Ridge, gave them a little cover. Col. Edmund C. Brabble's 32d Regiment advanced on the right.[12]

The 149th met Daniel's attack by waiting until his line reached the fence "within pistol shot" of the cut. Then Colonel Dwight shouted for his Bucktails to "rise up, aim and fire at the battle line of the charging foe." The 149th fired a "staggering volley" and reloaded as the Confederates climbed the fence. When Daniel's men reached to within thirty yards of the cut, the 149th gave them another volley before charging and driving the North Carolinians back beyond the fence in "utter confusion."[13]

Dwight expanded on Stone's account. He believed that the North Carolinians were unaware that the 149th was in the cut until they reached the rail fence. They then saw the 149th's colors off to the left, and a battalion blazed away at them, doing no harm to anyone. Dwight ordered the 149th to return the Rebel fire "by battalion." He recalled that the "effect on the enemy was terrible, he being at the time brigade *en masse*, at 9-pace interval." The enemy broke to the rear in confusion. The 149th reloaded, and the enemy rallied and advanced again. The Bucktails held their fire until it seemed that they could almost touch their attackers with the muzzles of their pieces. After firing a second volley, they blazed away as long as a man was seen moving in the field to their front. Dwight reported that the enemy's dead and wounded covered the ground there. On Daniel's right Colonel Brabble halted the 32d North Carolina's advance when he saw that the attacks of the 45th and the 2d Battalion had been beaten back.[14]

The 149th owed a share of its success to the 143d Regiment. The 143d covered the 149th's right and the trough between the two arms of McPherson Ridge — a natural avenue for advance that provided some cover from artillery and infantry fire from Oak Ridge and Seminary Ridge. Col. Edmund Dana wrote that Daniel had attacked the brigade's entire front, and though he credited the 149th for its advance to the cut, he insisted that both regiments had received the Tarheels with an effective fire that had driven them back in confusion.[15]

After the 149th repulsed the Confederate attack, it withdrew from the cut to the ditch south of the pike. Daniel thought that his attack had driven the 149th from the cut, but there was a better reason for its withdrawal. A Confederate battery on Herr Ridge had been firing down the railroad bed, making the cut a deadly place to be. Lt. Col. David McIntosh mentioned that the Union troops in the cut and along the road had afforded "a fine opportunity" for Confederate guns to rake them with enfilading fire. Cpl. Charles B. Fleet of Marye's battery credited Brander's battery with enfilading the cut. Fleet wrote that Marye's battery was too far to the right to fire into the mouth of the cut, but that Major Pegram ordered two guns of Brander's battery to do so. As they fired, Pvt. Martin Douglas, an Irish cannoneer, crossed himself before pulling the lanyard of his piece and muttered, "Lord be marsiful to their poor souls." It took only two or three shots to send the troops in the cut packing.[16]

Captain Jones thought that Brander's guns were firing canister, but the range was too great for that. Either case exploding in the cut or shot ricocheting through it would have made it untenable. Captain Bassler complained that the retreat to the pike was easy enough for the men in the swale on the right of the regiment, where the cut was shallow, and for Dwight, who was with them. But in the deep portion of the cut to the left, its sides were increasingly hard to scale. Some Bucktails were shot while trying to climb the steep south wall, and others lost their holds and slid to the bottom; some ran to the right to get out, and numbers on the left became prisoners because the Rebels were on them before they could get clear. A bullet hit Captain Jones in the leg on his way from the cut. At almost the same time a shell fragment struck the same leg and broke it. Jones fell to the ground, and the 149th went on to the pike. The field between the railroad bed and the pike became a no-man's land fired into by both sides. Jones wrote that "the rain of bursting shells and bullets was so thick about me that the entire hayfield was mown down as if a scythe had cut it off." Because of the confusion of the fight and of the retreat, the survivors of the 149th were scattered when they reached the pike. Having no colors to rally on, they formed on Dwight, who was tall and visible.[17]

When the 149th returned from the cut, Dwight berated them loudly for what he deemed to be their cowardice. Dwight's report blamed the regiment's rapid retreat for the loss of its colors, but this was not so. The flags had not been with the regiment and were still off to its left, neglected perhaps, but serving as a red herring rather than an inspiration and a rallying point. Perhaps Dwight's anger was rooted in alcohol, for Bassler wrote that Dwight's drunkenness during the fight "is well known to the men of his regiment."[18]

THE SECOND ATTACK OF DANIEL'S BRIGADE

Daniel's first attack had been costly; he had been unable to strike Oak Ridge in force because Stone's line along the pike forbade it. There was no time to waste, and he mounted another attack without delay. Apparently his plan was the same as for his first assault: the 45th Regiment and the 2d Battalion would again thrust toward the railroad bed and the pike, their assault aided by the 32d, which would cross the railroad bed to the west, wheel left, and take Stone's line in the flank. In the meantime the 53d would assail Oak Ridge off Iverson's right. The 43d would prepare to go to the aid of the 53d or the 2d Battalion as necessity demanded. Daniel wrote nothing of coordinating his attack with Hill's troops, so it seems likely that he believed that Heth's division was not yet ready to move.[19]

The 2d Battalion and the 45th "gallantly led by their commanders and supported by the rest of the line advanced at a charge." As Daniel saw it, they drove enemy troops from the cut in confusion, but it is likely that by this time most of the Union troops in it had already gone. The 143d and remnants of the 149th punished the advancing Tarheels severely with rifle fire. A fourth of the 45th jumped into the west cut while others pressed toward the pike. Colonel Wister, now in command of Stone's brigade, saw that the Rebel attack was losing its momentum and ordered a counterattack. The 149th charged. Colonel Dana of the 143d, which covered the swale between the two arms of McPherson Ridge, shouted, "Steady now my men. Every one of you pick your man, ready now, Fire." Their rifles spurted smoke and flame, the enemy's first line fell, and another took its place. It pushed close; Dana pointed toward the 143d's colors and shouted, "143d defend that flag." The enemy "with a determination that was brave, and which befitted a better cause" continued to advance, waver, and advance. Some Confederates were shot when climbing a fence, probably the one along the north side of the pike, and hung from it. Those who pushed toward the 143d's colors fell in a heap of dead and wounded in front of them. Private Harris believed that their bravery was "due to the Dutch whiskey they had found."[20]

The North Carolinians discovered that the deep portion of the cut was a trap—troops in it could neither advance nor shoot from it. Col. Wharton

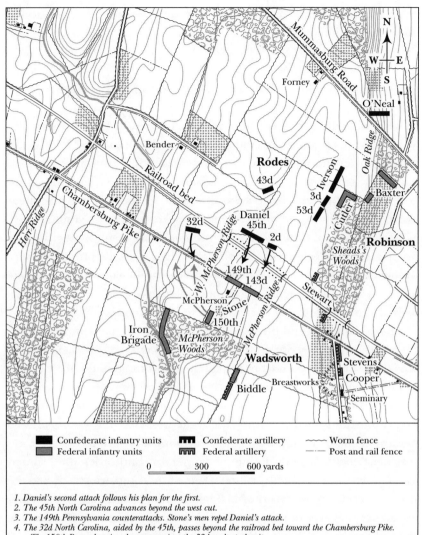

Map 15.2. Daniel's Second Attack

1. Daniel's second attack follows his plan for the first.
2. The 45th North Carolina advances beyond the west cut.
3. The 149th Pennsylvania counterattacks. Stone's men repel Daniel's attack.
4. The 32d North Carolina, aided by the 45th, passes beyond the railroad bed toward the Chambersburg Pike. The 150th Pennsylvania advances against the 32d and repulses it.

Green of Daniel's staff had picked up a rifle and gone into the deep area of the cut. He figured that he would be shot and that he should shoot someone in blue "to offset my own loss, which was deemed inevitable." After entering the cut, he laboriously scaled its south wall and saw the 149th advancing from behind a fence. He aimed at an officer in its front who was waving his hat to urge it on and shot at him. Green then slid to the bottom of the cut. In doing so, he lost his hat and ripped a pants leg from top to bottom. Nor was that all. When he stood up, a minié ball or shell fragment struck him and knocked him from the fight. In his zeal to shoot a Pennsylvanian, he had deprived Daniel of his services as a staff officer. It was said that Daniel's brigade had lost more men in "that death trap" in fifteen minutes than any other brigade lost during the three days' battle — a dubious claim but one that suggested that Daniel's casualties had been high.[21]

At some point during this action Pvt. Josiah Wolf approached Corporal Hubler and announced that he had loaded his rifle with two charges and was afraid to shoot it. Hubler, a good corporal, took the weapon from the fearful private and fired it. It kicked so hard that Hubler believed that it must have contained five or six cartridges rather than two. Hubler returned the rifle to Wolf and vehemently warned him never again to load his piece with more than one charge. The slaughter went on.[22]

During this portion of the fight, the 150th had been fronting west near the McPherson barn. When Colonel Stone fell wounded and was carried to the stable in the barn, an officer rode up to Colonel Wister with the message, "Roy Stone is badly wounded, and you have to take command of the brigade." He added that a large body of infantry was headed their way. Wister heard "furious musketry fire" along the brigade's entire line. He ordered Lt. Col. Henry S. Huidekoper to take command of the 150th in his stead. Wister divided the regiment into two wings, the right commanded by Huidekoper and the left by Maj. Thomas Chamberlin. Although Wister reported that he left Chamberlin's wing in position by the barn, Chamberlin and others wrote that both wings went to the pike to meet Daniel's thrust. The 150th halted along the pike to the left of the 149th.[23]

Rebel artillery firing from the west and north shot at the 150th when it reached its new position. Some of these projectiles, those from Napoleons no doubt, arced so slowly that they were visible to the naked eye. Most struck the ground and bounded off without exploding. One grazed the chest of Sgt. Maj. Thomas M. Lyon of the 150th, tore away his clothing, and bruised him, but it did not tear his flesh.[24]

As the 2d Battalion and the 45th Regiment advanced toward the cut and the pike, Colonel Brabble tried for the second time to swing the 32d North Carolina around the west cut "and get a position where he could reach the flank of the enemy, posted about the barn and in the woods in the rear of the barn." Aided by the fire of skirmishers in the railroad bed, the 32d flanked the cut and entered the wheat field that blanketed the west slope of McPherson Ridge between the cut and the pike. The right three companies of the 150th waited for the North Carolinians to approach within fifty yards. When they did, the Pennsylvanians fired a volley that so staggered them that the 150th got off a second round before the North Carolinians could shoot back. Then Wister ordered the 149th to attack. Drawing his sword, he crossed the fence at the pike into the wheat field and called for the 150th's right wing to follow him. Huidekoper wheeled the wing left and led it to within pistol range of the Confederates, where it fired three volleys. Although the Rebels fought back and inflicted casualties on the 150th, Huidekoper's companies prevailed. The North Carolinians retreated, and Huidekoper, in turn, moved his men back to their former position along the pike. At the same time, the men at the center and left of the 150th's line shot at a body of about seventy Confederates, possibly from Davis's brigade, 200 yards to the northwest at the foot of the ridge.[25]

As the 150th repulsed the 32d North Carolina on Stone's left, Lieutenant Colonel Dwight, in obedience to Wister's orders, launched a counterattack against the 45th and the 2d Battalion, many of whose men had halted in the cut or pushed beyond it against the Union line. Some passed Captain Jones, who must have been sure that his minutes were numbered. In spite of his wounded thigh, Dwight personally led the 149th in its assault, hobbling forward using his sword as a cane. Captain Bassler complained sourly that Dwight, "without taking time to form the regt. properly into line, headed a charge and carried the regt. back to the cut." The charge cleared the field north of the pike of Confederates and resulted in the recovery of Captain Jones and some other wounded soldiers, but it had no lasting effect because Daniel was already mounting his third attack.[26]

The fight was taking its toll on the senior officers of both sides. Stone had been shot in the hip, and though he had kept the field, Dwight had been wounded in the thigh. When walking from the brigade right where he had gone to check on the progress of the battle, Wister was shot in the mouth and face. The wound made his face a bloody mess; it prevented him from speaking and forced him to turn the brigade over to Colonel Dana of the 143d. On the Confederate side Daniel reported that his three right regiments "had met the heaviest efforts of the enemy." Lt. Col. Samuel Boyd, commander of the 45th, and Lt. Col. Hezikiah L. Andrews, commander of the 2d Battalion, had both been wounded. Capt. William C. Ousby was the only officer of the 43d killed by this time. A bullet had hit Ousby in the chest, and he died at once. His comrades wrapped him in a blanket and buried his body in a "bark coffin" under a headboard inscribed with his name, rank, and regimental number. After two hard tries, Daniel still had not seized Oak Ridge.[27]

THE THIRD ATTACK OF DANIEL'S BRIGADE

When he realized that the railroad cuts were a serious obstacle to his advance and that his second attack would fail, Daniel halted it. In "stentorian tones audible in command a quarter of a mile or more away," he ordered the 45th and the 2d Battalion to form on him forty or so paces back at the crest of the rise where they had formed before. They kept up a heavy fire from this area while Daniel prepared his third attack. After examining the terrain further, he "saw the necessity of carrying the hill [Oak Ridge] at all hazards." This could be done only by driving Stone's brigade from beyond the cut, something that he had twice failed to do. For the third time he ordered Brabble to take the 32d Regiment across the cut. Once there, it was to advance to the east with its left on the railroad bed so as to strike the Union infantry between McPherson's barn and the ridge.[28]

Daniel saw that Iverson's brigade had been bested, but he learned that Ramseur's brigade was preparing to attack the Federal position on Oak Ridge. He sent Capt. William M. Hammond to the left to order the 43d and 53d regiments to attack with the 2d Battalion and the 45th. The latter would go forward under his direct command, not head-on against Stone's line as before, but east toward the ridge. Obviously, he believed that if the 32d was successful, it would prevent Stone's troops south of the railroad bed from enfilading the line attacking the ridge. This was a large order for a 400-man regiment, heretofore unsuccessful, unless it had good support.[29]

Daniel must have known something that he did not mention in his report. Heth's division was stirring. Daniel probably saw what the troops of the 150th Pennsylvania had noticed: the tempo of the firing by the batteries of Hill's corps had increased, and its infantry was in motion. To meet the threat of an attack from the west, the 150th Pennsylvania turned its

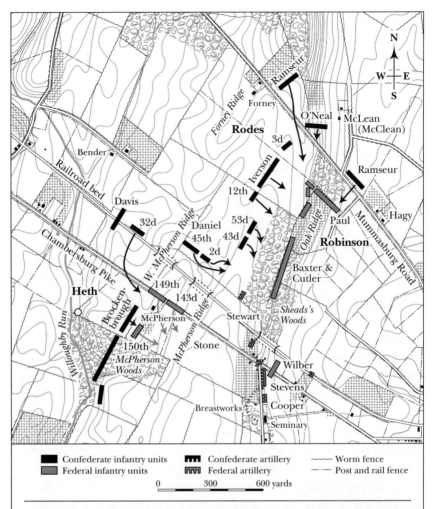

Map 15.3. Daniel's Third Attack

1. *Daniel learns that Heth will advance on his right and changes his attack plan. The brigade's major thrust will be east toward Sheads's Woods. However, the 32d North Carolina will advance beyond the railroad bed, connect with the left of Brockenbrough's brigade, and attack Stone's brigade.*

2. *When Brockenbrough and the 32d threaten their flank, the 149th and 143d Pennsylvania swing back their left, connect with the 150th, and retreat, fighting, to Seminary Ridge, where the First Corps forms a temporary line.*

3. *The remainder of Daniel's brigade, joined by Iverson's, Ramseur's, and O'Neal's brigades, drive the Federals from Sheads's Woods and into town.*

attention from the danger posed by the 32d North Carolina. "With no undue excitement, and in thoroughly good order," it fell back from the pike to its former position fronting west near the barn. As it did so, Major Chamberlin fell wounded in front of its new line. Lieutenant Colonel Huidekoper called for volunteers to rescue the major, and Sgt. William R. Ramsey and four others went back for him. The rescue party, being a good target, attracted the attention of Brockenbrough's Virginians and created the extra peril that makes such actions questionable. A shell fragment nearly hit Ramsey and the major and wounded one man in the party before burrowing into the earth. Fortunately there were no other casualties. They laid the major on the floor of the McPherson house. His calm demeanor impressed Ramsey. Chamberlin said, "Now boys, raise my head up, give me a drink of water and go out to your work." There was plenty of work to be done.[30]

In spite of their earlier successes the brigades of Cutler, Paul, Baxter, and Stone were ill prepared to meet attacks from both Daniel and Ramseur plus portions of the brigades of Iverson and O'Neal. This was at a time when the troops off their flanks were facing attacks by Early's, Heth's, and Pender's divisions. Cutler's brigade had left its position in Sheads's Woods and had fallen back to the railroad bed because it was out of ammunition. After getting more, Cutler received orders to send three regiments to the seminary area and the 6th Wisconsin and the 14th Brooklyn to support Stewart's battery at the east railroad cut. Baxter's and Paul's brigades of Robinson's division fell back to Sheads's Woods and took position north of the cut. Whether or not they received additional ammunition is not clear. The 12th Massachusetts apparently did not; it fixed bayonets instead. Stone's three regiments continued to have their hands full. They had to oppose the 32d North Carolina's attack as well as that of Brockenbrough's brigade.[31]

In probable response to Daniel's request, the 12th North Carolina of Iverson's brigade had advanced on Daniel's left. Lt. Col. William S. Davis, commander of the 12th, who was only twenty-three at the time, wrote of the 12th's attack but said nothing of either Daniel or Iverson. As the 170 men of the 12th waited in the swale without orders, Davis saw a Federal "vidette" run to the edge of Sheads's Woods in his front, look around, and dash back into the trees. Otherwise, Davis and his men saw no outposts in their front. If this was so, the Union forces in the woods seemed to be displaying little initiative and interest in their own security. Davis could hear firing on both his right and left and assumed that the Union troops in his front were hearing it too. He believed that they would run if the 12th surprised them with a yell and a charge. He told this to his company commanders and ordered them to prepare to attack. Then he sent Lt. William M. Sneed with fifteen men to establish a skirmish line in the woods about forty yards from the Union position — probably at the crest near where the avenue is today. Then the 12th itself entered the woods. When it reached Sneed's line, it charged with a loud Rebel yell. To Davis the 12th's success was "marvelous." As he saw it, the enemy fled without firing a shot, spreading panic right and left. If he was correct, it is no wonder that Union reports contained little about this part of their day.[32]

The 53d North Carolina, Daniel's left regiment, also entered the wood, joined the 12th, and then swung right and advanced to the east railroad cut. The 43d, on the 53d's right, charged toward Stewart's battery and ended its drive at the railroad cut, which blocked its movement. The 2d Battalion was next in line — Daniel had changed the direction of its advance and that of the 45th from south against the railroad bed to the southeast and parallel to it. Lt. Col. Hezikiah Andrews, who had already been wounded that day, fell in this final charge. Lt. Col. William G. Lewis of the 43d estimated that from 400 to 500 prisoners were captured by the brigade in addition to several colors, but he wrote modestly that he did not know if the 43d had captured any of the flags. Not so with Capt. James A. Hopkins of the 45th, who claimed the capture of 188 Union troops in addition to others taken earlier. The 45th also recovered the flag of the 20th North Carolina, which had been taken earlier by the 97th New York, and a "very fine flag staff and tassels." In addition, its men had seen remnants of what had been "a fine Yankee Flag." Likely this staff and scraps were from the flags of the 16th Maine.[33]

While Daniel attacked Oak Ridge, the 32d North Carolina tried again to flank the west cut. This time it had help on its right, for Heth's division was advancing and the 150th Pennsylvania, which had blocked its last try, had moved back beyond McPherson's barn and no longer barred its way. The 32d crossed the railroad bed and paused while Brockenbrough's brigade of Heth's division moved up on its right. Although the Iron Brigade fought in McPherson Woods, only Stone's three regiments defended the ground between the railroad bed and the woods.[34]

It was at this time, before the 150th left the barn area, that Lt. Benjamin Wilber's section of Reynolds's battery came from the rear and dropped trail on the 150th's left. Wadsworth had requested artillery support, and Wainwright had sent it there. It was a bad move; Huidekoper knew that

Confederates were in the woods to the left and warned Wilber to get his guns away. Protected by the 150th, probably at the cost of some casualties, Wilber's section pulled away without firing a shot. About this time a ball shattered Huidekoper's right arm, and he hurried to the barn to have it bandaged (he had already been wounded in the leg). Huidekoper had anticipated such a wound and carried a piece of rope for use as a tourniquet. A doctor took care of the wound without delay, and Huidekoper hurried back to the 150th. When he reached it, he saw that its right had been forced back on the colors and that a lot of men from the 149th had joined it.[35]

The Virginians of Brockenbrough's brigade had driven Stone's skirmishers from the fence down by Willoughby Run, and their bullets pelted the 150th's line like hail. Suddenly the firing stopped, and the Confederate line shifted right into the woods to avoid quarry holes unseen by officers of the 150th. The shift gave the Pennsylvanians a brief respite; but artillery fire replaced musketry, and another Rebel line moved toward Stone's men.[36]

The presence of the 149th's soldiers in the 150th's line suggests that regimental cohesion was breaking down. Most of the field officers had been wounded, though Huidekoper and Dwight were still with their regiments. The 32d North Carolina's pressure against the 149th and 143d had pried the left of their line loose from the pike, and its remnants formed between the McPherson buildings and the right of the 143d's position where the pike crossed the east arm of McPherson Ridge. In addition, soldiers of the 149th were sent to the McPherson barn to fire from its ventilation slits — this in spite of the barn's containing wounded men. After leaving Major Chamberlin in the McPherson house, Sergeant Ramsey went to the well for water and then searched for the 150th. It had moved, and possibly because of the smoke that must have clouded the area, he did not see it. He did meet Orderly Sgt. Elias Weidensaul, who had become separated from his company, and asked, "Where is the regt.?" Weidensaul pointed to a gap between the 149th's left and the barn and said, "To hell with the regt., let us go over there." The two sergeants and some others went to a ditch in the gap and fired from there until the Union line fell back. It seemed to Ramsey that every man was fighting on his own hook.[37]

Colonel Dana of the 143d, who now commanded Stone's brigade, reported that most of the brigade's officers had become casualties and that there had been heavy losses in the ranks as well. He deemed it necessary for the brigade to retire to "some point of support" to avoid capture or destruction. He faced the brigade to the rear. Although the men of the three regiments were mingled together, they withdrew in good order toward Seminary Ridge. When they reached the bottom of the swale in front of Seminary Ridge, they formed a line, gave the Rebels a volley when they appeared over the crest of McPherson Ridge, and charged them. This staggered the pursuing Confederates and delayed them; in fact, it must have been at this time that Scales's brigade passed over Brockenbrough's. By this time Sergeant Weidensaul had rejoined the 150th. Adjutant Richard Ashurst saw him bending over as if in pain and asked if he was wounded. "No," replied Weidensaul, "killed," and he fell dead.[38]

Dana's line continued its retreat, pausing halfway up the slope of Seminary Ridge momentarily before taking position in a peach orchard on its crest and west slope. There, amid Wainwright's batteries, Stone's brigade became a part of the First Corps line that made its final stand west of the town.[39]

Lt. Col. James A. L. Fremantle of Britain's Coldstream Guards was on the field with General Hill that afternoon. He watched Stone's brigade retreat and wrote later, "A Yankee color bearer floated his standard in the field and the regiment fought around it, and when at last it was obliged to retreat, the color bearer retreated last of all, turning around now and then to shake his fist in the face of the advancing Confederates. He was shot. General Hill was sorry when he met his fate." Fremantle did not name the man or his unit, and the incident was not recorded in regimental reports. Yet the veterans of the 143d were quick to identify him as Sgt. Benjamin H. Crippen, their color-bearer. Some members of the 150th disagreed, contending that the color-bearer seen by Fremantle was Color Sgt. Samuel L. Peiffer (also spelled Phifer) of the 150th, "a man of large stature and boundless courage." When fighting near the barn, Huidekoper moved the 150th forward, having Peiffer advance the colors. The Confederates fired at the flags, wounding three members of the color guard and mortally wounding two others. Peiffer fell with a mortal wound while "proudly flaunting the colors in the face of the foe." Major Chamberlin contended that the man mentioned by Fremantle must have been Peiffer because no other bearer would have been visible to him at that time.[40]

The veterans of the 143d did not agree. Private Harris wrote that the enemy attacked "firmly and steadily" but that "Crippen with the colors was loth to yield, and the Regiment . . . rallied upon him, and when he was forced to retire, he first shook his fist at the enemy, and defied them to take his colors, but brave boy as he was he goes down wrapped in the fold of his

Color Sgt. Samuel L. Peiffer (Chamberlin, *One Hundred and Fiftieth*, 103)

colors, and all but two of the Color guard were down, and one of the survivors wounded, when Owen Phillips the guard from our company, picks up both Flags, but nothing but the trumpets last call will raise brave young Crippen." According to Sergeant Ramsey, the 143d claimed that Crippen was the man seen by Fremantle twenty years before the 150th asserted that he had referred to Peiffer. On the basis of its claims, the 143d received permission from the battlefield commission to commemorate the incident on its monument. And so a granite likeness of Crippen still holds his flag and shakes his fist on McPherson Ridge today, whereas Peiffer has been all but forgotten.[41]

Stone's brigade had entered the battle with more than 1,315 men, and

The 143d Pennsylvania's memorial,
Sgt. Benjamin H. Crippen defies the Rebel foe (H. Pfanz)

by the battle's end had suffered 850 casualties — a rate of nearly 65 per-cent — most of which were sustained on 1 July. The 143d and 150th each had over 250 casualties on that day, and the 149th, which had fought longest and hardest, had 336.[42]

Daniel's regiments continued their stubborn fight by pursuing the retir-ing Federals until they reached the outskirts of the town. Daniel rested his brigade that night along the railroad bed. Although it had lost a third of its number in killed and wounded in the 1 July battle, it would take part in more fighting on Culp's Hill on 3 July. After the day's battle, Captain Hammond of Daniel's staff noticed a bullet hole in the crown of Daniel's hat above the center of his forehead. He called the general's attention to his narrow escape. Daniel replied simply, "Better there than an inch lower," and said no more about it.[43]

CHAPTER 16

Schurz Prepares
for Battle

Carl Schurz seemed an unlikely warrior. He had been born on 2 March 1829 in Liblar, a village on the Rhine near Cologne. His father was a school-master turned businessman; his mother, a farmer's daughter. Schurz's youthful ambition was to be a professor of history, and to that end he became a candidate for a doctorate at the nearby university at Bonn. But Schurz lived in a turbulent time and was caught up in the revolutionary movement that swept mid-nineteenth-century Germany. He became a disciple of Professor Gottfried Kinkel, one of the democratic movement's leaders, and gained prominence as a student orator. This led him to a lieutenancy in the revolutionary army and to the fortress at Rastatt just before it was surrendered to a victorious Prussian army. Fearing execution, young Schurz escaped Rastatt through its sewers and fled to Switzerland. Meanwhile Professor Kinkel had been confined in Berlin's Spandau Prison. Schurz planned and heroically effected Kinkel's rescue, and Schurz and his mentor escaped to England. He spent a few months in Paris until, in 1851, the French expelled him as a dangerous alien. Schurz returned to England, where he became acquainted with Lajos Kossuth and other revolutionaries who had taken refuge there. There he wed, and he and his bride embarked for America.

The Schurzes traveled in the East and Midwest and developed an interest in U.S. politics. They settled on a farm in Wisconsin but must have done little farming. Schurz became involved in Republican politics; he campaigned for Republican candidates including John C. Frémont and Abraham Lincoln. He was admitted to the Wisconsin bar. He became a power in

Maj. Gen. Carl Schurz
(CWLM)

the German immigrant community and the Republican Party and was "put forward" as governor of Wisconsin. Schurz campaigned for Lincoln for the presidency in 1860, and Lincoln rewarded him with the post of minister to Spain.

After a short stay in Spain, he returned to the United States to urge Lincoln to adopt a strong antislavery position and made speeches to that end. In April 1862 he resigned his diplomatic post to accept a commission of brigadier general of volunteers. It made little difference that his military experience was limited to service as a lieutenant in a revolutionary army; he had political influence and the president's gratitude. Like Dan Sickles, John McClernand, and Ben Butler, he received his reward. But the country was fortunate in his case. He was highly intelligent and developed into a capable officer. Nevertheless, he was an amateur in 1862. With only two months' service, he received command of a division in Franz Sigel's corps at Second Bull Run. In March 1863 he became a major general, a blatant political promotion that elevated him over senior brigadiers of demonstrated competence, including a fellow German and a division commander, Adolph von Steinwehr. General Howard, and others no doubt, knew that Schurz was Lincoln's friend and believed that he was working to have Franz Sigel returned to the command of the Eleventh Corps. This did not happen, and Howard retained the command.

Maj. Charles Howard described Schurz as gentlemanly and tall, with a broad forehead, curly brown hair, reddish brown whiskers, and strong spectacles. He displayed charm and ability. Schurz had been with the Eleventh Corps at Chancellorsville and vigorously defended the conduct of the corps there. The German troops in the Eleventh Corps were highly incensed at being scapegoats, and Schurz sought official investigations of their behavior that might clear them of blame. He urged also that the German regimental commanders be allowed to publish their reports and place their cases before the public, but all of this was denied them, to the detriment of their morale. This, then, was the second ranking general of the Eleventh Corps as it marched toward Gettysburg.[1]

Schurz led his and von Steinwehr's divisions to Gettysburg via the Taneytown Road. At about 10:00 A.M., near Horner's Mill, about four miles south of Gettysburg, Schurz received a request from Howard to hurry forward. He turned the command of his division over to Brig. Gen. Alexander Schimmelfennig, told him to bring the column on at a double-quick, and hurried ahead to report to Howard.[2]

Schurz met Howard on Cemetery Hill. From there they were able to see portions of the First Corps battling on McPherson Ridge a mile and a half to the northwest. Yet he and Howard knew little about the enemy they faced. At that time Howard received a message from Wadsworth that said the enemy was retiring; he thought that the Federals ought to attack. However, Wadsworth said too that the enemy might be moving around his right flank — an ominous forecast of what was to come. The message gave Howard and Schurz no idea of the size of the Rebel force that they faced. Howard decided that if the enemy force was small, they should push it back; if large, they should take up a defensive position and hold it until they were reinforced or were ordered back. To this end Howard ordered Schurz to take his and Barlow's divisions through the town and place them on the First Corps right while von Steinwehr's remained in reserve on Cemetery Hill.[3]

{ SCHURZ PREPARES FOR BATTLE }

Schimmelfennig led Schurz's division through town over Washington Street. It filed onto the fields north of the college under the watchful eye of General Rodes, whose division held the high ground that Schurz intended to occupy. Without delay Lt. Louis Fischer, who had charge of the pioneers of Schurz's division, put his men to work cutting gaps in fences between the college and the Hagy house on the Mummasburg Road so that Schurz's men could deploy in the area. At this time Howard learned from Buford that there were Confederates in strength to the northeast, a report confirmed by Schurz and Major Howard. On learning of this, General Howard ordered Schurz to halt his command, to push forward skirmishers to assist the First Corps right, and to take measures to prevent his right from being turned.[4]

Schurz ordered Schimmelfennig to deploy the Third Division in "two lines" east of the Mummasburg Road. As this was taking place, Rodes launched his first attack against the First Corps right on Oak Ridge. In response, the 45th New York of von Amsberg's (Schimmelfennig's) brigade, supported by Dilger's battery, assaulted O'Neal's left. While von Amsberg's left assisted Baxter's brigade in repulsing O'Neal's attack, the remainder of the Third Division reached the fields of the Gettysburg Plain north of the town.[5]

That portion of the Gettysburg Plain involved most directly in the battle of 1 July is approximately one mile square. It extends east from the foot of Oak Ridge to Rock Creek and from the north edge of the town and college north to the junction of the Carlisle and the Table Rock roads and to Blocher's Run. The plain is an undulating area and was covered with irregularly shaped fields of grain, hay, and pasture. It was halved by the north-south Carlisle Road and divided further by the Mummasburg Road to the northwest and the Harrisburg Road to the northeast. Both forked from the Carlisle Road about 200 yards north of Gettysburg's square. The Harrisburg Road passed the Crawford farm buildings about 0.3 mile northeast of the fork, by the Adams County Almshouse buildings a half-mile farther on, and over Rock Creek another half-mile beyond that. The dominating terrain feature within the area was Blocher's (later Barlow) Knoll. This hill rises about fifty feet above Rock Creek, which washes its north base. Other buildings in this area and along the Mummasburg Road belonged to the McLean, Hagy, and Kitsman farms. Two small streams ran from west to east across the plain into Rock Creek. Blocher's Run flows from near the McLean buildings and by the north side of Blocher's Knoll; an unnamed stream passed north of the Kitsman buildings and south of the almshouse. A third and larger stream, Stevens Run, was just south of the plain. It coursed east between the town proper and the college, passing Kuhn's brickyard and then running northeast into Rock Creek east of the Crawford buildings.

Brig. Gen. Alexander Schimmelfennig, acting commander of the Third Division, Eleventh Corps, was termed by one author as a "German victim" of the war. He had been born in 1824 in a "favored" German family in the Prussian province of Lithuania. After attending a military school in Berlin, he became a lieutenant in the Prussian army, participated in the Schleswig-Holstein War, and in six years became a captain. When the revolution of 1848 broke out, he left Prussia's service to enter the revolutionary army in the Palatinate, where he met Schurz. When the revolution was crushed, Schimmelfennig, like Schurz, fled to Switzerland and was sentenced to death in absentia by the Palatine government. He made his way to London, where he married, and in 1853 he emigrated to Philadelphia. While there, he wrote military history and secured a position as an engineer with the War Department in Washington. After the war began, he accepted the colonelcy of the German 74th Pennsylvania Regiment, which had been organized in Pittsburgh. His active service began badly when his horse fell on him and badly injured his ankle. Soon after, Schimmelfennig contracted smallpox and had a long convalescence. He was with the 74th at Second Bull Run, and when his commander, Brig. Gen. Henry Bohlen, was killed on 22 August at Freeman's Ford, Schimmelfennig received command of the brigade. On 29 November he became a brigadier general. He commanded his men at Chancellorsville and was caught up in the rout.[6]

When von Amsberg's brigade reached the fields north of Gettysburg, four companies pushed forward immediately as skirmishers to help the First Corps right as O'Neal's brigade attacked it. As they did so, Lt. Col. Adolphus Dobke, acting commander of the 45th New York, formed the remaining six companies east of the Mummasburg Road and 100 yards south of the later site of the 45th's memorial. Once formed, the 45th advanced along the road toward the First Corps right.[7]

General Schurz ordered Schimmelfennig to deploy the Third Division on the right of the First Corps, and this was done "with promptness and spirit." The 45th New York, the 61st Ohio, and the 74th Pennsylvania set up a skirmish line that extended from the Mummasburg Road toward the Carlisle Road. During this deployment the 157th New York was in a second line about 250 yards east of the Hagy buildings and in the rear of a portion of Dilger's battery.[8]

Brig. Gen. Alexander
Schimmelfennig (CWLM)

In fact, during this deployment and the fighting that followed, most regiments of the brigade claimed to have supported Dilger's battery. The battery had performed valiantly and well at Chancellorsville and would do well at Gettysburg. Yet its movements are hard to reconstruct because Dilger reported them poorly.[9]

Col. Wladimir Krzyzanowski's brigade, the Second Brigade of Schurz's division, followed the First to the field. Its four regiments halted between the Mummasburg and Carlisle roads just north of the college grounds. The 26th Wisconsin rested in an orchard, sergeants called the rolls, and Commissary Sgt. Ernst Damkoehler and other noncombatants went to the rear. They massed then in "double column on center" with the 82d Ohio on the left by the Mummasburg Road and the 75th Pennsylvania, the 119th New York, and the 26th Wisconsin in turn to the right in a wheat field. Capt. Alfred E. Lee of the 82d described the regiments as being in solid squares, deep formations that were especially vulnerable to artillery fire. Lee wrote that the Ohioans were in support of Dilger's Ohio battery and that projectiles fired at it struck men in his company. A "severe cannonade" likewise fell around the 119th New York and the 26th Wisconsin, and rifled guns pounded the 75th Pennsylvania. As the brigade waited, Krzyzanowski ordered the 119th to post a company as skirmishers to keep the enemy from a large barn, possibly on the Crawford farm.[10]

Doles's brigade and Maj. Eugene Blackford's battalion of Alabama sharpshooters confronted Schurz's division in the early stages of the fight. After driving off videttes and skirmishers of Devin's brigade, Blackford's sharpshooters ran into skirmishers of the Eleventh Corps who seemed to be making for Rodes's batteries. No doubt they were troops of the 45th New York and the 61st Ohio regiments. Doles's brigade stretched from near the foot of Oak Ridge east toward the Carlisle Road. Blackford's line extended across Doles's front from McLean's lane southeast along the Mummasburg Road to the Hagy orchard, then east across the fields to Blocher's Knoll. Blackford reported that his right company annoyed the Federal skirmishers greatly, but that his center met no more than a double line of skirmishers, which his men drove back. Page's battery of four Napoleons was on the slope above the McLean farm buildings, and Capt. William Reese's battery, with its four three-inch rifles, took position in a field of tall wheat in support of Doles's line. Reese's four guns probably were on the rise a short distance south of the Cobean buildings and about 1,500 yards north of the site of present-day Howard Avenue.[11]

While Robinson's division repulsed initial attacks, the 45th New York and Dilger's battery bore the brunt of the heavy action on Schurz's front. The 45th raked O'Neal's left when the Alabamians attempted to drive in the First Corps right, and Dilger's battery dueled with the batteries of Carter's battalion — particularly with Page's battery's guns near the McLean barn. Confederate shells directed at Dilger's guns flew over the battery and fell among the 157th New York, doing much injury. They frightened its field officers' horses so that the officers had to dismount and send their animals to the rear. According to an infantryman, Dilger soon exacted revenge. His first shot at the Rebel battery was high, and the Confederates yelled in derision. Dilger sighted the piece himself, and the second shot dismounted the targeted gun and killed some of its horses. Col. Philip P. Brown of the 157th New York shouted, "What effect Captain Dilger?" Dilger studied the targeted gun through his "glass" for a moment and replied, "I have spiked a gun for them, plugging it at the muzzle."[12]

This story is nonsense. Dilger did not claim such a lucky hit in his report, and a skeptic could wonder if Dilger could have seen the damage said to have been done to the muzzle through the smoky air even with a "glass." Further, the Confederates reported no such damage. Colonel Carter admitted that Dilger had delivered "destructive oblique fire" on Page's battery, but the corps ordnance report mentions no damage to materiel. According to Dilger, the Confederates brought up eight more guns during the duel, two of which approached to within 800–1,000 yards, and his battery damaged the carriages of five of them, "which they had to leave on the ground" after trying to take them off with "new horses."[13]

A half-hour after Dilger began firing, Lt. William Wheeler's 13th New York Battery's four three-inch rifles reached the field. Dilger had asked for help from the 13th because a battery of rifled guns, probably Reese's, had opened on him, and rifles were better than Napoleons for counterbattery fire. Wheeler's guns dropped trail to the right of Dilger's four rear guns, which must have been on the rise south of the unnamed stream. About this time, Wheeler recalled, the First Corps repulsed a Confederate attack, probably O'Neal's, and "everything looked auspicious." Wheeler opened on the offending battery of rifled guns to cover the advance of Dilger's four pieces to a rise west of the Carlisle Road 500 yards to the north. As soon as Dilger's guns began firing from there, Wheeler led his four pieces forward. As they neared the Ohio battery's new position, some Rebel guns opened on Dilger. The "overs" fell into Wheeler's battery. One shot killed two horses and took off their driver's leg. Things became worse when Wheeler's battery reached a fence that his cannoneers could not breech by hand. The battery had to halt under fire until cannoneers could bring up axes from the caissons and chop a gap in it. As they waited, Wheeler saw a shot take off an infantryman's leg. It whirled through the air until it hit one of Wheeler's caissons "with a loud whack." After the gap was opened in the fence, Wheeler's four guns rolled forward to the crest of a rise and began firing back.[14]

When Wheeler's rifled pieces joined him, Dilger sent Lt. Christian Weidman's section 600 yards to the right. At this time Wheeler saw "two gray clouds" moving from the right of Blocher's Knoll toward the infantry of the Eleventh Corps. The battle was taking another turn.[15]

Barlow's division of the Eleventh Corps followed Schimmelfennig's through the town and took position on its right. Although born in Brooklyn on 19 October 1834, Francis Channing Barlow was of New England stock and the son of a Unitarian minister. He spent his youth in New Hampshire and Massachusetts and graduated from Harvard in 1854 at the

Brig. Gen. Francis Barlow
(CWLM)

head of his class. He was admitted to the bar in New York City in 1856 and worked for the *New York Tribune*. Although he could easily have obtained a commission at the outbreak of the war, he enlisted in Daniel Butterfield's 12th New York Militia Regiment. After spending three weeks in its ranks, Barlow saw the desirability of having a commission and received an appointment as first lieutenant. He left the 12th Regiment in August, and on 9 November 1861 he became lieutenant colonel of the 61st New York Infantry Regiment. Four months later he became the 61st's colonel.

Barlow led the 61st on the Peninsula and at Antietam, where he was severely wounded. He became a brigadier general on 19 September 1862 in spite of not having commanded a brigade. When he rejoined the army in April 1863, he received command of the Second Brigade, Second Division, Eleventh Corps. On 24 May, with less than two months' experience as a brigade commander, he received command of the First Division, Eleventh Corps, which he would lead to Gettysburg.

Barlow was twenty-nine at Gettysburg, but his contemporaries said that he looked even younger — "boyish" was the term applied. A biographer described him as of "medium size, slender, with a smooth face, temperamentally enthusiastic and energetic." His youthful appearance was due in great part to his being clean shaven. Barlow obviously appreciated his own worth and was ambitious. He was also an ardent and cool warrior, brave and devoted to his duty. In addition, he was a firm disciplinarian, perhaps overly so; he carried what in a photograph appears to have been a cavalry saber rather than the smaller sword, because "when he hits a straggler he wants to hurt him." Carl Schurz saw virtue in these attributes but believed that Barlow could carry them to excess.[16]

Barlow did not like being in the Eleventh Corps. After Chancellorsville he wrote his mother of his "indignation & disgust of the miserable behavior of the 11th Corps," and he hoped that it was known that his brigade had not been involved in its rout. (It saw little action there.) He went on to say that he had "always been down on the 'Dutch'" and still was, though some of the "Yankee" regiments had behaved badly at Chancellorsville too. On 26 June he remarked that von Gilsa's brigade had been detached and that he did not care much if he did not have it in case of battle. After Gettysburg he admitted that some of the German officers had behaved well. Still, in August he wrote a friend that he had been "seduced" into taking over the First Division of the Eleventh Corps, and he observed that "these Dutch won't fight. Their officers say so & they say so themselves & they ruin all with whom they come in contact."[17]

Schurz ordered Barlow to place his division of two small brigades on the right of Schurz's division with Colonel von Gilsa's brigade connecting with Krzyzanowski's. Barlow's second brigade, that of Brig. Gen. Adelbert Ames, was to be held in echelon behind the right of von Gilsa. Schurz reported that the Mummasburg Road divided the two, but this could not have been correct; it seems likely that he meant the Harrisburg Road instead. Howard met Barlow as the latter division passed Cemetery Hill and accompanied him through the town. In fact, Howard recalled that he went with Barlow to Blocher's Knoll, but this could not have been so, for Blackford's Alabama sharpshooters occupied the hillock at that time.[18]

Barlow's two brigade commanders, Ames and von Gilsa, were very different fellows. Ames was a Maine man, twenty-eight years old and an 1861

Brig. Gen. Adelbert Ames
(CWLM)

graduate from West Point. He had commanded a section of Battery D, 5th Artillery, at Bull Run, where he was wounded in the thigh; yet he continued to direct his section from a seat on a caisson until he was too weak to do so. He commanded the entire battery during the Peninsular Campaign, and in August 1862 he became commander of the 20th Maine Regiment, which he led in the battle of Fredericksburg. Ames served as a volunteer aide to General Meade at Chancellorsville and then received command of the Eleventh Corps brigade that he led at Gettysburg. Colonel Wainwright called him "the best kind of man to be associated with." He was "cool and clear in his judgment," and he did not swear. Lt. Oscar D. Laidley of the 75th Ohio gave him a more earthy endorsement, rating Ames "far superior to any Dutchman in the army."[19]

Presumably that assessment included Col. Leopold von Gilsa. He had been a major in the Prussian army during the Schleswig-Holstein War before immigrating to the United States. He became a teacher in New York City and played a piano in some of its music and dance halls — hardly an elevated vocation for a former major in the best army in Europe. With war

Lt. Col. Douglas Fowler
(CWLM)

came opportunity, however, and in the summer of 1861 von Gilsa helped to organize the DeKalb Regiment, the 41st New York, which was composed of German immigrants. He became its colonel and led it at Cross Keys, where he was wounded. He served as Sigel's chief of staff at Second Bull Run and received command of his Eleventh Corps brigade just before Chancellorsville. His was the first Union brigade struck by Jackson's assault in spite of von Gilsa's having warned Howard of this danger. Afterward, when Howard sought to assuage his anger, von Gilsa exploded with such profanity that Howard thought him mad.

Howard nevertheless complimented his fine soldierly appearance on parade and at drills — faint praise perhaps. Schurz described his fellow German as "one of the bravest of men and an uncommonly skillful officer." Barlow called him "personally brave." Von Gilsa's soldiers apparently liked him, for they greeted him with cheers in Gettysburg after Barlow released him from arrest after a minor infraction.[20]

Barlow's two brigades entered the plain from Washington Street. They proceeded east along the north edge of the town, probably over land occupied by college buildings today, to the Harrisburg Road south of the Crawford buildings. The head of the column turned left on that road and followed it to the vicinity of the almshouse buildings. There Ames's brigade turned into a meadow on the east side of the road, and von Gilsa's formed west of it. Ames's brigade rested and watched the skirmishing between Blackford's men and some of Devin's cavalry. Lt. Col. Douglas Fowler, commander of the 17th Connecticut, ordered his men to load their pieces, and those having pistols fired them to make sure that the morning's dampness had not rendered them useless.[21]

It had not been a promising day for Fowler. On the march to Gettysburg, a staff officer had seen a man from the 17th leave ranks to dip a cup of water from a stream. The officer reported this to a general, either Barlow or Ames, who placed Fowler in arrest and sent him to the rear of his regiment. The men of the 17th waxed indignant over this and threatened not to fire a shot until Fowler was restored to his command. Fowler counseled patience. As the regiment approached Gettysburg, Schurz intervened and released Fowler from arrest; he would not have the regiment deprived of Fowler's leadership over a "mere unimportant pecadillo."[22]

Soon after reaching the meadow, General Ames requested Fowler to send a party forward to seize the bridge over Rock Creek about a half-mile north of the almshouse. At the same time he was to hold the brick Josiah Benner house just beyond the bridge on the west side of the road. Fowler asked for companies to volunteer, and four did so. Pvt. William Warren of Company C, who kept a log of the 17th's doings, wrote that the men of his company did not volunteer for this because they saw no use in it. Some of Devin's cavalry in a woods a mile to the front were being driven back; the fight would come to them.[23]

CHAPTER 17
Early's Division Attacks

Maj. Gen. Jubal A. Early's division left its bivouac east of Heidlersburg for Cashtown on 1 July about 8:00 A.M. The sun was three hours high, but there seemed to be no hurry. No one bothered to say how the division spent the hours since dawn; perhaps some officers and sergeants finished their work on the 30 June muster, and the soldiers cooked rations and performed other chores incidental to armies on the march. Early sent a reconnaissance party to examine the road to Hunterstown, which the division was to use before turning west to Mummasburg. It was fortunate that he did so. The scouts found that the road was in poor condition and not nearly as suitable for the division's march as the road west to Heidlersburg. Early therefore decided to go three miles to Heidlersburg, then south over the road to Gettysburg four and a half miles to the road to Mummasburg and Cashtown. After passing Heidlersburg, Early received a dispatch from Ewell telling him that Hill's corps was heading for Gettysburg, that Rodes's division had already turned south to there from Middletown (Biglerville), and that he should march to Gettysburg. Therefore, Early would follow the road that he was on (the Harrisburg Road) for a second visit to the town.[1]

We do not know the division's order of march. Some of White's Cavalry (the 35th Virginia Battalion) screened the advance, and Early and his staff followed close behind. Gordon's brigade probably led the main column, followed by Hoke's (Avery's) and Smith's brigades, Lt. Col. Hilary P. Jones's battalion of artillery, and the corps train — not necessarily in that order. Hays's brigade marched in the rear. About 10:00 A.M., soon after the division turned on to the Harrisburg Road, there was a heavy mist, and murky clouds covered the sky. A pessimist might have seen an omen in the lowering clouds; but there were few pessimists in Lee's army that morning, and the weather did not dampen the soldiers' ardor. White's cavalry met only a few Union cavalry videttes, who offered no real opposition. When about two miles north of Gettysburg, Lt. Thomas T. Turner of Ewell's staff, followed a short while later by Major Brown, reached Early with dispatches from Ewell. They informed him that Rodes's division was engaged. Early was to hurry his division forward and attack at once.[2]

Early and his staff passed by a woods to high ground from which they could see both the town of Gettysburg a mile and a half in their front and the hills behind it. Maj. John W. Daniel, Early's adjutant, waxed poetic over the scene. There were the town, the hills, and the bucolic landscape, to be sure, but there were also lines of infantry crossing the fields. More sinister, there was a battle in progress off to their far right. Barking cannons sent smoke billowing above the trees, and O'Neal's brigade could be seen battling on Oak Ridge. Daniel remembered hearing above "the sullen roar of musketry and cannon, the mechanical 'Hip, hip! hurrah!' of the Federal infantry, or . . . that sound once heard never to be forgotten, the clear, sonorous, hearty, soul-stirring ring of the Confederate cheer." General Early remembered seeing Union artillery on Cemetery Hill that could sweep "all of the ground on the enemy's right flank." (This would have been Wiedrich's New York battery and Heckman's Ohio battery, which at a range of two miles could have done Early's division little harm.) Early saw at once that he was approaching the enemy's right flank and resolved to strike it. He shouted to Daniel, "Tell Gordon, Hays, Avery, and Smith to double-quick to the front, and open the lines of infantry for the artillery to pass." Daniel galloped back to bring the division up.[3]

Gordon's brigade, which led the column, dashed forward. Five of its six regiments turned right from the road and formed for the attack in the Bringman farm lane. Their 1,200 officers and men, when in line of battle, must have occupied the entire lane between the road and Rock Creek. Jones's battalion "came thundering to the front with its horses at a run." Three of its batteries — Capt. William Tanner's Courtney (Virginia) Artillery, Charles E. Green's Louisiana Guard Artillery, and Asher W. Garber's Staunton (Virginia) Artillery, with eight rifled guns and four Napoleons — went into position east of the road about a hundred yards left of Gordon's line. The four Napoleons of Capt. James McD. Carrington's Charlottesville Artillery remained on the road ready to advance with Gordon's brigade. Hoke's brigade, commanded at Gettysburg by Col. Isaac Avery, dropped its packs and blankets, double-quicked forward, and formed behind Jones's guns. Hays's Louisiana brigade filed into a line on Avery's right. The 9th

Louisiana formed across the road with the 5th and 6th regiments in the fields to its right and the 7th and 8th to its left. As the 9th jogged to its position, a solid shot struck the road fifty yards in its front and ricocheted into trees on its right. This greeting must have convinced the Louisianians that the enjoyable part of their Pennsylvania excursion was over. The three regiments of Smith's brigade remained in reserve in Avery's rear. Smith's special task was to guard Early's flank and watch the road that led east a mile from Early's position to the York Pike, where Union cavalry was thought to lurk.[4]

As Jones's batteries and Gordon's brigade took their positions, Early saw that the Union troops in his front were not yet ready to receive his attack but were faced to strike Doles's left. Two Federal batteries, probably Wilke-son's and Wheeler's, rolled into position. The "glisten of bayonets could be seen above the undulations of the ground that concealed their bearers." There was the usual racket along Jones's gun line as trails dropped, the limbers wheeled to the rear of their pieces, and the crews prepared to fire. Then the guns opened, "Bang! bang! bang!" on their Federal targets. Early ordered Gordon to attack at once. Gordon was ready to go. He "drew his sword, the Georgians grasped their arms, and in a few minutes the line was moving through a field of yellow wheat like a dark gray wave in a sea of gold."[5]

Jones's guns fired first at the masses of infantry in their front. Then, as the Federal batteries opened on them, they directed their fire at the Union guns. One of the first Union shots in this duel was a remarkable one: it struck the face of the muzzle of one of Garber's Napoleons and put it out of commission. Captain Carrington wrote that such a shot was rare. He supposed it the "only occurence of the kind on record," and he was proba-bly right.[6]

As Early's division deployed to strike the Eleventh Corps right, Barlow's small division was preparing to defend it. One of Barlow's first acts was to send four companies of the 17th Connecticut forward from Ames's tempo-rary location east of the Harrisburg Road to the Josiah Benner farm build-ings on the west side of the road about 200 yards north of Rock Creek. Neither Barlow nor Ames explained this movement. It began at about the time that Early's division was arriving on the high ground 400 yards farther north and likely was intended to establish an outpost to guard the ap-proach over the Harrisburg Road. Maj. Allen G. Brady, who rode an "old yellow horse" instead of a better one that he had stabled in the town, led the four companies forward. Brady deployed two companies as skirmishers and the other two in a supporting line. They crossed Rock Creek downstream from the bridge beyond the left of the Confederate skirmish line. Once across, the four companies swung left toward the brick Benner house, "loading and firing as rapidly as possible." As they neared the house, Confederate artillery opened on them, slowed their advance, and set the Benner house afire. Brady got off his horse, walked to the front of his skirmish line, and led it forward. His men seized the house and denied it to the enemy's skirmishers. Brady claimed that his men shot five Confederates for every Connecticut man hit.[7]

Brady's advance to the Benner house was part of a larger movement by Barlow's two brigades. The terrain north of Gettysburg provided no strong defensive positions for the Eleventh Corps, so Schurz had to make the best of the ground available. Schimmelfennig's division occupied the higher ground east of the Hagy house, where Howard Avenue now intersects the Carlisle Road. A logical extension of a line here would have been east along the lane leading to the brick barn of the county almshouse and on to the Harrisburg Road. The almshouse's brick buildings might have provided a strong point along such a line. A slight rise between the Kitsman and Crawford farm buildings, an area now covered by buildings in the northern part of town, was a potential fall-back position in case the first line did not hold. Schurz did not order Barlow to a specific piece of ground, but he did order him to place one brigade on Krzyzanowski's right and the other in echelon behind it.[8]

Barlow made no report and gave no specific reasons for leaving the position assigned to him and moving to Blocher's Knoll and its environs. In a letter to his mother he wrote, "I had an admirable position. The country was an open one for a long distance around and could be swept by our artillery. . . . We ought to have held the place easily for I had my entire force at the very point where the attack was made." At the dedication of the Barlow memorial, Col. Lewis Stegman said, "Barlow, with characteristic vision, quickly realized that a knob in his front offered an invaluable salient for his two brigades and with characteristic daring he did not hesitate in trying to seize it." General Schurz wrote only that Barlow had misunderstood his order or had been "carried away by the ardor of the conflict." In truth, the knoll seemed an attractive prize; like the high ground at the Peach Orchard on 2 July, it seemed a fine place for both Union and Confederate artillery. Barlow certainly wished to keep it from the enemy. Further, it must have looked like a good place from which to attack Doles's line to its west. Unfortunately Barlow did not reckon well with Early's division.

He had blundered, and in doing so he had ensured the defeat of the corps that he so despised.[9]

Von Gilsa's brigade led Barlow's division toward the tempting knoll. The brigade had three regiments: the 54th and 68th New York and the 153d Pennsylvania — about 900 officers and men. The New York regiments numbered a bit over 200 men each and were made up of German immigrants. The 153d, a nine-month regiment recruited from the Bethlehem, Pennsylvania, area, numbered about 500 officers and men whose term of enlistment essentially ended.[10]

Von Gilsa's brigade followed Ames's to the Harrisburg Road. After Barlow decided to occupy the knoll area, it double-quicked to the barn at the north end of the almshouse cluster. At von Gilsa's order, the men of the brigade unslung their knapsacks, and the 153d tossed theirs into an outbuilding before the brigade formed en masse. As Rebel missiles whistled by them, Maj. John Frueauff addressed the men of the 153d. Pvt. Reuben Ruch recalled that Frueauff stated (wrongly) that their enlistments had expired and that they could leave the field if they desired. However, he pointed out that there would be a battle fought in their native state and that it was their duty to protect their homes. The men gave three cheers, and not one left the ranks.[11]

Lt. Clyde Miller of Company A asked Lt. Benjamin Shaum not to go into the fight. Shaum had just returned to the regiment while on parole from Libby Prison and could not legally do so. Shaum insisted on staying — "he would go in with the boys any how, parole or no parole." Since Shaum outranked Miller, Miller graciously offered him the use of his sword and command of the company. Shaum declined both, insisting that Miller must remain in command of the company. Miller then faced a problem. Somehow when Frueauff formed the 153d into a "division" (two company) front, the color division had gotten into the front line while the skirmish division formed in the rear. When von Gilsa ordered skirmishers out, the color division stepped forward. In the context of linear tactics this was a major error; a regiment's colors did not belong in the skirmish line. Von Gilsa saw what had happened and thundered, "What in —— is that color division deploying for?" This error gave Miller a chance to demonstrate his ability to command. He quickly marched the skirmish division, Companies A and F, from the rear by the left and right flanks until they were in the regiment's front. Then he double-quicked them to their place in the skirmish line. It was a heady time for the second lieutenant.[12]

Von Gilsa's task was to take Blocher's Knoll and move on to Rock Creek.

He deployed his two New York regiments and Companies A and F of the 153d as skirmishers and sent them forward, while the remaining eight companies of the 153d followed them in a support line about fifty yards in their rear. Von Gilsa rode between the two lines admonishing the skirmishers not to shoot until they had targets, for ammunition cost money and they must not waste it. Confederate skirmishers in the wheat field to their left and in woods to their front peppered von Gilsa's men with minié balls, and a battery fired at them. A shell passed so close to Lieutenant Miller's head that "the swing of the fuse" struck him across the face. A ball or fragment hit Lieutenant Shaum in the knee, and he was left wounded on the field. When von Gilsa saw men duck as minié balls zipped by them, he shouted that they should not mind the bullets; as long as they heard them, they were all right. (The same would not have applied to artillery rounds.) The skirmish line advanced at the double-quick. It rushed over the crest of the knoll, scattered the Confederates there, and dashed down the slope into the trees along Rock Creek. There von Gilsa's regiments formed a skirmish line. The 200 men of the 54th New York held the right near the Harrisburg Road. Miller's two companies of the 153d were next in line, and the 68th New York was on the left. The remaining eight companies of the 153d, about 400 men, formed a support line in the rear. It was a small force when compared with the Confederates confronting it, though the creek and its steep banks strengthened its position.[13]

About 11:00 A.M., an hour after Dilger reached the field, Battery G, 4th U.S. Artillery, arrived at a trot. Lt. Bayard Wilkeson, age nineteen, commanded it. He was the son of Samuel Wilkeson, a war correspondent of the *New York Times*. Maj. Thomas Osborn sent Lieutenant Wilkeson to report to General Barlow. The general ordered four Napoleons to the knoll; two under Lt. Christopher F. Merkle went east of the road to cover the division's right. Although the knoll provided a fine firing platform, it was within range of the more numerous guns of Jones's battalion only 1,200 yards away. Major Osborn, commander of the Eleventh Corps artillery, thought that the four guns on the knoll were "unfortunately near the enemy's line of infantry, with which they were engaged, as well as two of his batteries, the concentrated fire of which no battery could withstand." Wilkeson's guns opened at once and fired the shot that struck the muzzle of one of Garber's Napoleons. East of the road, Lieutenant Merkle's section fired at the guns of Jones's battalion before shifting to attacking Confederate infantry.[14]

Ames's brigade remained east of the Harrisburg Road for a half-hour

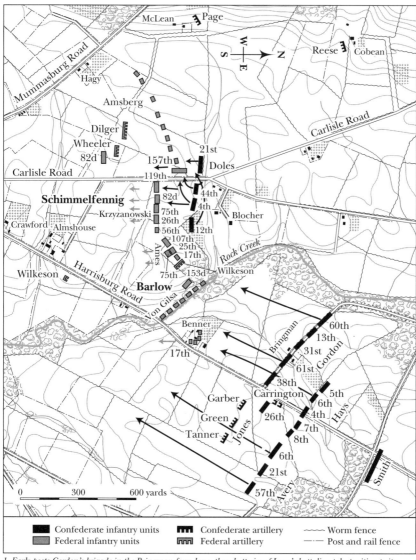

McLean Page

W N Reese Cobean
S E

Mummasburg Road

Hagy

Amsberg

Carlisle Road

Dilger

Wheeler

82d

157th 21st

Doles

119th

82d 44th
Krzyzanowski 4th
Schimmelfennig 75th
26th Blocher
Crawford Almshouse 56th 12th

107th
25th
Ames 17th
75th 153d Wilkeson
Rock Creek

Wilkeson

Harrisburg Road

Barlow

Von Gilsa

Benner 60th
13th
Bringman 31st
17th 61st Gordon

38th
5th
Garber Carrington 6th
Green 26th 4th
Jones 7th
Tanner 8th

6th
21st

57th Avery Hays Smith

0   300   600 yards

| ■ Confederate infantry units | ⊞ Confederate artillery | ⁓⁓ Worm fence |
| ▨ Federal infantry units | ⊞ Federal artillery | –·– Post and rail fence |

1. *Early posts Gordon's brigade in the Bringman farm lane; three batteries of Jones's battalion take position to its left, beyond the road. Carrington's battery is to advance with Gordon.*

2. *Hays's brigade is posted astride the Harrisburg Road, with Avery's brigade to its left. Smith's brigade is held in the rear in reserve.*

3. *Von Gilsa's brigade deploys in a skirmish line along Rock Creek. The 153d Pennsylvania forms a support line.*

4. *Four guns of Wilkeson's battery occupy Blocher's (Barlow) Knoll, and its remaining section drops trail "near the poorhouse."*

5. *Ames's brigade forms in two lines to Wilkeson's left rear.*

6. *Krzyzanowski's brigade advances from west of the Carlisle Road to form on Ames's left.*

7. *The 157th New York of von Amsberg's brigade strikes Doles's right. Much of von Amsberg's brigade is deployed as skirmishers. Their positions are conjectural.*

8. *Dilger's and Wheeler's batteries occupy the high ground just west of the Carlisle Road. The 82d Illinois supports them.*

9. *Gordon attacks, smashing von Gilsa's and Ames's lines in turn.*

10. *Doles's brigade shifts to the Carlisle Road and Gordon's right. After crushing the 157th New York, it strikes Krzyzanowski's left before moving right against the Union batteries and von Amsberg's brigade.*

11. *Early halts Gordon on the swell of ground south of the almshouse.*

Map 17.1. Early Attacks the Eleventh Corps's Right

or so after the departure of Major Brady and the four companies of the 17th Connecticut. Then the 25th Ohio moved to Blocher's Knoll to support Wilkeson's battery, and the rest of the brigade — the remaining six companies of the 17th Connecticut, plus the 75th and 107th Ohio regiments — double-quicked after the 25th to a field near the almshouse. Why did Barlow shift his Second Brigade from its post to the right rear of the corps, as ordered by Schurz, to the fields near the knoll? We can only conjecture. He probably did so to strengthen the position on the knoll and to tie it in with the remainder of the corps to the left.[15]

When the six companies of the 17th Connecticut reached the almshouse area, Colonel Fowler told his men to drop their knapsacks; they would pick them up later. Then, although the men were "all gone" after their morning's hike over the muddy roads leading to the field, the 17th "fussed & fooled around advancing & falling back, over fences and back again" for what seemed like almost an hour. All the while Colonel Fowler remained in the saddle. When his officers protested his doing so, he said that it might be deemed cowardly for him to dismount.[16]

Because of the shuffling, perhaps, the principal positions of Ames's regiments were not identified accurately. The brigade formed with its right behind Wilkeson's guns on the knoll. Its line extended downslope to the left rear of the battery and fronted generally northwest toward Doles's brigade. Col. Andrew L. Harris, commander of the 75th Ohio, wrote that the 17th Connecticut was on the right of the forward line and closest to the battery, and the 25th and 107th extended the brigade's line to the left. He placed his own regiment in the support line and later passed to the front by moving between the other Ohio regiments. Ames had 1,200 men in line.[17]

Like von Gilsa's brigade, Ames's came under fire from both infantry and artillery. Wilkeson's battery attracted fire to both itself and the infantry near it. Wilkeson, who has been depicted by Alfred R. Waud on horseback in front of his guns, "holding his battery to its work," fell soon after the battery opened fire. A shot mangled his right leg and killed his horse. He applied a tourniquet made from a handkerchief to the stump and amputated it. Four men from the battery carried him to the almshouse, where he died that night. Just before he died, he asked for water. Someone gave him a canteen. He was about to drink when a wounded man lying beside him begged, "For God's sake, give me some." Without drinking, Wilkeson passed the canteen to the man, who drank all of the water from it. "Wilkeson smiled on the man, turned slightly, and expired."[18]

When shells pounded the infantry's position, Colonel Fowler called

"Lieutenant Bayard Wilkeson holding his battery . . . to its work"
on Blocher's Knoll ("ARW," *B&L*, 3:109)

jokingly to his men, "Dodge the big ones, boys." It was timely advice, for one projectile hit ten feet in front of the 17th, kicked up dirt, and bounded over its line into a field behind it. Another shell wounded Pvts. Alonzo Scranton and William Dewhurst of Company D. Lt. Albert Peck, their company commander, demonstrated his inexperience by sending the two men to the rear escorted by a sergeant and a corporal. Peck later regretted his action, for one private could have taken care of both men, and under the circumstances even he ought not to have been spared. Cpl. W. Wallace Paynton observed of this time that "the bravado and bluster of camp life is all gone in the face of the enemy, and it is a remarkably courageous man that can look into the mouth of a twelve pound Parrott gun, or the muzzles of a regiment of infantry, and not feel a quiver of fear."[19]

As Barlow deployed, Schurz heard the sounds of battle swell on his left, a sign that the Confederates had renewed their attacks on the First Corps right. In order to better see what was going on, Schurz rode to the Hagy house, which was close behind the left of the corps skirmish line. He climbed to its roof, looked around, and saw that his fears had materialized: the Confederate force in his front was growing stronger. Worse, it was showing signs of advancing on his right. Schurz sent off a request to Howard for a brigade to guard that flank.[20]

Schurz returned to his headquarters, where he learned that Barlow had advanced to Blocher's Knoll and had broken his connection with Schimmelfennig's right. Further, in doing so he had moved Ames's brigade from its position in echelon to the corps' right rear. Schurz's situation was not unlike that which General Meade would face on the following day when he discovered that Sickles had advanced the Third Corps from Cemetery Ridge. Unlike Meade, Schurz had no reinforcements for his overextended corps line aside from a brigade that Howard might send him. He ordered General Schimmelfennig to advance Krzyzanowski's brigade to restore its contact with Barlow's left. At the same time he sent additional requests for help from Cemetery Hill. Schurz was in a sweat. He feared that the Confederates were preparing to flank his corps on the right and cut it off from the town. This suggested that he should "begin a movement to the rear"; but before he could order one, the Confederates attacked, and it was too late for an orderly withdrawal.[21]

Krzyzanowski's brigade consisted of four regiments plus two companies of a fifth. Its commander, Col. Wladimir Krzyzanowski ("Kriz" to some of his American colleagues), had come to America from a part of Poland governed by Prussia. He fled his native land after the revolt of 1848 failed, and he settled in New York, where he worked as a civil engineer. In August 1861 the secretary of war authorized him to recruit a multinational regiment that became the 58th New York, the "Polish Legion." Krzyzanowski and the 58th fought with Louis Blenker's division in the Valley and John Pope's Army of Virginia before the Eleventh Corps became a part of the Army of the Potomac. For a three-month period he was a temporary brigadier general, but he reverted to the grade of colonel in March 1863. Schurz cherished Krzyzanowski's friendship, and Brig. Gen. Alpheus Williams remarked that "he is a Pole but a good officer and speaks English well."[22]

After marching through the town, Krzyzanowski's brigade massed in the fields north of the college between the Mummasburg and Carlisle roads. Dilger's nearby guns drew Confederate artillery fire its way. The fire, wrote one soldier, was "lively, and their shot and shell ricocheted splendidly over the open fields." The shelling wounded two men of the 82d Ohio, causing the Buckeyes to shift their position. Orderly sergeants called rolls amid the artillery fire. Lt. Theodore Dodge, the adjutant of the 119th New York, had trouble controlling his mare, which bolted with him. When he returned, he saw that the field officers had dismounted because they could not control their horses. Dodge dismounted, and his mare galloped off not to be seen again.[23]

Col. Wladimir Krzyzanowski
(CWLM)

While waiting, the men of the brigade saw something of O'Neal's attack on Oak Ridge off to their left. They cheered as they watched the Alabamians "scampering like frightened sheep." But they began to have misgivings when they saw that the enemy had reserves. Like Schurz, they feared that they "were cunningly being dallied with." According to Maj. Benjamin A. Willis of the 119th New York, Barlow's division was already showing signs of being overwhelmed when the order came to close on its left. Krzyzanowski must have known this; it is no wonder that Capt. Alfred Lee of the 82d Ohio thought that the brigade commander's face became "pale and distressed." Orders were orders, however, and Krzyzanowski's brigade started through fields to the right crossed by fences that slowed the march and forced the brigade to halt under heavy fire. In later years Captain Lee complained that they tore down fences that might have given them some cover or furnished material for the construction of breastworks. As the brigade approached the 107th Ohio Regiment on Barlow's left, a gray line appeared from the ravine of Blocher's Run. "Their movements were firm and steady, as usual, and their banners bearing the blue Southern cross, flaunted impudently and seemed to challenge combat. On they came, one line after the other, in splendid array."[24]

Krzyzanowski posted his 1,200 officers and men east of the Carlisle Road in time to meet the Rebel attack. It formed on Barlow's left rear and is memorialized along the present Howard Avenue fronting to the north-west. But the memorials there mark approximate positions only. The 58th New York was on the right. It had just two companies on the field — less than fifty men — hardly enough to guard its colors. Lt. Col. August Otto, an immigrant from Schleswig-Holstein, commanded them. The remainder of the regiment was on a patrol south of Emmitsburg and would not reach Gettysburg in time to take part in the 1 July fight.[25]

The 26th Wisconsin, 75th Pennsylvania, 82d Ohio, and 119th New York regiments extended Krzyzanowski's line left toward the Carlisle Road. Col. James S. Robinson, commander of the 82d Ohio, insisted that his regiment had advanced 150 yards farther than the rest of the brigade and held its position until ordered back. Captain Lee agreed when he wrote that the 82d had passed over the site of its memorial to a point 125 yards to the north, where it confronted the enemy at a distance of about a hundred yards.[26]

And so it was when Early's division and Doles's brigade launched their attacks against Barlow's and Schurz's divisions of the Eleventh Corps. The numbers of attackers and defenders were approximately equal, but the position of the Eleventh Corps was poor, and most of its key commanders were new in their assignments. In contrast, the Confederates were veteran troops commanded by one of their army's best division commanders and by competent brigade commanders. As things stood, Early's division and Doles's brigade could strike Schurz's brigades one at a time with superior force. In retrospect, the result seems preordained.

CHAPTER 18

Gordon and Doles
Sweep the Field

Brig. Gen. John Brown Gordon, a thirty-year-old Georgian, a graduate of the University of Georgia, and a lawyer, was running a coal mining operation in Alabama when the war began. He entered the Confederate army as a captain and company commander of the "Raccoon Roughs." Soon he became colonel of the 6th Alabama. After Rodes was wounded at Seven Pines, Gordon commanded Rodes's brigade temporarily. He became a brigadier general and led his own Georgia brigade at Chancellorsville and Gettysburg. Gordon had ambition and conceit and could be careless with facts, but he proved to be an excellent brigade commander. In an often quoted remark, a soldier is supposed to have said of him, "He's the most prettiest thing you ever did see on a field of fight. It'ud put fight into a whipped chicken just to look at him." At Gettysburg Gordon rode a black stallion that had been captured at Winchester, and when he stood in his stirrups, "bareheaded, hat in hand, arms extended, and, in a voice like a trumpet, exhorting his men," one man thought that "it was superb; absolutely thrilling."[1]

The men of Gordon's brigade were "much fatigued" when they reached the field. Gordon advanced them slowly until they were within 300 yards of the enemy position. He rode just behind the skirmish line so that his men could see him and so that he could get a better view of the partially hidden enemy position. Gordon's skirmishers passed through the fringe of woods that lay along the south edge of the field adjoining Bringman's lane. Major Daniel heard "Pop! pop!, pop!" as Gordon's skirmishers met von Gilsa's out of view of the remainder of the division. The brigade passed over open

Brig. Gen. John B. Gordon
(CWLM)

bottomland that contained neither cover nor obstacles to the advance. Gordon's line moved steadily and well closed; it followed the skirmishers into the open field. There was a loud crash, a dense cloud of gray powder smoke rose over the trees, and a "wild startling cheer" was added to the noise of battle.[2]

The appearance of Gordon's brigade in serried ranks that stretched beyond their flanks must have been unnerving to the men who manned the thin Eleventh Corps line. The four companies of the 17th Connecticut at the Benner house were probably off to Gordon's left. That placed them in the path of Hays's line, which stretched across the road and threatened to envelop them. General Ames ordered them back before they were overrun, and they retired skirmishing east of the Harrisburg Road toward Cemetery Hill. Though they were ordered back, Major Brady had difficulty getting Company K away, "as they were so earnestly engaged and making such sad havoc among the rebels."[3]

The departure of the 17th's four companies from the Benner buildings further exposed von Gilsa's right to Gordon's onslaught. Von Gilsa's small numbers deployed along the creek as skirmishers rather than in a compact line of battle. As the Georgians approached, von Gilsa ordered up the brigade's reserve, eight companies of the 153d, to extend his skirmish line to the left. Approximately 900 Union soldiers along the creek faced nearly double their number of Confederates.[4]

Pvt. Reuben Ruch was lying in the woods on the knoll's slope about fifty feet from Rock Creek. Shells from Wilkeson's battery that passed over his head seemed so close that he thought he could feel heat from them. He saw Confederate attacks against von Gilsa's line to the left and knew that there would soon be attacks on his front. In the meantime, Lieutenant Miller, who commanded Ruch's part of the line, received orders to shift left. While Miller was trying to get the movement started, however, there were shots in his direction from his right rear. Miller assumed that they came from his own brigade, and they angered him. He sent a corporal back to the 153d's reserve line, thirty yards to the rear, to have the shooting stopped. The corporal returned soon with the disturbing news that the reserve was no longer there (it had gone to the left) and that the firing came from Rebels who had flanked the right of von Gilsa's line. About this time Sgt. Edward Kiefer told Miller that Rebels were in strength beyond the trees in their front; by bending down, Miller could see them too. Miller ran back up the slope to where the regiment had been and, like the corporal, found most of it gone; only Lt. Adam Reisinger was there with a small detachment. Then Capt. Howard Reeder appeared. Reeder told Miller to take his companies off to the left, but Miller convinced Reeder that the Confederates were about to attack. Not knowing what else to do, Reeder told Miller to get his men out as best he could. As Miller left, he saw Lt. Horatio Yeager of Company C, who, though down with a bad wound in the hip, urged his men to retreat before they were taken prisoner.[5]

While Lieutenant Miller tried to determine what was going on, Private Ruch studied the area around him. Rock Creek was about fifty feet in front of him and looked to be about twenty feet wide and three feet deep. Large trees beyond it limited his view to about forty yards. Soon the Union skirmishers in his front fell back, followed by what looked to be three lines of battle. Ruch fired his rifle. As he loaded a second cartridge, a man pitched forward from behind him and fell to his front. Ruch was able to see his face, and he fumbled with the cartridge while watching the man die. Moments later the man on his left was shot. Ruch thought that he might be next, yet he kept cool and described the battle around him as "good, solid

Pvt. Reuben Ruch (Kiefer, *One Hundred and Fifty-third*, 113)

fighting." After firing four or five shots, he heard Miller's order to fall back. At this time, as he recalled, the left of von Gilsa's line had been broken, and the Rebels were attacking them from the right.

Ruch saw a Rebel color-bearer crossing the stream in his front "yelling like an Indian." He paused to take a shot at the fellow, but as he capped his gun, he decided that the bearer of the "rebel rag" could do no harm, and that it would be better to shoot a man with a rifle. He saw one such fellow with his hand on a top rail climbing a low fence about thirty feet in his front. Ruch, who was kneeling, fired and saw the man clutch his side as he fell behind the fence. Ruch stood and was tearing a cartridge to reload when he saw that his comrades had fallen back about thirty feet and were firing as they withdrew. He saw a row of dead and wounded in blue off to the side and heard bullets zipping by. He started back, but he had not gone far before he felt a blow on his knee. Looking down he saw a hole in the knee of his pants. Then a bullet flicked his other knee and convinced him that he was in a crossfire. He kept going. As he did so, he saw Wilkeson's guns pulling off the knoll.[6]

Von Gilsa's brigade provided examples of personal bravery as well as efforts at self-preservation. As he was leaving the woods, Pvt. John Trombeam of the 153d stopped at an oak tree, rested his rifle against it, and said, "Come boys, let us give them what they deserve." Just then a bullet hit him in the right shoulder, and his rifle dropped. He did not quit. Instead he hoisted the weapon to his left shoulder, rested it against the tree, and took his shot.[7]

As Ruch ran back past the almshouse barn, he saw a Rebel line "a mile long"—the brigades of Hays and Hoke (Avery)—swinging around the Union right like a closing gate. To the west he saw Union soldiers "dropping like flies." Pvt. John Snyder of his company ran past him, head pulled down behind his knapsack and heels flying. Snyder was the only man that he saw running. His haste was all the more remarkable because he had usually moved too slowly even to participate in company drill, and he was hard of hearing. Therefore his soldiering had been confined to fatigue duty—doing chores. When the time came to fight, though, Snyder was put in line, "for he could stop a bullet as good as any body." Ruch also saw von Gilsa on foot, calling to some men to catch a riderless horse for him. They did so, and von Gilsa mounted and set off to try to form a line near the barn. He rode up and down amid a storm of lead, shouting "rally boys" and German epithets. His line did not last long.[8]

As the 153d fell back from its position near the creek, Pvt. William Kiefer, who had been shot in the knee and was lying on the right of the regiment's old line, watched Captain Reeder with apprehension and pride. Although the regiment had fallen back, Reeder remained behind, firing his pistol at the advancing enemy. Before running to rejoin his company, he emptied its cylinder when the Rebels were less than fifteen feet away. About the same time Pvt. John Rush, who had been shot in both shoulders and could not raise his arms, was walking to the rear. He met a lieutenant trying to rally the troops. Rush explained that though he still carried his rifle, he could not fire it. The lieutenant replied that he should break the gun, and Rush said that he was unable to do so. The lieutenant took the rifle, and the two stood at a gate; Rush held his open cap box in one hand and the cartridge box in the other while the lieutenant loaded the rifle and fired it. The Confederates captured Rush, but the lieutenant escaped. Rush nevertheless described him as having been made of "sterling stuff."[9]

Gordon's smashing attack drove von Gilsa's three regiments from the front of Blocher's Knoll and forced Wilkeson's four guns from the hill. Gordon wrote that his brigade had moved forward under heavy fire over plank-and-rail fences and had crossed a creek whose "banks were so abrupt as to prevent a passage excepting at certain points." The enemy made obstinate resistance until the colors marking the two lines were less than fifty paces apart. If the Georgia regimental commanders made reports, they have been lost, and only the 61st has a published history. It states that just these Georgians met a Union line at Rock Creek, probably the reserve from the 153d, and had a hard time moving it. The Georgians advanced with a Rebel yell, but the Federals stood firm until they came near. Then they retired shooting. One minié ball struck Capt. William L. McLeod, commander of the 38th Georgia, in the head as he grasped the colors and cheered his men on. The Georgians found that the Federals were harder to move than they had known them to be before. Yet the fate of von Gilsa's brigade was sealed. Its 900 men were greatly outnumbered, and its line was flanked. Its only viable option was to retreat and try to rally in a better position.[10]

As Jones's three batteries dueled with Eleventh Corps guns and as Gordon's brigade advanced, Carrington's battery waited restlessly north of the bridge over Rock Creek. When General Early rode by, the cannoneers voiced their desire to join the fight. Early replied that they need not be impatient, for there would be plenty for them to do after a while. A few minutes later Carrington saw Gordon's line beyond Rock Creek advancing gallantly toward the enemy. Soon Early told Carrington to cross the bridge and follow Gordon's line. Because Union artillery was shelling the bridge, Carrington feared that horses crossing it might be hit and block it, but he rushed his pieces across one at a time. After crossing, the battery turned right into a field between the road and the knoll. Early and Carrington rode after Gordon's line.[11]

Hays's and Avery's (Hoke's) brigades marked time for a short while as Gordon advanced. John Cabell Early, nephew of the general, happened to be with Hays's brigade along a side road that crossed the Harrisburg Road, perhaps today's Shealer Road. John was fifteen years old and the son of the general's brother Sam, a captain on his staff. The general had invited John to join his staff as a courier, but when he had seen him just a few hours before, he decided that he was too young for the job. The general then told his brother that a battle was impending and that he was to keep the boy out of it. John rode with his father to the rear of Hays's brigade, which was lying in the shelter provided by the road. When the troops saw Sam, they jumped to their feet and shouted, "There's old Sam! Hurrah! hurrah!

hurrah!" and "Hurrah for old Sam." John regarded this shouting as a welcome to his father, but it sounds a lot like leg-pulling.

Hays's troops were lying down to avoid artillery rounds that came their way, but John stayed with some officers who were on horseback behind their line. One shell whistled particularly close, causing John to duck behind his horse's neck. The others teased him, and John was pleased to admit to his father that the general was right—he was too young to be a courier. Soon the infantry line advanced, and John saw his first casualty. As a soldier climbed the fence in front of the line, the hammer of his rifle struck a rail; it fired, and the ball entered his chest and exited from the back of his head. After that, John helped a staff officer with wounded and prisoners.[12]

Soon after Gordon advanced, Hays and Avery received orders to do so. As they moved forward, Pvt. L. B. Barnard, on the Ninth's skirmish line, wore a "three story white silk hat," probably a souvenir of his visit to Pennsylvania. The hat made Barnard an obvious target, and a Union skirmisher shot him. Hays's brigade met no serious opposition, though, until it veered left and moved abreast of Gordon's line. It pressed toward the town in the fields east of the Harrisburg Road and opposite the almshouse buildings. With Avery's (Hoke's) brigade stepping along on its left, the Louisianians moved forward with great deliberation until they reached Rock Creek east of the almshouse. There Hays's troops came under both artillery and infantry fire, possibly from the four retreating companies of the 17th Connecticut and Merkle's section of Wilkeson's battery. Colonel Avery ordered his North Carolinians to double-quick. Although told to support the other brigades of the division, Smith's did not advance with them. Smith feared that Union cavalry might be off his left and watched for it.[13]

Before Early's arrival, von Gilsa's skirmishers had driven Blackford's sharpshooters from the knoll to the cover of the trees west of it. After firing from the shelter of the trees, the Alabamians deployed in a "very close skirmish line." At the same time Doles's brigade moved by its left flank to counter any attack that the enemy might make against its left and rear. The sharpshooters, with Doles in their support, pressed Ames's brigade when it arrived on the west slope of Blocher's Knoll. This must have drawn Barlow's attention from the threat that was looming along the Harrisburg Road.[14]

Confederate shells pounded Ames's brigade as it took position on the northwest slope of the hill, and soon it was hotly engaged. It was not long before Gordon's right swung around von Gilsa's left and joined Blackford's and Doles's line. The pressure on Ames's brigade increased so much that it began to waver.[15]

Barlow, Ames, and others of Ames's brigade saw von Gilsa's brigade in retreat. Pvt. William Warren wrote that when the 17th Connecticut was moving to the front, a "German regiment came back hallooing" through its line and scattered it. When he got between an officer and his company, the officer, whom he believed was drunk, swung his sword and threatened to split his head open. Colonel Andrew Harris of the 75th Ohio, with scant appreciation of the situation on his right, wrote that von Gilsa's brigade, "composed of Blenker's old division, true to their natural instinct, being hard pressed by superior numbers, gave way and thus left our Brigade, now equally engaged with the enemy in front and flank (and exposed) to an enfilading fire of the most terrible kind."[16]

Barlow's troops were in trouble. Yet Barlow and Ames "set an excellent example for the men," in the recollection of Pvt. Justice Silliman of the 17th. Barlow wrote that Ames had behaved with great coolness and courage and that he assumed that von Gilsa had also, although he had not seen him after the fight began. He admitted, too, that some of the German officers had behaved well. Barlow was a fighter, and instead of ordering a retreat at this critical time, he sent Ames's brigade forward to receive the enemy.[17]

Ames ordered Harris to have the 75th Ohio fix bayonets, to move up from the brigade's support line to a place in the forward line between the 107th and 25th Ohio Regiments, and to check the enemy's advance. The 75th pushed to the front, passed over the high ground "on which the line was first formed," and entered a thin woods. There it halted and opened fire. The little regiment of 200 men checked the Georgians in their front, but the enemy pressed around their exposed flanks. The regiment's strength was exhausted. Harris expected either reinforcements or an order to fall back, but neither came. There was no help to be had. Harris termed the 75th's effort "a fearful advance and made at a dreadful cost of life." Four of his twelve officers were dead, and four others were wounded; a fourth of his men were dead or mortally wounded, and half of the rest were wounded and could no longer fight. Harris formed his able men into a skirmish formation and ordered them to fall back.[18]

We know less of what Ames's other Ohio regiments did in this action. The Georgians attacked the 107th "yelling like Indians in making a savage charge." Lt. Col. Charles Mueller was shot in the right arm, Capt. August

Vignos lost his right arm, and Capt. Barnet Steiner received a mortal wound in the bowels. The 107th went into the fight with 434 "muskets," and by that evening only 171 were present. The 25th Ohio started the fight with about 220 men and had four commanders, but at day's end only about sixty men with its colors remained.[19]

The 17th Connecticut was on the brigade's right near the top of the knoll. At the order to advance, Lieutenant Colonel Fowler, still on his white horse, gestured with his sword and shouted, "Now, Seventeenth, do your duty! Forward, double quick! Charge bayonets!" His six companies "advanced with a will" but, at the crest, ran into a hail of iron and lead. A bullet or shell fragment hit Fowler in the head and spattered some of his brains on Lt. H. Whitney Chatfield, a "brave and fearless boy." Chatfield, who was the regiment's adjutant and on horseback, made a good target. A ball went through his hat, another passed through his sleeve, and a third hit his sword and snapped its blade off below the hilt. Chatfield also lost his horse. Within minutes Confederate fire cut the gallant 17th into pieces. Two bullets hit Capt. James E. Moore in the head. Moore, a veteran of the Mexican War, had expected to die. At Emmitsburg the night before, he had told Capt. Milton C. Daniel that he was weary and would soon be "at rest." He asked Daniel to take care of some personal matters for him and to see that Lt. Henry Quien, who would be wounded in the hand that day, received his meerschaum pipe.[20]

Like their Ohio comrades, the Connecticut men did not tarry long in their untenable position. Private Warren wrote that they fired a few volleys. By then he felt alone; his comrades had fallen back a few feet, and he followed them. An officer trying to form a new line stopped him, and Cpl. George Scott called out, "Don't run boys." In the meantime Sgt. Maj. C. Frederick Betts and Lieutenant Chatfield tried to drag Fowler's body from the field but were forced to leave it behind. Warren's halt at the new line was short—he did not even have time to load before the men in it started for the rear. Warren joined the flight. He had not gone far when Pvt. Rufus Warren, who was just ahead of him, threw up his hands and cried, "Oh dear, help me, help me," and fell to the ground. William Warren did not stop; the Rebels were too close behind him. As he ran toward the almshouse buildings, a bullet ripped a hole in his pants leg, and a spent one bruised his shoulder. He stopped first behind a haystack, where he found an officer of the 153d with a bad leg wound. While there, he saw an artillery horse, still in harness. The horse had a deep hip wound that bled profusely. It was in so much pain that it could not stand still and so ran off, probably to be shot or to bleed to death. Warren decided that the haystack provided little cover and left it for the shelter of a shed forty feet away. Inside he found Pvt. James Hannon, and the two bided their time there until Rebel skirmishers captured them.[21]

At roll call the next morning only 241 of the 386 officers and men of the 17th taken into the fight were present—a loss of 145. Most of the absentees, like Pvt. William Warren, were listed as captured or missing, and many of these no doubt lived to return to the Nutmeg State. The regiment's casualties might have been much greater had not four of its companies been skirmishing at the Benner buildings, thereby missing the fight on Blocher's Knoll.[22]

When struck by both Gordon's and Doles's brigades, Ames's brigade, like von Gilsa's, was greatly outnumbered and outflanked. The Confederates had hit Barlow's two brigades in tandem and had overwhelmed each in turn. They continued ahead against a third that was forming in their path.

In his overly brief report of the fight, General Ames stated that Barlow had been wounded and that the whole division was "falling back with little or no regularity, regimental organizations having become destroyed." Soon after the division's lines began to break, Barlow had attempted to rally his troops and to form another line in the rear—we do not know just where. As he turned his horse, a ball entered his left side halfway between his armpit and his thigh. He climbed from his horse and started to walk from the field among his fleeing men. Two men stopped to help him, and one was shot. A spent ball bruised Barlow in the back, and soon he was too faint to go on. He lay down. The Georgians fired in his direction; one ball hit his hat, and another grazed his finger. The area became more quiet after the Confederates passed through, and they helped him. One of Gordon's favorite and often told tales and a prime human interest story of the battle was of how he saw Barlow lying helpless on the ground. He stopped to assist him. At Barlow's request, he destroyed some personal letters that Barlow carried and promised that he would tell Mrs. Barlow, if opportunity offered, that her husband's last thoughts were of her. He then had litter bearers carry Barlow to shade in the rear—possibly to an aid station. At this time, perhaps, Lt. Andrew L. Pitzer, one of Early's aides, came on the scene. Pitzer had Barlow carried into some trees and placed on a bed of leaves. He lay there until Eleventh Corps prisoners carried him to the Benner house. The Confederates were kind to him, and their surgeons dressed his wounds. They and Union doctors brought to see him were pessimistic about his recovery; they feared that his intestines had been punctured and that peritonitis would set in. The next day they carried him to the Crawford house and made him comfortable. In due time it became apparent that there was no peritonitis and that he was recovering. Barlow had cheated death a second time.[23]

After Barlow was wounded, General Ames took command of the First Division and attempted to rally it without success. A message from Schurz urged him to set up a line at the edge of town, perhaps near the Crawford buildings. Von Gilsa must have had some initial success in forming this line, for Jubal Early made arrangements to attack it.[24]

Major Daniel had been riding with Early. The two saw Gordon's advancing line disappear into the trees along Rock Creek. Suddenly there was a wild yell, a crashing volley, and a cloud of smoke that masked the scene. Barlow's men fled "in wild confusion." Daniel described the slaughter as terrific and noticed that a line of dead and wounded marked where the Federal line had been. "The Federal flank had been shrivelled up as a scroll," he recalled, "and the whole force gave way." Daniel turned to Early and exclaimed, "General, this day's work will win the Southern Confederacy." Early did not reply and soon sent Daniel after Gordon. As he rode forward, Daniel passed Barlow lying wounded among the fallen of his division.[25]

Wheeler's and Dilger's batteries had been firing at the Confederate batteries opposing them. Afterward Wheeler boasted to his grandfather that his battery had gotten along "finely" and that neither battery suffered greatly, but both he and Dilger would soon have more than they could handle. Suddenly, from around Blocher's Knoll, Wheeler saw "two great gray clouds" that moved steadily toward the Federal infantry. Wheeler pivoted his two right guns toward the gray lines and fired canister at the red battle flags that marked the Confederate regiments; Weidman's section of Dilger's battery presumably did the same. Yet the canister charges that fit Wheeler's three-inch rifles were small and probably did little to delay the Confederate advance.[26]

The two gray clouds Wheeler saw must have been the brigades of Doles and Gordon as they advanced together against the Eleventh Corps right. Gordon's brigade had come like a whirlwind from across Rock Creek overlapping Blackford's left. Blackford's bugler summoned the sharpshooters to rally on the battalion's center and out of Gordon's zone. The battalion and Doles's brigade advanced with Gordon along the axis of the Carlisle Road. Col. John T. Mercer's 21st Georgia, on the right of Doles's line, moved west of the road, while Doles's three left regiments extended east of it. There they joined Gordon's men in their attack against Barlow's shattered regiments and those of Krzyzanowski's brigade who prepared feverishly to meet them.[27]

From his position near the left of Krzyzanowski's brigade line, Capt. Alfred Lee of the 82d Ohio saw the Rebels coming on in "splendid style" from both the front and left. The Federals held their fire until a Union officer shouted, "Let them have it."[28]

Smoke belched from the blue line, wrote Lee, and "quick as a flash the compliment was returned; bullets hummed about our ears like infuriated bees." The lines blazed away at each other at a distance of about seventy-five yards or even closer. Captain Lee thought that he might have read the battle honors inscribed on the Confederate battle flags had he had the time do so. For a brief time the Georgians stood and fired rather than advance. Pvt. George W. Nichols of the 61st Georgia mentioned that the Yankees had made a desperate stand near the almshouse, and that they had been harder to drive than ever before. He recalled "that their officers were cheering their men and behaving like heroes and commanders of the 'first water.'" General Gordon said little of this; the enemy had changed front to meet him, he remembered, and was driven back in "the greatest confusion."[29]

The 119th New York lost 100 men in fifteen minutes. Being on the left of Krzyzanowski's line, it probably received volleys "of musketry in swift succession, and a destructive fire of shot and shell" from Blackford's and Doles's men as well as Gordon's. Both Col. John T. Lockman and his adjutant, Theodore Dodge, were wounded. Sgt. Louis Morrell was struck in both an eye and his body while loading his rifle and a third time in the thigh as he lay upon the ground. It was claimed that the 119th held its ground until troops of both Barlow's division and von Amsberg's brigade on its left fell back. Somehow, the 119th lost its state flag to the 13th Georgia of Gordon's brigade. Two corporals listed as color-bearers were killed in action.[30]

The 82d Ohio lost about 150 of its 258 officers and men who went into the fight. The survivors mourned Lt. Stowell L. Burnham especially. Lt. Col. David Thomson described Burnham as a "brave and good officer above all, good and honest." The field officers of the 82d had gone into the fight mounted, but the horses of all but one man were shot. Thomson's "Charley" was hit three times before he fell and pinned Thomson to the ground. After this, Thomson noticed that the major was standing by his

horse. He asked the major to mount and look to the line, but the major refused — he could not manage the horse. Thomson, who had two light wounds, mounted the major's horse and rode along the 82d's line.[31]

On the other flank of the brigade, Sgt. Carl Wickesberg of the 26th Wisconsin described the bullets as coming as "thick as hail." Many men fell. The two ranking officers of the 26th Wisconsin, Lt. Col. Hans Boebel and Maj. Henry Baetz, were wounded. Boebel ignored a wound in his right leg made by a minié ball until a shell fragment sliced into the leg and fractured the bone. Lt. Albert Wallber, the regiment's adjutant, was knocked unconscious and was taken prisoner along with Sgt. Adam Muenzenberger and Capt. Bernhard Domschcke. Every member of the color guard was killed or wounded. The 26th lost over 100 men in fifteen minutes.[32]

The Confederates shot the horse of Col. Francis Mahler, commander of the 75th Pennsylvania, and then shot Mahler as he directed the 75th on foot. Schurz rode by Mahler's position and saw Mahler as he lay dying. They had had been comrades in the fortress of Rastatt in 1849. Schurz stopped. Mahler, "with death on his face," gave Schurz his hand and bade him a last goodbye in this Pennsylvania field far from the Rhine. Mahler's regiment lost 111 of its 194 men in a deadly fifteen minutes. This number included Lt. Louis Mahler, the colonel's brother.[33]

Krzyzanowski, too, had been riding the brigade's line shouting orders and encouragement. He recalled the troops as "sweaty, blackened by gunpowder, and they looked more like animals than human beings." They fought with bloodshot eyes, and to him the "portrait of battle was the portrait of hell." Soon a bullet struck his horse; the animal gave a shrill scream of pain and reared high into the air, pitching the colonel hard to the ground. Even though breathing was painful for him, Krzyzanowski remained on the field and conducted the remnants of his brigade to the rear.[34]

In no time Krzyzanowski's brigade had become a shadow and had to fall back. After the battle, there was the usual disagreement about which regiment had retreated first. Maj. August Ledig of the 75th Pennsylvania stated that the 82d Ohio on his left had been flanked and gave way. This accusation did not sit well with the Ohioans. Lieutenant Colonel Thomson insisted that his regiment had not fallen back until it was ordered to do so. Colonel Robinson, his commander, concurred, claiming that it had been farther forward than the others in the brigade and that it had fallen back "in fairly good order," firing as it it went. Captain Lee thought that the regiments on his right had fallen back first and took issue with Maj. Benjamin Willis's report for the 119th, which implied that it was the last regiment off the field. Lee believed that it was correct to say that the entire line went back, and the difference in the time of the 119th's doing so was not enough to be worth noting.[35]

The 119th New York had been flanked on front and flank and was fighting hard. Its men maintained that it held on until Barlow's division had left the field. Lt. Theodore Dodge, the 119th's adjutant, claimed that a supporting column on its left, presumably a regiment of Schimmelfennig's brigade, had given way and that there were Confederates within ten yards of that flank. He held also that the 119th was firing and retreating in good order, unlike some other regiments that were in confusion. Then Dodge felt a hard blow and fell. He kept his wits about him and realized that he could be hit by bullets from both friend and foe. To avoid them, he stretched flat on his back until the enemy line passed over him. Then he sat up to examine his wound and found that it was in his ankle. He cut off his boot and spur. Several Confederates passed by him; one asked for his sword, and a field officer asked him who commanded the Army of the Potomac. Dodge took satisfaction in saying that he did not answer this question. A captured sergeant of the 119th and a Rebel private assisted him to the rear, where the Confederates were kind to him. An officer gave him a canteen of water to pour on his wound, and a sympathetic doctor apologized for not taking care of it sooner because he had to give his first attention to bleeding men. Another Confederate stopped by, looking for spurs, but Dodge had only one to give him. Later the Confederates carried him to the Benner house. On the following Sunday, a Union army surgeon amputated his foot four inches above his ankle. He lived.[36]

Captain Lee of the 82d Ohio did not fall back with the brigade. Instead he picked up a rifle to take a personal parting shot at the Confederates. As he was doing this, a soldier fell at his side with the plea, "Oh help me!" The man took Lee's hand and tried to stand but could not. He murmured, "Oh, I'm gone, just leave me here." No sooner had this happened than Lee felt a sting and fell, "benumbed with pain" and utterly helpless. A soldier paused to help him, but he, too, was shot and limped away, leaving Lee behind. Lee watched the enemy line of battle come toward him, preceded by skirmishers, an indication, perhaps, that the Georgian leaders did not expect more firing by regimental formations. Some of the Georgians "seemed even disposed to be savage," for one of them threatened to shoot a wounded man who had raised himself on his elbow. Yet another man assured the wounded that they need not be afraid, but he took Lee's revolver.

After the Confederate line had passed, Lee looked around. One of the first persons that he saw was Lieutenant Burnham, who had been shot twice, had a mortal wound, and was in agony. As he surveyed the scene, Carrington's battery rolled up at a canter and dropped trail nearby.[37]

Captain Carrington and General Early had ridden slowly south from the knoll in Gordon's rear. Early watched the progress of the fighting ahead coolly and intently. At one point he told Carrington that if Gordon met opposition, Carrington was to unlimber his guns and prepare for action. They advanced some more, and when in the middle of the field, perhaps half the distance between the almshouse and the knoll on the rise where the Union line had been, Early turned to Carrington and in sharp tones told him to prepare for action. As the battery did so, there was a pause in Gordon's firing. Early rode on for about fifty yards; Carrington followed the general and stopped near him. As Carrington sat there, a sergeant rode up to him to say that a wounded Union officer wished to speak with him. Early heard the request and in a kindly voice told Carrington to see what he wanted.[38]

Carrington found the officer, whom he remembered as a lieutenant colonel, lying between one of his pieces and its caisson. The officer said that he was helpless and asked to be carried to a place of greater safety. Carrington had four cannoneers carry the officer to a nearby fence corner. There Carrington tried to arrange the man's coat into a comfortable bed. In gratitude for this kind treatment the man offered Carrington his binoculars. Carrington declined the offer, but the man insisted, saying that if he kept them, a straggler might knock him in the head for them. Carrington accepted the gift and returned to Early.

The officer that Captain Carrington had assisted was Captain Lee. Lee recalled that Carrington's men carried both him and Burnham to the side. Burnham was crying in agony in spite of the artillerymen's efforts to make him comfortable and quench his thirst. The battery moved on. Close behind came scroungers looking for loot and Good Samaritans who tried to assist the wounded. A young man, said to be a private at Ewell's headquarters, tried to be helpful, but he could do little. Burnham asked to be lifted up so that he could see the sunset, but this caused him great pain. He then asked the young Confederate to send his watch to someone, and as the daylight faded, he died. Soon after, the young Rebel brought a Union doctor to Lee. The doctor arranged to have Lee and a wounded German soldier carried to a house in the town.[39]

About this time there was action nearby on Doles's front. As Doles and Gordon approached Krzyzanowski's line, Schimmelfennig ordered Col. Philip P. Brown to take his 157th New York Regiment forward from the Hagy buildings to strike the right of Doles's line. All but one regiment of Doles's brigade were then east of the Carlisle Road in a wheat field south of Blocher's Run. Those of Doles's Georgians east of the road were advancing with a "soul stirring" Rebel yell toward the Union position and were unaware of the 157th's approach. Suddenly Doles's "powerful" horse took the bit in his teeth and galloped with the general toward the Union line. When about fifty feet from it, Doles slid from his saddle into the wheat, and the horse galloped on. Either the wheat and the smoke concealed Doles or the Union soldiers' attention was on the horse, for they paid Doles no heed. When about fifteen feet from the Union line, the horse wheeled and returned to his Confederate allegiance without having been shot.[40]

As Doles's left regiments advanced against Krzyzanowski's line, the 21st Georgia, still west of the road, saw the 157th New York approach its right. Colonel Mercer wheeled the 21st to the right, advanced into a wheat field, and opened fire on the attackers. The enemy returned the fire, and finding that the 21st had bitten off more than it could chew, Mercer pulled it back forty yards to a lane. There the regiment went to ground and awaited the blue line's approach in concealment.[41]

The 157th's 400 officers and men had gotten to within fifty yards of the flank of the unsuspecting enemy line before being spotted. They were able to do so because Doles had lost his horse and was not high enough to see them, and the other mounted officers were near the brigade's left. General Ewell had seen the 157th's approach, but he was on foot and alone. Since he had only one leg, he could neither send a warning to Doles's men nor mount his horse without help and take it himself. He was in despair until someone noticed the 157th's approach and Doles's regiments changed front to meet it.[42]

The 44th Georgia's flank was near the road, and when the 157th was only forty yards away, it wheeled to face the New Yorkers and opened fire. The 157th replied. The 4th Georgia, which was next in line, wheeled and joined the 44th on its left. The 12th Georgia, on the left of the line, moved by the right flank and came upon the 44th's right. The 21st Georgia then arose from its concealment off the 157th's left and fired into its flank. Cpl. Sidney J. Richardson of the 21st remembered that his regiment had dropped behind a fence. Just before the 157th reached it, the 21st fired a volley and charged as quickly as it could.[43]

Colonel Brown ordered the men of the 157th to fire at will. The noise of shells and bullets was terrible. Brown's men were falling rapidly, and the enemy line was becoming a semicircle embracing the 157th and concentrating its fire on it. To add to the horror, an enemy battery was enfilading the New Yorkers' line and doing "fearful execution." Lt. Col. George Arrowsmith was one of those hit. Colonel Brown described him as a brave man and a skillful officer, generous to a fault, and with a keen sense of honor.[44]

Brown looked back for support or for someone bearing an order for the 157th to retreat but saw neither. He spotted one of Schimmelfennig's aides at a distance; the man's horse had been shot, and he had removed the saddle and was carrying it to the rear. Although Brown learned later that the man had "hallooed" for him to retreat, Brown did not know this then. But seeing that his regiment would be destroyed if it remained where it was, he ordered it to retreat. The 157th did so. Corporal Richardson of the 21st Georgia was glad to see it go. Doles's Georgians continued to press the New Yorkers until they got away. The 157th lost 307 of its officers and men in the entire battle, almost all near the Carlisle Road; the casualties of Doles's brigade numbered only 179.[45]

It was said that on the morning of 2 July the wife of Lt. Col. David R. E. Winn, commander of the 4th Georgia, entered her parlor in Americus, Georgia. To her horror she saw that the portrait of Colonel Winn had fallen from the wall and struck a chair post, which punctured the colonel's face. She ran to a neighbor's house and told them that she believed that Winn had been killed in battle. When news of Gettysburg reached Americus, the list of killed included Colonel Winn, who had been shot in the face on 1 July.[46]

The fighting on the plain was almost over. Dilger sent all but two sections of his and Wheeler's batteries to the rear. One section from each battery covered the retreat. They went back over the Carlisle Road, Wheeler's guns going first because they were less useful in this situation than Dilger's large-bore Napoleons ought to be. A Confederate projectile struck one of Wheeler's pieces and knocked its barrel to the ground. Wheeler tried to haul the tube off by slinging it under a limber with a prolonge; but this did not work, and it had to be left behind. Dilger's two sections halted at the edge of the town, where they fired a few canister rounds before moving on. Capt. George Warren, who had brought Schurz's provost guard to the field, rode with Dilger. As they left, Warren saw the 76th New York of Cutler's brigade retreating toward the town. He considered this important in establishing the comparative times of retreat when veterans refought the battle in the postwar years.[47]

Wheeler's battery went through the town to Cemetery Hill. After a section of Wilkeson's battery relieved Dilger's section "on the Market road," probably Carlisle Street, Dilger saw that the streets of the town were crowded. He turned his battery onto a street to the left and passed around the town to the east. He reported that the battery had lost fourteen men and twenty-four horses, and that one piece was disabled. Wilkeson's battery was the last off the field. It halted north of Gettysburg to fill the chests of its gun limbers with ammunition from its caissons before retiring slowly through the town to Cemetery Hill. It suffered only ten casualties, including Wilkeson, and had twelve horses killed. It was probably Wilkeson's battery that covered the retreat by firing in the streets of the town.[48]

The 45th New York, the first Eleventh Corps regiment on the field, was among the last to leave. After aiding in the initial repulse of O'Neal's brigade, its men had fought as skirmishers on the corps left and had supported the 157th New York in its daring movement toward the Carlisle Road. When Schimmelfennig saw the First Corps retreating from Oak Ridge, he ordered the 45th to the rear. It moved in a deliberate fashion to the grounds of Gettysburg College and formed to fight there. After about fifteen minutes, Schimmelfennig's bugler sounded "Retreat" and then the call to double-quick. The 45th responded by jogging into the town and to further adventures.[49]

After stampeding the Union regiments from their position on the rise near the almshouse, Gordon's brigade halted there so that its men could fill their cartridge boxes. Early saw that the enemy was establishing another line among some houses on the edge of the town. He saw also that this line extended beyond Gordon's left and across the Harrisburg Road. After advancing east of the Harrisburg Road, Hays's and Hoke's (Avery's) brigades were pausing at Rock Creek. Early instructed Gordon to hold his brigade where it was and ordered Hays and Colonel Avery to attack the newly forming line. Early's division, with the aid of Doles's brigade and Blackford's sharpshooters, had overwhelmed and smashed von Gilsa's, Ames's, and Krzyzanowski's brigades in succession. As Carrington waited for Early's instructions, he saw Hays's and Avery's brigades move forward on the left beyond the Harrisburg Road and heard the noise of battle swell again. One more brigade awaited Early's attention. The last phase of the fighting north of the town had begun.[50]

CHAPTER 19

The Brickyard Fight

Maj. Gen. Carl Schurz was anxious. He had deployed his two Eleventh Corps divisions across the plain north of Gettysburg, Rodes's Confederates were already engaged with Robinson's division of the First Corps on his left, and Doles's brigade stretched across his front. More to the point, though, the Confederates seemed stronger than they had been when the afternoon's battle opened a short time before. Further, there were signs that more of them were approaching his right over the Harrisburg Road. To counter such a move, Schurz requested that General Howard send him one of von Steinwehr's brigades then in reserve on Cemetery Hill. He would place it at the northeast edge of the town, where it would be available to oppose an attempt by the enemy to turn his right. Howard replied that he had no troops to spare; he needed both of Steinwehr's brigades to secure Cemetery Hill.[1]

Schurz's anxiety increased when Barlow advanced his division to Blocher's Knoll, further exposing his division and the corps to potential envelopment by the Confederates arriving over the Harrisburg Road. Schurz ordered Schimmelfennig's right brigade, Krzyzanowski's, to Barlow's support. He also sent Captain Winkler back to bring up the brigade that he had requested from Cemetery Hill, perhaps not realizing that Howard had declined to send it to him. After two or three requests and the appearance of Early's division, von Steinwehr, with Howard's approval, ordered Col. Charles R. Coster to take his brigade to assist Schurz.[2]

The brigade, which had been commanded by Col. Adolphus Buschbeck at Chancellorsville, numbered four regiments: the 27th Pennsylvania commanded by Lt. Col. Lorenz Cantador, a fifty-three-year-old former Prussian officer and merchant; the 73d Pennsylvania under Capt. Daniel F. Kelly, a twenty-six-year-old watchmaker; and two New York regiments—the 134th commanded by Lt. Col. Allan H. Jackson, an experienced officer and lawyer, and the 154th under Lt. Col. Daniel B. Allen, a twenty-four-year-old lawyer. Colonel Coster, the brigade commander, was from New York City and had begun his war service as a private in the 7th New York Militia Regiment. He was likely backed by men of influence, for he received a commission in the 12th U.S. Infantry in May 1861 and became a captain in May 1862. He served with his regiment on the Peninsula and had been wounded at Gaines's Mill. Coster became colonel of the newly organized 134th New York in October 1862 and led it at Chancellorsville, where it was in Barlow's brigade. After that battle, the 134th was transferred to the First Brigade, where in Buschbeck's absence Coster's rank elevated him to its command. Therefore, the brigade left Cemetery Hill under an acting commander—a colonel—and with regiments led by three lieutenant colonels and a captain.[3]

At Schurz's request Captain Winkler galloped through the town in search of Coster's brigade. When he reached Cemetery Hill, he found that it had not yet started to Schurz's aid. Coster did not explain the delay, but it must have taken some time to call in the regiments deployed as outposts in front of Cemetery Hill. No one described the route taken by the brigade through the town, though Pvt. Charles W. McKay of the 154th wrote of going over Stratton Street and of "confusion and disaster" all around. On the other hand, Sgt. John Wellman of the 154th told of marching at a quick-step down a main street, crossing a railroad track and a bridge. A historian of the 134th mentioned that the brigade passed up Baltimore Street, which is quite likely, and that it continued along Carlisle Street, but he might well have meant Stratton Street instead. The column came under artillery fire, probably not directed at it, but according to Sergeant Wellman, the men hurried along in ranks without being intimidated.[4]

By the time Coster's brigade reached the north edge of the town, Barlow's division had been crushed. Schurz mused later that had Coster's brigade been available at the onset of Early's attack, he could have sent it against Early's left and rear. (This seems like wishful thinking. Hays's and Avery's (Hoke's) brigades had no other significant opposition and could readily handle such a small force.) As it was, Schurz could only try to rally Ames's brigade in the hope that it might cover the corps' retreat. While Schurz was trying to do this, he learned from Captain Winkler that Coster's brigade was at hand. Schurz left Barlow's retreating men to others and rode back to post Coster's troops.[5]

Col. Charles R. Coster
(CWLM)

Winkler rode to a cluster of retreating Union troops and found that they belonged to Krzyzanowski's brigade. There were 30 or so men among them from the 26th Wisconsin — his own regiment. He learned also that though the Badgers had no officers with them, they had the regiment's colors — a dire situation indeed. The colors of a regiment of 500 in the custody of only 30 men in retreat suggested heavy casualties and disorder. With Schurz's permission, Winkler remained with the 30 and their flag, but he sent his horse to the rear. He formed the Wisconsin men into two ranks and placed them in the Carlisle Road near the left of Coster's position. Although the rest of Krzyzanowski's brigade continued its retreat, Winkler held his little force in place. He knew that Coster's brigade was off to the right, and he had no orders to fall back. The enemy paid Winkler's force little heed, giving him time to look at them. He saw a long line of battle on each side of the Harrisburg Road; the one west of the road had no Union opposition, while that east of it headed for his troops and for Coster's little brigade.[6]

260   { THE BRICKYARD FIGHT }

The 134th New York led Coster's march through the town, followed in turn by the 154th New York and the 27th Pennsylvania. The 73d Pennsylvania halted "near the square," probably in an open area near the railroad tracks. With this detachment of the 73d and an earlier one from the 154th to make a reconnaissance south from Emmitsburg, Coster had only about 900 officers and men when he arrived to help Schurz hold off the brigades of Hays and Avery. In addition the brigade had the support of the four Napoleons of Capt. Lewis Heckman's Ohio battery, which took position off the brigade's left.[7]

Schurz directed Coster's brigade to an area on the northeast edge of town bounded on the west by Stratton Street and on the east and south by Stevens Run. Three wheat fields adjoined the property beyond a post-and-rail fence, 700 feet long on its north and northeast sides. The Kuhn house stood on the east side of Stratton Street within the property, and there were three brick kilns directly east of it. The tract contained fenced enclosures for animals or gardens. Unfortunately for its defenders, the area sloped downhill from Stratton Street southeast to Stevens Run in such a way that the brigade's left was higher than its right and could not be seen from the right. More important, though, higher ground on the left bulged across the front of the position and shortened the forward view of the troops in the center of the line. Coster's three regiments entered Kuhn's property through a "carriage gateway" beside the house that led to the kilns. Once inside the brickyard, they formed lines and advanced to the post-and-rail fence edging the wheat fields on its northern and eastern sides.[8]

The 27th Pennsylvania, a regiment of German immigrants, occupied the left of the line and had its flank near Stratton Street. The 154th New York was on the 27th's right in the center of the line, and the 134th was on the right. The 134th's right fronted to the northeast and extended beyond Stevens Run. After taking their positions, the 134th and 154th had a gap between them. Probably at Coster's suggestion, Colonel Cantador plugged it with fifty men of the 27th under Lt. Adolphus D. Vogelbach. After taking position, Colonel Allen of the 154th, who was near the right of his line, realized that he could not see beyond the higher ground held by the 27th on the 154th's immediate left. Yet because Colonel Coster was on that part of the line and probably could see the enemy, Allen assumed that he would be warned of any danger from that direction. Pvt. Charles McKay of the 154th wrote that on reaching the fence, they received an order to kneel and to hold their fire until it would be effective. He saw, too, that the

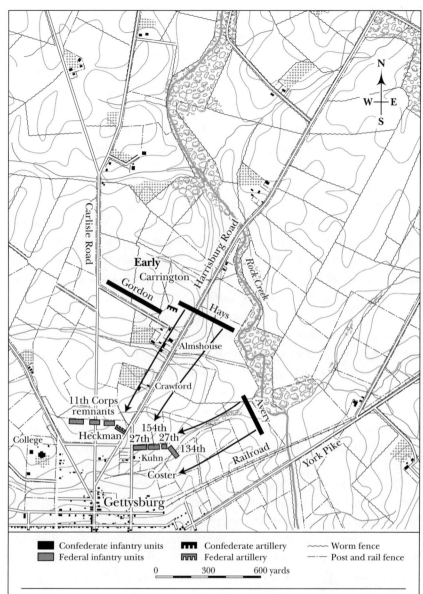

Map 19.1. The Brickyard Fight

Legend:
- Confederate infantry units
- Federal infantry units
- Confederate artillery
- Federal artillery
- Worm fence
- Post and rail fence

0   300   600 yards

1. General Schurz posts three regiments of Coster's brigade in Kuhn's brickyard to cover the retreat of the Eleventh Corps's right. Heckman's battery's four guns are on the brigade's left, west of the Harrisburg Road. Remnants of the corps rally briefly on the swell of ground west of the Harrisburg Road.
2. Early halts Gordon's advance. He orders Hays's and Avery's brigades to attack Heckman and Coster.
3. Hays attacks down the Harrisburg Road, routs the Eleventh Corps line, captures two of Heckman's guns, and drives off the left of Coster's line.
4. Avery's brigade crosses Rock Creek and envelopes the right of Coster's line, capturing many men.

ground in the 154th's front was "gently rising until, 40 rods away" and "was perhaps 20 feet above us and covered with wheat just ready for the sickle."[9]

Coster's brigade was hardly in position before the enemy, double its number, attacked. To Private McKay it seemed as though the enemy's line had battle flags every few rods; this meant to him that "their formation was in a solid column." As was customary, the enemy advanced in "splendid style." General Hays reported little of his attack; his brigade, perhaps, was too far to the west to bear the brunt of Coster's opposition. Col. Archibald C. Godwin, reporting for the dead Colonel Avery, found the enemy behind a strong fence. The North Carolina brigade had advanced with great deliberation until it reached Rock Creek about 200 yards from Coster's position. As the North Carolinians waded Rock Creek, canister and deadly rifle fire hit them. The canister probably came from Heckman's guns, and the infantry fire from the 134th New York on Coster's right.[10]

Colonel Allen, who could not see what happened to his left, thought that the 154th was holding the enemy in check, and McKay believed that they executed well and stopped the enemy line in their front. Lt. Alanson Crosby described the 154th's stand as being as "firm as the pyramids, fighting with the desperation of a forlorn hope." Edwin D. Northrup claimed that the men of the 154th fired from six to nine rounds each, a respectable amount considering what was taking place around them.[11]

It was not the attack against the front of the 154th that would decide the fate of Coster's brigade. The 134th on the brigade's right was putting up a hard but only brief fight. Avery's brigade's advance was unstoppable. The 134th gave the North Carolinians a volley at a range of about sixty yards. Before being wounded, Sgt. William G. Glen fought with "determined resistance until unable to fight longer." Lt. Ben Shelton sent Glen to the rear; as he walked off, another ball struck him, "and he fell with his face to the ground, a corpse." Avery's brigade swung right to the right and rear of the 134th's position, forcing the New Yorkers back. The North Carolinians shot many men of the 134th as they left the cover of the fence.[12]

Meanwhile, Hays's right moved against Coster's left and attacked the troops along Stratton Street and the Harrisburg Road. Hays met little or no opposition until his line came abreast of Gordon's brigade, and he found the enemy in "considerable strength." He might have been thinking of Heckman's battery and the 27th Pennsylvania, for as Winkler wrote, the other infantry there did not remain long. Winkler's small force tarried, but Hays's men did not fire at it — probably they were still too far away, and with all that was happening, the Wisconsin men were an insignificant target. Winkler saw one of Krzyzanowski's staff officers ride by, and he asked what the orders were. The officer replied, "Fall back." Winkler took his men as far as a nearby cottage, where they halted and fired a volley. After this parting salute, the Wisconsin men joined the retreat into the town, leaving Winkler behind. Winkler's staying was a personal thing; he had been back and forth through the town three times that day and had been cheered by the townfolk. Now he felt ashamed. He stood defiantly in the street for a few minutes, but when the Rebels paid him no attention, he, too, started back to Cemetery Hill and to Schurz. His duty was there.[13]

Winkler wrote nothing of Heckman's battery, which had probably come with Coster's brigade through the town and had gone into position near the Carlisle Road. In spite of his four Napoleons not being able to shoot while fleeing Union troops were between them and the enemy, Heckman reported that his battery fired for about thirty minutes and shot 113 rounds, an average of 28 per gun and mostly canister. On his way to the rear, Colonel Robinson of the 119th New York paused at the battery and was wounded there as he pointed out targets for its guns. In spite of Heckman's canister, Hays's brigade pushed ahead. It overran the battery. When the enemy got close, Heckman ordered his sections to limber up and haul out, but the order came too late for his men to save two of the battery's guns.[14]

Just as Avery's brigade turned the flank of the 134th New York on Coster's right, so Hays's brigade turned the flank of the 27th Pennsylvania on Coster's left. Neither Coster, who was at that end of the brigade line, nor Colonel Cantador made a report of what happened there. After the war Colonel Allen of the 154th expressed the belief that the ground rising to the brigade's left kept the 27th from firing in that direction; if so, it could not have slowed Hays's onslaught. Hays suggested that his brigade met little opposition, and Union accounts do not contradict him. Yet Capt. Michael O'Connor of the 6th Louisiana wrote of stubborn resistance. Pvt. J. Arthur Taylor credited the Federals in front of the 8th Louisiana for making a better stand than he had ever seen before, but the 8th was on the left of Hays's line and probably struck the 154th. Taylor observed that Avery's brigade had reached Coster's line before Hays's came up and was exchanging fire with the Federals from behind a fence. When Hays's men appeared, they went over the fence without halting and pushed after the Federals. When the Confederates were within thirty yards of them, the men in blue "raised up like a flock of blackbirds" and fled. Hays's men poured a terrible fire into the fleeing New Yorkers.[15]

Pvt. Charles Comes,
8th Louisiana Infantry,
killed 1 July (LC)

When Colonel Allen saw Avery's line curling around the brigade's right, he ordered the 154th to fall back to the left toward Stratton Street. It had come this way, and it was away from the flanking force to its right rear. When he reached the position of the 27th, Colonel Allen found, to his surprise, that it was no longer there and that the enemy was blocking his way. He had received no warnings of danger. In fact, he had heard firing to the left when his regiment had taken its position, and he had assumed wrongly that his men "were joined onto something" there — troops that would give them protection on that flank. After all, they had come forward to cover the corps' right. But Allen was disillusioned, for he found that the enemy had outflanked the brigade on the left as well as on the right. After the battle, Allen, who must have been angry as hell, learned that Coster had sent an order for the 154th and 134th to retreat when the 27th withdrew. Unfortunately, the order did not reach Allen, and although Colonel Jackson of the 134th might have received one, it came too late to save Allen's regiment. Lieutenant Colonel Cantador may also have neglected to inform Lieutenant Vogelbach of his own regiment of the pullout. Vogelbach's detachment remained on the 154th's right. The Confederates shot Vogelbach when he tried to leave the brickyard and captured his men.[16]

Lt. John Mitchell, commander of Company C, did not obey Allen's order immediately. Company C was doing well, and he did not appreciate the seriousness of the threat. Most of his men started off when they heard of Allen's order; but Mitchell shouted, "Boys, let's stay right here," and they did. For another five or ten minutes they fired as fast as they could. Mitchell then saw that it was suicidal to stay longer and shouted, "Boys, we must get out of here." The boys ran back to the kilns at once, and Private McKay and others each fired another round before heading for the gateway to Stratton Street. At the gateway McKay saw two men on horseback and Capt. Simeon V. Poole and most of Company B sitting on the ground. When Pvt. Addison Scott approached one of the horsemen, a mounted man shouted, "Throw down your gun; surrender." When Scott hesitated, the Confederate officer on the horse struck Scott's head with his sword. McKay suddenly realized, as had others before him, that Hays's men were in Stratton Street and that there was no escape in that direction. He and Pvt. Albert E. Hall ran for Stevens Run and, sheltered by its bank, made their way to a part of Stratton Street closer to the town and ahead of Hays's men.[17]

Lieutenant Crosby, the 154th's adjutant, was among those who reached Stratton Street before the Confederates blocked the gate. There "a fierce hand to hand conflict ensued. The opposing forces were mixed in promiscuous confusion. Four color-bearers in the 154th were shot down in rapid succession. The only resource left was to cut through the enemy's ranks. The bayonet was used, but alas, what could a mere handful of men do against the thousands that surrounded us on all sides? A few in the confusion escaped, but the majority were either killed, wounded or captured." Of the 270 soldiers in the 154th, the Confederates captured or killed all but 3 officers and 15 enlisted men. The afternoon of 1 July 1863 was a sad one for Cattaraugus and Chautauqua counties.[18]

The 27th Pennsylvania's casualties numbered 111 out of a strength of 300 for the entire battle, and it sustained most of them on 1 July. No accounts of the 27th's part in the 1 July fight have been found, but we can assume that the main body of the regiment battled Hays's troops briefly before retreating over Stratton Street. Half of the 27th's casualties must have been in Vogelbach's detachment.[19]

The 134th New York probably did not hold its position as long as the 154th did, but its fight was just as lethal. Avery's Tarheels had it in a crossfire that killed about 40 of the 134th and wounded some 150 before it was able to leave the field. Lieutenant Colonel Jackson, who "displayed great coolness and determination," was among those who escaped capture. He wrote to friends that the regiment was "horribly cut to pieces," all of its officers being wounded except himself and four others. He had never imagined such a rain of bullets, but he claimed that the 134th held its position until ordered back. Orderly Sgt. William H. Howe of Company F was among those captured. He avoided captivity by nursing the 134th's wounded. He announced that all of the regiment's dead were buried near where they fell in a "nice place" by a fence in a pasture.[20]

Coster and his regimental commanders survived the battle. Colonel Jackson escaped capture by hiding for two days in the loft of the house of Henry Meals on York Street. Mrs. Meals helped Jackson disguise his uniform. In the darkness of night Jackson and Pvt. Levi More, who was also hiding in the Meals's house, "ran the enemy's pickets" and rejoined the 134th on Cemetery Hill.[21]

A regiment's colors embodied its honor. The 27th's colors probably were carried off without difficulty, but the New York regiments were not so fortunate. Color Sgt. Lewis Bishop and Color Cpl. Albert Mericle of the 154th were both shot as they fled the brickyard with their flags. Mericle, who carried the state flag, fell on Stratton Street at the bridge over Stevens Run. First Sgt. James Bird took Mericle's flag and carried it to Cemetery Hill. A soldier of the 134th recovered the 154th's national flag and carried it from the field.[22]

Sgts. John J. Carroll and Robert O. Seaman, color-bearers of the 134th, also had a perilous time. A bullet wounded Seaman in the arm, and he was unable to carry the state flag. Carroll took both flags and headed for Cemetery Hill. After being shot three times during his flight, he fell. "The rebel hordes were close behind, and bent on obtaining the colors, but they were foiled." Sergeant Carroll tore the state flag from its staff and wrapped it around his body underneath his clothes, where he concealed it for the four days that he was a wounded prisoner. Capt. Matthew Cheney of the 154th picked up the 134th's national flag, thinking that it was the banner of his own regiment, and carried it through a hail of minié balls, one of which wounded him as he crossed the railroad track. Although Cheney reached Cemetery Hill, the wound ended his service. Sergeant Bishop and Corporal Mericle died in Gettysburg hospitals before the month was out, but Carroll rejoined the 134th with its state flag on 4 July, "as happy as a King." A general, probably von Steinwehr, and the regiment thanked him for his brave deed.[23]

In his report of the day's action Schurz observed that Coster's brigade and Heckman's battery succeeded in checking the enemy long enough to permit Barlow's division to "enter the town without being seriously molested on its retreat." It might have held Hays's and Avery's brigades up long enough to accomplish some of that mission, and perhaps it is just as well to assume that Schurz's statement was correct. The cost of the brief delaying action, however, was enormous — on the order of 550 casualties, a number comparable to that of each of Barlow's brigades. Three hundred of Coster's brigade casualties became prisoners of war, and 172 of them were from the 154th. Of these, 60 would experience the horrors of Andersonville and Belle Isle prisons before dying in them. One of the men killed, Sgt. Amos Humiston, fell at the corner of York and Stratton streets and died with a photograph of his three children in his hand. The Humiston family's story would embody the tragedy at Gettysburg in the years to come (see Appendix C).[24]

CHAPTER 20

Heth Attacks

Amelia Harmon, a young lady in her teens, and her aunt were alone at the "Old McLean Place," the Harmon farm, on the Old Mill Road about 250 yards west of Willoughby Run. When they heard the boom of Confederate cannon off to the west, they rushed to a window and saw "hundreds" of galloping horses. The riders were shouting to one another as they rode by the Harmon farmyard toward the woods 400 yards to the west. There were a few shots, and the riders returned pell-mell to the shelter of the farm buildings. The women quickly locked the house's doors and went to the second floor to look from a west window. As they peered toward Herr Ridge, a minié ball struck a shutter by the aunt's ear. At the same time, below the window, a bullet hit an officer's horse, sending both the horse and its rider to the ground. One glance to the west revealed "hundreds of gray crouching figures" stealthily advancing through the timothy field between the Harmon barn and the woods. The women "fairly shrieked" down to the officer who was arising from the ground. "Look, the field is full of Confederates." "Leave the window," he shouted, "or you will be killed!" They did so at once but climbed to the cupola of the house, from which they could get a better view but were in greater danger.[1]

The gray figures were skirmishers from Heth's division. Heth placed his main line south of the pike facing the Federal strong point in McPherson Woods. Pettigrew's 2,500-man brigade, probably the largest in Lee's army, stood in the center of this line. Its right was near the Old Mill Road, and its single two-rank line extended north along the east front of the Springs Hotel Woods to the area opposite the center of McPherson Woods. Heth placed Archer's battered brigade, now commanded by Col. Birkett Fry, in the woods on Pettigrew's right between the Old Mill Road and the Finnefrock buildings. Heth's left brigade, commanded by Col. John Brocken-brough, extended north from Pettigrew's left through the woods and into the open fields beyond. No one recorded the hour that Heth's three brigades reached their positions; but deploying a division in trees and fields was complicated, and it must have taken considerable time. Federal skirmishers greeted their arrival with a hail of bullets, and the Confederates sent out skirmishers of their own to return the greeting.[2]

Lt. Col. John R. Lane of the 26th North Carolina wrote that the men of his regiment were allowed to lie down and be as comfortable as possible during their long wait. Details went back for water. The water at Willoughby Run was in Union hands and beyond their reach. There was the usual joking, but because there were no chaplains at hand, there were no religious services. All the while the enemy skirmishers reminded them "that they had better cling to the bosom of old mother earth." Lane had his own problems: he had become nauseous from drinking bad water and was vomiting. He asked Col. Henry K. Burgwyn's permission to go to the rear, but Burgwyn would not hear of it. Burgwyn gave Lane a swig of brandy that he carried for such occasions, and in a little while Lane felt able to advance with the regiment.[3]

Some sniping from the Harmon buildings, to the 26th's right, annoyed Colonel Burgwyn, who was already edgy because of the long delay in attacking. Lt. John A. Lowe of Company G volunteered to shoot a sniper who was behind a chimney of the house. Lowe crept close to the culprit by following a fence, perhaps the one that paralleled the woods about 200 yards to the east. Although Lowe silenced the sniper, there would be further annoyance from the Harmon house that day.[4]

In the hours between Archer's repulse and A. P. Hill's afternoon attack, the Iron Brigade consolidated its position in McPherson Woods, the designated strong point of the Union front. On its north side the woods rose abruptly above Willoughby Run. The stream's banks were lined with willows, brush, and briers that made it an obstacle to an attacking force, but the woods itself was open and had little underbrush to limit vision and maneuvers. It favored the troops who defended it but offered no insurmountable obstacle to an attacker.[5]

The 7th Wisconsin was on the Iron Brigade's right with its right at the fence that bordered the north side of the woods. Its line ran midway along the slope of the west arm of McPherson Ridge for about 100 yards. To the 7th's left, the 24th Michigan's line curved about 130 yards across the slope and down to the bottomland along the run occupied by the 19th Indiana

{ HETH ATTACKS }

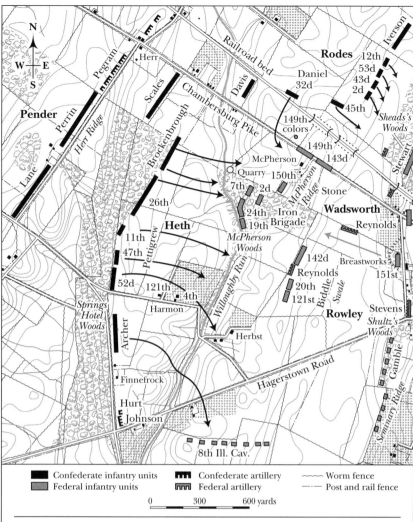

N
W E
S

Railroad bed

Pegram

Herr

Scales

Davis

Chambersburg Pike

Rodes 12th
53d
Daniel 43d
32d 2d
45th

Iverson

Sheads's
Woods

Pender

Perrin

Herr Ridge

Brockenbrough

149th
colors

149th

McPherson
Quarry 150th
7th 2d

Stone

143d

Stewart

Wadsworth

26th

24th Iron
19th Brigade

Reynolds

Heth

11th

47th

McPherson
Woods

Pettigrew

52d 121th 4th

Harmon

Springs
Hotel
Woods

Archer

142d

Reynolds
20th
121st

Herbst

Breastworks

151st

Biddle Swale

Stevens
Rowley Shultz's
Woods

Finnefrock

Hurt

Johnson

Hagerstown Road

Willoughby Run

Seminary Ridge

Gamble

8th Ill. Cav.

| ■ Confederate infantry units | ▥ Confederate artillery | ∼ Worm fence |
| ▨ Federal infantry units | ▥ Federal artillery | -·- Post and rail fence |

0   300   600 yards

1. The Iron Brigade occupies McPherson Woods. The 150th Pennsylvania of Stone's brigade is at the McPherson buildings. Biddle's brigade is on McPherson Ridge south of the woods. Its 151st Pennsylvania Regiment is in reserve at the seminary. Gamble's cavalrymen, dismounted, form a line in Shultz's Woods and along the ridge to the south.
2. Cooper's battery is on Biddle's line; it is replaced by Reynolds's battery. Soon all of the Union batteries fall back to Seminary Ridge.
3. Heth's division forms on the east slope of Herr Ridge. Pettigrew's brigade is in its center, along the east edge of Springs Hotel Woods. Archer's brigade is to Pettigrew's right, Brockenbrough's brigade to its left. Pender's division is deployed in Heth's rear.
4. Pettigrew attacks the Iron Brigade in front and on the left; Brockenbrough strikes its right front. The Iron Brigade falls back, occupying lines in the woods, behind the woods, and at the bottom of the swale.
5. Pettigrew's right regiments drive Union troops from the Harmon buildings and advance on Biddle. The 151st Pennsylvania advances to the right of Biddle's line. The line is flanked on the left and right and retreats to Seminary Ridge.
6. Archer's brigade and the 52d North Carolina guard Heth's right from the 8th Illinois Cavalry.
7. Heth's line halts at the crest of McPherson Ridge. Pender's division passes over it.

Map 20.1. Heth's Afternoon Attack

on the brigade left. The Hoosier line, which measured about 100 yards from flank to flank, was in the trees on the narrow floodplain. The brigade's fourth regiment, the 2d Wisconsin, which had been in the fields to the right of the 7th, moved to the 7th's rear after Stone's brigade occupied the ridgeline north of the woods.[6]

The high ground west of Willoughby Run dominated the left of the Iron Brigade. Several times the commanders of the 19th Indiana and the 24th Michigan asked for permission to shift to more defensible ground, but to no avail. Doubleday intended to hold the woods as long as possible, and they were to hold their positions "at all hazards." Col. Samuel J. Williams of the 19th Indiana announced, "Boys, we must hold our colors on this line or die under them." In spite of such an order it is both ironic and instructive that, though the writings of Iron Brigade veterans told of their waiting three hours in their position — a wait that embraced care of the wounded, eating, and skirmishing — the Iron Brigade made no significant effort to strengthen its vital position by entrenching or erecting breastworks.[7]

Col. Chapman Biddle, acting commander of Rowley's brigade, was a Philadelphia Biddle. The forty-one-year-old officer had been a lawyer in civilian life and active in the prewar militia. Biddle and his brigade supported the left of the Iron Brigade. After forming in the swale behind McPherson Ridge, it moved across the ridge and down to Willoughby Run to the left of the 19th Indiana's position in McPherson Woods. No one said who ordered the brigade to this position or why; possibly Doubleday or Rowley deemed it desirable to extend the line of the Iron Brigade along the run. The trees of McPherson Woods afforded the Iron Brigade some shelter, but Biddle and his men had little cover. The grainfields to the west "were alive with" concealed Confederate skirmishers who fired down on the hapless Federals who could neither see nor shoot them. Soon the brigade fell back to the reverse slope of the ridge, except the 20th New York Militia remained on its crest. Many men of the 20th complained about their exposed location. Theodore B. Gates or Biddle calmed them by appealing to their vanity — telling them that they held an important position and that General Wadsworth, who had once been their brigade commander, had wanted them to man it.[8]

Wadsworth, who seemed to have no fear and expected others to share his dedication and fearlessness, was responsible for one of the bold small-unit actions of the battle. He directed Colonel Gates to send a company of the 20th New York to clear the Confederate skirmishers from his front and from Harmon's stone barn. The Rebel skirmishers there were sniping at

Rowley's brigade and Cooper's battery. Colonel Gates sent his K Company, thirty men commanded by Capt. Ambrose N. Baldwin, "a most capable and courageous officer," to do the job. Baldwin deployed his company as skirmishers. They dashed forward, and after a "spirited contest," drove the Confederates from the Harmon farmyard and its buildings.[9]

This farmyard was about 700 yards west of Gates's position on McPherson Ridge, 250 yards west of Willoughby Run, and about 400 yards east of the Confederate position in Springs Hotel Woods. While there, Company K was much closer to the Confederate position than to its comrades on McPherson Ridge. Its men occupied the house, the stone barn, a two-story brick washhouse, a smokehouse, and a corncrib. The house was a large brick building topped with a cupola and had at least four rooms on its first floor and five on the second.

From the house's cupola, Amelia Harmon saw the approach of the Eleventh Corps — "a dark sinuous line winding around the distant hills beyond the town like a huge serpent." After awhile, a "violent commotion and uproar" replaced the sounds of skirmishing and summoned the women to the lower floor. Men pounded on the kitchen door with fists and gun butts, shouting, "Open, or we'll break down the doors." One of the women drew the bolt and "in poured a stream of maddened, powder-blackened blue coats, who ordered us to the cellar, while they dispersed to the various west windows throughout the house." From the cellar the women could hear the crack of rifles, yelling troops, and occasional cannon fire.[10]

The racket continued for well over an hour as irritated Confederates tried to destroy this hornets' nest. As the pressure on Company K grew to beyond handling, Baldwin sent Lt. Jack Young back to the 20th's position on McPherson Ridge with a request for help. Young was a wild fellow, the sort who could be a blessing or a curse. He had been a sergeant in the war with Mexico and had helped capture a cannon at Cerro Gordo. When he became roaring drunk and riotous, he often bellowed a "bawdy ballad" at the top of his voice. His superiors tolerated his behavior because "he was too good a man in a fight to be left out." As Young approached the 20th's line of "men lying down almost rigidly nervous under the prolonged exposure and shot and shell," he roared an obscene verse from his ballad and shouted to Gates, "Colonel, its d——d hot out there." This broke the tension of the men nearby, but Young's report was not good. The enemy was in force in front of Baldwin's company, and Baldwin would soon be unable to hold the buildings. Gates asked Young to tell Baldwin to hang on as long as possible, and Young returned to Company K. Soon Gates sent

Maj. Gen. Henry Heth (LC)

Capt. William Cunningham's Company G to reinforce Company K at the Harmon buildings.[11]

The men of the 26th North Carolina looked toward McPherson Woods, where they could see the soldiers of the Iron Brigade in their "tall bell crowned black hats which made them conspicuous in the line." By this time Rodes's division of Ewell's corps had reached the field and engaged the Eleventh Corps and Robinson's division of the First Corps north of Gettysburg. "Never was a grander sight beheld," wrote Lieutenant Colonel Lane as he recalled seeing Ewell's corps engaged in battle to his left. In Lane's memory the "roar of artillery, the crack of musketry, and the shouts of the combatants added grandeur and sublimity to the scene."[12]

Although Lane thought the scene on Ewell's front sublime, General Lee probably found it less so. The details of Lee's movements and actions on the afternoon of 1 July seem impossible to reconstruct, yet some of them may be assumed. Maj. Campbell Brown met Lee east of Cashtown early that afternoon to report on Ewell's movements. Brown found Lee greatly concerned with Stuart's absence, and Lee stated that he did not want a general engagement brought on until his entire army had come up. After this conversation, Brown returned to Ewell, and Lee rode on toward Gettysburg and to "Hill's front," which Brown believed to be about three miles to the east. When Brown reached Ewell, he found him and Rodes posting Carter's batteries. This could have been about 2:00 P.M. and the time of Rodes's advance. It seems safe to assume, then, that Lee reached Hill's front at Belmont Ridge or Herr Ridge at the same time. Lee must have viewed the Confederate deployment with concern and anxiety, for the premature battle that he feared seemed at hand. We can assume that Hill briefed him on the morning's fight and told him what was known of the enemy in his front. We may assume also that Lee urged caution on Hill even as Ewell's skirmishers were opening the battle on Oak Ridge.

Major Venable of Stuart's staff had reached Ewell soon after Brown's return, and Ewell sent him at once to Lee. Therefore, as Ewell's attack began, Lee would have been conversing with Venable about Stuart and would have ordered Stuart to Gettysburg.[13]

In his report General Hill had little to say of this portion of the battle; he wrote only that at 2:30 P.M. Ewell's right wing appeared to his left and formed at a right angle with his line. Fortunately Heth had more to say. He reported that after being in position for an hour or more, he received orders to attack. In a later account he wrote that after hearing heavy firing on Ewell's front, he rode to his artillery's first position, possibly Belmont Ridge at the Chambersburg Pike, where he found Lee and Hill. He told them that Rodes seemed to be heavily engaged and suggested that his division had better "go in." Lee replied that he did not wish to bring on a general engagement that day, for Longstreet was not up.

Heth returned to his division, and the battle continued. Heth might have seen the repulse of Iverson's brigade and perhaps the opening of Daniel's fight at the railroad bed. Then he saw troops in his front, Stone's brigade, shifting to confront Daniel. He rode again to where he had left Hill and Lee and found Lee. Apparently Hill had gone elsewhere. Heth told Lee that he believed that troops were being shifted from his front to engage Rodes and again asked permission to attack. This time Lee told him to "wait awhile and I will send you word when to go in." Heth returned to his division, and soon an order came for him to attack.[14]

Who sent this order? Lee reported that Hill had ordered Heth's advance, but neither Hill nor Heth said where the directive originated. Certainly if Hill ordered it, he would not have done so without Lee's permission. Lee's hopes to avoid a general engagement were fading fast.[15]

At Pettigrew's command, "Attention," his 2,500 North Carolinians stood. Pettigrew rode his gray horse along the line, the officers took their posts, and color-bearers, like Sgt. Jefferson B. Mansfield of the 26th, strode four paces to the front of their regiments and halted. When all seemed ready, Pettigrew shouted, "Forward, march!" and the brigade advanced toward Willoughby Run and destiny.[16]

On the right, the "trigger pullers" of the 47th North Carolina stepped out with forty rounds of ammunition. They felt like conquerors, but their confidence may have wavered when Federal batteries opened on them as they emerged from the woods. A round killed three men in one company and felled its file closers. In Lieutenant Colonel Lane's memory, "all to a man stepped off, apparently willingly and as proudly as if they were on review." The Union troops tended to fire high, but the Carolinians "kept the step and made as pretty and perfect a line [as] any regiment ever made, every man endeavoring to keep dressed on the colors." Lt. Louis G. Young, Pettigrew's adjutant, echoed Lane's observation, writing, perhaps with some exaggeration, that Pettigrew's brigade "marched out in perfect alignment, and under as hot a fire as was ever faced, moved steadily through the wheat." Good alignment signified good discipline and training and was necessary if a unit was to have maximum fire power. There could have been no grander compliment or greater boast than these words of Lane and Young.[17]

Pvt. William Roby Moore of the 19th Indiana saw the Rebels coming from the woods in three lines that extended far beyond the left of the Union position. "They kept coming steadily on, and in as good line as ever troops did upon parade, and their muskets a glittering. It was an awe-inspiring sight to observe them." Other Union soldiers recalled that the Confederates had advanced in two or more lines. Colonel Morrow of the 24th Michigan, Colonel Biddle, and Colonel Gates reported seeing two lines; Colonel Williams of the 19th Indiana saw three lines. In short, the Union soldiers saw Heth's division coming on in at least two lines that extended beyond their left.[18]

Yet Confederate sources suggest that the Confederates advanced in a single line. Heth reported that his division formed in "line of battle," while Lieutenant Colonel Lane wrote that Pettigrew's four regiments formed in "line by echelon," with the 26th on the left, but that "as the fight progressed," they formed one line. Lane went on to observe that the echelon lineup appeared to the enemy as several lines of battle, whereas there was only one.[19]

There are other explanations, of course, for the Confederates appearing to be in two or more lines. An obvious answer is that there actually were two lines — Heth's and Pender's. Although Pender's division followed some distance in the rear and was distinct from Heth's, the Union soldiers might have remembered the two as one formation. This, and to a lesser extent the deployment of Hill's troops prior to Pickett's Charge, would be the only instances at Gettysburg when one Confederate division advanced behind another. We do not know the interval between Heth's and Pender's lines; but as an example, Daniel formed 200 yards behind Iverson that afternoon, and on 2 July the second line of Hood's division was posted 400 yards behind its first line. If following at an interval of 200 yards, Pender's line of battle might give the Confederate advance the appearance of a double line.[20]

Federal artillery opened on the Confederate line as it left the trees. Probably only a few guns were firing, primarily the four of Reynolds's battery in position near Biddle's (Rowley's) brigade. Colonels Williams and Morrow of the Iron Brigade ordered their men to hold their fire until the Confederates were well within range, even as close as Willoughby Run itself. This did not mean that everyone obeyed the order. Private Moore of the 19th Indiana wrote that "there was not a man in our ranks but realized the futility of endeavoring to turn back that horde." His officers seemed dazed to him and gave no orders to fall in and to fire. Moore and Pvt. Roswell Root of the 24th were of the same mind. Root shared Moore's awe of the Rebel lines. He asserted later that he saw no virtue in the orders they had received to "hold at all hazards." They were "shamefully ordered to stand there without support of either troops or cannon," and this is what the Iron Brigade tried to do.[21]

The soldiers of both the Iron Brigade and the 150th Pennsylvania Regiment, on their right between the woods and the McPherson buildings, saw something inexplicable. As the Pennsylvanians recalled, Heth's and Pender's divisions descended rapidly and magnificently toward Willoughby Run. Suddenly, instead of pressing forward, Brockenbrough's Virginians ceased firing, fell back, obliqued to the right, and disappeared into McPherson Woods.

This movement puzzled the officers of the 150th Pennsylvania on whose front it occurred. After the war, Captain Ashurst visited the field and discovered the answer. Brockenbrough's brigade had maneuvered right to avoid a large quarry hole that had been dug into the hillside overlooking the run just north of the woods. Had they shifted left to miss it, they would have moved toward Daniel's brigade and left a gap in the division's front.[22]

Rodes's arrival and artillery fire from Oak Hill had compelled Biddle's brigade, which was behind McPherson Ridge, to change front to face the artillery fire from the north and avoid being enfiladed by it. The brigade fell back to the Hagerstown Road, but thirty minutes later, when Heth's division began its attack, it moved again. First it formed in two lines with the 121st and 142d regiments in the first line and the 20th New York and the 151st Pennsylvania in their rear. Col. Chapman Biddle took charge of the 121st and the 142d, while Colonel Gates commanded the troops in the second line. The brigade advanced north in the swale until it was opposite the seminary. There the two demibrigades wheeled left to take position on McPherson Ridge. However, during this maneuver General Doubleday detached the 151st Pennsylvania and posted it in reserve behind the works at the seminary.[23]

Colonel Biddle found artillery occupying the ridge. After a shell from Oak Hill struck a pointing ring on one of Cooper's pieces, Colonel Wainwright had ordered Cooper's battery back to the seminary. Then, at a request by General Wadsworth for more artillery support, Wainwright sent Wilber's section of Reynolds's battery to the orchard at the McPherson house. He put its two remaining sections under Lt. William H. Bower on McPherson Ridge south of the woods. Wainwright stayed awhile with Bower's guns and watched the Rebels file from the woods in two strong columns and march to the left until they extended beyond the Federal position by nearly a third of a mile. Then they came on in a double line of battle, and Bower's four guns opened on them. It was then that Biddle's brigade returned to the ridge and, in trying to take position, blocked the fire of the guns. These movements confirmed Wainwright's low opinion of the infantry's ability to work with artillery. He made a quick assessment of the situation and decided that "there was not the shadow of a chance of our holding this ridge even had our Third Division commanders had any idea what to do with their men, which they had not." Therefore, when the enemy line was about 200 yards yards away, Wainwright ordered Bower's two sections back to a stone wall 100 yards south of the seminary, leaving Biddle's brigade to meet the attack alone.[24]

In its new alignment the 142d Pennsylvania, on the brigade right, was at or near the site occupied by its memorial today. To the regiment's left was a gap of perhaps twenty yards where the four cannons had been, then the

20th New York and the 121st Pennsylvania. Biddle remained on the right of the brigade line, and Colonel Gates took command of the two regiments on the left. There the brigade waited while enemy units filed across its front and formed a line that extended far beyond its left. This done, the Confederates moved slowly against the Union flank. During the wait General Rowley rode up to the 142d and shouted, "Stand up for the Old Key Stone. There the Rebels are coming — give it to them." The men of the 142d replied with a shout, and Rowley rode back to their rear.[25]

Before their advance against Biddle's line, the Confederates had swept by the Harmon buildings toward Willoughby Run. From their refuge in the house's gloomy cellar, Amelia Harmon and her aunt listened to the noise of battle and awaited its outcome with suspense and fear. Suddenly they heard the pounding of feet on the floor above, a clatter on the stairs, and the slamming of doors. Silence followed. "With sickening dread," the women awaited what was to come.

The cellar had grated windows at ground level that provided a little light and a limited view. Through them the women heard a swishing noise like that of scythes mowing hay. They also heard the thudding of many feet and saw dark shadows and the passing knees of soldiers in gray. Rushing up the stairs to their kitchen, they saw that their barn was on fire and found Confederates in the house. The Rebels were heaping books, rags, and pieces of furniture on a pile of burning newspapers. They were torching the house. The two women tried to put out the fire and begged for help, "but there was no pity in those determined faces. They were 'Louisiana Tigers,' they boasted, and tigers indeed they were."

The women fled from the burning house. They saw a Rebel line fighting along Willoughby Run and that a second was just then abreast of the barn and was being shelled. Probably those along the run were Heth's men, and Pender's were coming up. Of course, the men who set fire to the house were North Carolinians and not Louisianians. The only Louisiana infantrymen on the field were with Ewell's corps. The infamous Tigers (Wheat's battalion) were no more than an unhappy memory whose ill repute persisted. The women had to flee, but they could not go toward Gettysburg, for there was fighting in that direction. They had to run west through the second line of troops and the gunfire directed at them. Soon they met a group of newspapermen and officers. A London *Times* correspondent, probably Francis Lawley, took them in hand; they were given food and placed in a cottage with a Confederate guard who protected them until the Confederate army slipped away.[26]

As the Harmon women fled west, Baldwin's and Cunningham's companies tried to return to the 20th New York's position. To avoid the Confederates who were threatening them on three sides, they fell back to Willoughby Run's ravine. Because they would make fine targets for their pursuers if they climbed the slope of McPherson Ridge, they filed south along the run under the cover of the cavalry's fire and into the cavalry's lines. Finally, they returned to the 20th on Cemetery Hill. The "capable and courageous" Captain Baldwin survived this adventure only to die two days later during the repulse of Pickett's Charge.[27]

The 19th Indiana and the 24th Michigan regiments, at the apex of the Federal salient in McPherson Woods, were closer to the enemy than other units along the Union line. They were the first to meet Heth's assault. The Confederate advance had been orderly, deliberate, and unhurried. Pvt. Charles H. McConnell of the 24th Michigan thought that the Confederates advanced in splendid alignment, as "if on dress parade, slowly, steadily, resistlessly — closing up the gaps made by our guns, the slow advance not being checked in the least — banners flying proudly, voices ringing out defiantly above the roar of artillery." He deemed it magnificent. Except for one fence that crossed the Confederate front, there were no obstacles in the attackers' path short of Willoughby Run. Some artillery fire raked their lines, but not enough to stop them, and the Union infantry tended to shoot over their heads. Lt. Louis Young estimated that the advance from the Springs Hotel Woods to McPherson Woods, a distance of only 400 yards, "would not ordinarily take over 20 to 30 minutes." That would have been more than ample time.[28]

By the time that Pettigrew's 26th and 11th regiments reached Willoughby Run, the Iron Brigade opened a lethal fire. That against the left of the brigade and the left of the 26th was especially galling. The terrain, the briers and brush along the run, and the hail of lead from McPherson Woods disrupted the Confederate line. As was often the case, the troops tended to crowd toward the centers of their regiments and their colors. The large battle flag of the 26th was an attractive target for Iron Brigade marksmen, and color-bearers fell in quick succession. No sooner would one fall than another would snatch the flag and carry it forward.[29]

The left flank of the 19th Indiana was in the air and vulnerable to enemy attack. The nearest troops on its left were Biddle's men near the crest of the ridge 300 yards to the rear. Private Moore wrote that when the Rebel line drew near, the Hoosier soldiers opened fire of their own accord. Yet Colonel Williams reported that the regiment fired at his command,

and Lieutenant Colonel Dudley boasted that at the 19th's initial volley the enemy's first line "disappeared from view." Dudley claimed that for one hour no Rebel crossed Willoughby Run and lived, but that was more braggadocio than truth. The 19th was in a hot fight that began on its front and extended around its unprotected left. Sgt. Burlington Cunningham, the regiment's color-bearer, had been shot and rendered unconscious in the morning's battle but revived before the afternoon attack and insisted on carrying the colors again. Hardly had the 19th been called to attention to meet the Confederate attack when a bullet struck Cunningham's right leg and knocked him down. He was the first of the regiment's five color-bearers to fall that afternoon.[30]

The Confederates enfolded the 19th's left. Soon 20 men lay dead and 100 wounded along its line. Colonel Williams realized that disaster was in store for the 19th if it remained in place, and he ordered it to retire firing to a second position 100 yards to the rear. Again the North Carolinians threatened to envelop the 19th's flank. Williams ordered it back to the remnants of a fence off the left flank of the 7th Wisconsin. In their retreat many of the men took cover behind the large trees on the slope, sometimes as many as four or five at each tree, and they popped away at the enemy.[31]

As the regiment started back, someone shouted to Capt. William W. Macy, "The flag is down." Macy answered, "Go and get it." The soldier replied, "I won't do it." Captain Macy hurried to the downed flag, and with the help of Lt. Crockett East, put the cover over it to make it less conspicuous until it could be carried to relative safety. The Confederates killed East, and Macy bore the flag toward the rear. Sgt. Maj. Asa Blanchard saw Macy with the flag and asked him for it. Macy replied, "No, there's been enough men shot with it." Blanchard appealed to Colonel Williams, who gave him the responsibility for selecting men to carry it. The regiment retreated to the rear of the woods, losing other color-bearers as it went. Lieutenant Colonel Dudley saw the flag shot down, picked it up, and was shot. Blanchard secured two men to help Dudley to the rear, further depleting the strength of the regiment's line. He picked up the sheathed flag himself, jerked off its cover, tied it around his waist, and shouted, "Rally, boys," as he waved it. A Confederate bullet hit him in the groin, severing an artery there. As his blood spurted out and his life ebbed away, Blanchard said to a Private Jackson, "Don't stop for me. Tell mother I never faltered." Capt. William Murray took the flag from Blanchard's grasp and the cover from around his body and started off with it, but Pvt. Burr M. Clifford took the flag from Murray and bore it from the field. Colonel Williams had no idea how many Hoosiers had carried the 19th's flag that afternoon. He was able to report, however, that "in their hands the honor of our flag and of our State is safe."[32]

While lying prone to the 19th's right, the men of the 24th Michigan saw and heard the Rebels coming, "yelling like demons." Colonel Morrow "called them up" and, when the Rebels drew near, gave the order to fire at will. In spite of heavy losses, the 26th pressed ahead halfway up the hill. Lt. Louis Young wrote of a delay caused by obstinate Union resistance and by the configuration of the ground — the base of the hill had been cut away leaving a perpendicular slope. The steep bank created such comfortable cover for the attackers that many were loath to leave it to brave the hail of lead farther up the slope. About this time Lieutenant Colonel Lane walked from his position behind the right of the 26th to see if all was well elsewhere along the line. Colonel Burgwyn told him that "it is all right in the center and on the left; we have broken the first line of the enemy." Yet by this time ten color-bearers had fallen and the regiment's entire color guard had been shot. Undaunted, the Tarheels pushed toward the enemy's second line.[33]

The 24th was fighting hard, but the attackers' pressure was too great. When the 19th Indiana was flanked on its left and had to give way, the left of the 24th became vulnerable to assault. Private McConnell recorded that this exposed the flank of the 24th, and its men "fell like grass before the scythe." Capt. William J. Speed attempted to refuse its left to meet that threat and died for his pains before the movement could be completed. Lt. Gilbert Dickey, who was in the first graduating class at Michigan State University, also died while trying to set up a line to defend the left.[34]

The second Union line was a place of desperate fighting. While attacking it, Capt. Thomas J. Cureton first appreciated the extent of the 26th's losses. Lieutenant Young, speaking for Pettigrew, had ordered him to close his company on Company F to the right. When he did so, he found only two or three soldiers there who had had not been killed or wounded. About this time he saw Colonel Burgwyn with the regiment's colors. Burgwyn asked him if he would provide a bearer for them. Cureton detailed Pvt. Frank Hunneycutt to the honor.[35]

Henry King Burgwyn Jr., age twenty-one, had attended the University of North Carolina and graduated from the Virginia Military Institute. He was the lieutenant colonel of the 26th in August 1862 when Zebulon Vance, its colonel, resigned to become the governor of North Carolina. Burgwyn

Col. Henry K. Burgwyn Jr.
(W. Clark, *Histories*, 2:302)

succeeded to the command. Now he was leading it in one of the bloodiest fights of the war. At this critical moment, when the 26th's attack was stalling on the slope in front of the 24th's second position, Capt. William McCreery, Pettigrew's ordnance officer, reached Burgwyn with a compliment from Pettigrew: the 26th had covered itself with glory. After delivering this message, and perhaps others of more substance, McCreery seized the regiment's flag, which Hunneycutt had not yet taken, and waved it. He drew fire. McCreery, who had impatiently awaited a command assignment that he deemed worthy of his West Point training, took a bullet in his heart and fell, "bathing the flag in his life's blood."

Lt. George Wilcox of Company H pulled the flag from beneath McCreery's body and advanced a few steps with it before falling with two wounds. The flag and the 26th had to advance — it was suicidal not to do so. Burgwyn seized the flag from the fallen Wilcox and started forward shouting, "Dress on the colors." It was then that Hunneycutt reached Burgwyn and asked for the flag. As Burgwyn turned to give it to him, a ball tore through his side, spun him around, and knocked him to the floor of

McPherson Woods. Hunneycutt, reckoned to be the thirteenth bearer of the banner, fell soon with a bullet though his head.[36]

Lieutenant Colonel Lane went to Burgwyn's side and asked if he was "severely hurt." Burgwyn's only answer was a squeeze of his hand. Lane, now in command of the regiment, hurried to the right, where he told Capt. John C. McLauchlin of Company K, "Close your men quickly to the left. I am going to give them the bayonet." Lane hurried to the left with the same order and then returned to the center. There he saw Hunneycutt's body lying across the colors. "It is my turn to take them now," Lane said. He picked up the flag and shouted, "Twenty-sixth, follow me." The Carolina line surged forward with a cheer.[37]

Lt. Louis G. Young, Pettigrew's adjutant, was on horseback and was prominent that day. Young rode behind and above Pettigrew's line amid the thick and oily smoke that darkened the scene of carnage. He could see along the brigade's line and tried to keep its attack going. Young had close calls; Iron Brigade bullets twice knocked the hat from his head. A member of the 24th Michigan remembered seeing a mounted "colonel" who rode along the Confederate line yelling, "Give 'em hell, boys," and saw a bullet tear the rider's hat from his head. He caught the hat with one hand, clapped it back on, and continued to urge the Tarheels forward.[38]

The 24th Michigan fell back to its third position east of the ravine in the east end of the woods. As it did so, Pvt. Charles McConnell lingered to take another shot. Resting his rifle against a tree, he took a bead on Lieutenant Colonel Lane, who was carrying the 26th North Carolina's colors. McConnell fired; the ball struck Lane in the back of the neck and smashed through his jaw and mouth. The colors of the 26th fell for the fourteenth time.[39]

The veterans of the 2d and 7th Wisconsin regiments on the 24th's right and in the western portion of the woods related little of their afternoon fight. They faced Brockenbrough's brigade, whose officers and men likewise wrote virtually nothing extant of their part in the 1 July battle. The Virginia brigade numbered about 800 "muskets" and would have had a narrow front. It faced the 150th Pennsylvania, the only portion of Stone's brigade then fronting west, and the 2d and 7th Wisconsin regiments in the woods. First Brockenbrough's men drove in the 150th's skirmishers, who retreated into the cover of McPherson Woods. Then they obliqued toward the woods and the Iron Brigade to avoid the quarry hole and disappeared from the 150th's view. Brockenbrough's temporary disappearance gave these Bucktails breathing time, but in the lull they saw the right regiments of the Iron Brigade fall back 200 yards, probably to a line corresponding to the 24th Michigan's position behind the ravine in the east end of the woods. This created a gap between it and the 150th. When Brockenbrough's line shifted right, it unmasked the line of fire from the batteries on Herr Ridge, which again reopened on the 150th and the nearby troops of Stone's brigade. This fire did not last long; it ceased when the Virginians renewed their assault.[40]

The fire was extremely hot. Huidekoper, who had been wounded in the leg, took another bullet in the arm and had to turn the regiment over to Capt. Cornelius Widdis. Lt. Richard Ashurst, the 150th's adjutant, who had been the dominant figure on the 150th's left, was shot in the shoulder and hit by a spent ball on a shin, and a third ball struck his sword's scabbard. Nevertheless he remained at his post. By this time half of the regiment had been killed or wounded. Daniel's brigade assailed it on the right and Brockenbrough's in the front. In the midst of this carnage Wilber's section of Reynolds's battery rolled up. It was no place for artillery; the infantrymen warned it to get out of there and then had to protect it as it did so. When the 150th finally received an order to retreat, Sgt. George Bell complained to Ashurst, "Adjutant, it is damn cowardice; we have beaten them and will keep on beating them back." Bell's ardor had warped his judgment.[41]

Union troops in the McPherson barn fired at the 55th Virginia as it pushed by them. The Virginians had assumed that the occupants of the barn, being behind their line, were their prisoners and did not take kindly to this discourtesy. Maj. Charles N. Lawson of the 55th took two companies to straighten the matter out. Lawson saw an officer at the door of the barn and ordered him to surrender. Instead the officer fired his pistol at Lawson but missed him and killed a man behind him. In response Sgt. Arthur Allen shot the foolish officer. "After some sharp passages," the 55th captured 350 men at the barn, many of whom were wounded. Heth, former commander of Brockenbrough's brigade, reported that its officers and men behaved with their usual gallantry.[42]

The 2d and 7th Wisconsin regiments, on the right of the Iron Brigade's line, contested the advance of Brockenbrough's brigade. When the afternoon's fight began, the two regiments occupied the nose of McPherson Ridge, the 7th down the forward slope and the 2d near the crest. The men of the two regiments "waited with stern determination the impending conflict." Yet the brunt of the battle was to their right, where Brockenbrough's men contended with the 150th Pennsylvania, and to the left, where the 19th Indiana and the 24th Michigan were flanked and forced to fall back—the 24th to the slope overlooking the ravine that passed through the eastern portion of the woods. When Lt. Col. John Callis saw the Confederates split to the 7th's right and left, he remarked to Capt. Henry F. Young, "Capt. they are going to flank us on both flanks." Young replied, "in his peculiar way, 'let them flank and be d——d we are giving them h—l in front.' " But not for long. After the 24th retired, an officer, possibly Capt. Hollon Richardson of the brigade staff, ordered the Wisconsin men to fall back and form a new line of battle, probably near the 24th and overlooking the ravine. There the two Wisconsin regiments formed in a single line with the 2d on the left. They received a "galling fire" from the Confederate line behind the crest of the ridge's nose where the 2d had been before its short retreat. The Union position was untenable. Robinson took seven of his companies back to the ridgeline east of the woods, leaving three of the 7th's companies behind on the right of the 2d, which now "was battling in terrible fury with their Rebel foes" and holding those to their front in check. But the flank fire that had forced back the regiments to their left ate into their strength also; they had to fall back slowly until they came to the open ridgeline where the 7th had formed a new line in "splendid style."[43]

Brig. Gen. Solomon Meredith was one of the casualties of this fight. Meredith, a North Carolinian by birth and six feet, six inches tall, had entered the service as commander of the 19th Indiana. He became a brigadier general in October 1862 and had commanded the Iron Brigade at Fredericksburg and at Chancellorsville. Soon after the opening of the afternoon's attack, the Confederates shot his horse; the horse and Meredith fell, and the general sustained internal injuries that forced him to turn the brigade over to Col. William W. Robinson of the 7th Wisconsin. Meredith recovered eventually but did not return to the Iron Brigade.[44]

A bullet struck Pvt. Emanuel Markle of the 2d Wisconsin in the heel during the morning's charge and "knocked him as flat as a board." But he remained in the woods instead of going to the rear. When the 2d fell back, he could not go and continued to shoot from behind a tree. A spent bullet struck him in the pocket that contained his wallet and did him no harm. Another struck his left breast pocket where a folded handkerchief kept him from being hurt. A third tore a hole in his clothes, and a fourth struck him in the right hand. With two wounds and two narrow escapes, Markle was "used up." A Rebel soldier said, "We've got you, Yank," and Markle replied, "Well you haven't got very much." The Rebel said that he would just as soon kill him as look at him, to which Markle responded that there were 60,000 to 80,000 men in his front, and he had better try his hand on them. Markle went on to tell his captors that the whole army was "up and dressed for action." The Rebel did not kill him.[45]

Orderly Sergeant Wheeler of the 2d Wisconsin had the wits scared out of him during the fight. A shell burst directly over his head, and the concussion knocked him to his knees. When he discovered that he had not been wounded, he became ashamed for his "unaccountable and unnecessary dodge." (In those days brave men, officers especially, were supposed to not flinch from the dangers of enemy fire.) A while later, while he was shooting his rifle, a bullet struck the shank of its fixed bayonet. It drove particles of metal into his ear and caused it to ring. A short time later a rifle fired behind him, and he felt the wind of its bullet. Sgt. Billy Wager, a file closer, ran to him with apologies, and Wheeler swore at him for his carelessness. By now Wheeler felt demoralized, but since "running was not good," he stayed to see things through.[46]

A historian of the Iron Brigade wrote that at this point in the battle each regiment of the brigade was fighting on its own and that none seemed to know what others were doing. He also tried to present the 24th's retreat in an orderly way that placed it in five successive lines of battle before it made a final stand at the seminary. It formed its third line in the east end of the woods above the ravine; its fourth line in the open, probably east of the woods on McPherson Ridge; and the fifth somewhere to the rear. Probably the fifth position corresponded to one taken by the 2d Wisconsin near the bottom of the swale between McPherson Ridge and Seminary Ridge. From there the 2d gave the Johnnies a hot reception as they burst from the woods and advanced down the slope. Capt. Robert K. Beecham did not remember receiving any help from the artillery while the 2d was in the swale. He did find the hollow "hot with the incessant hum of the bees of battle." He also remembered their withdrawing without orders in the manner of a flock of birds that "are seen to quit their tree at the same instant."[47]

An unusual incident occurred while the Iron Brigade was falling back to the seminary. Wadsworth's division had an ammunition train of about forty wagons that had been left in the rear as the division hiked ahead to Gettysburg. After hearing the sound of artillery fire for about a half-hour, Ordnance Sgt. Bert O'Connor was told to take ten wagons loaded with ammunition to the division. O'Connor selected the wagons and put two extra men into each. Six mules (three pair) pulled each wagon, and their driver rode the near (left) horse of the wheel pair. The ten wagons set off for the division. They rolled fast, the drivers whipping their mules to a run. The wagons passed through the town. When they reached the seminary, a major advised O'Connor to go no farther for fear that the wagons would be captured. Since the major did not belong to Wadsworth's division, the sergeant elected not to take his advice. Confederate cannons opened on the wagons as they crossed the ridge, but they reached the Iron Brigade line, which was probably in the swale. The men riding in three wagons threw boxes of cartridges from them, and O'Connor chopped them open with an axe. He dropped off about 70,000 rounds. All the while Confederate guns shelled the wagons, putting holes in their canvas covers. When they had finished unloading, the teamsters ran their wagons back toward the town under increasing enemy fire. A solid shot tore off the hind legs of a "saddle mule," and the mule sank to its stumps. A soldier shot the mule, and others cut its carcass from the team's harness. A second mule received a flesh wound while this was being done, and a cannon shot collapsed the wagon's rear wheels. About this time a retreating regiment passed and took ammunition from the wagon. Pulled by five horses, it moved off on its two front wheels with its rear end dragging. Sergeant O'Connor issued ammunition in the town until the Confederates drove him to Cemetery Hill. Every wagon had been hit, some many times.[48]

As Brockenbrough's brigade and the 11th and 26th North Carolina regiments attacked on Heth's center and left, the 47th and 52d North Carolina advanced on Biddle's brigade from Pettigrew's right. Beyond the Mill Road and to Pettigrew's right, Archer's small and battered brigade guarded the division's right from harassment by Gamble's troopers. Archer's brigade operated essentially on the defensive during the afternoon, and its members wrote but little of what they had done. Lt. Col. Samuel Shepard reported only that the brigade changed front to protect the flank and that the enemy did not advance against it. Another account held that the brigade was in line of battle with its right refused to protect the flank. Capt. Jacob B. Turney of the 1st Tennessee Regiment merely recalled that it deployed as a "body of observation." In short, Archer's brigade played a passive role. Yet its presence opposite Biddle's left flank constituted a threat that Rowley, the division commander; Biddle; and Gates could not ignore.[49]

To the men of Biddle's brigade and to Capt. John Cook of the 20th New York, Pettigrew's North Carolinians appeared as a long butternut line. Its soldiers were "as dirty, disreputable and unromantic as can well be imagined" and "exhibited no more of 'the pomp and circumstance of glorious war' than so many railroad section hands." But Cook freely admitted "they could shoot all right and as they stood out there in line in the open field and poured in a rapid fire of musketry they gave us no time to criticize their appearance. Our men sprang to their feet, returned their fire, and the battle was on."[50]

After crossing Willoughby Run, the 47th North Carolina climbed the west slope of McPherson Ridge, assailed briefly by artillery fire until Reynolds's guns displaced to the seminary. The Carolinians spoke of attacking in two lines — perhaps one was composed of skirmishers — and they were having a hard time. The day was hot. When they tried to load their rifles, the sweat on their hands made their ramrods so slick that they could not shove their cartridges home. As an expedient, they pushed their ramrods against the ground and, in stopping to do so, "undressed" their advancing line. Near the crest of the ridge, they entered a field of breast-high wheat. Suddenly the enemy appeared above the wheat less than seventy-five yards off, with rifles glistening and flags waving. The men in the Union line "leveled their shining line of gun barrels on the wheat heads." Both lines fired. The Tarheels believed that they had the drop on their enemies, and after firing, they rushed them. "The earth just seemed to open and take in that line which five minutes ago was so perfect." Maj. Alexander Biddle, acting commander of the 121st Pennsylvania, remembered it differently. According to Biddle, the 121st fired into the faces of the attacking Confederates when they appeared over the crest and nearly annihilated them. Yet the enemy was able to swing around the 121st's left and poured on a heavier fire than the Pennsylvanians were able to return.[51]

On Pettigrew's right the 52d North Carolina passed through the Harmon barnyard, and Gamble's 8th Illinois Cavalry Regiment threatened it. No one explained why Archer's brigade failed to cover the 52d's right, yet it apparently did not do so. At one point Col. James Marshall formed the 52d North Carolina into a square, presumably as a defense against Gamble's mounted men, and its Company B deployed to guard the regiment's flank from the Union horsemen. Gamble's small force thus occupied both Archer's brigade and the 52d regiment, a notable accomplishment.[52]

As Pettigrew's right regiments attacked Biddle's line, the 26th North Carolina and Brockenbrough's brigade forced the Iron Brigade to the rear of McPherson Woods. To fill a gap between the Iron Brigade's left and Biddle's right, Doubleday told General Rowley to send Col. George McFarland's 151st Pennsylvania Regiment forward to McPherson Ridge from its place in reserve at the seminary. McFarland posted it on the right of the brigade between the rear edge of McPherson Woods and the 142d Pennsylvania's right. As the 151st took position, the Confederates greeted it with a volley that brought down several men. Soon after, McFarland saw Iron Brigade regiments retreat from the woods and reform in the swale to his rear. He thought that their leaders regarded the 460-man 151st Pennsylvania as "a *relief*." He remembered seeing Iron Brigade officers moving up and down their line in the swale with "coolness and bravery."[53]

When the Iron Brigade fell back, it permitted the Confederates in the woods to move against the front and right of the 151st. The Confederate fire was "severe and destructive." Further, since the Confederates were downhill and among trees, McFarland did not order volley fire in return. His men had new Springfield rifles and had had a lot of target practice; therefore, each man was to choose a Confederate as a target and take deliberate aim at him. Nevertheless the Confederates outgunned them, and soon a third of the 151st was down.[54]

The Confederates pressed the brigade's front and flanks. Colonel Biddle rode back and forth along its line "cheering his men and urging them through that fiery ordeal, his words unheard in the roaring tempest, but, as well by gesture and the magnificent light of his countenance, speaking encouragement to the men on whom he well knew he could place every reliance." The 142d Pennsylvania Regiment lost heavily. At one point Colonel Biddle seized its flag and led it in a "charge" against the left flank of the 47th North Carolina. Scattered Federals swarmed around Biddle and his flag like bees around their queen. As this mass of Union soldiers approached the 47th North Carolina's left, fire from all directions cut it to pieces. An officer of the 142d described the charge as hopeless, "an act of personal gallantry . . . but unwise, rash, leading to misfortune which might not otherwise have occurred."[55]

The fire received from both front and flank dominated the memories of veterans of Biddle's two left regiments — Colonel Gates's command. It came from the 47th North Carolina in the front and from the 52d regiment to the left. Although the accounts from the 52d deal primarily with its confrontation with Gamble's cavalrymen, it would have been on the 121st's flank and capable of giving it deadly attention. Like von Gilsa's brigade on Blocher's Knoll, Biddle's was flanked and doomed. In retrospect, Gates and others wrote of holding on until the artillery moved off, but if Reynolds's guns pulled away when the advancing Confederates were 200 yards away, as Wainwright said, the artillery would not have detained them long.[56]

The initial fire into the 121st Pennsylvania's flank created havoc within its ranks. Bullets riddled Color Sgt. William Hardy's flag and broke its staff into three pieces. Capt. J. Frank Sterling remarked that had the regiment remained in its position for a few more minutes, not a man would have been unscathed. The officers tried to reform their companies without success. A minié ball struck Captain Sterling in the thigh as he tried to rally the men around the colors. He set off for a hospital and had to walk alone a half-mile to reach a doctor who could remove the ball. Although Sterling did not consider his wound serious, he died from its complications four months after the battle. As Sterling made his way to the rear, the 121st, "broken and scattered," retreated to the seminary grounds, where it prepared for more fighting. By day's end only a fourth of the regiment and two officers were still with its colors.[57]

The 20th New York was in no better shape. It, too, was the target of Confederate riflemen in its front and to its left. As its men fell, the survivors crowded toward its flag. Captain Cook and a lieutenant in his company had agreed to give special attention to four men of doubtful courage. Each would keep his eye on two. When the shooting began, the captain saw one man turn to run; he threatened to shoot him. As the man turned back toward the line, he received a mortal wound. He grasped the captain's legs and begged for help, but Cook could only let him die. About the same time one of the lieutenant's men started to run. The lieutenant stopped him with his sword, and a bullet stopped him permanently. In the ensuing confusion, the other two cowards disappeared; Cook assumed that they went to hospitals and avoided returning to the ranks.[58]

Colonel Gates saw that the 20th could not hold its position. From atop his horse he reached down, took the flag from the color-bearer, rested it across his shoulder, and shouted for the men to stand by him. He then ordered a parting volley at the closest Confederates to give them pause and started the 20th back toward the seminary. Its men fought "so obstinately as they moved off that the enemy's pursuit was cautious and tardy." Gates recalled with satisfaction that the 20th lost no prisoners except wounded who had to be left behind. On the other hand, Lt. William H. Blount of the 47th North Carolina boasted that though the fight had cost the regiment the lives of many of its best men, "in the fight we showed the superiority of southern soldiers over Yankee hirelings."[59]

Colonel Gates noted that the two regiments on the brigade's right departed first, but Colonel McFarland of the 151st did not agree. As McFarland recalled it, the Iron Brigade fell back to his right, and Gates's wing

Capt. Romulus M. Tuttle
(W. Clark, *Histories*, 1:341)

and the 142d Pennsylvania retreated from his left. Their departure exposed the 151st to a savage crossfire. This accounted for its heavy casualties—67 percent of its officers and 77 percent of its enlisted men. He thought first to fall back to the left of the Iron Brigade in the swale but saw that it had retreated to the seminary. To prevent the 151st from being surrounded, he started it to the rear, and with the rest of the brigade, it took position at the seminary.[60]

Heth's division did not seriously dispute the Federal retreat. It was worn out. A minié ball struck General Heth in the head as he rode across the nose of the west arm of the ridge. Fortunately a folded paper placed behind the sweat band of his oversized hat cushioned the blow. He fell unconscious at the climax of the fight, and command of the division passed to General Pettigrew.[61]

After driving the Federals from McPherson Ridge, Heth's attack stalled. He claimed that his division had lost 2,300 men in thirty minutes. Pettigrew's brigade, which had borne the brunt of the afternoon's fight, had lost over 1,000 men in killed and wounded, including 250 of 550 in the 11th North Carolina and 549 of 800 men in the 26th. Capt. Romulus M. Tuttle's Company F of the 26th suffered the most astounding loss. Every man in the fight was killed or wounded. It went into action with 3 officers and 88 enlisted men; 31 were killed or mortally wounded, and the remainder were wounded. Tuttle had a bad leg wound.[62]

Apart from their casualties, Heth's brigades were out of ammunition and halted their advance. The men of the 26th scrounged ammunition from cartridge boxes lying on the field in order to continue their fight. As they prepared to advance again, Pender's division came up from the rear and passed over their line. Pender's arrival signaled the end of Heth's division's battle on 1 July and the beginning of the day's last round.[63]

CHAPTER 21

Retreat from McPherson Ridge

Shortly before 4:00 P.M. Maj. Gen. Abner Doubleday assessed the state of the Union First Corps west of the town. He saw the enemy overwhelming its center, pressing hard on its right, and overlapping its left. It seemed as if Lee's entire army was at hand. In contrast, his own men were exhausted from their morning's march and their subsequent fighting. Their casualties were high, they had no reserves, and they were falling back. Any further orders to hold their positions would be demanding the impossible. Therefore he ordered them to withdraw to Cemetery Hill south of the town. There would be a pause on Seminary Ridge by the Iron Brigade and Biddle's (Rowley's) brigade in particular to support the First Corps batteries on the ridge and to cover the retreat of the corps to Cemetery Hill. Doubleday's order only ratified and gave some direction to what already was taking place.

A few minutes earlier, General Howard had answered Doubleday's calls for reinforcements by replying, "Hold out, if possible, a little longer, for I am expecting General Slocum every moment." But although Slocum and his Twelfth Corps were nearby, they did not come. Howard sent another message to Doubleday at 4:00 P.M. telling him that if they could no longer hold the ground, they must fall back to Cemetery Hill. He also asked Buford to make a show of force with his cavalry against the enemy right. Then, recognizing that the positions west and north of Gettysburg had to be abandoned, Howard, at 4:10 P.M., ordered both Doubleday and Schurz to fall back fighting to Cemetery Hill. In later years Doubleday claimed no recollection of having received such an order until he was passing through town. He maintained that it had come too late; had his troops remained in position until he received it, the Confederates would have captured them all.[1]

In retrospect, Doubleday thought that his regiments might have had less loss had they not halted at the seminary to support the First Corps batteries placed there by Colonel Wainwright. The colonel, not knowing that there was a "Cemetery Hill," had assumed that "cemetery" was "seminary" and had placed his batteries on Seminary Ridge. Doubleday saw, too, that the attack against his left offered Buford an opportunity to take Rebels in the flank. He claimed that he directed Buford to do this.[2]

The position that Doubleday chose utilized Seminary Ridge's crest and west slope between the Hagerstown Road and the east railroad cut—a distance of just over 700 yards. The cut and Sheads's Woods beyond covered its right. Shultz's Woods and the Hagerstown Road defined the left. Its principal feature was the large, three-story brick building that housed classrooms and dormitory rooms of the Lutheran seminary and a basement apartment for its caretaker. It stood midway between the Hagerstown Road and the Chambersburg Pike. There were other buildings in the area also: the brick houses of the Reverend Simon Schmucker, president of the seminary, and of the Reverend Charles Krauth, a seminary professor. There was a cluster of buildings at the pike, including the story-and-a-half stone house of Mary Thompson on the ridge's crest north of the pike and the James Thompson house south of that road. The large Dustman house was just east of the crest and the Mary Thompson house. Each had outbuildings. As was usually the case, the five houses and their outbuildings received little or no mention in the recollections of the men who fought around them.[3]

There were two orchards on the west slope of the ridge, one between the pike and the railroad cut and another that extended about 200 yards south from the pike. More importantly, a large open grove of trees blanketed 200 yards of the west slope of the ridge opposite the seminary building and the Schmucker house. There were also fences and a stone wall that ran along the crest for 200 yards south of the pike and in front of the Krauth house. Amid these features was the breastworks, a semicircular structure about two feet high of fence rails and debris. The works arced west across the front of the seminary building and back to the stone wall west of the Krauth house.[4]

The 1 July battle was a challenge for the commanders of the First Corps batteries. Lt. George Breck, acting commander of Reynolds's New York

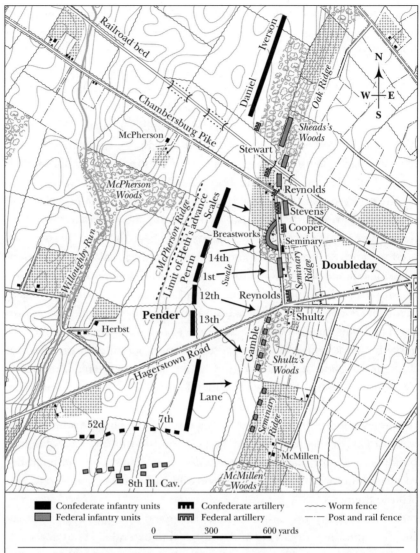

Railroad bed

Chambersburg Pike

McPherson

Stewart

Daniel

Iverson

Oak Ridge

Sheads's Woods

N
W E
S

Reynolds

McPherson Woods

Stevens

Cooper

Scales

Breastworks

Seminary

14th

Doubleday

1st

Perrin

Limit of Heth's advance

McPherson Ridge

Swale

12th

Reynolds

Seminary Ridge

Pender

13th

Shultz

Herbst

Gamble

Shultz's Woods

Willoughby Run

Hagerstown Road

Lane

Seminary Ridge

52d

7th

McMillen

8th Ill. Cav.

McMillen Woods

| ■ Confederate infantry units | ⊓⊓⊓ Confederate artillery | ∿∿ Worm fence |
| ▨ Federal infantry units | ⊓⊓⊓ Federal artillery | —·— Post and rail fence |

0   300   600 yards

1. The Iron Brigade and Stone's and Biddle's brigades fall back behind the batteries on Seminary Ridge and the breastworks there. All have sustained heavy casualties and are disorganized.
2. Pender's division advances behind Heth with Perrin's, Scales's, and Lane's brigades. They pass over Heth's line on McPherson Ridge.
3. Scales's brigade reaches the bottom of the swale. Union fire forces it to halt.
4. Perrin's brigade, on Scales's right, advances to the bottom of the swale. It reforms in a ravine there before attacking the Union position in its front.
5. Perrin orders his 1st and 14th South Carolina regiments to attack the Union troops near the seminary, and the 12th and 13th South Carolina regiments to attack Gamble's cavalry line in Shultz's Woods to his right front.
6. Lane's brigade on the right attacks the cavalry line.
7. The 1st South Carolina breaks into the Union position south of the seminary building. The Union troops retreat to Cemetery Hill.

Map 21.1. Pender's Division Attacks

battery, wrote that "matters seemed to be, at times, very much at 'log-gerheads,' lacking a controlling, directing head in the movements and dispositions of our forces." Breck probably wrote of the First Corps as a whole, but the same applied to its batteries. Generals liked to post batteries even though many knew little about artillery. General Wadsworth had authorized Lieutenant Stewart to post his battery astride the railroad cut, and Doubleday had ordered Stevens's Maine battery to unlimber north of the seminary building. Wainwright, who should have been controlling these batteries, was with Cooper's and Reynolds's batteries at the time and did not know what Wadsworth and Doubleday had done. When Wain-wright turned his attention to Stevens's and Stewart's batteries, they were firing, and there was no time for changes even had he wanted to make them.[5]

Stewart's U.S. battery, manned in part by infantrymen from the Iron Brigade, had three Napoleons just north of the railroad bed in the corner of the woods about 200 yards down from the ridge's crest. They could fire west along the railroad bed and the pike and still be sheltered by the woods from enfilading fire from Oak Hill. Stewart's other three guns were be-tween the cut and the pike; they could shoot across the fields to the west.[6]

Colonel Wainwright sent Cooper's Pennsylvania battery back from McPherson Ridge to Seminary Ridge. Its four three-inch Ordnance rifles stood in front of the seminary building and in the rear of the breastworks. Soon after, Cooper's guns dueled with Brander's battery, which was north of the Isaac Bender farm buildings. It fired also at Daniel's regiments as they attacked Stone's brigade.[7]

Stevens's 5th Maine battery was on Cooper's right. Wainwright had placed its six Napoleons by the Hagerstown Road, but Doubleday had ordered them north of the seminary. Two three-inch Ordnance rifles be-longing to Wilber's section of Reynolds's battery were on Stevens's right. When this section had fallen back from near the McPherson house, Lt. Benjamin W. Wilber placed his two guns there—one on the pike itself. Artillerymen recalled that the guns on this line were packed tightly, only five yards apart rather than at the prescribed fifteen-yard intervals. Actu-ally they might have had more room than that.[8]

When Pettigrew's men threatened Biddle's line on McPherson Ridge, Wainwright placed two sections of Reynolds's battery behind a wall on Seminary Ridge near the Hagerstown Road. After he became elderly, Ser-geant Shelton remembered this move: how the limbers had swung around to the gun trails in "beautiful curve[s]," hooked up, and went off at a "sharp trot," with the cannoneers running alongside, some trying to put the implements in their places on the guns as they ran. The battery passed into the swale, "a low stubble field, into which the wheels of the carriages sink heavily and through which the galloping horses flounder." He remembered also the gun sections' implements: "the buckets and chains swinging to and fro and the sponges and wormers trembling on their hooks." The officers and sergeants, on their horses, rode in their places, and the guidon bearer on his gray horse was to the right of the line with his "fluttering flag." Enemy shells fell behind the battery, "striking in the soft ground and throwing up fountains of black earth."

During this retreat Pvt. John Conn ran to Shelton with a bleeding head, crying, "For God's sake, Sergeant, save me." Shelton grabbed Conn by the arm and pulled him onto his horse as it galloped away. When they reached Seminary Ridge, Shelton turned Conn over to the care of his tent mate; but Conn had a mortal wound, and he died at Gettysburg.[9]

The infantry of Stone, Biddle, and the Iron Brigade followed the cannons back to the ridge. They seemed to fall back in no particular order. Probably the 150th Pennsylvania, the 2d Wisconsin, and the 151st Pennsylvania were the last in their brigades to retreat, but this is not certain. After moving over the east arm of McPherson Ridge, several regiments paused in the bottom of the swale to reform their lines. They shot at the Confederates who had followed them as far as the crest of McPherson Ridge about 300 yards to the west.[10]

A portion of Stone's brigade, now under Colonel Dana, fell back to a peach orchard on the west slope of the ridge. Because there were no fences or works for them to rally behind, some men went on to Stevens's battery. For a time they masked its front and prevented it from firing. Sergeant Hubler of the 143d Pennsylvania heard a battery commander, probably Stevens, shout, "My G—d, boys, save my guns." They obliged by lying down by his and Wilber's pieces, where some of them must have interfered with the cannoneers. One young fellow was keyed up; he stood and watched the Confederate shells striking the ground around them and called out, "Come boys, don't you hear the music, the ball is going to open, why don't you get up and choose your partners?"[11]

The Iron Brigade occupied the ridge to the left of Stevens's battery and manned the breastworks there. As its men took cover behind the works, artillery forty yards behind them fired over their heads. Colonel Morrow of the 24th Michigan was wounded in the head before he reached this barricade. He asked "Colonel" John G. Stephenson to help him. Stephenson, the Librarian of Congress, had taken a leave of absence from his collections to serve as a volunteer aide to General Meredith. Stephenson replied, "Get on my horse and go to the rear, and I will rally your boys." Capt. Albert Edwards took Morrow's place as commander of the 24th. Seizing his regiment's flag from a severely wounded color-bearer, Edwards rallied the Michigan men "under a murderous fire."[12]

The 19th Indiana, "reduced to a mere handful," also formed behind the barricade. There, in Williams's words, it made its "last and hopeless stand."[13]

The 2d Wisconsin was the last Iron Brigade regiment back to Seminary Ridge. It retired in good order, firing, and when halfway there, probably in the swale, it halted and feigned a counterattack as if to dare the Confederates to come on. Again the enemy threatened its left flank, and Major Mansfield led it to the breastworks. The 2d formed on the right of the brigade near a small outbuilding. A section of Stevens's battery stood nearby. Captain Beecham looked back across the fields, where he saw Confederates hurrying down McPherson Ridge, yelling like demons, in seeming hope of reaching the dead zone in front of the Federal batteries before they were blown to kingdom come.[14]

As Biddle's brigade fell back to the right, its left crumbled. Colonel Gates, who commanded its two left regiments, wrote that the right regiments under Colonel Biddle fell back first and that the two under his command, the 20th New York and the 121st Pennsylvania, retreated slowly in perfect order. This was not entirely true. Maj. Alexander Biddle described his 121st as having been "broken and scattered," mixed together and not in proper ranks. Yet he claimed that the troops were not disheartened and displayed no panic or "unseemly apprehension." They fell back without being greatly troubled by the Confederates and took position toward the left of Doubleday's line but still within the works in front of the seminary building. There, in the brief period of quiet that followed, they tried to strengthen the barricade.[15]

Colonel McFarland, on the right of Biddle's brigade, claimed that the 151st Pennsylvania was the last regiment to leave McPherson Ridge. The 151st retreated to the barricade with the enemy following it closely but cautiously for some distance. When it reached the works, it formed on the brigade right beside the 19th Indiana Regiment. Soon after, a mounted officer brought McFarland a flag that he presumed belonged to the 151st. McFarland determined that it belonged to the 142d Pennsylvania. After the death of Col. Robert P. Cummins, the 142d was in some disorder. McFarland turned the flag over to the 142d and prepared for more fighting.[16]

Pender's division, supported by McIntosh's battalion of artillery, had followed Heth's toward Gettysburg. When it reached Marsh Creek, Pender learned that Heth was engaged and deployed his division astride the Chambersburg Pike and along the present Knoxlyn Road. McGowan's South Carolina brigade, commanded at Gettysburg by Col. Abner M. Perrin, formed along this cross road, leaving room for Scales's brigade between its left and the pike. Perrin deployed skirmishers off his right to protect the division's flank. Lane's and Thomas's brigades formed to the left, beyond the pike. With its brigades in line of battle, the men of the division tramped east across the fields in Heth's support.[17]

The division advanced for a half-mile. It halted, probably at a small stream that crossed its front so that its men could fill their canteens and rest. After a pause of an hour, they heard the sound of skirmishing and increased artillery fire. They advanced another half-mile. The day was "cloudy and close." Lt. James F. J. Caldwell recalled that "these advances in line of battle are the most fatiguing exercises I had in the army. . . . The perspiration poured from our bodies." Yet they could see the Bluecoats fleeing in some disorder, and to this time, "everything went as merry as a marriage bell." Perrin's and Lane's brigades halted to the rear of the Confederate batteries on Herr Ridge; Scales's brigade stopped behind the batteries on the ridge for a short while and then moved downhill in front of the guns, its left holding to the pike. While there, Scales's men watched the battle in their front, particularly the fighting between Stone's and Daniel's brigades at the west railroad cut.[18]

Union shells directed at the batteries on Herr Ridge fell among Scales's men, and several were wounded. A shell fragment bloodied a captain's head. He jumped up and started for the rear, hollering, "I'm dead, I'm dead." His colonel called to a couple of stretcher bearers to "go and take that dead man off — if you can catch him."[19]

Pender became concerned about cavalry demonstrations against his flank and shifted Lane's brigade from the left of the pike to the division's right near the Hagerstown Road. General Hill ordered Thomas's brigade to remain in reserve north of the pike in support of the batteries on Herr Ridge. This assignment took that Georgia brigade out of the fight.[20]

Lane's brigade became involved with the cavalry of Gamble's brigade in a perplexing way. When the First Corps relieved Gamble's brigade, much of the brigade went to the rear. Gamble posted the 8th Illinois Regiment

Maj. Gen. William D. Pender
(CWLM)

south of the Hagerstown Road to guard the Federal left. The 8th was still there when the Confederates began their afternoon assault. It covered the retreat of Captain Baldwin's companies from the Harmon buildings and then confronted the Confederate infantry on the right of Heth's and Pender's lines.[21]

The horsemen threatened to charge the 52d North Carolina. Col. James K. Marshall was said to have formed the 52d into a square to guard against such an attack; if true, it was an extreme reaction to a limited threat by a small force that could have attacked the regiment from only one direction. Marshall deployed Company B also to guard that flank. About the same time the remnant of Archer's brigade, now commanded by Col. Birkett Fry, advanced on the right rear of Pettigrew's line. The 8th Illinois threatened its flank, and Fry changed the brigade's front to protect it. Col. John Fite of the 7th Tennessee remembered that the brigade actually fell back about 200 yards.[22]

General Lane took over the burden of guarding the Confederate right. Lane had been born in Virginia in 1833 and was reared in North Carolina. He graduated from the Virginia Military Institute and attended the University of Virginia for a year. After working on a hydrographic survey of the James River, he joined the faculty of the Virginia Military Institute. When war came, he joined the 1st North Carolina Regiment and fought at Big Bethel. Lane became its lieutenant colonel in September 1861, and a few days he later succeeded Daniel H. Hill as commander of the 28th North Carolina. He led a brigade at Antietam and became a brigadier in November 1862. However, in spite of his early rise and a solid record of competency, he never received a division command. After the war, "The Little General" taught at four universities and ended his career as a professor of mathematics at Alabama Polytechnic Institute.[23]

On receiving the order to go to Pender's right, Lane simply faced his line right and marched it off in column. After reaching Pender's flank, he deployed his 7th North Carolina into a strong line of skirmishers facing the enemy cavalry on a rise about a half-mile to the right. At this time Archer's brigade was still with Heth's line in Pender's front. When Heth advanced, Lane's line followed in its support. The 7th Regiment kept up by moving by its left flank. After the brigade passed through Springs Hotel Woods, Lane saw, to his surprise, that Archer was no longer in his front and that his line was "unmasked." No troops stood between his and the enemy. The advance continued, Lane thought, for about a mile, but it cannot have been quite that far. Because of the "threatening attitude of the cavalry," the 7th halted, and the remainder of the brigade went ahead without it. As it did so, Lane sent Company G of the 37th as skirmishers to the right to hold some dismounted cavalry there at arm's length. By this time Lane's main line was approaching Shultz's Woods. As it did so, it left a strong line of flankers in its wake. The 52d North Carolina of Pettigrew's brigade and the 7th North Carolina were watching the 8th Illinois Cavalry Regiment, which continued to menace the right of Hill's lines.[24]

There was another Confederate unit somewhere on the right whose activities are not well reported. This was the 1st South Carolina Sharpshooter Battalion, a provisional unit that had been organized in June 1863 from McGowan's brigade. Maj. William T. Haskell commanded its 7 officers and 120 enlisted men. It was to assemble when a special task or skirmishing was to be done. Because Haskell was killed on 2 July, no one made a report of the battalion's activities. We know of its doings on 1 July only by a letter of Acting Sergeant Barry Benson. Benson stated that the battalion screened McGowan's (Perrin's) brigade's flank for a while during its approach march. After the afternoon attack began, it neared some Union cavalry outposts that were probably on the far right. A few sharpshooters ran the cavalry off and took possession of thirty head of cattle, a horse, and a pig. At this time, according to Benson, a "*tremendous*" battle was raging to the left—Heth's and Pender's divisions were well engaged. The battalion remained where it was for an hour, then Haskell sent Benson to Pender with a note. Benson passed the smoldering Harmon buildings on his way and somehow acquired some clean clothes. He delivered the note, and Pender ordered that Haskell return his battalion to the division.[25]

When General Buford saw that the First Corps was retreating before the onslaught of Heth's and Pender's divisions, he ordered Colonel Gamble to take his remaining three regiments forward to support Doubleday's left. Gamble led the 8th New York, the 3d Indiana, and the 12th Illinois regiments forward at a trot from their resting place south of the town to Shultz's Woods on Seminary Ridge. Half of the cavalrymen dismounted to fight on foot and left their horses with mounted men behind the ridge. A short while earlier Sergeant Shelton of Reynolds's battery passed a squadron of them and remembered their being mounted on gray horses and facing Shultz's Woods "as stolid as the stones under their horses noses." So long as Gamble's men held the wall in Shultz's Woods, Lane's brigade could not readily flank the left of Doubleday's line and bar its retreat to Cemetery Hill.[26]

Pender advanced Scales's and McGowan's brigades behind Brockenbrough's and Pettigrew's as they crossed Willoughby Run and climbed McPherson Ridge. When near Willoughby Run, Scales saw a regiment of Confederates north of the pike, probably the 32d North Carolina of Daniel's brigade, giving way before Stone's men in his front. He started his brigade to the 32d's assistance. The intimidated Pennsylvanians fell back, and Scales's men approached Brockenbrough's line, which was lying down. Before reaching it, Scales received an order from Pender to halt and wait for the rest of Pender's line to advance. Meanwhile McGowan's brigade pushed close to Pettigrew's. When near Willoughby Run, the South Carolinians met wounded and stragglers coming from the front. Since Heth's line seemed stalled, Pender sent Maj. Joseph A. Engelhard to Heth to ask if his division was in need of help. Heth replied that his division was pushing the enemy from one position to another. Therefore, Pender kept his line in supporting distance and bided his time.[27]

Heth's men "seemed much exhausted and greatly reduced" by their efforts that afternoon, and when Heth fell stunned, someone — Hill or Pender — decided that it was time for Pender's line to take over. Pender ordered his brigades to pass over Heth's if they were halted. Lane's brigade had already passed Archer's on the right. When Scales's line reached the east crest of McPherson Ridge, it found Heth's men lying down. Their officers told Scales that they were out of ammunition and would go no farther. Perrin's South Carolinians (McGowan's brigade) pressed ahead with renewed vigor, passing over Pettigrew's line on ground that was "grey with dead and disabled." As they did so the Tarheels shouted, "Go in, South Carolina! Go in, South Carolina!" Perrin's line descended into the swale in front of Seminary Ridge. Perrin halted it there in the shelter of a "ravine," the bed of the headwaters of Pitzer's Run. The South Carolinians reformed their line, caught their breath, and prepared for the final push toward Doubleday's line on Seminary Ridge.[28]

Lt. Col. Joseph N. Brown, commander of the 14th South Carolina Regiment, looked from the bottom of the swale in front of Seminary Ridge toward its crest 400 yards away. Just ahead was a grove of trees and, behind it, the seminary's large brick classroom and dormitory building. It was being "changed from the halls of learning to a scene of bloodshed and carnage." Among the trees Brown likely saw the breastworks manned by troops that had been "pressed back but not defeated." Torn flags marked the Union line, and First Corps cannons supported it. A weaker Union line extended along the crest toward the right across the front of McGowan's (Perrin's) brigade. Behind the large trees there, Brown might have seen four three-inch rifles from Reynolds's battery behind a wall between Schmucker's house and the Hagerstown Road. He also might have seen dismounted Union cavalrymen in Shultz's Woods beyond the Hagerstown Road on the front of Lane's brigade. He must have regarded what he saw with much apprehension, for he deemed it "the fairest field and finest front for destruction on an advancing foe that could well be conceived."[1]

Pender's attack on the Union forces on the ridge's crest would be the work of two brigades: Perrin's (McGowan's) on the right and Scales's on the left. Their 3,000 men would occupy the space between the Chambersburg Pike and the Hagerstown Road. Brig. Gen. Alfred M. Scales, born in 1827, had pursued a successful career as a lawyer and politician before the war. He entered Confederate service as a captain in the 13th North Carolina in the spring of 1861 and became its colonel in October 1861. He commanded the 13th in the various battles of the Army of Northern Virginia and was wounded at Chancellorsville. When Pender received command of the division, Scales became the brigade's commander. He joined

The Lutheran seminary (GNMP)

it during its march to Gettysburg. Scales and the brigade were one, for he had shared its fortunes, was proud of it, and was confident of victory as he led it to Gettysburg.[2]

When ordered to pass Heth's line and press home the attack against the Union forces on Seminary Ridge, Scales marched his men over Brockenbrough's prone brigade as it regrouped behind the crest of the east arm of McPherson Ridge. Scales's men crossed the ridge's broad crest and descended at a double-quick into the swale. Scales credited his men with keeping as good a line during this advance as he had ever seen. Then disaster struck.[3]

It came from the large muzzles of the twelve Napoleons of Stevens's and Stewart's batteries, from the three three-inch rifles of Cooper's battery, and from the two of Wilber's section at the pike. Union infantrymen added to the carnage. The Union troops had fired at Pettigrew's and Brockenbrough's lines at the climax of Heth's charge; now Pender's line would be their target.

Stevens's battery first fired spherical case and shells over the heads of the Union infantrymen behind the works in its front. Then, when the infantry fell back from the works, they swung the muzzles of their guns to the right and fired canister. The gunners had difficulty seeing targets because of a haze of blue smoke that settled in the swale. At the same time, clouds of white smoke enveloped the cannons. The artillerymen fired as fast as they were able. Sergeant Hubler of the 143d Pennsylvania, who was near the gun line, saw that the artillerymen worked "heroically" with small concern for their safety. When the guns became hot, the cannoneers fired them by thumbing their vents: "one man would hold a piece of leather [a thumbstall] over the vent while another would ram home the charge. As soon as he would remove his thumb from the vent the charge would be exploded." Sergeant Wheeler of the 2d Wisconsin was near a battery watching the effects of its fire. Suddenly a corporal of his company jerked him aside just in time to get him away from a gun's muzzle blast. The wind from the shell nearly bowled him over. The experience so unnerved Wheeler that he went behind the guns and sat down. Yet he had one more contribution to make that day.[4]

After watching the three pieces in his left half-battery fire at Heth's line, Lieutenant Stewart told Lieutenant Davison to use the same tactics if the Confederates advanced again. He then hurried to his three guns north of the cut. These pieces should have been firing at Daniel's formations, but Stewart made no mention of their doing so in his account of the battle. Stewart decided to concentrate on Pender's attack. He ordered his right guns to swing their muzzles left and to fire charges of double canister into the swale south of the pike when the Confederates renewed their attacks. When Scales's line appeared, Stewart's entire battery opened on it.[5]

From a vantage point near Stewart's guns, Lieutenant Colonel Dawes watched Pender's and Rodes's brigades advance. He evaluated what took place. "For a mile up and down the open fields before us the splendid lines of the veterans of the Army of Northern Virginia swept down upon us. Their bearing was magnificent. They maintained their alignments with great precision. In many cases the colors of the regiments were advanced several paces in front of the line." Stewart's guns fired shell until the Confederates crossed McPherson Ridge, then the Southerners came on with a rush. Federal infantry opened fire on them, and Stewart's men worked their pieces "with the regularity of a machine." Stewart wrote of repulsing two or three Confederate lines.[6]

Scales's brigade had passed over Brockenbrough's used-up line below the crest of McPherson Ridge, crossed the ridge's crest, and begun its descent into the swale. There it encountered an onslaught of canister and shell from Stewart's guns on its left and from canister and musketry in its front that played "sad havoc" with the North Carolinians' line. They double-quicked ahead until they reached the bottom of the swale halfway between the ridges. They could go no farther, nor could they go back—to do so would have been suicidal. Scales had been wounded by a shell fragment, the brigade line was shattered, and "only a squad here and there marked the place where regiments had rested." All of the field officers but two, Col. William L. J. Lowrance and Lt. Col. George T. Gordon, both of the 34th North Carolina, had been wounded and were out of the fight. Of the 1,400 Tarheels who had begun the charge, only 500 were able to go on, and many companies were without officers "to lead them or inquire after them."[7]

Lt. George Mills of the 16th North Carolina recalled that at the beginning of the advance every man stood at the command "attention," grasped his rifle with a firm grip, and at the command to march, moved off at the quickstep. Soon shells and minié balls struck around them, and men began to fall. Among the casualties were Sgt. John H. Bradley and Lt. John Ford, who must have been in the file closer's rank to Mills's left and right. Mills had just helped Bradley pull a stuck ramrod from his rifle's barrel, but Bradley did not get a chance to use his weapon. Mills tried to get the regiment's surgeon to help Ford before he bled to death, but the "doughty" doctor was on horseback riding with the regiment's line instead of tending to the wounded—until he was shot in the head. A shell fragment tore into Mills's right thigh as Scales's line crossed the rivulet in the bottom of the swale, and the line moved on without him. After recovering a little from his shock, Mills started for the rear using a stick for a crutch. He saw that both Ford and Bradley had disappeared from where they had fallen, but Ford had not gone far. He was barely alive but gestured that he wanted to leave the field and escape the mayhem around him. Mills could not find litter bearers to carry him off, and John Ford died on McPherson Ridge.[8]

Scales's brigade halted about seventy-five yards from the Federal line. Scales was down; his brigade had lost its formation, about 60 percent of its strength, and its momentum. Some men scattered while others halted and returned the enemy's fire. Union soldiers, pleased momentarily with their success, taunted them with shouts of "Come on, Johnny! Come on!" and probably other less hospitable greetings. Pender and the wounded Scales worked to rally the remaining 500 and to get the 55th Virginia of Brockenbrough's brigade to come up on Scales's left. Scales's troops had attracted

Col. Abner Perrin (CWLM)

a lot of the lethal artillery fire that might otherwise have raked the ranks of Perrin's South Carolinians. As Perrin's regiments pushed ahead, Scales's remnant kept up fire on their left.[9]

Perrin, born in 1827, was a lawyer from South Carolina's Edgefield District. He had been a lieutenant during the war with Mexico and had entered the Confederate service as a captain in the 14th South Carolina. He succeeded to the command of the 14th and became a colonel in February 1863 when Samuel McGowan took command of the brigade. After McGowan was wounded at Chancellorsville, Perrin received acting command of the brigade and led it to Gettysburg.[10]

When the brigade halted in the "ravine" in the bottom of the swale to prepare for its push against the Federals on Seminary Ridge, Perrin gave his regimental commanders orders for the coming attack: they were to press forward and close with the enemy, and they were not to stop and fire until Perrin ordered them to do so. Obviously Perrin believed it was essential that they maintain the momentum of the advance. In commenting on this, Lieutenant Caldwell observed that though Pettigrew's men had fought well, like most soldiers with little experience they had been content to stand and shoot instead of charging. Perrin was not going to make that mistake.[11]

The South Carolina brigade advanced with the 14th Regiment on its left, initially keeping pace with Scales's brigade and its 1st, 12th, and 13th regiments in order to its right. Like Scales's brigade, the left of Perrin's line was raked with "a furious storm of musketry and shells" when it began its ascent of Seminary Ridge. The hail of iron and lead hit the 14th particularly hard, and it hesitated. Capt. Washington P. Shooter of the 1st South Carolina wrote that the left and center of the 14th faltered and gave way; Perrin wrote that the 14th seemed to follow Scales's example but soon resumed its charge. Colonel Brown said nothing of a pause but observed, "To stop was destruction. To retreat was disaster. To go forward was 'orders,' " and the 14th went forward. Perrin boasted that his brigade scrupulously observed the orders he had given it not to halt and fire, and that it had received the enemy's fire without faltering.[12]

The first punishing fire came from the batteries, those north of the seminary building and from Reynolds's four guns near the Hagerstown Road. After that the Confederates had to reckon with the Union infantry. Some men on the 14th's left could hear officers telling their men not to shoot until the command to fire was given. Then it came. The Union soldiers stood, took deliberate aim, and shot thirty-four of thirty-nine men in Company K. Just where the 14th was when this happened, we do not know. Perrin reported that as his brigade was crossing a fence about 200 yards from the Union position at the seminary, the Union rifles blazed, subjecting the South Carolinians to the most destructive fire that he had experienced. Three weeks later Perrin wrote petulantly that Scales's brigade had given way and that he had heard no more of it until the next day. Actually, that brigade had sustained artillery fire that might otherwise have been directed at the South Carolinians. He owed them gratitude rather than censure.[13]

Soon after Biddle's brigade reached Seminary Ridge, Colonel Gates of the 20th New York rode back to the west edge of the grove in front of the seminary and looked for the attackers. He saw Confederates to the right and left but none in his immediate front. This was the brief lull remembered by the men of the 121st Pennsylvania. Possibly it occurred while

Perrin's brigade formed for its attack in the ravine at the bottom of the swale. After Gates assessed the situation in his front, he returned to the rear of the Union line and spoke with Colonel Biddle, the acting brigade commander. As they talked, a spent ball struck Biddle in the head with a distinct "pop" that suggested that he had been injured seriously. A surgeon dressed the wound, and Biddle returned to the brigade after a few minutes. Gates had no wounds, but his horse had four.[14]

After the Confederates closed on the Union position, the fighting did not last long. Colonel McFarland estimated that they resisted the Confederate assault from behind the breastworks and in the grove for "ten or more minutes," and that they broke the Carolinians' line. He thought that the 14th South Carolina was opposite the 151st Pennsylvania. If so, Biddle's three other battered regiments must have been the only troops facing the rest of Perrin's line. The Iron Brigade and Stone's men contended with the remnant of Scales's brigade, now led by Lieutenant Colonel Gordon. Some of Brockenbrough's and Daniel's men may have joined Scales's attack.[15]

On the Iron Brigade front, Captain Beecham remembered that like the artillery, the infantrymen fired so fast that their rifles became hot, and the smoke around them became so thick that it was as if "darkness, as of night," had settled upon them. Then the firing subsided, the smoke thinned, and "only the dead and dying remained on the bloody slopes of Seminary Ridge." The men on the ridge had beaten off a frontal attack, and for the moment all was quiet. Capt. Nathaniel Rollins directed the attention of the 2d Wisconsin's officers to their colors carried by Cpl. Rasselas Davidson. He announced that Major Mansfield, the regiment's commander, wanted all of the regiment's survivors to consider themselves its color guard. Then he looked at his watch and announced that it was four o'clock. No sooner had he said this than someone pointed toward the Eleventh Corps front and shouted, "Look there! What troops are those?" They saw that the troops referred to carried the "saucy battle-flags of the Confederacy." (How they determined this at such a distance Beecham did not say.) They also saw U.S. flags retiring into the town. The Eleventh Corps, like the First, was pulling back.[16]

The lull on the Union front was only momentary. The rifles of the infantry and the carbines of the cavalry beyond the Hagerstown Road raked the South Carolinians, who in obedience to Perrin's orders did not halt to return the fire that so punished them. As the South Carolinians neared the edge of the woods in front of the Union position, another blast staggered the 14th. Its line wavered. Perrin saw that the situation demanded a display of personal leadership. Brandishing his sword, he spurred his horse forward through the ranks of the 1st South Carolina and led the charge. In response to this action, wrote Lieutenant Caldwell, "filled with admiration for such courage as defied the whole fire of the enemy . . . the brigade followed, with a shout that was itself half a victory."[17]

Perrin saw that his brigade should flank the force firing in his front as well as strike it head on. He ordered Lieutenant Colonel Brown to continue straight ahead and hold the Union defenders in position and directed Maj. C. W. McCreary to oblique his 1st South Carolina to the right toward what appeared to be a lightly defended section of the ridge. That reached, he was to wheel it left against the flank of the troops behind the works and in front of the 14th. About this time he ordered the 12th and 13th regiments to oblique right and attack the cavalry line south of the road.[18]

The regiments did as ordered. It must have been this movement that so puzzled the troops of the 20th New York. The New Yorkers saw the 1st South Carolina's column moving across their front, and some fired at it. In the smoke that clouded the field the column appeared almost ghostlike, and in the confusion some officers believed it to be Union and ordered a cease-fire. Suddenly the column halted, faced the Union position, and blazed away. Captain Cook of the 20th New York hurried to the left to direct the fire of the troops there against the flanking South Carolinians. Suddenly his men stopped firing and began to run away. Cook looked behind him and saw the 20th's flag going to the rear. He and his men hurried to join it. As this was happening, the 12th and 13th regiments on the right of McGowan's line turned their attention toward their right and the cavalrymen in Shultz's Woods.[19]

About 4:00 P.M. the Federal units on Seminary Ridge, like the Eleventh Corps troops north of the town, began their retreat to Cemetery Hill. It was not an orderly withdrawal on the whole, but under the circumstances it was probably done as well as could have been expected. When the Confederates entered the grove in their front, General Wadsworth told Captain Stevens to take his battery to the rear. Stevens was preparing to leave when Colonel Wainwright countermanded Wadsworth's order — Wainwright was still under the impression that his guns were to defend Seminary Ridge. He compounded his error further by riding along the gun line to see that they remained there.

In the meantime Orderly Sergeant Wheeler was lying behind the guns trying to recover from having nearly been blown away by a muzzle blast. He looked to the north and saw a line of battle moving across the Gettysburg Plain. He called Capt. George Otis's attention to it. Otis thought that it must be an Eleventh Corps unit. They pointed out the line to Colonel Wainwright, who looked at it through his binoculars. After lowering his glasses, he saw that portions of Wadsworth's and Robinson's divisions were filing back over the railroad bed — in fact much of these divisions had already gone. Wainwright quickly ordered his batteries to limber up and get out.[20]

It was high time. A Rebel color-bearer planted his flag on the breastwork within fifty yards of Cooper's guns. Having fired about 400 rounds of ammunition, most of them from just three guns, Cooper's battery limbered up and started off. About the same time Confederates, probably Scales's men, reached the works in front of Stevens's Napoleons. One placed his hand on one of its pieces and shouted, "This gun is mine." In reply a cannoneer shouted, "D—n you, take it then." He pulled the lanyard, the gun fired, and it blew the Rebel into pieces. Fortunately, smoke must have concealed the guns from the Carolinians, and they were able to escape. Cooper's guns wheeled to the right, north of the seminary building, and headed for the pike. Stevens's Napoleons started off at the same time, and "little Cooper" shouted to Lt. Edward Whittier, "Hell's to pay, Ned!" This was an understatement.[21]

Reynolds's four guns near the Hagerstown Road had already pulled away. The two sections there had run out of ammunition. Lieutenant Bower had sent Sergeant Shelton and his caissons back for more ammunition and to get a horse for a sergeant whose mount had been shot. Shelton was returning from the artillery park with loaded caissons when he met the battery's excited quartermaster sergeant, who told him that the enemy was attacking from all directions and that he would be unable to get back to the guns. Only half believing him, Shelton halted his caissons and rode ahead to see for himself. He passed in front of some cavalry as he neared Shultz's Woods and proceeded to the end of their line. Then he saw a dust-covered body of infantry, which he assumed to be Union, climbing a fence and forming about 300 yards to the front. He paid it little attention until it fired at him and the cavalry. Its shots went into the trees, sending leaves fluttering down, but they did no obvious damage. The firing spooked Shelton's horse; it took the bit in its teeth, jumped the stone wall by the woods, and bolted to the rear.[22]

When pressed by the South Carolinians, Bower escaped with his four guns to the Taneytown Road. They moved behind the cavalry line and across the fields over the route by which they had come. This left Wainwright with the task of getting Stevens's and Cooper's batteries, Wilber's section, and Stewart's left half-battery to safety. Fortunately, all of their caissons except Stewart's had already gone. Wainwright instructed the batteries to move at a walk down the pike; he feared that if they moved faster, they would create panic among the infantrymen who were crowding the road. Yet as they moved off, he could see Rebels not far away and was sure that he would soon "go to Richmond." The drivers itched to let their teams out, to go at a trot at least, and escape the bullets that zipped around them. As the last of Stewart's caissons arrived, a body of Confederate infantry, probably the 14th South Carolina, appeared around the south end of the seminary building and opened fire at the Union troops on the pike. This drove the infantry north from the pike to the railroad bed and left the pike for use by the batteries. As the road cleared, Wainwright shouted, "Trot," and then, "Gallop." The drivers yelled to their teams and applied their whips, and the guns and caissons, three abreast, rolled toward the town.[23]

Stewart's three guns north of the cut were the last away. Stewart had not realized that the First Corps was withdrawing until one of General Robinson's aides rode up with orders for him to fall back. Then, he wrote, he appreciated for the first time the horror of war — he had no way of carrying off his wounded. Although their beseeching looks unnerved him, he had to leave them behind. He took his three pieces back along the north side of the cut to the more level ground to the east before attempting to cross the railroad bed. Two of his pieces crossed it, but the third hung up on some rocks. The limber's pintle hook broke as they tried to pull it off, and the gun's trail dropped to the ground. The crew tried to tie the trail to the limber with its prolonge, but it was not quickly done. As they struggled, enemy infantry came to within 100 yards and shot at them. The two other guns opened on these Rebels to hold them off. As the crew dragged the third gun from the cut, the enemy dashed forward to within 60 yards of the disabled piece, fired, and wounded its wheel pair's driver and two horses. Finally the three pieces reached the pike and started into the town and to Cemetery Hill. As they headed off, Stewart went back to where his left guns had been. Near the crest of the ridge he met Confederates who demanded his surrender. In answer he turned his horse and galloped toward the town.[24]

The sequence in which the infantry regiments left the ridgeline is not readily apparent. The 121st Pennsylvania, whose casualties approached 70 percent and had only two officers left when it reached Cemetery Hill, followed the tactic of "get up and get." To avoid threatened capture, these Pennsylvanians left the ridge as individuals without "a semblance of order." The 151st began its retreat in a much more orderly way. Colonel McFarland led some of its remaining 100 soldiers around the north end of the seminary building, where they briefly found shelter from the 1st South Carolina's flanking fire. McFarland paused about twenty feet from the building and stooped to look beneath the smoke for the enemy. As he squatted, the 14th South Carolina fired a volley and wounded him in both legs. Pvt. Lyman Wilson carried him into the seminary building though its north door as the Confederates entered at its south end. The 151st, now under Capt. Walter Owens, went on to Cemetery Hill.[25]

Colonel Gates believed that his 20th New York left the ridge in the rear of the brigade. When it did so, Gates saw 400 to 500 mounted cavalrymen beyond Hagerstown Road, and not knowing the situation in their front, he could not understand why they did not charge the Confederate flank. As Captain Cook left the seminary position, he found Capt. Dan McMahon with a shattered thigh. A soldier who tended McMahon was unwilling to abandon him. Cook and others tried to carry the captain to a house on the edge of town, but a party of Confederates fired on them before they reached it and wounded two of Cook's helpers. Cook placed McMahon in a ditch, tried to make him comfortable, and bade him goodbye. Soon after, he saw General Wadsworth and his staff gallop across the bridge over Stevens Run, and a battery rumbled across it behind them. Wadsworth was probably one of the last ranking officers to leave the ridge.[26]

At 3:45 Wadsworth saw that the Iron Brigade was hard pressed. It was nearly out of ammunition and was flanked on right and left. It would be a pleasure to say that this renowned unit marched off "as if on parade," but this was not quite so. Colonel Williams of the 19th Indiana reported without apology, for none was needed, that he ordered the 19th to retreat, but that the regiments of the brigade were so intermixed that it was impossible to form them as a unit. Therefore they retired "each to care for himself through the town." Capt. Hollon Richardson of the brigade staff, who had been a prominent officer on the field, relayed an order to retreat to Colonel Robinson along with the order that the 7th Wisconsin was to be the brigade's rear guard. Robinson marched the brigade to the right through an orchard to the pike and away from McGowan's brigade. It went to the east side of the ridge, where there must have been less enemy fire; formed;

and marched through the town. Lieutenant Colonel Dudley described this march as "trying and perilous." When the 7th left the ridge and before it reached the town, a body of South Carolinians fired into its right. Another line from Rodes's division shot into its left at long range. While running this gauntlet, the 7th suffered its greatest losses of the day.[27]

The 6th Wisconsin was north of the east railroad cut in support of Stewart's guns when Lt. Clayton Rogers of Wadsworth's staff rode up to Lieutenant Colonel Dawes. Rogers bent down and in a quiet voice said, "The orders, colonel, are to retreat beyond the town. Hold your men together." Dawes was surprised at the order. He had just heard shouts of defiance from along the First Corps line, but when he looked toward the Eleventh Corps front, he could see Confederates sweeping across the plain "without let or hindrance." He quickly faced the 6th to the rear and marched it down the ridge's east slope in line of battle, its right holding to the railroad bed. "With the flag of the Union and of Wisconsin held aloft, the little regiment marched firmly and steadily." The Wisconsin men could see the oncoming lines of Rodes's men, but fortunately they reached the college grounds without being fired on. They crossed Washington Street and turned south toward Cemetery Hill and into the confusion of the town. Oddly enough, Dawes wrote nothing of the doings of Stewart's battery as the 6th left the ridge, nor did Stewart mention the 6th. Since Stewart had a brush with advancing Confederates soon after his guns left the ridge and Dawes did not, it seems likely that Stewart's right half-battery was still in position when the 6th pulled out. By the same token, the 6th must have reached the shelter of the town at the college before the rest of the brigade left the ridge and ran the Confederate gauntlet.[28]

Stone's brigade, now under Colonel Dana of the 143d Pennsylvania, had been on the ridge in the orchard near Stewart's left pieces and Wilber's section of Reynolds's battery. There it made a desperate stand, the men firing the ammunition issued them after they reached this position. Like others, they believed that they were the last organized body of troops to leave the field. After the batteries had gone, the brigade retreated over the nearby railroad bed and the pike. Private Harris described their retreat as "without semblance of military order with every man for himself and the Rebs take the hindmost." Going off that way, Harris believed that the enemy captured only a few of the unwounded men of the regiment.[29]

As the 143d neared the town, Colonel Dana overtook Cpl. Owen Phillips, who was carrying both flags of the 143d in addition to his rifle. Dana said, "Why corporal, drop your gun. What are you bringing that off the field for with both flags?" Phillips replied, "Well Colonel, I am drilled to the use of my gun, but not the Flag drill." To this Dana responded, "Well, Well! Drop your gun and hand me the State Flag, and don't let any man take those colors from you while you are alive, and remember brave Crippen." Harris commented that such "promotion upon the field of action is honor doubly won."[30]

In his report Doubleday credited Capt. James Glenn and Company D of the 149th Pennsylvania for being the last troops to defend the Seminary Ridge position. Company D was the headquarters guard for Doubleday's division. It formed first in a skirmish line south of the seminary building across the Hagerstown Road and in front of the Shultz house. For a time, at General Rowley's order, the company gathered stragglers and sent them back to their units. Although few stragglers came its way so long as Biddle's brigade held its position on McPherson Ridge, it was busy thereafter. As Pender's line approached, Company D opposed it with the help of Reynolds's four pieces and a "squad" of cavalry. But after a while the battery ran out of ammunition and moved off, and the cavalry also left. The company fell back. General Rowley, who was with it, told its men to hold the position for the sake of Allegheny County. Some men feared that he would be captured and insisted that he leave. Their retreat was disorganized; they fled as individuals to avoid capture. A few men went back along the road with Captain Glenn, some took to the fields, and one man rode a cavalry horse to Cemetery Hill. As the men of Company D fled, the Confederates seemed content to fire at them from the ridge; after all, they were a small target when compared with other units streaming toward the town. When Glenn reached Stevens Run, he insisted that the half-dozen men with him stop there to fight, but they continued into the town, where they joined the retreating mass on Chambersburg Street. The last infantry company defending Seminary Ridge had gone.[31]

Cavalrymen of Gamble's brigade had opened the battle of 1 July west of the town, and there was poetic justice to their being present at its close. From the fields south of the Hagerstown Road, Major Beveridge and the 8th Illinois Regiment had covered the retreat of Captain Baldwin's skirmishers from the Harmon buildings; it had aided the departure of Biddle's brigade from McPherson Ridge; and it had occupied the attention of Confederate brigades that might have been used gainfully against the First Corps lines. Before the infantry fell back to Seminary Ridge, the remainder of the brigade was in reserve somewhere to the east.

When the infantry fell back to Seminary Ridge, General Buford ordered Colonel Gamble to take his reserve forward at a trot to cover the First Corps left south of the Hagerstown Road. At this time Gamble had a force of about 1,000 troopers, from the 3d Indiana, the 8th Illinois, and the 12th Illinois regiments. He placed half of them behind the ridge with the horses, and many of the remaining 500 formed in Shultz's Woods behind a low stone wall along the ridge crest. Unfortunately we know little of their deployment, but they must have had a heavy line in the woods opposite the most threatening Confederate force. Eventually Gamble's line extended south another 500 to 600 yards to McMillan Woods.[32]

When the dismounted cavalrymen reached the woods, they opened sharp and rapid carbine fire at the advancing South Carolinians of McGowan's brigade. The 3d Indiana poured "volley after volley into them and they returned them as liberally." The 8th Illinois delayed Lane's brigade so much that it could not attack to the front. This caused Perrin to complain that Lane's brigade "never came up until the Yankees were clear out of reach." Perrin's right received a "constant and withering fire" from the woods and took measures to cope with it. He ordered his 12th and 13th regiments to oblique to the right and attack. The 12th pushed to the crest of the ridge on the right of the 1st South Carolina and then wheeled to strike the flank of the cavalry line. At the same time the 13th drove against its front. The cavalrymen were no match for the veteran infantry regiments. Gamble ordered them back to their horses, to mount and retire to Cemetery Ridge. The cavalry's casualties were light compared with those of the infantry who fought west of the town that day. The 3d Indiana's casualty list, which numbered about 10 percent of its strength, was the highest in the brigade. Its dead included Maj. Charles Lemmon, a "most efficient and zealous officer," who "fell mortally wounded, while gallantly urging the men to hold their position against the advancing foe."[33]

Colonel Gamble reported that the stand of his brigade on Seminary Ridge had prevented the left flank of the Union position at the seminary from being turned, and this is probably so. It is ironic, then, that the cavalry veterans and their friends stressed their skirmishing at the opening of the battle but virtually ignored their stand on Seminary Ridge.[34]

After they had driven the Union regiments from Seminary Ridge, Colonel Perrin ordered the 1st and 14th regiments to push ahead toward the town. Lieutenant Colonel Brown led the left wing of the 14th around the north end of the seminary building, where it fired on Colonel McFarland and the 151st Pennsylvania, while Maj. Edward Croft led the 14th's right around the building's south side. Men from the 14th entered the seminary building. "The brilliant, fearless, and magnetic Major McCreary" called for volunteers to go into the town, and they went to a man.[35]

Capt. Washington P. Shooter, in his enthusiasm, wrote that the 1st South Carolina entered the town a half-mile ahead of any other regiment, a boast that the 14th could not have tolerated. Major Croft's men pushed for Wilber's piece that sat in the pike because four of its six horses had been shot. Croft, "with an eye for the immediately useful secured the only uninjured horse, which he mounted with harness still on." Croft lent the horse to the gallant Capt. T. Pinckney Alston, commander of the 1st's skirmishers, so that he could lead them into the town.[36]

Unlike Shooter, Brown wrote that the 1st and 14th entered Gettysburg at the same time with flags unfurled. The 1st went in over Chambersburg Street; the 14th, by a route between "north boundary street" and the railroad bed. The two regiments probably met at the square. The 1st South Carolina claimed that it raised the first Confederate flag in the town. Pender joined the two regiments there and complimented each on a "glorious day's work." Since Rodes's division was to occupy the west half of the town, Pender ordered the 1st and 14th regiments to rejoin the 12th and 13th between the town and Seminary Ridge.[37]

We cannot readily know the number of casualties sustained by Pender's division on 1 July, for its official casualty figures are for both 1 July and Pickett's Charge. McGowan's brigade's casualties did not "fall short of 500," this of about 1,800 engaged. Lieutenant Colonel Brown estimated that more than 600 of 1,500 men of that brigade had fallen in front of the Union position and gave the 14th South Carolina's loss as more than 200 of the 475 taken into the fight. General Scales reported a loss of 545 killed, wounded, and missing. Yet Lieutenant Colonel Lowrance, who took command of the brigade after the day's battle, reported having only 500 men of the 1,400 taken into the conflict. General Lane reported his 1 July casualties as "slight," and Thomas's brigade ought to have had none.[38]

General Hill wrote that the enemy had been routed entirely and that the First Corps had been annihilated. The Confederates would learn differently later. Hill reported that Heth's and Pender's divisions had been exhausted by "six hours' hard fighting" and were necessarily in some disorder. This being so, prudence had led Hill not to push them farther lest they encounter fresh troops of the enemy.[39]

Neither Hill nor General Lee, who was at hand, had seen fit to order Anderson's division into the fight. Anderson's division had arrived, and Anderson had been ordered to post it in line of battle where Pender's division had been — on Herr Ridge or, perhaps, on Belmont Ridge just to its rear. Hill also ordered Anderson to guard the army's right by placing a brigade and a battery there. (Wilcox's brigade took position on Herr Ridge at the Hagerstown Road.) General Lee reported that the four divisions present were weakened and exhausted. Yet in this reckoning he did not include Anderson's division and Thomas's brigade of Pender's division, which had been in reserve and had done no fighting. Neither Lee nor Hill explained this decision in his report, but after the war Anderson observed that Lee had said that he did not know the strength of the enemy in his front and that "a reserve in case of a disaster was necessary."[40]

In spite of having this reserve at hand, Hill has escaped the criticism given Ewell for not pushing on to Cemetery Hill. Apart from that, hindsight suggests that Hill might have used his artillery more aggressively at the close of the day's battle when the Federals were falling back to Cemetery Hill. Lieutenant Colonel McIntosh believed that Hill's batteries could have occupied the positions taken on 2 July and shelled Cemetery Hill from them. Such a shelling, he believed, might have caused the Federals to abandon the hill. On the other hand, McIntosh's fellow artillery commander, Lt. Col. John J. Garnett, wrote that when his battalion reached Gettysburg, Lee, who was just west of the seminary, ordered him to place his battalion at the seminary and fire on a body of Union troops moving toward the Emmitsburg Road. He was to disperse them or determine where they were going. He did so; he determined that they simply were retreating to Cemetery Hill. In the meantime, his pieces drew fire from Union guns on the hill.[41]

CHAPTER 23

Retreat through the Town

The early morning of 1 July was a time of calm in the borough of Gettysburg. The rumors that had disturbed the townsfolk since the Confederates had crossed the Potomac and the recent visits of Jubal Early and Gordon's brigade were behind them. Although they had seen Confederate campfires on South Mountain and had a near visit by Pettigrew's brigade, the presence of Buford's troopers gave them a sense of security—with such protectors all would be well. There was some excitement, of course; the cavalry camps on the edge of the town and Buford's headquarters in the Eagle Hotel were unusual, as were the visits of cavalry officers that morning in search of breakfast and groceries for their messes. It must have been like having a county fair, particularly for boys who went to the cavalry bivouacs to mingle with the soldiers and get a look at army life.

But matters took a serious turn. Bugle calls interrupted the routine in the cavalry bivouacs, and squadrons rode off to the west. Soon the citizens on that side of the town heard the distant popping of carbines and rifles and, about 10:00 A.M., the thudding of distant cannon fire. This was something new. Some of the more curious folks went west of the town or to their rooftops to see what was going on; others sat on their doorsteps, "their hearts beating with anxiety, looking at one another mutely"; still others prepared to leave the town for safety elsewhere. Some residents later remembered General Reynolds passing through the town and his staff urging them to go to their cellars. About noon the Eleventh Corps passed north over Washington Street to the fields beyond the college. Things began to have a serious aspect.

By this time it was apparent that deadly business had been transacted in the fields to the west. May McAllister remembered one of the first casualties brought into the town, a cavalryman with a leg wound whose blood reddened the flank of his gray horse. Soon Christ Lutheran Church, the courthouse, the railroad depot, and other public buildings became hospital sites, and many women of Gettysburg became volunteer nurses and cooks. As the day progressed, these facilities became inadequate; wounded soldiers crowded into private dwellings, where host families tried to care for them. During this growing misery, a band, probably from the Eleventh Corps, played patriotic airs in the Diamond—the town square. Robert McLean thought the music incongruous with the occasion, and his wife, Elizabeth, considered its rendition of "The Star-Spangled Banner" a dirge.

Civilian morale received a boost before noon when prisoners from Archer's and Davis's brigades passed under guard through the town and out Baltimore Street to holding areas on the Baltimore Pike. Occasionally an artillery projectile whistled into the town. One smashed the balcony of Catherine Foster's house at the corner of High and Washington streets. Catherine and Belle Stewart had been watching the battle to the west from there; fortunately they had left earlier to go down to the street to watch the Eleventh Corps march through the town. Another projectile, probably from a rifled piece with a careless crew, hit the roof of Christ Lutheran Church to the dismay of wounded inside. Although such shell fire killed no civilians, it must have hurried many of them to their cellars.

Stragglers and wounded men wandered into the town. As the afternoon wore on, the number of fugitives increased. Salome Myers and others became especially alarmed toward 4:00 P.M. when caissons and wagons passed back through town at rapid gaits. About the same time officers rode through the streets shouting, "Women and children to the cellars. The Rebels will shell the town." This was a harbinger of what was to come.[1]

Devin's cavalry brigade was probably the first organized unit back through the town. Its squadrons had been picketing the roads leading into Gettysburg from the north and, after lively skirmishing, had fallen back before Ewell's corps. The 17th Pennsylvania's last picket lines had been across the Harrisburg Road, where they supported the 6th and 9th New York Cavalry regiments. After the arrival of the Eleventh Corps, Devin's brigade formed just east of the town (Bachelder's map placed them west of Rock Creek and south of the York Pike), and Devin placed videttes out the York Pike. They remained there until shells fired from Cemetery Hill by Wiedrich's battery fell among them. When the Union forces began their retreat, Buford ordered Devin to join Gamble's brigade west of Cemetery Ridge. In response, the brigade moved west and south by an unrecorded route to the junction of the Emmitsburg and Taneytown roads. During this march the 17th "moved with unbroken column and, by its steady bearing and example exerted a wholesome influence upon some of the disorganized troops." Actually it might have been the other way around. The brigade would have filled the streets during its passage and, if the retreat was in full swing, would probably have created a jam. Yet since none of the infantrymen mentioned seeing Devin's horsemen, they probably passed by before the retreat was well under way.[2]

Wiedrich's battery had fired at Howard's request. Its target was a Confederate battery, though its shells fell short, allegedly because of the poor quality of its ammunition. In his report Captain Wiedrich wrote only that his battery fired at an unknown Confederate battery near the York Pike. Later it was said that Wiedrich's guns had fired at masses of troops in the distance until a staff officer demanded that the battery cease firing. Some of the cannoneers thought that the officer was a Rebel in disguise.[3]

Although the retreat of the First and Eleventh Corps to Cemetery Hill is often termed a rout, it was not quite that. Yet if Howard and Doubleday took measures in advance to ensure an orderly movement, no one recorded it. Captain Cook of the 20th New York did mention hearing cries of "First Corps this way" and "Eleventh Corps this way" when he reached either Washington or Baltimore streets, but he was one of a crowd and could not see who was yelling and did not understand what the shouters wanted him to do.[4]

Colonel Hofmann of the 56th Pennsylvania wrote that Wadsworth's division, perhaps only Cutler's brigade, moved to the town over the railroad bed, and that the head of the column met the Eleventh Corps at Baltimore Street. (He did not say why the column did not turn down Washington Street instead.) This meeting checked their progress and caused the men at the rear of the column to be captured. Once in the town, many units became mixed and lost their identities until they reached Cemetery Hill. Lt. Thomas Miller, Cutler's aide, recalled that the Union forces passed through the town in three columns; the artillery kept to the middle of the streets and the infantry walked along the sides. He agreed that Cutler's brigade had become "somewhat entangled" with other troops as it passed through the town, but this in itself did not constitute a rout. Lt. Col. Edward Salomon led the 82d Illinois and the 61st Ohio of Schimmelfennig's brigade back into the town and claimed, perhaps wrongly, that they were the last units to enter it from the north. He found great confusion and crowding and termed it a rout. Yet he insisted that his own men were under control enough to guard cross streets and open a cul-de-sac before they reached Cemetery Hill as a unit — among the last to do so.[5]

At the height of the retreat the crowds in the main streets were like a river in flood. Masses of blue-clad soldiers moved inexorably away from the yelling Confederates. Colonel Wainwright, who rode within this mass toward Cemetery Hill, saw little organization, except that men of the Eleventh Corps seemed to walk on one side of the street while those of the First used the other. They did not appear to be panic stricken, and most seemed to be talking and joking as they moved along. (Perhaps they were similar to a large crowd walking from a stadium after an exciting game.) General Schurz saw numerous stragglers. Many, like those of the 19th Indiana, had been told to fall back as individuals because their officers could not reform them in their units. Schurz saw particular disorder where wagons in the street obstructed the flow, but he saw no dissolution.[6]

There must have been a lot of wagons in the streets: those belonging to civilians, ammunition wagons, and ambulances. Pvt. Jacob Smith of the 107th Ohio wrote that he and other ambulance drivers had been ordered to go through the town to pick up Eleventh Corps wounded. When they reached its center, they met Union soldiers falling back in confusion, crowding the streets so that ambulances could neither go against the tide nor turn around. More than half of Smith's party were captured, but he and others got away by turning into an alley and breaking through some fences. At one time the stream of retreating soldiers was so strong on Chambersburg Street that it pushed Mary McAllister a half-block when she tried to cross the street in front of Christ Lutheran Church. Anna Garlach watched the blue mass pouring down Baltimore Street in front of her home. So crowded was the street that she thought she could have crossed it by stepping on men's heads.[7]

There were scores of individual episodes during the retreat, particularly among men closest to the Confederates. Catherine Foster saw the last Union soldiers hurrying along Washington Street harassed by Confederate bullets and ducking "into every nook and corner." One of these was a Lieutenant Wilcox, regiment unknown, who entered the Fosters' rear door. Catherine sent him to their cellar and gave him some civilian clothes. He avoided detection. Lieutenant Colonel Dawes observed that the streets were crowded with skulkers who were awaiting an opportunity to surrender. He could not recall seeing a First Corps badge on any of these fellows — perhaps he had a selective memory.[8]

Pvt. Franklin Pratt of the 76th New York was getting food from a house for wounded men when he saw Confederates chasing Union soldiers. Some of the fugitives entered the house. It occurred to Pratt that a house full of wounded and stragglers was bound to draw the attention of the Confederates, so he exited through a rear window, jumped a fence, and entered the house of Samuel Forney, a druggist. The Forneys welcomed him, gave him some civilian clothing, and like Wilcox, he escaped detection.[9]

About the same time Corporal Hubler and two other men, one from the 6th Wisconsin, were hurrying along a side street west of Baltimore Street when a party of Rebels, probably from the 1st South Carolina, demanded their surrender. They ran, and the Confederates shot at them. One of the balls passed through Hubler's hair and hit the Wisconsin man in the back of his head. It cracked like a pistol shot, the man fell, and Hubler saw his oozing brains. An instant later a ball struck Hubler's cartridge box, causing him to think that he had been shot in the hip. Nevertheless, he hurried along until he saw a man exiting a house with a cup of water. He decided to get some for himself but noticed a Confederate aiming his rifle at a Union soldier. As he glimpsed this, he saw another Rebel loading his rifle and giving him a "ferocious look." Hubler dashed into Baltimore Street, and there "a charge of canister came crashing along." It missed him but struck some wounded men in an ambulance. When he neared the foot of Cemetery Hill, a man from his company with a wounded arm called to him from a barn. Hubler bound the man's wound with a handkerchief and then spotted the knapsack of a New York artilleryman who was hiding here. He took tobacco, writing paper, and an artillery jacket from it. Hubler remained in the barn with his wounded comrade and with skirmishers from the 55th Ohio of Orland Smith's brigade until next day.[10]

After the 88th Pennsylvania began its retreat from Oak Ridge, Lieutenant Boone and others went to Stewart's position and found that the battery, like the corps, was retreating. Boone hurried east along the north side of the railroad bed until he ran into the right of a Confederate skirmish line. (This timing suggests that the Eleventh Corps had just left that area.) To escape it, he crossed the bed and entered the town. He had to pause at Chambersburg Street because the Confederates were firing down it from the square. He made his way south through yards and over fences until he reached Baltimore Street at the Garlach house. By this time there was quiet; the retreat was essentially over, and Hays's brigade was occupying the area east of Baltimore Street. Boone bumped into a Tiger, who demanded his sword. Boone took it off and threw it to the side rather than give it to him. His captor did not take offense and ordered him to the rear. A short distance back he met a half-dozen "wild, unrestrained, excited men who were now whooping 'go in Tigers.' " He tried to avoid them by crossing the street, but one headed him off and expressed interest in his watch. Then a party of Union soldiers appeared; their uniforms were so dusty that the Confederates could not make them out. Boone told them that they were Confederates, but the Tigers shot at them anyhow. The Union troops fired back. In the excitement Boone ducked into a side street that turned out to be a blind alley. As he climbed a fence to leave it, he heard, "git back thar, git back." He had run into a Rebel skirmish line and was a prisoner again. Soon he would be walking to Virginia.[11]

A spent ball bruised Pvt. Avery Harris of the 143d Pennsylvania in the side and made his breathing painful. Nevertheless, he hurried to the rear over Chambersburg Pike between board fences that enemy bullets were turning into kindling. It was a dangerous route, and his bruised side did not permit him to walk erect; yet he carried his prized Enfield rifle all the way. Turning into a side street, he met two comrades who were getting water from a pump that had a crank rather than a handle. They filled their canteens, and Harris poured water over the wound of Pvt. Stephen Miller. A blast of "canister" sent his friends on their way, but Harris remained behind to get more water. He continued to the rear through rifle fire and canister until a log breastworks blocked his way. A head wearing a blue kepi appeared over the works, and the Union soldier beneath it hauled Harris over as another charge of canister came "cracking and snapping." He climbed painfully to the top of the hill and sat on a wall to get his breath. An officer on a horse asked if he had been hit. Before Harris could answer the officer remarked, "I guess by God you are by the looks of your gun." Glancing at his Enfield, he saw that the ball which had bruised him had shattered its stock and bent its barrel. He had not noticed this and had taken a great deal of trouble to carry the rifle with him. In later years, he wondered why those whom he had met had not mentioned it.[12]

Among the most inspirational vignettes of the day took place during the retreat of the 7th Wisconsin through the town. The survivors of the 7th, which was acting as a rear guard for the division, followed three caissons of Stewart's battery, marching with their colors uncased and with rifles at "right shoulder shift." Rebels fired at them from less than 200 yards away. When Color Sgt. Daniel McDermott entered the town, a charge of "grape and canister" wounded him and shattered the staff of his flag. McDermott's comrades placed him on a caisson, and McDermott rode on it at the head of the 7th still flaunting his tattered flag in defiance at the enemy.[13]

The First Corps batteries did not pass through Gettysburg unscathed. One of Stewart's caissons broke an axle, and all of its crew but one cannoneer abandoned it. Stewart encountered the caisson and the cannoneer on his way into the town and learned that the cannoneer had stayed behind to destroy the caisson's powder bags. Stewart asked the man if he had been ordered to do this. "No," he replied, "but the Rebs are following us up pretty hard, and if the caisson fell into their hands they would use the ammunition on us."[14]

Both Stevens's and Reynolds's batteries had breakdowns. As Stevens's guns were rolling at a trot, a wheel spun off one, and its axle dropped to the road. This called for quick action. The wheel was not damaged, so cannoneers lifted the axle of the 1,250-pound Napoleon and slid the wheel back over the end of the axle. Captain Stevens secured the wheel by using the handle of a gunner's pincers for a linchpin.[15]

The Eleventh Corps batteries had less trouble in their retreat. Dilger's Napoleons moved east around the town without difficulty. After losing three pieces north of the town, Wheeler's and Heckman's batteries reached the hill without giving up more. Wilkeson's battery covered the retreat as no other had done. After halting at the north edge of town, where its cannoneers filled the guns' limber chests from the caissons, the battery retreated slowly through the town, sometimes by prolonge. Its reports do not mention firing in the town, but one account states that a battery fired from the Diamond; from his basement window at Baltimore and High streets, Albertus McCreary saw a Union gun fire down Baltimore Street toward the square, making much dust and noise.[16]

The Confederates captured a number of Union officers of rank, including General Barlow and Colonels Morrow and Fairchild, all of whom were wounded. They captured about ninety men of the 97th New York as they left Oak Ridge with Colonel Wheelock. In the hope of avoiding capture, Wheelock took refuge in the cellar of Carrie Sheads's Oak Hill Seminary on the Chambersburg Pike. Confederate infantry found him there, and a sergeant demanded his surrender. Instead of turning over his sword, Wheelock tried to break it across his knee. This angered the sergeant who threatened to shoot him. Wheelock dramatically bared his chest and dared the sergeant to do so. Elias Sheads, father of Carrie, stepped in and tried to calm the two. Someone called the sergeant away, and Carrie made off with the sword in the folds of her ample skirt and hid it. After being a prisoner for a few days, Wheelock escaped his captors and returned to retrieve the sword.[17]

General Rowley obtained notoriety for allegedly being drunk during the retreat. Rowley, who had been an acting division commander during the fight, claimed to be the commander of the First Corps. General Cutler encountered Rowley haranguing some retreating troops. Rowley asked for Cutler's name, though he must have known it. He said that Cutler was of no account and vowed to attend to him another day. Colonel Robinson thought that Rowley was drunk also. After asking Robinson for his name, he told him that his men were "damned good fighting men" but that his officers were worthless and that he should keep them with the regiment. Robinson replied that all were there except those who had been killed and wounded. Rowley continued his unseemly behavior after he reached Cemetery Hill. Colonel Dawes wrote that he was "raving and storming and giving wild and crazy orders." Lt. Clayton Rogers, provost marshal of Wadsworth's division, placed Rowley under arrest and asked Dawes to enforce the order. Rowley was court-martialed in April 1864, and the court recommended that he be dismissed from the service. However, because there were those who attested to Rowley's sobriety and the testimony was mixed, the recommendation was not upheld. Rowley resigned eight months later.[18]

Some people have scoffed at General Schimmelfennig because of his misfortune during the retreat. After his Third Division had fallen back toward town in good order, the general tried to reach Cemetery Hill by riding south over Washington Street. He attempted to cross east to Baltimore Street through an alley that took him to the Garlach's barn and then turned north to Breckenridge Street and the Confederates. He was in a trap. After pursuing Confederates shot his horse, the general tried to reach Baltimore Street by climbing a board fence into the Garlach yard. When he saw Confederates in Baltimore Street, he returned to the yard and hid in a culvert there. After dark he sought a better hiding place behind two swill barrels and between a woodshed and some stacked wood that he rearranged to give him better cover. When Mrs. Garlach went into the yard that night to slop her hogs, the general made his presence known to her. (He was not in the hog pen.) On 2 July Mrs. Garlach returned to the yard with a bucket and pretended to feed her pigs. Instead the bucket contained bread and water for the general. This was the last food that she gave him because she was afraid that she would cause him to be discovered. The general remained in his hiding place until the morning of 4 July when the Confederates left the area. When Schurz rode up Baltimore Street early that morning, Schimmelfennig greeted him from the doorway of one of the houses, and the two shared a breakfast of fried eggs.[19]

There were units that retained order and cohesion in the congested town. Major Brady deployed the remains of the 17th Connecticut in the street, and they fired several volleys, which, according to Brady, cleared one of the principal streets several times. Finally, the enemy proved too much for them, and they retreated to Cemetery Hill. From the other side of the Eleventh Corps, the 45th New York was ordered back to the college, where it prepared to make a stand. In twenty minutes the brigade bugler sounded "Retreat" and "double quick," and the greater portion of the brigade, under von Amsberg's direction, fell back slowly toward the town. The head of the 45th pushed to Washington Street where it met a crossfire that wounded Maj. Charles Koch. It returned to Chambersburg Street and cut south from it on each side of Christ Lutheran Church over fences, through yards and alleys, and finally to the safety of Cemetery Hill. While six companies escaped, four under Captain Irsch had taken shelter in buildings opposite the church from Rebel fire coming from the square a half-block to the east. There they and others held out until 5:30 P.M. At that time the Confederates persuaded Captain Irsch to come out and see that the town was firmly in their control. After consultation among its officers, this remnant of the 45th broke its firearms and surrendered.[20]

The 150th Pennsylvania was not so fortunate. The Rebels captured some of its officers and men before they reached the town. Adjutant Ashurst, who had been wounded, escaped capture by avoiding streets until he met troops from Robinson's division and an ambulance that followed them. He climbed into the ambulance and rode to Cemetery Hill. Confederate skirmishers followed it for a time, and one of their shots wounded another soldier in the ambulance. Capt. George Jones, whose Company B had been on the 150th's skirmish line, followed a southerly route through the town. A Confederate officer riding at the head of troops that intercepted the company's route ordered the company to halt. In response Pvt. Terrence O'Connor remarked as he shot the man, "We take no orders from the likes of you!" and the company went on.[21]

Alice Powers, who lived at the intersection of Washington and High streets, witnessed a fight involving the 150th Pennsylvania. Skirmishers from Ramseur's brigade under Lt. Frank M. Harney of the 14th North Carolina attacked the Pennsylvanians. Harney seized their flag from Cpl. Rodney Connor before being mortally wounded by a bullet in the bowels.

Before dying, Harney asked that the captured colors be sent to Jefferson Davis. This was done, and the flag was found within the baggage of President Davis when he was captured at the end of the war.[22]

After leaving Seminary Ridge, the 6th Wisconsin retreated in line of battle and with colors flying to the college grounds. It crossed Washington Street and came face-to-face with enemy soldiers. Dawes headed his men south, probably in a column if not in a ragged file, until they reached Chambersburg Street, which was swept by enemy fire. Beyond the street there was a board fence with a "hog hole" where missing boards had been. Telling his men to follow him at a run in single file, Dawes took the flag and dashed for the hole. The remainder of the 6th followed in turn until all but two who had been shot gathered within the confines of the yard. They reformed, and Dawes led them to South Washington Street, which was crowded with fleeing soldiers, some "sound in body but craven in spirit." Dawes formed the 6th in two lines across the street, and they exchanged fire with nearby Confederates. By this time they were hot and thirsty; sweat streamed from their powder blackened faces. As they fired at the pursuing Confederates, an "old citizen" came from a nearby house carrying two buckets of water and gave it to the men. After this brave and compassionate act, Dawes called for a cheer, and the men of the 6th, amid the chaos that surrounded them, gave three "hearty cheers for the Old Sixth and the good cause."[23]

The shooting had cleared the street, and the 6th hurried on. Finally its men saw "the colors of the Union, floating over well ordered line of men in blue, who were arrayed along the slope of Cemetery hill." It was the 73d Ohio of Col. Orland Smith's brigade, von Steinwehr's division. The brigade's presence and its flags raised the spirits of the retreating troops and discouraged their pursuers. Howard's decision to man and hold the hill as a Union rallying point was being vindicated.[24]

CHAPTER 24
Cemetery Hill

At 4:30, after riding slowly through Gettysburg, Maj. Gen. Abner Double-day approached Cemetery Hill and General Howard. Howard asked him to place his corps to the west of the Baltimore Pike on the left of the Eleventh Corps. The hill provided an excellent position. Not only did it dominate the fields east and west of the town, but it had a gentle forward slope that could be swept by artillery and fences and stone walls that made good shelter for infantry. Orland Smith's brigade of von Steinwehr's division had three regiments posted along the Taneytown Road facing in the direction of Hill's potential attack, and some of Coster's troops were occupying the houses south of the town at the foot of the hill. Later, when Dawes's 6th Wisconsin Regiment arrived, its men fell exhausted among the cemetery's graves. As they did so, Dawes saw defeated Union soldiers spread over the hill in "much disorder" and a stream of stragglers and wounded men passing over it. Pvt. Avery Harris observed that "there will always be a few that don't seem to know where or when to stop, if the movement is to the rear." As Pvt. Jacob Smith reached the hill in his Eleventh Corps ambulance, he passed through a line of soldiers and realized for the first time that the retreating troops were to rally there. He thought that many of the soldiers assumed that they had been defeated and were trying to get as far from the enemy as possible. If they did not know that they were to make a stand, they soon learned differently from units of cavalry and infantry posted behind the hill to prevent able-bodied men from going farther to the rear.[1]

Howard and Doubleday and their subordinates worked to bring order to the arriving mass. Howard and an aide met a German regiment ascending the hill, its colonel growling something that Howard could not understand. Seeing its color-bearer, Howard called out, "Sergeant, plant your flag down there in the stone wall." The sergeant, who seemed not to recognize him, replied, "All right, if you will go with me, I will!" Howard took the flag and set it against the wall, and the regiment rallied on it. About the same time he went to the 17th Connecticut, which had formed a line nearby, and asked if there were men in it who had the courage to advance across a lot to a stone wall closer to the town. Major Brady replied, "Yes, the Seventeenth Connecticut will," and it did so. Shortly thereafter it advanced again to a fence even closer to the town. Capt. Edward Culp of Barlow's staff saw Howard as he rallied the arriving troops and spoke briefly with him. He wrote that this meeting "taught me what a cool and confident man could do. No hurry, no confusion in his mind. He knew that if he could get his troops in any kind of order back of those stone walls the country was safe, and that upon the succeeding days Lee would meet his great defeat."[2]

Lt. Jacob Slagle of Doubleday's staff rode to the hill in search of General Rowley. He saw a "pitiable sight; the tired, worn out remnants of our fine regiments, who had gone so proudly into the field in the morning, were collecting together, and when all was told, — what a miserable remnant. One regiment was a sample of all the rest, they went in with companies having from thirty-five to fifty-five men and not one had more than a dozen men and only five officers to the whole regiment." Lt. Col. John D. Musser of the 143d Pennsylvania recalled that they "sat down to rest, but could not sit still. Officers and men shook hands in silence great tear drops standing in their undaunted eyes, as they thought of the dead and wounded left in the hands of the cursed Rebels. We were almost afraid to ask each other where the rest of our regt. were, we knew most of them were either killed or wounded." The 143d Pennsylvania, which had entered the battle with nearly 500 officers and men, had 27 killed, 150 wounded, and 60 or 70 missing.[3]

The troops of the First Corps did not think well of the "Flying Dutchmen." It was written, perhaps apocryphally, that a First Corps officer stood by the road directing men to their units. A "big German" asked where the Eleventh Corps was forming. The officer replied, "Don't know. Nor does anybody else either I guess." He continued with his directions, "1st Corps goes to the right & 11th Corps go to *hell*."[4]

Eventually the men who halted on the hill and on Cemetery Ridge adjacent to it found their places. As Schurz described it, von Steinwehr's division was behind the stone walls west of the cemetery; his own division was "immediately opposite the town," and Barlow's division was on the right east of the pike. Insofar as the First Corps was concerned, the Iron Brigade would go to Culp's Hill, and Cutler's rested behind the hill. Robinson's division occupied the north end of Cemetery Ridge facing the Emmitsburg Road, and Doubleday's was on the west slope of the hill along the Taneytown Road.[5]

How many troops were on the hill? In truth, there is no way of knowing — there are only estimates. Most commanders did not report their strengths on the evening of 1 July, and many numbers reported could not have been correct. Stragglers and men detached to other duties rejoined their units throughout the following hours. Schurz's division went into the fight with about 3,100 troops, but it had only about 1,500 on the hill that evening. Lt. Peter Young, adjutant of the 107th Ohio, wrote that the 107th had 434 muskets when the battle opened and that evening had only 171. Young estimated that each of the three other regiments of Ames's brigade had less than 100 men each. General Doubleday reported that the First Corps had gone into battle with 8,200 officers and men and had 2,450 at the end of the day. Howard offered a casual estimate; he wrote that about 6,000 men of the Eleventh Corps were engaged and that it lost 3,195, leaving about 2,800. When Orland Smith's 1,600 men are added to that number, it seems likely that there were about 4,400 Eleventh Corps troops on the hill. Therefore, if Howard and Doubleday were essentially correct, less than an estimated 7,000 infantrymen were on Cemetery Hill and on the west slope of Culp's Hill before reinforcements arrived. Colonel von Gilsa did not reach his brigade until after dark. Captain von Fritsch met him. After greetings, von Fritsch pointed to some flags surrounded by sleeping soldiers and announced, "You can now command your Brigade easily with the voice, my dear Colonel, this is all that is left."[6]

The Federal trump card was its artillery. When the ten Federal batteries of the two corps reached Gettysburg, they had fifty-four guns. On 1 July the Confederates killed or wounded eighty-three men and eight officers — approximately the strength of one battery. The Rebels captured one gun from Reynolds's battery, two of Stewart's pieces lost their pointing rings and could not be used until they were replaced, and three of Hall's guns were disabled. One gun in Cooper's battery had a broken axle, but the battery seems to have had all four of its pieces on the hill. The Eleventh Corps left one of Wheeler's guns on the field, and the Confederates captured two of Heckman's, leaving that corps with twenty-three pieces. At Howard's request Colonel Wainwright took command of the batteries of

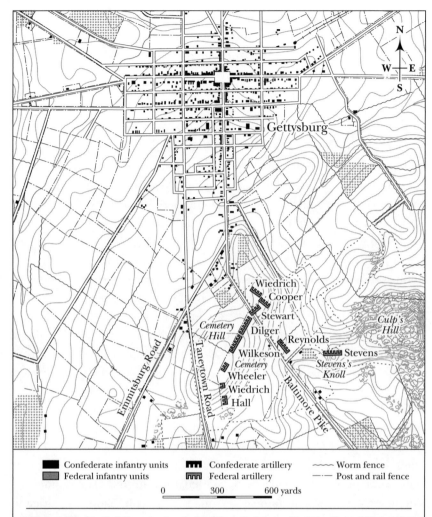

N
W — E
S

Gettysburg

Wiedrich
Cooper
Stewart
Cemetery Hill
Dilger
Reynolds
Wilkeson
Cemetery
Wheeler
Wiedrich
Hall

Culp's Hill

Stevens
Stevens's Knoll

Emmitsburg Road

Taneytown Road

Baltimore Pike

■ Confederate infantry units   ▥ Confederate artillery   ∿∿ Worm fence
▦ Federal infantry units   ▥ Federal artillery   —·— Post and rail fence

0   300   600 yards

1. *After retreating from the fields west and north of Gettysburg, the batteries of the Union First and Eleventh Corps join Wiedrich's battery on Cemetery Hill. Forty-three pieces defend the hill. Union infantry occupies the slopes in their front and on their flanks.*

2. *Stewart's, Wiedrich's, Cooper's, and Reynolds's batteries, with seventeen guns, occupy Cemetery Hill east of the Baltimore Pike. They cover the streets leading out of town and the approaches to the hill east of the town.*

3. *The six Napoleons of Stevens's battery are on "Stevens Knoll," between Culp's Hill and Cemetery Hill. They cover the approach to the Union position from the north and east.*

4. *Dilger's, Wilkeson's, Wheeler's, and Hall's batteries, as well as a section of Wiedrich's, are on Cemetery Hill west of the Baltimore Pike. Their twenty pieces cover the approaches from town and from the fields to the west; they can shell Seminary Ridge.*

Map 24.1. Artillery Positions, Cemetery Hill

Cemetery gatehouse and Stewart's battery's lunettes (GNMP)

both corps. Wainwright took personal charge of those posted east of the Baltimore Pike (perhaps he thought the greater danger was there), and Major Osborn commanded those west of it—most of which were in the cemetery. At the retreat's end Osborn had twenty guns of the two corps in the cemetery, and Wainwright had twenty-three on East Cemetery Hill and Stevens Knoll. All were amply supplied with ammunition from the Eleventh Corps train.[7]

After the batteries were ready for action, Wainwright saw that there was about an hour of daylight left. He feared that an attack from the town would force him to fire into it and harm the civilians and wounded there. He cautioned his officers not to waste ammunition and "not to take orders from any man with a star on his shoulders who might choose to give them."[8]

But one general had already given some orders. When Cooper's and Stevens's batteries reached Cemetery Hill, a portly major general on a horse by the arched cemetery gate shouted in a commanding voice for the captain of "that brass battery." Stevens reported to him. The general

Maj. Gen.
Winfield S. Hancock
(CWLM)

pointed toward Culp's Hill and to a knoll rising from the saddle between it and Cemetery Hill. He told Stevens to post his battery to "stop the enemy from coming up that ravine." "By whose order?" asked Stevens. "General Hancock's," the general replied. Stevens took his six Napoleons to the knoll from which they could cover the eastern approaches to Cemetery Hill.[9]

Hancock was thirty-eight years old, a West Point graduate with nineteen years of service as an officer of the 6th Infantry and as a quartermaster. He had been a captain when the war began. Fate, politics, and the army had provided him a star twenty days after Howard had become a general. He had served with distinction and had been given the nom de guerre "The Superb." Like Howard, Hancock received his second star on 29 November 1862, but because Howard had become a brigadier general before Hancock had received that grade, Howard outranked him. Unlike Howard, Hancock was outgoing and proficient in profanity, and he had the confidence of the rank and file and of Meade as well. In 1863 he came about as close to being a model major general as anyone in either army.[10]

When Meade learned that Reynolds had been wounded, he sent for Hancock, whose corps had reached Taneytown at about 11:00 A.M. From their previous conversations, Hancock knew of Meade's intentions. Meade did not feel free to go to Gettysburg at that time; most of his army had not yet gone there, and he had not yet decided to fully implement the Pipe Creek Circular. Since he was not acquainted with the Gettysburg area, he sent Hancock to evaluate the situation and Gettysburg's potential as a place to fight. Should he find that Reynolds was incapacitated, Hancock was to take command of the left wing.

Hancock knew that Howard outranked him. When he reminded Meade of this, Meade replied that he knew Hancock better than Howard, and that he could trust him in a crisis. Hancock also knew of Meade's plans and could represent him on the field. Further, Meade had the authority to make appointments in emergencies regardless of seniority, and he would not be deterred by questions of legality. At Meade's request, Chief of Staff Daniel Butterfield wrote an order, timed 1:10 P.M., giving Hancock authority to go to Gettysburg and, in event of Reynolds's death, to take command of the army's left wing. He was also to advise Meade if Gettysburg was a more suitable place to give battle than the proposed Pipe Creek line.[11]

Hancock and Lt. Col. Charles H. Morgan, his chief of staff, rattled off in an ambulance over the rough and winding Taneytown Road. They studied maps of the area for a time, and when the ambulance could "not keep pace with the General's anxiety," they mounted horses and hurried on. After passing Horner's Mill, they found wagons blocking the road. Hancock ordered these to the rear. They reached Cemetery Hill about 4:30 and saw what must have been First Corps regiments going to the rear. (Doubleday probably would not have agreed, for his report suggests that First Corps dispositions had already been made by the time Hancock arrived.) Hancock rode along the line of Smith's brigade, which needed no rallying, and then proceeded toward the pike. He met Stevens's battery as it arrived and sent it to the knoll that now bears Stevens's name. Hancock's report states that he gave orders to establish a position on Cemetery Hill, which was already partially occupied. He suggested that he had labored hard to get the Eleventh Corps in position. However, in his testimony before the Committee on Conduct of the War, Hancock stated that Howard had already posted one of his divisions before he arrived.[12]

Hancock and Howard exhibited two forms of behavior. According to Sgt. Jerome Watrous, who retreated to the hill with the First Corps ammunition train, Howard sat on his horse "with as much coolness as though he was watching a Fourth of July parade." In contrast Hancock was "all excitement — not nervous — looking in a thousand ways every minute and giving directions as carefully and precisely as though he was preparing for a great parade . . . he was saying to this man and to that: 'Take your guns in that direction'; 'Collect your men'; 'Prepare for immediate action.' " Watrous reported to Hancock, who quizzed him. He told Watrous that he had done well and asked him to report back to him in a half-hour. Sgt. Bert O'Connor, who must have been there, recalled that Hancock said that the train's experience was the first "Mule Train Charge" that he had heard about. In writing of this, Watrous observed that Hancock's bluff behavior toward them was "one of the things that a non-commissioned, or a commissioned officer would never forget when we take into account the character of a man that Hancock was."[13]

Hancock's meeting with Howard created one of many postwar squabbles. In his report Hancock stated simply that upon arriving at Gettysburg, he "assumed the command." On Cemetery Hill he met Howard, who had attempted "to stop and form some of his troops there." He told Howard that he had orders authorizing him to take command at the front, but he did not show him the orders. Nevertheless, Howard acquiesced. Lieutenant Colonel Morgan, who might have been present, wrote that Howard waived seeing the written orders and expressed satisfaction at Hancock's arrival.[14]

Doubleday, who became peeved with Howard, gave another version. He wrote that after Hancock announced that he was assuming command, Howard said, "Why, Hancock, you cannot give any orders here! I am in command and I rank you!" According to Doubleday, Howard refused to acknowledge Hancock's authority. Hancock replied that he would go back to army headquarters and report, but Howard asked him to remain and help him organize the troops. Then Hancock went to see Doubleday, who was lower in rank than Hancock and was pleased to serve under him.[15]

Howard cherished yet another view. In his report Hancock said that

Meade had sent him forward and had given him instructions under the assumption that he was Howard's senior. Nothing was said of the written order, and both agreed that it was no time for talking. Hancock would take care of troops on the left of the Baltimore Pike, while Howard would see to those on the right. In 1864 Howard insisted that he had been in command of forces on the field until 7:00 P.M., when he turned the command over to the newly arrived Slocum. Twelve years later Howard repeated the story given in his report with the addition that he assumed that Hancock was doing no more than acting as "temporary chief of staff for Meade." Later, in his autobiography, Howard wrote that he had not received any intimation that Hancock, who was his junior in rank, had been placed in command until he saw the written order at 7:00 P.M. Howard's Gettysburg service was dear to him, and he could not force himself to admit anything that would diminish it.[16]

After leaving Howard, Hancock rode to Doubleday. It was then, apart from the inspiration of his presence perhaps, that he made his greatest contribution to the Federal rally. He asked Doubleday to send Wadsworth and the Iron Brigade to the west slope of Culp's Hill beyond Stevens's battery. Doubleday claimed that he had no problem with this, but there was delay and confusion because Howard had wanted them posted elsewhere. Howard later wrote that "it was just the thing to do," and it was. But this time Doubleday did not get off without criticism. Colonel Morgan, who had little good to say of any of the generals at Gettysburg that day except Wadsworth and Buford, wrote that when he carried Hancock's order to Doubleday, Doubleday displayed the "beaten demeanor that characterized some persons on that field." He protested that his men were worn out and short of ammunition. Hancock overheard part of Doubleday's protests and ordered the movement.[17]

Maj. Gen. Henry W. Slocum and two divisions of the Twelfth Corps were also in the area. Maj. Charles Howard of General Howard's staff met General Slocum on the Baltimore Pike a mile from Gettysburg and gave him General Howard's message. It told of the dire situation at Gettysburg and asked Slocum to send one division to the right and another to the left. Howard asked Slocum to come in person to Cemetery Hill. Slocum replied that he had sent divisions to the flanks and that he did not wish to come to Gettysburg and take responsibility for the fight. Later Slocum told Colonel Morgan that when he saw Eleventh Corps stragglers, he thought that Gettysburg might be another Chancellorsville and that it would be prudent for him to deploy his troops to check the imagined rout. He did not wish to take over from Hancock, who had been assigned to the command by Meade, and he did not wish to assume a command that might make him responsible for matters over which he had no control.[18]

But the interview with Morgan happened later. About 4:00 P.M. Brig. Gen. Alpheus Williams's division of the Twelfth Corps was poised to attack Benner's Hill and the Confederate left from the east, but Slocum ordered it back when he learned that the Union troops had retreated to Cemetery Hill. Williams retired his division to a bivouac a half-mile northeast of the Baltimore Pike, where it spent the night. At the same time Slocum ordered Brig. Gen. John Geary to leave a brigade and a section of artillery in reserve and to take his two other brigades forward to report to Howard. By this time, though, Hancock had reached the field. Hancock told Geary to place his two brigades on his extreme left, and Geary put two regiments on or near the Round Tops. The Third Corps was also on the way and would arrive later that evening.[19]

When the Federal forces were in their assigned positions and things had settled down, Hancock sat on a stone wall at the brow of the hill. Schurz, who claimed to be the last general officer to reach the hill, joined him there, and the two watched the enemy through their binoculars. Some of the movements that they saw puzzled them. Schurz became nervous, for he knew that their infantry lines were "woefully thin." It soothed his pride when Hancock admitted that he was nervous too, but Hancock thought that the artillery could enable them to hold out until help came. As the minutes passed, they became more calm. The Union forces had a strong position, and their strength was growing. With each hour, their situation became more secure.[20]

The Confederate movements observed by Hancock and Schurz must have been those of Ewell's corps. Doles's brigade and portions of Ramseur's and O'Neal's brigades swept the town west of Baltimore Street; Hays's brigade cleared the streets to the east. Doles had attempted to cut off First Corps units retreating from Seminary Ridge and along the railroad bed by swinging his left forward, but it did not move fast enough to do so. Colonel Grimes claimed that his 4th North Carolina was the first regiment to enter the town, but it halted at Middle Street. When the town was secure, Doles's, Iverson's, and Ramseur's brigades formed a line on Middle Street between Baltimore Street and the seminary.[21]

The civilians took shelter as the Confederates cleared their streets. Sarah Broadhead peered at them from her house on Chambersburg Street and discovered the Southerners to be a "dirty, filthy set" who wore a varied garb.

Some were barefooted and wounded. Catherine Foster watched them from a cellar window of her house at the corner of Washington and High streets. She saw one unit with a hatless leader that was "yelling furiously and firing, curdling one's blood." As Henry Jacobs watched from a cellar window of his house at the corner of Washington and Middle streets, he saw a lone Union soldier run by pursued closely by some Confederates and gasping for breath. One of the pursuers yelled, "Shoot him, shoot him"; a rifle cracked, and the fleeing soldier dropped dead in the street. As the firing subsided, the Confederates searched the houses for Union soldiers. This brought them into direct contact with some of Gettysburg's women, some of whom gave Capt. Thomas Hightower of the 21st Georgia and others "a hard battle with their tongues, which . . . they are capable of doing."[22]

Hays's Louisiana brigade captured many prisoners, whom were disarmed and sent to the rear. Hays complained later that Rodes's division corralled many of these men and took credit for their capture. After "driving them like chaff through the town," Hays halted, formed his main line along East Middle Street, and sent Company I of the 8th Regiment forward as skirmishers. These soldiers, under Lt. J. Warren Jackson, deployed at the foot of Cemetery Hill, where they sweated in the heat and endured the sniping of Union skirmishers posted on higher ground in their front. That afternoon Jackson spent two hours "as miserably as I ever did in my life." Things would not be better for him the next day. "Loud and furious were the curses for not allowing us to go on and take Cemetery Hill that day."[23]

After Avery's North Carolina brigade stampeded the right of Coster's ill-fated line, it continued south along the edge of the town to the railroad track. It reformed there, then filed left about 400 yards to clear the town's buildings before facing right toward Cemetery Hill. While at the railroad, the brigade came under fire from Wiedrich's battery on Cemetery Hill. The brigade advanced toward the hill still under artillery fire and passed by the Culp buildings. The fire, recalled one Tarheel, was "proving very effective." Wiedrich's fire and a lack of support prompted Col. Isaac Avery, the brigade commander, to halt the brigade in the ravine of Winebrenner's Run at the base of Cemetery Hill. Some Union troops considered Avery's approach an attack that they had repulsed, but the North Carolinians deemed it an opportunity missed. The men of the 57th North Carolina were certain that the war would have soon been over had a final push been made. Those of the 6th Regiment thought that Wiedrich's battery was just arriving and could see no infantry on the hill. In their recollections, tinted by time, they were anxious to proceed and take possession of the hill but stopped only because they received positive orders to do so. Skirmishers went forward to cover their front.[24]

The retreat of the Union forces demanded that the Confederate commanders make decisions about the action they should take. Obviously, none had been made prior to their success. The ranking generals had been influenced by General Lee's often expressed wish that a general engagement be avoided until "the rest of the army came up." But a battle had begun, the Confederates had prevailed over the Union forces at hand, and further action seemed in order. Yet none of the Confederates knew the whereabouts of the remaining units of the Army of the Potomac. For his part, General Hill considered the casualties suffered by Heth's and Pender's divisions, their exhaustion, and their disorganization as reasons to halt his advance. He believed that the enemy had been routed, and he was content with what had been gained.[25]

Not so with Generals Lee and Ewell. After Rodes's attack was under way, Ewell rode east toward Early's front. As he passed William P. Carter's battery, a shell exploded nearby. The one-legged Ewell fell to the ground. Protesting that he was not hurt, Ewell mounted again and continued on. Soon after, he observed Doles's assault on the 157th New York. As the Federals retreated toward the town, Ewell and his staff gathered on a rise, probably that west of the Carlisle Road where Dilger's guns had been, and watched the end of the fighting north of the town. During that pause, Maj. Henry Kyd Douglas of General Johnson's staff rode up. He reported that Johnson and his division were about an hour's march away and that it could go into battle as soon as it arrived. General Gordon was present. He volunteered to join his brigade with Johnson's division in the attack. Together, he claimed, they could take Cemetery Hill before dark. (If said, this was a brash statement made by a general who was well over a mile from the hill and who would have known nothing about the difficulties involved in attacking it.) In response Ewell remarked that he had brought his troops to Gettysburg as ordered by General Lee, and that Lee had given him no further orders. Without additional instructions, he did not feel justified in continuing the advance. He then asked that Johnson bring his division "well to the front, to halt and wait for orders." There was silence, and according to Major Douglas, Maj. "Sandie" Pendleton, Ewell's chief of staff, muttered, "Oh, for the presence and inspiration of Old Jack for just one hour!"[26]

Rodes entered the town after Doles's and Ramseur's brigades, but he did not prepare his division for a further attack. He justified this lack of aggressive action by his belief that General Lee did not want a general engagement. His division *alone* was in no condition to attack the formidable Union position on Cemetery Hill, and he saw no troops on his right preparing to do so. On his left, Early, whom he saw thirty minutes later, was still awaiting instructions.[27]

"Elated with the success," Early had followed Hays's brigade into town. He saw Union troops on his right falling back and sent for Smith's brigade and a battery of artillery. The latter did not arrive in time, and the former did not come at all. Hays's and Avery's brigades were deploying, and Early observed that the hillside in front of the North Carolinians was rugged and crossed by stone walls and plank fences. An advance from the town would have to be made over narrow streets in columns, which could be plowed by a destructive fire from batteries on the hill. Early saw this in a glance and concluded that he could not advance from his front "with advantage." Any advance would have to be from his right by Rodes or the divisions of A. P. Hill.[28]

Yet as soon as he saw that Hays's and Hoke's brigades were in position, Early searched for Ewell, Rodes, and even Hill. He wanted to urge an immediate advance "before the enemy should recover from his evident dismay." Early requested also that Smith bring his brigade forward to the support of Hays and Avery. Smith replied that a large force of the enemy was advancing on the York Road and that he thought it "proper to detain his brigade to watch that road." Early did not accept this explanation initially, for he sent for Smith's brigade a second time. Early surely knew that Smith was a brave and natural leader, but he did not trust his judgment under such circumstances. Yet Smith had been a congressman and a governor of Virginia, and he was Virginia's governor-elect. He received deference even from Jubal Early.[29]

Early rode to the right into Rodes's zone. There he met an unidentified staff officer of Pender's division. Seemingly ignoring Ewell's prerogatives, he asked this officer to tell Hill that if he would send a division forward, then they could take the hill. Nothing came of this. He then encountered Col. Abner Smead of Ewell's staff, who told him that Ewell wished to discuss the use of Johnson's division with him. At this time some Union shells fell around them. Then a peculiar thing happened: Lt. Fred Smith, General Smith's son and a member of his staff, galloped up "under great excitement." He told Early that a large Federal force was approaching over the York Pike against Ewell's left flank and that Smith's brigade could not hold it off. Early wrote later that he had no faith in the report, yet he sent

Gordon's brigade to Smith's support. He placed Gordon in charge of the two with orders to stop the "stampeding." Thus Early squandered half his strength to answer a request in which he professed later to have had no faith. In doing this he seriously reduced Ewell's ability to capture Cemetery Hill.[30]

Ewell followed his troops into Gettysburg and waited in the square while Hays and Doles secured the town. According to an account written by Lt. James P. Smith, a staff officer, Ewell chatted as time slipped away. But in a later article Smith wrote that Ewell was "earnestly engaged in receiving reports from all his command, giving directions as to the disposition of his troops, directing supplies of ammunition and making disposition of a large number of prisoners that had fallen into our hands." Ewell talked also with Rodes and Early. He learned that they favored a continuation of the attack if Hill's corps would join them. He agreed. Summoning Lieutenant Smith, who had come to Gettysburg with General Lee, he said, "You have lately been with General Lee; perhaps you can find him again. Please tell him what Generals Early and Rodes wish to say." After listening to the generals' opinions, Smith set out to find Lee.[31]

Soon after Smith's departure, Capt. Walter H. Taylor, Lee's adjutant, arrived with an oral message to Ewell from Lee. According to Taylor's recollection, Lee said that the enemy was fleeing in confusion and that it was only necessary for Ewell to press him in order to take Cemetery Hill. But neither Lee nor Ewell recalled it that way. Lee's recollection was that he instructed Ewell to attack *if practicable* but that he was *to avoid a general engagement* until the arrival of the other divisions of the army. Ewell's memory of the message was that he was to attack only if he could do so "to an advantage." When he returned to Lee, Taylor was under the correct impression that Ewell intended to attack, but Ewell began to change his mind.[32]

Leaving Ewell, Lt. James P. Smith rode to Seminary Ridge and south along it until he found Lee and Longstreet at a fence near McMillan Woods. Both knew Smith and greeted him courteously. Smith relayed Ewell's message that "if General Lee would send troops to support them on their right, they could at once advance to occupy the cemetery hill in front of the town; and that it would be well for General Lee to occupy at once the higher ground in front of our right, which seemed to command the cemetery hill." In reply Lee handed the lieutenant his binoculars and pointed to the front, saying, "I suppose . . . this is the higher ground to which these gentlemen refer. . . . You will see that some of those people are there now." He went on to say that "our people are not all up yet, and I have no troops with which to occupy this higher ground." Turning to Longstreet he asked where his troops were and how soon they could be brought to the front. Longstreet replied that his leading division was six miles away. Beyond that he was noncommittal. In one account Lieutenant Smith wrote that Lee then asked him to tell Ewell that he regretted that the troops coming in from the west were not in a position to support him on the right, but that he wished him to take Cemetery Hill if possible. Yet at this time Anderson's division was on Herr Ridge, and Thomas's fresh brigade of Pender's division was nearby. In short, Lee's message to Ewell was that if he attacked he would get no help from Hill and Longstreet.[33]

Perhaps it was at this time that Lee and Longstreet discussed the merits of an assault against the Union position on Cemetery Ridge, and Longstreet advocated a turning movement instead. Col. Armistead Long, Lee's "Military Secretary," a West Point graduate who had been an artillery lieutenant in the Old Army, heard this exchange. When it was finished, Lee asked Long to make a reconnaissance of the Federal position on Cemetery Ridge. Long did so and reported that Federals occupied the ridge in "considerable force." In later years Long wrote Jubal Early that "an attack at that time, with the troops then at hand, would have been hazardous and of very doubtful success." After he made his report to Lee, Long heard no further mention of an attack that evening.[34]

After Smith departed to carry Ewell's request to General Lee, Generals Ewell, Early, and Rodes and their staffs rode south from the square along Baltimore Street, passed High Street, and crossed over the crest just south of the alley beyond. There they attracted the attention of Federal skirmishers about 500 yards away in the Wagon Hotel and in other buildings at the foot of the hill. Bullets zipped around the horsemen, one hitting the stirrup leather of a staff officer. The party turned into the shelter of the alley and obtained a good view of Cemetery Hill from the cover of buildings along High Street.[35]

Ewell must have been impressed by the strength of the Union position, particularly by the batteries ranged along the hill's crest. Presumably Rodes told him of his division's casualties and that his men were not then in a condition to attack. Early would have mentioned that he had only two brigades at hand and that the other two were off to the east. In addition, Ewell saw no good artillery positions within his zone — his left had not yet encompassed Benner's Hill. Still, Major Brown wrote that Ewell had begun to prepare for an attack. He ceased doing so only when he was told that the enemy was advancing toward his left flank.[36]

We do not know what troops General Smith thought he saw on the York Pike. There were no Federal units there — at least none of consequence. Some unidentified guns, probably from Cemetery Hill, shelled Smith's column when it moved to its new position, but that was all. Lt. Cyrus B. Coiner of the 52d Virginia heard the general ask his son and aide, Fred, to tell Early that the Union forces were advancing and that he needed help. Coiner did not know the reason for Smith's alarm and thought that he might have mistaken a distant fence for a line of troops. Gordon's brigade soon arrived at a double-quick but halted before it reached Smith's position.[37]

Ewell, Early, and Rodes went east on the York Pike until they could see it extending off two or three miles to the northeast. Smith's regiments were deployed in the foreground. Early, who had allowed Smith to be there and had sent Gordon to join him, related what happened next. He said that he placed no confidence in the rumor of an enemy advance over the York Pike, but that Rodes was inclined to believe it, and Ewell did not know what to think. As they surveyed the scene, they saw a line of infantry. Rodes exclaimed, "There they are now," but Early disagreed. Early sent two aides to reconnoiter. They found that the infantry line belonged to Smith's brigade and that Gordon was shifting them about. Although they saw no enemy, Ewell and Early left both brigades there to guard the road. The brigades remained until the following day.[38]

While Ewell concerned himself with events in and around Gettysburg, Johnson's division approached the town over the Chambersburg Pike. Other units got in its way and slowed its march; at other times its men moved at a double-quick. They heard the sounds of battle from Cashtown, and as they neared the field, they met casualties going to the rear. Francis R. Nicholls's Louisiana brigade led the march. When it reached one of the swales on the afternoon's battlefield, it filed left from the pike to the unfinished railroad bed and followed it into the town. By this time, of course, the fighting on that part of the field was over, and dead and wounded were everywhere. Johnson's rear brigade arrived shortly before darkness — two hours or more after Major Douglas had told Ewell that the division was an hour away and would soon be up.[39]

The division halted for a time on the railroad bed west of the Gettysburg station and waited for orders. In the meantime, General Johnson had ridden ahead and met with Ewell and Early, who by now had returned from the York Pike. Ewell had decided already that Johnson should occupy Culp's Hill in order to threaten the Union right and rear on Cemetery

Hill. Its very presence, he thought, would oust the Federals from their strong position — perhaps without a fight. We do not know just when Ewell decided to occupy Culp's Hill; certainly it was after he entered the town and saw that Cemetery Hill could not be had for the asking. Early claimed that he suggested to Colonel Smead that Culp's Hill should be occupied by Johnson's division even before he saw Ewell in the town. Yet in his report he mentioned that when he saw Ewell, Ewell told him that he was determined to occupy the hill with Johnson's division when it arrived.[40]

Isaac Trimble had something to say about this. In an account written in 1883, Trimble claimed that while the Confederates occupied the town and Ewell paced in indecision in a yard near the almshouse, he examined the terrain "on the northern and north eastern" side of the city and saw the value of Culp's Hill. He told Ewell of his reconnaissance and urged him to occupy the hill at once with a brigade and with artillery. Trimble went on to say that if the Confederates did not seize the hill, the Union forces would. According to Trimble, Ewell replied to his suggestions with petulance, saying, "When I need advice from a junior officer, I generally ask it."[41]

About two hours after the Confederates entered the town, Ewell sent Lt. Thomas Turner and Robert D. Early, a volunteer aide on General Early's staff, on a reconnaissance of Culp's Hill. By this time the Iron Brigade must have gone to the west slope of the hill, though the 7th Indiana probably had not yet extended its line to the hill's crest. The two aides claimed that they went to the top of the hill, probably by ascending its gentler east slope, without meeting an enemy soldier. From the hill they could see the Union line stretched out before them. But somehow they did not see the line of the nearby Iron Brigade — perhaps it was hidden by trees. They rode back to tell Ewell that the hill was not occupied and that its possession by the Confederates would make "the enemy's position untenable."

The two aides found Ewell sitting in a fence corner between Rodes and Early. After hearing their report, Ewell asked Rodes what he thought about sending Johnson's division there that night. Rodes, who might have been unwell, replied that the men were tired and footsore and that he did not think "that it would result in anything one way or the other." Early's reply was just the opposite. He said, "If you do not go up there tonight, it will cost you ten thousand men to get up there tomorrow." The result of this conversation, wrote Turner, was that Ewell ordered Johnson to move his division to the vicinity of Culp's Hill and to take possession of it if he found it to be unoccupied.[42]

Maj. Campbell Brown, who drafted Ewell's reports, summarized this decision by writing simply that because of "the inactivity of the troops under Gen'l Lee's own eye, those of Hill & Longstreet . . . that Gen'l Ewell finally decided to make no direct attack, but to await for Johnson's coming up & with his fresh troops seize & hold the high peak to our left of Cemetery Hill."[43]

General Johnson seems not to have participated in the decision that involved him and his division. When Ewell told Johnson of it, an argument took place between Johnson and Early in which the language used "was more forceful than elegant." Time had blurred the reasons for the exchange; both men had positive personalities and were tired, and Johnson had been angered by Longstreet's corps being in his division's way during its march to Gettysburg. Perhaps it was only a trivial thing (the generals of the Army of Northern Virginia could be a prickly lot), yet such squabbles could inhibit communication and cooperation. Nevertheless, Johnson's division resumed its movement toward Culp's Hill. Its men stumbled their way in the semidarkness over the railroad's ties and tracks to the railroad bridge over Rock Creek. (The bridge had been wrecked by Gordon's brigade during its visit the week before.) They forded the creek and continued along the tracks to the Hunterstown Road crossing. Turning right there to the York Pike, they crossed it and filed into the lane of the George Wolf farm. By this time the moon was rising, and by its light the division formed a line in a depression that ran southeast to Benner's Run.[44]

Based on Jubal Early's writings, it has been generally accepted that Lee talked with Ewell, Rodes, and Early that evening in a meeting dominated by Early's comments. In this meeting Lee and the generals discussed matters relating primarily to 2 July and the possibility of Ewell making an attack on his front. Ewell and his generals were reluctant to do this, and when Lee suggested that Ewell's corps might be moved to the right, they opposed that too. When Lee left, Ewell and his generals believed that the main attack on 2 July would be made by Longstreet's corps against the Union left.[45]

They were in for a surprise. Lee later sent word by Col. Charles Marshall that unless Ewell could carry the position in his front, he intended to move Ewell's corps to the right. This prompted a visit by Ewell to Lee's headquarters. There Ewell presumably told Lee of his hope that Johnson's division would be able to occupy Culp's Hill and force the enemy from his position on Cemetery Hill. Ewell was persuasive, and Lee permitted his corps to remain in place.[46]

It was after midnight when Ewell returned to his headquarters; 1 July was over, but the events of that day had not yet played out. Ewell had not heard of Johnson's progress and sent orders to him by Lieutenant Turner for his division to take possession of Culp's Hill if it had not already done so.

Turner found Johnson preparing to advance, but Johnson had bad news. After his division had formed east of the town, he had sent a reconnaissance party to the hill to determine if the enemy was on or near it. When this party neared the top of the hill, the enemy fired on it. The 7th Indiana Regiment had taken position on the right of the Iron Brigade and had extended the Union line to the hill's summit. Col. Ira Grover, its commander, had placed a picket line first on the east slope of the hill and then had pickets on the hill's south slope beneath its crest. These men heard the Confederates approaching and fired at them. The Hoosiers captured an officer and a soldier, and the rest of the party fled. So ended the Confederate attempt to occupy Culp's Hill.[47]

On their return from the hill, the reconnaissance party captured a Union courier bearing a dispatch sent at midnight by Maj. Gen. George Sykes, commander of the Union Fifth Corps, to General Slocum. In it Sykes stated that his corps had bivouacked along the Hanover Road about four miles east of Gettysburg and that it would resume its march to Gettysburg at 4:00 A.M. Turner delivered the captured dispatch to Ewell with the message from Johnson saying that he would remain in place until further orders. This was a discouraging postscript to what many had deemed a Confederate victory. Ewell wrote its epitaph, and that of his fine reputation and career, when he reported, "Day was now breaking, and it was too late for any change of place." Ewell's corps would stay where it was, and the Confederates would have to fight for the hills in their front.[48]

CHAPTER 25
Epilogue

Many men who fought on 1 July would not be able to fight again at Gettysburg. According to the Army of the Potomac's "Return of Casualties," the First Corps units, which fought on 1 July and numbered about 9,500, suffered more than 5,600 casualties, including 1,600 men captured and missing. The Eleventh Corps, which had about 7,000 men in the battle north of the town, lost 3,400, with 1,490 captured and missing. Almost all of these casualties would have been sustained on 1 July. Neither corps would recover from its losses, and the days of each were numbered. The First Corps disbanded when the Army of the Potomac reorganized in March 1864. The First Division (Barlow's) of the Eleventh Corps quit the corps for the South Carolina coast in August 1863, and the corps' remaining two divisions left the Army of the Potomac for Tennessee in September. There, in April 1864, the two divisions were melded with the Twelfth Corps into the new Twentieth Corps commanded by Joseph Hooker.[1]

On the Confederate side General Ewell reported that his corps had "less than 2,900 killed, wounded, and missing" on 1 July, and Rodes stated that 2,500 of them came from his division. Rodes's figure included 179 in Doles's brigade. Of the 400 that Early's division apparently sustained, Gordon reported that 350 came from his brigade.[2]

Hill made no comparable report for the two divisions of his corps in the 1 July battle. However, in postwar writings Heth gave two casualty figures for his division in the afternoon's battle: in one account he wrote of losing 2,300 of his men killed or wounded in thirty minutes of fighting and, in another, 2,700 men killed or wounded in twenty-five minutes. Obviously Heth was using round numbers, and his figures did not include Archer's and Davis's men shot or taken prisoner in the morning's fight. Maj. Joseph

Engelhard, reporting for Pender's division, gave no casualty figures, but Colonel Perrin wrote that as a result of his 1 July attack, his four regiments in the fight were reduced to less than half the number of men (about 1,500) taken into the battle, and that the number did not "fall short of 500." Lane's brigade's casualties were "slight" on 1 July, but Scales reported a loss of 545 out of his 1,400. Yet Colonel Lowrance reported that fewer than 500 men were in line when he took command of Scales's brigade after the 1 July fight, thus suggesting that the number reported by Scales ought to have been larger.[3]

The heavy losses sustained by both armies led to errors in their casualty figures. The Confederates compounded this difficulty for future students of the battle by not listing as casualties those soldiers captured or slightly wounded. Some students of the battle have believed that the casualty figures reported for Heth's division in particular were too low. Further, there was no effort made in some units to differentiate between the casualties of 1 July and those suffered on 2 or 3 July. As a consequence, casualty figures must be viewed with skepticism.[4]

On the basis of the figures above, it seems likely that the 9,500 soldiers of the First Corps on the field inflicted the 5,900 casualties sustained by Heth's, Pender, and Rodes's division less Doles's brigade, and that 6,000 men of the Eleventh Corps on 1 July were responsible for the 400 sustained by Early's division plus the 200 more probably sustained by Doles's and O'Neal's brigades. Although these figures are approximate at best, they suggest that the First Corps put up a much better fight on 1 July than the Eleventh Corps. This was so, but there were extenuating circumstances.[5]

The north-south ridges occupied by the First Corps plus the woods in its sector provided good defensive positions, whereas there was little good defensive terrain on the Eleventh Corps front. Certainly men occupying strong positions can be expected to fight longer and inflict heavier casualties that men who fight from a weak position that is dominated by high ground and can be, and was, easily turned. Such was the plight of the Eleventh Corps.

It would be difficult to compare the leadership of the two corps. Because of their poor position and inadequate numbers to defend it, the Eleventh Corps commanders faced an impossible situation. Probably few, if any, commanders could have done much better under similar circumstances. It is ironic that the defeat of the corps, which was criticized for its lack of desire to fight, was hastened by Barlow's aggressive action that thinned the corps line and exposed its right to Early's onslaught.

Many of the survivors of the First Day's battle fought again on 2 or 3 July. When Johnson's division attacked the Twelfth Corps on Culp's Hill on the evening of 2 July, units of both the First and the Eleventh Corps hurried to aid the Twelfth. Three regiments of Wadsworth's division went from the western slope of that hill to the Twelfth Corps works on its south slope. These regiments — the 6th Wisconsin, the 14th Brooklyn, and the 147th New York — are probably the only regiments on the field that participated in heavy fighting on all three days of the battle.[6]

Schurz sent the 45th New York and the 82d Illinois to the aid of Greene's brigade on the evening of 2 July. After the fighting on Culp's Hill ebbed, an unknown officer approached Lieutenant Colonel Salomon of the 82d in the darkness. Not knowing to whom he spoke, he complimented Salomon by saying, "If you were here yesterday instead of that d——d 11th Corps, we would not have been driven back."

To this Salomon shot back, "You are a miserable hound, sir. I and my regiment belong to that same 11th Corps you are speaking of, and we did no worse fighting yesterday."[7]

On the evening of 2 July, Hays's and Avery's brigades attacked the Union position on East Cemetery Hill defended by the remnants of Barlow's division. Although a few of the attackers reached the crest of the hill and the cannons there, troops of the division and artillerymen, with the help of regiments of Krzyzanowski's and Coster's brigades, repelled their assault. Colonel Avery died alone near the hill from a mortal wound. With his last strength he scrawled a note that spoke for many North Carolinians: "Tell my father I died with my face to the enemy."[8]

Rodes's division was to have attacked Cemetery Hill from the west on the evening of 2 July, but the movement started late and was stopped. Junius Daniel then led his and O'Neal's brigades to the aid of Johnson's division on Culp's Hill, where they took part in the fighting there on 3 July.[9]

The most questionable use of the veterans of 1 July took place on 3 July in Pickett's Charge. In spite of their heavy casualties, General Lee, with Hill's concurrence no doubt, selected the four brigades of Heth's division, commanded then by General Pettigrew, to form the left wing of the assault column that would attack the Union center. Lane's and Scales's brigades, under General Trimble, were to advance in their support. All but Brockenbrough's brigade went forward gallantly. Many reached the wall that sheltered the Union Second Corps line. Heth's division's casualties that day numbered about 60 percent; Lane's and Scales's, about 50 percent. Archer's brigade lost four flags at The Angle, and the fifth was saved only because a captain removed it from its staff and carried it off beneath his coat. Trimble received a leg wound, and bullets wounded Pettigrew in the hand and killed his horse. Pettigrew was mortally wounded at the Potomac crossing eleven days later. The 28th North Carolina of Lane's brigade would be the last Confederate unit to cross the pontoon bridge back into Virginia.[10]

Four generals commanded Heth's and Pender's divisions at Gettysburg. Of these, Pettigrew and Pender were mortally wounded before the end of the campaign, and Trimble lost his leg and became a prisoner of war. Only Heth, who had been put out of action by a bullet that struck him in the head, would command his division until it was surrendered at Appomattox Courthouse.[11]

A. P. Hill commanded his corps until the last days of the war, although his health had deteriorated markedly by that time. A Federal bullet killed him near Petersburg a week before Lee's surrender.[12]

Robert Rodes led his division until he was killed on 19 September 1864 at the Third Battle of Winchester. In the meantime, Jubal Early had become commander of Ewell's old corps, which he led to the Shenandoah Valley. After Early's 1864 raid on Washington, Philip Sheridan defeated Early's command at Winchester and virtually destroyed it at Waynesboro in March 1865. Lee then relieved his "bad old man" from duty. After the war, when president of the Southern Historical Society, Early refought the war with pen and printing press. He extolled Lee as *the* peerless commander and smote those, like Longstreet, whom he deemed responsible for mishaps leading to Confederate defeat. Many historians have taken issue with some of Early's writings in recent years, but they will continue to influence interpretations of the war for a long time to come.[13]

After Gettysburg, Richard Ewell's star dimmed. He performed well at the Wilderness and less so at Spotsylvania, where he commanded the troops at the Bloody Angle. At Spotsylvania his horse was shot, and he had a bad fall. By this time Lee was worried about his physical condition and seems to have lost confidence in his ability to continue with the Second Corps. He relieved Ewell of command of the corps and gave it to Early. Ewell then commanded the garrison of Richmond and its defenses. When the army evacuated that city at the end of the war, Ewell took the field again and was captured at Saylor's Creek on 6 April 1865. Unlike the officers who were surrendered at Appomattox Courthouse three days later and paroled, Ewell was imprisoned in Boston's Fort Warren for nearly four months. After his release, he became a prosperous farmer near Nashville, Tennessee. He died in January 1872.[14]

Brave Wadsworth led a division in the Fifth Corps in the Wilderness, was mortally wounded there, and died on 8 May 1864. He was brevetted a major general for his service at Gettysburg and at the Wilderness. John Robinson was commanding another Fifth Corps division when he lost his left leg at Spotsylvania. He was brevetted a brigadier general in the Regular Army for his service at Gettysburg, Spotsylvania, and the Wilderness and a major general for his war service. He retired from the army in 1869 in the grade of major general. He returned to Binghamton and served a term as lieutenant governor of New York. He also was a commander of the Grand Army of the Republic and president of the Society of the Army of the Potomac, and in 1894 he received a Medal of Honor. Robinson died in Binghamton in 1897.[15]

Thomas Rowley received no honors. His drunken behavior on 1 July resulted his court-martial and the recommendation that he be dismissed. A review board did not accept this recommendation, but Rowley's days were numbered. He resigned his commission in December 1864. He later practiced law and was a federal marshal.[16]

The postbattle fates of Barlow and Schimmelfennig were very different. Barlow recovered from his Gettysburg wound and returned to active service in March 1864. In spite of his excessive aggressiveness at Gettysburg and his lack of experience as a division commander, he received command of a division of the Second Corps. He led it from the Wilderness to Petersburg, where he became ill and was forced to take leave. He returned to the army in time to command a division at Appomattox. He was brevetted a major general for his service at Spotsylvania and was promoted to that grade in May 1865. After resigning his commission in November 1865, he practiced law in New York City and was active in Republican politics. He became New York's attorney general and prosecuted the Tweed Ring before his death in 1896.[17]

General Schimmelfennig continued in misfortune after Gettysburg. He left the Eleventh Corps to command a brigade in South Carolina. This was tedious, unhealthy duty, but Schimmelfennig had one moment of triumph. When the Confederate army evacuated Charleston in February 1865, he accepted the city's surrender. In April 1865 he went to his home in Pennsylvania in a fruitless attempt to restore his health. He died of tuberculosis in August 1865, leaving his family in dire straits. He is buried in Reading, Pennsylvania.[18]

Schimmelfennig's friend Carl Schurz prospered after Gettysburg. He continued to command the Third Division, Eleventh Corps, so long as the corps existed. In 1864 he went on inactive status and made speeches urging Lincoln's reelection. He returned to the army toward the end of the war as chief of staff of Slocum's Army of Georgia. After resigning his commission in May 1865, he toured the South at the request of President Andrew Johnson and reported to him on conditions found there. Subsequently he worked as a newspaperman. He was a senator from Missouri and served as an outstanding secretary of the interior under President Rutherford B. Hayes. He died in 1906.[19]

Abner Doubleday held no field commands after Gettysburg, but he was brevetted both a brigadier general and a major general in the Regular Army. After the war he remained with the Regular Army as a colonel of infantry until he retired in 1873. He was never reconciled to Meade's relieving him as acting commander of the First Corps in favor of Maj. Gen. John Newton, who was his junior in rank, and the reproach that it implied. He wrote of his experiences in letters, articles, and books, particularly his *Chancellorsville and Gettysburg*. He died on 25 January 1893.[20]

Hancock was the Union hero of Gettysburg; no one contributed more to the Union victory than he and his Second Corps. Hancock received the thanks of Congress for his service there. Unfortunately he was wounded at the climax of Pickett's Charge. After convalescence, he led the Second Corps in its 1864 campaigns, and he closed out the war in less active commands. He received the usual brevets and was made a major general in the Regular Army in 1866. After the war he held positions commensurate with his rank in New Orleans, the Dakotas, and finally New York. Unfortunately he had strained relations with General Grant, which must have affected his career. Yet, ironically, it was Hancock who had the responsibility to plan and execute Grant's New York funeral. Hancock was the unsuccessful Democratic candidate for president in 1880. He died in New York in 1886. It seems doubtful that he gave much serious thought to the events of 1 July after that day had passed.[21]

But Howard did. He was proud of his service at Gettysburg and continued to be rankled at being replaced by Hancock, his junior in rank, as commander of the left wing there. Yet he had an illustrious career. He led the Eleventh Corps in its Chattanooga battles and commanded the Fourth Corps and the Army of the Tennessee in the Atlanta Campaign, in the March to the Sea, and in the Carolinas. This was after many of his Gettysburg peers had been killed or were no longer in high commands. During

Reconstruction he headed the Freedman's Bureau, and he founded Howard University in the District of Columbia. He conducted the Nez Percé campaign in a lackluster manner, but he later headed the prestigious Military Division of the East. He retired in 1894 and died in 1909. Although he was never a popular general, few of Howard's contemporaries rose so high.[22]

The site of the Eleventh Corps headquarters on Cemetery Hill, like all Union corps headquarters at Gettysburg, is marked by an iron cannon barrel standing vertically in a granite base. We can assume that Howard would be glad to see it there. He might be less pleased to see the equestrian statue that stands about forty paces southeast of it almost opposite the cemetery gate. It is of Hancock; the Commonwealth of Pennsylvania placed it there in 1896. It might just as well have been placed on Cemetery Ridge at a suitable site on the Second Corps line where Hancock had commanded so well on 2 and 3 July and had been wounded. Yet the commonwealth chose to place it on Eleventh Corps turf on East Cemetery Hill.

Hancock is depicted in the act of rallying troops as they fell back to Cemetery Hill. He is alert, and he gestures with his right arm and hand as if to tell a regimental or battery commander where to place his unit. The horse reflects the rider. Its head is erect, and its left hoof is raised in a nervous movement. Hancock's is one of the most dynamic memorials on the field.

Hancock's statue laid uncontested claim to the East Cemetery Hill location until 12 November 1932, when the State of Maine belatedly erected an equestrian statue of General Howard there. It stands northeast of the Hancock memorial, about thirty paces beyond the headquarters marker and closer to the town. The bronze one-armed Howard sits quietly on his horse. He looks intently toward the town and the enemy. The statue's bronze horse reflects its rider. It stands with all four hooves planted firmly, as if it and its rider were there to stay. The two statues are separate entities that seem to ignore each other. They suggest that the echoes of the 1 July battle and the controversies associated with it still reverberated in 1932. They promise also that these squabbles as well as the accounts of the battle's heroics and blunders will continue well after us into the new millennium.

In his report of the First Corps battle of 1 July, Maj. Gen. Abner Doubleday wrote, "My thanks are specially due to a citizen of Gettysburg named John Burns, who, although over seventy years of age, shouldered his musket, and offered his services to Colonel Wister, One hundred and fiftieth Pennsylvania Volunteers. Colonel Wister advised him to fight in the woods, as there was more shelter there, but he preferred to join our line of skirmishers in the open fields. When the troops retired, he fought with the Iron Brigade. He was wounded in three places."[1]

Who was this septuagenarian who received over seven lines of praise in Doubleday's report, a mention that hundreds of soldiers would have coveted and scores who earned it did not receive?

Burns arrived about noon at the position of the 150th Pennsylvania in the area between the McPherson barn and the woods. He was "of rather bony frame and more than average stature," and he came from the direction of the town, walking with a "deliberate step, carrying in his right hand an Enfield rifle at a 'trail.' " He was marked by age and by his dress, which Maj. Thomas Chamberlin described as consisting of dark trousers and waistcoat, a blue swallowtail coat with brass buttons, and a high black silk hat. It was as though Rip Van Winkle had come down from South Mountain.

Burns went to Major Chamberlin and asked if he could fight with his regiment. Chamberlin referred him to Colonel Wister. Wister asked Burns if he could shoot. Burns replied that he had been a soldier in the War of 1812 and had fought at Lundy's Lane. Wister asked him if he had ammunition for his gun, and Burns slapped a pocket that bulged with cartridges. Wister gave him permission to fight on the Union line, but he recommended that Burns go into nearby McPherson Woods where he would find some shelter from the sun and from bullets. According to Chamberlin, Burns reluctantly complied. Chamberlin wrote that Burns's visit "did much to create good feeling and stimulate the courage of the regiment."[2]

Burns entered McPherson Woods, where he talked with Lt. Col. John Callis of the 7th Wisconsin. Callis's description of Burns was much the same as that given by Chamberlin. When Callis told Burns that he should go to the rear or he might be shot, Burns replied, "Tut, I've heard the whistle of bullets before." Callis gave Burns a rifle, and Burns consented to try it. He walked to the front of the skirmish line and took a bead on a Rebel officer riding toward him at full speed. Burns fired, the man fell from the saddle, and the horse ran into the Union lines.[3]

After his stay with the 7th Wisconsin, Burns went farther left to the 24th Michigan near the eastern edge of the woods. There, according to that regiment's history, Burns was shot three times, and Asst. Surg. Alex Collar dressed his wounds. On 15 July the 24th's chaplain called on Burns, presumably at his house on the west side of Gettysburg. The chaplain observed that he was quite comfortable and commented that "he is made of the right kind of stuff."[4]

Bret Harte wrote a poem titled *John Burns of Gettysburg*. In it Harte described Burns as "the only man who didn't back down" and "who held his own in the fight next day, When all of the townfolk ran away." Burns, a cobbler and onetime constable, was reputed to have been a controversial fellow, and he must have become even more so. On 1 July 1903 Pennsylvania dedicated a memorial erected by the state in his honor. The Reverend E. J. Wolf of Gettysburg made the dedicatory address, and in it he commented on certain highlights of Burns's life. He told his audience that "John Burns is no myth" and castigated the "mediocre critics" who strived to "extinguish the personality of 'the hero of Gettysburg.'" Wolf presented Burns as a patriot who had served in the War of 1812. He spoke of the fight in McPherson Woods and how Burns, after being shot, got rid of his gun and buried his ammunition so that the Confederates would not know that he, a civilian, had fought them.[5]

On 19 November Gettysburg's civilian hero met President Lincoln and walked arm in arm with him from the square to the Presbyterian church. Then, according to Dr. Wolf, both the United States and Pennsylvania placed him on their pension rolls. Residents of Germantown, Pennsylvania, sent him a gift of $100, and perhaps there were similar rewards from others. In addition he sold copies of a photograph of himself sitting in a chair with a musket and crutches nearby. It was said that this varied income enabled him to pay $1,800 for a farm east of Gettysburg.[6]

John Burns was no myth, but some of his fame was made by tellers of myths. Obviously he could not have fought with the Iron Brigade and remained in the open as Doubleday suggested, and Callis's story about his shooting a Confederate from his horse from the Iron Brigade's skirmish line with a rifle that he had not fired before raises some doubts. Perhaps such details are immaterial. He did exist, he fought on McPherson Ridge, and he was wounded. He died in February 1872, and he and Mrs. Burns are buried in Gettysburg's Evergreen Cemetery.[7]

APPENDIX B
The Color Episode of the 149th P.V.I.

The regimental colors, a silken U.S. flag and often the flag of the state to which the regiment belonged, had a very special meaning to units of Civil War armies. Like the standards of the Roman legions, they embodied the souls and honor of their regiments. The U.S. flag had the regiment's number emblazoned on its stripes along with the names of the principal battles in which the regiment had fought. A regiment's colors identified it, marked its location on the field, led it in the charge, and served as a rallying point in event of retreat. The regiments' commanders accepted these flags from local officials and other dignitaries, and they promised to defend them, their honor, and the values that they represented. From that time until the regiment was mustered out of the service, the colors were the special responsibility of the regiment's color company and its color guard. It was considered a great feat of arms to capture an enemy's colors; on the other hand, it was considered a disgrace for a regiment to lose its flags unless under highly extenuating circumstances.[1]

The Confederate colors were more varied than their Union counterparts in both fabric and design. Regiments in the Army of Northern Virginia at the time of Gettysburg commonly carried the well-known battle flag. Yet they might have flaunted the official Confederate flag — the Stars and Bars — and one regiment carried the new Stainless Banner. The regiments of Pickett's division are said to have carried Virginia's state flag.[2]

The two flags carried by Union regiments measured six by six and a half feet; the Confederate battle flag was four feet square. All were carried on polished wood staffs. A gilded eagle topped the staff of the U.S. flag. The army's drill manual required that a "color-bearer" or color sergeant carry the national flag; he was escorted by a color guard of eight corporals (it did not provide for a state flag). These men were selected for their bearing and character. Their place in a ten-company regiment was at the left of the right center company, therefore, near the center of the regiment's line. Ideally the color-bearers, flanked by two ranking corporals, were in the first rank; three corporals formed behind them in the second rank; and three more corporals were in the rear with the file closers. This format, however, did not take into account that most volunteer regiments would have had two flags in the front line, that there might be fewer than ten companies in the regiment, and that attrition would have made the prescribed color guard a luxury that regiments could not afford. In addition, the exceptionally large number of casualties among the color guard meant that it might well be composed of privates rather than corporals. It will be apparent in the text below that the color guard of the 149th Pennsylvania did not conform to the ideal prescribed by the army's drill manual.[3]

The ordeal of the color guard of the 149th Pennsylvania on 1 July was described in a paper prepared by Capt. John H. Bassler, commander of Company C, the color company of the 149th at Gettysburg. It was titled "The Color Episode of the One Hundred and Forty-ninth Regiment, Pennsylvania Volunteers at Gettysburg, July 1, 1863." It was published first by the Lebanon County Historical Society in October 1907 and republished by the Southern Historical Society with Confederate additions in 1909. The latter version is probably the more accessible of the two today. The Bassler account is the basic source for the text of this appendix and will not normally be cited.

This unique incident began on the afternoon of 1 July. Most of the 149th formed in the lane between the McPherson barn and the pike, and the remaining third was in the ditch along the south side of the pike and faced north. When Carter's batteries opened from Oak Hill, some shells crashed through the branches of the cherry trees lining the lane and proclaimed that Carter's batteries could enfilade the troops posted there. Lt. Col. Walton Dwight, commander of the 149th, ordered the portion of the regiment in the lane to move to the left of the companies in the ditch by the pike and face north. This would not only give them cover, but it would prevent their being enfiladed by the batteries on Oak Hill.[4]

As the left of the 149th was taking position along the pike, however, it extended to the crest of the west arm of McPherson Ridge and was seen by Confederate artillerymen on Herr Ridge. Soon Pegram's batteries were enfilading the 149th's line from that direction. To prevent this, Col. Roy Stone, the brigade commander, decided to try to deceive the enemy by moving the colors from the 149th's line to where the enemy might readily see them but away from the 149th's position. After receiving instructions from an officer of Dwight's staff, Color Sgt. Henry G. Brehm, a native of Myerstown and a descendant of Conrad Weiser, the famed Pennsylvania pioneer, led his men to the left and front to a chevron of piled fence rails. The chevron consisted of two piles of rails that had been heaped up by cavalry pickets. The piles were about 50 yards north of the pike and 115 yards south of the west cut. They were in the east edge of a wheat field that covered the west slope of the ridge between the pike and the railroad bed. The tall, ripe wheat, untrampled at the east end of the field, concealed the rail piles and the men behind them from the enemy on Herr Ridge. Yet, as was intended, the flags propped against the rails were visible above the wheat. Sergeant Brehm had custody of the national flag, and Cpl. Franklin Lehman carried the state flag. There were four other members of the color guard with them: Cpl. John Friddell and Pvts. Frederick Hoffman, John H. Hammel, and seventeen-year-old Henry H. Spayd. Like Brehm, all were from the Myerstown area except Hoffman, who was from nearby Newmanstown.[5]

The six Pennsylvanians reached the rail pile without trouble. Brehm and Lehman propped their flags against the rails, and the guards stretched prone behind the rails where the Confederates could not see them. The piles were off to the left of the 149th and protected by the west railroad cut from direct attack from the north. Thus they did not become involved with the seesaw fighting between the 149th and Daniel's troops at the cut. We cannot know their real contribution to the 149th's fight, but Captain Bassler believed that the fire from Pegram's guns on Herr Ridge had been diverted from the regiment's line and that Colonel Stone's diversion was a success. Further, Bassler thought that the Confederates supposed that there was a regiment beneath the flags and that Colonel Brabble of the 32d North Carolina believed this when he advanced to flank the Union troops along the pike. His concern enabled the 150th Pennsylvania to repulse the 32d with comparatively few troops. Bassler was pleased to quote Col. John Nicholson, chairman of the battlefield commission, who allegedly said that a minute gained by Brehm's bluff had been worth a regiment.

The color squad remained behind the rails during Daniel's first two attacks against Stone's brigade. They must have been worried about the possibility of an attack from the west, but fortunately Davis's nearby bri-

Color Sgt. Henry G. Brehm
(Bassler, "Color Episode,"
85)

gade was not aggressive and did not advance. Nevertheless, as the Confederate threat grew, the men behind the rails had a "hot discussion" over whether they should remain there or fall back to the regiment's position at the pike. But Brehm refused to leave — they had been ordered there, and they would remain there until they were recalled. By this time, though Brehm did not know it, both Bassler and Stone had been wounded and carried back to the McPherson buildings. Colonel Dwight had his hands full leading the regiment in its fight against Daniel and gave no orders for the flag's removal.[6]

Brehm's men worried about both the artillery fire that fell around them and Confederate snipers. They kept down, but occasionally one of them would raise his head above the rails to try to see what the Rebels were doing. During one such look they saw Brockenbrough's brigade advancing toward McPherson Ridge beyond the pike as Heth's division attacked. Perhaps they saw the 32d North Carolina flanking the Chambersburg Pike line as well. At this Brehm relented and sent Private Hoffman to find Stone or Dwight to tell them of the color guard's perilous situation and to ask for orders. Hoffman dashed off, but before he could find Dwight, Stone's brigade was retreating, and Confederates blocked Hoffman's return to the color guard. Hoffman therefore remained with the brigade.[7]

In the meantime the 149th's flags had attracted the attention of men of Davis's brigade lying to the west. They were beyond Willoughby Run and were recovering from their morning's ordeal rather than supporting Daniel's brigade in its attacks. But some alert Mississippians had noticed that the colors had not moved during the ebb and flow of battle, and they decided to try to capture them. These men included Lt. Atlas K. Roberts of the 2d Mississippi, Sgt. Frank Price, and another man named Johnson from the 42d. Unseen by the color guard, they crept forward, concealed by the tall wheat, toward the tantalizing flags. They moved quietly until they neared the rails, then they made a fatal error. In their enthusiasm, they whooped a Rebel yell. This alerted the color guard, and Brehm's men jumped to their feet to greet them.[8]

The Confederates grabbed for the two flags, which rested against the west-facing rail pile. The man who reached for the national colors shouted, "This is mine." Brehm shouted back, "No, by G—d, it isn't." Brehm seized the Confederate, probably Sergeant Price, by the throat, threw him to the ground, and fell on him. In a twinkling Brehm got to his feet, flag across his shoulder, and began running to the rear. Corporal Friddell shot one nearby Rebel, and Hammel shot another. Possibly one of the men shot was Lieutenant Roberts and the other was Johnson, who was wounded in the shoulder. Friddell and Hammel followed Brehm, but they did not go far. When they neared McPherson's lane at the pike, they saw to their dismay that it was occupied by Confederates. Brehm dashed through the gray line. Friddell and Hammel attempted a diversion in Brehm's favor; Friddell was shot in the right lung, and Hammel was wounded in the abdomen.[9]

As Brehm struggled to hold on to the national flag before leaving the rail pile, Lehman fought to keep the state flag. When he jumped up, he bumped against Brehm and fell to his knees. He grasped the state flag, which was lying across the rail pile, with his right hand as a Confederate tugged at it from across the pile. At the same time, with his left hand he grasped the barrel of a rifle that another man was pointing at him and tried to shove it aside. In these seconds Spayd shot a man, and the Confederate jerked the state flag from Lehman's hand. Lehman had had enough; he stood and headed for the rear. Then Spayd clubbed his empty rifle and hurled it at the man with the state flag. As the man loosed his hold on the flag, Spayd seized it. Spayd tried to furl it to make it easier to carry, and like Brehm he dashed for the rear.[10]

Spayd saw that the site formerly occupied by the Union line was held by Confederates, and he swerved to avoid them. In the meantime Sergeant Price had recovered from his struggle with Brehm. He picked up a rifle and set off in pursuit. When Spayd had gone about 100 feet and Price was close behind him, someone shot Spayd, and he fell. Price later denied that he had done this. Other Confederates came up about this time; they took the flag from the downed Spayd back to Price's company and awarded it to Price.[11]

While this fracas was going on, Lt. William R. Bond of Daniel's staff was returning from carrying a message to Heth when he saw a man running with a strange flag. Bond jumped from his horse, picked up one of the numerous rifles lying around (which must have been loaded), and fired it at the running man. He missed, and he later decided that the man must have been Price. In this he must have been wrong, for Price had not carried a flag.[12]

At the time of Brehm's retreat, Captain Bassler was lying wounded in the southeast corner of McPherson's barnyard. Brockenbrough's brigade and the 32d North Carolina on its left had just passed him, driving Stone's brigade ahead of it. The 143d and 149th regiments had swung back from along the pike and, with the 150th, were trying to form a line on the east arm of McPherson Ridge. Yet by this time Stone's line must have passed beyond the crest of the ridge, for Bassler could not see it. While lying amid the tumult, Bassler saw Brehm dashing with his flag across the smoky field. Brehm crossed the pike into the field east of the McPherson buildings. He ran with long strides toward the rear of the advancing Confederate line hoping to dash through it and into the Union ranks beyond. Bassler watched Brehm prayerfully until he disappeared from view.[13]

At this time a portion of Davis's brigade was following Brockenbrough's in a support line. Pvt. James A. Lumpkin of the 55th North Carolina, on the right of the brigade, and some others shot at Brehm. Lumpkin pursued Brehm and was close to him when an exploding shell gave Brehm a mortal wound. Lumpkin seized the flag and hurried with it back to his regiment's line. He passed not far from where Bassler was lying, and Brehm was following him. As Bassler remembered, Brehm "though mortally wounded, he carried his head high, as became the undismayed warrior he was. His eyes were still ablaze with the fire of battle. He looked neither to the right nor to the left. His gaze was fixed on his beloved flag."[14]

Brehm died in a Philadelphia hospital some weeks later. However, Bassler survived and returned to Myerstown to recuperate. He was there when

Brehm's body was brought home for his funeral and burial. Through his open window, Bassler could hear a choir sing at the funeral. Friddell recovered from the wound in his chest. After the day's fighting ended, in spite of his wound, Friddell searched the area west of the town for a sponge with which to bathe Bassler's wound. It was Friddell who first gave Bassler an account of the color guard's adventure. Lehman, Spayd, and Hoffman all survived and in 1907 gave affidavits telling of their parts in the fight. Spayd not only recovered, but he returned to the 149th that winter and served as the regiment's color sergeant until it was mustered out in June 1865. Later he became a superintendent of schools. Lumpkin, who captured Brehm's flag, became a Methodist minister in North Carolina, and Frank Price became a farmer in Mississippi.[15]

Bassler placed the principal blame for the loss of the colors on Colonel Dwight, "a brave and forceful man" who, he wrote, was drunk during the fight. If so, it might have affected Dwight's memory and judgment to some degree, but it did not impair his other fighting qualities. Bassler had other concerns too. After the war this episode over the colors became a cause for dispute. Lieutenant Colonel Huidekoper of the 150th Pennsylvania claimed that the 150th had recovered the colors of the 149th and had returned them to it. Dr. Harry M. Kieffer, an eminent cleric who had been a drummer boy with the 150th, wrote of this incident and the 150th's claim in his popular "Recollections of a Drummer Boy," which was published in the *St. Nicholas Magazine*. Bassler did not take this claim lightly and, with the aid of Sgt. William Ramsey of the 150th, got Huidekoper and Kieffer to recant. Though lamentable in themselves, such squabbles elicited accounts of the battle that otherwise would not have been written.[16]

APPENDIX C

Children of the Battlefield

Sometime soon after the battle, one of the daughters of Benjamin Shriver noticed that there was a dead Union soldier in the yard of Judge Samuel R. Russell, in the northeast corner of Stratton and York streets. The dead soldier held a photograph in his hand. It was an ambrotype, an image on glass, and probably was in a metal case. The photo was of three small children, two boys and a girl, seated side by side and looking seriously into the camera lens. It was an interesting and unique souvenir of the battle, and the finders took it from the dead man's hand. Unfortunately the children were not identified, and it was said that the soldier had no identification on his person that the civilians could recognize. Possibly the corpse's pockets had been emptied by battlefield scavengers, and they might also have taken his shoes and other portions of his clothing. At any rate the soldier was unknown. Soon his decomposing corpse was interred in the yard until a permanent burial place was available.[1]

At that time the sentimental story of a dead soldier spending his dying moments gazing at a photograph of his children aroused great human interest. Thus we can assume that many people saw the photograph in the days following the battle. One who did so was Dr. John Francis Bourns, a Philadelphia physician. Bourns realized the possibility of determining the children's identity and that of their father through newspaper publicity and asked for the use of the photograph to that end.

Bourns took the picture to Philadelphia and persuaded that city's newspapers, particularly the *Inquirer* and the *Press*, to publish the interesting but sad story. This meant that the ambrotype was reproduced, and copies in the form of *cartes de visite* were made for public distribution. As was common then, other newspapers copied the story and circulated it. One of these was the *American Presbyterian*; it printed an article but did not print the photograph.

In the meantime Philinda Humiston, wife of Sgt. Amos Humiston of the 154th New York Regiment, Coster's brigade, von Steinwehr's division, of the ill-fated Eleventh Corps, cared for her three small children at her home in Portville, New York. She anxiously awaited word and money from Sergeant Humiston, but months passed without news from or of him. They were difficult months, and Philinda made ends meet by working as a seamstress and by receiving allotments from a local benevolence fund established for the care of needy families of soldiers. Perhaps this cruel lack of information about her husband's fate resulted from disorganization within the 154th, which had more than 150 of its members captured or missing.

The family's fate was partially revealed when a copy of the 29 October 1863 issue of the *American Presbyterian* reached Portville. Although the paper passed from hand to hand among the Presbyterians of the community, it was several days before a reader saw a connection between the story of the dead soldier and the Humiston family. But when Philinda read the story, she realized that the children in the photo could well be her own Frank, Alice, and Fred.

Portville friends took up her cause and wrote to Bourns of Philinda's belief that the dead soldier might be her husband. Bourns sent her a *carte de visite*. He had many on hand that he sold to interested people for inclusion in photograph albums, and religious organizations sold them with the intention of turning their profits over to the bereaved family should it be found. Bourns also sent copies to widows who believed that they might be the soldier's wife. Such a photo was sent to the postmaster of Portville, and it proved that the dead soldier was Philinda's husband.

The Humistons became celebrities of a sort as newspapers published articles about them. Further, the previously unknown soldier was taken from the Russell yard and buried under his own name in grave 14, section B, of the New York plot in Gettysburg's newly established Soldiers' National Cemetery.

This ended the first part of the saga. The Humistons, their photograph, and songs and poems composed about them were used by Bourns and others working through the Homestead Association to establish an orphanage for soldiers' orphans at Gettysburg.[2] The site selected for it was the John

Myers house on Baltimore Street a few yards north of the gate of Soldiers' National Cemetery. The Humiston children were among the first admitted to it, and Philinda was employed there as a "wardrobe mistress."

The orphanage was to exist through 1877 and, like many such institutions, had both good and troubled times. The Humiston children and their story brought it much favorable publicity. Although Philinda remarried in 1869 and moved to Becket, Massachusetts, the children remained at the orphanage until the spring of 1871. They then rejoined their mother and began new lives. In the summer of 1993 an Amos Humiston Memorial, financed by private donations, was erected on Stratton Street not far from the place of the sergeant's death. In addition, an account of the family's travail and the orphanage's history has been recently published.

APPENDIX D
Order of Battle

*The First and Eleventh Corps and the First and Second Brigades, First Division,
Cavalry Corps, and Supporting Batteries, Army of the Potomac, 1 July 1863*

FIRST ARMY CORPS.§
Maj. Gen. Abner Doubleday.
Maj. Gen. John Newton.

GENERAL HEADQUARTERS.
1st Maine Cavalry, Company L, Capt. Constantine Taylor.

FIRST DIVISION.
Brig. Gen. James S. Wadsworth.

First Brigade.	*Second Brigade.*
Brig. Gen. Solomon Meredith.	Brig. Gen. Lysander Cutler.
Col. William W. Robinson.	7th Indiana, Col. Ira G. Grover.
19th Indiana, Col. Samuel J. Williams.	76th New York:
24th Michigan:	Maj. Andrew J. Grover.
Col. Henry A. Morrow.	Capt. John E. Cook.
Capt. Albert M. Edwards.	84th New York (14th Militia),
2d Wisconsin:	Col. Edward B. Fowler.
Col. Lucius Fairchild.	95th New York:
Maj. John Mansfield.	Col. George H. Biddle.
Capt. George H. Otis.	Maj. Edward Pye.
6th Wisconsin, Lieut. Col. Rufus R.	147th New York:
Dawes.	Lieut. Col. Francis C. Miller.
7th Wisconsin:	Maj. George Harney.
Col. William W. Robinson.	56th Pennsylvania (nine companies),
Maj. Mark Finnicum.	Col. J. William Hofmann.

§Maj. Gen. John F. Reynolds, of this corps, was killed July 1, while in command of the left wing of the army; General Doubleday commanded the corps July 1, and General Newton, who was assigned to that command on the 1st, superseded him July 2.

The Order of Battle for the Union First and Eleventh Corps and Buford's division of cavalry is from *OR* 27 (1):155–57, 164–66; the Order of Battle for the Second and Third Corps of the Army of Northern Virginia is from *OR* 27 (2):285–90.

Brig. Gen. John C. Robinson.

First Brigade.

Brig. Gen. Gabriel R. Paul.
Col. Samuel H. Leonard.
Col. Adrian R. Root.
Col. Richard Coulter.
Col. Peter Lyle.
Col. Richard Coulter.

16th Maine:
Col. Charles W. Tilden.
Maj. Archibald D. Leavitt.

13th Massachusetts:
Col. Samuel H. Leonard.
Lieut. Col. N. Walter Batchelder.

94th New York:
Col. Adrian R. Root.
Maj. Samuel A. Moffett.

104th New York, Col. Gilbert G. Prey.

107th Pennsylvania:
Lieut. Col. James MacThomson.
Capt. Emanuel D. Roath.

Second Brigade.

Brig. Gen. Henry Baxter.

12th Massachusetts:
Col. James L. Bates.
Lieut. Col. David Allen, Jr.

83d New York (9th Militia), Lieut. Col.
Joseph A. Moesch.

97th New York:
Col. Charles Wheelock.
Maj. Charles Northrup.

11th Pennsylvania:*
Col. Richard Coulter.
Capt. Benjamin F. Haines.
Capt. John B. Overmyer.

88th Pennsylvania:
Maj. Benezet F. Foust.
Capt. Henry Whiteside.

90th Pennsylvania:
Col. Peter Lyle.
Maj. Alfred J. Sellers.
Col. Peter Lyle.

*Transferred, in afternoon of July 1, to the First Brigade.

THIRD DIVISION.
Brig. Gen. Thomas A. Rowley.
Maj. Gen. Abner Doubleday.

First Brigade.

Col. Chapman Biddle.
Brig. Gen. Thomas A. Rowley.
Col. Chapman Biddle.

80th New York (20th Militia):
Col. Theodore B. Gates.

121st Pennsylvania:
Maj. Alexander Biddle.
Col. Chapman Biddle.
Maj. Alexander Biddle.

142d Pennsylvania:
Col. Robert P. Cummins.
Lieut. Col. A. B. McCalmont.

151st Pennsylvania:
Lieut. Col. George F. McFarland.
Capt. Walter L. Owens.
Col. Harrison Allen.

Second Brigade.

Col. Roy Stone.
Col. Langhorne Wister.
Col. Edmund L. Dana.

143d Pennsylvania:
Col. Edmund L. Dana.
Lieut. Col. John D. Musser.

149th Pennsylvania:
Lieut. Col. Walton Dwight.
Capt. James Glenn.

150th Pennsylvania:
Col. Langhorne Wister.
Lieut. Col. H. S. Huidekoper.
Capt. Cornelius C. Widdis.

ARTILLERY BRIGADE.
Col. Charles S. Wainwright.

Maine Light, 2d Battery (B), Capt. James A. Hall.
Maine Light, 5th Battery (E):
Capt. Greenleaf T. Stevens.
Lieut. Edward N. Whittier.
1st New York Light, Battery L:*
Capt. Gilbert H. Reynolds.
Lieut. George Breck.
1st Pennsylvania Light, Battery B, Capt. James H. Cooper.
4th United States, Battery B, Lieut. James Steward.

*Battery E, 1st New York Light Artillery, attached.

ELEVENTH ARMY CORPS.*
Maj. Gen. Oliver O. Howard.

GENERAL HEADQUARTERS.
1st Indiana Cavalry, Companies I and K, Capt. Abram Sharra.
8th New York Infantry (one company), Lieut. Hermann Foerster.

FIRST DIVISION.
Brig. Gen. Francis C. Barlow.
Brig. Gen. Adelbert Ames.

First Brigade.	*Second Brigade.*
Col. Leopold von Gilsa.	Brig. Gen. Adelbert Ames.
	Col. Andrew L. Harris.
41st New York (nine companies),	
Lieut. Col. Detleo von Einsiedel.	17th Connecticut:
54th New York:	Lieut. Col. Douglas Fowler.
Maj. Stephen Kovacs.	Maj. Allen G. Brady.
Lieut. Ernst Both [?].	25th Ohio:
68th New York, Col. Gotthilf Bourry.	Lieut. Col. Jeremiah Williams.
153d Pennsylvania, Maj. John F.	Capt. Nathaniel J. Manning.
Frueauff.	Lieut. William Maloney.
	Lieut. Israel White.
	75th Ohio:
	Col. Andrew L. Harris.
	Capt. George B. Fox.
	107th Ohio:
	Col. Seraphim Meyer.
	Capt. John M. Lutz.

*During the interval between the death of General Reynolds and the arrival of General Hancock, on the afternoon of July 1, all the troops on the field of battle were commanded by General Howard, General Schurz taking command of the Eleventh Corps, and General Schimmelfennig of the Third Division.

SECOND DIVISION.
Brig. Gen. Adolph von Steinwehr.

First Brigade.
Col. Charles R. Coster.

134th New York, Lieut. Col. Allan H. Jackson.
154th New York, Lieut. Col. D. B. Allen.
27th Pennsylvania, Lieut. Col. Lorenz Cantador.
73d Pennsylvania, Capt. D. F. Kelley.

Second Brigade.
Col. Orland Smith.

33d Massachusetts, Col. Adin B. Underwood.
136th New York, Col. James Wood, Jr.
55th Ohio, Col. Charles B. Gambee.
73d Ohio, Lieut. Col. Richard Long.

THIRD DIVISION.
Maj. Gen. Carl Schurz.

First Brigade.
Brig. Gen. Alex. Schimmelfennig.
Col. George von Amsberg.

82d Illinois, Lieut. Col. Edward S. Salomon.
45th New York:
 Col. George von Amsberg.
 Lieut. Col. Adolphus Dobke.
157th New York, Col. Philip P. Brown, Jr.
61st Ohio, Col. Stephen J. McGroarty.
74th Pennsylvania:
 Col. Adolph von Hartung.
 Lieut. Col. Alexander von Mitzel.
 Capt. Gustav Schleiter.
 Capt. Henry Krauseneck.

Second Brigade.
Col. W. Krzyzanowski.

58th New York:
 Lieut. Col. August Otto.
 Capt. Emil Koenig.
119th New York:
 Col. John T. Lockman.
 Lieut. Col. Edward F. Lloyd.
82d Ohio:
 Col. James S. Robinson.
 Lieut. Col. David Thomson.
75th Pennsylvania:
 Col. Francis Mahler.
 Maj. August Ledig.
26th Wisconsin:
 Lieut. Col. Hans Boebel.
 Capt. John W. Fuchs.

ARTILLERY BRIGADE.
Maj. Thomas W. Osborn.

1st New York Light, Battery I, Capt. Michael Wiedrich.
New York Light, 13th Battery, Lieut. William Wheeler.
1st Ohio Light, Battery I, Capt. Hubert Dilger.
1st Ohio Light, Battery K, Capt. Lewis Heckman.
4th United States, Battery G:
 Lieut. Bayard Wilkeson.
 Lieut. Eugene A. Bancroft.

CAVALRY CORPS.
Maj. Gen. Alfred Pleasonton.

Brig. Gen. John Buford.

First Brigade.
Col. William Gamble.

8th Illinois, Maj. John L. Beveridge.
12th Illinois (four cos.), ⎫ Col. George H.
3d Indiana (six cos.),   ⎭ Chapman.
8th New York, Lieut. Col. William L.
  Markell.

Second Brigade.
Col. Thomas C. Devin.

6th New York Maj. Wm. E. Beardsley.
9th New York, Col. William Sackett.
17th Pennsylvania, Col. J. H. Kellogg.
3d West Virginia (two companies),
  Capt. Seymour B. Conger.

Reserve Brigade.
Brig. Gen. Wesley Merritt.

6th Pennsylvania, Maj. James H. Haseltine.
1st United States, Capt. Richard S. C. Lord.
2d United States, Capt. T. F. Rodenbough.
5th United States, Capt. Julius W. Mason.
6th United States:
  Maj. Samuel H. Starr.
  Lieut. Louis H. Carpenter.
  Lieut. Nicholas Nolan.
  Capt. Ira W. Claflin.

Early's and Rodes's Divisions, Second Corps, and Heth's and Pender's Divisions, Third Corps, and Supporting Batteries, Army of Northern Virginia, 1 July 1863.

SECOND ARMY CORPS.
Lieut. Gen. Richard S. Ewell.

Escort.
Randolph's Company Virginia Cavalry, Capt. William F. Randolph.

EARLY'S DIVISION.
Maj. Gen. Jubal A. Early.

Hays' Brigade.
Brig. Gen. Harry T. Hays.

5th Louisiana:
  Maj. Alexander Hart.
  Capt. T. H. Biscoe.
6th Louisiana, Lieut. Col. Joseph Hanlon.
7th Louisiana, Col. D. B. Penn.
8th Louisiana:
  Col. T. D. Lewis.
  Lieut. Col. A. de Blanc.
  Maj. G. A. Lester.
9th Louisiana, Col. Leroy A. Stafford.

Smith's Brigade.
Brig. Gen. William Smith.

31st Virginia, Col. John S. Hoffman.
49th Virginia, Lieut. Col. J. Catlett
  Gibson.
52d Virginia, Lieut. Col. James H.
  Skinner.

374   { APPENDIX D }

Hoke's Brigade.
Col. Isaac E. Avery.
Col. A. C. Godwin.

6th North Carolina, Maj. S. McD. Tate.
21st North Carolina, Col. W. W. Kirkland.
57th North Carolina, Col. A. C. Godwin.

Gordon's Brigade.
Brig. Gen. J. B. Gordon.

13th Georgia, Col. James M. Smith.
26th Georgia, Col. E. N. Atkinson.
31st Georgia, Col. Clement A.
  Evans.
38th Georgia, Capt. William L.
  McLeod.
60th Georgia, Capt. W. B. Jones.
61st Georgia, Col. John H. Lamar.

Artillery.
Lieut. Col. H. P. Jones.

Charlottesville (Virginia) Artillery, Capt. James McD. Carrington.
Courtney (Virginia) Artillery, Capt. W. A. Tanner.
Louisiana Guard Artillery, Capt. C. A. Green.
Staunton (Virginia) Artillery, Capt. A. W. Garber.

RODES' DIVISION
Maj. Gen. R. E. Rodes.

Daniel's Brigade.
Brig. Gen. Junius Daniel.

32d North Carolina, Col. E. C. Brabble.
43d North Carolina:
  Col. T. S. Kenan.
  Lieut. Col. W. G. Lewis.
45th North Carolina:
  Lieut. Col. S. H. Boyd.
  Maj. John R. Winston.
  Capt. A. H. Gallaway.
  Capt. J. A. Hopkins.
53d North Carolina, Col. W. A. Owens.
2d North Carolina Battalion:
  Lieut. Col. H. L. Andrews.
  Capt. Van Brown.

Iverson's Brigade.
Brig. Gen. Alfred Iverson.

5th North Carolina:*
  Capt. Speight B. West.
  Capt. Benjamin Robinson.
12th North Carolina, Lieut. Col. W. S.
  Davis.
20th North Carolina:†
  Lieut. Col. Nelson Slough.
  Capt. Lewis T. Hicks.
23d North Carolina:‡
  Col. D. H. Christie.
  Capt. William H. Johnston.

*The four captains present (West, Robinson, James M. Taylor, Thomas N. Jordan) were reported as wounded July 1; Robinson and Taylor as having rejoined July 2, but it does not appear who commanded during Robinson's absence.

†Lieutenant-Colonel Slough and Maj. John S. Brooks reported as wounded at 4 P.M. July 1.

‡Colonel Christie, Lieut. Col. R. D. Johnston, Maj. C. C. Blacknall, and the senior captain (Abner D. Peace), reported as wounded early in the fight, July 1.

Doles' Brigade.
Brig. Gen. George Doles.

4th Georgia:
  Lieut. Col. D. R. E. Winn.
  Maj. W. H. Willis.
12th Georgia, Col. Edward Willis.
21st Georgia, Col. John T. Mercer.
44th Georgia:
  Col. S. P. Lumpkin.
  Maj. W. H. Peebles.

Ramseur's Brigade.
Brig. Gen. S. D. Ramseur.

2d North Carolina:
  Maj. D. W. Hurtt.
  Capt. James T. Scales.
4th North Carolina, Col. Bryan
  Grimes.
14th North Carolina:
  Col. R. Tyler Bennett.
  Maj. Joseph H. Lambeth.
30th North Carolina:
  Col. Francis M. Parker.
  Maj. W. W. Sillers.

O'Neal's Brigade.
Col. E. A. O'Neal.

3d Alabama, Col. C. A. Battle.
5th Alabama, Col. J. M. Hall.
6th Alabama:
  Col. J. N. Lightfoot.
  Capt. M. L. Bowie.
12th Alabama, Col. S. B. Pickens.
26th Alabama, Lieut. Col. John C. Goodgame.

Artillery.
Lieut. Col. Thomas H. Carter.

Jeff. Davis (Alabama) Artillery, Capt. W. J. Reese.
King William (Virginia) Artillery, Capt. W. P. Carter.
Morris (Virginia) Artillery, Capt. R. C. M. Page.
Orange (Virginia) Artillery, Capt. C. W. Fry.

THIRD ARMY CORPS.
Lieut. Gen. Ambrose P. Hill.

HETH'S DIVISION.
Maj. Gen. Henry Heth.
Brig. Gen. J. J. Pettigrew.

First Brigade.
Brig. Gen. J. J. Pettigrew.
Col. J. K. Marshall.

11th North Carolina, Col. Collett
Leventhorpe.
26th North Carolina:
Col. Henry K. Burgwyn, Jr.
Capt. H. C. Albright.
47th North Carolina, Col. G. H.
Faribault.
52d North Carolina:
Col. J. K. Marshall.
Lieut. Col. Marcus A. Parks.

Second Brigade.
Col. J. M. Brockenbrough.

40th Virginia:
Capt. T. E. Betts.
Capt. R. B. Davis.
47th Virginia, Col. Robert M. Mayo.
55th Virginia, Col. W. S. Christian.
22d Virginia Battalion, Maj. John S.
Bowles.

Third Brigade.
Brig. Gen. James J. Archer.
Col. B. D. Fry.
Lieut. Col. S. G. Shepard.

13th Alabama, Col. B. D. Fry.
5th Alabama Battalion, Maj. A. S. Van
de Graaff.
1st Tennessee (Provisional Army),
Maj. Felix G. Buchanan.
7th Tennessee, Lieut. Col. S. G.
Shepard.
14th Tennessee, Capt. B. L. Phillips.

Fourth Brigade.
Brig. Gen. Joseph R. Davis.

2d Mississippi, Col. J. M. Stone.
11th Mississippi, Col. F. M. Green.
42d Mississippi, Col. H. R. Miller.
55th North Carolina, Col. J. K.
Connally.

Artillery.
Lieut. Col. John J. Garnett.

Donaldsonville (Louisiana) Artillery, Capt. V. Maurin.
Huger (Virginia) Artillery, Capt. Joseph D. Moore.
Lewis (Virginia) Artillery, Capt. John W. Lewis.
Norfolk Light Artillery Blues, Capt. C. R. Grandy.

PENDER'S DIVISION.

Maj. Gen. William D. Pender.
Brig. Gen. James H. Lane.
Maj. Gen. I. R. Trimble.
Brig. Gen. James H. Lane.

First Brigade.
Col. Abner Perrin.

1st South Carolina (Provisional
Army), Maj. C. W. McCreary.
1st South Carolina Rifles, Capt.
William M. Hadden.
12th South Carolina, Col. John L.
Miller.
13th South Carolina, Lieut. Col. B. T.
Brockman.
14th South Carolina, Lieut. Col.
Joseph N. Brown.

Second Brigade.
Brig. Gen. James H. Lane.
Col. C. M. Avery.
Brig. Gen. James H. Lane.
Col. C. M. Avery.

7th North Carolina:
Capt. J. McLeod Turner.
Capt. James G. Harris.
18th North Carolina, Col. John D.
Barry.
28th North Carolina:
Col. S. D. Lowe.
Lieut. Col. W. H. A. Speer.
33d North Carolina, Col. C. M. Avery.
37th North Carolina, Col. W. M.
Barbour.

Third Brigade.
Brig. Gen. Edward L. Thomas.

14th Georgia.
35th Georgia.
45th Georgia.
49th Georgia, Col. S. T. Player.

Fourth Brigade.
Brig. Gen. A. M. Scales.
Lieut. Col. G. T. Gordon.
Col. W. Lee J. Lowrance.

13th North Carolina:
Col. J. H. Hyman.
Lieut. Col. H. A. Rogers.
16th North Carolina, Capt. L. W.
Stowe.
22d North Carolina, Col. James
Conner.
34th North Carolina:
Col. William Lee J. Lowrance.
Lieut. Col. G. T. Gordon.
38th North Carolina:
Col. W. J. Hoke.
Lieut. Col. John Ashford.

Artillery.

Maj. William T. Poague.

Albemarle (Virginia) Artillery, Capt. James W. Wyatt.
Charlotte (North Carolina) Artillery, Capt. Joseph Graham.
Madison (Mississippi) Light Artillery, Capt. George Ward.
Virginia Battery, Capt. J. V. Brooke.

ARTILLERY RESERVE.

Col. R. Lindsay Walker.

McIntosh's Battalion.	*Pegram's Battalion.*
Maj. D. G. McIntosh.	Maj. W. J. Pegram.
	Capt. E. B. Brunson.
Danville (Virginia) Artilery, Capt. R. S. Rice.	
	Crenshaw (Virginia) Battery.
Hardaway (Alabama) Artillery, Capt. W. B. Hurt.	Fredericksburg (Virginia) Artillery, Capt. E. A. Marye.
2d Rockbridge (Vriginia) Artillery, Lieut. Samuel Wallace.	Letcher (Vriginia) Artillery, Capt. T. A. Brander.
Virginia Battery, Capt. M. Johnson.	Pee Dee (South Carolina) Artillery, Lieut. William E. Zimmerman.
	Purcell (Vriginia) Atrillery, Capt. Joseph McGraw.

NOTES

ABBREVIATIONS

The following abbreviations are used in the notes and illustration credits.

ACHS
    Adams County Historical Society, Gettysburg, Pennsylvania
ADAH
    Alabama Department of Archives and History, Montgomery
Bachelder Map
    John B. Bachelder, *Position of Troops, First Day's Battle* (New York: Office of the
    Chief of Engineering, U.S. Army, 1876)
BAS
    Bruce A. Suderow Collection, Washington, D.C.
BC
    Bowdoin College Library, Special Collections and Archives, Brunswick, Maine
B&L
    Robert U. Johnson and Clarence C. Buel, *Battles and Leaders of the Civil War*, vol.
    3 (New York: Thomas Yoseloff, 1956)
BLC
    Arnold Blumberg Collection, Baltimore, Maryland
BP
    David L. Ladd and Audrey J. Ladd, eds., *The Bachelder Papers*, 3 vols. (Dayton:
    Morningside, 1994–95)
BPL
    Bridgeport Public Library, Bridgeport, Connecticut
BR
    Bassler-Ramsey File, 150th Pennsylvania Regiment
BrC
    Robert L. Brake Collection
CAT
    Cattaraugus County Historical Museum and Research Center, Little Valley,
    New York
CCW
    U.S. Congress, *Report of the Joint Committee on the Conduct of the War at the Second
    Session, Thirty-eighth Congress, Army of the Potomac, General Meade . . .*
    (Washington, D.C.: U.S. Government Printing Office, 1865)

CWLM

Civil War Library and Museum, Military Order of the Loyal Legion of the United States, Philadelphia, Pennsylvania

CWMC

Civil War Miscellaneous Collection

DAB

Allen Johnson and Dumas Malone, eds., *Dictionary of American Biography*, 20 vols. (New York: Charles Scribner's Sons, 1928–36)

DU

Duke University, Rare Book, Manuscript, and Special Collections Library, Durham, North Carolina

FM

Franklin and Marshall College, Shadek-Fackenthal Library, Special Collections, Lancaster, Pennsylvania

GC

Gettysburg College, Musselman Library, Gettysburg, Pennsylvania

GDAH

Georgia Department of Archives and History, Atlanta

GNMP

Gettysburg National Military Park, Gettysburg, Pennsylvania

GP

Ken Bandy and Florence Freeland, *The Gettysburg Papers*, 3 vols. (Dayton: Morningside, 1978)

HCWRTC

Harrisburg Civil War Round Table Collection

HL

Huntington Library, San Marino, California

IHS

Indiana Historical Society, Indianapolis

ISL

Indiana State Library, Manuscript Section, Indianapolis

LC

Library of Congress, Washington, D.C.

MC

Museum of the Confederacy, Eleanor S. Brockenbrough Library, Richmond, Virginia

McElfresh Map

Gettysburg Battlefield: The First Day's Battlefield (Olean, N.Y.: McElfresh Map Co., 1994).

MCLL

Massachusetts Commandery, Military Order of the Loyal Legion of the United States, United States Army Military History Institute, U.S. Army Collection, Carlisle Barracks, Pennsylvania

MGC

Maine Gettysburg Commission

MHS
   Massachusetts Historical Society Library, Boston
MWC
   Michael Winey Collection
NA
   National Archives, Washington, D.C.
NCDAH
   North Carolina Department of Cultural Resources, Division of Archives and
   History, Raleigh
NYHS
   New-York Historical Society, New York
NYMC
   New York Monuments Commission
OHS
   Ohio Historical Society, Columbus
OR
   U.S. War Department, *The War of the Rebellion: A Compilation of the Official Records of
   the Union and Confederate Armies*, 128 vols. (Washington, D.C.: U.S. Government
   Printing Office, 1890–1901). All citations are to volumes in Series 1.
PSA
   Pennsylvania Historical and Museum Commission, Pennsylvania State
   Archives, Harrisburg
PU
   Princeton University Library, Manuscripts Division, Department of Rare Books
   and Special Collections, Princeton, New Jersey
RBC
   Ronald Boyer Collection
RU
   Rutgers University Library, Special Collections and University Archives, New
   Brunswick, New Jersey
SCL
   South Caroliniana Library, University of South Carolina, Columbia
SHC
   University of North Carolina, Wilson Library, Southern Historical Collection,
   Chapel Hill
SHSP
   Southern Historical Society Papers, Southern Historical Society, Richmond,
   Virginia
SHSW
   State Historical Society of Wisconsin, Madison
TSL
   Tennessee State Library and Archives, Tennessee Civil War Collection, Nashville
UGL
   University of Georgia Libraries, Hargrett Rare Book and Manuscript Library,
   Athens

USAMHI

U.S. Army Military History Institute, U.S. Army Collection, Carlisle Barracks, Pennsylvania

UV

University of Virginia, Special Collections Department, Alderman Library, Charlottesville

VHS

Virginia Historical Society, Division of Special Collections and Archives, Richmond

Warren Map

U.S. Army, Engineer Department, *Map of the Battlefield of Gettysburg, Surveyed and drawn under the direction of Bvt. Maj. Gen. G. K. Warren*

WHGS

Wyoming Historical and Genealogical Society, Wilkes-Barre, Pennsylvania

YU

Yale University Library, Civil War Manuscripts Collection, Manuscripts and Archives, New Haven, Connecticut

INTRODUCTION

1. W. Clark, *Histories*, 2:343; Robertson, *General A. P. Hill*, 200; *OR* 27 (2):652.

2. The casualty figures are from Bigelow, *Chancellorsville*, 473.

3. D. S. Freeman, *Lee's Lieutenants*, 3:703–6; Coddington, *Gettysburg Campaign*, 24; Hunt, "First Day," 258.

4. *OR* 27 (2):305, 313.

5. Bigelow, *Chancellorsville*, 437, 487; Coddington, *Gettysburg Campaign*, 36–38, 611–12.

6. Coddington, *Gettysburg Campaign*, 32–33; *OR* 27 (1):30–31.

7. Coddington, *Gettysburg Campaign*, 32–33; Bigelow, *Chancellorsville*, 476–80.

8. Hunt, "First Day," 259–61.

9. *OR* 27 (1):34, 904, (3):27.

10. *OR* 27 (2):305, 313, 440, (3):878.

11. *OR* 27 (2):306, 440–42.

12. Ibid., 305–7, 313–15, 358, 613, 692.

13. *OR* 27 (1):42, 50, 53, (3):93, 94, 101, 120, 145, 147.

14. *OR* 27 (1):54.

15. Wallace Journal, 17–21, PSA; "Memoirs of Jonathan W. W. Boynton, 157th N.Y.," CWMC, USAMHI; F. B. Jones, "Excerpt," GNMP; Tevis, *Fighting Fourteenth*, 77, 78.

16. *OR* 27 (1):43, 45.

17. Ibid., 47.

18. Ibid., 55.

19. *OR* 27 (3):208, 209, 228, 233, 246, 283, 310, 311, 313, 314, 316, (1):53.

20. *OR* 27 (3):28, 291, 305–7, (1):147.

21. *OR* 27 (1):15, 58, 59, 60; Coddington, *Gettysburg Campaign*, 128–33.

1. *OR* 27 (2):442, 548; Schuricht, "Jenkins' Brigade," 339–40. The Union troops in Greencastle had probably retreated from Martinsburg or Winchester.

2. Shevchuk, "Wounding of Albert Jenkins," 52–54.

3. *OR* 27 (2):306, 316, 443, 464; W. Clark, *Histories*, 1:194.

4. *OR* 27 (3):905, 914.

5. Ibid., 914–15.

6. Ibid., 912–13.

7. Shevchuk, "Wounding of Albert Jenkins," 74; Schuricht, "Jenkins' Brigade," 340.

8. *OR* 27 (2):211, (3):161, 162; Shevchuk, "Wounding of Albert Jenkins," 55. David McConaughy, an attorney from Gettysburg, was involved in gathering intelligence in the Cumberland Valley. He reported to Maj. Gen. Darius Couch in Harrisburg of the Confederate cavalry's arrival in Greencastle at 6:00 P.M. on the sixteenth. See *OR* 27 (3):162.

9. *OR* 27 (2):551; Shevchuk, "Wounding of Albert Jenkins," 55.

10. *OR* 27 (2):358, 613, 677; Littlejohn, "Recollections," GNMP.

11. H. H. Hall, *Johnny Reb Band*, 39.

12. Wilson, *Confederate Soldier*, 110–11; G. W. Nichols, *Soldier's Story*, 114–15.

13. Marye, "First Gun," 1226.

14. *OR* 27 (2):464–66, 551.

15. Hoke, *Historical Reminiscences*, 56.

16. Nicholson, *Pennsylvania*, 2:779–80; *OR* 27 (2):443, 466–67, 491–92.

17. S. S. Rogers, *Ties*, 161.

18. Gordon, *Reminiscences*, 147–48; J. A. Early, *Autobiographical Sketch*, 259, 261, 262.

19. Hoke, *Historical Reminiscences*, 48–49.

20. *OR* 27 (2):443, 465, 466; John Stumbaugh to son, 9 July 1863, HCWRTC, USAMHI.

21. A. Taylor to W. S. Taylor, 9 July 1863, GNMP; Marye, "First Gun," 1229.

22. *OR* 27 (2):677; Chamberlayne, *Ham Chamberlayne*, 191–92.

23. J. Warren Jackson to R. Stark Jackson, 20 July 1863, in T. L. Jones, "Going Back," 12–13.

24. Fite, "Memoir," 83–89, TSL. The Order of Battle does not list Fite as commander of the 7th Tennessee at Gettysburg, but a listing of 31 July does. Yet he was captured at Gettysburg. His memoirs state that he was at Gettysburg with his regiment until captured during Pickett's Charge. See *OR* 27 (2):289, (3):1061; Krick, *Lee's Colonels*, 125.

25. Hufham, "Gettysburg," 451–52; T. B. Reed, *Private in Gray*, 41.

26. Wilson, *Confederate Soldier*, 114.

27. William W. Hassler, *General to His Lady*, 254; Tom to Lou, 28 June 1863, Hightower Papers, GDAH; Runge, *Four Years*, 49.

28. Battle, "Third Alabama Regiment," 143, VHS; Gordon, *Reminiscences*, 148–49. A handwritten copy of Battle's "Third Alabama Regiment" is held by the ADAH.

29. T. L. Jones, "Going Back," and *Seymour*, 68–69.

30. *OR* 27 (2):443, 551; D. C. Pfanz, *Ewell*, 299–301; Park, *Twelfth Alabama*, 53; Betts, *Experiences*, 38; H. Pfanz, *Culp's Hill*, 13.

31. W. Clark, *Histories*, 2:525–26; Polk to wife, 28 June 1863, Polk Papers, SHC; Hufham, "Gettysburg," 452; Shevchuk, "Wounding of Albert Jenkins," 55–56.

32. Schuricht, "Jenkins' Brigade," 343–44; Shevchuk, "Wounding of Albert Jenkins," 56; C. B. Nesley to parents, 11 July 1863, HCWRTC, USAMHI.

33. *OR* 27 (2):443; Shevchuk, "Wounding of Albert Jenkins," 56–57; Schuricht, "Jenkins' Brigade," 344–45.

CHAPTER 2

1. Coddington, *Gettysburg Campaign*, 182–83; H. W. Pfanz, *Second Day*, 3; *OR* 27 (2):297, 307, 316. David G. McIntosh observed that if Lee wrote to Ewell on 28 June at 7:30 A.M. that Hooker was reported to have crossed the Potomac and was advancing via Middletown, he wanted Ewell to move to Gettysburg via Heidlersburg as stated in a dispatch on the previous night. He inferred then that the story that Lee first heard of the Federal army's crossing the Potomac from a spy on the twenty-eighth must be incorrect. See McIntosh, "Gettysburg Campaign," 31, VHS. Lee's orders to Ewell dated 28 June at 7:30 A.M., at least twelve hours before Harrison made his report, are in *OR* 27 (3):943–44. This dispatch has received little notice and is not supported by Lee's and Ewell's reports. According to a footnote added to it, the letter was "copied from memory," and perhaps its date is incorrect.

2. *OR* 27 (2):443, 552; Trimble to Bachelder, 8 Feb. 1883, *BP*, 2:926–27.

3. *OR* 27 (2):443, 467, 503, 552; Park, *Twelfth Alabama*, 53; Pickens Diary, 30 June 1863, GNMP; Green Diary, 30 June 1863, SHC; Grace, "Rodes's Division," 614; McDonald, *Make Me a Map of the Valley*, 156; W. Clark, *Histories*, 2:234.

4. W. Clark, *Histories*, 4:238. Wharton stated that the legal officer with him was a Col. D. M. Carter. A Col. David M. Carter had held such a post, but according to Krick, *Lee's Colonels*, 74, he had resigned in December 1862 because of wounds received at Seven Pines.

5. *OR* 27 (2):606, 613; McIntosh, "Gettysburg Campaign," 34, VHS. In his reports Lee suggested that Hill's orders were changed immediately, but Hill's reports and actions suggest otherwise. See *OR* 27 (2):307, 317.

6. *OR* 27 (2):317; "Account of the Movements of Co. G, 52d Regt. N.C.," Little Papers, SHC; W. Clark, *Histories*, 3:236; W. S. Christian to Daniel, 24 Oct. 1903, Daniel Papers, UV; *OR* 27 (1):926. The 55th could have occupied the cemetery at Flohr's Church, or perhaps it was farther east at McKnightstown.

7. Wilson, *Confederate Soldier*, 115.

8. J. S. Harris, *Seventh Regiment*, 34; William W. Hassler, *General to His Lady*, 253–54; W. Clark, *Histories*, 1:698.

9. Morrison, *Memoirs of Henry Heth*, 173; W. Clark, *Histories*, 5:115; H. H. Hall, *Johnny Reb Band*, 45; Fite, "Memoir," 85, TSL. Colonel Fite was about thirty years old at Gettysburg, and his recollections suggest that he was a hard-drinking hell-raiser. Perhaps his memory betrayed him on occasion.

10. W. Clark, *Histories*, 5:515; H. H. Hall, *Johnny Reb Band*, 45.

11. W. S. Christian to Daniel, 24 Oct. 1903, Daniel Papers, UV. Christian's account is not supported by others. Christian wrote that his regiment was recalled after contact was made with the Union cavalry and when they were in sight of Gettysburg.

12. W. Clark, *Histories*, 5:115. The spy's report of Buford's presence in Gettysburg is inexplicable. By most Union accounts Buford should not have been in Gettysburg this soon.

13. O'Neal, "Battle of Gettysburg." O'Neal was a Virginian by birth. Since his recollections place him near Pettigrew on 30 June, it seems strange that Lieutenant Young did not mention him. Perhaps Young assumed him to be a Knight of the Golden Circle. O'Neal might also have been remembered by a soldier of the 47th North Carolina as a civilian on a farm horse who was said to have warned Pettigrew of an ambush.

14. Ibid.; W. Clark, *Histories*, 5:115–16; *OR* 27 (2):317, 607, 637.

15. W. Clark, *Histories*, 5:116–17; *OR* 27(2):637; Heth, "Letter," 157; Morrison, *Memoirs of Henry Heth*, 173; Robertson, *A. P. Hill*, 206. The quotations of Heth and Hill are from Heth's account in *SHSP*, 4:157. Similar quotations are in Heth's memoirs. For some reason Heth took the reported word of Lee's scouts over that of one of his brigade commanders.

16. W. Clark, *Histories*, 2:342–43. The bivouac might have been near the hamlet of Seven Stars, which was by a small stream about a half-mile west of Marsh Creek.

17. *OR* 27 (2):358; Welch, *Confederate Surgeon's Letters to His Wife*, 61–63; Littlejohn, "Recollections," 5, GNMP.

18. Lecture text of Gen. A. M. Scales, Scales Papers, DU.

CHAPTER 3

1. *OR* 27 (1):61, (3):369. The general order was No. 194, 27 June 1863.

2. *OR* 27 (1):61; Benjamin, "Hooker's Appointment and Removal," 243. A bronze plaque affixed to a large rock from Devil's Den at Gettysburg is located in Frederick at the junction of the Ballenger Creek Road and U.S. Route 340. It indicates where Meade took command.

3. *OR* 27 (1):61–62.

4. Henry P. Clare to William, 30 June 1863, Clare Papers, DU; C. E. Davis, *Thirteenth Massachusetts*, 221.

5. For comments on Meade's appointment see Coddington, *Gettysburg Campaign*, chap. 9, and Benjamin, "Hooker's Appointment and Removal," 247. Benjamin, a clerk for Seth Williams at Army of the Potomac headquarters, claimed to have overheard Meade and Reynolds's conversation.

6. *OR* 27 (1):114, 143–44.

7. *OR* 27 (3):351, 354, 372; Weld, *War Diary*, 224–29.

8. Weld, *War Diary*, 224–29.

9. Tevis, *Fighting Fourteenth*, 79–80; Hubler, "Just a Plain Unvarnished Story"; Nicholson, *Pennsylvania*, 2:745.

10. *OR* 27 (1):243, 733, (3):397; Nicholson, *Pennsylvania*, 2:745; Schurz, *Remi-*

niscences, 3:3; O. O. Howard, *Autobiography*, 1:402; Avery Harris Papers, 83, BrC, USAMHI.

11. Grayson, "Frederick City to Gettysburg"; Herdegen and Beaudot, *Bloody Railroad Cut*, 154–55.

12. *OR* 27 (1):67–68, (3):414–15.

13. *OR* 27 (1):243–44; O. O. Howard, *Autobiography*, 402; Avery Harris Papers, 83, BrC, USAMHI; Boone, "Personal Experiences," MWC, USAMHI.

14. Tevis, *Fighting Fourteenth*, 80; Besancon Diary, 30 June 1863, DU; Hofmann, "56th Pennsylvania"; Nicholson, *Pennsylvania*, 2:245. Myers Mill was on Marsh Creek about a half-mile downstream from the Emmitsburg Road crossing.

15. *OR* 27 (3):312, 313, 315, 334, 337, 370; Longacre, *Cavalry at Gettysburg*, 163; S. S. Rogers, *Ties*, 161; Bennett, *Days*, 16; Broadhead Diary, GNMP. Stahel's division had three brigades commanded by Brig. Gen. Joseph T. Copeland and Cols. Butler Pierce and Othneil DeForest. See Dyer, *Compendium*, 1:378.

16. *OR* 27 (3):373, 376, (1):58, 59–60.

17. Weigley, "John Buford," 15–16; Wittenberg, "John Buford," 19–23, and "Analysis," 11–12.

18. Wittenberg, "Analysis," 12, 14.

19. *OR* 27 (1):143–44, 926, (3):373, 376; Dyer, *Compendium*, 1:324; Beveridge, "First Gun," 170.

20. *OR* 27 (1):926, 943; Beveridge, "First Gun," 170; Nicholson, *Pennsylvania*, 2:875.

21. *OR* 27 (1):926; Hard, *Eighth Cavalry*, 255.

22. *OR* 27 (1):926; Hall and Besley, *Sixth New York*, 133; Hard, *Eighth Cavalry*, 255–56; W. Clark, *Histories*, 3:236; "Account of the Movements of Co. E, 52d N.C. Troops," Little Papers, SHC.

23. Jacobs, "Meteorology of the Battle"; Moyer, *Seventeenth Regiment*, 58; Rosengarten, *William Reynolds . . . John Fulton Reynolds*, 17.

24. *OR* 27 (1):926; Gamble to Church, 10 Mar. 1864, BLC; Harter, *Erinnerungen*, 181–82; Cheney, *Ninth Regiment*, 102; Hall and Besley, *Sixth New York*, 133; Bennett, *Days*, 17–18.

25. Gamble to Church, 10 Mar. 1864, BLC; Beveridge, "First Gun," 172.

26. Gamble to Church, 10 Mar. 1864, BLC; Beveridge, "First Gun," 172.

27. Beveridge, "First Gun," 172; Moyer, *Seventeenth Regiment*, 49–50; Hall and Besley, *Sixth New York*, 134. Kross, "Gettysburg Vignettes," deals extensively with the location of picket or vidette posts.

28. *OR* 27 (1):922, 923.

29. Ibid., 922, 924; Hard, *Eighth Cavalry*, 256.

30. Hall and Besley, *Sixth New York*, 136; Weigley, *John Buford*, 21.

CHAPTER 4

1. Meade, *Life and Letters*, 2:12, 14; *OR* 27 (2):67. The dispatch to Halleck probably did not reach him in a timely way. The message was sent by a courier whose body was found in Glen Rock, Pennsylvania.

2. Boatner, *Dictionary*, 539; *OR* 27 (3):410; Nicholson, *Pennsylvania*, 2:1000; J. B. Young, *Gettysburg*, 338. In his biography of Reynolds, *Toward Gettysburg*, Edward J. Nichols seems to stress rivalry between Reynolds and Meade and Meade's presumed jealousy of Reynolds. He also suggests that Reynolds was familiar with the Gettysburg area because he had hunted there. I see no reason for these views.

3. Butterfield Testimony, *CCW*, 36; Meade Testimony, *CCW*, 329–30; Warren Testimony, *CCW*, 376. Mention is made of Meade's views in a letter from John C. Ropes to John C. Gray, 16 Apr. 1864. See Ropes and Gray, *War Letters*, 316–17.

4. *OR* 27 (1):143, 144, (3):372, 402.

5. *OR* 27 (3):415, 419–20.

6. Ibid., 416, 420, (1):68–69.

7. *OR* 27 (3) 415–17; Meade, *Life and Letters*, 2:18, 27–29.

8. *OR* 27 (1):70–71, (3):420, 458; Humphreys Testimony, *CCW*, 388–89; Warren Testimony, *CCW*, 376–77; Hunt, "First Day," 274. A discussion of the Pipe Creek Line, "Meade's Pipe Creek Line," by Frederick Shriver Klein, was published in the *Maryland Historical Magazine*, June 1962.

9. O. O. Howard, *Autobiography*, 1:302–3; H. W. Pfanz, *Culp's Hill*, 16. Moritz Tavern is a large brick house on the Emmitsburg Road at Bull Frog Road. It is a mile and a quarter south of Marsh Creek and just north of the U.S. 15 Business interchange.

10. The information on Reynolds is from a variety of sources, including E. J. Nichols, *Toward Gettysburg*; Nicholson, *Pennsylvania*, 2:212–13, 1090–99; and Boatner, *Dictionary*, 464.

11. O. O. Howard, *Autobiography*, 1:403–5; E. J. Nichols, *Toward Gettysburg*, 196; *OR* 27 (1):923–24.

12. O. O. Howard, *Autobiography*, 1:404; *OR* 27 (3):416, 419–20.

13. Meade, *Life and Letters*, 2:33.

14. *OR* 27 (3):458, 491; Meade, *Life and Letters*, 2:33–34.

15. *OR* 27 (1):460–61. Busey and Martin, *Regimental Strengths*, gives a force of 79,880 for the Army of Northern Virginia as of 30 June 1863; this includes 12,358 cavalry (see pp. 129, 194).

CHAPTER 5

1. Robertson, *A. P. Hill*, 205–6; *OR* 27 (2):307, 317, 607, 637; Morrison, *Memoirs of Henry Heth*, 173. In his *Memoirs*, p. 173, Heth stated that Hill's reply was "Do so."

2. W. Clark, *Histories*, 5:116–17.

3. *OR* 27 (2):307, 308, 317, 444, 607.

4. Ibid., 637; W. Clark, *Histories*, 3:343; Marye, "First Gun," 1228; Fleet, "Fredericksburg Artillery," 340; Fulton, "Fifth Alabama," 379, and *War Reminiscences*, 76; Fulton to Owen, 10 Aug. 1910, ADAH; Van de Graaff to wife, 8 July 1863, GNMP; Lindsley, "Battle of Gettysburg," 294; McIntosh, "Gettysburg Campaign," 43, VHS.

5. Kelley, "Account"; Beveridge, "First Gun," 172; Dodge, "Lieut. Jones"; Ketcheson, "Who Fired the First Shot?," in NYMC, *Final Report*, 3:1145; Willet, "A Comrade"; Abner B. Frank Diary, 1 July 1863, CWMC, USAMHI.

6. Kelley, "Account"; Ketcheson, "Who Fired the First Shot?," in NYMC, *Final Report*; Lindsley, "Battle of Gettysburg," 243.

7. Krolick, "First Shot," GNMP; Dodge, "Lieut. Jones"; Beveridge "First Shot."

8. Beveridge, "First Gun," 173; Ditzler, "First Gun"; Kelley, "Account"; A. B. Jerome to Hancock, 18 Oct. 1865, *BP* 1:201.

9. Doubleday, *Chancellorsville*, 126.

10. Cheney, *Ninth Regiment*, 106; Bentley to Illinois Commandery, n.d., GNMP; W. G. Bentley, "First Shot"; NYMC, *Final Report*, 3:1153, 1376; *OR* 27 (2):934, 938. In his article "The First Union Shot at Gettysburg," James L. McLean Jr. examined claims made by five different soldiers, including Corporal Hodges and Lieutenant Jones, to having fired the first shot. He concluded that only Jones had a valid claim.

11. Fulton, "Fifth Alabama," 279; Lindsley, "Battle of Gettysburg," 246; Boland, "Beginning," 308. Private Boland described Marsh Creek as a wooded swampland clothed in a misty rain.

12. *OR* 27 (2):677; Coco, *Vast Sea of Misery*, 135; Marye, "First Gun."

13. Turney, "First Tennessee," 535; Fulton, "Fifth Alabama," 379, and *War Reminiscences*, 791; Boland to Owen, 21 May 1906, ADAH; Boland, "Beginning," 308; Hard, *Eighth Cavalry*, 256; Beveridge, "First Gun," 174–75; Storch and Storch, " 'What a Deadly Trap,' " 118. The 8th Illinois Regiment was armed principally with Sharps carbines. All regiments of the division had single-shot carbines including Sharps, Merrill, Smith, and Gallaghers. See Busey and Martin, *Regimental Strengths*, 202–3.

14. *OR* 27 (2):637, 646; Kelley, "Account"; B. D. Fry to Bachelder, 26 Jan., 10 Feb. 1878, *BP*, 2:1932, 3:522.

15. Pleasonton Testimony, *CCW*, 359; *OR* 27 (1):927.

16. Calef, "Gettysburg Notes," 42–44.

17. Ibid., 47–48; *OR* 27 (1):1030–31.

18. Gamble to Church, 10 Mar. 1864, BLC; Beveridge to Bachelder, 21 June, 2 July 1890, *BP*, 3:1736, 1747–48. The memorials of the regiments of Gamble's brigade are on the east arm of McPherson Ridge (Reynolds Avenue). The diary of Col. George H. Chapman of the 3d Indiana Cavalry states that the 3d was on the right of the 8th Illinois and the "battery in the center." It is not clear if the 3d was behind Roder's section. See Chapman Diary, 1 July 1863, IHS.

19. *OR* 27 (1):938; Hall and Besley, *Sixth New York*, 138; Cheney, *Ninth Regiment*, 107.

20. *OR* 27 (2):637; Turney, "First Tennessee," 535. Archer's protest was well founded, as the result of the charge would prove.

21. *OR* 27 (1):1031, (2):677–78; Calef, "Gettysburg Notes," 48; Fleet, "Fredericksburg Artillery," 240; Marye, "First Gun," 1229; Purifoy, "Artillery at Gettysburg," 424; Goolsby, "Crenshaw's Battery," 358; Carmichael, *Purcell, Crenshaw, and Letcher Artillery*, 185. The report of Pegram's battalion stated that only one section unlimbered. See *OR* 27 (2):272.

On his 1 July map Bachelder placed McGraw's and Zimmerman's batteries north of the pike and Marye's and the Crenshaw batteries south of it. McIntosh's batteries were to the right of Pegram's battalion. McIntosh's battalion moved to

Gettysburg in front of Pender's division and must have halted behind Brocken-brough's and Pettigrew's brigades, which were in reserve at this time. I infer that McIntosh's battalion did not deploy until Heth's division did so. See *OR* 27 (2):674 and McIntosh, "Review of the Gettysburg Campaign," 43.

22. Bird, *Stories*, 6; Boland, "Beginning," 308; Moon, "Beginning," 449; Bachelder Map, 1 July.

23. Fulton, "Fifth Alabama," 379, and *War Reminiscences*, 79.

24. *OR* 27 (2):649; Belo, "Battle," 65; Wilson, *Confederate Soldier*, 116; Holt, "Gettysburg." The 11th Mississippi was left in the rear to guard the division's trains.

25. *OR* 27 (2):649; J. M. Stone to J. R. Davis, n.d., *BP*, 3:328–30; Holt, "Gettysburg." W. B. Murphy of the 2d Mississippi stated that the 2d was north of the railroad bed. See Murphy to Dearborn, 29 June 1900, Bragg Papers, SHSW.

26. Belo, "Battle," 65; Hall and Besley, *Sixth New York*, 138; Cheney, *Ninth Regiment*, 107–8; Heermance, "Cavalry at Gettysburg," 200. Cpl. Cyrus W. James of the 9th New York Cavalry was killed in this fight. The New Yorkers considered him to be the first Union soldier killed in the battle. See NYMC, *Final Report*, 1:10.

27. Calef, "Gettysburg Notes," 48.

28. Moon, "Beginning," 449.

29. Ibid.; Bird, *Stories*, 7.

30. Moon, "Beginning," 449; Turney, "First Tennessee," 535; Mockbee, "14th Tenn.," MC.

31. Hard, *Eighth Cavalry*, 256–57; Beveridge, "First Gun," 174–75; Harter, *Erinnerungen*, 187. The fields described are shown on the McElfresh Map. On the "Crop Map" the field in which the 8th Illinois deployed is shown as a cornfield.

32. Flavius Bellamy Diary, 1 July 1863, and F. L. Bellamy to parents, 3 July 1863, Bellamy Collection, ISL; Moyer, *Seventeenth Regiment*, 62; Nicholson, *Pennsylvania*, 2:878; Willet, "A Comrade."

33. *OR* 27 (1):1031; Calef, "Gettysburg Notes," 49. Corporal Watrous lost his leg.

34. Bird, *Stories*, 7; Moon, "Beginning," 449; *OR* 27 (2):646. Maj. Felix Buchanan is listed as the 1st Tennessee's commander in the Order of Battle. However, Lt. Col. Newton George was said by Moon to have been the commander, and in Krick, *Lee's Colonels*, 138, George is said to have been captured at Gettysburg.

35. *OR* 27 (1):185, 230, 927, 934. Gamble to Church, 10 Mar. 1864, BLC; Regimental History, n.p., IHS; F. L. Bellamy to parents, 3 July 1863, Bellamy Collection, ISL; NYMC, *Final Report*, 3:1145.

CHAPTER 6

1. Riddle to LeBouvier, 4 Aug. 1863, Reynolds Papers, FM; Weld, *War Diary*, 229.

2. *OR* 27 (3):416, 457, (1):701.

3. Nevins, *Diary*, 232.

4. Wadsworth Testimony, *CCW*, 413; C. E. Rogers, "Gettysburg Scenes"; Rosengarten to Bates, 31 Jan. 1871, Bates Papers, PSA; *OR* 27 (1):244. There is a question about the order of Reynolds's activities. Doubleday reported that Reynolds

had briefed him between 7:00 and 8:00 A.M. and that he had already ordered Wadsworth to lead the march.

5. Boatner, *Dictionary*, 216–17.

6. Curtis, *Twenty-fourth*, 155; Mickey of Company K, "Charge of the Iron Brigade"; "Report of Col. Samuel J. Williams," in Gaff, "Here Was Made," 29; Marsh Diary, 1 July 1863, IHS; *OR* 50 (1):1066.

7. Hofmann, "General Hofmann Replies"; Nolan, *Iron Brigade*, 234; Meade Diary, 1 July 1863, SHSW; Hughes, "Report of the Movements of the Second Wisconsin," 1 July 1863, SHSW; Otis Diary, 1 July 1863, SHSW.

8. Mickey of Company K, "Charge at Gettysburg"; Otis, "Second Wisconsin Regiment"; Curtis, *Twenty-fourth*, 155.

9. C. Wheeler, "Reminiscences," 200–201.

10. Cutler's order of march is from Nicholson, *Pennsylvania*, 1:340; the Iron Brigade's is in Colonel Dudley's report of 28 Dec. 1878 in Hewett, Trudeau, and Suderow, *Supplement*, 137, and in Nolan, *Iron Brigade*, 233. The strength figures are based on those given in Busey and Martin, *Regimental Strengths*, 239. Those given here exclude 434 members of the 7th Indiana Regiment who were not present.

11. Ellie Reynolds to brother, 5 July 1863, Reynolds Papers, FM. E. J. Nichols, *Toward Gettysburg*, gives an account of Reynolds's last hours. Nichols places the Rosengarten incident west of Gettysburg after Rosengarten had been in the town.

12. Veil to McConaughy, 7 Apr. 1864, McConaughy Collection, GC. Charles H. Veil, Reynolds's orderly, wrote at least two accounts of this part of the battle. This one is first and probably the most accurate. In Veil's later account, titled "An Old Boy's Personal Recollections and Reminiscences of the Civil War" (GNMP), he stated that on receipt of the message that Buford was engaged, Reynolds immediately sent staff officers to Meade and to Generals Howard and Sickles. I deem this unlikely because at this time Reynolds knew little of the situation confronting him, and other accounts do not support it.

The George house is on the west side of the road, now Steinwehr Avenue, south of Washington Street.

13. A. B. Jerome to Hancock, 18 Oct. 1865, *BP*, 1:201. Edwin Coddington, in *Gettysburg Campaign*, 682 n. 14, stated that Jerome's account is not convincing, and I agree. Jerome stated that at a distance of two miles he identified the corps by its flag. This seems unlikely especially if the flag was hanging limply from its staff; this seems probable because there was no heavy breeze that day. Further, he would have seen only Cutler's brigade. It must have been known that only the First Corps would have been coming over the Emmitsburg Road. Jerome also states that he was in the seminary building's cupola when Reynolds arrived. No other accounts mention this, and it seems unlikely.

14. Veil to McConaughy, 7 Apr. 1864, McConaughy Collection, GC; Rosengarten to Bates, 13 Jan. 1876, Bates Papers, PSA; Rosengarten, *William Reynolds . . . John Fulton Reynolds*; Weld, *War Diary*, 231–32. Maj. Henry Tremain of Sickles's staff wrote that he spoke with Reynolds at Gettysburg and that Reynolds stated, "Tell General Sickles I *think* he had better come up." See Tremain, *Two Days of War*, 14.

15. Weld, *War Diary*, 252; *OR* 27 (3):458.

16. H. W. Pfanz, *Culp's Hill*, 20, 411 n. 15.

17. Veil to McConaughy, 7 Apr. 1864, McConaughy Collection, GC; Wadsworth Testimony, *CCW*, 413; Hofmann, *Remarks*, 3–4; NYMC, *Final Report*, 3:990; Cooke, "First Day," 278; Pierce to Bachelder, 1 Nov. 1882, *BP*, 2:910; Curtis, *Twenty-fourth*, 156; "Newspaper Account Enclosed by Coe," *BP*, 3:1566. Reynolds might have been looking at a wall map of Adams County that was published in 1858.

18. *OR* 27 (1):265, 267; Hofmann, *Remarks*, 4; Parkhurst, "Heroism of the 147th N.Y."; Snyder, *Oswego County*, 59; Cooke, "First Day," 242; Curtis, *Twenty-fourth*, 156; William W. Dudley Report, n.d., *BP*, 2:940; A. P. Smith, *Seventy-sixth*, 237; Lyman Diary, 1 July 1863, GNMP.

19. *OR* 27 (1):359; Hall to Bachelder, 29 Dec. 1869, *BP*, 1:385–89; MGC, *Maine at Gettysburg*, 16. Hall did not specify whether or not he took his battery north through the swale in front of the seminary or in the swale behind McPherson Woods and the battery's position. Since the former was at hand, it seems likely that he used it. Hall reported that six cannons fired at his battery when it took position.

20. MGC, *Maine at Gettysburg*, 19; *OR* 27 (1):266; Coey, "Cutler's Brigade."

21. Hofmann, *Remarks*, 4; Cutler to Governor of Pennsylvania, 5 Nov. 1863, in "Picket Shots," *National Tribune*, 9 May 1912; A. P. Smith, *Seventy-sixth*, 237; Hofmann, "Fifty-sixth Regiment."

22. Tevis, *Fighting Fourteenth*, 82, 132–33; NYMC, *Final Report*, 2:616, 733.

23. *OR* 27 (1):24–45; Nevins, *Diary*, 232–33. In his report Doubleday wrote that the officer sent to Reynolds was Lt. Benjamin T. Marten. However, in *Chancellorsville* he wrote that the officers sent were Maj. Eminel P. Halstead and Lt. Meredith L. Jones. It was at this time, according to his report, that Doubleday urged the Iron Brigade to hold the position "to the last extremity," to which they are supposed to have replied, "If we can't hold it, where will you find men who can?" This is alleged to have been said to other units, too, but it seems unlikely that their orders would have been identical.

24. *OR* 27 (1):244, 273; Dudley, "Report," 129; Beecham, "Corporal and the General." Dudley reported that Reynolds sent Capt. Craig Wadsworth to the 2d Wisconsin; Major Mansfield wrote that it was Lieutenant Colonel Kress. Since Mansfield was the most closely involved, the officer probably was Kress.

25. *OR* 27 (1):273; C. Wheeler, "Reminiscences," 210; "Incomplete Draft Report, Col. Lucius Fairchild," n.d., Fairchild Papers, SHSW.

26. Veil to McConaughy, 7 Apr. 1864, McConaughy Collection, GC. Veil's account was first recorded by Ellie Reynolds in a letter to her brother dated 5 July 1863, in Reynolds Papers, FM. She stated that Reynolds rode in the rear of the infantry line and shouted, "Forward, Forward Men, drive those fellows out of there, Forward, for God's sake forward." In his letter to McConaughy, Veil wrote that Reynolds had ordered the 19th Indiana " 'Forward into line' at a double quick and ordered them to charge into the woods, leading the charge personally." In his "Old Boy's Personal Recollections," GNMP, Veil stated that Reynolds had ridden toward the seminary, met the lead regiment of the brigade, and led it into McPherson Woods. There he ordered it to charge and led the charge, riding in advance.

The regiment veered to the right, leaving Reynolds alone. Reynolds then rode back to the edge of the woods, where he was shot.

In the postwar years several people claimed to have shot Reynolds. The men of Marye's battery thought that he had been killed by one of their volleys, and there were individuals who claimed to have done the deed. Such claims have no credibility. Bullets fired at the 2d Wisconsin must have been flying all around.

In his letter to McConaughy, Veil wrote that only Capts. Robert W. Mitchell and Edward C. Baird were present. Neither of these men wrote accounts of this insofar as I know.

Veil was from the 9th Regiment, Pennsylvania Reserves.

27. Veil to McConaughy, 7 Apr. 1864, McConaughy Collection, GC; H. Lyman, "Data Concerning 147th N.YV.," *BP*, 1:322. Veil is the principal source of information on the details of Reynolds's death.

28. Veil to McConaughy, 7 Apr. 1864, McConaughy Collection, GC; Veil, "Old Boy's Personal Recollections," GNMP; Rosengarten to Bates, 13 Jan. 1876, Bates Papers, PSA; Ellie Reynolds to brother, 5 July 1863, and Jennie Reynolds to brother Will, 5 July 1863, Reynolds Papers, FM; Weld, *War Diary*, 230, 234–37.

CHAPTER 7

1. NYMC, *Final Report*, 3:1343–44, and *In Memoriam: James Samuel Wadsworth*, 53, 59; Boatner, *Dictionary*, 882–83; O. O. Howard, *Autobiography*, 1:407; Nevins, *Diary*, 172; J. Hall to Bachelder, 27 Feb. 1867, *BP*, 1:307. Wadsworth had two sons who served as aides during the battle; Charles was on his father's staff, and Craig was aide to Buford and to the First Corps commanders.

2. Snyder, *Oswego County*, 59–61; Coey, "Cutler's Brigade." The accounts in *Oswego County* are also in NYMC, *Final Report*, 3, in the section dealing with the 147th New York Infantry Regiment. McLean, *Cutler's Brigade*, covers this whole action well.

3. Snyder, *Oswego County*, 59, 61, 63; Bartlett Affidavit, 23 Nov. 1889, GNMP; Lyman to Bachelder, n.d., *BP*, 1:330. For the location of the McPherson buildings see the Warren Map. Edward M. McPherson, chief clerk in the U.S. House of Representatives, owned the farm. At the time of the battle John Slentz and his family lived there.

4. *OR* 27 (1):285; Edward Haviland to mother, 11 Aug. 1863, 76th New York Vol. Inf., RG 94, NA; Kellogg to Bachelder, 1 Nov. 1865, *BP*, 1:204; W. Clark, *Histories*, 1:297.

Col. John Kerr Connally was twenty-three years old at the time of the battle. He had attended the U.S. Naval Academy but did not graduate. He became a captain in the 21st North Carolina on 12 May 1861 and colonel of the 55th on 19 May 1862. He was captured at Gettysburg and was exchanged in March 1864. He was wounded again at Cold Harbor and resigned on 7 March 1865. See Krick, *Lee's Colonels*, 86.

5. Edward Haviland to mother, 11 Aug. 1863, 76th New York Vol. Inf., RG 94, NA; NYMC, *Final Report*, 3:616. It is not clear if the 76th began firing with the 56th

or was delayed until Major Grover was convinced that the men shooting after them were Confederates.

6. Snyder, *Oswego County*, 59, 60.

7. *OR* 27 (1):266, 282; Lyman, "Gen. Howard Criticized"; NYMC, *Final Report*, 3:991.

8. Snyder, *Oswego County*, 60; *OR* 27 (1):359.

9. Snyder, *Oswego County*, 60, 62; NYMC, *Final Report*, 3:992–93, 1001; Coey, "Cutler's Brigade."

10. Snyder, *Oswego County*, 60, 62; NYMC, *Final Report*, 3:991–92.

11. Snyder, *Oswego County*, 62, 63; Bartlett Affidavit, 23 Nov. 1889, GNMP.

12. Coey, "Cutler's Brigade."

13. Snyder, *Oswego County*, 60, 61, 63.

14. *OR* 27 (1):282; NYMC, *Final Report*, 3:992, 1002; Hofmann, "Fifty-sixth Regiment."

15. Cooke, "First Day," 280. According to Lieutenant Pierce, Sergeant Wyburn received a commission in recognition of his bravery on 1 July.

General Cutler reported that the 147th New York, with a strength of 380 officers and men, sustained 207 casualties; the 76th New York's 375 officers and men had 169 casualties; and the 56th Pennsylvania suffered 52 casualties from its strength of 252. See *OR* 27 (1):282.

16. *OR* 27 (1):359; Hall to Bachelder, 27 Feb. 1867, 29 Dec. 1869, *BP*, 1:306, 386.

17. *OR* 27 (1):359; MGC, *Maine at Gettysburg*, 16–17.

18. *OR* 27 (1):1031; Calef, "Gettysburg Notes," 39. This incident is presented in greater detail in Chapter 5.

19. *OR* 27 (1):354–55, 359; MGC, *Maine at Gettysburg*, 18–19; Hall to Bachelder, 29 Dec. 1869, *BP*, 1:386–88. Sgt. Charles E. Stubbs, who was with Hall's right section, wrote that the attacking Rebels wore "talmers," a kind of cape. Stubbs wrote also that the Rebels fired explosive bullets. See Stubbs to Bachelder, 3 July 1882, *BP*, 2:891–92.

CHAPTER 8

1. *OR* 27 (2):1030; Beecham, *Gettysburg*, 65. Although gray was to have been the color of Confederate uniforms, butternut, a shade of brown made from butternut dye, was common.

2. J. B. Young, *Gettysburg*, 442; F. S. Harris, "Gen. Jas. J. Archer"; Hopkins, "Archer Letters," 352.

3. *OR* 27 (1):273; "Incomplete Draft Report, Col. Lucius Fairchild," n.d., Fairchild Papers, SHSW; Otis, "Second Wisconsin Regiment"; Storch and Storch, " 'What a Deadly Trap,' " 21.

4. Warren Map. Colonel Fairchild described the woods as "thinly studded with trees of large growth." See "Incomplete Draft Report, Col. Lucius Fairchild," n.d., Fairchild Papers, SHSW.

5. *OR* 27 (1):273; C. Wheeler, "Reminiscences," 202–3; Wheeler Manuscript, Wheeler Papers, SHSW; Hughes Diary, 1 July 1863, SHSW.

6. Wheeler Manuscript, Wheeler Papers, SHSW; Markle, "Story of Battle," GNMP.

7. Moon, "Beginning," 449.

8. *OR* 27 (2):646; Turney, "First Tennessee"; F. S. Harris, "From Gettysburg"; Moon, "Beginning," 449; Lindsley, "Battle of Gettysburg," 246.

9. Moon, "Beginning," 449. Lt. Col. Newton J. George was about twenty-three years old at Gettysburg. He was captured there and spent the rest of the war as a prisoner. See Krick, *Lee's Colonels*, 137–38.

10. *OR* 27 (1):279.

11. Ibid.

12. Williams, "Report," 136; Dudley, "Report," 129; M. C. Barnes to W. W. Dudley, 28 Mar. 1883, *BP*, 2:937.

13. *OR* 27 (1):267; Curtis, *Twenty-fourth*, 156–57; R. Root to Grandfather, 23 Aug. 1863, HCWRTC, USAMHI.

14. Col. Lucius Fairchild Notes, *BP*, 1:335–36; "Incomplete Draft Report, Col. Lucius Fairchild," n.d., Fairchild Papers, SHSW; *OR* 27 (1):273–74. Fairchild's left arm was shattered just above the elbow. It was "succesfully amputated leaving an elegant stump." His brother Charles found "Lushe" ensconced in the seminary president's back parlor and as "jolly as a king." See Charles Fairchild to mother, 6 July 1863, Fairchild Papers, SHSW.

15. Harries, "Iron Brigade," 187; Dailey to Doubleday, 24 Mar. 1891, *BP*, 3:1806; *OR* 27 (2):274, Storch and Storch, " 'What a Deadly Trap,' " 25. The large quarry hole was dug sometime before the battle. I do not know what was taken from it.

16. *OR* 27 (1):279; Callis, " 'Iron Brigade,' " 140; Dudley, "Report," 129; M. C. Barnes to W. W. Dudley, 28 Mar. 1883, *BP*, 2:937; Hawkins, "Blanchard," 214.

17. *OR* 27 (1):279; S. D. G., "From the Twenty-fourth"; Callis, " 'Iron Brigade,' " 140; Moon, "Beginning"; Boland, "Beginning," 308; "Dick Huftill and the Flag"; Bird, *Stories*, 7.

18. *OR* 27 (1):267, 279; Curtis, *Twenty-fourth*, 156–57, 24; Hawkins, "Blanchard," 274. Storch and Storch, " 'What a Deadly Trap,' " 25–27, analyzes the brigade's casualties; the book's tables suggest that the brigade had a maximum of 373 casualties on 1 July, the 13th Alabama had 168, and the 5th Alabama Battalion suffered only 5.

19. *OR* 27 (1):267; Curtis, *Twenty-fourth*, 157.

20. D. S. Freeman, *Lee's Lieutenants*, 3:80; Moon, "Beginning," 450; Castleberry, "Thirteenth Alabama," 338; *OR* 27 (2):646; Herndon, *Reminiscences*, 15. Apparently the division reserve was not prepared to render Archer and Davis effective support. In this Heth erred. He did not address this failure in his report.

21. *OR* 27 (1):245, 274; Dailey to Doubleday, 24 Mar. 1891, *BP*, 3:1806–7; Harries, "Iron Brigade"; Gaff, *George Otis*, 274–75.

22. Dailey to Doubleday, 24 Mar. 1891, *BP*, 3:1806–8.

23. *OR* 27 (1):275; Halstead, "Incidents," 285; Harries, "Iron Brigade," 186–87; Gaff, *George Otis*, 274.

CHAPTER 9

1. Dawes, *Service with the Sixth*, 164, and "Align on the Colors"; Dawes to Bachelder, 18 Mar. 1868, *BP*, 1:322–23. A brigade guard had been established by General Meredith to perform sentry and other duties for the brigade and the division. On the approach to Gettysburg its 100 officers and men marched at the rear of the brigade, probably serving as a provost guard. See Herdegen and Beaudot, *Bloody Railroad Cut*, 147–48, 166.

2. Dawes, *Service with the Sixth*, 166, and "Align on the Colors"; Dawes to Bachelder, 18 Mar. 1868, *BP*, 1:323–24; Fairfield to Watrous, n.d., Watrous Papers, SHSW; Grayson, "Iron Brigade"; Herdegen and Beaudot, *Bloody Railroad Cut*, 178–89. In his report General Doubleday stated that he formed the 6th in line and directed it to attack. See *OR* 27 (1):246. Dawes wrote that he alone was responsible for the 6th's movements and that Doubleday "had nothing to do whatsoever with this 'placing' of the regiment on the enemy's flank." See Dawes, "Align on the Colors."

"Grayson" was the pen name for Lt. Lloyd G. Harris; "Mickey of Co. K" was that of Sgt. James P. Sullivan.

3. Dawes, *Service with the Sixth*, 166–67, and "Align on the Colors"; Dawes to Bachelder, 18 Mar. 1868, *BP*, 1:323–24; Mickey of Co. K, "Charge of the Iron Brigade"; Herdegen and Beaudot, *Bloody Railroad Cut*, 182.

4. *OR* 27 (2):649; NYMC, *Final Report*, 3:1016; Belo, "Battle," 165; W. Clark, *Histories*, 3:298; Murphy to Dearborn, 29 June 1900, Bragg Papers, SHSW.

5. NYMC, *Final Report*, 2:681–89, 733–40; Memorandum, "Dress of the Troops of the Second Brigade, 1st Division, 1st Army Corps at the Battle of Gettysburg," Rothermel Papers, PSA; H. W. Pfanz, *Culp's Hill*, 306.

6. *OR* 27 (1):286–87; Tevis, *Fighting Fourteenth*, 132–33.

7. Van de Graaff to wife, 8 July 1863, GNMP.

8. Tevis, *Fighting Fourteenth*, 83, 133; *OR* 27 (1):286–87. Fowler's men might have driven Confederates from the gun, but Captain Hall was adamant in his claim that his men hauled the gun from the field after their return from Cemetery Hill. See *OR* 27 (1):360.

9. *OR* 27 (1):276; Dawes, *Service with the Sixth* and "Align on the Colors"; Grayson, "Iron Brigade"; Dawes to Bachelder, 18 Mar. 1868, *BP*, 1:324; Mickey of Company K, "Charge at Gettysburg"; Herdegen and Beaudot, *Bloody Railroad Cut*, 84. Each of Dawes's accounts has slight variations in its quotations.

Sgt. George Fairfield stated that the fence on the south side of the road was an old one that they pulled down, but the one on the north side was a new post and rail fence that they had to climb. The battle account suggests the opposite, and the Warren Map shows the reverse. See Fairfield, "Capture at the Railroad Cut."

10. *OR* 27 (1):276; Dawes to Bachelder, 18 Mar. 1868, *BP*, 1:324.

11. *OR* 27 (1):276; Dawes, *Service with the Sixth*, 168; Waller statement in E. M. Rogers, "Settled Question"; Fairfield, "Capture at the Railroad Cut"; Rogers to Watrous, n.d., Watrous Papers, SHSW; Herdegen and Beaudot, *Bloody Railroad Cut*, 192–94.

12. Dawes to Bachelder, 18 Mar. 1868, *BP*, 1:324; Herdegen and Beaudot,

Bloody Railroad Cut, 189, 193; Mickey of Company K, "Charge at Gettysburg"; Grayson, "Asleep at His Post." Sergeant Sullivan wrote that Captain Ticknor's nickname was "Jerkey."

13. Dawes, "Align on the Colors"; Herdegen and Beaudot, *Bloody Railroad Cut*, 192, 212–13. Kelly is buried in the Gettysburg National Cemetery.

14. Murphy to Dearborn, 29 June 1900, Bragg Papers, SHSW.

15. Remington, "Remington's Story." The accounts of the melee at the colors of the 2d Mississippi reflect the confusion that must have existed at that time.

16. Herdegen and Beaudot, *Bloody Railroad Cut*, 194–96.

17. E. M. Rogers, "Settled Question."

18. *OR* 27 (1):276, 287; Dawes, *Service with the Sixth*, 169.

19. Fairfield, "Sixth Wisconsin"; Rogers to Watrous, n.d., Watrous Papers, SHSW; Herdegen and Beaudot, *Bloody Railroad Cut*, 200.

20. Dawes, *Service with the Sixth*, 169; Dawes to Bachelder, 18 Mar. 1868, *BP*, 1:325; Mickey of Company K, "Charge of the Iron Brigade."

21. Belo, "Battle," 165; W. Clark, *Histories*, 3:297–98; Blair to Lyman, 6 Sept. 1888, NYMC, *Final Report*, 3:1005.

22. Fairfield, "Capture at the Railroad Cut" and "Sixth Wisconsin."

23. *OR* 27 (1):246, 266, 287–88; Tevis, *Fighting Fourteenth*, 134; Kellogg to Bachelder, 1 Nov. 1865, *BP*, 1:205; Fairfield, "Sixth Wisconsin."

24. Herdegen and Beaudot, *Bloody Railroad Cut*, 294–95. The strength figures given on their Gettysburg memorials are 6th, 340; 14th, 356; and 95th, 261. Numbers given in Busey and Martin, *Regimental Strengths*, 239, are 6th, 344; 14th, 318; and 95th, 241. These figures are of those present at or near Gettysburg, not necessarily those at the railroad cut.

25. Dawes, *Service with the Sixth*, 170–72, and "Align on the Colors."

26. Grayson, "Adventures of a Rebel Flag"; Herdegen and Beaudot, *Bloody Railroad Cut*, 208, 221–23. Some questions arise concerning Sergeant Evans's stay at the Jacob Hollinger house. One is how did he get there? A man on makeshift crutches with wounds in both legs would be expected to seek treatment in the closest available hospital, yet Evans passed hospitals and houses in the center of Gettysburg in order to reach the Hollinger house on the east of the town. Lieutenant Harris explained that he and Lieutenants Remington and Beeley went there after their wounds were dressed. At their request a hospital orderly, possibly a man from the 6th, had found accommodations for them at the Hollinger house. However, Evans had preceded them there and was in his bed before they arrived.

There was a minor dispute after the battle about the staff of the captured flag. Dawes stated several times that Evans left the railroad cut area using rifles for crutches and with the flag wrapped around his waist. Yet Waller tried to bolster his own claim by branding statements written by Sergeant Okey as false. Okey held that after he had captured the flag, he was wounded and gave it to another man. This man was wounded in turn but had kept the butt end of the staff as a souvenir and had given it to Okey. Waller attacked Okey's claim by stating that Okey's souvenir was false, for Evans had told him (Waller) that he had taken the staff to the Hollinger house, where he had concealed it by breaking it in half and placing its parts in his bed. Harris wrote that Jacob Hollinger had made firewood of it. See Waller statement in E. M. Rogers, "Settled Question"; Okey, "After That Flag"; Grayson, "Adventures of a Rebel Flag"; Herdegen and Beaudot, *Bloody Railroad Cut*, 279–85. This raises more questions. One is how Evans on makeshift crutches could have carried the flag staff and why Dawes specifically stated that Evans wrapped the flag around his body. Further, Private Okey, whose credibility is in doubt, claimed that he had a part of the staff. One other factor must also be considered. Private Murphy of the 2d Mississippi, who claimed to be the color-bearer from whom it was captured, stated that the staff had been splintered before it was captured. This would imply that there was no complete staff and would add credence to Okey's claim. It could explain, too, why Dawes wrapped the flag around Evans's waist. It seems likely that the truth of this detail cannot be known.

Lieutenant Harris must have had an active imagination. In his (Grayson's) article "Adventures of a Rebel Flag" he stated that "Mississippi brigade" members made frequent visits to the Hollinger house. This seems unlikely. That brigade did not enter the town on 1 July; it was in the Springs Hotel Woods with Heth's division on 2 July and participated in Pickett's Charge on 3 July. Any troops straggling in that area must have belonged to either Hays's or Gordon's brigades, and they would not have known of the capture of the Mississippi flag at the railroad cut and would have been looking for it at the Hollinger house.

CHAPTER 10

1. Robertson, *A. P. Hill*, 209.

2. This biographical information on Hill is based primarily on ibid., which is the source of much additional information, and on references in D. S. Freeman, *Lee's Lieutenants*, vols. 1 and 2.

3. *OR* 27 (2):638, 642–43; W. Clark, *Histories*, 2:348, 5:118. The woods is approximately 2,500 feet wide along its east side. The 26th North Carolina was on the left of Pettigrew's line opposite the north half of McPherson Woods.

Lt. J. Rowan Rogers wrote that the 47th led the march toward Gettysburg and that about a mile or so west of Herr Ridge dismounted cavalrymen fired at both sides of the head of the column. The brigade put out flankers and drove the cavalry off. Federal accounts do not mention this. See W. Clark, *Histories*, 3:103–4.

4. *OR* 27 (2):646; Boatner, *Dictionary*, 317–18.

5. *OR* 27 (2):638; Krick, *Lee's Colonels*, 60; Mayo, "Report," 414; Report of Col. Robert T. Mayo for Heth's Brigade, 13 Aug. 1863, Heth Papers, MC. There was a woods about 500 yards west of the Springs Hotel Woods.

6. *OR* 27 (2):638.

7. Ibid., 656, 661, 665, 669.

8. Ibid., 610, 652, 678; Fleet, "Fredericksburg Artillery." Brander had two Napoleons and two ten-pounder Parrotts; Maurin had six rifled pieces from Garnett's battalion. The two Whitworth guns in Hurt's battery were imported from England. There were only two on the field, and one was out of service much of the time.

9. McIntosh, "Review of the Gettysburg Campaign," 43; *OR* 27 (2):674–75.

Johnson's battery had two Napoleons and two three-inch rifles; Hurt's other section had two three-inch Ordnance rifles, and Wallace had four three-inch rifles. If any Federal guns fired at the Confederate ordnance along the pike, they would have been from either Cooper's or Reynolds's batteries. Even they would have had better targets.

10. *OR* 27 (2):610, 653, 673; Garnett, *Gettysburg*, 18. There was always a need for horses to graze when opportunity afforded. Keeping horses in usable condition was a never-ending job.

11. *OR* 27 (1):244–47; Doubleday, *Chancellorsville*, 134. Doubleday wrote of the alleged significance of Gettysburg's road net and the town's strategic importance, and the adverse effect of a withdrawal on the rest of the army, especially the Eleventh Corps.

12. NYMC, *In Memoriam: Abner Doubleday*, 61–62; Nevins, *Diary*, 172, 233; Coddington, *Gettysburg Campaign*, 696 n. 82.

13. *OR* 27 (1):268, 274, 279; Report, Col. Samuel J. Williams to Capt. J. D. Wood, 16 Nov. 1863, in Storch and Storch, "Unpublished Gettysburg Reports"; Cornelius Wheeler Speech Draft, n.d., Wheeler Papers, SHSW; Curtis, *Twenty-fourth*, 157–58.

14. *OR* 27 (1):282; A. P. Smith, *Seventy-sixth*, 239; Hofmann, "Fifty-sixth Regiment"; Snyder, *Oswego County*, 61.

15. *OR* 27 (1):356, 1032; Calef, "Gettysburg Notes," 50.

16. Tevis, *Fighting Fourteenth*, 85. It is not clear if the two regiments supporting Calef's right were north or south of the cut. In his "Gettysburg Notes" Calef suggested that they were on the north side, yet Corporal Forrester, who was wounded in the morning's charge, must have been shot south of it.

17. *OR* 27 (1):244, 354; Pumping Station Road is the present name. In 1863 it might have been Nunemah(k)er Mill Road. See Nicholson, *Pennsylvania*, 2:659.

18. Strong, *121st Regiment*, 44, 119, 149; Osborne, *Civil War Diaries of Theodore B. Gates*, 91; Nicholson, *Pennsylvania*, 2:659.

19. *OR* 27 (1):319, 329; Strong, *121st Regiment*, 119.

20. Cook, *Personal Reminiscences*, 125–26. The "sharpshooters" in this case were probably skirmishers. The 80th New York's state designation was the 20th Regiment State Militia, and it seemed to prefer that.

21. *OR* 27 (1):312, 313, 315, 317, 326–27; Biddle, "Supplemental Account," 149–50; Cook, *Personal Reminiscences*, 126; Slagle to brother, 13 Sept. 1863, GNMP; F. B. Jones, "Excerpt," GNMP.

22. Nicholson, *Pennsylvania*, 2:738, 745; Chamberlin, *One Hundred and Fiftieth*, 108–9; Avery Harris Papers, 85, BrC, USAMHI.

23. Nicholson, *Pennsylvania*, 2:745; Huidekoper, *Short Story*, 4–5; Avery Harris Papers, 85, BrC, USAMHI.

24. Avery Harris Papers, 85, BrC, USAMHI; Chamberlin, *One Hundred and Fiftieth*, 110–11.

25. *OR* 27 (1):331; Avery Harris Papers, 86, BrC, USAMHI; Chamberlin, *One Hundred and Fiftieth*, 111; Shelton Autobiography, 74, NYHS.

26. *OR* 27 (1):329, 331–32; 334–35; Chamberlin, *One Hundred and Fiftieth*, 111.

27. *OR* 27 (1):329, 331–32, 334–35; Chamberlin, *One Hundred and Fiftieth*, 112; Hubler, *Narrative*, 3.

28. Hubler, *Narrative*, 3.

29. Jacob Slagle to brother, 13 Sept. 1863, 149th Pennsylvania File, CWMC, USAMHI; Cook, *Personal Reminiscences*, 126; *OR* 27 (1):317, 320; Gates, *Ulster Guard*, 433.

30. Nevins, *Diary*, 230–31; J. Stewart, "Battery B," 363.

31. J. Stewart, "Battery B," 367. Stewart's account conflicts with Wainwright's, which states that he placed the battery initially south of the seminary. See *OR* 27 (1):356; Nevins, *Diary*, 232.

32. *OR* 27 (1):355, 361–62; Nevins, *Diary*, 233–34; Shelton Autobiography, 75, NYHS.

33. *OR* 27 (1):281, 295, 300, 307, 309; C. E. Davis, *Thirteenth Massachusetts*, 225; I. Hall, *Ninety-seventh Regiment*, 132. I assume that Baxter's brigade led the march.

34. Northrop, "Going into Gettysburg." Josephine Miller, the granddaughter, later baked bread for Third Corps troops posted near the house. See H. W. Pfanz, *Second Day*, 144.

35. *OR* 27 (1):247–48, 289, 307; Small, *Road to Richmond*, 98; Robinson, "First Corps." Both Doubleday and Robinson wrote that they had ordered the construction of the works.

Robinson's articles in the *National Tribune* are disappointing; they give general accounts of the battle rather than descriptions of his division's actions.

36. *OR* 27 (1):295, 299, 301; C. E. Davis, *Thirteenth Massachusetts*, 226; Nicholson, *Pennsylvania*, 1:560; Small, *Sixteenth Maine*, 116, and *Road to Richmond*, 99.

37. Small, *Sixteenth Maine*, 117, and *Road to Richmond*, 99; MGC, *Maine at Gettysburg*, 4.

CHAPTER 11

1. Carpenter, *Sword*, 1–19; *DAB*, 4:279.

2. Carpenter, *Sword*, 19; *DAB*, 4:279; Harwell and Racine, *Fiery Trail*, 100; H. W. Pfanz, *Culp's Hill*, 7.

3. Carpenter, *Sword*, 27.

4. Ibid., 38–39; H. W. Pfanz, *Culp's Hill*, 7–9.

5. O. O. Howard, *Autobiography*, 1:349, 536–37; C. Howard to mother, "Before Gettysburg," Howard Papers, BC; McFeely, *Yankee Stepfather*, 14; Pula, *Sigel Regiment*, 102. I went into this matter in greater detail in *Culp's Hill*, 9–10.

6. O. Howard to mother, 27 Dec. 1863, Howard Papers, BC; Hitz, *Letters of Winkler*, 43.

7. Hunt, "First Day," 256; Hitz, *Letters of Winkler*, 61; Bigelow, *Chancellorsville*, 478–80.

8. *OR* 27 (3):418, 419, (1):715, 733, 739; O. O. Howard, *Autobiography*, 1:402; Wallace Journal, 30 June 1863, PSA; Fox to Harris, 14 Nov. 1885, *BP*, 2:1144.

9. O. O. Howard, *Autobiography*, 1:402; Schurz, *Reminiscences*, 3:4; Domschcke, *Twenty Months*, 27; Hitz, *Letters of Winkler*, 67–68.

10. Muenzenberger to wife, 30 June 1863, Muenzenberger Papers, SHSW; Jacob Smith, *Camps and Campaigns*, 85; Kiefer, *One Hundred and Fifty-third*, 139–41; Company Officer, "Reminiscences," 54.

11. O. O. Howard, "Personal Reminiscences"; *OR* 27 (1):457, 701; O. Howard to Jacobs, 22 Mar. 1864, Howard Papers, BC. A transcript of a letter from Reynolds to Howard stated that Reynolds was moving up to Gettysburg. He asked Howard where he would move and where his headquarters would be and to send a staff officer to him at Gettysburg. In a letter to S. P. Bates, Captain Rosengarten of Reynolds's staff stated that Howard had been ordered to Cemetery Hill. Howard denied this. Rosengarten named Weld as the aide who had gone to Howard, but Weld had gone to Meade. See Rosengarten to Bates, 14 Apr. 1874, Bates Papers, PSA.

12. *OR* 27 (1):701, 727. In his "Personal Reminiscences," O. O. Howard gave 2:30 P.M. as the time of arrival of his message. In his *Autobiography*, 1:408, he gave 8:30 A.M. for the beginning of the corps march.

13. O. O. Howard, *Autobiography*, 1:410.

14. *OR* 27 (1):359; Hall to Bachelder, 29 Dec. 1869, *BP*, 1:387.

15. *OR* 27 (3):703; O. O. Howard, *Autobiography*, 1:412; Kiefer, *One Hundred and Fifty-third*, 120–21; H. W. Pfanz, *Culp's Hill*, 22–23; W. A. Bentley, "Howard at Gettysburg." The other Gettysburg civilians on the roof included Daniel Skelly's father, Mrs. Edward G. Fahnstock, and Isaac Johns.

Howard remembered the orderly as a Lieutenant Quinn. Skelly identified him as George Guinn, a resident of the Gettysburg area. See Skelly, *Boy's Experiences*, 12; H. W. Pfanz, *Culp's Hill*, 412.

16. O. O. Howard, *Autobiography*, 1:413; C. Howard, "First Day," 314, 316. Howard recalled that Maj. William Riddle brought him word of Reynolds's death. Later he decided that Capt. Daniel Hall had brought him the news. See O. Howard, "Address to Graduating Class, Syracuse University," 10 June 1903, and O. Howard to Edward S. Fowler, 20 July 1888, Howard Papers, BC.

17. *OR* 27 (1):702; O. O. Howard, *Autobiography*, 1:413; H. W. Pfanz, *Culp's Hill*, 23–24, 92–93; O. O. Howard, "Personal Reminiscences."

18. *OR* 27 (1):702, (3):463; H. W. Pfanz, *Culp's Hill*, 92–93, 422–23.

19. W. A. Bentley, "Howard at Gettysburg"; O. Howard to Bates, 14 Sept. 1875, Bates Papers, PSA.

20. *OR* 27 (1):701, 727; Schurz, *Reminiscences*, 3:4–5. Whether Cemetery Hill was a good place for Howard's headquarters at this time is questionable. It might have been better had it been closer to the fighting.

21. Kiefer, *One Hundred and Fifty-third*, 208; NYMC, *Final Report*, 2:568; Southerton Reminiscences, 4–5, OHS; Marcus, *New Canaan Private*, 39; Harris to Lough, 11 July 1863, A. L. Harris Papers, OHS; Newel Burch Diary, 1 July 1863, BrC, USAMHI; Dunkelman and Winey, *Hardtack Regiment*, n.p.; Hurst, *Seventy-third Ohio*, 65. Schurz stated that the march began at 7:30 A.M. See Schurz, "Battle," 273.

22. *OR* 27 (1):230, 701, 747, 748; Hitz, *Letters of Winkler*, 66–67; W. Wheeler, *In Memoriam*, 408. Whether Wilkeson's battery was with Barlow or with the other batteries is not clear. Howard placed it with Barlow; Major Osborn was with the rest of the batteries. The battery's reports do not say.

23. W. Wheeler, *In Memoriam*, 408.

24. *OR* 27 (1):702, 727, (3):463; O. Howard to Bates, 14 Sept. 1875, Bates Papers, PSA.

25. *OR* 27 (1):727; Schurz, "Battle," 274–75.

26. *OR* 27 (1):702, 727–28; Schurz, *Reminiscences*, 3:8; O. O. Howard, "Personal Reminiscences."

27. Southerton Reminiscences, 8, OHS; W. H. Warren, "Seventeenth Connecticut," 56–57, BPL; Warren Letters, 56, YU; Nicholson, *Pennsylvania*, 1:434; Jacobs, "Eyewitness," n.p., GNMP; Simmers and Bachschmid, *Volunteers' Manual*, 28; Applegate, *Arrowsmith*, 211. Many officers, even those of high rank such as A. P. Hill, were placed under arrest by their commanders for perceived infraction of orders or procedures. Arrests usually meant they were deprived of their commands for the periods of arrest and, when on the march, traveled at the rear of their commands. Such arrests seemed not to affect their status in a permanent way, but the practice, often cavalier, must have made for bad relations and must have affected the officers' status.

28. *OR* 27 (1):702; O. O. Howard, "Campaign," 56, and *Autobiography*, 1:414.

29. O. O. Howard, *Autobiography*, 1:414; *OR* 27 (1):266; Wadsworth Testimony, *CCW*, 414; O. O. Howard, "Campaign," 56.

30. *OR* 27 (1):702; O. Howard to Bates, 14 Sept. 1875, and Doubleday to Bates, 3 Apr. 1874, Bates Papers, PSA.

31. *OR* 27 (1):703; Halstead, "Incidents," 285.

32. *OR* 27 (1):702; Slocum, *Life and Services*, 102; O. O. Howard, "Battle of Gettysburg."

33. Slocum, *Life and Services*, 102; Slocum to T. H. Davis, 8 Sept. 1875, Bates Papers, PSA; H. W. Pfanz, *Culp's Hill*, 93.

34. C. Howard, "First Day," 325–26; Hall to Howard, 19 Feb. 1877, Howard Papers, BC.

35. *OR* 27 (1):758–59; C. Howard, "First Day," 258. Charles Howard stated that Slocum's words to him were "I'll be damned if I will take the responsibility of this fight."

36. *OR* 27 (1):126, 758–59, (3):465.

CHAPTER 12

1. D. S. Freeman, *Lee's Lieutenants*, 1:85–86; H. W. Pfanz, *Culp's Hill*, 64–66.

2. D. S. Freeman, *Lee's Lieutenants*, 1:247–48, 2:xxxviii, 3:xlvi; H. W. Pfanz, *Culp's Hill*, 276–77; Ledford, *Reminiscences*, 79.

3. *OR* 27 (3):943–44, (2):307, 317, 444. McIntosh, "Gettysburg Campaign," 3–4, VHS, states that Lee must have learned that the Army of the Potomac was in nearby Maryland on 27 June. He based his opinion on the reference to an earlier message made in Lee's dispatch to Ewell dated 28 June (see *OR* 27 [3]:943–44). He observed also that a dispatch sent off on 28 June could not have reached Early via Carlisle on the twenty-ninth.

McIntosh raised good questions. I have used the traditional accounts in spite of doubts about them. Lee stated in both of his reports that he learned of the presence of the Army of the Potomac from Harrison on the night of the 28th (see *OR* 27 [2]:307, 316). Had a courier been sent to Ewell on the night of the 28th, I assume that Ewell's message for Early could have reached Early by the evening of the 29th. Further, the dispatch from Lee to Ewell dated 7:30 A.M., when being copied from memory, might have been misdated the 28th when the 29th was intended (see *OR* 27 [3]:943, 944).

4. D. S. Freeman, *Lee's Lieutenants*, 2:414–16, 700–701; Boatner, *Dictionary*, 849; H. W. Pfanz, *Culp's Hill*, 31–32; Trimble to Bachelder, 8 Feb. 1883, *BP*, 2:926; Trimble, "Battle."

5. Trimble to Bachelder, 8 Feb. 1883, *BP*, 2:926–27; Trimble, "Battle," 120. In the *SHSP* article Trimble wrote that it was on the night of the thirtieth that Ewell received orders from Lee to concentrate. It had to be the night of the twenty-ninth. Even had Ewell offered Trimble the use of a brigade from Rodes's division, which he probably would not have seriously considered doing, it seems highly unlikely that Rodes would have agreed to such an arrangement.

6. McDonald, *Make Me a Map of the Valley*, 156; *OR* 27 (2):468, 503, 552.

7. Trimble to Bachelder, 8 Feb. 1883, *BP*, 2:927.

8. *OR* 27 (2):444, 468, 552; C. Brown, "Personal Narrative," Hunt Papers, LC; E. M. Daniel, *Speeches*, 80; H. W. Pfanz, *Culp's Hill*, 33, 38.

9. Trimble to Bachelder, 8 Feb. 1883, *BP*, 2:927–28; Trimble, "Battle," 122, and "Campaign," 211.

10. C. Brown, "Memoir," n.p., Brown and Ewell Papers, TSL; C. Brown, "Personal Narrative," 1–2, Hunt Papers, LC. Brown was the son of Ewell's widowed first cousin and new wife, Lizinka Campbell Brown. She was probably the wealthiest woman in Tennessee.

Brown wrote that Lee said that he had heard nothing *from or of* Stuart in three days and that he had learned from a paper that he had been near Washington. He stated that Ewell should "send out to his left" and try to communicate with Stuart. Lee had been told that firing had been heard near Hanover Junction and thought that Stuart might have been there.

According to Brown, the battery posted by Ewell and Rodes drew fire from a battery near the seminary. The fire of the Federal battery killed many horses and "made our seats behind it rather uncomfortable." If they were fired on from the seminary, it must have been one of the batteries on Oak Hill — Carter's or Fry's.

11. *OR* 27 (2):552.

12. Boatner, *Dictionary*, 429; Krick, "Three Confederate Disasters," 129–31.

13. *OR* 27 (2):552, 581, 596; Pickens Diary, 1 July 1863, GNMP.

14. *OR* 27 (2):444, 552; Trimble to Bachelder, 8 Feb. 1883, *BP*, 2:928; Trimble, "Campaign," 172; Purifoy, "With Ewell," 464. Trimble suggested that Doles's brigade was deployed in the plain after Rodes was engaged. Rodes's and Ewell's reports state otherwise, but neither report confirms that Trimble was involved in the deployment of Rodes's division.

15. *OR* 27 (1):938–39: Moyer, *Seventeenth Regiment*, 60–62; Bean, "17th Penna. Cavalry"; Myers, *Comanches*, 196.

16. *OR* 27 (2):552, 579.

17. Thompson, "Reminiscences of the Autauga Rifles," ADAH; Pickens Diary, 1 July 1863, GNMP. Former lieutenant J. C. Irvin of the 5th North Carolina described the position of Iverson's brigade to battlefield commissioner William C. Robbins. See Robbins Journal, 16 Apr. 1895, GNMP.

18. *OR* 27 (2):553, 581, 597; Willis, "Report," 404–5; Grace, "Rodes's Division," 614; Boatner, *Dictionary*, 243.

19. *OR* 27 (2):552, 566; W. Clark, *Histories*, 2:255; Kenan, *Sketch of the Forty-third Regiment*, 9.

20. *OR* 27 (2):587; William Calder to mother, 8 July 1863, Calder Family Papers, SHC; Norman, *Portion of My Life*, 185.

21. *OR* 27 (2):552, 602, (1):356, 364, 1032.

CHAPTER 13

1. *OR* 27 (1):356, 352, 364; Calef, "Gettysburg Notes," 50–51; Nicholson, *Pennsylvania*, 2:897; McKelvey, "George Breck's Civil War Letters," 127; Wainwright Journal, 215, HL.

2. *OR* 27 (1):248, 329.

3. Hofmann, "Fifty-sixth Regiment"; Tevis, *Fighting Fourteenth*, 84; Nicholson, *Pennsylvania*, 1:311; Snyder, *Oswego County*, 61, 62; A. P. Smith, *Seventy-sixth*, 239. The order of Cutler's regiments in line from the left were probably 96, 75, 56, 147.

4. *OR* 27 (1):266, 282, 285–86.

5. Ibid., 702, 727; Schurz, "Battle," 275. Mention has often been made of a "gap" between the two corps. There probably was a gap between Cutler's right and the Eleventh Corps left, but Baxter's brigade would have narrowed it. Likely the gap had little real impact on the outcome of the fight on Oak Ridge because whatever gap existed was not exploited until Ramseur's assault, and by that time the Union forces were falling back.

6. *OR* 27 (1):734; NYMC, *Final Report*, 1:374, 374, 378. See Hartwig, "11th Army Corps," 33–40, for an excellent short account of these events.

The McLean farm's resident was a J. Martin; its owner was Moses McClean, a prominent Gettysburg resident. I have employed the McLean spelling here and below because it was used on the Warren Map and has been in common usage.

7. *OR* 27 (1):248–49, 289, 292, 307, 309; I. Hall, *Ninety-seventh Regiment*, 135–36, and "Iverson's Brigade," 26 June 1884; Boatner, *Dictionary*, 51. The high rail fence between the wheat field and the hay field was recorded by Capt. Isaac Hall. Apparently it was damaged during the battle and perhaps was not replaced. It was not recorded on the Warren Map or on subsequent army maps. Hall showed its location and discussed it and its important role in the battle in his *Ninety-seventh Regiment* and in his letter to Col. John Bachelder, 15 Aug. 1884, *BP*, 2:1061. The McElfresh Map shows the fence.

The 11th Pennsylvania Regiment had a mascot, a mongrel dog named Sallie. Sallie is portrayed in bronze on the front (west) side of the 11th's memorial. Elsie

Singmaster, a Gettysburg woman who wrote fiction about Gettysburg, had a piece on Sallie published in an E. P. Dutton anthology titled *For Love of Country*.

8. *OR* 27 (1):292, 307, 309; Boatner, *Dictionary*, 51; I. Hall, *Ninety-seventh Regiment*, 136, and "Iverson's Brigade," 26 June 1884. Captain Hall, a dogmatic veteran, made errors when he wrote of other regiments, but I believe that he was essentially correct when writing about the 97th New York.

9. *OR* 27 (1):282; Hofmann, "Fifty-sixth Regiment"; A. P. Smith, *Seventy-sixth*, 239–40; Grant, "First Army Corps," 261; Look to Bachelder, 17 Feb. 1884, enclosure, *BP*, 2:1021.

10. *OR* 27 (2):444; C. Brown, "Personal Narrative," Hunt Papers, LC.

11. *OR* 27 (2):444, 552.

12. Ibid., 581, 597.

13. Boatner, *Dictionary*, 608; Krick, "Three Confederate Disasters," 122; Sifakis, *Who Was Who*, 497. O'Neal's brigade was often referred to as "Rodes's old brigade."

14. *OR* 27 (2):553, 592. On p. 553 Rodes stated that he ordered the Alabama brigade to form on Iverson's left, but that he ordered the 3d Alabama to form on the left of Daniel and the brigade to form on it. Since Daniel was behind Iverson, this would place O'Neal's line behind Iverson's.

If the 6th Alabama was on the east slope of the hill, it could not have been hit by fire from the First Corps batteries. Therefore, the casualties must have been caused by Dilger's fire and would have been taken after the Eleventh Corps arrived.

15. Ibid., 592; May, "First Confederates," 620; May, "Reminiscences," 284–85, GDAH.

16. *OR* 27 (2):592.

17. Ibid., 553, 592, 595; Battle, "Third Alabama Regiment," 80, VHS.

18. *OR* 27 (2):579, 587; W. Clark, *Histories*, 1:633, 2:235; Robbins Journal, 16 Apr. 1895, GNMP. Only in the Robbins Journal is there a specific statement about the location of Iverson's brigade. In the account of the 23d North Carolina regiment, however, it is said that the brigade formed across the Mummasburg Road and faced east. See W. Clark, *Histories*, 2:235.

19. *OR* 27 (2):583, 597.

20. Ibid., 553, 579.

21. Ibid., 553, 592, 595; Battle, "Third Alabama Regiment," 80, VHS.

22. Griffin, "Rodes on Oak Hill," 36; Krick, "Three Confederate Disasters," 120, 129, 131.

23. *OR* 27 (2):553.

24. Ibid., 592, 602–3.

25. Ibid., 553–54.

26. Ibid., 601; David Ballenger to mother, 18 July 1863, Ballenger Letters, SCL; Park, *Twelfth Alabama*, 53–54.

27. Pickens Diary, 1 July 1863, GNMP.

28. Warren Map; McElfresh Map.

29. *OR* 27 (1):307; Todd, *Ninth Regiment*, 270; Wehrum, "Iverson's Brigade"; Nicholson, *Pennsylvania*, 1:477, 487; Grant, "First Army Corps," 49; Lash, "Bax-

ter's Brigade," 14; quotes from Vautier, "At Gettysburg: The Eighty-eighth Pennsylvania in the Battle."

30. NYMC, *Final Report*, 1:374, 378; *OR* 27 (2):397. The use of Remington rifles is from NYMC, *Final Report*, 1:378.

Blackford's right was described by the New Yorkers as having "stretched along the lane at the foot of Oak Hill to the apple orchard, at or near Hagy's Farm, close to the Mummasburg Road on our left, and some of them in a skirmish line in the wheat or rye fields . . . in our front." See NYMC, *Final Report*, 1:378.

31. *OR* 27 (1):754. Dilger's fame as an artilleryman cannot rest on his nebulous Gettysburg report. He claimed that this action took place between the Baltimore and Taneytown roads rather than between the Mummasburg and Carlisle roads.

32. *OR* 27 (2):603; T. H. Carter to D. H. Hill, 1 July 1885, Lee Family Papers, VHS. Carter was Thomas Henry Carter.

33. *OR* 27 (2):592–93, 603; NYMC, *Final Report*, 1:374, 375, 379. Fischer, "First Day's Work," mentions seeing the 45th and 157th New York regiments aiding in the repulse of Rebels attacking the Union position in the oak grove.

34. NYMC, *Final Report*, 1:380.

35. W. Clark, *Histories*, 1:634.

36. Montgomery, *Days of Old*, 26; Robbins Journal, 12 Sept. 1897, GNMP. William M. Robbins, the battlefield commissioner, escorted Montgomery and his wife to Iverson's position. He identified Montgomery as a justice on the North Carolina Supreme Court. Robbins noted that the 12th was on the right of the brigade and did not suffer like the others because "its line was slightly refused and partly sheltered by the knoll there; so that the flank fire of Cutler's brigade on the right did not strike this Regiment, which was also too remote to be much hurt by the Union fire on the left flank of the brigade which almost destroyed Iverson's 5th, 20th, & 23rd Reg'ts."

37. Blacknall, "Memoirs of Charles C. Blacknall," 31, Blacknall Papers, NCDAH; W. Clark, *Histories*, 1:635, 2:235. Blacknall stated that E. A. Fuller was shot as he climbed "a mortised rail fence running east and west."

38. *OR* 27 (1):289, 307; Robinson, "First Corps"; Todd, *Ninth Regiment*, 270.

39. Warren Map; I. Hall, *Ninety-seventh Regiment*, 136–37; Cooksey, "They Died," 95.

40. I. Hall, "Iverson's Brigade," 26 June 1884 and 10 Sept. 1885, and *Ninety-seventh Regiment*, 136–37; Todd, *Ninth Regiment*, 270; NYMC, *Final Report*, 2:678.

41. Vautier, *Eighty-eighth*, 106; W. Clark, *Histories*, 2:235; *OR* 27 (2):553.

42. I. Hall, *Ninety-seventh Regiment*, 137.

43. Todd, *Ninth Regiment*, 270; Vautier, *Eighty-eighth*, 106; Grant, "First Army Corps," 261; NYMC, *Final Report*, 2:678; Hanna, "Day."

44. Hanna, "Day"; Todd, *Ninth Regiment*, 270; W. Clark, *Histories*, 1:635. Colonel Moesch was killed in the Wilderness on 6 May 1864. His grave is near the gate of Fredericksburg National Cemetery.

45. Blacknall, "Memoirs of Charles C. Blacknall," 22, Blacknall Papers, NCDAH; Coghill to Pappy et al., 9, 31 July 1863, Coghill Letters, SHC; W. Clark, *Histories*, 2:236.

46. Blacknall, "Memoirs of Charles C. Blacknall," 22, Blacknall Papers, NCDAH; W. Clark, *Histories*, 2:236; Vautier, *Eighty-eighth*, 106–7.

47. Boone, "Personal Experiences," 22, MWC, USAMHI; Boone, "Captured at Gettysburg."

48. Blacknall, "Memoirs of Charles C. Blacknall," 22, Blacknall Papers, NCDAH; Montgomery, *Days of Old*, 26.

49. Robbins Journal, 12 Sept. 1897, GNMP; *OR* 27 (2):580; W. Clark, *Histories*, 1:637.

50. Wehrum, "Iverson's Brigade"; Grant, "First Army Corps," 262.

51. I. Hall, *Ninety-seventh Regiment*, 138, and "Iverson's Brigade," 26 June 1884.

52. George Kimball, "Iverson's Brigade"; Wehrum, "Iverson's Brigade." I cannot identify the troops said by Wehrum to have been shifted toward the Union left.

53. I. Hall, "Iverson's Brigade," 10 Sept. 1885; Wehrum, "Gettysburg."

54. George Kimball, "Iverson's Brigade"; Boone, "Captured at Gettysburg"; Boone, "Personal Experiences," 22, MWC, USAMHI; Grant, "First Army Corps," 262; I. Hall, "Iverson's Brigade," 26 June 1884; W. Clark, *Histories*, 2:236–37.

55. *OR* 27 (1):289, 307, 310, (2):342, 579; I. Hall, *Ninety-seventh*, 136; W. Clark, *Histories*, 1:636.

56. Grant, "First Army Corps," 263. Grant wrote that the officer killed was a captain. However, only lieutenants were killed.

57. Beyer and Keydel, *Deeds of Valor*, 221; Medal of Honor, Edward L. Gilligan File, R&P, 325-121, NA.

58. J. F. Coghill to Pappy et al., 9, 10 July 1863, and to sister, 31 July 1863, Coghill Letters, SHC; Boone, "Personal Experiences," 22–23, MWC, USAMHI. Among those hit by the Confederate fire was Pvt. Rial Stewart of the 23d North Carolina, Coghill's friend.

59. J. F. Coghill to Pappy et al., 10 July 1863, and to sister, 31 July 1863, Coghill Letters, SHC.

60. W. Clark, *Histories*, 1:637–38; *OR* 27 (2):554, 558; *Sketch of the Life*, 10–13.

61. W. Clark, *Histories*, 2:235; Blacknall, "Memoirs of Charles C. Blacknall," 31, 32, Blacknall Papers, NCDAH; Hufham, "Gettysburg," 454; Krick, "Three Confederate Disasters," 132; Patterson, "Death of Iverson's Brigade," 15.

62. Blacknall, "Memoirs of Charles C. Blacknall," 34, Blacknall Papers, NCDAH; Patterson, "Death of Iverson's Brigade," 17. Blacknall stated that Christie was at the P. W. B. Hankey house on the Mummasburg Road.

63. *OR* 27 (2):579–80.

64. Ibid., 444–45, 553–54, 559.

65. W. Clark, *Histories*, 2:235.

CHAPTER 14

1. Wakelyn, *Biographical Dictionary*, 158; Boatner, *Dictionary*, 222; W. Clark, *Histories*, 2:255, 525; 3:5; 4:514; Kenan, *Sketch of the Forty-third Regiment*, 8.

2. *OR* 27 (2):566.

3. W. Clark, *Histories*, 2:255; J. Bennett, "Junius Daniel." Capt. William M. Hammond was the adjutant of Daniel's brigade.

4. *OR* 27 (2):566, 571, 574, 578, 595; Battle, "Third Alabama Regiment," 80, VHS.

5. *OR* 27 (2):566; H. W. Pfanz, *Second Day*, 175.

6. *OR* 27 (2):566, 579; Bates, *Pennsylvania Volunteers*, 2:896; Hartwig, "11th Army Corps," 37. It is not clear if the force threatening Iverson's right was Cutler's brigade or Stone's.

7. OR 27 (2):554, 566–67.

8. Robinson's life is discussed in NYMC, *In Memoriam: Abner Doubleday*. New York memorialized Robinson and its other division commanders as standing figures. Corps commanders are on horseback.

9. *OR* 27 (1):289, 292, 307, 311; Todd, *Ninth Regiment*, 271; Nicholson, *Pennsylvania*, 1:342; Hofmann, "Fifty-sixth Regiment."

10. I. Hall, *Ninety-seventh Regiment*, 139, 141; *OR* 27 (1):310.

11. Beyer and Keydel, *Deeds of Valor*, 221; Sellers to unknown, 9 July 1863, GNMP; Sellers to Ainsworth, 13 Sept. 1895, Medal of Honor File, 2791-VS-1879, NA. The Confederates were probably from O'Neal's brigade.

Sellers's action was not mentioned in the regiment's report or in his address at the dedication of the regiment's memorial. It seems likely that he actively sought the Medal of Honor award. In Beyer and Keydel, *Deeds of Valor*, it was stated that his action saved the Eleventh Corps from "annihilation." This seems preposterous.

12. Boatner, *Dictionary*, 24.

13. *OR* 27 (1):295, 299; Small, *Road to Richmond*, 99; MGC, *Maine at Gettysburg*, 41; A. W. Stratton, "What Became of the Flag?"; Root, letter to editors.

14. NYMC, *Final Report*, 2:756.

15. Thirteenth Massachusetts Regiment, *Circular 15*, 16–17, BrC, USAMHI; W. S. Kimball, "13th Massachusetts."

16. NYMC, *Final Report*, 2:756; "Brigadier General Gabriel R. Paul"; Root, letter to editors. Colonel Root was captured. His captors belonged to the 33d North Carolina Regiment, some of whom his brigade had captured at Fredericksburg the previous December. They treated him like an honored guest and took him to see A. P. Hill, who gave him supper. Hill gave Root permission to use captured men from the 94th to gather Union wounded from the field and take care of them. When the Confederates departed Gettysburg, Root was left behind on parole. While assisting the wounded, Root met a Confederate officer whom he had known in school in Buffalo.

17. *OR* 27 (1):295, 297, 299, 301; Nicholson, *Pennsylvania*, 1:560; Thirteenth Massachusetts Regiment, *Circular 15*, 17, BrC, USAMHI; C. E. Davis, *Thirteenth Massachusetts*, 227; Stearns, *Three Years*, 179; NYMC, *Final Report*, 2:756.

18. A. P. Smith, *Seventy-sixth*, 240; Nicholson, *Pennsylvania*, 1:342; "Recollections of Henry Lyman," in Snyder, *Oswego County*, 62; Lyman, "Data Concerning 147th N.Y.V.," BP 1:331; Tevis, *Fighting Fourteenth*, 85, 135. I have not identified the officer who is said to have lost a hand. Perhaps this was hearsay.

19. *OR* 27 (1):307; Vautier, *Eighty-eighth*, 108; Locke, *Story of the Regiment*, 230; Todd, *Ninth Regiment*, 271; Robert S. Coburn Diary, 1 July 1863, *Civil War Times Illustrated* Collection, USAMHI; Dawes, *Service with the Sixth*, 175; J. Stewart, "Battery B," 186.

20. *OR* 27 (2):554, 566.

21. Ibid., 566, 595; Battle, "Third Alabama Regiment," 90, VHS.

22. *OR* 27 (2):576.

23. Ibid., 587, 593, 595, 601.

24. NYMC, *Final Report*, 2:756–57.

25. Stearns, *Three Years*, 179–80; C. E. Davis, *Thirteenth Massachusetts*, 227; W. H. Freeman, *Letters*, 79; Thirteenth Massachusetts Regiment, *Circular 15*, 17, BrC, USAMHI. If the men captured were from North Carolina, they must have been from Ramseur's brigade. Yet its casualties do not suggest such a loss.

26. Nicholson, *Pennsylvania*, 1:560–61.

27. Small, *Road to Richmond*, 200, and *Sixteenth Maine*, 119; Battle, "Third Alabama Regiment," 81.

28. Sifakis, *Who Was Who*, 529; Boatner, *Dictionary*, 677; Ledford, *Reminiscences*, 78.

29. *OR* 27 (2):587; May, "Reminiscences," 285, GDAH; "Battle of Gettysburg," in Pierce's Memorandum Account Book, Gorman Papers, NCDAH; Harris to Burton, 14 Aug. 1863, in M. W. Taylor, "Ramseur's Brigade," 31.

30. *OR* 27 (2):554, 587, 589; W. Clark, *Histories*, 2:237; John J. McLendon, "Reminiscences," bk. 3, p. 285, Smith Papers, DU; Blacknall, "Memoirs of Charles C. Blacknall," 33, Blacknall Papers, NCDAH; W. A. Smith, *Anson Guards*, 206. Several of the above sources mention Lieutenant Crowder's warning and some include a Lieutenant "Dugger" as well. I have not yet located a Lieutenant Dugger and assume that he was identified incorrectly.

31. *OR* 27 (1):290, 295; Small, *Sixteenth Maine*, 118, and *Road to Richmond*, 101; MGC, *Maine at Gettysburg*, 42–43.

32. Small, *Sixteenth Maine*, 118, and *Road to Richmond*, 101; MGC, *Maine at Gettysburg*, 43.

33. R. T. Bennett to Judge Phillips, 28 May 1891, Bennett Papers, NCDAH.

34. May, "Reminiscences," 285, GDAH; Phillips to Schenck, 27 Oct. 1891, and Parker to Phillips, 29 May 1891, typescript, Ramseur Collection, NCDAH; R. T. Bennett to Judge Phillips, 28 May 1891, Bennett Papers, NCDAH; Betts, *Experiences*, 40–41; Harris to Burton, 24 Aug. 1863, in M. W. Taylor, "Ramseur's Brigade," 34; Gallagher, *Ramseur*, 72.

35. *OR* 27 (2):589–90; Fischer, "First Day's Work"; NYMC, *Final Report*, 1:379.

36. *OR* 27 (1):295; MGC, *Maine at Gettysburg*, 43–44; A. W. Stratton, "What Became of the Flag?," 96; Small, *Road to Richmond*, 102, 239. Lt. Frederick Beecher was one of the officers who escaped that day and was wounded later on 2 July. After the war he entered the Regular Army and served with the 3d Infantry Regiment. He was killed in September 1868 by the Cheyenne Indians at the Battle of Beecher's Island, in the Arikara Fork of the Republican River in Colorado.

1. Raus, *Generation*, 136, 138, 139. The 13th Reserves, the original Bucktails, was also designated the 42d Pennsylvania Regiment and was called the 1st Rifles. It served at Gettysburg with the First Brigade, First Division, Fifth Corps, and fought north of Devil's Den on 2 July.

2. *OR* 27 (1):329, 341, 349–50; Bassler, "Color Episode," *SHSP*, 267; Matthews, *149th Pennsylvania*, 80–81. Matthews states that the 149th occupied a sunken farm lane rather than a ditch.

3. *OR* 27 (1):329, 545; Bassler, "Color Episode," *SHSP*, 268–69.

4. *OR* 27 (1):329; Bassler, "Color Episode," *SHSP*, 268–69; Spayd, "Colors of the 149th"; Bassler to Bachelder, 17 Dec. 1881, *BP*, 2:762, 765. The color guard's story is peripheral to the regiment's subsequent movements and is told in Appendix B.

5. *OR* 27 (2):566, (1):342; F. B. Jones, "Excerpt," 3, GNMP.

6. Matthews, *149th Pennsylvania*, 83.

7. *OR* 27 (1):330, 341, 342; Hubler, "Just a Plain Unvarnished Story."

8. *OR* 27 (2):566–67, 574, 578; W. Clark, *Histories*, 2:255; Green, *Recollections*, 175.

9. *OR* 27 (1):342; Gearhart, "In the Years of '62–'65," GNMP; F. B. Jones "Excerpt," 6, GNMP.

10. Avery Harris Papers, 87, BrC, USAMHI.

11. *OR* 27 (1):330; Bassler, "Color Episode," *SHSP*, 284–85.

12. *OR* 27 (2):566–67, 571–72, 573, 574. Stewart made no report for his battery, and his and Wainwright's writings say nothing of the battery's firing at Daniel's men. I infer it doing so from Confederate sources.

Brabble was in Harvard's class of 1857.

13. *OR* 27 (1):330; F. B. Jones, "Excerpt," 5, GNMP.

14. *OR* 27 (1):342, (2):572; F. B. Jones, "Excerpt," 5, GNMP. Captain Jones wrote that the slaughter took place while the 149th was at the pike and before it went to the cut. Since this does not comport with both Dwight's and Stone's reports, I have used it in that context.

15. *OR* 27 (1):335.

16. *OR* 27 (2):675; F. B. Jones, "Excerpt," 6, GNMP; Fleet, "Fredericksburg Artillery," 241; Avery Harris Papers, 87, BrC, USAMHI. In 1910 Colonel McIntosh looked west along the west cut from the bridge over the center cut and observed that to rake it, guns must have crossed to the north of the pike. See McIntosh, "Ride on Horseback," n.p., VHS. Marye's battery of Pegram's battalion probably enfiladed the cut.

17. *OR* 27 (1):342–45; F. B. Jones, "Excerpt," 6, GNMP; Bassler to Bachelder, Feb. 1882, *BP*, 2:830.

18. *OR* 27 (1):342; Avery Harris Papers, 88, BrC, USAMHI; Bassler, "Color Episode," *SHSP*, 286, 288.

19. *OR* 27 (2):567, 572, 573. In the broad sense, Daniel's brigade made three attacks, and this was the second. Probably the distinction was not so clear on the field.

20. *OR* 27 (2):567, (1):330, 335, 343; Avery Harris Papers, 88, BrC, USAMHI.

21. Green, *Recollections*, 176; W. Clark, *Histories*, 2:175.

22. Hubler, "Just a Plain Unvarnished Story."

23. Kensill to Bachelder, 14 Feb. 1882, *BP*, 2:833; Chamberlin, *One Hundred and Fiftieth*, 117.

24. *OR* 27 (1):332–33; Chamberlin, *One Hundred and Fiftieth*, 117; Chamberlin to Bachelder, 8 June 1889, *BP*, 3:1593.

25. *OR* 27 (2):566, 572, (1):333, 335; Chamberlin, *One Hundred and Fiftieth*, 117–19.

26. *OR* 27 (1):332, 343; Bassler to Bachelder, Feb. 1882, *BP*, 2:830.

27. *OR* 27 (2):568, 570, 573, 574, 578; Malon to Ousby, 28 July 1863, Ousby Papers, NCDAH.

28. *OR* 27 (2):567, 572, 575; W. Clark, *Histories*, 2:256. Daniel reported a battery near the McPherson barn. There should have been no battery there unless it was Wilber's section, which was there only momentarily.

29. *OR* 27 (2):567.

30. Chamberlin, *One Hundred and Fiftieth*, 119–20; Ramsey to Bachelder, 16 Apr. 1883, *BP*, 2:948–49. Chamberlin wrote that the 150th Pennsylvania charged the 32d North Carolina "just prior to the advance of Heth's division from the west." See Chamberlin to Bachelder, 1 June 1889, *BP*, 3:1593.

31. *OR* 27 (1):282, 286, 292, 307; A. P. Smith, *Seventy-sixth*, 240; Dawes to Bachelder, 18 Mar. 1868, and Kellogg to Bachelder, 1 Nov. 1885, *BP*, 1:326, 206; J. Stewart, "Battery B," 370.

32. W. Clark, *Histories*, 2:637–38. After the war Davis became a Methodist minister. See Krick, *Lee's Colonel*, 101.

33. *OR* 27 (2):570, 573, 575, 576, 578; Small, *Road to Richmond*, 239.

34. *OR* 27 (2):572.

35. *OR* 27 (1):341, 346, 362; Nicholson, *Pennsylvania*, 2:751. Huidekoper remained with the 150th until he was too weak to do so. His arm was amputated at Gettysburg; later he received the Medal of Honor.

36. Nicholson, *Pennsylvania*, 2:750; Chamberlin, *One Hundred and Fiftieth*, 120; "Memorandum of Lt. Col. Huidekoper," in *GP*, 2:951–52.

37. *OR* 27 (1):336, 338, 343; Ramsey to Bachelder, 16 Apr. 1883, *BP*, 2:949; Nicholson, *Pennsylvania*, 2:752; —— to Gamble, 15 Mar. 1906, BR, USAMHI.

38. *OR* 27 (1):336, 358; Ashurst, *First Day's Fight at Gettysburg*, 16; Nicholson, *Pennsylvania*, 2:752; Chamberlin, *One Hundred and Fiftieth*, 124; Hubler, "Just a Plain Unvarnished Story."

39. *OR* 27 (1):336, 338; Musser to ——, 15 Sept. 1863, and to Ribu, 10 Dec. 1863, Musser Papers, USAMHI; Ramsey to Bachelder, 16 Apr. 1883, *BP*, 2:949.

40. Nicholson, *Pennsylvania*, 2:696 (includes Fremantle quotation); Chamberlin, *One Hundred and Fiftieth*, 122–23.

41. Avery Harris Papers, 90, BrC, USAMHI; "Deductions and Conclusions," in Ramsey to Bassler, 3 Aug. 1906, BR, USAMHI.

42. *OR* 27 (1):337–38; Busey and Martin, *Regimental Strengths*, 24.

43. *OR* 27 (2):567; J. Bennett, Junius Daniel."

1. *DAB*, 8:470; C. Howard to mother, "Before Gettysburg," n.d., Howard Papers, BC; H. W. Pfanz, *Culp's Hill*, 26–28; Bigelow, *Chancellorsville*, 478.

2. *OR* 27 (1):727; Schurz, *Reminiscences*, 3:4–5; Hartwig, "11th Army Corps," 33; H. W. Pfanz, *Culp's Hill*, 24.

3. *OR* 27 (1):702, 707, (3):463; Schurz, *Reminiscences*, 3:6.

4. *OR* 27 (1):702, 728; Fischer, "First Day's Work."

5. *OR* 27 (1):727, 734.

6. Lonn, *Foreigners*, 196–97; Raphelson, "Unheroic General," 26.

7. *OR* 27 (1):735; NYMC, *Final Report*, 1:15, 374, 375, 378.

8. *OR* 27 (1):727, 734, 738; Raus, *Generation*, map 4; P. P. Browne to Bachelder, 4 Apr. 1864, *BP*, 1:136. Browne located his position by reference to a map. Perhaps it is that shown for the 157th on the 1 July Bachelder map. The positions shown for some other units on this map are obviously incorrect. P. P. Browne's name is spelled "Brown" in the *Official Records*, and I shall spell it so in the text.

9. *OR* 27 (1):754.

10. Ibid., 742, 744, 745, 746; Dodge Journal, 2 July, 2:00 P.M., LC; Company Officer, "Reminiscences," 55; Pula, *Sigel Regiment*, 161–62.

11. *OR* 27 (2):553, 581, 597; NYMC, *Final Report*, 1:378; Purifoy, "Battle of Gettysburg," 23, 138; "Jeff Davis Artillery," 48–49, ADAH; McIlhenny, "Cobean History," n.p., ACHS. Capt. William Reese had been a dentist in Montgomery, Alabama. After the war he moved to Galveston, Texas.

Doles's brigade had a provisional sharpshooter unit also, but I have found nothing that tells of its use at Gettysburg. Capt. Shepherd G. Pryor commanded Doles's sharpshooters at Gettysburg. He and three other officers are mentioned in Doles's report. See *OR* 27 (2):582–83 and S. G. Pryor to Penelope, 16 July 1863, Pryor Collection, UGL.

12. Applegate, *Arrowsmith*, 212; *OR* 27 (1):734.

13. *OR* 27 (1):754, (2):458, 603. Confederate reports say nothing of damage to carriages but state that one limber was damaged. See *OR* 27 (2):458.

Lieutenant Fischer of Schurz's pioneer detachment stated that he saw Dilger blow up two or three caissons and disable one or two guns. See Fischer, "First Day's Work."

14. *OR* 27 (1):753, 754; W. Wheeler, *In Memoriam*, 409.

15. W. Wheeler, *In Memoriam*, 409. In his report, *OR* 27 (1):754, Dilger stated that he advanced Weidman's section about "600 yards on our right, on the Baltimore and Harrisburg road, and returned from there the other four pieces of my battery on the left, under protection of Lieutenant Wheeler's fire, about 400 yards." Weidman's position is marked southeast of the intersection of the Carlisle Road and Howard Avenue.

16. NYMC, *In Memoriam: Francis Channing Barlow*, 60–62, and *Final Report*, 3:1353–54; Boatner, *Dictionary*, 44; Schurz, *Reminiscences*, 3:8. Howard, Schurz, Barlow, and Ames each advanced to general officer rank with minimal command experience. We cannot know if this lack of experience had an effect on the performance of the corps.

17. Barlow to mother and brother, 8 May 1863; to Richard, 26 June 1863; to mother, 7 July 1863; to Bob, 12 Aug. 1863, Barlow Papers, MHS.

18. *OR* 27 (1):727–28; Schurz, *Reminiscences*, 3:7, 9.

19. H. W. Pfanz, *Culp's Hill*, 245–46; Sifakis, *Who Was Who*, 8; Boatner, *Dictionary*, 11–12; NYMC, *In Memoriam: Francis Channing Barlow*, 60–66, 135–36; Becker and Thomas, *Hearth and Knapsack*, 147.

20. H. W. Pfanz, *Culp's Hill*, 245–46; Lonn, *Foreigners*, 217; O. O. Howard, *Autobiography*, 1:349; Schurz, *Reminiscences*, 3:10; Bigelow, *Chancellorsville*, 288. After Gettysburg, von Gilsa and his brigade were transferred with the division to the Carolinas, and he returned to the command of the 41st New York Regiment. He was mustered out with it in June 1864. Although he had commanded a brigade in two major battles, he did not receive a brevet.

Captain Baron von Fritsch wrote that von Gilsa had been relieved from command shortly before the battle for allowing more than one man at a time to leave the ranks for water. See Butts, *Gallant Captain*, 62. His relief might also have been because at Middletown he had received conflicting orders from Howard and Barlow and elected to obey Howard. See H. W. Pfanz, *Culp's Hill*, n. 34, 413.

21. *OR* 27 (1):727–28; O. O. Howard, *Autobiography*, 3:414; Browne to Bachelder, 8 Apr. 1864, *BP*, 1:148; W. H. Warren, "Seventeenth Connecticut," 57, BPL. The area traversed by Barlow's division is covered by streets and houses in the north end of the town, particularly by East Broadway and East Lincoln Avenue. The Crawford house, which then was surrounded by farmland, is in the northwest corner of the intersection of Lincoln Avenue with the Harrisburg Road.

22. Paynton, "From Virginia," in W. H. Warren, "Seventeenth Connecticut," 126–27, BPL; Schurz, *Reminiscences*, 3:8.

23. Warren Diary, 1 July 1863, YU; W. H. Warren, "Seventeenth Connecticut," 56–57, BPL; Hamblen, *Connecticut Yankees*, 18.

CHAPTER 17

1. *OR* 27 (2):444, 468; J. W. Daniel, "Account," 1, VHS. This has been cited elsewhere as "Memoirs of Gettysburg."

The road connecting the Harrisburg road with Mummasburg is now named Schriver's Corner Road. Early's division would have bivouacked on the Heidlersburg–East Berlin Road (Rte. 234) west of the Carlisle Pike (Rte. 94).

2. J. W. Daniel, "Account," 1, VHS; C. Brown, "Personal Narrative," Hunt Papers, LC; C. Brown, "Memoir," n.p., Brown and Ewell Papers, TSL; *OR* 27 (2):479. Ewell made it a custom to send duplicate messages with two couriers during battles in the hope that at least one would arrive. The practice had its origin at First Bull Run, where he did not receive a dispatch sent to him by Beauregard because the single courier did not reach him.

3. J. A. Early, *War Memoirs*, 267; E. M. Daniel, *Speeches*, 80; J. W. Daniel, "Account," 2, VHS; Early to Bachelder, 23 Mar. 1876, *BP*, 1:459; Garber to Daniel, 13 Feb. 1909, Daniel File, GNMP.

4. *OR* 27 (2):469, 479, 484, 489, 495, 497; Early to Bachelder, 23 Mar. 1871, *BP*,

1:459–60; W. Clark, *Histories*, 3:413; R. J. Hancock to Daniel, 27 Jan. 1904, Daniel Papers, UV; R. J. Hancock, "William Singleton," 499; Gannon, "6th Louisiana," 89. Gordon's 26th Georgia was detached to support artillery, leaving five regiments in line.

The Jacob Kime family lived at the Bringman farm. See Hofe, *That There Be No Stain*, 12–13.

Garber's battery had four Napoleons; Tanner's, four three-inch Ordnance rifles; and Green's, two three-inch Ordnance rifles and two ten-pounder Parrotts.

The road guarded by Smith is the Shealer Road today.

The identity of the battery that fired the round that hit the road near the 9th Louisiana is unknown. Likely it was from either Wilkeson or Dilger.

5. *OR* 27 (2):468; J. W. Daniel, "Account," 2–3, VHS; J. W. Daniel, "Commentary on John B. Gordon's *Reminiscences*," 1, Daniel Papers, UV.

The mention of glistening bayonets was probably only poetry. Why would the Federals have fixed bayonets?

6. *OR* 27 (2):495, 497, 498, (1):752, 754, 756; Applegate, *Arrowsmith*, 211. Lt. Col. Hilary P. Jones reported that while in this position three guns were disabled because their own shots stuck in their bores—an indication that the Confederates had faulty ammunition—and a Napoleon was disabled when it was hit in the muzzle by a solid shot. J. W. Daniel, in his "Commentary on John B. Gordon's *Reminiscences*" (Daniel Papers, UV), stated that he and Early were nearby when one of the enemy's first shots hit the gun's muzzle. It might be assumed that the reputation of Dilger's battery was responsible for the belief that it did this. Yet its closest guns were a mile away. See also Carrington, "First Day," 330.

7. *OR* 27 (1):717.

8. Ibid., 727.

9. Barlow to mother, 7 July 1863, Barlow Papers, MHS; NYMC, *In Memoriam: Francis Channing Barlow*, 29; Schurz, *Reminiscences*, 3:9. Col. Lewis R. Stegman was a member of the NYMC. He was a captain in the 102d New York Regiment, Twelfth Corps, at Gettysburg. After his colonel was wounded on 2 July, he commanded the regiment.

The assumption that Barlow must have considered the knoll a place from which to attack Doles is mine. But see NYMC, *In Memoriam: Francis Channing Barlow*, 29.

10. Raus, *Generation*, 62, 68, 140.

11. Kiefer, *One Hundred and Fifty-third*, 180, 210; Simmers and Bachschmid, *Volunteers' Manual*, 29; Miller to Bachelder, 2 Mar. 1884, *BP*, 2:1025. The 153d was not mustered out until 24 July 1863.

12. Miller to Bachelder, 2 Mar. 1884, 2 Mar. 1886, *BP*, 2:1025, 1211. The term "division," as used by Miller, referred to two companies.

13. Kiefer, *One Hundred and Fifty-third*, 140, 210–11; Miller to Bachelder, 2 Mar. 1886, *BP*, 2:211. I do not know what Miller meant by "swing of the fuse." Perhaps a burning fuse gave off a trail of sparks that brushed his face.

14. *OR* 27 (1):748, 756, 757; War Department Tablet, Battery G, 4th Artillery, on Barlow Knoll. Lt. Eugene A. Bancroft wrote that Merkle's section was on the south side of the York (Harrisburg) Road near the "poor-house," while the other

sections were north of the road and eastward of the almshouse. In his report Merkle wrote that Wilkeson sent his section to a position three-quarters of a mile northwest of the almshouse. Both reports must have been written without reference to a map.

It was said that Wilkeson was the youngest battery commander in the Army of the Potomac.

15. *OR* 27 (1):719; NYMC, *In Memoriam: Francis Channing Barlow*, 29.

16. Warren Diary, 1 July 1863, YU; W. H. Warren, "Seventeenth Connecticut," 57, BPL; Peck, "First Day," and Paynton, "From Virginia," in W. H. Warren, "Seventeenth Connecticut," 95, 128, BPL; Culp, *25th Ohio*, 77.

17. Harris to Bachelder, 14 Mar. 1881, and M. Browne to Bachelder, 8 Apr. 1869, *BP*, 2:743, 1:148.

18. Waud sketch, "Lieutenant Bayard Wilkeson," *B&L*, 3:289; Raus, *Generation*, 165. Wilkeson was said to have cut the lower portion of his leg from the stump. He was brevetted a lieutenant colonel posthumously. There is a drawing of Wilkeson and his battery in *B&L* 3:288 and a watercolor of the same in C. Clark, *Gettysburg*, 58.

19. Warren Diary, 1 July 1863, YU; W. H. Warren, "Seventeenth Connecticut," 58, BPL; Hamblen, *Connecticut Yankees*, 19; Paynton, "From Virginia," in W. H. Warren, "Seventeenth Connecticut," 127–28, BPL. There was no "twelve-pound Parrott" at Gettysburg, only ten- or twenty-pounders.

20. *OR* 27 (1):727, 728; Schurz, *Reminiscences*, 3:9. Scott Hartwig identified the Hagy house roof as Schurz's observation post, and I believe that he was right. Schurz's headquarters could have been at the Kitsman buildings.

In his report (*OR* 27 [1]:727) Schurz stated that the connection between the First and Third Divisions was west of the Carlisle Road. I believe that he meant east instead.

21. *OR* 27 (1):728; Schurz, *Reminiscences*, 3:9.

22. Lonn, *Foreigners*, 233–34; Sifakis, *Who Was Who*, 368–69; Quaife, *From the Cannon's Mouth*, 206. Krzyzanowski was brevetted a brigadier general in March 1865.

23. Robert Brewster entry, 20 July 1863, in Dodge Journal, LC; Company Officer, "Reminiscences," 54.

24. *OR* 27 (1):742; Company Officer, "Reminiscences," 56.

25. *OR* 27 (1):739–40; Raus, *Generation*, 63, map 1.

26. *OR* 27 (1):739–40; Robinson to Bachelder, 9 Apr. 1888, and Lee to Bachelder, 16 Feb. 1888, *BP*, 3:1526.

CHAPTER 18

1. Stiles, *Four Years*, 211–12; Boatner, *Dictionary*, 348. Gordon, an aggressive and capable brigade commander, seems to have had a penchant for exaggerating and bending the truth for the sake of a good story or to serve his ambitions.

2. *OR* 27 (2):492; J. W. Daniel, "Account," 3, VHS.

3. *OR* 27 (1):717.

4. Von Gilsa probably sent his reserve to the left, since he did not extend his line to the right. Comment on this is made in Miller to Bachelder, 2 Mar. 1884, 2 Mar. 1886, *BP*, 2:1026, 1211.

5. Ibid.; Kiefer, *One Hundred and Fifty-third*, 140–41, 211. Miller wrote that he was told to take his men to the left to support the 41st New York; he apparently meant the 68th.

6. Kiefer, *One Hundred and Fifty-third*, 211–13.

7. Ibid., 213–14.

8. Ibid., 214–15.

9. Ibid., 178, 251–52. Unfortunately von Gilsa and Barlow made no reports, and I did not find accounts by members of the 54th and 68th regiments.

10. *OR* 27 (2):492; G. W. Nichols, *Soldier's Story*, 116; Gordon, *Reminiscences*, 151; *Atlanta Constitutionalist*, 5 Sept. 1863, in Hofe, *That There Be No Stain*, 40.

11. Carrington, "First Day," 328; J. W. Daniel, "First Day."

12. J. C. Early, "Southern Boy's Experiences at Gettysburg," 414, 418. John Early wrote that he was with "Peck's Brigade." There was no brigade with that designation; however, his description suggests Hays's brigade. A William R. Peck was in the 9th Louisiana and became the brigade's commander late in the war.

13. *OR* 27 (2):469, 479, 484; T. B. Reed, *Private in Gray*, 42.

14. *OR* 27 (2):582, 597.

15. Harris to Bachelder, 14 Mar. 1881, *BP*, 2:744; *OR* 27 (2):496, 582, 597.

16. W. H. Warren, "Seventeenth Connecticut," 58, BPL; Warren Letters, 1 July 1863, 85, YU; Harris to Lough, 11 July 1863, A. L. Harris Papers, OHS. I have added punctuation to the Harris quotation.

17. Barlow to mother, 1 July 1863, Barlow Papers, MHS; Marcus, *New Canaan Private*, 41; *OR* 27 (1):715.

18. *OR* 27 (1):715, 717; Harris to Bachelder, 14 Mar. 1881, *BP*, 2:744.

19. Jacob Smith, *Camps and Campaigns*, 92, 225; Peter Young to Bachelder, 12 Aug. 1867, *BP*, 1:311; Culp, *25th Ohio*, 78.

20. Hamblen, *Connecticut Yankees*, 24; Warren Letters, 1 July 1863, 88, YU; Paynton, "From Virginia," Peck, "First Day," and McDaniel Letter, in W. H. Warren, "Seventeenth Connecticut," 58–60, 64, 95, 128, BPL. Chatfield's sword was a straight-blade, silver mounted sword of Revolutionary War vintage. See Peck to Powell, 16 Dec. 1889, Peck letter, ISL.

21. W. H. Warren, "Battle of Gettysburg," 58–60, and Paynton, "From Virginia," 128, in W. H. Warren, "Seventeenth Connecticut," BPL.

22. *OR* 27 (1):183, 719; Hamblen, *Connecticut Yankees*, 31.

23. *OR* 27 (1):712; Barlow to mother, 7 July 1863, Barlow Papers, MHS.

In his "Memoirs" (Brown and Ewell Papers, TSL) Campbell Brown wrote of seeing a knot of horsemen, one carrying a large white flag near Wilkeson's battery. A Rebel shell dispersed the party, killing at least one man who was carried off. The large white flag was probably the flag of the First Division, Eleventh Corps — Barlow's. Soon after, the battery limbered up and left the field. It is natural to believe that the man hit was Barlow, yet Barlow's account suggests otherwise.

"The Barlow-Gordon Incident" has been one of the often told human interest stories of the battle. It originated with Gordon, who related it somewhat as given in the text. He went on to say that many years later, when both were in Washington, the two men met and renewed their acquaintance. The story has been questioned, probably because Barlow did not substantiate it in writing and because Gordon's credibility is often in doubt. I believe it to be essentially true because Barlow must have known of it (the two met on Blocher's Knoll in 1888) and did not refute it. See Gordon, *Reminiscences*, 151–53, and *New York Times*, 4 July 1888.

At this time Barlow's wife was Arabella Griffith. Like wives of some other ranking officers, she stayed near or with the army. She nursed the general after his Antietam wound and apparently cared for him at Gettysburg also. We do not know if Gordon was instrumental in her reaching him. Captain von Fritsch and others mentioned seeing her on Cemetery Hill and passing through the lines to reach the general. Barlow made no mention of her in his Gettysburg letters cited, although one has pages missing. Nor was she mentioned in the talks made at the dedication of the Barlow statue. See Scrymser, *Extracts and Personal Reminiscences*, 5–6; Butts, *Gallant Captain*, 79–80; O. O. Howard, "After the Battle"; Flavius J. Bellamy to Frank, 11 July 1863, Bellamy Papers, IHS.

24. *OR* 27 (1):713; Kiefer, *One Hundred and Fifty-third*, 215.

25. E. M. Daniel, *Speeches*, 81; J. W. Daniel, "Commentary on John B. Gordon's *Reminiscences*," Daniel Papers, UV.

26. *OR* 27 (1):752–53, 754; W. Wheeler, *In Memoriam*, 409–10; G. L. Warren, "Eleventh Corps."

27. *OR* 27 (2):582, 597; Grace, "Rodes's Division," 614. Doles reported that the enemy was behind a rock fence. There are none in this immediate area.

28. Company Officer, "Reminiscences," 56; A. E. Lee to Bachelder, 16 Feb. 1888, *BP*, 3:1525–26.

29. Company Officer, "Reminiscences," 56; G. W. Nichols, *Soldier's Story*, 116; Carrington, "First Day," 330–31.

30. *OR* 27 (1):742; Pula, *For Liberty*, 101; Whitehead, *119th New York*, 9–10.

31. Thomson to Mary, 16 July 1863, Thomson Letters, OHS; Thomson to General, 28 Feb. 1888, *BP*, 3:1529.

32. Pula, *Sigel Regiment*, 163–64, 166–67, 378; Wallber, "From Gettysburg," 354. Sgt. Muenzenberger died in prison in Richmond on 3 December 1863.

33. *OR* 27 (1):745; Pula, *History of a German-Polish Brigade*, 78–91; Schurz, *Reminiscences*, 3:12.

34. Pula, *For Liberty*, 102, and *History of a German-Polish Brigade*, 79.

35. *OR* 27 (1):742, 745; Company Officer, "Reminiscences," 56; Thomson to Bachelder, 28 Feb. 1888, and Lee to Bachelder, 15 Feb. 1888, *BP*, 3:1529, 1526.

36. Dodge Journal, 1 July 1863, and Robert Brewster account in Dodge Journal, 20 July 1863, LC; Whitehead, *119th New York*, 7–8.

37. Company Officer, "Reminiscences," 56–57.

38. Carrington, "First Day," 330–31.

39. Ibid.; Company Officer, "Reminiscences," 57–58.

40. Brown to Bachelder, 4 Apr. 1864, *BP*, 1:137; Thomas, *Doles-Cook Brigade*, 8–9; Grace, "Rodes's Division," 614; Applegate, *Arrowsmith*, 216.

41. *OR* 27 (2):584–85.

42. Grace, "Rodes's Division," 615.

43. *OR* 27 (2):582, 584–85, 586; Richardson to father and mother, 8 July 1863, GDAH.

44. Applegate, *Arrowsmith*, 217.

45. Ibid., 217; Richardson to father and mother, 8 July 1863, GDAH.

46. "Gettysburg Incident."

47. *OR* 27 (1):753, 754; W. Wheeler, *In Memoriam*, 410; G. L. Warren, "Eleventh Corps," 887.

48. *OR* 27 (1):748.

49. Ibid., 735; NYMC, *Final Report*, 1:376, 380.

50. *OR* 27 (2):332, 469; Carrington, "First Day," 332.

CHAPTER 19

1. *OR* 27 (1):721, 728.

2. Ibid.

3. Ibid., 164; Raus, *Generation*, 81, 85, 111, 122; H. W. Pfanz, *Culp's Hill*, 430; Sifakis, *Who Was Who*, 146. Coster resigned his commission in May 1864 to become provost marshal of New York's South District. He died in 1888. See Conklin, "Long March," 56.

4. Hitz, *Letters of Winkler*, 70; McKay, "Three Years," 131; Wellman, letter; Dunkelman, "Hardtack Regiment," 19–20; NYMC, *Final Report*, 2:918. I believe that the brigade followed Baltimore Street to the center of town, possibly to the railroad, and then turned east to Stratton Street. According to the Warren Map the railroad extended to the west end of the town; however, the McElfresh Map shows it only to Carlisle Street. If McElfresh and Sergeant Wellman are correct, the column would not have crossed the railroad on Carlisle Street.

5. *OR* 27 (1):729.

6. Hitz, *Letters of Winkler*, 70–71; Pula, *Sigel Regiment*, 171.

7. Warren Map; McKay, "Three Years," 131; Inscription, 73d Pennsylvania Infantry Regiment Memorial, GNMP, in Raus, *Generation*, 122; Dunkelman, "Hardtack Regiment," 20; Nicholson, *Pennsylvania*, 1:420; Conklin, "Long March," 51; *OR* 27 (1):748, 755.

8. Dunkelman, "Hardtack Regiment," 20; McKay, "Three Years," 131; Warren Map; McElfresh Map. The Kuhn house is at 221 North Stratton Street. The area occupied by the left of Coster's line is now covered with buildings.

9. Dunkelman, "Hardtack Regiment," 20–21; McKay, "Three Years," 130; NYMC, *Final Report*, 2:130, 3:1051; Bates, *Pennsylvania Volunteers*, 1:390.

10. McKay, "Three Years," 131; *OR* 27 (2):484.

11. NYMC, *Final Report*, 3:1051, 1055; Alanson Crosby to Sam. Glover, 28 Feb. 1864, *Jamestown Journal*, 18 Mar. 1864; Allen Report, July 1863, CAT. Edwin Northrup was an eccentric who did not serve in the 154th; yet he attempted to write a history of the regiment, and apparently material collected by him was used by the NYMC. See Dunkelman to Pfanz, 23 Aug. 1999.

12. "Col. Jackson"; Sheldon, "Our Boys at Gettysburg."

13. *OR* 27 (2):479; Hitz, *Letters of Winkler*, 71. Fred Winkler became major of the 26th Wisconsin on 17 November 1863 and commanded the regiment in Georgia and the Carolinas. He received brevet ranks to colonel and brigadier general.

14. *OR* 27 (1):230, 748, (2):479; A. T. Lee to Bachelder, 16 Feb. 1888, *BP*, 3:1527; Taylor to father, 9 July 1863; T. L. Jones, *Seymour*, 71. After this fight Heckman's battery was deemed too unserviceable for further fighting, though it had one section of guns available. See *OR* 27 (1):748.

15. Allen Report, July 1863, CAT; NYMC, *Final Report*, 3:1051; Taylor to father, 9 July 1863.

16. Allen Report, July 1863, CAT; NYMC, *Final Report*, 3:1053; Dunkelman, "Hardtack Regiment," 21; Bates, *Pennsylvania Volunteers*, 5:391; "Col. Jackson."

17. Dunkelman, "Hardtack Regiment," 23; McKay, "Three Years," 121.

18. Crosby to Glover; NYMC, *Final Report*, 3:1055. The 270 figure is based on that shown on the regiment's memorial, which is 274.

19. *OR* 27 (1):721, 183; Bates, *Pennsylvania Volunteers*, 1:391. Vogelbach survived the war and in the *National Tribune*, 10 Oct. 1888, wrote a letter in praise of von Steinwehr.

20. *OR* 27 (1):183; "Col. Jackson."

21. *Gettysburg Compiler*, 30 Sept. 1902.

22. Dunkelman, "Hardtack Regiment," 22; NYMC, *Final Report*, 3:1155; Crosby to Glover; Clinton Brown, letter to editor; A. J. Kelly, *134th Regiment*, 29; Clinton Brown, letter to editor.

23. Dunkelman, "Hardtack Regiment," 26.

24. *OR* 27 (1):183, 729; Dunkelman, "Hardtack Regiment," 25, 26; Raus, *Generation*, 81, 85, 111. The rounded total of those missing and/or held prisoner is from the Gettysburg memorials of three regiments in the fight.

CHAPTER 20

1. Sheads, "Burning of the Home," GNMP; Amelia Miller account, *Gettysburg Compiler*, 1 July 1915. The Harmon farm buildings had been built by Rev. Charles G. McLean, whose wife was the aunt of Eleanor Junkin, Stonewall Jackson's first wife. Amelia's father was in the Union army. The Harmon's hired man had taken the family's horses away from the farm.

2. *OR* 27 (2):638, 642–43; W. Clark, *Histories*, 2:348, 5:118; Mayo, "Report," 414. See also Chapter 10 above. Archer's brigade probably numbered about 800 men at this time, and portions of it must have been disorganized. See Storch and Storch, " 'What a Deadly Trap,' " 26.

3. Address of Col. John R. Lane, *News and Observer* clipping, 5 July 1903, Lane Papers, SHC; W. Clark, *Histories*, 2:368. Lane made a point to write that neither he nor Burgwyn drank during the war.

4. Address of Col. John R. Lane, *News and Observer* clipping, 5 July 1903, Lane Papers, SHC.

5. *OR* 27 (2):643; W. Clark, *Histories*, 236; Young to Burgwyn, 22 Aug. 1903,

Burgwyn Papers, NCDAH; Beecham, *Gettysburg*, 72. Lt. Louis G. Young stated that the bank had been "cut squarely down" for the mining of marl.

6. *OR* 27 (1):247, 268, 274, 279; Curtis, *Twenty-fourth*, 157, 159; Doubleday, *Chancellorsville*, 130.

7. Dudley, "Report," 133–34; *OR* 27 (1):268, 274; William W. Dudley Report, n.d., *BP*, 2:941; Dudley to Blanchard, 9 Aug. 1877, in Hawkins, "Blanchard," 215; Moore Papers, 2:365, IHS; D. L. Smith, *Twenty-fourth Michigan*, 129; Beecham, *Gettysburg*, 71–72; Gaff, "Here Was Made," 31.

8. Nicholson, *Pennsylvania*, 2:663; Gates, *Ulster Guard*, 433; Cook, *Personal Reminiscences*, 127. Colonel Gates, in a letter to Bachelder, 30 Jan. 1864, *BP*, 1:81–83, stated that Rowley's brigade occupied the following positions on or near McPherson Woods on 1 July:

a. In the swale east of McPherson Ridge.

b. In the Willoughby Run ravine.

c. Reverse slope of McPherson Ridge — the Twentieth was on the crest of the ridge for twenty minutes.

d. In the Hagerstown Road facing north.

e. Brigade in two lines facing north. Marched north and then into position on McPherson Ridge.

f. With 121st Pennsylvania on McPherson Ridge on left of the brigade line supporting Cooper's battery. Fought there.

g. Retreated to seminary grove.

At some point, probably after item e, the 151st Pennsylvania was placed in reserve at the seminary and then, in item f, advanced to the right of the brigade line.

9. *OR* 27 (1):247, 317, 320, 355, 364; Gates, *Ulster Guard*, 433. Doubleday stated that Rowley was in charge of this part of the Union line. Yet Gates stated that Wadsworth had ordered him to send skirmishers to the Harmon buildings. Perhaps Wadsworth, who outranked Rowley, assumed authority over his part of the line.

10. Harrison, "Significance of the Harmon Farm," 4, 6; Sheads, "Burning of the Home," GNMP.

11. *OR* 27 (1):317, 320; Cook, *Personal Reminiscences*, 128.

12. Address of Col. John R. Lane, *Charlotte News and Observer* clipping, 5 July 1903, Lane Papers, SHC.

13. C. Brown, "Personal Narrative," Hunt Papers, LC.

14. *OR* 27 (2):607; Heth, "Letter," 158; Morrison, *Memoirs of Henry Heth*, 173.

15. *OR* 27 (2):317.

16. Address of Col. John R. Lane, *Charlotte News and Observer* clipping, 5 July 1903, Lane Papers, SHC.

17. W. Clark, *Histories*, 2:351, 3:89, 5:119; "Address of Col. John R. Lane," *Charlotte News and Observer* clipping, 5 July 1903, Lane Papers, SHC.

18. *OR* 27 (1):268, 315, 317; "Report of Col. Samuel J. Williams," 16 Nov. 1863, in Gaff, "Here Was Made," 29; Moore Papers, 2:365, IHS; Dudley to Blanchard, 9 Aug. 1887, in Hawkins, "Blanchard," 215.

19. *OR* 27 (2):638; W. Clark, *Histories*, 2:348.

20. *OR* 27 (2):566, 630; W. Clark, *Histories*, 2:348; H. W. Pfanz, *Second Day*, 174.

21. *OR* 27 (2):268; "Report of Col. Samuel J. Williams," 16 Nov. 1863, in Gaff, "Here Was Made," 29; Dudley, "Report," 137; Roswell Root, 24th Michigan, to grandfather, 23 Aug. 1863, Coco Collection, USAMHI; Moore Papers, 2:365, IHS.

22. *OR* 27 (1):346–47; Nicholson, *Pennsylvania*, 2:746, 752; Chamberlin, *One Hundred and Fiftieth*, 112, 115, 120; Report, Major Mark Finnicum to Gov. Salomon, 24 July 1863, in Storch and Storch, "Unpublished Gettysburg Reports," 20; *OR* 27 (1):274; Ashurst, *First Day's Fight at Gettysburg*, 12–13. The quarry holes are in the steep slope of west McPherson Ridge just north of McPherson Woods and on the east side of Willoughby Run. The largest could hold a small house, and there is a smaller one north of it. Neither is shown on the Warren Map, but one is shown on the McElfresh Map of the First Day's battlefield. The largest is mentioned as a place of refuge for some of Archer's men, in Storch and Storch, " 'What a Deadly Trap,' " 25.

23. *OR* 27 (1):315, 317, 320, 323; Gates to Bachelder, 30 Jan. 1864, and McFarland to Bachelder, 12 Aug. 1866, *BP*, 1:82, 271. Although Rowley was acting commander of the Third Division, First Corps, there is no indication that he spent any time on the front of Stone's brigade. Rather, he seems to have remained on the left with his (Biddle's) brigade.

24. *OR* 27 (1):248, 315, 323, 356, 362; Nevins, *Diary*, 235. In his report Colonel Wainwright wrote that Battery L opened on the Confederates, but Lieutenant Breck reported that no fire was opened. Colonel Gates wrote that the battery fired a few rounds. See Bates to Bachelder, 30 Jan. 1864, *BP*, 1:82, and *OR* 27 (1):326.

In his report Wainwright notes Reynolds's guns being under Wilber and Bowers at this time, but no mention is made of Breck, who was in command of the battery.

25. *OR* 27 (1):315, 323; Gates, "Report," 144, and *Ulster Guard*, 440; "Court Martial of Brig. Gen. Thos. Rowley," 11, 12, Dana Papers, WHGS, typescript copy, GNMP.

26. Amelia Miller account, *Gettysburg Compiler*, in Sheads, "Burning of the Home," GNMP. Sheads includes material from the *Adams Sentinel and Advertizer*, 8 Dec. 1863, that states that Amelia attempted to stop the burning of the house by saying that her mother had been a southern woman. One "ruffian" asked her to prove it by hurrahing for the Confederacy.

Capt. Benjamin F. Little stated that the house had been burned by order of Col. James K. Marshall of the 52d to get the sharpshooters out of it. See "Account of Captain Benjamin F. Little, 52d North Carolina," Little Papers, SHC. Snipers in the second story of the house had greatly annoyed the men of the 52d. See W. Clark, *Histories*, 5:236.

27. *OR* 27 (1):320; Gates, *Ulster Guard*, 433–34.

28. Young to Burgwyn, 22 Aug. 1903, Burgwyn Papers, NCDAH; W. Clark, *Histories*, 5:120; interview with John R. Lane, Burgwyn Papers, NCDAH; Address of John R. Lane, *Charlotte News and Observer* clipping, 5 July 1903, Lane Papers, SHC; McConnell, "First and Greatest." This advance took about the same amount of time as Pickett's Charge, which covered 1,300 yards.

29. W. Clark, *Histories*, 2:351, 5:119.

30. Moore Papers, 1:n.p., 2:366, IHS; Dudley, "Report," 133; Williams, "Report," 137; Marsh, "Nineteenth Indiana," 3, ISL.

31. Williams, "Report," 138; Marsh, "Nineteenth Indiana," 4, ISL; Williams to Morton, 30 July 1863, in Gaff, "Here Was Made," 31.

32. Williams, "Report," 138, 140; Moore Papers, 1:n.p., 2:4, IHS; Marsh, "Nineteenth Indiana," 4, ISL; Hawkins, "Blanchard," 215–16.

33. *OR* 27 (1):268; Curtis, *Twenty-fourth*, 160; W. Clark, *Histories*, 2:352; Cureton to Col. J. R. Lane, n.d., Lane Papers, SHC; Young to Burgwyn, 22 Aug. 1903, Burgwyn Papers, NCDAH.

34. Curtis, *Twenty-fourth*, 160; D. L. Smith, *Twenty-fourth Michigan*, 130–31; McConnell to mother, 2 July 1863, *Detroit Advertiser and Sentinel*, 7 July 1863, BrC, USAMHI.

35. Cureton to Col. J. R. Lane, n.d., Lane Papers, SHC.

36. W. Clark, *Histories*, 2:352; G. Wilcox to W. H. S. Burgwyn, 21 June 1900, Burgwyn Papers, NCDAH; Louis G. Young to Major W. J. Bala, 10 Feb. 1864, Grimes Papers, ser. 2, NCDAH; Krick, *Lee's Colonels*, 65; A. K. Davis, *Boy Colonel*, 334–37. Burgwyn was buried in a crude coffin under a tree by an unidentified stone house. Others, including Captain McCreery, were buried nearby.

37. W. Clark, *Histories*, 2:352–53; Cureton to Col. J. R. Lane, n.d., Lane Papers, SHC.

38. Young to Burgwyn, 22 Aug. 1903, Burgwyn Papers, NCDAH; Curtis, *Twenty-fourth*, 160.

39. McConnell, "First and Greatest"; W. Clark, *Histories*, 2:353–54.

40. Mayo, "Report," 415; Nicholson, *Pennsylvania*, 2:750–51; Chamberlin, *One Hundred and Fiftieth*, 122–25.

41. *OR* 27 (1):346; Chamberlin, *One Hundred and Fiftieth*, 120–22; Nicholson, *Pennsylvania*, 751.

42. *OR* 27 (2):638; Col. W. S. Christian to Daniel, 24 Oct. 1903, Daniel Papers, UV.

43. *OR* 27 (1):274, 279; Report, Major Mark Finnicum to Gov. Salomon, 24 July 1863, in Storch and Storch, "Unpublished Gettysburg Reports," 21–22; Report of Lt. Col. John Callis, n.d., *BP*, 1:141.

44. *OR* 27 (1):254; Report of Lt. Col. John Callis, n.d., *BP* 1:141; Boatner, *Dictionary*, 543. Three of Meredith's sons served in the Union army. Two were killed. After the war he farmed in Indiana and was surveyor general of Montana Territory.

45. Markle, "Story of Battle," GNMP.

46. Cornelius Wheeler Speech Draft, n.d., 40, Wheeler Papers, SHSW.

47. Beecham, *Gettysburg*, 76–77.

48. Watrous, "Mule Train Charge"; *OR*, atlas, plate 174.

49. *OR* 27 (2):646; Lindsley, "Battle of Gettysburg," 244; Turney, "First Tennessee," 535. If Heth's division extended beyond the First Corps left, it was because Archer's brigade was included. The right of Pettigrew's brigade should have been approximately opposite Rowley's left.

50. Cook, *Personal Reminiscences*, 128.

51. W. Clark, *Histories*, 3:89–90, 106; Biddle, "Supplemental Account," 151; *OR* 27 (1):323.

52. W. Clark, *Histories*, 3:236–37. Why Colonel Marshall had to form a square against what was likely only the 8th Illinois Cavalry Regiment is difficult to understand. An infantry regiment ought not to have been greatly threatened by a comparable body of cavalry, particularly since there would have been other supporting infantry nearby.

53. *OR* 27 (1):327; McFarland, "Movements of the 151st Penn. Vols.," *BP*, 1:271; McFarland, "Report of the Movements," 300–301.

54. *OR* 27 (1):327; Nicholson, *Pennsylvania*, 2:327.

55. Strong, *121st Regiment*, 46; H. N. Warren, *142d Regiment*, 60; W. Clark, *Histories*, 3:90.

56. *OR* 27 (1):318, 356; Strong, *121st Regiment*, 121; Gates, *Ulster Guard*, 441.

57. *OR* 27 (1):323; Sterling to father, RU; Strong, *121st Regiment*, 46.

58. Cook, *Personal Reminiscences*, 329.

59. Gates, *Ulster Guard*, 442; *OR* 27 (1):321; William Blount to Miss Bettie, 2 Aug. 1863, Steed and Phipps Family Papers, SHC.

60. *OR* 27 (1):327–28; McFarland, "Report of the Movements," 301; Strong, *121st Regiment*, 47–48; Nicholson, *Pennsylvania*, 2:763; McFarland to Editor, *Juniata Tribune*, in Dreese, *Imperishable Fame*, 131–32.

61. *OR* 27 (2):638; Heth, "Letter," 158; Morrison, *Memoirs of Henry Heth*, 174; Robbins Journal, 24 July 1894, GNMP. Robbins wrote that Heth pointed out the site of his wounding. It was a few feet south of Meredith Avenue and about fifty yards east of the 7th Wisconsin's memorial. See Henry Heth, "Marking Battle Sites," in Robbins Journal, 18 Aug. 1894, GNMP.

62. W. Clark, *Histories*, 5:120, 601; "The Pennsylvania Campaign," *Richmond Dispatch*, 17 Mar. 1864; Tuttle, "Unparalleled Loss," 199–203. Figures often vary. In a letter written in June 1877 to Rev. J. William Jones, Heth stated that in twenty-five minutes his division lost 2,700 men. See Heth, "Letter," 158. According to Tuttle one man of his company had been left in the rear to guard packs.

63. *OR* 27 (2):643.

CHAPTER 21

1. *OR* 27 (1):250, 703–4; Doubleday, "Journal," 103; C. Howard, "First Day," 329–30.

2. Doubleday, "Journal," 102–3; Nevins, *Diary*, 235.

3. Warren Map; McElfresh Map, 1 July 1863; T. H. Smith, *Lee's Headquarters*. The Dustman house is gone. The Mary Thompson house is said to have been Lee's headquarters on 2–4 July. However, a marker indicates that the headquarters were in the orchard south of the pike.

4. Warren Map; McElfresh Map, 1 July 1863. The breastworks is mentioned in Small, *Sixteenth Maine*, 116, and *Road to Richmond*, 98, and MGC, *Maine at Gettysburg*, 38, 45.

5. McKelvey, "George Breck's Civil War Letters," 129; Nevins, *Diary*, 255.

6. J. Stewart, "Battery B," 368–69; *OR* 27 (1):356.

7. *OR* 27 (1):356, 364–65; Nicholson, *Pennsylvania*, 2:898. Cooper's battery might have had three pieces here rather than four.

8. *OR* 27 (1):361, 362. The distance between the seminary building and the pike is approximately 330 yards. Ideally, each piece would have occupied 16 yards. If so, fifteen guns in this space would have taken up 240 yards. Therefore, if they were packed in, it seems likely that 90 yards was not usable either because of a lack of space for the pieces or because of a lack of fields of fire, possibly because of the orchard south of the pike. For information on space and intervals see Coggins, *Arms and Equipment*, 71.

9. *OR* 27 (1):356, 363; Shelton Autobiography, NYHS.

10. *OR* 27 (1):274, 336, 343; Avery Harris Papers, 89, BrC, USAMHI; Hubler, "Just a Plain Unvarnished Story"; Ramsey to Bachelder, 7 May 1883, *BP*, 2:958.

11. *OR* 27 (1):269; Hubler, "Just a Plain Unvarnished Story"; Avery Harris Papers, BrC, USAMHI.

12. Curtis, *Twenty-fourth*, 163, 165; N. Davidson's Dispatch, *New York Herald*, 7 July 1863, in McPherson Papers, box 98, LC.

13. Williams, "Report"; Williams to Morton, 30 July 1863, in Gaff, "Here Was Made," 50–51.

14. *OR* 27 (1):274; Beecham, *Gettysburg*, 78–80.

15. *OR* 27 (1):313, 315, 317, 321; A. Biddle to Strong, 16 Dec. 1892, in Strong, *121st Regiment*, 161; Cook, *Personal Reminiscences*, 147; Biddle, "Supplemental Account," 151.

16. *OR* 27 (1):328; McFarland, "Report of the Movements," 301.

17. *OR* 27 (2):656, 665, 669.

18. Ibid., 656, 661, 665, 668; Caldwell, *History*, 97; Shooter, "Letter to McIntyre"; Mills, *16th North Carolina*, 36.

19. W. Clark, *Histories*, 4:178.

20. *OR* 27 (2):656, 665, 668.

21. Beveridge, "First Gun," 177, 179; Gates, *Ulster Guard*, 434.

22. W. Clark, *Histories*, 3:236; Fite, "Memoir," TSL; Turney, "First Tennessee," 535.

23. Boatner, *Dictionary*, 471; Cox, *Address on the Life and Services of James M. Lane*, 2, 21; Hartwig, "Never Have I Seen Such a Charge," 2, GNMP.

24. *OR* 27 (2):665; J. S. Harris, *Seventh Regiment*, 34; W. Clark, *Histories*, 2:660–61; Beveridge, "First Gun," 97. Lane's line had the 37th North Carolina on its right followed left by the 28th, 18th, and 33d regiments.

25. *OR* 27 (2):661; Benson to brother, July 1863, Benson Papers, SHC.

26. *OR* 27 (1):927, 934; Chapman to Bachelder, 30 Mar. 1864, *BP*, 1:130; NYMC, *Final Report*, 3:1145; Shelton Autobiography, NYHS. In his report Buford made no mention of being requested by Howard or Doubleday to support Doubleday's left. He implies that he did so under his own initiative.

27. *OR* 27 (2):656, 669; Scales to Bachelder, 2 Feb. 1890, *BP*, 3:1697. In his letter to Bachelder, Scales mentioned that a "heavy shell" passed near him and made a hole in the ground big enough to bury a man. Since the only guns used by

Union troops that day fired twelve-pounder or three-inch shells, his comment is inexplicable.

28. *OR* 27 (2):656–57, 661, 670; Caldwell, *History*, 97; B. F. Brown, "Some Recollections," 33; Morrison, *Memoirs of Henry Heth*, 175.

CHAPTER 22

1. V. D. Brown, *Colonel at Gettysburg*, 78–79. The large seminary building, which contained dormitory rooms and classrooms, had no special name at this time. Therefore, I have referred to it only as the seminary building.

2. Boatner, *Dictionary*, 724; lecture text of Gen. A. M. Scales, Scales Papers, DU.

3. *OR* 27 (2):671; Scales to Bachelder, 22 Feb. 1890, *BP*, 3:1697.

4. *OR* 27 (1):361, 364; MGC, *Maine at Gettysburg*, 84; Nicholson, *Pennsylvania*, 898; J. Stewart, "Battery B," 185; Hubler, "Just a Plain Unvarnished Story"; Cornelius Wheeler Speech Draft, Wheeler Papers, SHSW. Cooper's battery opened the battle with four guns; one was damaged, and at this time it may have had only three in action.

The practice described by Hubler was called "thumbing the vent." The Number 3 cannoneer wore a leather thumbstall to protect his thumb from being burned when he covered the vent with it while the piece was being loaded. This was to prevent sparks being drawn from the vent to the powder when the sponge and rammer were removed. When the gun was being fired fast and was hot, it was possible to ignite the powder simply by uncovering the vent.

Wheeler must have been more endangered by the muzzle blast than the shell.

5. J. Stewart, "Battery B," 185–86; Felton, "Iron Brigade," 60–61. Stewart's account says nothing of having fired at Daniel's men, who would have been directly in its front. Yet it is inconceivable that it did not do so.

6. Dawes, "With the Sixth Wisconsin" and *Service with the Sixth*, 175.

7. *OR* 27 (2):659, 670–71. Colonel Lowrance had also been wounded on 1 July but not severely. Lowrance, who was twenty-six at the time of the battle, survived the war and became a merchant, a member of the Mississippi legislature, and a Presbyterian minister. Gordon, an Englishman with prior service in the British army, had served as an aide to A. P. Hill and others. He joined the 34th as major in December 1862. He was wounded in the leg during Pickett's Charge and wounded twice afterward before retiring to the Invalid Corps in November 1864. See Krick, *Lee's Colonels*, 146, 224; W. Clark, *Histories*, 2 692.

8. W. Clark, *Histories*, 2:692.

9. *OR* 27 (2):658; Dawes, *Service with the Sixth*, 175; N. S. Smith, "Letter," 463–64. The 60 percent figure is based on Lowrance's statement that only 500 men were available that night. According to Smith, Scales tried to get the 55th Virginia to come up on his left to fill the gap between it and the road. It apparently did.

10. Boatner, *Dictionary*, 642; V. D. Brown, *Colonel at Gettysburg*, 78.

11. *OR* 27 (2):661; Perrin to Governor, 29 July 1863, in Bonham, "Little More Light," 522; Shooter, "Letter to McIntyre." The ravine is a continuation of the intermittent stream in the low point of this swale. At a point 1,000 feet north of

the Hagerstown Road and directly west of the seminary building the stream bed deepens into a trenchlike ditch. Possibly this erosion is caused by a spring located at the head of the ditch.

12. *OR* 27 (2):661–62; Perrin to Governor, 29 July 1863, in Bonham, "Little More Light," 522; Shooter, "Letter to McIntyre"; V. D. Brown, *Colonel at Gettysburg*, 79–80.

13. Tompkins, *Company K*, 19–20; Perrin to Governor, 29 July 1863, in Bonham, "Little More Light," 522. The 14th South Carolina also received criticism from Perrin and Shooter, who neglected to mention that its casualties were much larger than those of the brigade's other regiments.

14. Gates, *Ulster Guard*, 443; Strong, *121st Regiment*, 48.

15. Nicholson, *Pennsylvania*, 2:763.

16. Beecham, *Gettysburg*, 88–89. Since there was little or no wind on 1 July and flags must have hung limply from their staffs, it seems unlikely that Union troops on Seminary Ridge could have distinguished between Union and Confederate flags carried by troops north of the town.

17. Caldwell, *History*, 97–98; V. D. Brown, *Colonel at Gettysburg*, 80.

18. *OR* 27 (2):662; Perrin to Governor, 29 July 1863, in Bonham, "Little More Light," 522; Caldwell, *History*, 98. Major McCreary's name was Commillus Wycliff, but he went by his initials. McCreary became colonel of the 1st South Carolina on 4 January 1864. He was wounded at Spotsylvania, killed at Five Forks, and buried at Williston, South Carolina. See Krick, *Lee's Colonels*, 229–30.

19. Strong, *121st Regiment*, 48; Cook, *Personal Reminiscences*, 129–30.

20. *OR* 27 (1):357; Nevins, *Diary*, 236; Cornelius Wheeler Speech Draft, n.d., Wheeler Papers, SHSW.

21. *OR* 27 (1):361, 365; Nicholson, *Pennsylvania*, 2:899; Nevins, *Diary*, 230; Whittier to Bachelder, Dec. 1883, *BP*, 3:1939; Hubler, "Just a Plain Unvarnished Story." A similar story about a Confederate who reached for the gun was told relating to Wiedrich's battery on Cemetery Hill on 2 July, except the cannoneer spoke German. See H. W. Pfanz, *Culp's Hill*, 269.

22. Shelton Autobiography, 77, NYHS. The location of the First Corps artillery park at this time was not given. In his report Lieutenant Breck stated that it was along the Emmitsburg Road. See *OR* 27 (1):363. Later the army's artillery park was east of the Taneytown Road and south of Granite Schoolhouse Lane.

23. *OR* 27 (1):357; Nevins, *Diary*, 236.

24. J. Stewart, "Battery B," 187–88.

25. *OR* 27 (1):323, 328; Strong, *121st Regiment*, 49; Nicholson, *Pennsylvania*, 2:763.

26. Gates, *Ulster Guard*, 444, and "Report," 147; Cook, *Personal Reminiscences*, 130.

27. *OR* 27 (1):266; "Report of Col. Samuel J. Williams," 16 Nov. 1863, in Gaff, "Here Was Made," 30; Dudley, "Report," 134.

28. *OR* 27 (1):277; Dawes, *Service with the Sixth*, 176, and "With the Sixth Wisconsin," 229.

29. *OR* 27 (1):336; Avery Harris Papers, 91, BrC, USAMHI. Colonel Dana

reported that the brigade had exhausted the ammunition at the Seminary Ridge position in addition to the sixty rounds brought to the field.

30. Avery Harris Papers, 91, BrC, USAMHI.

31. *OR* 27 (1):336; Testimony of Maj. James Glenn, "Court Martial of Brig. Gen. Thos. Rowley," 15, Dana Papers, WHGS; Nesbit, *General History of Company D*, 14–15. One of those killed was Capt. Ambrose N. Baldwin, who had led the fight at the Harmon buildings. A marker at the intersection of the Hagerstown Road and West Confederate Avenue commemorates Baldwin and Company D.

32. *OR* 27 (1):927, 934, (2):665; Busey and Martin, *Regimental Strengths*, 257. In his report for Pender's division, Major Engelhard stated that Lane's brigade met an unnamed force in McMillan Woods — that occupied by Pegram's battalion on 2 July. This could have been the 8th Illinois as it retired at the end of the fight.

In his report Colonel Gamble stated specifically that half of his troopers were dismounted.

33. *OR* 27 (1):927, 934, (2):657, 662; Pickerill, *Third Indiana*, 82; Bellamy to Parents, 3 July 1863, Bellamy Papers, IHS; Regimental History, IHS; Perrin to Governor, 29 July 1863, in Bonham, "Little More Light," 29, 522. Busey and Martin, *Regimental Strengths*, 257, gives losses for the 3d Indiana at 10.2 percent, the 8th Illinois at 1.5 percent, the 12th Illinois at 8.6 percent, and the 8th New York at 6.9 percent. These figures suggest that the Confederates on the right did not press the 8th Illinois.

34. *OR* 27 (1):935.

35. *OR* 27 (2):607, 662; B. F. Brown, "Some Recollections," 53; Caldwell, *History*, 99.

36. Shooter, "Letter to McIntyre"; V. D. Brown, *Colonel at Gettysburg*, 81.

37. V. D. Brown, *Colonel at Gettysburg*, 82; Caldwell, *History*, 99.

38. *OR* 27 (1):663, 667; W. Clark, *Histories*, 5:120; V. D. Brown, *Colonel at Gettysburg*, 96.

39. *OR* 27 (2):607; Robertson, *A. P. Hill*, 213–15; Pender's and Heth's divisions had a tiring day, but they could not have had "some six hours' hard fighting."

40. *OR* 27 (2):317, 607, 613, 616; Campbell, "Richard Anderson's Division in the Gettysburg Campaign," 108, GNMP.

41. In McIntosh, "Gettysburg Campaign," VHS, Lt. Col. David G. McIntosh observed that it was "entirely practicable" to have placed thirty or forty guns on Seminary Ridge, where they would have been posted on 2 July. He believed that their fire from there on the Union troops falling back to Cemetery Hill would have been disastrous and probably would have caused them to abandon that position. He also believed, however, that Ewell should have attacked the hill.

However, Lt. Col. John J. Garnett wrote that General Lee had ordered him to place his batteries on Seminary Ridge and that they had drawn fire. In his report he said nothing of this. It was natural that they would have drawn fire; it seems likely that a lot of artillery fire from Seminary Ridge could have caused the Union troops on Cemetery Hill great difficulty. Whether or not it would have caused them to go elsewhere we do not know. Probably not. See Garnett, *Gettysburg*, 20.

1. The incidents related to civilians cited here are from Bennett, *Days*. Those relating to 1 July are from pp. 20–40. Rosengarten's efforts are mentioned in E. J. Nichols, *Toward Gettysburg*, 202–3.

2. *OR* 27 (1):939; Moyer, *Seventeenth Regiment*, 64; Nicholson, *Pennsylvania*, 2:878.

3. *OR* 27 (1):703, 751; NYMC, *Final Report*, 3:1247. Wiedrich must have been wrong about firing at a battery on the York Pike. There should have been no Confederate battery there.

4. Cook, *Personal Reminiscences*, 131.

5. Hofmann, *Remarks*, 6; Salomon, *Gettysburg*, 7.

6. Nevins, *Diary*, 237; Schurz, *Reminiscences*, 3:12–13.

7. Jacob Smith, *Camps and Campaigns*, 87–88; Bennett, *Days*, 29–30.

8. Bennett, *Days*, 31; Dawes, *Service with the Sixth*, 178.

9. Pratt to parents, 4 July 1863, ACHS; Seventy-sixth New York File, BrC, USAMHI.

10. Hubler, "Just a Plain Unvarnished Story." Hubler became a physician after the war.

Some Union troops mentioned being fired at by canister while in the town. Carrington's battery, which entered the town with Early's division, did not fire. John Purifoy stated that Reese's battery of Carter's battalion entered the town. He did not mention its firing while there, but it could have done so. It is possible that the supposed canister was shrapnel from case shot. See Carrington, "First Day," 332; Purifoy, "Battle of Gettysburg," 24–25.

11. Boone, "Personal Experiences," 26–27, MWC, USAMHI; Boone, "Captured at Gettysburg."

12. Avery Harris Papers, 98–99, BrC, USAMHI.

13. *OR* 27 (1):254, 281; Henry F. Young to father, 11 July 1863, Young Papers, SHSW.

14. J. Stewart, "Battery B," 372–73.

15. MGC, *Maine at Gettysburg*, 86.

16. *OR* 27 (1):742, 756; "Battery (G) 4th U.S.," *BP*, 3:1974; Bennett, *Days*, 33. Since both Wilkeson's and Dilger's batteries were armed with Napoleons, it would have been easy to have confused the two.

A battery retired by prolonge when it was hard pressed and firing and did not have time to limber up. The prolonge was attached between the pintle on the limber and a ring on the end of the trail. This permitted the gun to be dragged and fired without limbering and unlimbering.

17. *Gettysburg Compiler*, 30 Sept. 1902; I. Hall, *Ninety-seventh Regiment*, 142–43; Bennett, *Days*, 34.

18. "Court Martial of Brig. Gen. Thos. Rowley," 3–5, Dana Papers, WHGS; C. E. Rogers, "Gettysburg Scenes"; Herdegen, "Lieutenant Who Arrested a General," 29–30; Coddington, *Gettysburg Campaign*, 706.

19. Kitzmiller, "Story of a Brig. Gen." There are several versions of this story, including Schurz, *Reminiscences*, 3:35–36; Raphelson, "Unheroic General"; and

"General Schimmelfennig's Headquarters." Some have Schimmelfennig hiding in a pig sty and eating scraps fed to the pigs, and one had him fed by Henry Garlach. The Anna Garlach Kitzmiller version seems the most reliable. Unfortunately the "pig sty" versions, which denigrated the general, have circulated widely and have unfairly made him a subject of ridicule by armchair soldiers.

20. *OR* 27 (1):717; NYMC, *Final Report*, 1:380.

21. *OR* 27 (2):587; Chamberlin, *One Hundred and Fiftieth*, 128; Nicholson, *Pennsylvania*, 2:753; Bennett, *Days*, 33.

22. Bennett, *Days*, 33; W. Clark, *Histories*, 1:719.

23. *OR* 27 (1):277; Dawes, *Service with the Sixth*, 176–78.

24. Dawes, *Service with the Sixth*, 178–79.

CHAPTER 24

1. *OR* 27 (1):251–52, 721, 724; Doubleday, "Journal," 103, and *Chancellorsville*, 150; Avery Harris Papers, 88, BrC, USAMHI; Jacob Smith, *Camps and Campaigns*, 88.

2. *OR* 27 (1):718; O. O. Howard, *Autobiography*, 1:219; Culp, "Gettysburg."

3. Slagle to brother, 13 Sept. 1863, GNMP; Musser to unnamed, 15 Sept. 1863, Musser Papers, USAMHI.

4. John Vautier Diary, 1 July 1863, Vautier Papers, USAMHI. Vautier was not at Gettysburg. Therefore his Gettysburg entries must have been based on information provided by others.

5. *OR* 27 (1):251, 282, 290, 322, 336, 358, 697, 730.

6. Ibid., 251; Warren Hassler, *Crises*, 146–50; Busey and Martin, *Regimental Strengths*, 253–54; Young to Bachelder, 12 Aug. 1867, GP, 1:36–37; Butts, *Gallant Captain*, 88. The Comte de Paris estimated that there were 5,000 men "in fighting condition" on the hill. Edward Coddington gave the number as about 12,000, including 2,700 of Buford's cavalry off to the left. See Comte de Paris, *Battle of Gettysburg*, 120, and Coddington, *Gettysburg Campaign*, 321.

7. *OR* 27 (1):230, 357, 748, 755; Nevins, *Diary*, 237–38. Although two of Heckman's guns were brought from the field, they were not posted on the hill because the battery was "so severely disabled." Wainwright's report suggests that Cooper's battery had four guns on the hill. Wainwright had Stewart's battery with four Napoleons, Wiedrich's and Cooper's batteries each with four three-inch rifles, Reynolds's with five three-inch rifles, and Stevens's battery on the knoll with six Napoleons. Osborn had Dilger's and Wilkeson's batteries each with six Napoleons, Hall's battery with three Napoleons, Wheeler's battery with three three-inch rifles, and a section from Wiedrich's battery with two three-inch rifles.

8. Nevins, *Diary*, 238.

9. MGC, *Maine at Gettysburg*, 88–89.

10. Boatner, *Dictionary*, 372; H. W. Pfanz, *Second Day*, 37–38.

11. *OR* 27 (1):252, 268, 367–68, 704; Hancock Testimony, CCW, 404–5; Report of Lt. Col. Charles H. Morgan, *BP*, 3:1351.

12. Report of Lt. Col. Charles H. Morgan, *BP*, 3:1350; Cooper to Mac, 14 June

1868, Hancock Papers, USAMHI; Hancock Testimony, *CCW*, 405. Hancock gave 3:00 P.M. as his time of arrival at Gettysburg in his report and 3:30 in his testimony. Although the times seem to fit well with his leaving Taneytown soon after 1:00 P.M., if he did, he did not reach the field until about 4:30 P.M.

13. Herdegen and Beaudot, *Bloody Railroad Cut*, 228; Watrous, "Mule Train Charge."

14. *OR* 27 (1):368; Hancock Testimony, *CCW*, 405; W. S. Hancock, "Gettysburg," 822–23; Report of Lt. Col. Charles H. Morgan, *GP*, 3:1351.

15. Doubleday, *Chancellorsville*, 151; E. P. Halstead of Doubleday's staff, who was no admirer of Howard, had a slightly different version that presents Howard as adamant and Hancock as yielding. See Halstead, "Incidents," 285. Perhaps Doubleday's problem with Howard was partially due to a statement in Hancock's dispatch to Butterfield on 1 July that stated that Howard had said that "Doubleday's command gave way." What this refers to is not clear. See *OR* 27 (1):366.

16. *OR* 27 (1):704; Howard to Coppee, 14 Mar. 1864, Howard Papers, BC; O. O. Howard, "Campaign," 59.

17. *OR* 27 (1):252, 704; O. O. Howard, "Campaign," 58–59; Report of Lt. Col. Charles H. Morgan, *BP*, 3:1351–52.

18. *OR* 27 (1):704; C. Howard, "First Day," 330; Report of Lt. Col. Charles H. Morgan, *BP*, 3:1351–52.

19. *OR* 27 (1):258, 271, 773, 777, 811, 825; A. S. Williams to Bachelder, 10 Nov. 1865, *BP*, 1:213; H. W. Pfanz, *Culp's Hill*, 96–97.

20. Schurz, "Battle," 277–78.

21. *OR* 27 (2):582, 585, 586, 587; Thomas, *Doles-Cook Brigade*, 9; Lt. William Calder letter, 8 July 1863, Calder Family Papers, SHC.

22. Bennett, *Days*, 32–33; H. W. Pfanz, *Culp's Hill*, 63; Capt. Thomas M. Hightower to Lou, 7 July 1863, Hightower Papers, GDAH.

23. *OR* 27 (2):499, 479; M. E. Reed, "Gettysburg Campaign," 188; R. J. Hancock to Daniel, Daniel Papers, UV. I suspect that most of the Confederates would have voiced such a desire to attack more loudly after the event than at the time.

24. *OR* 27 (2):469, 484; NYMC, *Final Report*, 1247; W. Clark, *Histories*, 1:312, 3:414. Hoke's brigade's left was about thirty yards west of the Culp farm's springhouse, and its right was about 300 yards to the west. See H. W. Pfanz, *Culp's Hill*, 127.

In his report (*OR* 27 [1]:704) General Howard stated that the enemy made a single attempt to turn the Union right but that his line was broken by Wiedrich's battery.

25. *OR* 27 (2):444, 555, 607.

26. William P. Carter to Daniel, 17 Mar. 1904, Daniel Papers, DU; William P. Carter to Colonel, 17 Mar. 1904, Peters Collection, USAMHI; Grace, "Rodes's Division," 615; Douglas, *I Rode with Stonewall*, 238–39. Douglas's comments have been accepted as generally accurate and are often quoted, but it is possible to be skeptical about them. Gordon's remark, if made, seems like an enthusiastic outburst not to be taken seriously. Pendleton's remark seems unfortunate considering that he was Ewell's chief of staff and should have supported him in his dilemma.

27. *OR* 27 (2):555.

28. Ibid., 469; J. A. Early, *War Memoirs*, 269, and "Leading Confederates," 253.

29. *OR* 27 (2):469; J. A. Early, *War Memoirs*, 270, and "Leading Confederates," 255.

30. *OR* (2):255; J. A. Early, *War Memoirs*, 269, and "Leading Confederates," 255. Col. Abner Smead, a Georgian, had graduated from West Point in 1854 and had been a lieutenant in the Old Army. He entered Confederate service as a lieutenant of artillery but soon became major of the 19th Mississippi. He transferred to the 12th Georgia in June 1861 and became its lieutenant colonel in December 1861. He joined Edward Johnson's staff in May 1862. He then became the inspector general on the staffs of Stonewall Jackson and Ewell. He was transferred to Wilmington, North Carolina, in November 1864. He became a colonel of artillery in August 1862. After the war Smead became a physician in Harrisonburg, Virginia. He died in 1904. See Krick, *Lee's Colonels*, 323–24.

31. J. P. Smith, "General Lee at Gettysburg," 14–45, and "With Stonewall Jackson," 56. Smith had just returned to the army after escorting Mrs. Jackson to the general's funeral and to her parents' home in North Carolina. In citing Smith as an authority for Ewell's presence in the square at Gettysburg, Douglas S. Freeman used only that in *SHSP* 33 rather than both accounts. This account gives the impression that Ewell frittered away his time when in the square.

32. W. H. Taylor, *Four Years*, 95–96; *OR* 27 (2):318, 345; C. Brown, "Reminiscences," 33, Brown and Ewell Papers, TSL.

33. J. P. Smith, "General Lee at Gettysburg," 145, and "With Stonewall Jackson," 57.

34. Long, *Memoirs of Robert E. Lee*, 276–77; Long to Early, 5 Apr. 1876, Early Papers, LC.

35. C. Brown, "Reminiscences," 3, Brown and Ewell Papers, TSL; J. W. Daniel, "Commentary on John B. Gordon's *Reminiscences*," Daniel Papers, UV. In his *Reminiscences*, 157, Gordon stated that it was during this ride that Ewell was shot in his wooden leg. In his *Memoirs* entry for 3 July, Capt. William Seymour of Hays's brigade stated that Ewell and Capt. Henry B. Richardson were shot on 3 July at the same time; Richardson was hit in the body. This took place off Hays's brigade's left, near Liberty Street. See T. L. Jones, *Seymour*, 79, and H. W. Pfanz, *Culp's Hill*, 357.

36. *OR* 27 (2):445; Campbell Brown to Henry Hunt, 7 May 1885, Hunt Papers, LC.

37. *OR* 27 (2):489; Driver, *52d Virginia*, 38; H. W. Pfanz, *Culp's Hill*, 78.

38. J. A. Early, "Leading Confederates," 256. It may be wondered why Ewell did not have Jenkins's brigade rather than two brigades of infantry picket the York Pike area.

39. *OR* 27 (2):503–4; H. W. Pfanz, *Culp's Hill*, 78–79. In his *Soldier's Recollections*, 295–96, Lt. Randolph McKim mentioned seeing dead Union soldiers in this area but said nothing of dead Confederates, which must have been numerous.

In his report General Johnson stated that his division had been held up by Longstreet's wagons. It would seem doubtful that wagons were in his way after he cleared the Cashtown area. However, Campbell Brown stated that Johnson's division was halted to allow two of Longstreet's divisions to pass and that this made him angry. If so, it should have. See *OR* 27 (2):504; C. Brown, "Reminiscences," 35, Brown and Ewell Papers, TSL.

40. *OR* 27 (2):445; J. A. Early, "Leading Confederates," 255.

41. Trimble to Bachelder, 8 Feb. 1883, *BP*, 3:930–31. Trimble appears to have been a pest, and his commentary, written when he was in his eighties, seems devoted to enhancing his own importance. In his "Campaign and Battle of Gettysburg," 212, he stated only that Ewell made "some impatient reply." Culp's Hill is southeast of Gettysburg.

42. "Personal Narrative, T. T. Turner," in C. Brown, "Personal Narrative," Hunt Papers, LC. Rodes's lackadaisical reply was reflected in his division's movements on 2 July.

Culp's Hill is bounded on the east by Rock Creek and on the west by the Baltimore Pike. It has two crests separated by a saddle. Its north crest is the higher of the two. Its west slope toward Stevens Knoll was occupied by the Iron Brigade.

A few hours later Capt. Samuel Johnston, Lee's engineering officer, made a reconnaissance of Little Round Top. Like Early and Turner he missed seeing Union troops in that area. See H. W. Pfanz, *Second Day*, 106.

43. C. Brown, "Reminiscences," 34, Brown and Ewell Papers, TSL.

44. *OR* 27 (2):465, 504, 509, 513, 526, 531; "Would Have Saved Officers." This article, based on the recollections of Maj. J. W. Bruce of Brig. Gen. John M. Jones's staff, said that Ewell had ordered Early to move his division to the "heights beyond the town." When he learned that it would be an hour before Johnson arrived, Early complained that his division had been doing all of the marching and hard fighting and was in no condition to go. This provoked a "tart reply" from Johnson and hot words. It seems unlikely that Hays's and Hoke's brigades would have been moved.

45. Campbell Brown to Henry Hunt, 6 May 1885, Hunt Papers, LC; H. W. Pfanz, *Culp's Hill*, 89; J. A. Early, "Leading Confederates," 273–74. Major Brown wrote that General Early maintained that this meeting was on the evening of 1 July; Maj. Charles R. Venable of Lee's staff said that it was on the morning of 2 July. Major Brown "could not fit it into either hour" and declared it "inconsistant" with the "movements of these officers." See Campbell Brown to Henry J. Hunt, 6 May 1885, Hunt Papers, LC.

46. Marshall to Early, 13 Mar. 1878, Early Papers, LC; J. A. Early, "Leading Confederates," 271–73; H. W. Pfanz, *Culp's Hill*, 84–85.

47. *OR* 27 (1):284–85, (2):446; "Personal Narrative, T. T. Turner," in C. Brown, "Personal Narrative," Hunt Papers, LC; H. W. Pfanz, *Culp's Hill*, 86.

48. *OR* 27 (2):318, 446.

CHAPTER 25

1. *OR* 27 (1):173–74, 182–83; Busey and Martin, *Regimental Strengths*, 239–41, 253–55; Boatner, *Dictionary*, 188, 193. These figures are the corps totals revised less those of Stannard's brigade in the First Corps, Smith's brigade in the Eleventh, and the 7th Indiana and 73d Pennsylvania regiments.

2. *OR* 27 (2):445, 493, 555, 583.

3. Ibid., 607, 657, 663, 670, 671; Heth, "Letter," 158; Morrison, *Memoirs of Henry Heth*, 175.

4. Confederate casualties inflicted by the Union First Corps are those of Heth's and Pender's divisions, less Lane's brigade, and all but Doles's brigade of Rodes's division. Krick, in his *Gettysburg Death Roster*, notes that Heth's and Pender's divisions failed to report captured and missing men, though this number must have been significant. For instance, Archer's brigade reported 517 missing. Alfred Young of Burtonsville, Maryland, who has studied Confederate casualties, stated to me that he believed that the casualties were significantly greater than reported. See also Alfred Young to Pfanz, 30 Aug. 1999.

5. Coddington, in his *Gettysburg Campaign*, 305–8, gives his views on casualties and corps performance.

6. H. W. Pfanz, *Culp's Hill*, 213.

7. Ibid., 213–14; Schurz to Frank Mason, 6 June 1865, De Coppet Collection, PU.

8. H. W. Pfanz, *Culp's Hill*, 258–59.

9. *OR* 27 (2):447, 556, 568, 588.

10. Ibid., 642, 647, 667; G. Stewart, *Pickett's Charge*, 37–38, 225–27.

11. McIlhenny, "Cobean History," n.p., ACHS.

12. Robertson, *A. P. Hill*, 318.

13. Boatner, *Dictionary*, 254–55; *DAB*, 2:568. Many of Early's views and sources were presented by D. S. Freeman in his *R. E. Lee* and *Lee's Lieutenants*.

14. *DAB*, 3:220; Ewell's postwar life is discussed at length in D. C. Pfanz, *Ewell*.

15. Boatner, *Dictionary*, 704, 822–23; NYMC, *In Memoriam: James Samuel Wadsworth*, 91–92; NYMC, *In Memoriam: Abner Doubleday*, 154, 156; NYMC, *Final Report*, 3:1343–45, 1347–49.

16. Boatner, *Dictionary*, 711.

17. Ibid., 44; NYMC, *In Memoriam: Francis Channing Barlow*, 35, 136; NYMC, *Final Report*, 3:1353–55.

18. Raphelson, "Unheroic General," 28–29.

19. Boatner, *Dictionary*, 727.

20. Ibid., 244; NYMC, *In Memoriam: Abner Doubleday*, 97–99; NYMC, *Final Report*, 3:1341–43.

21. Nicholson, *Pennsylvania*, 2:1067–82.

22. Boatner, *Dictionary*, 413.

APPENDIX A

1. *OR* 27 (1):255.

2. Chamberlin, *One Hundred and Fiftieth*, 113; Nicholson, *Pennsylvania*, 2:746–47.

3. Callis, " 'Iron Brigade,' " 141; Nicholson, *Pennsylvania*, 2:935.

4. Curtis, *Twenty-fourth*, 183. Other accounts say that Burns was treated by a Confederate doctor and that Dr. Charles Horner of Gettysburg took care of him.

See Bennett, *Days*, 59; Nicholson, *Pennsylvania*, 936; *Gettysburg Star and Sentinel*, 9 Feb. 1872, McPherson Papers, LC. Casper Dustman, who lived on the east slope of Seminary Ridge, said that on 1 July Burns had reached a nearby house and asked Dustman to have Mrs. Burns get a wagon and carry him home. Dustman claimed that he had a passing wagon take Burns home. See T. H. Smith, *Lee's Headquarters*, 37–38.

5. Nicholson, *Pennsylvania*, 2:931–38; Stevenson, *Poems of American History*, 493–94.

6. Nicholson, *Pennsylvania*, 936; article in *Germantown Telegraph* cited in the *New York Evening Post*, n.d., BAS. Richard Sauers, in his "Gettysburg Controversies," 114, states that in 1877 the Commonwealth of Pennsylvania acquired Burns's musket, a model 1816 piece manufactured by Marine T. Wickham. This is the musket that appears in the photo of Burns sitting on the porch of his house. Sauers states also that "Burns has escaped the scrutiny of Gettysburg buffs." This is so. For instance, if Burns was wounded and captured by the Confederates, how was he able to retain his musket? If wounded, he would have been unable to search McPherson Woods for it.

Burns added to his myth by claiming that a local Copperhead told the Confederates of Burns's part in the battle and that two Rebel officers questioned him. He gave them "little satisfaction," and they left. Soon after, two shots were fired into his window, one nearly hitting him. He claimed that this was an assassination attempt. See Bennett, *Days*, 59–60.

7. *Gettysburg Star and Sentinel*, 9 Feb. 1872, McPherson Papers, LC.

APPENDIX B

1. U.S. War Department, *U.S. Infantry Tactics*, 10–11; Coggins, *Arms and Equipment*, 25. At Gettysburg some of the "Irish" regiments carried green flags emblazoned with Irish symbols. Because the flag of the 56th Pennsylvania was in Philadelphia to have lettering placed on it, at Gettysburg the regiment carried a flag of blue bunting with its numerical designation and the First Corps insignia on it. See Hofmann, "Fifty-sixth Regiment."

2. G. Stewart, *Pickett's Charge*, 309–10.

3. U.S. War Department, *U.S. Infantry Tactics*, 10–11; Coggins, *Arms and Equipment*, 25.

4. Bassler, "Color Episode," *SHSP*, 268. Bassler implied that thirty-four guns could have fired at the 149th from Herr Ridge. This is probably an exaggeration.

5. Whether the rail piles were in the wheat field or on the edge of it is open to question. Corporal Lehman and Private Spayd both stated that the Confederates dashed out of it. I have presumed that the rails were at the east edge of the wheat field and not in it. See Bassler, "Color Episode," *SHSP*, 272–73.

6. Matthews, *149th Pennsylvania*, 89; *OR* 27 (1):342; Bassler, in "Color Episode," *SHSP*, 286, said that Dwight was drunk.

7. Affidavit of Fred Hoffman, 11 May 1907, in Bassler, "Color Episode," *SHSP*, 274–75.

8. Brig. Gen. Joseph Davis reported that Lt. Atlas K. Roberts led the party and was killed. Heth also mentioned this. See *OR* 27 (2):638, 650; Frank Price to Bond, 27 Jan. 1878, *BP*, 1:524.

9. Bassler, "Color Episode," *SHSP*, 276–81; Frank Price to Bond, 27 Jan. 1878, *BP*, 1:524.

10. Sergeant Price, if he was the man pursued by Spayd, gave a different account. He wrote that he became entangled in the flag and fell and was chased by a man with a bayonet. See Frank Price to Bond, 27 Jan. 1878, *BP*, 1:526.

11. This is a combination of Spayd's and Price's accounts. See Bassler, "Color Episode," *SHSP*, 273–74; Frank Price to Bond, 27 Jan. 1878, *BP*, 1:526.

12. Bassler, "Color Episode," *SHSP*, 278–79.

13. Ibid., 262, 272–77, 279, 283; Frank Price to Bond, 27 Jan. 1878, *BP*, 1:524–27.

14. *OR* 27 (1):346; Ramsey (Bill) to Bassler, 12 Mar. 1884, BR, USAMHI.

15. Bassler, "Color Episode," *SHSP*, 285–86, 290–93, 298–301.

16. Ibid., 286, 288–90, 294, 298–99.

APPENDIX C

1. The text of this appendix is based on Dunkelman, *Gettysburg's Unknown Soldier*, an authoritative and thorough account of the Humiston story.

2. Two of the songs published about the Humistons are J. G. Clark's "The Children of the Battlefield" and Wilson G. Horner's and W. H. Hayward's "The Unknown Soldier." See Dunkelman, *Gettysburg's Unknown Soldier*, 246–51.

BIBLIOGRAPHY

A bibliography of sources used in the preparation of this study appears below. It includes the reports that were published in the *Official Records*, unit histories, and personal accounts from the *National Tribune*, the *Confederate Veteran*, the *Southern Historical Society Papers*, the *Bachelder Papers*, and other organs.

Of particular interest are the articles published in the last decade in the *Gettysburg Magazine* published by Bob and Mary Younger's Morningside House, Inc. A few of these are primary sources, others are secondary, but all merit attention.

In my previous books I have mentioned the comparative lack of good Confederate sources. That continues to be true. However, the most frustrating deficiency, insofar as this study is concerned, has been the dearth of good reports and accounts of the operations of the German American regiments of the Eleventh Corps. I have been pleased to learn that James Pula and others are making special efforts to locate and present extant writings of members of these units.

As before, I have frequently used and have been helped by a variety of reference sources. Those used in this work include publications of Mark M. Boatner III, John W. Busey and David G. Martin, Robert K. Krick, Edmund J. Raus, and Richard A. Sauers. These and others are listed below.

As always, the battlefield itself is an essential source. It is a sad fact that much of the arena of 1 July has been obliterated or compromised by modern development. This has made the maps cited below even more essential to the understanding of the events of that day.

MANUSCRIPT SOURCES

Adams County Historical Society, Gettysburg, Pennsylvania
   Mrs. Hugh McIlhenny, "Cobean History," paper, 2 November 1948
   Franklin Pratt to parents, 4 July 1863
Alabama Department of Archives and History, Montgomery
   Cullen A. Battle, "The Third Alabama Regiment"
   E. T. Boland to Thomas M. Owen, 21 May 1906, 13th Alabama Regiment File
   William F. Fulton to Thomas M. Owen, 10 August 1910, 5th Alabama Regiment File
   J. M. Thompson, "Reminiscences of the Autauga Rifles," 16th Alabama Regiment File

Arnold Blumberg Collection, Baltimore, Maryland (Private)
William Gamble to W. S. Church, 10 March 1869
Bowdoin College Library, Special Collections and Archives, Brunswick, Maine
Charles Henry Howard Papers
Oliver Otis Howard Papers
Bridgeport Public Library, Historical Collections, Bridgeport, Connecticut
William Henry Warren, "History of the Seventeenth Connecticut Volunteers . . .
1862–1865: The Battle of Gettysburg As Seen by the Writer"
Cattaraugus County Historical Museum and Research Center, Little Valley, New
York
Report of Lt. Col. Daniel B. Allen, Regimental Letterbook, 154th New York
Volunteers
Duke University, Rare Book, Manuscript, and Special Collections Library,
Durham, North Carolina
Civil War Diary of Henry Besancon, 1863
William Keating Clare Papers
John W. Daniel Papers
Alfred M. Scales Papers
William Alexander Smith Papers, 1858–1864
Franklin and Marshall College, Shadek-Fackenthal Library, Special Collections,
Lancaster, Pennsylvania
Reynolds Family Papers
Georgia Department of Archives and History, Atlanta
Capt. Thomas M. Hightower Papers
W. H. May, "Reminiscences of the War between the States," Confederate
Letters, Diaries, and Reminiscences, 1860–65, vol. 10
Sidney Jackson Richardson to Father and Mother, 8 July 1863
Gettysburg College, Special Collections, Musselman Library, Gettysburg,
Pennsylvania
McConaughy Collection
Gettysburg National Military Park, Gettysburg, Pennsylvania
John Bartlett Affidavit, 23 November 1889, 149th New York Regiment File
W. A. Bentley to the Illinois Commandery, Opening Shots File
George Breck to *Rochester Union*, 13 July 1863, 1st New York Light Artillery File
Sarah Broadhead, "The Diary of a Lady of Gettysburg"
Eric A. Campbell, "Richard Anderson's Division in the Gettysburg Campaign"
A. W. Garber to John W. Daniel, 24 February 1904, John W. Daniel File
Edwin R. Gearhart, "In the Years of '62–'63: Personal Recollections of Edwin R.
Gearhart, a Veteran," *Daily Times*, Stroudsburg (Pennsylvania), 149th
Pennsylvania Regiment File
Kathleen Georg, "Significance of the Harmon Farm," 1 March 1991
D. Scott Hartwig, "Never Have I Seen Such a Charge: Pender's Light Division at
Gettysburg," draft, n.d.
Edward Haviland to mother, 11 August 1883, 76th New York Regiment File

Henry Jacobs, "How an Eyewitness Watched the Battle," typescript

Francis B. Jones, "Excerpt from the Chronicles of Francis Bacon Jones, pp. 26–41, Covering the Battle of Gettysburg," 149th Pennsylvania Regiment File

Marshall Krolick, "First Shot," typescript, 8th Illinois Cavalry File

Emanuel Markle, "Story of Battle Told by a Survivor," 2d Wisconsin Regiment File

Thomas M. Littlejohn, "Recollections," 13th South Carolina Regiment File

H. H. Lyman Diary, 147th New York Regiment File

Samuel Pickens Diary, 5th Alabama Regiment File

William McK. Robbins Journal

William McK. Robbins Scrapbook

Alfred Sellers to unknown, 9 July 1863, 90th Pennsylvania Regiment File

Jacob M. Sheads, "The Burning of the Home of General 'Stonewall' Jackson's Uncle during the First Day's battle of Gettysburg, 1 July 1863," typescript, 29 July 1939

Jacob F. Slagle to brother, 13 September 1863, 149th Pennsylvania Regiment File

A. Taylor to W. S. Taylor, 9 July 1863, 8th Louisiana Regiment File

David G. Thompson to Mary, 16 July 1863, 82d Ohio Regiment File

A. S. Van de Graaff to wife, 8 July 1863, 5th Alabama Regiment File

Charles H. Veil, "An Old Boy's Personal Recollections and Reminiscences of the Civil War"

Huntington Library, San Marino, California

Charles Shiels Wainwright Journal, 1 October 1861–30 June 1865

Indiana Historical Society, Indianapolis

George Henry Chapman Diary

Henry C. Marsh Papers

William Roby Moore Papers, 1 and 2

Indiana State Library, Manuscript Section, Indianapolis

Flavius J. Bellamy Collection

Henry C. Marsh, "The Nineteenth Indiana at Gettysburg"

A. W. Peck to John T. Powell, 16 December 1889

Regimental History, 3d (Indiana) Cavalry

Library of Congress, Washington, D.C.

Journal of Theodore Dodge, 1862–63

Jubal A. Early Papers

Richard S. Ewell Papers

Papers of E. N. Gilpin

Diary of George Washington Hall

Jedidiah Hotchkiss Papers

Henry J. Hunt Papers

Edward McPherson Papers

Massachusetts Historical Society Library, Boston

Francis Channing Barlow Papers

Museum of the Confederacy, Ellen S. Brockenbrough Library, Richmond,
   Virginia
   Henry Heth Papers
   R. T. Mockbee, "Historical Sketch of the 14th Tenn. Regt. of Infantry, C.S.A.,
     1861–1865"
National Archives, Washington, D.C.
   RG 94
New-York Historical Society, New York
   William Henry Shelton Autobiography
North Carolina Department of Cultural Resources, Division of Archives and
   History, Raleigh
   Joseph Bennett Papers
   Oscar W. Blacknall Papers
   William Hyslop Sumner Burgwyn Papers
   Thomas M. Gorman Papers
   Bryan Grimes Papers
   William Clark Ousby Papers
   Stephen D. Ramseur Collection
   Alfred M. Scales Papers
Ohio Historical Center, Archives/Library Division, Columbus
   Andrew Leitner Harris Papers
Pennsylvania Historical and Museum Commission, Pennsylvania State Archives,
   Harrisburg
   Samuel Penniman Bates Papers (MG-17)
   J. Horace McFarland Papers (MG-85)
   Peter F. Rothermel Papers (MG-108)
   Stephen Wallace Journal (MG-6), Diaries and Journals Collection
Princeton University Library, Manuscripts Division, Department of Rare Books
   and Special Collections, Princeton, New Jersey
   De Coppet Collection
Rutgers University Library, Special Collections and University Archives, New
   Brunswick, New Jersey
   Capt. J. Frank Sterling to Father, 2 July 1863
South Caroliniana Library, University of South Carolina, Columbia
   Civil War Letters of David Ballenger
State Historical Society of Wisconsin, Madison
   Papers of E. S. Bragg
   Rufus Dawes Papers
   Henry Dillon Papers
   Fairchild Papers
   Robert Hughes Diary
   Capt. Robert H. Hughes, "Report of the Movements of the Second Wisconsin"
   Sidney B. Meade Diary
   Adam Muenzenberger Papers
   Diary of Captain George H. Otis

Jerome A. Watrous Papers

Cornelius Wheeler Papers

Henry Falls Young Papers

Bruce A. Suderow Collection, Washington, D.C. (Private)

Col Adrian R. Root to Editors, *Commercial Advertiser*, Washington, D.C., 14 July
1863

Tennessee State Library and Archives, Tennessee Civil War Collection, Nashville

Campbell Brown and Richard S. Ewell Papers

John A. Fite, "Memoir of Colonel John A. Fite"

Thomas Herndon, "Reminiscences of the Civil War"

U.S. Army Military History Institute, U.S. Army History Collection, Carlisle
Barracks, Pennsylvania

Bassler-Ramsey File, 150th Pennsylvania Regiment

Ronald Boyer Collection

Robert L. Brake Collection

Civil War Miscellaneous Collection

Civil War Times Illustrated Collection

Gregory A. Coco Collection

W. S. Hancock Papers

Harrisburg Civil War Round Table Collection

John D. Musser Papers

Leigh Peters Collection

Save the Flag Collection

John D. Vautier Papers, 88th Pennsylvania Infantry Regiment File

Michael Winey Collection

University of Georgia Libraries, Hargrett Rare Book and Manuscript Library,
Athens

Shepherd Green Pryor Collection

University of North Carolina, Wilson Library, Southern Historical Collection,
Chapel Hill

Berry Greenwood Benson Papers (#2636)

Calder Family Papers (#125)

John Fuller Coghill Letters (#1724)

James E. Green Diary (#2678)

Francis Milton Kennedy Diary (#3008)

John Randolph Lane Papers (#411)

Benjamin F. Little Papers (#3954)

Peek Family Papers (#4710)

Leonidas La Fayette Polk Papers (#3708)

Steed and Phipps Family Papers (#3960)

George Whitaker Wills Letters (#2269)

University of Virginia, Special Collections Department, Alderman Library,
Charlottesville

Papers of John W. Daniel (MSS 158)

Virginia Historical Society, Division of Special Collections and Archives, Richmond

Cullen A. Battle, "The Third Alabama Regiment," typescript

John W. Daniel, "Account of Gettysburg"

———, "Commentary on John B. Gordon's Reminiscences of the Civil War"

———, "Memoir of the Battle of Gettysburg"

Lee Family Papers

David Gregg McIntosh, "The Gettysburg Campaign"

———, "A Ride on Horseback in the Summer of 1910 over Some Battlefields of the Great Civil War"

Wyoming Historical and Geological Society, Wilkes-Barre, Pennsylvania

Edmund L. Dana Papers

Yale University Library, Civil War Manuscripts Collection, Manuscripts and Archives, New Haven, Connecticut

William H. Warren Diary

MAPS

Bachelder, John B. *Position of Troops, First Day's Battle*. New York: Office of the Chief of Engineering, U.S. Army, 1876.

Battle of Gettysburg Field Map. Gettysburg: Friends of the National Parks at Gettysburg, 1998.

Gettysburg Battlefield: The First Day's Battlefield. Olean, N.Y.: McElfresh Map Co., 1994.

Gettysburg National Park Commission. *Map of the Battlefield of Gettysburg*. Gettysburg: Gettysburg National Park Commission, 1901.

U.S. Army, Engineer Department. *Map of the Battlefield of Gettysburg, Surveyed and drawn under the direction of Bvt. Maj. Gen. G. K. Warren*. (See page xcv of the Atlas to U.S. War Department, *The War of the Rebellion: A Compilation of the Official Records of the Union and the Confederate Armies*.)

BOOKS, ARTICLES, AND PAMPHLETS

Applegate, John S. *Reminiscences and Letters of George Arrowsmith of New Jersey*. Red Bank, N.J.: John H. Cook, 1893.

Ashurst, R. L. *First Day's Fight at Gettysburg*. Military Order of the Loyal Legion of the United States paper. Philadelphia: Press of Allen, Lane, and Scott, 1897.

Bandy, Ken, and Florence Freeland. *The Gettysburg Papers*. 3 vols. Dayton: Morningside, 1978.

Bassler, J. H. "The Color Episode of the One Hundred and Forty-ninth Regiment, Pennsylvania Volunteers at Gettysburg, July 1, 1863." *Papers and Addresses of the Lebanon County Historical Society* 4 (1907): 77–110.

———. "The Color Episode of the One Hundred and Forty-ninth Regiment, Pennsylvania Volunteers at Gettysburg, July 1, 1863." *Southern Historical Society Papers* 37 (1909): 266–301.

Bates, Samuel P. *History of the Pennsylvania Volunteers*. 5 vols. Harrisburg: D. Singerly, 1869.

"Battle of Gettysburg." *Gettysburg Compiler*, 5 July 1905.

Bean, Theodore. "The 17th Penna. Cavalry . . . in the Gettysburg Campaign." *Philadelphia Weekly Press*, 27 June 1866.

Becker, Carl M., and Ritchie Thomas. *Hearth and Knapsack: The Laidley Letters, 1858–1880*. Athens: Ohio University Press, 1958.

Beecham, Robert K. "The Corporal and the General." *Milwaukee Sunday Telegraph*, 14 December 1884.

———. *Gettysburg: The Pivotable Battle of the Civil War*. Chicago: A. C. McClung, 1911.

Belo, A. H. "The Battle of Gettysburg." *Confederate Veteran* 8 (1900): 165–68.

Benjamin, Charles F. "Hooker's Appointment and Removal." In Johnson and Buel, *Battles and Leaders*, 3:239–43.

Bennett, Gerald R. *Days of "Uncertainty and Dread."* Littlestown, Pa.: Gerald R. Bennett, 1994.

Bennett, Joseph. "Junius Daniel, Oration of Hon. Joseph Bennett, May 10, 1888." *Raleigh News and Observer*, 11 May 1888.

Bentley, W. A. "Howard at Gettysburg." *National Tribune*, 12 February 1885.

Bentley, W. G. "The First Shot at Gettysburg." *National Tribune*, 21 August 1913.

Betts, Rev. Alexander D. *Experiences of a Confederate Chaplain, 1861–64*. N.p., n.d.

Beveridge, John L. "The First Gun at Gettysburg." In Bandy and Freeland, *Gettysburg Papers*, 1:161–80.

———. "First Shot at Gettysburg." *National Tribune*, 31 July 1902.

Beyer, W. F., and O. F. Keydel. *Deeds of Valor*. Detroit: Perrien-Keydel, 1906.

Biddle, Alexander. "Supplemental Account of Major Alexander Biddle, One Hundred Twenty-first Pennsylvania Volunteers, on the Gettysburg Campaign, July 1 and 2, 1863." In Hewett, Trudeau, and Suderow, *Supplement*, 27:145–52.

Bigelow, John, Jr. *The Campaign of Chancellorsville*. New York: Konecky and Konecky, 1995.

Bird, W. H. *Stories of the Civil War, Company C, 13th Regiment of Alabama Volunteers*. Columbiana, Ala.: Advocate Print, n.d.

Boatner, Mark M., III. *Civil War Dictionary*. New York: David McKay, 1959.

Boland, Pvt. E. T. "Beginning of the Battle." *Confederate Veteran* 14 (1906): 308–10.

Bonham, Milledge Louis. "A Little More Light on Gettysburg." *Mississippi Valley Historical Review* 29 (1937–38): 519–25.

Boone, Samuel G. "Captured at Gettysburg." *National Tribune*, 27 January 1910.

"Brigadier General Gabriel R. Paul." *New York Herald*, 16 July 1883.

Brown, B. F. "Some Recollections of Gettysburg." *Confederate Veteran* 31 (1923): 53.

Brown, Clinton. Letter to the editor. *Schenectady Evening Star and Times*, 9 July 1863.

Brown, Varina Davis. *A Colonel at Gettysburg and Spotsylvania*. Columbia: State Co., 1931.

Busey, John W., and David G. Martin. *Regimental Strengths and Losses at Gettysburg*. Hightstown, N.J.: Longstreet House, 1986.

Butts, John Tyler. *A Gallant Captain of the Civil War, from the Extraordinary Adventures of Friederich Otto, Baron von Fritsch*. New York: F. Tennyson Neely, 1902.

Caldwell, James F. J. *The History of a Brigade of South Carolinians*. Marietta, Ga.:
Continental Book Co., 1951.

Calef, John H. "Gettysburg Notes: The Opening Gun." *Journal of the Military
Services Institution of the United States*, January/February 1907, 40–58.

Callis, John. " 'The Iron Brigade,' 7th Wis. Infantry at Gettysburg, Pa." In Ladd
and Ladd, *Bachelder Papers*, 1:139–46.

Carmichael, Peter S. *The Purcell, Crenshaw, and Letcher Artillery*. Lynchburg: H. E.
Howard, 1990.

Carpenter, John A. *Sword and Olive Branch: Oliver Otis Howard*. Pittsburgh:
University of Pittsburgh Press, 1964.

Carrington, James McD. "First Day on the Left at Gettysburg." *Southern Historical
Society Papers* 37 (1909): 326–37, and *Richmond Times Dispatch*, 19 February
1905.

Castleberry, W. A. "Thirteenth Alabama: Archer's Brigade." *Confederate Veteran* 19
(1911): 338.

Chamberlayne, C. G. *Ham Chamberlayne, Virginian*. Richmond: Dietz, 1932.

Chamberlin, Thomas. *History of the One Hundred and Fiftieth Regiment, Pennsylvania
Volunteers*. Philadelphia: Lippincott, 1895.

———. "Letter of Maj. Thomas Chamberlin, 8 June 1889." In Ladd and Ladd,
Bachelder Papers, 3:1593–94.

Chapman, George H. "Letter of Colonel George H. Chapman, 30 Mar. 1864." In
Ladd and Ladd, *Bachelder Papers*, 1:129–31.

Cheney, Newell. *History of the Ninth Regiment New York Volunteer Cavalry, War of
1861–1865*. Jamestown, N.Y.: Martin Merz and Son, 1901.

Clark, Champ. *Gettysburg: The High Tide*. Alexandria, Va.: Time-Life, 1985.

Clark, Walter, ed. *Histories of the Several Regiments and Battalions from North Carolina
in the Great War, 1861–'65*. 5 vols. Raleigh: State of North Carolina, 1901.

Coco, Gregg. *A Vast Sea of Misery*. Gettysburg: Thomas, 1988.

Coddington, Edwin B. *The Gettysburg Campaign*. Dayton: Morningside, 1979.

Coe, Algernon S. "Letter of Dr. Algernon Coe, 28 Dec. 1888." In Ladd and Ladd,
Bachelder Papers, 3:1563–72.

Coey, James. "Cutler's Brigade: The 147th N. Y's. Magnificent Fight on the First
Day at Gettysburg." *National Tribune*, 15 July 1915.

Coggins, Jack. *Arms and Equipment of the Civil War*. New York: Fairfax Press, 1963.

"Col. Jackson." *Schenectady Evening Star and Times*, 13 July 1863.

A Company Officer [Alfred E. Lee]. "Reminiscences of the Gettysburg Battle."
Lippincott's Magazine, July 1883, 54–60.

Comte de Paris. *The Battle of Gettysburg*. Philadelphia: Winston, 1907.

Conklin, George W. "The Long March to Stevens Run: The 134th New York
Volunteer Infantry at Gettysburg." *Gettysburg Magazine* 21 (July 1999): 45–56.

Cook, John D. S. *Personal Reminiscences of Gettysburg*. Read before the Kansas
Commandery of the Military Order of the Loyal Legion of the United States,
12 December 1903, 123–44. Reprinted in *Gettysburg Sources*, by James L.
McLean and Judy W. McLean, 912–35. Baltimore: Butternut and Blue, 1987.

Cooke, Sidney G. "The First Day at Gettysburg." In Bandy and Freeland, *Gettysburg Papers*, 1:239–54.

Cooksey, Paul Clark. "They Died As If On Dress Parade." *Gettysburg Magazine* 20 (January 1999): 89–112.

Cox, William Ruffin. *Address on the Life and Services of James M. Lane, Richmond Va. December 4, 1908*. N.p., n.d.

Crosby, Alanson, to Maj. Sam Glover, 28 February 1864. *Jamestown (New York) Journal*, 18 March 1864.

Culp, Edward C. "Gettysburg." *National Tribune*, 19 March 1885.

———. *The 25th Ohio Vet. Vol. Infantry*. Topeka: Geo. W. Crane, 1885.

Curtis, Orson B. *History of the Twenty-fourth Michigan*. Detroit: Winn and Hammond, 1891.

Cutler, Lysander. "Cutler to Governor of Pennsylvania, 5 Nov. 1892." *National Tribune*, 9 May 1912.

Dailey, Dennis B. "Letter of Lt. Dennis B. Dailey, 24 Mar. 1891." In Ladd and Ladd, *Bachelder Papers*, 1:1806–8.

Daniel, Edward M. *Speeches and Orations of John W. Daniel*. Lynchburg: J. P. Bell, 1911.

Daniel, John W. *The Campaign and Battle of Gettysburg: Address . . . Richmond, Virginia, October 28, 1875*. Lynchburg: Bell, Browne, 1875.

———. "First Day on the Left at Gettysburg." *Richmond Times Dispatch*, 19 February 1905.

Davis, Archie K. *Boy Colonel of the Confederacy: The Life and Times of Henry King Burgwyn, Jr.* Chapel Hill: University of North Carolina Press, 1985.

Davis, Charles E. *Three Years in the Army: The Story of the Thirteenth Massachusetts Volunteers*. Boston: Estes and Lauriat, 1894.

Dawes, Rufus R. "Align on the Colors." *Milwaukee Sunday Telegraph*, 27 April 1890.

———. "Letter of Lt. Col. Rufus Dawes, 18 Mar. 1868." In Ladd and Ladd, *Bachelder Papers*, 1:322–27.

———. *Service with the Sixth Wisconsin Volunteers*. Madison: Historical Society of Wisconsin, 1962.

———. "With the Sixth Wisconsin at Gettysburg." In Bandy and Freeland, *Gettysburg Papers*, 1:214–38.

"Dick Huftill and the Flag." *Milwaukee Sunday Telegraph*, 10 July 1881.

Ditzler, O. H. "The First Gun at Gettysburg." *National Tribune*, 22 May 1902.

Dodge, H. O. "Lieut. Jones . . . Fired the First Shot at Gettysburg." *National Tribune*, 24 September 1891.

Domschcke, Bernhard. *Twenty Months in Captivity*. Rutherford, N.J.: Fairleigh Dickinson University Press, 1987.

Doubleday, Abner. *Chancellorsville and Gettysburg*. New York: Charles Scribner's Sons, 1908.

———. *Gettysburg Made Plain*. New York: Century, 1909.

———. "Journal of Major General Abner Doubleday, June 4–August 28, 1863." In Hewett, Trudeau, and Suderow, *Supplement*, 27:84–115.

Douglas, Henry Kyd. *I Rode with Stonewall*. Atlanta: Mockingbird, 1976.

Dreese, Michael A. *An Imperishable Fame: The Civil War Experiences of George Fisher McFarland*. Mifflintown, Pa.: Juniata County Historical Society, 1997.

Driver, Robert J., Jr. *52d Virginia Infantry*. Lynchburg: H. E. Howard, 1986.

Dudley, William W. "Report of Lieutenant Colonel William Wade Dudley, Nineteenth Indiana Volunteers, on Operations Around Gettysburg, Pennsylvania, June 28–July 3, 1863." In Hewett, Trudeau, and Suderow, *Supplement*, 27:128–36.

Dunkelman, Mark H. *Gettysburg's Unknown Soldier: The Life, Death, and Celebrity of Amos Humiston*. Westport, Conn.: Praeger, 1999.

———. "The Hardtack Regiment in the Brickyard Fight." *Gettysburg Magazine* 8 (January 1993): 17–30.

Dunkelman, Mark H., and Michael J. Winey. *The Hardtack Regiment*. East Brunswick, N.J.: Fairleigh Dickinson University Press, 1981.

Dyer, Frederick H. *A Compendium of the War of the Rebellion*. 2 vols. Dayton: Morningside, 1878.

Early, John Cabell. "A Southern Boy's Experiences at Gettysburg." *Journal of the Military Services Institution of the United States*, January/February 1911, 415–23.

Early, Jubal A. *Autobiographical Sketch and Narrative of the War between the States*. Philadelphia: Lippincott, 1912.

———. "Leading Confederates on the Battlefield: A Review by General Early." *Southern Historical Society Papers* 4 (1877): 241–81.

———. *War Memoirs*. Bloomington: Indiana University Press, 1960.

Ellis, Franklin. *History of Cattaraugus County*. Philadelphia: L. H. Everts, 1879.

Fairchild, Lucius. "Notes from a Conversation with Col. Lucius Fairchild." In Ladd and Ladd, *Bachelder Papers*, 1:335–36.

Fairfield, George. "The Capture at the Railroad Cut." *National Tribune*, 1 September 1910.

———. "The Sixth Wisconsin." *National Tribune*, 14 December 1905.

Felton, Silas. "The Iron Brigade at Gettysburg." *Gettysburg Magazine* 11 (July 1994): 57–67.

Fischer, Louis. "First Day's Work of the Eleventh Corps." *National Tribune*, 12 December 1889.

Fleet, C. B. "The Fredericksburg Artillery." *Southern Historical Society Papers* 32 (1904): 241.

———. "The Fredericksburg Artillery Boys." *Richmond Times Dispatch*, 8 July 1904.

Freeman, Douglas S. *Lee's Lieutenants*. 3 vols. New York: Charles Scribner's Sons, 1949–51.

———. *R. E. Lee: A Biography*. 4 vols. New York: Charles Scribner's Sons, 1934–35.

Freeman, Warren Hapgood. *Letters from Two Brothers Serving in the War for the Union*. Cambridge, Mass.: Printed for Private Circulation, 1871.

Fulton, William F. "The Fifth Alabama Battalion at Gettysburg." *Confederate Veteran* 31 (1923): 379–80.

———. *The War Reminiscences of William Frierson Fulton*. Gaithersburg, Md.: Butternut Press, 1986.

Gaff, Alan D. "Here Was Made Our Last and Hopeless Stand." *Gettysburg Magazine* 2 (January 1990): 25–31.

———, ed. *George Otis: The Second Wisconsin Infantry*. Dayton: Morningside, 1984.

Gallagher, Gary W. *The First Day at Gettysburg*. Kent: Kent State University Press: 1992.

———. *Stephen Dodson Ramseur: Lee's Gallant General*. Chapel Hill: University of North Carolina Press, 1985.

Gannon, James P. "The 6th Louisiana Infantry at Gettysburg." *Gettysburg Magazine* 21 (July 1999): 88–99.

Garnett, John J. *Gettysburg*. New York: J. M. Hill, 1888.

Gates, Theodore B. "Report of Colonel Theodore Burr Gates, Twentieth New York State Militia, on the Battle of Gettysburg, Pennsylvania, July 1–3, 1863, dated August 13, 1863." In Hewett, Trudeau, and Suderow, *Supplement*, 27:143–48.

———. *The Ulster Guard*. New York: Benjamin H. Tyrel, 1879.

"General Schimmelfennig's 'Headquarters.'" *Civil War Times Illustrated* 10 (January 1994): 18–19.

"Gettysburg Incident." *Gettysburg Compiler*, 11 October 1887.

Goolsby, P. C. "Crenshaw's Battery, Pegram's Battalion, Confederate States Artillery." *Southern Historical Society Papers* 28 (1900): 336–76.

Gordon, John B. *Reminiscences of the Civil War*. Dayton: Morningside, 1985.

Grace, C. D. "Rodes's Division at Gettysburg." *Confederate Veteran* 5 (1894): 614–15.

Grant, George W. "The First Army Corps on the First Day in Gettysburg." In Bandy and Freeland, *Gettysburg Papers*, 1:257–70.

Grayson. "Adventures of a Rebel Flag." *Milwaukee Sunday Telegraph*, 29 February 1888.

———. "Asleep at His Post." *Milwaukee Sunday Telegraph*, 6 June 1880.

———. "Frederick City to Gettysburg." *Milwaukee Sunday Telegraph*, 25 January 1885.

———. "The Iron Brigade Guard at Gettysburg." *Milwaukee Sunday Telegraph*, 22 March 1885.

Green, Wharton J. *Recollections and Reflections*. Richmond: Edwards and Broughton, 1906.

Griffin, D. Massy. "Rodes on Oak Hill." *Gettysburg Magazine* 4 (January 1991): 33–48.

Hall, Harry H. *A Johnny Reb Band from Salem*. Raleigh: North Carolina Centennial Commission, 1963.

Hall, Hillman, and W. B. Besley. *History of the Sixth New York Cavalry*. Worcester, Mass.: Blanchard Press, 1908.

Hall, Isaac. *History of the Ninety-seventh Regiment, New York Volunteers*. Utica, N.Y.: L. C. Childs and Son.

———. "Iverson's Brigade." *National Tribune*, 26 June 1884.

———. "Iverson's Brigade." *National Tribune*, 10 September 1885.

Hall, James A. "Letter of Capt. James A. Hall, 29 Dec. 1869." In Ladd and Ladd, *Bachelder Papers*, 1:385–89.

Halstead, Eminel. "Incidents of the First Day's Battle." In Johnson and Buel, *Battles and Leaders*, 3:284–85.

Hamblen, Charles P. *Connecticut Yankees at Gettysburg*. Edited by Walter L. Powell. Kent: Kent State University Press, 1993.

Hancock, R. J. "William Singleton." *Confederate Veteran* 14 (1906): 499.

Hancock, Winfield S. "Gettysburg, Reply to General Howard." *Galaxy* 22 (1876): 821–31.

Hanna, Thomas L. "A Day at Gettysburg." *National Tribune*, 23 May 1911.

Hard, Abner. *History of the Eighth Cavalry Regiment, Illinois Volunteers*. Aurora, Ill.: n.p., 1868.

Harries, William H. "The Iron Brigade in the First Day's Battle at Gettysburg." In Bandy and Freeland, *Gettysburg Papers*, 1:183–96.

Harris, F. S. "From Gettysburg." *Lebanon Democrat*, 10 August 1899.

———. "Gen. Jas. J. Archer." *Confederate Veteran* 3 (1895): 18.

Harris, J. S. *Historical Sketch of the Seventh Regiment, North Carolina Troops*. Mooresville, N.C.: Mooresville Printing Co., 1893.

Harrison, Kathleen Georg. "The Significance of the Harmon Farm and Springs Hotel Woods." Typescript, Gettysburg National Military Park, 1991.

Harter, F. A. *Erinnerungen aus dem amerikanischen Buergerkrieg*. Chicago: Verlag von F. A. Harter, 1885.

Hartwig, D. Scott. "The 11th Army Corps on July 1: The Unlucky 11th." *Gettysburg Magazine* 2 (January 1990): 33–49.

Harwell, Richard, and Philip N. Racine, eds. *The Fiery Trail: A Union Officer's Account of Sherman's Last Campaign*. Knoxville: University of Tennessee Press, 1986.

Hassler, Warren W. *Crises at the Crossroads: The First Day at Gettysburg*. Gaithersburg, Md.: Butternut Press, 1986.

Hassler, William W., ed. *The General to His Lady: The Civil War Letters of William Dorsey Pender to Fanny Pender*. Chapel Hill: University of North Carolina Press, 1965.

Hawkins, Norma Fuller. "Sergeant Major Blanchard at Gettysburg." *Indiana Magazine of History* 34, no. 2 (June 1938): 212–16.

Heermance, William L. "The Cavalry at Gettysburg." In Bandy and Freeland, *Gettysburg Papers*, 1:414–24.

Herdegen, Lance J. "The Lieutenant Who Arrested a General." *Gettysburg Magazine* 4 (January 1991): 25–32.

Herdegen, Lance J., and J. K. Beaudot. *In the Bloody Railroad Cut at Gettysburg*. Dayton: Morningside, 1990.

Herndon, Thomas. *Reminiscences of the Civil War*. N.p., n.d.

Heth, Henry. "Letter from Major-General Henry Heth." In "Causes of Lee's Defeat," *Southern Historical Society Papers* 4 (1877): 151–60.

Hewett, Janet B., Noah Andre Trudeau, and Bryce A. Suderow. *Supplement to the Official Records of the Union and Confederate Armies*. Pt. 1, vol. 5, series 5, Addendum, vol. 27. Wilmington, N.C.: Broadfoot, 1995.

Hitz, Louise W., ed. *The Letters of Frederick C. Winkler*. Privately printed, 1963.

Hofe, Michael W. *That There Be No Stain upon My Stones*. Gettysburg: Thomas Publications, 1995.

Hofmann, J. William. "The 56th Pennsylvania at Gettysburg." *National Tribune*, 20 March 1884.

———. "The Fifty-sixth Regiment, Pennsylvania Volunteers in the Gettysburg Campaign." *Philadelphia Weekly Press*, 13 January 1886.

———. "General Hofmann on the Action of the 147th New York at the Opening of the Battle." *National Tribune*, 5 June 1884.

———. "General Hofmann Replies to the Second Wisconsin's Claim." *National Tribune*, 19 June 1884.

———. *Remarks on the Battle of Gettysburg*. Paper read before the Historical Society of Pennsylvania, 18 March 1880. Philadelphia: A. W. Auner, 1880.

Hoke, Jacob. *The Great Invasion of 1863*. Dayton: W. J. Shirey, 1887.

———. *Historical Reminiscences of the War*. Chambersburg, Pa.: M. A. Foltz, 1884.

Holt, Joseph. "Gettysburg: Reminiscences of the Great Battle as Told by an Assistant Surgeon." *New Orleans Times Democrat*, 22 June 1913.

Hopkins, C. A. Porter, ed. "The James J. Archer Letters." *Maryland Historical Magazine* 56 (December 1961): 352–83.

Howard, Charles. "The First Day at Gettysburg." In Bandy and Freeland, *Gettysburg Papers*, 1:310–36.

Howard, Oliver Otis. "After the Battle: Some Incidents and Observations." *National Tribune*, 31 December 1885.

———. *Autobiography of Oliver Otis Howard*. 2 vols. New York: Baker and Taylor, 1902.

———. "The Battle of Gettysburg." *Army and Navy Journal*, 8 July 1876, 770.

———. "The Campaign and Battle of Gettysburg." *Atlantic Monthly*, July 1876, 48–71.

———. "General O. O. Howard's Personal Reminiscences of the War of the Rebellion." *National Tribune*, 27 November 1877.

Howe, William H. Letter to editor, 6 July 1863. *Schenectady Evening Star and Times*, 13 July 1863.

Hubler, Simon. "Just a Plain Unvarnished Story of a Soldier in the Ranks." *New York Times*, 29 June 1913.

———. *Narrative of Simon Hubler, First Sergeant of Co. I, 143 Reg. Pa. Vol. Inf.* N.p., n.d.

Hufham, J. D., Sr. "Gettysburg." *Wake Forest Student* 7 (April 1897): 451–56.

Huidekoper, Henry S. *A Short Story of the First Day's Fight at Gettysburg*. Philadelphia: Bicking Print, 1906.

Hunt, Henry J. "The First Day at Gettysburg." In Johnson and Buel, *Battles and Leaders*, 3:255–84.

Hurst, Samuel H. *Journal-History of the Seventy-third Ohio Volunteer Infantry*. Chillicothe, Ohio: n.p., 1866.

Iobst, Richard W., and Louis H. Manarin. *The Bloody Sixth*. Durham, N.C.: Christian Printing Co., 1965.

Jacobs, Michael. "Meteorology of the Battle." *Gettysburg Star and Sentinel*, 30 July 1885.

Jerome, Aaron B. "Letter of First Lt. Aaron Brainard Jerome." In Ladd and Ladd, *Bachelder Papers*, 1:200.

"John Burns." *Gettysburg Star and Sentinel*, 9 February 1872.

Johnson, Allen, and Dumas Malone, eds. *Dictionary of American Biography*. 20 vols. New York: Charles Scribner's Sons, 1928–36.

Johnson, Robert U., and Clarence C. Buel, eds. *Battles and Leaders of the Civil War*. 4 vols. New York: Thomas Yoseloff, 1956.

Jones, Terry L. *The Civil War Memoirs of Captain William Seymour*. Baton Rouge: Louisiana State University Press, 1991.

——. "Going Back into the Union at Last." *Civil War Times Illustrated* 29 (January/February 1991): 12, 55–60.

Kelley, T. Benton. "An Account of Who Opened the Battle by One Who Was There." *National Tribune*, 31 December 1891.

Kelly, Andrew W. *History of the 134th Regiment, N.Y.S. Vol.* Schenectady, N.Y.: J. S. Marlett, n.d.

Kenan, Thomas. *Sketch of the Forty-third Regiment, North Carolina Troops*. Raleigh: n.p., 1895.

Ketcheson, John C. "The First Shot at Gettysburg." *National Tribune*, 25 December 1913.

Kiefer, William A. *History of the One Hundred and Fifty-third Regiment, Pennsylvania Volunteers*. Easton, Pa.: Chemical Pub. Co., 1909.

Kimball, George. "Iverson's Brigade." *National Tribune*, 1 October 1885.

Kimball, W. S. "The Thirteenth Massachusetts at Gettysburg." *National Tribune*, 14 May 1885.

Kitzmiller, Anna Garlach. "Story of a Brig. General." *Gettysburg Compiler*, 9 August 1905.

Klein, Frederick Shriver. "Meade's Pipe Creek Line." *Maryland Historical Magazine* 57 (June 1962): 133–49.

Krick, Robert K. *The Gettysburg Death Roster*. Dayton: Morningside, 1981.

——. *Lee's Colonels*. Dayton: Morningside, 1979.

——. "Three Confederate Disasters on Oak Ridge." In Gallagher, *First Day at Gettysburg*, 92–139.

Kross, Gary. "Gettysburg Vignettes." *Blue and Gray Magazine*, February 1995, 9–22.

Krumwiede, John F. "A July Afternoon on McPherson's Ridge." *Gettysburg Magazine* 21 (July 1999): 21–24.

Ladd, David L., and Audrey J. Ladd, eds. *The Bachelder Papers*. 3 vols. Dayton: Morningside, 1994–95.

Lash, Gary G. "Brig. Gen. Henry Baxter's Brigade at Gettysburg, July 1." *Gettysburg Magazine* 10 (January 1994): 7–27.

Ledford, P. L. *Reminiscences of the Civil War, 1861–1865*. Thomasville, N.C: News Printing House, 1909.

Leon, Louis. *Diary of a Tarheel*. Charlotte: Stone Pub. Co., 1913.

Lindsley, John B. "The Battle of Gettysburg." In *The Military Annals of Tennessee, Confederate*, 244–53. Spartanburg, S.C.: Reprint Co., 1974.

Locke, William Henry. *The Story of the Regiment*. New York: James Miller, 1877.

Long, Armistead L. *Memoirs of Robert E. Lee*. New York: J. M. Stoddard, 1887.

Longacre, Edward G. *The Cavalry at Gettysburg*. Cranberry, N.J.: Associated University Press, 1986.

Lonn, Ella. *Foreigners in the Union Army and Navy*. Baton Rouge: Louisiana State University Press, 1952.

Look, Benjamin F. "Letter of Maj. Benjamin Look, 17 Feb. 1884" and enclosure. In Ladd and Ladd, *Bachelder Papers*, 2:1019–23.

Lyman, H. H. "At Gettysburg." *National Tribune*, 13 October 1892.

———. "Gen. Howard Criticized." *National Tribune*, 12 March 1885.

McConnell, Charles H. "First and Greatest Day's Battle of Gettysburg." *National Tribune*, 13 July 1916.

McDonald, Archie P. *Make Me a Map of the Valley*. Dallas: Southern Methodist University Press, 1973.

McFarland, "Report of the Movements of 151st Pennsylvania." In Ladd and Ladd, *Bachelder Papers*, 1:300–304.

McFeely, William S. *Yankee Stepfather: O. O. Howard and the Freedman's Bureau*. New York: W. W. Norton, 1970.

McIntosh, David Gregg. "Review of the Gettysburg Campaign." *Southern Historical Society Papers* 37 (1909): 74–143.

McKay, Charles W. "Three Years or During the War with the Crescent and the Star." In *The National Tribune Scrapbook, No. 2*, 121–66. Washington, D.C.: National Tribune, n.d.

McKelvey, Blake, ed. "George Breck's Civil War Letters from Reynolds' Battery." *Rochester Historical Society Publication* 22 (1944): 91–199.

McKim, Randolph. *A Soldier's Recollections*. New York: Longman's Green, 1910.

McLean, James L., Jr. *Cutler's Brigade at Gettysburg*. Baltimore: Butternut and Blue, 1987.

———. "The First Union Shot at Gettysburg." *Lincoln Herald* 82 (spring 1980): 318–22.

Maine Gettysburg Commission. *Maine at Gettysburg*. Portland, Maine: Lakeside Press, 1898.

Marcus, Edward, ed. *A New Canaan Private in the Civil War: Letters of Justus W. Silliman, 17th Connecticut Volunteers*. New Canaan, Conn.: New Canaan Historical Society, 1984.

Marye, John L. "The First Gun at Gettysburg." *American Historical Register* 11 (July 1895): 1225–32.

Matthews, Richard E. *The 149th Pennsylvania Volunteer Infantry Unit in the Civil War*. Jefferson, N.C.: McFarland, 1994.

May, William H. "First Confederates to Enter Gettysburg." *Confederate Veteran* (1897): 620.

Mayo, Robert Murphy. "Report of Colonel Robert Murphy Mayo, 47th Virginia Infantry." In Hewett, Trudeau, and Suderow, *Supplement*, 27:414–16.

Meade, George G., Jr. *The Life and Letters of George Gordon Meade*. 2 vols. New York: Charles Scribner's Sons, 1913.

Mickey of Company K. "The Charge at Gettysburg." *Milwaukee Sunday Telegraph*, 20 January 1884.

———. "The Charge of the Iron Brigade at Gettysburg." *Milwaukee Sunday Telegraph*, 20, 28 December 1884.

Miller, J. Clyde. "Letter of Second Lt. J. Clyde Miller, 2 Mar. 1884." In Ladd and Ladd, *Bachelder Papers*, 2:1025–28.

———. "Letter of Second Lt. J. Clyde Miller, 2 Mar. 1886." In Ladd and Ladd, *Bachelder Papers*, 2:1213–14.

Mills, George H. *History of the 16th North Carolina Regiment in the Civil War*. Hamilton, N.Y.: Edmonston, 1992.

Montgomery, Walter Alexander. *The Days of Old and the Years That Are Past*. N.p., n.d.

———. "William D. Pender." In *Lives of Distinguished North Carolinians*, compiled by W. J. Peeler. Raleigh: North Carolina Pub. Co., 1898.

Moon, W. H. "Beginning of the Battle of Gettysburg." *Confederate Veteran* 33 (1925): 449–50.

Morgan, Charles H. "Report of Lt. Col. Charles H. Morgan." In Ladd and Ladd, *Bachelder Papers*, 3:1351–69.

Morrison, James L., Jr., ed. *The Memoirs of Henry Heth*. Westport, Conn.: Greenwood Press, 1974.

Moyer, Henry P. *History of the Seventeenth Regiment, Pennsylvania Volunteer Cavalry*. Lebanon, Pa.: Sowers, 1911.

Myers, Frank M. *The Comanches: A History of White's Battalion, Virginia Cavalry*. Marietta, Ga.: Continental Book Co., 1986.

Nesbit, John W. *General History of Company D, 149th Pennsylvania Volunteers*. Oakdale, Pa.: Oakdale Printing and Pub. Co., 1908.

Nevins, Allan, ed. *A Diary of Battle: The Personal Journal of Colonel Charles S. Wainwright*. New York: Harcourt, Brace and World, 1962.

New York Monuments Commission. *Final Report of the Battlefield of Gettysburg*. 3 vols. Albany: J. B. Lyon, 1902.

———. *In Memoriam: Abner Doubleday, 1810–1893, and John Cleveland Robinson, 1817–1897*. Albany: J. B. Lyon, 1918.

———. *In Memoriam: Francis Channing Barlow, 1834–1896*. Albany: J. B. Lyon, 1923.

———. *In Memoriam: James Samuel Wadsworth, 1807–1864*. Albany: J. B. Lyon, 1916.

Nichols, Edward J. *Toward Gettysburg: A Biography of General John F. Reynolds*. State College: Pennsylvania State University Press, 1958.

Nichols, G. W. *A Soldier's Story of His Regiment*. Kennesaw, Ga.: Continental Book Co., 1961.

Nicholson, John P. *Pennsylvania at Gettysburg*. 2 vols. Harrisburg: Wm. Stanley Ray, 1904.

Nolan, Alan T. *The Iron Brigade: A Military History*. New York: Macmillan, 1961.

Norman, William M. *A Portion of My Life*. Winston-Salem: John F. Blair, 1959.

Northrop, Rufus. "Going into Gettysburg." *National Tribune*, 11 October 1906.

Okey, C. W. "After That Flag." *Milwaukee Sunday Telegraph*, 29 April 1883.

O'Neal, J. W. C. "Battle of Gettysburg." *Gettysburg Compiler*, 5 July 1905.

Osborn, Thomas W. "The Artillery at Gettysburg." *Philadelphia Weekly Press*, 31 May 1879.

Osborne, Seward R. *Holding the Left at Gettysburg*. Hightstown, N.J.: Longstreet House, 1990.

——, ed. *The Civil War Diaries of Theodore B. Gates, 20th New York State Militia*. Hightstown, N.J.: Longstreet House, 1991.

Otis, George H. "Second Wisconsin Regiment." *Milwaukee Sunday Telegraph*, 29 August 1880.

Park, Robert Emory. *Sketch of the Twelfth Alabama Infantry*. Richmond: William Ellis Jones, 1906.

Parkhurst, D. E. "Heroism of the 147th N.Y." *National Tribune*, 1 November 1888.

Patterson, Gerard A. "The Death of Iverson's Brigade." *Gettysburg Magazine* 5 (July 1991): 13–18.

Pfanz, Donald C. *Richard S. Ewell: A Soldier's Life*. Chapel Hill: University of North Carolina Press, 1998.

Pfanz, Harry W. *Gettysburg: Culp's Hill and Cemetery Hill*. Chapel Hill: University of North Carolina Press, 1993.

——. *Gettysburg: The Second Day*. Chapel Hill: University of North Carolina Press, 1987.

Pickerill, W. N. *History of the Third Indiana Cavalry*. Indianapolis: Aetna Printing Co., 1906.

Pierce, J. Volney. "Letter of Lt. J. Volney Pierce, 1 Nov. 1882." In Ladd and Ladd, *Bachelder Papers*, 2:910–13.

Pula, James S. *For Liberty and Justice: The Life and Times of Wladimir Krzyzanowski*. Chicago: Polish-American Congress Charitable Foundation, 1978.

——. *The History of a German-Polish Brigade*. San Francisco: R&E Research Associates, 1976.

——. *The Sigel Regiment*. Campbell, Calif.: Savas Pub. Co., 1998.

Purifoy, John. "The Artillery at Gettysburg." *Confederate Veteran* 32 (1924): 424–27.

——. "The Battle of Gettysburg, July 1, 1863." *Confederate Veteran* 31 (1923): 22–25, 138–42.

——. "With Ewell and Rodes in Pennsylvania." *Confederate Veteran* 30 (1930): 462–64.

Quaife, Milo, ed. *From the Cannon's Mouth: The Civil War Letters of General Alpheas S. Williams*. Detroit: Wayne State University Press, 1959.

Ramsey, William R. "Letter of Sgt. William R. Ramsey, 16 April 1883." In Ladd and Ladd, *Bachelder Papers*, 2:947–51.

Raphelson, Alfred C. "The Unheroic General." *German-American Review* 29 (October–November 1962): 26–29.

Raus, Edmund J. *A Generation on the March: The Union Army at Gettysburg*. Lynchburg: H. E. Howard, 1987.

Reed, Merl E. "The Gettysburg Campaign: A Louisiana Lieutenant's Eye Witness Account." *Pennsylvania History* 30 (April 1963): 185–91.

Reed, Thomas Benton. *A Private in Gray*. Camden, Ark.: Thomas B. Reed, 1905.

Remington, William N. "Wm. N. Remington's Story." *Milwaukee Sunday Telegraph*, 29 April 1883.

Robertson, James I. *General A. P. Hill: The Story of a Confederate Warrior*. New York: Random House, 1987.

Robinson, John C. "The First Corps." *National Tribune*, 21 April 1887.

Rogers, Clayton E. "Gettysburg Scenes: Captain Clayton E. Rogers Justly Takes Exception to a *Century* Article." *Milwaukee Sunday Telegraph*, 13 May 1887.

Rogers, Earl M. "A Settled Question." *Milwaukee Sunday Telegraph*, 29 July 1883.

Rogers, Sarah Sites, ed. *The Ties of the Past: The Gettysburg Diaries of Salome Myers Stewart, 1834–1922*. Gettysburg: Thomas Publications, 1996.

Root, Adrian. Letter to editors, 14 July 1863. *Buffalo Commercial Advertizer*, 18 July 1863.

Ropes, John C., and John C. Gray. *War Letters of John Chipman Gray and John Codman Ropes*. Boston: Houghton Mifflin, 1927.

Rosengarten, Joseph G. *William Reynolds, Rear Admiral U.S.N., John Fulton Reynolds, Major General, U.S.V., Colonel, Fifth Infantry, A Memoir*. Philadelphia: Lippincott, 1880.

Runge, William H., ed. *Four Years in the Confederate Artillery: The Diary of Private Henry Robinson Berkeley*. Chapel Hill: University of North Carolina Press for the Virginia Historical Society, 1961.

Salomon, Edward S. *Gettysburg*. War Paper No. 24, Military Order of the Loyal Legion of the United States, California Commandery. San Francisco: Shannon Conmy, 1913.

Sauers, Richard Allen. *The Gettysburg Campaign, June 3–August 1, 1863: Comprehensive Selected Annotated Bibliography*. Westport, Conn.: Greenwood Press, 1962.

———. "Gettysburg Controversies." *Gettysburg Magazine* 3 (January 1991): 113–23.

Scales, Alfred M. "Letter of Brig. Gen. Alfred M. Scales." In Ladd and Ladd, *Bachelder Papers*, 3:1696–98.

Schuricht, Herman. "Jenkins' Brigade in the Gettysburg Campaign." *Southern Historical Society Papers* 24 (1896): 329–51.

Schurz, Carl. "The Battle of Gettysburg." *McClure's Magazine*, July 1907, 272–85.

———. *The Reminiscences of Carl Schurz*. 3 vols. New York: McClure, 1906.

Scrymser, James A. *Extracts and Personal Reminiscences of James A. Scrymser in Time of Peace and War*. N.p., n.d.

S. D. G. "From the Twenty-fourth." *Detroit Free Press*, 14 July 1863.

Sheldon, Ben F. "Our Boys at Gettysburg." *Schenectady Evening Star and Times*, 13, 23 July 1863.

Shevchuk, Paul M. "The Wounding of Albert Jenkins." *Gettysburg Magazine* 3 (July 1990): 51–53.

Shooter, Washington P. "Letter to McIntyre." *Drumbeat*, Charleston Civil War Round Table, June 1989.

Sifakis, Stewart. *Who Was Who in the Civil War*. New York: Facts on File, 1986.

Simmers, William, and Paul Bachschmid. *The Volunteers Manual*. Easton, Pa.: D. H. Neiman, 1863.

Skelly, Daniel M. *A Boy's Experiences during the Battle of Gettysburg.* Gettysburg: n.p.,
1932.

A Sketch of the Life of Capt. Don P. Halsey of the Confederate States Army. Richmond:
Wm. Ellis Jones, 1904.

Slocum, Charles E. *The Life and Services of Major-General Henry Warner Slocum.*
Toledo: Slocum Pub. Co., 1913.

Small, Abner. *The Road to Richmond: Civil War Memoirs of Major Abner Small of the
Sixteenth Maine Volunteers.* Edited by Harold Adams Small. Berkeley: University
of California Press, 1939.

———. *The Sixteenth Maine Regiment in the War of the Rebellion.* Portland, Maine: B.
Thurston, 1886.

Smith, Abram P. *History of the Seventy-sixth Regiment, New York Volunteers.* Cortland,
N.Y.: Truair, Smith and Miles, 1867.

Smith, Donald L. *The Twenty-fourth Michigan of the Iron Brigade.* Harrisburg:
Stockpole, 1962.

Smith, Jacob. *Camps and Campaigns of the 107th Regiment, Ohio Volunteer Infantry.*
N.p., n.d.

Smith, James Power. "General Lee at Gettysburg." *Southern Historical Society Papers*
33 (1905): 135–60.

———. "With Stonewall Jackson." *Southern Historical Society Papers* 43 (1920): 1–
105.

Smith, Nathaniel S. "Letter, undated, of Adjutant Nathaniel S. Smith, Thirteenth
North Carolina Infantry on the Battle of Gettysburg, Pennsylvania, July 1–3,
1863." In Hewett, Trudeau, and Suderow, *Supplement,* 27:462–65.

Smith, Timothy H. *The Story of Lee's Headquarters.* Gettysburg: Thomas
Publications, 1995.

Smith, William A. *The Anson Guards, Company C, Fourteenth Regiment, North Carolina
Volunteers.* Charlotte: Stone Pub. Co., 1914.

Snyder, Charles McCool. *Oswego County, New York, in the Civil War.* Yearbook of the
Oswego County Historical Society, 1962.

Spayd, Henry H. "The Colors of the 149th Pa. at Gettysburg." In Ladd and Ladd,
Bachelder Papers, 2:762–64.

Stearns, Austin C. *Three Years with Company K.* Cranberry, N.J.: Fairleigh Dickinson
University Press, 1976.

Stevenson, Burton Egbert. *Poems of American History.* Cambridge, Mass.: Riverside
Press, 1950.

Stewart, George. *Pickett's Charge.* Boston: Houghton Mifflin, 1959.

Stewart, James. "Battery B, Fourth U.S. Artillery at Gettysburg." In Bandy and
Freeland, *Gettysburg Papers,* 1:364–77.

Stiles, Robert. *Four Years under Marse Robert.* Dayton: Morningside, 1977.

Storch, Marc, and Beth Storch. "Unpublished Gettysburg Reports by the 2d and
7th Wisconsin Infantry Regimental Officers." *Gettysburg Magazine* 17 (July
1997): 20–25.

———. " 'What a Deadly Trap We Were In': Archer's Brigade on July 1, 1863."
Gettysburg Magazine 6 (January 1992): 13–27.

Stratton, Albion W. "What Became of the Flag?" *Maine Bugle*, April 1896.

Strong, William W., ed. *History of the 121st Regiment, Pennsylvania Volunteers.* Philadelphia: Burke and McFetridge, 1893.

Taylor, J. Arthur, to father, 9 July 1863. *Richmond Daily Whig*, 23 July 1863.

Taylor, Michael W. "Ramseur's Brigade in the Gettysburg Campaign: A Newly Discovered Account by Capt. James I. Harris, Co. I, 30th Regt. N. C. T." *Gettysburg Magazine* 17 (July 1997): 26–40.

Taylor, Walter H. *Four Years with General Lee.* New York: Appleton, 1877.

Tevis, C. V. *The History of the Fighting Fourteenth.* New York: Brooklyn Eagle Press, 1911.

Thomas, Henry W. *History of the Doles-Cook Brigade.* Atlanta: Franklin, 1903.

Todd, William, ed. *History of the Ninth Regiment, N. Y. S. M. . . . (Eighty-third N. Y. Volunteers).* New York: J. S. Oglivee, 1889.

Tompkins, Daniel A. *Company K, 14th South Carolina Volunteers.* Charlotte: Charlotte Observer Printing and Publishing House, 1897.

Tremain, Henry E. *Two Days of War: A Gettysburg Narrative and Other Excursions.* New York: Bonnel, Silver and Bowers, 1905.

Trimble, Isaac R. "The Battle and Campaign of Gettysburg." *Southern Historical Society Papers* 26 (1898): 116–28.

———. "The Campaign and Battle of Gettysburg." *Confederate Veteran* 25 (1917): 209–13.

———. "Letter of Maj. Gen. Isaac R. Trimble, Feb. 8 1863." In Ladd and Ladd, *Bachelder Papers*, 2:921–34.

Turney, J. B. "The First Tennessee at Gettysburg." *Confederate Veteran* 8 (1900): 535–27.

Tuttle, R. M. "Unparalleled Loss, Company F, Twenty-sixth N.C. at Gettysburg." *Southern Historical Society Papers* 28 (1900): 199–205.

U.S. Congress. *Report of the Joint Committee on the Conduct of the War at the Second Session, Thirty-eighth Congress, Army of the Potomac, General Meade . . . .* Washington, D.C.: U.S. Government Printing Office, 1865.

U.S. War Department. *U.S. Infantry Tactics . . . .* Philadelphia: Lippincott, 1862.

———. *The War of the Rebellion: A Compilation of the Official Records of the Union and Confederate Armies.* 128 vols. Washington, D.C.: U.S. Government Printing Office, 1880–1901.

Vautier, John D. *History of the Eighty-eighth Pennsylvania Volunteers.* Philadelphia: Lippincott, 1894.

Wakelyn, Jon L. *Biographical Dictionary of the Confederacy.* Westport, Conn.: Greenwood Press, 1977.

Wallber, Albert. "From Gettysburg to Libby Prison." In Bandy and Freeland, *Gettysburg Papers*, 1:353–62.

Warren, George L. "The Eleventh Corps." *National Tribune*, 21 July 1877.

Warren, Horatio N. *Two Reunions of the 142d Regiment, Pa. Vols.* Buffalo: Courier, 1890.

Watrous, J. A. "Some Army Sketches: The Mule Train Charge at Gettysburg." *Milwaukee Sunday Telegraph*, 30 July 1882.

Wehrum, Charles C. "Gettysburg." *National Tribune*, 10 December 1888.

——. "Iverson's Brigade." *National Tribune*, 21 August 1884.

Weigley, Russell F. "John Buford: A Personality Profile." *Civil War Times Illustrated* 5 (June 1966): 14–23.

Welch, Spencer G. *A Confederate Surgeon's Letters to His Wife*. Marietta, Ga.: Continental Book Co., 1954.

Weld, Stephen M. *War Diary and Letters of Stephen Minor Weld, 1861–1865*. Cambridge, Mass.: Riverside Press, 1979.

Wellman, John F. Letter to Dear Comrades of the 154 Regiment, 10 August 1888. *Ellicottville Post*, 5 September 1888.

Wheeler, Cornelius. "Reminiscences of the Battle of Gettysburg." In Bandy and Freeland, *Gettysburg Papers*, 1:197–212.

Wheeler, William. *In Memoriam: Letters of William Wheeler of the Class of 1855, YC*. Cambridge, Mass.: H. G. Houghton, 1873.

Whitehead, Ralph J. *The 119th New York Vols. and Their Participation in the Gettysburg Campaign, June 12–July 4, 1863*. N.p., 1980.

Willett, Frank M. "A Comrade Who Says the Eighth N. Y. Cav. Opened the Great Battle." *National Tribune*, 1 December 1889.

Williams, Samuel J. "Report of Colonel Samuel J. Williams, Nineteenth Indiana Volunteers, on the Battle of Gettysburg, Pennsylvania, July 1–3, 1863." In Hewett, Trudeau, and Suderow, *Supplement*, 27:137–40.

Willis, Edward. "Report of Colonel Edward Willis, Twelfth Georgia Infantry, July 19, 1863." In Hewett, Trudeau, and Suderow, *Supplement*, 27:403–5.

Wilson, Le Grand James. *The Confederate Soldier*. Edited by James W. Silver. Memphis: Memphis State University Press, n.d.

Wittenberg, Eric J. "An Analysis of the Buford Manuscripts." *Gettysburg Magazine* 15 (July 1996): 17–23.

——. "John Buford and the Gettysburg Campaign." *Gettysburg Magazine* 11 (July 1994): 19–55.

"Would Have Saved Officers." *Charlottesville Daily Progress*, 22 March 1904.

Young, Jesse Bowman. *The Battle of Gettysburg*. New York: Harper and Brothers, 1913.

Young, Louis G. Letter to Maj. W. S. Baker, 10 February 1864. *Richmond Enquirer*, 18 March 1864.

INDEX

11; at Chambersburg, 12; at Mechanicsburg, 20; at Harrisburg, 20

Lane's, 119, 300, 302, 303; order of, 425 (n. 24)

O'Neal's, 152, 153, 162, 166, 171, 178, 188, 340, 406 (n. 14); position of, 162; advance of, 165, 188

Perrin's (McGowan's), 119, 300, 303; reforms, 309; casualties in, 319

Pettigrew's, 1, 25, 27, 41, 52, 269, 399 (n. 3); casualties in, 292

Ramseur's, 18, 156, 164, 186, 188, 189, 190, 340

Scales's, 119, 300, 305, 307, 308, 311, 319, 351, 426 (n. 9); halts, 30

Smith's, 229, 343

Thomas's, 119, 300

— ARTILLERY BATTALIONS:

Carter's, 155, 156, 160, 195, 404 (n. 10)

Garnett's, 119, 320

Jones's, 228, 229, 415 (nn. 4–6)

Lane's, 120

McIntosh's, 52, 119, 200, 300, 391 (n. 21), 399 (n. 9)

Pegram's, 52, 66, 399 (n. 8); deployment of, 60–61, 390 (n. 21)

Poague's, 120

— BATTERIES:

Brander's, 61, 119, 123, 200, 297

Carrington's, 228, 244, 429 (n. 10)

Carter's, W. P., 156, 160, 165, 179, 195

Crenshaw, 61

Fry's, 156, 160, 195, 196

Garber's, 228, 229, 232

Green's, 228

Hurt's, 119

Jackson's, 20

Johnson's, 120

McGraw's, 119

Marye's, 52, 57, 60, 200

Maurin's, 25, 119

Page's, 165, 168, 220

Reese's, 165, 220, 413 (n. 11), 429 (n. 10)

Rice's, 119

Tanner's, 228

Wallace's, 120

Zimmerman's, 63

Army of the Potomac, 1, 5, 6, 8, 33, 45

— CORPS:

First (Reynolds's and Doubleday's), 8, 33, 35, 44, 45, 48, 135, 160; ordered to Gettysburg, 48, 70; ammunition of, 189; at Cemetery Hill, 331, 333; casualties in, 350; future of, 350; casualties inflicted by, 351

Second (Hancock's), 8

Third (Sickles's), 8

Fifth (Sykes's), 8, 349

Eleventh (Howard's and Schurz's), 4, 8, 33, 35, 45, 48, 134, 191; route to Gettysburg of, 69; reputation of, 134–35; and roads, 138; in Gettysburg, 141; position of, 238; at Cemetery Hill, 331, 333; casualties in, 350; future of, 350; casualties inflicted by, 351

Twelfth (Slocum's), 8, 138, 142, 144

— CAVALRY DIVISIONS:

Buford's, 37, 40, 41, 52, 67

Stahel's, 35, 37

— INFANTRY DIVISIONS:

Barlow's, 134, 158, 221, 229, 258; route to Gettysburg of, 135, 140; position of, 140; orders for, 223; deploys, 226

Robinson's, 35, 142, 189, 170–71, 313

Rowley's (Doubleday's), 35

Schimmelfennig's (Schurz's), 134, 135, 136, 140, 158, 230, 333

Steinwehr's, 135, 216, 258, 331, 333

Emmitsburg Road, 39, 46, 69, 74, 123, 125, 126, 136, 138, 141
Engelhard, Joseph A., 303
Evans, Harry, 173
Evans, William, 114, 398 (n. 26)
Ewell, Richard S., 2, 22, 148, 149, 162, 227, 342, 344, 345, 346, 347, 348–49, 386 (n. 1); Lee's orders for, 11, 13, 148; at Heidlersburg, 149; attacks, 161; Lee's afternoon orders for, 342, 344; in town, 344; favors Cemetery Hill attack, 345; at Culp's Hill, 347; casualties under, 348; remains in place, 348; visits Lee, 348; later career of, 353

Fairchild, Lucius, 77, 92, 98; shot, 98, 396 (n. 14)
Fairfield, George, 109, 112, 113
Fairfield (Millerstown), Pa., 33, 38
Finnefrock buildings, 118, 128
"First shots," 53, 56, 76
Fischer, Louis, 217
Fite, John, 17, 25, 301, 385 (n. 24), 386 (n. 9)
Flags, 435 (n. 1)
Fleet, Charles B., 200
Ford, John, 308
Forney, Samuel, 325
Forney farm, 64
Forney Ridge, 64, 181
Forney's Woods, 155, 156, 163, 170, 179
Forrester, George W., 123
Foster, Catherine, 322, 324, 341
Fountaindale, Pa., 38, 40
Fowler, Douglas, 226, 234, 247
Fowler, Edward, 35, 76, 105, 106, 113,
Fremantle, James A. L., 210
Frueauff, John, 231
Fry, Birkett D., 58, 118, 301
Fulton, William F., 63

Gamble, William, 37, 56, 59, 303, 318
"Gap" between corps, 405 (n. 5)

Garlach, Anna, 324, 430 (n. 19)
Garlach, Catherine, 328
Garnett, John J., 120, 320, 428 (n. 41)
Gates, Theodore, 272, 273, 276, 279, 290, 291, 299, 310, 315
"General Order 72," 12, 16, 22
George, Newton J., 68, 96, 396 (n. 9)
George house, 73, 78, 392 (n. 12)
Georgia infantry regiments:
    4th, 255, 256
    12th, 255
    13th, 250
    21st, 249, 255, 341
    38th, 244
    44th, 255
    61st, 244, 250
Gettysburg College, 257
Gettysburg Plain, 151, 152, 217–18
Gilligan, Richard L., 176
Gilsa, Leopold von, 4, 41, 231, 243, 333; biography of, 224–25, 414 (n. 20)
Glen, William G., 263
Glenn, James, 195, 317
Godwin, Archibald, 263
Gordon, George T., 308, 426 (n. 7)
Gordon, John B., 229, 248, 342, 344; biography of, 239
Graaff, Albert van de, 106
Green, Wharton J., 180, 201–3
Greencastle, Pa., 10, 14, 17
Grimes, Bryan, 192
Grover, Andrew J., 83
Guinn, George, 137

Hagerstown, Md., 11, 12, 17
Hagerstown Road, 77, 120, 124, 278, 295, 297, 305, 311, 313, 315, 317, 318
Hagy house, 168, 217, 218, 230, 235
Hall, Daniel, 136, 137, 143
Hall, Isaac, 159, 174–75, 182
Hall, James A., 75, 85, 88, 89, 393 (n. 19), 397 (n. 8); Reynolds's orders for, 75

McPherson Ridge: east, 67, 83, 89, 96, 97, 209, 210, 211, 273, 277, 278, 287, 288, 289, 298, 299, 304, 306, 307; west, 26, 58, 63, 67, 77, 92, 105, 127, 194, 195, 204, 270, 285

McPherson Woods, 57, 60, 62, 65, 66, 76, 77, 91, 92, 95, 97, 122, 194, 208, 269, 270, 272, 284, 289; description of, 92; ravine in, 92, 97

Mahler, Francis, 251–52

Maine infantry regiment: 16th, 182, 185, 188, 189, 208, 410 (n. 36); ordered to hold, 191

Maloney, Patrick, 100

Mansfield, Jefferson B., 276

Mansfield, John, 98, 299, 311

Markle, Emanuel, 93, 286–87

Marshall, James K., 301, 422 (n. 26)

Marsh Creek, 35, 45, 46, 52, 53, 57, 124, 300

Marston, A. Richard, 109–10

Martinsburg, Va., 6, 10

Marye, Edward A., 52

Marye, John L., 13, 16

Massachusetts infantry regiments: 12th, 170, 171, 172, 174, 207 13th, 31, 188, 191

May, William H., 163

Meade, George G., 9, 32, 34, 45, 50, 127, 337; advances army, 34; biography of, 43–44; intentions of, 43; letters of to wife, 43, 46; instructs Reynolds, 45; Circular of 30 June, 45–46; hunts for position, 46; Pipe Creek Circular, 46; plans of, 49; relies on Reynolds, 49

Meals, Henry, 267

Mercer, John T., 249, 255

Meredith, Solomon, 70, 98, 101, 122, 286, 423 (n. 44)

Mericle, Albert, 267

Merkle, Christopher F., 232, 245

Meysenburg, Theodore, 133, 136

Michigan infantry regiment: 24th, 71, 97–98, 122, 270, 271, 280, 284, 286

Middleburg, Va., 6

Middle Street, 340

Middletown, Md., 8, 32

Middletown (Biglerville), Pa., 149

Miller, Clyde, 135, 231, 241, 415 (n. 12)

Miller, Francis, 82, 83, 85

Mills, George, 308

Mississippi infantry regiments: 2d, 23, 63, 67, 83, 110, 391 (n. 25); ordered into railroad bed, 104 42d, 63, 64, 67, 104

Mitchell, John, 265–66

Mitchell, Robert W., 78, 79

Moesch, Joseph A., 172

Montgomery, Walter, 170

Moon, William H., 66, 94, 96

Moore, Jack, 96

Moore, Roby, 276, 277, 280

Morgan, Charles H., 337, 339

Moritz Tavern, 46, 69, 135, 389 (n. 9)

Morrell, Louis, 250

Morris, Roland G., 184

Morrow, Henry, 98, 101, 271, 276, 277, 282, 298

Muenzenberger, Adam, 135, 251

Muldoon, Henry, 190

"Mule Train Charge," 338

Mummasburg, Pa., 149

Mummasburg Road, 64, 153, 159, 161, 165, 168, 169, 171, 173, 181, 184, 185, 187, 188, 191, 196, 217, 218, 223

Murphy, William B., 110

Musser, John D., 332

Myers, Salome, 14–15

Newman, Joseph, 60, 67

New York cavalry regiments: 6th, 38, 60, 64, 322 8th, 60, 303, 318 9th, 56, 64, 153, 322, 391 (n. 26)